Search through the complete book in PDF!

- Access the entire *CIW: Security Professional Study Guide*, complete with figures and tables, in electronic format.
- Search the *CIW: Security Professional Study Guide* chapters to find information on any topic in seconds.
- Use Adobe Acrobat Reader (included on the CD-ROM) to view the electronic book.

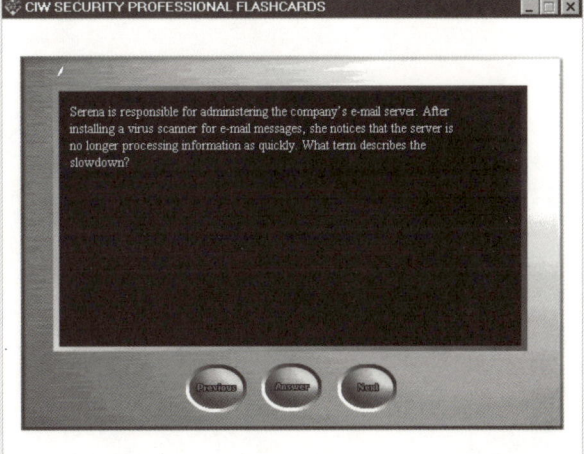

Use the Electronic Flashcards for PCs or Palm devices to jog your memory and prep last minute for the exam!

- Reinforce your understanding of key concepts with these hardcore flashcard-style questions.

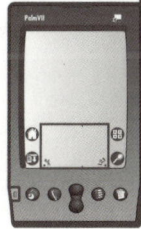

Prepare for the Security Professional exam on the go with your handheld device!

- Download the Flashcards to your Palm device and go on the road. Now you can study for the CIW Security Professional exam anytime, anywhere.

CIW: Security Professional Study Guide

Exam 1D0-470

OBJECTIVE GROUP	CHAPTER NUMBER
Network Security and Firewalls	
Define the significance of network security, and identify various elements of an effective security policy, including but not limited to: risk factors, security-related organizations, key resources to secure, general security threat types, access control.	1
Define encryption and the encryption methods used in internetworking.	2, 6
Use universal guidelines and principles of effective network security to create effective specific solutions.	2, 4
Apply security principles and identify security attacks.	3, 4
Identify firewall types and define common firewall terminology.	5, 6
Plan a firewall system that incorporates multiple levels of protection, including but not limited to: firewall system design, proactive detection, setting traps, security breach response, security alerting organizations.	5, 6, 7
Operating System Security	
Identify key principles for securing an operating system, including but not limited to: industry evaluation criteria, Unix and Windows servers, security management, default settings.	8
Identify the mechanisms, security parameters, and techniques necessary for securing Windows and Unix accounts.	8, 9
Identify, assign, and use file system permissions for Windows and Unix servers.	9
Assess common risks associated with Windows and Unix servers, including but not limited to: operating system attacks, system scanning, NIS, NFS, Trojans.	10
Reduce risk by modifying system parameters and locking down services.	10

OBJECTIVE GROUP	CHAPTER NUMBER
Security Auditing, Attacks, and Threat Analysis	
Identify security auditing principles, including but not limited to: security auditor's duties, network risk factor analysis, audit steps.	11
Define the security auditing and discovery processes, plan an audit, and install and configure network-based and host-based discovery software.	11
Identify penetration and control strategies and methods, including but not limited to: potential attacks, router security, threat containment, intrusion detection.	3, 7, 12, 13
Implement intrusion-detection systems in an enterprise environment.	13
Conduct log analysis, establish a user activity baseline, and implement auditing for various services and systems.	14
Identify ways to improve security policy compliance and create an assessment report.	15
Install operating system add-ons, including but not limited to: personal firewalls, native auditing SSH.	15

CIW:
Security Professional
Study Guide

CIW™:
Security Professional
Study Guide

James Stanger, Ph.D.
Patrick Lane
Tim Crothers

San Francisco • London

Associate Publisher: Neil Edde
Acquisitions and Developmental Editor: Heather O'Connor
Editor: Liz Welch
Production Editor: Molly Glover
Technical Editors: Liam Noonan, Donald Fuller
Book Designer: Bill Gibson
Graphic Illustrator: Tony Jonick
Electronic Publishing Specialist: Interactive Composition Corporation
Proofreaders: Emily Hsuan, Dave Nash, Laurie O'Connell, Yariv Rabinovitch
Indexer: Jack Lewis
CD Coordinator: Dan Mummert
CD Technician: Kevin Ly
Cover Designer: Archer Design
Cover Illustrator/Photographer: Jeremy Woodhouse, PhotoDisc

This book was developed and published by SYBEX Inc. under a license from ProsoftTraining. All Rights Reserved.

Original Security Professional training material © 2001 ComputerPREP, Inc.

Copyright © 2002 SYBEX Inc., 1151 Marina Village Parkway, Alameda, CA 94501. World rights reserved. No part of this publication may be stored in a retrieval system, transmitted, or reproduced in any way, including but not limited to photocopy, photograph, magnetic, or other record, without the prior agreement and written permission of the publisher.

Library of Congress Card Number: 2002100061

ISBN: 0-7821-4084-X

SYBEX and the SYBEX logo are either registered trademarks or trademarks of SYBEX Inc. in the United States and/or other countries.

The CIW logo and ComputerPREP, Inc. are trademarks of ProsoftTraining.com.

Some screen reproductions made using Jasc® Paint Shop Pro® Copyright © 1992–2002 Jasc Software, Inc. All Rights Reserved.

Some screen reproductions produced with FullShot 99. FullShot 99 © 1991–1999 Inbit Incorporated. All rights reserved. FullShot is a trademark of Inbit Incorporated.

The CD interface was created using Macromedia Director, COPYRIGHT 1994, 1997–1999 Macromedia Inc. For more information on Macromedia and Macromedia Director, visit http://www.macromedia.com.

Netscape Communications, the Netscape Communications logo, Netscape, and Netscape Navigator are trademarks of Netscape Communications Corporation.

Netscape Communications Corporation has not authorized, sponsored, endorsed, or approved this publication and is not responsible for its content. Netscape and the Netscape Communications Corporate Logos are trademarks and trade names of Netscape Communications Corporation. All other product names and/or logos are trademarks of their respective owners.

Internet screen shot(s) using Microsoft Internet Explorer version 5 reprinted by permission from Microsoft Corporation.

TRADEMARKS: SYBEX has attempted throughout this book to distinguish proprietary trademarks from descriptive terms by following the capitalization style used by the manufacturer.

The author and publisher have made their best efforts to prepare this book, and the content is based upon final release software whenever possible. Portions of the manuscript may be based upon pre-release versions supplied by software manufacturer(s). The author and the publisher make no representation or warranties of any kind with regard to the completeness or accuracy of the contents herein and accept no liability of any kind including but not limited to performance, merchantability, fitness for any particular purpose, or any losses or damages of any kind caused or alleged to be caused directly or indirectly from this book.

Manufactured in the United States of America

10 9 8 7 6 5 4 3 2 1

To Our Valued Readers:

The Certified Internet Webmaster (CIW) program from ProsoftTraining™ has established itself as one of the leading Internet certifications in the IT industry. Sybex has partnered with ProsoftTraining to produce Study Guides—like the one you hold in your hand—for the Associate, Master Administrator, and Master Designer tracks. Each Sybex book is based on official courseware and is exclusively endorsed by ProsoftTraining.

Just as ProsoftTraining is committed to establishing measurable standards for certifying IT professionals working with Internet technologies, Sybex is committed to providing those professionals with the skills and knowledge needed to meet those standards. It has long been Sybex's desire to help bridge the knowledge and skills gap that currently confronts the IT industry.

The authors and editors have worked hard to ensure that this CIW Study Guide is comprehensive, in-depth, and pedagogically sound. We're confident that this book will meet and exceed the demanding standards of the certification marketplace and help you, the CIW certification candidate, succeed in your endeavors.

Good luck in pursuit of your CIW certification!

Neil Edde
Associate Publisher—Certification
Sybex, Inc.

Software License Agreement: Terms and Conditions

The media and/or any online materials accompanying this book that are available now or in the future contain programs and/or text files (the "Software") to be used in connection with the book. SYBEX hereby grants to you a license to use the Software, subject to the terms that follow. Your purchase, acceptance, or use of the Software will constitute your acceptance of such terms.

The Software compilation is the property of SYBEX unless otherwise indicated and is protected by copyright to SYBEX or other copyright owner(s) as indicated in the media files (the "Owner(s)"). You are hereby granted a single-user license to use the Software for your personal, noncommercial use only. You may not reproduce, sell, distribute, publish, circulate, or commercially exploit the Software, or any portion thereof, without the written consent of SYBEX and the specific copyright owner(s) of any component software included on this media.

In the event that the Software or components include specific license requirements or end-user agreements, statements of condition, disclaimers, limitations or warranties ("End-User License"), those End-User Licenses supersede the terms and conditions herein as to that particular Software component. Your purchase, acceptance, or use of the Software will constitute your acceptance of such End-User Licenses.

By purchase, use or acceptance of the Software you further agree to comply with all export laws and regulations of the United States as such laws and regulations may exist from time to time.

Reusable Code in This Book

The authors created reusable code in this publication expressly for reuse for readers. Sybex grants readers permission to reuse for any purpose the code found in this publication or its accompanying CD-ROM so long as all of the authors are attributed in any application containing the reusable code, and the code itself is never sold or commercially exploited as a stand-alone product.

Software Support

Components of the supplemental Software and any offers associated with them may be supported by the specific Owner(s) of that material, but they are not supported by SYBEX. Information regarding any available support may be obtained from the Owner(s) using the information provided in the appropriate read.me files or listed elsewhere on the media.

Should the manufacturer(s) or other Owner(s) cease to offer support or decline to honor any offer, SYBEX bears no responsibility. This notice concerning support for the Software is provided for your information only. SYBEX is not the agent or principal of the Owner(s), and SYBEX is in no way responsible for providing any support for the Software, nor is it liable or responsible for any support provided, or not provided, by the Owner(s).

Warranty

SYBEX warrants the enclosed media to be free of physical defects for a period of ninety (90) days after purchase. The Software is not available from SYBEX in any other form or media than that enclosed herein or posted to www.sybex.com. If you discover a defect in the media during this warranty period, you may obtain a replacement of identical format at no charge by sending the defective media, postage prepaid, with proof of purchase to:

SYBEX Inc.
Product Support Department
1151 Marina Village Parkway
Alameda, CA 94501
Web: http://www.sybex.com

After the 90-day period, you can obtain replacement media of identical format by sending us the defective disk, proof of purchase, and a check or money order for $10, payable to SYBEX.

Disclaimer

SYBEX makes no warranty or representation, either expressed or implied, with respect to the Software or its contents, quality, performance, merchantability, or fitness for a particular purpose. In no event will SYBEX, its distributors, or dealers be liable to you or any other party for direct, indirect, special, incidental, consequential, or other damages arising out of the use of or inability to use the Software or its contents even if advised of the possibility of such damage. In the event that the Software includes an online update feature, SYBEX further disclaims any obligation to provide this feature for any specific duration other than the initial posting.

The exclusion of implied warranties is not permitted by some states. Therefore, the above exclusion may not apply to you. This warranty provides you with specific legal rights; there may be other rights that you may have that vary from state to state. The pricing of the book with the Software by SYBEX reflects the allocation of risk and limitations on liability contained in this agreement of Terms and Conditions.

Shareware Distribution

This Software may contain various programs that are distributed as shareware. Copyright laws apply to both shareware and ordinary commercial software, and the copyright Owner(s) retains all rights. If you try a shareware program and continue using it, you are expected to register it. Individual programs differ on details of trial periods, registration, and payment. Please observe the requirements stated in appropriate files.

Copy Protection

The Software in whole or in part may or may not be copy-protected or encrypted. However, in all cases, reselling or redistributing these files without authorization is expressly forbidden except as specifically provided for by the Owner(s) therein.

Acknowledgments

First, I would like to thank Liz Welch for making it such a pleasure to work on this book. Editors with your talent and eye for detail are hard to come by. And, yes, I know I could have tightened up the prose on that last sentence just a little bit more. I also wish to thank Molly Glover, whose flexibility and good humor have made the often bumpy process of putting a book together truly enjoyable. To Liam Noonan, thank you for your acumen as a technical editor. Rarely have I had a chance to work with such a consummate professional. I wish to give special thanks to Heather O'Connor. Not only are you a true Bugs Bunny fan, but I am truly impressed with your skill in putting together such a fine collection of publishing talent. Rarely have I seen such a complex project proceed so smoothly. Kudos to you!

I also want to take the time to thank Tim Crothers, who first piqued my interest in network security. I want to thank you for your patience, your time, and the knowledge you have shared with me. Finally, I wish to thank my family. To my wife Sandi, as well as James, Jacob, Joel, and now Joseph (yeah, I know that's a lot of names that start with "J"), you have shown amazing patience with me as I have worked on this book.

—James Stanger

I want to thank my family, Lori, Emily, Ben, and Jacob, for supporting me while I put in the extra time to write the original materials. I'd like to especially thank James Stanger for his efforts far beyond what was required on the original materials. I'd also like to thank Jud Slusser and his crew for an excellent support team on the original material authoring.

—Tim Crothers

Patrick Lane would like to thank his wife, Susan, for her support and ability to make him see the lighter side of life during the time-consuming development of the CIW Foundations, CIW Internetworking Professional, and CIW Security Professional books. He would also like to thank Jud Slusser for his wisdom and long-view approach toward certification, and James Stanger for his technical expertise. He would also like to thank Heather O'Connor for the opportunity to author CIW books for Sybex.

Contents at a Glance

Introduction   *xxiii*

Assessment Test   *xxxiii*

Chapter 1	What Is Security?	1
Chapter 2	Applied Encryption	55
Chapter 3	Types of Attacks	107
Chapter 4	General Security Principles	155
Chapter 5	Firewalls Roles and Types	193
Chapter 6	Firewall Topologies and Virtual Private Networks	243
Chapter 7	Detecting and Distracting Hackers	281
Chapter 8	Operating System Security	315
Chapter 9	File System Security	351
Chapter 10	Assessing and Reducing Risk	389
Chapter 11	The Auditing Process	433
Chapter 12	Auditing Penetration and Control Strategies	481
Chapter 13	Intrusion Detection	515
Chapter 14	Auditing and Log Analysis	555
Chapter 15	Recommending Solutions and Generating Reports	595
Appendix A	Sample Security Audit Report	641
Appendix B	A Sample Enterprise Scanner Report	649
Appendix C	Internet Security Resources	657
Glossary		661

Index   *695*

Contents

Introduction		*xxiii*
Assessment Test		*xxxiii*
Chapter 1	**What Is Security?**	**1**
	Defining Security	3
	Complete Security Is a Myth	3
	Security as Balance	4
	"White Hat" and "Black Hat" Hackers	4
	Understanding Black Hat Hackers	5
	Protecting Resources	6
	Security Standards	7
	ISO 7498-2	7
	ITSEC Document BS 7799	9
	Trusted Computer Systems Evaluation Criteria (TCSEC)	10
	Common Criteria (CC)	13
	The Health Insurance Portability and Accountability Act (HIPAA)	14
	Practical Security Elements	15
	The Security Policy	15
	Encryption	24
	Authentication	26
	Access Control	33
	Auditing	35
	Summary	43
	Exam Essentials	43
	Key Terms	44
	Review Questions	46
	Answers to Review Questions	52
Chapter 2	**Applied Encryption**	**55**
	Creating Trust Relationships	56
	Encryption Terminology	57

	Symmetric-Key Encryption	58
	Symmetric-Key Algorithms	59
	The Advanced Encryption Standard (AES)	64
	Asymmetric-Key Encryption	67
	Backing Up the Private Key	69
	Asymmetric-Key Encryption Elements	69
	Hash Encryption	69
	Hash Encryption and Signing	70
	MD2, MD4, and MD5	71
	Secure Hash Algorithm	71
	Implementing Hash Algorithms with the MD5sum Command	72
	Applied Encryption Processes	73
	Encryption and E-mail	74
	Summary	96
	Exam Essentials	97
	Key Terms	98
	Review Questions	99
	Answers to Review Questions	104
Chapter 3	**Types of Attacks**	**107**
	Specific Attacks	109
	Spoofing	111
	Man-in-the-Middle Attacks	113
	Denial-of-Service (DoS) Attacks	116
	Insider Attacks	122
	Bug-based Attacks	123
	Keylogging	132
	Brute-Force Attacks	133
	Trojan	136
	Viruses	139
	Worms	141
	Summary	142
	Exam Essentials	142

		Key Terms	144
		Review Questions	146
		Answers to Review Questions	152
Chapter	**4**	**General Security Principles**	**155**
		Be Suspicious of All Network Activity	157
		Minimizing Vulnerabilities	157
		You Must Have a Security Policy	158
		No System or Technique Stands Alone	159
		Minimize Damage When Possible	160
		Verifying Backups	160
		Deploy Companywide Enforcement	162
		Provide Training	162
		Use an Integrated Security Strategy	163
		Place Equipment According to Needs	165
		Conducting a Needs Assessment Audit	165
		Identify Business Issues	167
		Chargeback	167
		Business Issues and Network Latency	169
		Consider Physical Security	170
		Maintenance Personnel	171
		Surveillance Methods	171
		Physical Attack Strategies	172
		Creating Effective Solutions	179
		Summary	180
		Exam Essentials	181
		Key Terms	182
		Review Questions	183
		Answers to Review Questions	189
Chapter	**5**	**Firewalls Roles and Types**	**193**
		The Role of a Firewall	195
		Firewall Terminology	196
		Packet Filter	197

		Proxy Server	197
		Bastion Host	199
		Network Address Translation	199
		Operating System Hardening	202
		Screening and Choke Routers	203
		Demilitarized Zone (DMZ)	203
	Firewall Configuration Defaults		204
	Creating Packet Filter Rules		205
		The Packet Filter Process	205
		Stateful Multilayer Inspection	210
	Using *ipchains* and *iptables*		214
		Creating Rules	215
		ipchains	216
		Using *iptables*	218
		Logging with *iptables* and *ipchains*	221
	Configuring Proxy Servers		227
		Proxy Server Advantages and Features	228
	Summary		230
	Exam Essentials		231
	Key Terms		232
	Review Questions		234
	Answers to Review Questions		239
Chapter	**6**	**Firewall Topologies and Virtual Private Networks**	**243**
	Design Principles		244
	Types of Bastion Hosts		246
		Hardware Issues	247
		Operating System	248
		Services and Daemons	249
	Common Firewall Designs		250
		Screening Routers	251
		Screened Host Firewall (Single-Homed Bastion)	252
		Screened Host Firewall (Multihomed Bastion)	253
		Screened Subnet Firewall, with Demilitarized Zone	254

	ICMP and Firewalls	255
	ICMP Message Types	256
	Remote Access and Virtual Private Networks (VPNs)	258
	Internet Protocol Security (IPsec)	260
	Public-Key Infrastructure (PKI)	262
	PKI Standards	262
	Summary	270
	Exam Essentials	270
	Key Terms	272
	Review Questions	273
	Answers to Review Questions	278
Chapter 7	**Detecting and Distracting Hackers**	**281**
	Proactive Detection	282
	Automated Security Scans	283
	Login Scripts	283
	Personal Firewalls	284
	Automated Audit Analysis	285
	Distracting the Hacker	286
	Dummy Accounts	286
	Dummy Files	287
	Checksums and Tripwires	287
	Jails	290
	Punishing the Hacker	292
	Methods	292
	Creating an Attack-Response Plan	295
	Decide Ahead of Time	295
	Do Not Panic	296
	Document Everything	296
	Assess the Situation	297
	Stop or Contain Activity	298
	Execute the Response Policy	298
	Analyze and Learn	300
	Summary	302

Contents xv

		Exam Essentials	303
		Key Terms	304
		Review Questions	305
		Answers to Review Questions	311
Chapter	**8**	**Operating System Security**	**315**
		Windows 2000 Security Components	316
		Windows 2000 Objects	317
		The Windows 2000 Security Subsystem	321
		Linux Security Architecture	324
		Pluggable Authentication Modules (PAMs)	325
		Account Security in Windows 2000 and Linux	330
		Passwords	331
		Windows 2000 and Strong Passwords	331
		Linux and Strong Passwords	333
		Windows 2000 Account Policies	334
		Password Aging in Linux	336
		Timing Out Users	337
		Removing Accounts	337
		Renaming Default Accounts	338
		Summary	339
		Exam Essentials	340
		Key Terms	342
		Review Questions	343
		Answers to Review Questions	348
Chapter	**9**	**File System Security**	**351**
		Windows 2000 File System Security	352
		Drive Partitioning in Windows 2000	361
		Copying and Moving Files	362
		Remote File Access Control	362
		Combined Local and Remote Permissions	364
		Linux File System Security	365
		Reviewing Files Permissions	365

The *umask* Command		370
The *chmod* Command		371
UIDs and GIDs		373
The Set Bits: Setuid, Setgid, and Sticky Bits		374
Summary		379
Exam Essentials		380
Key Terms		381
Review Questions		382
Answers to Review Questions		387

Chapter 10 Assessing and Reducing Risk — 389

Reducing Risks in Windows 2000	390
Windows 2000 Registry Security	392
Disabling and Removing Unnecessary Services in Windows 2000	399
Miscellaneous Windows 2000 Configuration Changes	406
Microsoft Service Packs	408
Reducing Risks in Unix Systems	409
Disabling *rlogin*	409
The *hosts.equiv* File and *rlogin*	410
NIS Security Concerns	411
The Network File System (NFS)	413
Updating Linux Binaries	415
xinetd and *inetd*	417
TCPWrappers	420
Stand-Alone Services	421
Summary	422
Exam Essentials	422
Key Terms	424
Review Questions	425
Answers to Review Questions	430

Chapter 11 The Auditing Process — 433

What Is an Auditor?	434
What Does an Auditor Do?	435
Auditor Roles and Perspectives	444

Auditing Steps and Stages	446
Discovery	446
Penetration	447
Control	448
Discovery Tools and Methods	448
DNS Tools	449
Finger, SNMP, and Trivial TCP/IP Services	459
Vulnerability Scanners	460
Common Vulnerability Scanners	460
Network Scanning Issues	461
Vulnerability Scanners and Reporting	464
Additional Auditing Strategies	465
Education and Social Engineering	466
The Next Step: Research	466
Summary	470
Exam Essentials	470
Key Terms	472
Review Questions	473
Answers to Review Questions	478

Chapter 12   Auditing Penetration and Control Strategies   481

Compromising Network Elements	483
Firewalls	483
Control Phase	485
Gaining Root Access	485
Creating Additional Accounts	486
Obtaining Additional Information	488
John the Ripper and Crack	497
What Happens After Control Is Established?	501
Auditing and the Control Phase	503
Summary	503
Exam Essentials	504
Key Terms	505

	Review Questions	506
	Answers to Review Questions	511
Chapter 13	**Intrusion Detection**	**515**
	Understanding Intrusion Detection	517
	IDS Terminology	517
	IDS Applications and the Incident Response Team	521
	IDS Application Strategies	523
	Intrusion-Detection Architectures	523
	Network-Based IDS Applications	524
	Host-Based IDS Applications	525
	Creating Rules for an IDS Application	529
	IDS Applications and Slow Scanning Attacks	529
	IDS Concerns	530
	Purchasing an IDS	534
	IDS Application Vendors	536
	Summary	543
	Exam Essentials	543
	Key Terms	545
	Review Questions	546
	Answers to Review Questions	551
Chapter 14	**Auditing and Log Analysis**	**555**
	Baseline Creation	556
	Searching for Normative Activity	557
	Detecting Suspicious Activity	557
	Achieving Balance with Log Files	559
	Analyzing Log Files	560
	Firewall and Router Logs	560
	Operating System Log Files	561
	Filtering Information	571
	Filtering Logs in Windows 2000	571
	Filtering Logs in Linux	572
	Securing Log Files	574
	Remote Logging	575
	Customizing Log-File Size	576

		Third-Party Logging	577
		The Benefits of Managed Security Providers	578
		Choosing the Right Provider	578
		Summary	584
		Exam Essentials	584
		Key Terms	586
		Review Questions	587
		Answers to Review Questions	592
Chapter	**15**	**Recommending Solutions and Generating Reports**	**595**
		Recommending Solutions	596
		Improving Perimeter Security	597
		Enhancing Intrusion Detection	599
		Operating System Changes	601
		Compliance-Monitoring Software	608
		Replacing and Updating Services	610
		Generating Reports	625
		The Importance of a Written Report	626
		Steps for Continued Auditing and Strengthening	627
		Summary	628
		Exam Essentials	629
		Key Terms	630
		Review Questions	631
		Answers to Review Questions	637
Appendix	**A**	**Sample Security Audit Report**	**641**
		Executive Report	642
		Overview	642
		Summary of Penetration Risk	643
		Detailed Findings for the IT Department	643
		Security Assessment Procedures	643
		Conclusions	644
		Recommendations	645

Appendix B	**A Sample Enterprise Scanner Report**		**649**
	Scan Results		650
	Information-Gathering Modules		650
	SNMP Module		653
	Port-Scanning Modules		653
Appendix C	**Internet Security Resources**		**657**
	General		658
	Computer Emergency Response Team (CERT)		658
	Other Sources		658
	Unix		659
	Windows 2000		659
Glossary			**661**
Index			*695*

Table of Exercises

Exercise 1.1	Implementing Authentication and Access Control in Apache Server	36
Exercise 2.1	Reviewing Symmetric-Key Encryption Algorithms	65
Exercise 2.2	Installing PGP 7.0.3 in Windows 2000	78
Exercise 2.3	Exporting and Signing Public Keys Using PGP for Windows 2000	81
Exercise 2.4	Exchanging Encrypted Messages Using PGP for Windows 2000	84
Exercise 2.5	Generating a Key Pair Using GNU Privacy Guard (GPG) for Red Hat Linux	85
Exercise 2.6	Exchanging and Signing Public Keys in Linux	87
Exercise 2.7	Encrypting and Decrypting Files Using GPG	89
Exercise 2.8	Creating a Signature File	91
Exercise 3.1	Sending Fake E-Mail	130
Exercise 4.1	Exploiting and Protecting Red Hat Linux Single-Boot Mode Using LILO	174
Exercise 4.2	Conducting a Physical Attack Against a Windows 2000 Server	176
Exercise 5.1	Configuring Packet-Filtering Rules	211
Exercise 5.2	Using the *ipchains* Command to Create a Personal Firewall in Linux (for Kernels 2.2 and Lower, or for Systems Running the *ipchains* Module)	222
Exercise 5.3	Using the *iptables* Command to Create a Personal Firewall in Linux (for Kernels 2.3 and Higher)	224
Exercise 6.1	Obtaining an IPsec Certificate from a CA	265
Exercise 6.2	Configuring a Windows 2000 System for IPsec	267
Exercise 7.1	Setting a Logon Tripwire Script in Windows 2000	289
Exercise 8.1	Understanding the */etc/securetty* File	329
Exercise 9.1	Assigning Advanced NTFS Permissions	356
Exercise 9.2	Finding Setuid and Setgid Programs in Your Linux System	376
Exercise 9.3	Testing the *umask* Command in Linux	378
Exercise 10.1	Auditing the Windows 2000 Registry	398
Exercise 10.2	Removing Unnecessary Services and Protocols in Windows 2000	400
Exercise 10.3	Controlling SMB Connectivity in Windows 2000	405
Exercise 10.4	Updating Red Hat Linux and Disabling the *cron* and *at* Services	416
Exercise 11.1	Deploying eEye Retina 3.0	468
Exercise 12.1	Using L0phtCrack 3 (LC3) to Crack a Local Windows 2000 SAM Database	490

Exercise 12.2	Using Pwdump3 to Access Remote SAM Databases	493
Exercise 12.3	Using L0phtCrack 3 to Crack a Remote SAM Database	494
Exercise 12.4	Using L0phtCrack 3 to Sniff Passwords	496
Exercise 12.5	Using John the Ripper in Linux	498
Exercise 13.1	Installing Computer Associates' eTrust Intrusion Detection	536
Exercise 13.2	Becoming Familiar with eTrust Intrusion Detection	537
Exercise 13.3	Viewing Host Network Activity in eTrust Intrusion Detection	540
Exercise 13.4	Scanning for eTrust Intrusion Detection Activity on Your Network and Generating a Report	542
Exercise 14.1	Auditing Boot and Login Entries in Windows 2000	579
Exercise 14.2	Enabling Directory Auditing in Windows 2000	580
Exercise 14.3	Using Linux Log-Auditing Tools	582
Exercise 15.1	Installing a Personal Firewall in Windows 2000	604
Exercise 15.2	Installing SSH Server as a Replacement for Telnetd, *rlogind*, and FTP	614
Exercise 15.3	Installing an SSH Client in Windows 2000	616
Exercise 15.4	Using a Windows 2000 SSH Client to Encrypt Transmissions and Authenticate with an SSH Server	616
Exercise 15.5	Transferring Files with the SSH Secure FTP Client	618
Exercise 15.6	Establishing a Trust Relationship between Linux Clients	620
Exercise 15.7	Using Public-Key Encryption to Authenticate a Linux Client	621
Exercise 15.8	Generating a Key Pair in Secure Shell Terminal Client for Windows 2000	623

Introduction

The Prosoft CIW (Certified Internet Webmaster) certification affirms that you have the essential skills to create, run, and update a website. These skills are exactly what employers in today's economy are looking for, and you need to stay ahead of the competition in the current job market. CIW certification will prove to your current or future employer that you are serious about expanding your knowledge base. Obtaining CIW certification will also provide you with valuable skills, including basic networking, web page authoring, internetworking, maintaining security, and website design, and expose you to a variety of vendor products made for web design and implementation.

This book is meant to help you prepare for the Certified Internet Webmaster Security Professional Exam 1D0-470. The Security Professional exam is the final exam for the entire Master CIW Server Administrator track. It covers essential and advanced network security concepts, including how to use strong encryption, secure operating systems, deploy firewalls, and audit networks. It also discusses how to configure intrusion-detection systems and improve a network's security profile. Once you pass the CIW Security Professional exam, you achieve CIW Master Administrator status. With this certificate in hand, you can then approach your duties as a network security analyst and consultant with confidence.

The Certified Internet Webmaster Program

The CIW Internet skills certification program is aimed at professionals who design, develop, administer, secure, and support Internet- or intranet-related services. The CIW certification program offers industry-wide recognition of an individual's Internet and web knowledge and skills, and certification is frequently a factor in hiring and assignment decisions. It also provides tangible evidence of a person's competency as an Internet professional; holders of this certification can demonstrate to potential employers and clients that they have passed rigorous training and examination requirements that set them apart from non-certified competitors. All CIW certifications are endorsed by the International Webmasters Association (IWA) and the Association of Internet Professionals (AIP).

CIW Associate

The first step toward CIW certification is the CIW Foundations exam. A candidate for the CIW Associate certification and the Foundations exam has the basic hands-on skills and knowledge that an Internet professional is expected to understand and use. Foundations skills include basic knowledge of Internet technologies, network infrastructure, and web authoring using HTML.

The CIW Foundations program is designed for all professionals who use the Internet. The job expectations of a CIW Associate, or person who has completed the program and passed the Foundations exam, include:

- Understanding Internet, networking, and web page authoring basics
- Application of Foundations skills required for further specialization

There are a few prerequisites for becoming a CIW Associate. For instance, although you need not have Internet experience in order to start Foundations exam preparation, you should have an understanding of Microsoft Windows.

Table I.1 shows the CIW Foundations exam and the corresponding Sybex Study Guide that covers the CIW Associate certification.

TABLE I.1 The CIW Associate Exam and Corresponding Sybex Study Guide

Exam Name	Exam Number	Sybex Study Guide
Foundations	1D0-410	*CIW: Foundations Study Guide* (ISBN 0-7821-4081-5)

CIW accepts score reports from CIW Associate candidates who have passed the entry-level CompTIA i-Net+ exam (IKO-001) and will award Foundations certification to these individuals. For more information regarding the i-Net+ and other CompTIA exams, visit www.comptia.org.

After passing the Foundations exam, students become CIW Associates and can choose from four Master CIW certification tracks, by selecting a path of interest and passing the required exams:

- Master CIW Designer
- Master CIW Administrator
- CIW Web Site Manager
- Master CIW Enterprise Developer
- CIW Security Analyst

Master CIW Designer

The Master Designer track is composed of two exams, each of which represents a specific aspect of the Internet job role:

- Site Designer
- E-Commerce Designer

Site Designer Exam   The CIW Site Designer applies human-factors principles to designing, implementing, and maintaining hypertext-based publishing sites. The Site Designer uses authoring and scripting languages, as well as digital media tools, plus provides content creation and website management.

E-Commerce Designer Exam   The CIW E-Commerce Designer is tested on e-commerce setup, human-factors principles regarding product selection and payment, and site security and administration.

Table I.2 shows the CIW Site Designer and E-Commerce Designer exams and the corresponding Sybex Study Guide for each of these steps toward the CIW Master Designer certification.

TABLE I.2   The Master Designer Exams and Corresponding Sybex Study Guides

Exam Names	Exam Numbers	Sybex Study Guide
Site Designer	1D0-420	*CIW: Site and E-Commerce Design Study Guide* (ISBN 0-7821-4082-3)
E-Commerce Designer	1D0-425	*CIW: Site and E-Commerce Design Study Guide* (ISBN 0-7821-4082-3)

Master CIW Administrator

The CIW Administrator is proficient in three areas of administration:

- Server
- Internetworking
- Security administration

After passing each test, you become a CIW Professional in that specific area.

Server Administrator Exam   The CIW Server Administrator manages and tunes corporate e-business infrastructure, including web, FTP, news, and mail servers for midsize to large businesses. Server administrators configure, manage, and deploy e-business solutions servers.

Internetworking Professional Exam   The Internetworking Professional defines network architecture, identifies infrastructure components, and monitors and analyzes network performance. The CIW Internetworking Professional is responsible for the design and management of enterprise TCP/IP networks.

Security Professional Exam   The CIW Security Professional implements policy, identifies security threats, and develops countermeasures using firewall systems and attack-recognition technologies. As a CIW Security Professional, you are responsible for managing the deployment of e-business transactions and payment security solutions.

The Exams in the Master Administrator track are listed in Table I.3.

TABLE I.3   The Master Administrator Exams and Corresponding Sybex Study Guides

Exam Names	Exam Numbers	Sybex Study Guide
Server Administrator	1D0-450	*CIW: Server Administrator Study Guide* (ISBN 0-7821-4085-8)
Internetworking Professional	1D0-460	*CIW: Internetworking Professional Study Guide* (ISBN 0-7821-4083-1)
Security Professional	1D0-470	*CIW: Security Professional Study Guide* (ISBN 0-7821-4084-X)

Other CIW Certifications

Prosoft also offers three additional certification series in website management, enterprise development, and security analysis.

Master CIW Web Site Manager   The Web Site Manager certification is composed of two Internet job role series exams (Site Designer 1D0-420 and Server Administrator 1D0-450) and two additional language exams (JavaScript 1D0-435 and Perl Fundamentals 1D0-437 from the CIW Web Languages series).

Master CIW Enterprise Developer   The Enterprise Developer certification is composed of three Internet job role series (Application

Developer 1D0-430, Database Specialist 1D0-441, and Enterprise Specialist 1D0-442) and three additional language/theory series (Web Languages, Java Programming, and Object-Oriented Analysis).

CIW Security Analyst   The Security Analyst certification recognizes those who have already attained a networking certification and demonstrated (by passing the CIW Security Professional 1D0-470 exam) that they have the in-demand security skills to leverage their technical abilities against internal and external cyber threats.

For more information regarding all of Prosoft's certifications and exams, visit **www.ciwcertified.com**.

Special Features in This Book

What makes a Sybex Study Guide the book of choice for over 500,000 certification candidates across numerous technical fields? We take into account not only what you need to know to pass the exam, but what you need to know to apply what you've learned in the real world. Each book contains the following:

Objective Information   Each chapter lists at the outset which CIW objective groups are going to be covered within.

Assessment Test   Directly following this Introduction is an Assessment Test that you can take to help you determine how much you already know about configuring firewalls, securing operating systems, and auditing networks. Each question is tied to a topic discussed in the book. Using the results of the Assessment Test, you can figure out the areas where you need to focus your study. Of course, we do recommend you read the entire book.

Exam Essentials   To review what you've learned, you'll find a list of Exam Essentials at the end of each chapter. The Exam Essentials section briefly highlights the topics that need your particular attention as you prepare for the exam.

Key Terms and Glossary   Throughout each chapter, you will be introduced to important terms and concepts that you will need to know for the exam. These terms appear in italic within the chapters, and a list of the Key Terms appears just after the Exam Essentials. At the end of the book, a detailed glossary gives definitions for these terms, as well as other general terms you should know.

Review Questions, complete with detailed explanations   Each chapter is followed by a set of Review Questions that test what you learned in the chapter. The questions are written with the exam in mind, meaning that they are designed to have the same look and feel of what you'll see on the exam.

Hands-on Exercises   Throughout the book, you'll find exercises designed to give you the important hands-on experience that is critical for your exam preparation. The exercises support the topics of the chapter, and they walk you through the steps necessary to perform a particular function.

Interactive CD   Every Sybex Study Guide comes with a CD complete with additional questions, flashcards for use with a palm device or PC, and a complete electronic version of this book. Details are in the following section.

What's on the CD?

Sybex's *CIW: Security Professional Study Guide* companion CD includes quite an array of training resources and offer numerous test simulations, bonus exams, and flashcards to help you study for the exam. We have also included the complete contents of the study guide in electronic form. The CD's resources are described here:

The Sybex Ebook for the *CIW: Security Professional Study Guide*   Many people like the convenience of being able to carry their whole study guide on a CD. They also like being able to search the text via computer to find specific information quickly and easily. For these reasons, the entire contents of this study guide are supplied on the CD, in PDF format. We've also included Adobe Acrobat Reader, which provides the interface for the PDF contents as well as search capabilities.

The Sybex CIW Edge Tests   The Edge Tests are a collection of multiple-choice questions that will help you prepare for your exam. There are three sets of questions:

- Two bonus exams designed to simulate the actual live exam
- All the Review Questions from the Study Guide, presented in an electronic test engine. You can review questions by chapter or by objective area, or you can take a random test.
- The Assessment Test

Sybex CIW Flashcards for PCs and Palm Devices The "flashcard" style of question offers an effective way to quickly and efficiently test your understanding of the fundamental concepts covered in the exam. The Sybex CIW Flashcards set consists of 150 questions presented in a special engine developed specifically for this study guide series. We have also developed, in conjunction with Land-J Technologies, a version of the flashcard questions that you can take with you on your Palm OS PDA (including the Palm and Visor PDAs).

How to Use This Book

This book provides a solid foundation for the serious effort of preparing for the exam. To best benefit from this book, you may wish to use the following study method:

1. Take the Assessment Test to identify your weak areas.

2. Study each chapter carefully. Do your best to fully understand the information.

3. Study the Exam Essentials and Key Terms to make sure you are familiar with the areas you need to focus on.

4. Answer the review questions at the end of each chapter. If you prefer to answer the questions in a timed and graded format, install the Edge Tests from the book's CD and answer the chapter questions there instead of in the book.

5. Take note of the questions you did not understand, and study the corresponding sections of the book again.

6. Go back over the Exam Essentials and Key Terms.

7. Go through the study guide's other training resources, which are included on the book's CD. These include electronic flashcards, the electronic version of the chapter review questions (try taking them by objective), and the two bonus exams.

To learn all the material covered in this book, you will need to study regularly and with discipline. Try to set aside the same time every day to study, and select a comfortable and quiet place in which to do it. If you work hard, you will be surprised at how quickly you learn this material. Good luck!

Exam Registration

CIW certification exams are administered by Prometric, Inc. through Prometric Testing Centers and by Virtual University Enterprises (VUE) testing centers. You can reach Prometric at (800) 380-EXAM or VUE at (952) 995-8800, to schedule any CIW exam.

You may also register for your exams online at www.prometric.com or www.vue.com.

Exams cost $125 (U.S.) each and must be paid for in advance. Exams must be taken within one year of payment. Candidates can schedule exams up to six weeks in advance or as late as one working day prior to the date of the exam. To cancel or reschedule an exam, contact the center at least two working days prior to the scheduled exam date. Same-day registration is available in some locations, subject to space availability. Where same-day registration is available, registration must occur a minimum of two hours before test time.

When you schedule the exam, the testing center will provide you with instructions regarding appointment and cancellation procedures, ID requirements, and information about the testing center location. In addition, you will receive a registration and payment confirmation letter from Prometric or VUE.

Tips for Taking the CIW Security Professional Exam

Here are some general tips for achieving success on your certification exam:

- Arrive early at the exam center so that you can relax and review your study materials. During this final review, you can look over tables and lists of exam-related information.

- Read the questions carefully. Don't be tempted to jump to an early conclusion. Make sure you know *exactly* what the question is asking.

- For questions you're not sure about, use a process of elimination to get rid of the obviously incorrect answers first. This improves your odds of selecting the correct answer when you need to make an educated guess.

- Mark questions that you aren't sure of and return to them later. Quite often something in a later question will act as a reminder or give you a clue to the correct answer of the earlier one.

Contacts and Resources

Here are some handy websites to keep in mind for future reference:

Prosoft Training and CIW Exam Information	www.CIWcertified.com
Prometric	www.prometric.com
VUE Testing Services	www.vue.com
Sybex Computer Books	www.sybex.com

Assessment Test

1. Which of the following terms describes the time it takes for a server to fulfill a request from a client?

    A. Lag time

    B. Latency

    C. Media verification

    D. Delay

2. Which of the following operating system elements can a host-based IDS application augment?

    A. System authentication

    B. Data confidentiality

    C. System logging

    D. Data integrity

3. During an audit, which of the following can be used to responsibly provide proof of a system compromise?

    A. Web graffiti

    B. Locked-out user accounts

    C. Screen shots of penetrated resources

    D. Creation of user accounts

4. Which type of encryption scrambles text so that it is theoretically not recoverable?

    A. Public-key encryption

    B. Private-key encryption

    C. Symmetric encryption

    D. Hash encryption

5. Which of the following security elements creates perimeter security?

    A. A network vulnerability scanner

    B. An intrusion-detection system

    C. A packet-filtering firewall

    D. A server-based antivirus application

6. Which of the following can automatically detect an intrusion on a Unix system?

    A. Tripwire

    B. Top

    C. A login script

    D. Crond

7. What Windows 2000 element holds the security settings for a particular object, such as a network share?

    A. A security identifier (SID)

    B. An access control list (ACL)

    C. An access token (AT)

    D. A security descriptor (SD)

8. A packet-filtering firewall has been able to detect a port scan, and has stored this information into a database. It has then reconfigured itself to block all connections from the scanning host. What term describes the ability for a packet-filtering firewall to detect port scans?

    A. Packet filtering

    B. Reverse circuit-level proxying

    C. Chaining

    D. Stateful multilayer inspection

9. Serena is using the Pretty Good Privacy (PGP) application. She has just received a public key from a friend and wishes to use it. What must she first do in order to use her friend's public key?

    A. Place it into her e-mail client.

    B. Sign it with her public key.

    C. Use the ODBC applet to register it.

    D. Import the key into her key ring.

10. Which of the following is not a feature provided by personal-firewall software?

    A. Logging of packets sent to the host

    B. Notification of an attack on the host

    C. Notification of low password levels

    D. Blocking of packets sent to the local host

11. What is the benefit of placing the operating system on one partition and the data files on another?

    A. It protects against system bugs and buffer overflows.

    B. It ensures that the operating system files cannot be overwritten.

    C. It ensures that hackers cannot penetrate the system.

    D. It helps contain a security breach.

12. Sandi has been asked to allow all SMTP, POP3, and IMAP traffic to pass from the internal network out to the Internet. She is configuring a proxy server to allow this traffic. The proxy server blocks all traffic unless it is explicitly permitted. Which ports will she have to open?

    A. TCP ports 21, 110, and 143

    B. TCP ports 25, 110, and 143

    C. UDP ports 21, 110, and 143

    D. UDP ports 25, 110, and 143

13. Jason changes his system's `umask` value from 002 to 200 on his Linux system. What permissions will newly created files have?

    A. 664

    B. 400

    C. 466

    D. 477

14. Eric wishes to encrypt transmissions between all of the hosts on his LAN. What can he use to do this?

    A. IPsec

    B. A firewall

    C. Symmetric-key encryption

    D. Public-key encryption

15. Ian is using his web browser to access the following URL: www.goodstuff.com/purchase/niceprogram.exe. However, the purchase directory is protected by an access control list (ACL). What step must take place before Ian is allowed to access the niceprogram.exe file?

    A. He must provide an access token.

    B. He must authenticate.

    C. He must provide a password.

    D. He must activate the execution control list.

16. Which of the following files can you edit without restarting the `xinetd` daemon?

    A. /etc/hosts.deny

    B. /etc/xinetd.conf

    C. /etc/xinetd.d/telnet

    D. /etc/xinetd.d/wu-ftpd

17. Jimmy has just placed a packet-filtering firewall on the other side of the DMZ from the choke router. What is a common name for this packet-filtering firewall element?

A. A circuit-level gateway

B. A proxy server

C. A screening router

D. A subnet firewall

18. What stage involves the hacker's ability to spread to other systems?

    A. Discovery

    B. Penetration

    C. Control

    D. Identification

19. What is another name for a resource in Windows 2000?

    A. A SID

    B. A token

    C. A session key

    D. An object

20. Peter has just gained control of a system. Before he logs off, what will he likely do?

    A. Erase the log file.

    B. Tamper with the log file.

    C. Erase the operating system.

    D. Load a Trojan.

21. Jeff has employed L2TP and PPTP on his firewalls to ensure data privacy. What category do these two items belong to?

    A. PKI protocols

    B. IKE protocols

    C. IPsec protocols

    D. Tunneling protocols

22. Which of the following Windows 2000 snap-ins allows you to add and remove users?

    A. User Manager

    B. User Manager for Domains

    C. Computer Management

    D. Local Security Policy

23. Steven has downloaded, installed, and configured the Tripwire application from www.tripwire.org. Which of the following will this installation allow Steven to accomplish?

    A. Packet traces

    B. Physical-line traces

    C. Retaliation against hackers

    D. Checksum analysis

24. Steve has double-clicked a file he received from a friend as an e-mail attachment. The attachment was a game that he was able to play. However, after playing the game, he discovers that several new files have been created on his hard drive, and he also discovers that any user can now log on to his server and bypass his server's authentication mechanisms. What has occurred?

    A. Steve has been attacked by a root kit.

    B. Steve has ignored his company's security policy.

    C. Steve has been attacked by an illicit server.

    D. Steve has engaged in an unacceptable activity.

25. Which of the following is capable of listening on multiple ports, and can then permanently drop a host from a routing table if the connections are deemed suspicious?

    A. The Windows 2000 login service

    B. telnetd

    C. The Linux login daemon

    D. A port listener

26. Don has used the `tcpdump` application to capture packets and learn his manager's username and password for his e-mail account. What threat category does Don's activity fall into?

    A. Active threat

    B. Passive threat

    C. Social engineering

    D. Brute force

27. You want to become root on a Linux system. What command would you issue?

    A. `su -c root`

    B. `su admin`

    C. `su`

    D. `user root`

28. Which of the following is often used by `xinetd` to control access to the daemons that it starts?

    A. Portmapper

    B. TCPWrappers

    C. A page file

    D. /etc/securenets

29. Which of the following presents a classic case of firewall avoidance?

    A. Social engineering

    B. Brute-force attacks

    C. Dictionary attacks

    D. Physical attacks

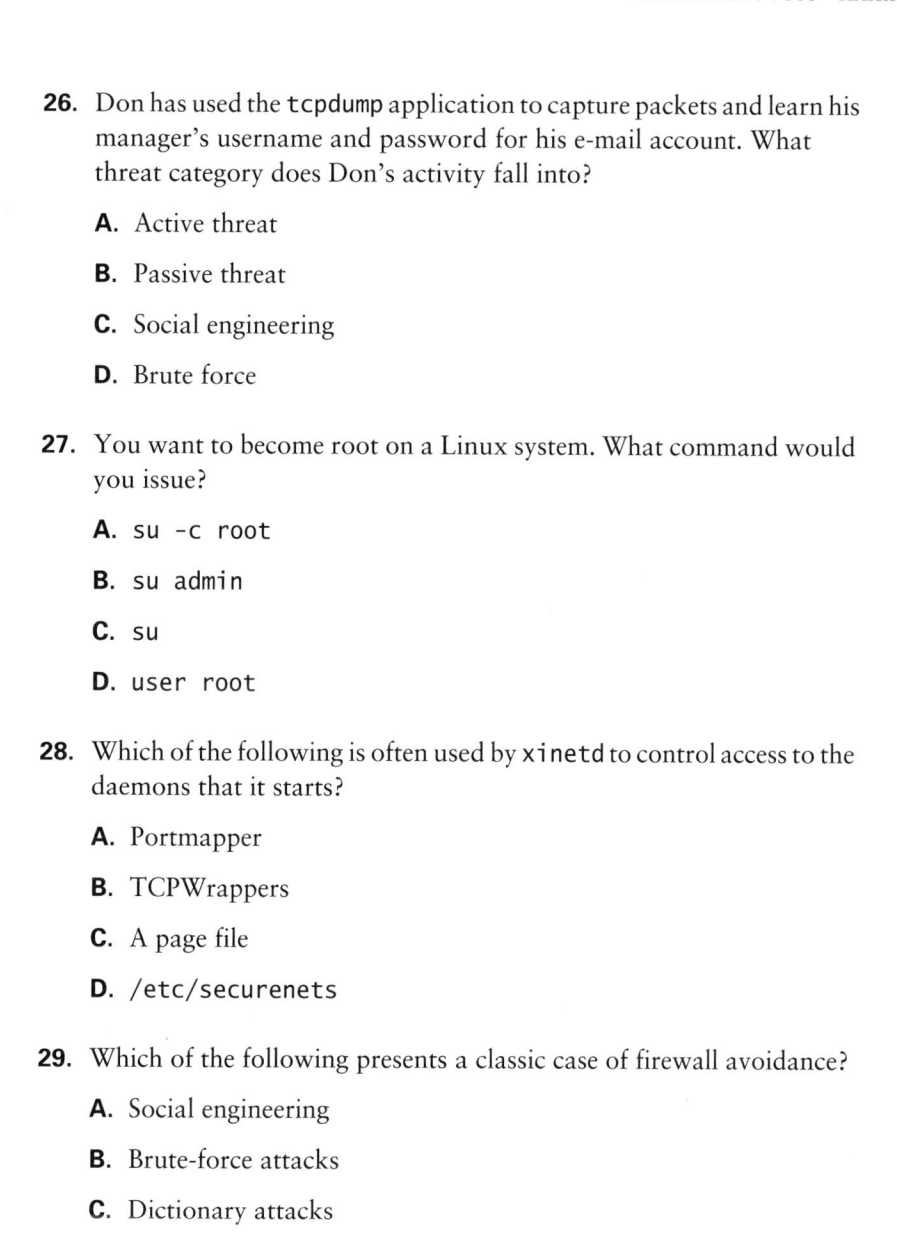

30. Which of the following is a man-in-the-middle attack?

    A. Connection hijacking

    B. Keylogging

    C. Denial-of-service

    D. Spoofing

31. In the `/etc/xinetd.d/telnet` file, Shirley has created the entry
    `only_from = 10.100.100.50`
    What host or hosts are allowed to connect to Shirley's system using FTP?

    A. Only a host with the IP address of 10.100.100.50

    B. Only hosts from the 10.100.100.50 network

    C. All hosts

    D. No hosts

32. Paul has been asked to add the following code to the `/etc/lilo.conf` file on a Linux system:

    ```
    restricted
    password=password
    ```

    Which of the following principles has Paul implemented on this system?

    A. Superzapping

    B. Media verification

    C. Threat minimization

    D. Physical security

33. Robert has deployed a network-based vulnerability scanner. What applications or services are involved in this type of management structure?

    A. Log daemons and port scanners

    B. Ping scanners and port scanners

    C. Trivial IP services and clients

    D. Managers and agents

34. Which of the following attacks exploits traffic at TCP port 53?

    A. ARP poisoning

    B. DNS poisoning

    C. A Teardrop2 attack

    D. A Smurf attack

35. What is another name for a compliance audit?

   A. A risk analysis

   B. A gap analysis

   C. A port scan

   D. A vulnerability scan

36. Which of the following does an IDS application have trouble responding to?

   A. HTTP traffic

   B. E-mail traffic

   C. Denial-of-service traffic

   D. Encrypted traffic

37. A month ago, ago, Mike used the MD5SUM application to create a signature of the /etc/shadow file on his Linux system. He has just used MD5SUM again to compare the original signature, and he has noticed that the values are different. What problem does this indicate?

   A. The system has been compromised.

   B. The /etc/shadow file has been altered.

   C. The /etc/shadow file is corrupted.

   D. The application is not functioning.

38. Which of the following can be caused by a host-based IDS application?

   A. System latency

   B. Network latency

   C. Increased login traffic

   D. Firewall crashes

39. Amanda wants to configure her system to accept connections from remote logging daemons. Her server will store the log files for three remote systems. She wants to create an entry in her Linux system's syslogd configuration file. Which of the following options allows her to configure her logging daemon to accept connections?

A. -l

B. -r

C. -x

D. -s

40. Which of the following is the first security element to look for when securing a network?

A. A security policy

B. A firewall

C. A security matrix

D. Physical security

41. Which of the following is an element of an IT-level report?

A. Brief recommendations concerning defensive strategies

B. A brief analysis of upward and downward trends in the network's security

C. A brief overview of basic terms used in the report

D. Brief instructions on how to solve the problem you have found

42. Which of the following will greatly enhance the usefulness of log files on your Windows 2000 systems?

A. Regularly purging log files

B. Scheduling a regular review time

C. Capturing only application-log traffic

D. Capturing only security-log traffic

43. Which of the following allows a user to use SSH to connect to a remote system named rogers.dentist.com as the user named steve?

A. /usr/local/bin/ssh -l steve rogers.dentist.com

B. /usr/local/bin/ssh rogers.dentist.com -l steve

C. /usr/local/bin/ssh rogers.dentist.com steve

D. /usr/local/bin/ssh -l rogers.dentist.com steve

44. Which of the following symmetric-key algorithms was chosen by the United States to become the Advanced Encryption Standard (AES)?

   A. Twofish

   B. Rijndael

   C. RC5

   D. MARS

45. You suspect that several users are attempting a buffer overflow attack on your Windows 2000 web server. This attack is designed to crash your web server. You are using the web server provided by IIS, so you open Windows 2000 Event Viewer to learn more about the attack. Which of the following log files will give you information about service failures for this system?

   A. Application

   B. Security

   C. System

   D. DNS Server

Answers to Assessment Test

1. **B.** Whenever a client asks a server to fulfill a request, the server takes a certain period of time to fulfill it. This period of time is described by the term *latency*. Security applications can increase latency, due to the checks and restrictions that they impose on the server or client. For more information, see Chapter 4.

2. **C.** An IDS application can augment a system's ability to log connections. This is especially the case with host-based IDS applications. An IDS application has no direct impact on the ability to keep data secret (data confidentiality) or unchanged (data integrity). Furthermore, it cannot enhance a system's ability to authenticate users. For more information, see Chapter 13.

3. **C.** It is always necessary to show proof of an audit. However, you should try not to change system settings. Thus, locking out user accounts, changing web pages, and adding user accounts may not be the best methods. However, showing a screen shot of a desktop may help prove to management and IT professionals that security needs to be upgraded. For more information, see Chapter 12.

4. **D.** Hash encryption can take a piece of text and encrypt it so that it is not recoverable. Hash encryption is highly dependent on the contents of the file that it encrypts. For more information, see Chapter 1.

5. **C.** A firewall is the primary means of enforcing perimeter security. It helps you implement your security policy. Network scanners and anti-virus applications are all important, but they address security issues related to individual hosts inside the network perimeter. Likewise, an intrusion-detection system detects and deters attacks that take place on the internal network and generally do not implement a network perimeter. For more information, see Chapter 5.

6. **A.** Tripwire is a series of scripts designed to scan for any and all changes to an operating system. It can detect the files that have been altered and then send you a report. For more information, see Chapter 7.

7. **D.** Every object within Windows 2000 has a security descriptor as part of its properties. The security descriptor holds that object's security settings. The security descriptor consists of the object owner SID, a group SID for use by the POSIX subsystem, a discretionary access control list, and a system access control list. For more information, see Chapter 8.

8. **D.** Stateful multilayer inspection describes the ability to examine packets in context and then determine that they are part of a continuing connection. Blocking packets is not part of stateful inspection but is a viable firewalling option. For more information, see Chapter 5.

9. **D.** Before you can use a public key in the PGP application, you must first import it into the application's key ring. For more information, see Chapter 2.

10. **C.** Personal-firewall software is not designed to notify users that a workstation's password level is low. However, this type of firewall can log packets, notify the administrator that a port scan is under way, and block connections. For more information, see Chapter 15.

11. **D.** Separating operating system and data files helps ensure that a hacker cannot easily move from one system element to another. Thus, it helps contain a security breach. This strategy does not do anything to protect against system bugs and buffer overflows, nor does it ensure that operating system files remain completely safe. Nevertheless, it does help make the operating system more stable, and can help slow down a hacker's progress through your system. For more information, see Chapter 9.

12. **B.** The e-mail server ports discussed in the question all use TCP. SMTP uses TCP port 25, POP3 uses TCP port 110, and IMAP uses TCP port 143. When taking the CIW Security Professional exam, you should have a good understanding of ports used by popular servers. Also, notice that the proxy server has been configured to block all traffic except for that which is explicitly allowed. As a result, clients will not be allowed to open ephemeral ports (i.e., ports above 1023) to hosts outside the firewall. Thus, Sandi will have to open the ephemeral ports. This specific question doesn't ask you for this information, but keep that fact in mind. For more information, see Chapter 5.

13. **C.** The umask command determines the value of files created on a Linux/Unix system. The umask value is subtracted from the value of 666. For more information, see Chapter 9.

14. **A.** IPsec is an add-on to IPv4, the current version of IP. It enables hosts to automatically encrypt transmissions using symmetric- and public-key encryption. Thus, IPsec is the more correct answer. A firewall does not encrypt transmissions on a LAN. It can, however, form a VPN, which enables one LAN to encrypt transmissions to another. For more information, see Chapter 6.

15. B. Before an access control list or execution control list can be consulted and acted on, authentication must take place. For more information, see Chapter 1.

16. A. `xinetd` automatically reads the contents of both the `/etc/hosts.allow` and `/etc/hosts.deny` files upon each connection. A restart is not necessary if changes are made to these files. For more information, see Chapter 10.

17. C. A screening router is a packet filter that resides between the public network and other firewall elements. For more information, see Chapter 6.

18. C. Whenever a hacker is able to spread to other systems, he or she has already entered the control stage. For more information, see Chapter 11.

19. D. Windows 2000 refers to all resources as objects. Doing so enables Windows to consistently apply policies across the entire operating system, as well as across multiple machines. Microsoft 2000 and XP systems use domains to control multiple machines across a LAN or WAN. The CIW Security Professional exam spends little time discussing domains. However, it is important to understand that in a Windows NT/2000 system, domain-wide settings often take precedence over local settings. For more information, see Chapter 8.

20. B. Most skilled hackers will try to do everything they can to hide evidence that they have control of a system. One way to do this is to erase evidence of the login from the system logs. Completely erasing the log file can alert a systems administrator that a breach has occurred. Erasing the operating system would constitute a rather unlikely denial-of-service attack. A hacker may launch a Trojan upon logout, but the priority is to erase all evidence of penetration and control. For more information, see Chapter 12.

21. D. L2TP and PPTP are tunneling protocols. They encrypt various protocols (TCP/IP and NetBEUI, among others) so that data remains confidential. They are not IPsec protocols, which include the Internet Key Exchange (IKE) and OAKLEY protocols. PKI involves the use of certificates, not protocols. For more information, see Chapter 6.

22. C. The Computer Management snap-in provides an interface to the Local Users and Groups utility. Using this utility, it is possible to add and remove users and groups. It is also possible to change the password using this utility. For more information, see Chapter 9.

23. D. The Tripwire application creates signatures, or checksums, that systems administrators can then analyze. Tripwire does not enable a packet trace; it only informs you when the file was changed. It does not truly enable physical-line traces, because Tripwire reports may not be generated until after the connection has ended. Finally, Tripwire is not capable of retaliating against hackers. For more information, see Chapter 7.

24. C. An illicit server is capable of allowing a client to bypass a system's authentication and access control measures and take control of the system. A classic e-mail virus does not allow the user to take control of the system, in the sense that the malicious user has the ability to obtain valuable data and competely compromise the system. Rather, it simply exploits messaging elements of an end user's operating system and uses it as a platform to stage or continue the attack. As far as security policies are concerned, the scenario does not give enough information concerning the security policy at Steve's place of work in order to determine whether or not he violated any of its rules. For more information, see Chapter 1.

25. D. A port listener is an application, service, or daemon that is capable of listening for connections to various ports on the system. A port listener can be configured to automatically add a host to a database of hosts that will not be allowed to connect to the system again. The Windows 2000 and Linux login daemons do not listen on multiple ports, nor can they permanently drop a connection, unless a great deal of customization is involved. Likewise, `telnetd` cannot permanently drop suspicious connections. For more information, see Chapter 7.

26. B. Network sniffing is categorized as a passive threat. Instead of obtaining and altering packets, or trying to actively defeat an authentication mechanism by repeatedly logging on, Don is simply eavesdropping on connections and passively gathering information. For more information, see Chapter 3.

27. C. Without arguments, the `su` command is used to allow a user to become root. It is also possible for the `su` command to take arguments. For example, the following command would allow any user (for example, root or non-root user) to become the user named james: `su james`. Additional arguments to `su` exist. For instance, if you wanted to become root simply to issue one command, you could use the `-c` option. For example, the command `"su -c /etc/rc.d/init.d /httpd restart"` allows the user named james to assume root permissions and start Apache Server. For more information, see Chapter 8.

28. B. The TCPWrappers package enables `xinetd` to control connections to any daemon that it launches. The Portmapper daemon is not related to `xinetd`, although it is used to handle requests from applications and daemons on remote hosts. A page file is a Windows 2000 term referring to virtual memory, whereas the `/etc/securenets` file is used to control connections to NIS servers. For more information, see Chapter 10.

29. A. Most hackers will try to find a way to avoid a firewall, rather than trying to defeat it. Social engineering presents an attractive alternative, because it enables the hacker to gain information and enter the network without having to attack a formidable resource, such as a firewall. For more information, see Chapter 12.

30. A. Active man-in-the-middle attacks include connection hijacking. Keylogging is not a man-in-the-middle attack, because it does not involve manipulating packets as they cross over a network. Denial-of-service attacks only send packets across the network; this type of attack does listen in on connections. Although spoofing attacks involve the creation of bogus packets on the network, they do not involve actually capturing and manipulating packets. For more information, see Chapter 3.

31. C. The `only_from` entry has been added to the `/etc/xinetd.d/telnet` file, and thus it does not apply to FTP connections. If users on remote hosts were to use Telnet clients to connect to Shirley's system, then only a host with the IP address of 10.100.100.50 would be able to connect to her system. For more information, see Chapter 10.

32. D. The entries discussed in this question invoke access control for a Linux system so that individuals cannot easily access the Linux single-user mode. Linux single-user mode activates the operating system, but only at a low level. Networking is not enabled, for example. Because single-user mode is accessible only by physical means, Paul is protecting this server against a physical attack. For more information, see Chapter 4.

33. D. Network-based vulnerability scanners use both managers and agents. It is very important to understand that networks will have various management structures already in place. These structures apply not only to vulnerability scanners, but also to an intrusion-detection system (IDS). For more information, see Chapter 11.

Answers to Assessment Test

34. B. DNS servers use TCP port 53 to conduct zone transfers. DNS poisoning is the activity of injecting packets into a zone transfer that is taking place. The result is that the slave server contains bogus DNS information for that particular zone. For more information, see Chapter 3.

35. B. A gap analysis, or compliance audit, enables the auditor to determine the difference between actual employee practice and the practices mandated by the security policy. For more information, see Chapter 11.

36. D. An IDS application can sniff encrypted traffic, but it cannot respond to it properly. If the traffic is encrypted, the IDS application will not be able to read it and match it to its signature database. As long as traffic is not encrypted or otherwise masked, an IDS application can read and respond to various types of traffic, including denial-of-service, HTTP, and FTP traffic. For more information, see Chapter 13.

37. B. The MD5SUM application uses the MD5 hash algorithm to generate signatures for files. Like all hash algorithms, MD5 generates values that are highly dependent on the contents of the file. If a signature has changed, this means that the contents of the file have changed, as well. The /etc/shadow file contains a list of encrypted passwords for the system. Even though a change has occurred to the file, you do not have enough evidence to justify thinking that the system has been compromised or that the file is corrupted. It very easily could be that a legitimate user has been added. For more information, see Chapter 2.

38. B. Host-based applications rarely cause significant latency problems for the system they reside on. However, they can cause network latency problems if multiple agents residing across a slow WAN link detect and act on an attack. Consider what would happen if 100 agents all respond to a port-scanning attack by sending pages, e-mails, and Windows "pop-up" alerts to a system across the slow WAN link. All of this activity could cause enough network traffic to affect other traffic. It is unlikely that manager/agent traffic will cause a firewall to crash. For more information, see Chapter 13.

39. B. The -r option instructs the Linux syslogd daemon to accept remote connections. The -l option allows you to log connections by simple hostname and not the fully qualified domain name (FQDN). The -x option disables name lookups, and the -s option allows domain names to be stripped off logging information. For more information, see Chapter 14.

40. A. A security policy is the first thing to check for when securing a network. It is also the first tool to consult when a security breach occurs. For more information, see Chapter 4.

41. D. An IT-level report will contain brief instructions on how to solve the problem you have found. It will also contain detailed information about the nature of the problem, including the name of the server, its IP address, and a list of the vulnerabilities found. Generally, the IT department is not interested in learning the overall defensive strategies; its job is to implement specific changes in the servers it administers. For more information, see Chapter 15.

42. B. Log files are useful only if they are analyzed. Thus, scheduling a regular review time is essential for ensuring that log files remain useful. It is often necessary to purge log files from a system to ensure that they do not occupy too much hard drive space or otherwise hinder system performance. However, the log files should be purged only after they have been read. Capturing only certain types of traffic may make sense for certain servers, depending on how they are used. However, not enough information is given in this question to warrant choosing only one log traffic type. For more information, see Chapter 14.

43. A. The syntax for using SSH is as follows: `/usr/local/bin/ssh2 -l username hostname`. You cannot change this syntax. The `-l` option allows you to specify a username. This option is useful, because it allows you to log onto a remote system under a different account than the one you are using on the local system. For more information, see Chapter 15.

44. B. The NIST, a standard body for the U.S. government, chose *Rijndael* as the official symmetric algorithm for AES. You can learn more about Rijndael/AES, as well as the reasons for its adoption, at `http://csrc.nist.gov/encryption/aes`. For more information, see Chapter 2.

45. C. The log file that would most plausibly contain evidence of a server crash is the System log. It contains entries generated by various system services. The Application log contains entries generated by applications that access system resources. The Security log file contains entries on successful and failed login types, but not about server crashes. The DNS Server log contains information relevant to the DNS server. For more information, see Chapter 14.

Chapter 1

What Is Security?

THE CIW EXAM OBJECTIVE GROUPS COVERED IN THIS CHAPTER:

- ✓ Define the significance of network security, and identify various elements of an effective security policy, including but not limited to: risk factors, security-related organizations, key resources to secure, general security threat types, access control.

So much has been written about network security and network intrusions, yet one question never seems to get answered: What is it about the Internet that allows so many attacks to take place? Several technical explanations exist. However, the creators of the CIW Security Professional exam have found that the chief reason is that the Internet, which includes the World Wide Web and many other networks and services, was originally designed as an *open network*. An open network is a group of clients and servers that can freely access each other using protocols such as the Transmission Control Protocol/Internet Protocol (TCP/IP).

In the beginning, it was something of a challenge for military and academic engineers to get the Internet up and running. They met this challenge head on, creating hardware and protocols that are *scalable* and reliable and have remained fundamentally the same for 20 years. For example, the parameters for TCP, as found in Request for Comment (RFC) 793, have remained largely unchanged since 1981. When this protocol was created, the developers were happy that it worked so well. Little or no effort was given to ensuring privacy or identity verification.

With the advent of corporate acceptance of the Internet, its open nature has introduced several challenges. Because TCP/IP has little or no built-in capacity for securing information, users of the Internet can send messages to each other without first verifying their identity. Servers can participate on the network even though they have not been configured for optimal security. These examples of easy access have made it possible for abuses to take place. Relatively simple programs, written by individuals with little or no formal training, have been used to attack e-mail and web servers. These applications, often called viruses, have been unleashed on the Internet and have caused serious damage. Malicious users, often called "hackers," have written and disseminated code specially designed to exploit vulnerable servers, including those created by Microsoft, Sun, and all Linux vendors.

Notable achievements have been made in securing systems. Today, it is much easier to scramble network transmissions through encryption. It's much easier to verify a user's identity. It's also easier to isolate networks and control what comes in and out of them. Nevertheless, changing the fundamentally open nature of the Internet remains somewhat of a struggle.

In spite of the difficulty, businesses and individuals still want to use the Internet. They want to use it to transmit sensitive information and communicate quickly. This has introduced a new challenge: Protect sensitive data and allow only authorized personnel to use Internet-enabled systems, but make such use as easy as possible. In this chapter, we will discuss security on the Internet, as well as security standards and mechanisms that can help you secure network transactions.

Defining Security

Security in an open networking environment is the ability to do two things:

- Differentiate your LAN or WAN from other networks.
- Identify and then eliminate threats and vulnerabilities.

It is a security professional's job to ensure the above two duties are properly carried out. Remember these two duties as you safeguard organizational assets.

Complete Security Is a Myth

There is no such thing as a system that is completely secure. *Connectivity* always implies risk. If you allow legitimate users to access your computers or networks, whether from a local or remote location, the opportunity exists for abuse. One popular saying is that the only secure computer is one that has been disconnected from the network, shut off, and locked in a safe. Although this solution secures the computer from intrusions, it also defeats the purpose for having a networked computer in the first place.

Although you can never reach a point of complete security, you can achieve a level that prevents all but the most determined and skilled hackers from accessing your system. Proper security techniques can minimize the negative effects of hacker activity on your organization. They can deter even the most determined hacker. Regarding Internet security, you can usually restrict legitimate user accounts just enough so users can accomplish their tasks but have no more access than necessary. The result of this simple measure is that even if a hacker can steal a legitimate user's identity and enter the system, the hacker will be able to gain only the level of access authorized for that user. Such a restriction will confine any possible damage that the hacker might cause using the stolen username and password.

Security as Balance

A key security principle is to use solutions that are effective but that do not burden legitimate users who want access to needed information. It is quite easy to employ security techniques that become so onerous that legitimate users disregard—or even circumvent—your security protocols. For example, a security policy that requires users to change their password each week might cause them to write down their passwords and leave them in accessible places (such as under their keyboards or in the traditional sticky note on a monitor). Hackers are always ready to capitalize on such seemingly innocent activity. Thus, having an overzealous security policy could result in less effective security than if you had no security policy at all. Always consider the effect that your security policy will have on legitimate users. In most cases, if the effort required by your users is greater than the resulting increase in security, your policy will actually reduce your company's effective level of security.

"White Hat" and "Black Hat" Hackers

The term *hacker* originated from a term given to a gifted programmer who was able to put, or "hack," together an application to solve a problem. These days, a hacker is most often defined as someone who illegally scans and penetrates a computer network to access and manipulate data. Some security professionals make the distinction between a "hacker," who is supposed to be a skilled user, and a "cracker," who is a malicious user. With one exception, the CIW exam generally uses the term hacker to refer to a malicious user. The exception is as follows: The CIW exam makes the distinction between *white hat hackers* (i.e., "good guys") and *black hat hackers* (sometimes called "crackers"). A white hat hacker is a person who is specifically employed to test a computer network's security. A black hat hacker is a person who breaks into a system without warning to take advantage of your systems and gain information. In either case, a hacker's ultimate goal is to discover and take advantage of information stored on a network.

Understanding Black Hat Hackers

Two types of black hat hackers exist. The *casual hacker* is a person who is simply curious, or is a cyberspace "thrill seeker" who enters a system "because it's there." The casual hacker category can be further broken down into two subcategories. Skilled casual hackers are able to create their own custom applications to take advantage of a vulnerability they discover. Other casual attackers are less experienced. These types of users are often called "script kiddies," because they rely on the work of others to exploit a vulnerability. This type of hacker will often leave behind traces of his or her activity.

It is important to understand that all modern network operating systems keep log files that track user logins. Experienced attackers will modify the log files, if possible, to eliminate any trace of activity. However, some attackers intentionally leave behind evidence of an attack. Examples of this type of activity include web graffiti, which is where the legitimate contents of a web site are replaced with images and other files of the hacker's own choosing. Hackers often leave behind web graffiti as an attempt to demonstrate their supposed skill.

The second type of black hat hacker is the *determined hacker*. This type of hacker is bent on attacking your network, often due to financial or ideological motivation, and often employs sophisticated techniques so that the attack cannot be traced. Such stealth makes the determined attacker quite difficult to catch. A determined attacker usually has enough skill and resources to penetrate unless you take extreme measures that can greatly inconvenience you and your employees. One example of a determined hacker is the corporate spy, who can devote enough time and money so that eventually, your system will likely be compromised unless you take extremely expensive countermeasures. Determined hackers are capable of taking advantage of improperly configured systems, as well as flaws in the services run by these systems. They can also take advantage of careless employees who can unwittingly provide sensitive information. Determined hackers can also apply for a job with that company and obtain inside access.

Protecting Resources

Now that you understand the nature of open networks, as well as the types of hackers, it is important to know how the CIW Security Professional exam categorizes resources:

End-user resources   Includes client workstations and their associated peripherals. Employees remain largely unaware of the hazards involved in double-clicking attachments from e-mails apparently sent from friends, for example. Still others have not enabled password-protected screensavers to prevent people from mapping the contents of a system's hard drive while the employee is out of the office for even short periods of time. This hacker activity is often known as system snooping. If left unsecured, this type of resource can become a platform where an illicit user can stage an attack on other systems.

Network resources   Routers, switches, hubs, wiring closets, and the wiring in the walls all count as network resources. If a hacker obtains control of these resources, then your network is no longer under your control. A hacker can obtain control of these resources either by logging into them remotely or by physically tampering with them. Once a hacker is able to compromise an unlocked wiring closet, he or she can begin taking control of your network.

Server resources   Your World Wide Web, e-mail, and File Transfer Protocol (FTP) servers are vulnerable to attacks designed to crash the server so that its services are unavailable. As with end-user resources, server resources become a target because compromising one of these resources often allows hackers to move on and control other resources.

Information storage resources   A database server often stores the most important information in a network—information that hackers prize highly. A database can contain credit card numbers, human resources information, and sensitive invoice information.

Security Standards

You have now identified what security means on the CIW Security Professional exam, and you have identified the resources that commonly need to be secured. The CIW Security Professional exam requires that you understand the terminology, or nomenclature, used in these documents.

ISO 7498-2

The International Organization for Standardization (ISO) 7498-2 Security Architecture document defines *security* as minimizing the vulnerabilities of assets and resources. An *asset* is defined as anything of value. A *vulnerability* is any exploitable weakness that allows entry. A *threat* is a potential security violation.

ISO further classifies threats as either accidental or intentional, and either active or passive. Accidental threats are those that exist with no premeditated intent. Such threats as natural disasters, as well as system malfunctions, fall within this group. Intentional threats range from the casual examination of computer or network data to sophisticated attacks using special system knowledge. Passive threats do not modify information contained in the systems; neither the operation nor the state of the system is changed. Alteration of information or changes to the system's state or operation is considered an active threat to the system. The ISO 7498-2 document defines several security services, as summarized in Table 1.1.

TABLE 1.1 Security Services

Service	Purpose
Authentication	Authentication is the process of proving a person's or server's identity.
Access control	This process determines which system resources a user or service can use, view, or change. Once a user is authenticated, access control occurs.
Data confidentiality	This service protects data from unauthorized disclosure, usually through encryption. Data confidentiality protects from passive threats, which include users who read data from the network wire using a *packet sniffer*.

TABLE 1.1 Security Services *(continued)*

Service	Purpose
Data integrity	Data integrity services protect against active threats (such as altering data) by verifying or maintaining the consistency of information.
Non-repudiation	Repudiation is the ability to deny participation in all or part of a transaction. In networking, one can repudiate an e-mail message or a piece of data, such as a traceroute ping packet or SYN packet, by saying "I did not send that." Non-repudiation services provide proof of origin and/or proof of delivery concerning any service, process, or piece of information.

Security mechanisms are used to implement security systems. Two forms of mechanisms exist: specific and wide. A *specific* mechanism applies to levels of the Operating Systems Interconnection Reference Model (OSI/RM), as well as to protocols used on the Internet. A *wide* mechanism applies to entire applications and operating systems.

Specific Security Mechanisms

During network communication, certain techniques can be implemented to provide security. Security mechanisms include:

Encipherment   Encrypts the data moving among systems on a network (or between two processes on a local host).

Digital signature mechanisms   Very much like encryption, but with the added advantage that a third party has verified that the sender and the contents are authentic. Unlike with simple encryption mechanisms, a third party verifies the transaction.

Access control   Simple checks to ensure that the sender or receiver is authorized to carry out a task or procedure. For example, network access may be allowed for prequalified users when logging on remotely.

Data integrity   Techniques to ensure that each data piece (such as several parts of a transaction being sent over a network) is sequenced, numbered, and time-stamped.

Authentication Can include simple or complex operating system and network password schemes. Authentication can be used for individual applications, too, requiring each access to be authenticated and reducing the chances for global access if unauthorized entry is gained.

Traffic padding Additions to the network packets flowing in and out, to prevent network watchers from exploiting their knowledge about packet sizes and trends to gain access. To illustrate, when a new login session is established, certain known packet sizes are transmitted and received at the beginning of the session. Analysis of the headers can alert these network watchers to capture the next few packets (due to their small size and the presence of certain fields in the headers). Padding can make all packets look the same size, so one can avoid being singled out for analysis.

Wide Security Mechanisms

Other mechanisms are not limited to any specific layers or levels. These mechanisms are as follows:

Trusted functionality A procedure that establishes that certain services or hosts are secure in all aspects and can be trusted. This can be a piece of software or other operating system add-on that strengthens an existing mechanism.

Security labels Can be applied to indicate the data's level of sensitivity. Security labels are used in addition to other measures. For example, a file may get an additional label, besides the read/write privilege, that allows access only to those who log on with account levels matching or exceeding those of that label.

Audit trails Usually employed at various levels and monitored for exceptions to facilitate intrusion detection and security violations. For example, daily examination of the Linux system file log to search for patterns of text may point to attempts to access certain accounts.

Security recovery A set of rules to apply when dealing with a security event.

ITSEC Document BS 7799

In Europe, the Information Technology Security Evaluation Criteria (ITSEC) document British Standard (BS) 7799 outlines network threats and various *controls* you can implement to reduce the likelihood of a crippling attack. It defines *vulnerability* as something for which the systems administrator is responsible. It characterizes a *threat* as something over which you have little control. The BS 7799 document was rewritten in 1999 and details the following procedures that you can implement:

- Auditing processes
- Auditing file systems
- Assessing risks
- Maintaining virus controls
- Properly managing IT information in regard to daily business and security issues

Additional concerns include e-commerce, legal issues, and reporting methods.

> **NOTE** For more information on ITSEC, visit www.cesg.gov.uk/assurance/iacs/itsec/index.htm.

Trusted Computer Systems Evaluation Criteria (TCSEC)

In the United States, the National Computer Security Center (NCSC) is responsible for establishing the security criteria for trusted computer products. The NCSC created the Trusted Computer Systems Evaluation Criteria (TCSEC), Department of Defense (DoD) Standard 5200.28, for establishing trust levels. The criteria, which are intended to indicate a system's potential security capabilities, consist of security functionality and effectiveness. This standard has been known as the "Orange book," because it once shipped in a book with an orange cover.

TCSEC designates several security ratings, called *security levels*, which range from Level A to Level D, with Level A being the highest. Levels A, B, and C have numeric sublevels. For example, Level A has A1 and so forth; Level B has B1, B2, and B3; and Level C has C1 and C2. See Table 1.2.

TABLE 1.2 TCSEC Security Levels

Security Level	Description
D	No inherent security. A classic example is an MS-DOS system.
C1	Discretionary security protection. At this level, the system need not differentiate between users. It can provide rudimentary access control. An example of this level might be a small departmental desktop publishing system, with files for common use and an area for individual use.
C2	Discretionary access security. At this level, the system does differentiate between users but treats them uniquely. System-level protection exists for resources, data, files, and processes. Certain implementations of Windows 2000 and Linux can be made C2-compliant.
B1	Labeled security protection. At this level, the system provides more protection, such as varied security levels. Also, mandatory access controls beyond those levels place resources in compartments, isolating users in cells and thus offering further protection. An example is AT&T System V, which is a precursor to Solaris.
B2	Structured protection. This level supports hardware protection. Memory areas are virtually segmented and rigidly protected. Examples are Trusted XENIX and Honeywell MULTICS.
B3	Security domains. This level offers data hiding and layering, preventing all interaction between layers. An example is Honeywell Federal Systems XTS-200.
A1	Verified design. This level requires rigorous mathematical proof that the system cannot be compromised and provides all the features listed in lower levels. An example is Honeywell SCOMP.

Level C is often implemented in commercial environments. It requires that owners of data must be capable of determining who can access the data, a privilege called *discretionary access control*:

- Level C1 requires users to log on and allows group IDs.
- Level C2 requires individual users to log on to the network with a password and requires an audit mechanism.

TCSEC is similar to ITSEC. However, ITSEC rates functionality (F) and effectiveness (E) separately. The TCSEC Level C2 is equivalent to the ITSEC Level F-C2, E2.

Level C2 and F-C2, E2 Requirements

The key requirements for C2 and F-C2, E2 classification are that a system have certain aspects of discretionary access control, object reuse, identification and authentication, and auditing.

Discretionary access control This term means that the owner of a resource must be able to control access to that resource.

Object reuse The operating system must control object reuse. Therefore, any time a program or process uses an object, such as memory, that was previously used by another program or process, the object's previous contents cannot be determined by that object's new user. The criteria require object control in the disk, monitor, keyboard, mouse, and all other devices attached to the system.

Identification and authentication The criteria require that each user be uniquely identified to the operating system and that the operating system be able to track all that user's activities by the identification.

Auditing The final major requirement of C2/F-C2, E2 status is that the systems administrators be able to audit all security-related events and individual users' actions. Furthermore, the auditing data must be accessible only to the systems administrators.

> **NOTE** You can obtain a copy of the National Computer Security Center publication "Department of Defense Trusted Computer System Evaluation Criteria," which defines the evaluation process in complete detail, at www.radium.ncsc.mil.

Common Criteria (CC)

The *Common Criteria* (CC) is a standard that unifies the various regional and national security criteria, such as the ITSEC and TCSEC, into one document standardized by ISO. The CC is currently ISO International Standard (IS) 15408, which is ISO's version of the CC 2.1. The two documents are technically identical.

The CC specifies and evaluates the security features of computer products and systems. The first internationally accepted standard for IT security, it is based on the ITSEC and TCSEC documents, and is intended to replace them as a worldwide standard.

The CC provides two basic functions:

- A standardized way to describe security requirements, such as security needs, the products and systems to fulfill those needs, and the analysis and testing of those products and systems.

- A reliable technical basis for evaluating the security features of products and systems.

Key Common Criteria Concepts

Three concepts are essential for understanding the CC. The concepts are largely used for communication and process purposes in determining the correct security product and system for a given situation.

Protection Profile (PP) A document created by IT administrators, users, product developers, and other parties that defines a specific set of security needs. The PP document communicates the needs to the manufacturer.

Security Target (ST) A statement from the manufacturer that describes the security an IT product or system can provide. It contains product-specific information that explains how the particular product or system meets the needs of the PP.

Target of Evaluation (TOE) The IT product or system to be evaluated. The product must be evaluated using the specific security requirements listed in the PP and ST documents. To comply with the CC, the product must be analyzed and tested by an accredited third party.

NOTE Download the latest CC standard at the Computer Security Resource Clearinghouse at http://csrc.nist.gov/cc, or visit the ISO at www.iso.ch.

The Health Insurance Portability and Accountability Act (HIPAA)

The Health Insurance Portability and Accountability Act (HIPAA) was passed by the U.S. government in 1996. A mandatory set of regulations for all health care organizations (hospitals, clinics, and so forth), it is intended to ensure confidentiality for all patient records. While not technically a standard, the HIPAA requires that health care providers take sufficient measures to control access to information. Many different ways exist to implement HIPAA regulations, including the use of standards and practices previously discussed. The CIW Security Professional exam may require you to understand the following facts about the HIPAA:

- Specific HIPAA rules: The HIPAA created several rules, including the Transactions and Privacy Rules.

- Rule time limits: Whenever a HIPAA rule is published, it becomes an effective rule after 60 days. After a rule becomes effective, a health care facility must implement this rule within 24 months. For example, the Privacy Rule was published on December 28, 2000, but because of an administrative problem on the part of the Health Care Financing Administration, who oversees the HIPAA, it did not become effective until April 14, 2001. Thus, a health care facility will not need to adhere to this rule until April 14, 2003.

- HIPAA-compliant standard code sets: All organizations must adopt a single terminology and coding system when discussing injuries, accidents, diseases, and other medical issues regarding a patient.

To learn more about the HIPAA, you can consult the following websites:

- HIPAA.org (www.hipaa.org)
- The Health Care Financing Administration (www.hcfa.gov/medicaid/hipaa/content/more.asp)

NOTE Many different security organizations exist, but the most respected are the Computer Emergency Response Team (www.cert.org) and the System Administration, Networking, and Security (SANS) Institute (www.sans.org).

Practical Security Elements

Now that you understand some of the concepts and terminology used in the security industry, it is time to learn more about how to implement them in a practical way. Figure 1.1 provides a representation of the most important security elements. It also shows the hierarchy into which these elements are organized.

FIGURE 1.1 Elements of effective security

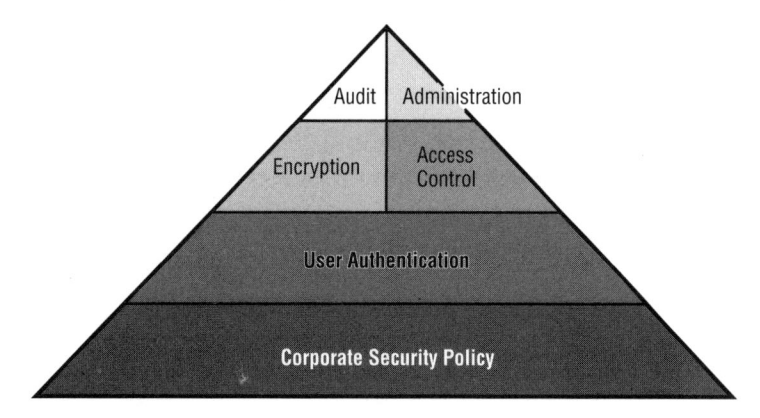

Pyramid diagram showing, from top to bottom: Audit | Administration; Encryption | Access Control; User Authentication; Corporate Security Policy.

Each of these elements operates in conjunction with the others to ensure that an organization can communicate as efficiently as possible.

The Security Policy

Notice that Figure 1.1 lists the security policy at the bottom of the pyramid. It is appropriate that the policy lies at the bottom, because the policy establishes the foundation of any successful security system. Having a security policy in place does not guarantee that you will eliminate intrusions and loss of information. However, a security policy does provide a foundation for all your subsequent actions, and it allows you to establish procedures so that you can carefully audit your network.

A security policy allows you to build an effective security infrastructure. Without an effective security policy, your overall implementation (e.g., your use of firewalls, intrusion-detection services, and scanning activities) will not be as successful. Your security policy must do the following:

- Clearly indicate the individual or group of individuals responsible for creating, altering, and implementing the policy.

- Secure resources, including the actual systems themselves, as well as the information stored on them.

- Allow employees to do their jobs as quickly as possible.

- Define the proper equipment and measures necessary to implement your policy. For example, it can determine which traffic your firewall will permit or deny, and identify which network servers will be scanned and audited more frequently than others.

Your security policy must provide guidelines for the entire organization and is the first line of defense in establishing secure systems use. Do not get too carried away, however, with simply countering threats and locking down systems when creating your security policy. Your security policy must not conflict with the goals and practices of your business. Therefore, you must assign a reasonable amount of protection to your resources.

To determine exactly how much protection a resource requires, you must also decide how much risk it is exposed to. To reduce risk, you should take the following steps, in order:

1. Classify your systems.
2. Determine the risk and prioritize your resources.
3. Assign risk factors.
4. Define acceptable and unacceptable activities.
5. Educate all employees according to their role in the company.
6. Determine who will administer your policy.

Let's look at each of these concepts in detail.

Classify Your Systems

As mentioned above, the first step is to effectively allocate security resources and develop a sound security infrastructure. You must identify and then classify systems and data based on their importance to the organization.

Often, dividing system resources into three categories is useful:

Level I   Systems that are central to the business's operation. For example, an e-commerce company might categorize its web server as a Level-I system. Employee databases, user account databases, and e-mail servers all count as Level-I resources. Do not categorize all systems as Level I.

Level II Systems that are needed but are not critical to daily operation. Though they cannot be down for long, a day or two of lost time would not cripple the company. For example, if the database of employee-pager numbers were down for two days, the loss would be an inconvenience, but not a fatal problem.

Level III A local desktop computer would be a Level-III category, as long as this computer does not affect systems in Levels I and II.

See Table 1.3 for a summary of this classification scheme.

TABLE 1.3 Typical Tri-Level Classification Scheme

Security Classification Hierarchy Level	Data	Systems	Security
Level III: routinely essential	Operational data	Normal systems whose loss would not stop the company from doing business (e.g., systems that have backup systems, and systems that can tolerate at least one week of downtime in case of emergency). These are typically end-user machines.	Normal security policy and defenses (usually 75 percent of an organization's systems).
Level II: significant	Data that could cause damage to the company if it is no longer available or falls into the wrong hands (customer information, product lists, dealer prices, and so forth)	Operational systems, line-of-business-level systems, systems that can tolerate up to 48 hours of downtime. These are typically internal servers that are not directly connected to the Internet.	Normal security plus a special monitoring, audit, and recovery procedure (usually 20 percent of systems).

TABLE 1.3 Typical Tri-Level Classification Scheme *(continued)*

Security Classification Hierarchy Level	Data	Systems	Security
Level I: critical	Critical data needing high data integrity (trade secrets, designs, customer lists, patient information, time-sensitive business documents, and so forth)	Mission-critical systems, systems with high availability requirements, or systems that cannot tolerate more than a few hours of downtime (such as certificate servers, or registration and customer billing systems). These are often publicly exposed servers.	Security analysis, extra security measures, dedicated system-level audit, monitoring, and other security functions. Usually, 5 percent of systems (research and development facilities, hospitals, and other health care facilities).

Determine Risk and Prioritize Resources

After you have classified all of your company's resources, identify which are experiencing the most *risk*. Determine which ones are most likely to be attacked, and then create a prioritized list and an action list, prioritized by system, in your security implementation plan. Your priorities must be based on the importance of each system and its information, including the availability of redundant systems and so forth. This prioritized list is essential, because during a crisis, staff members should not be forced to decide what to save first. Expecting them to make choices in such a situation is an undue burden and will damage your company's overall security. Few IT departments have enough employees and resources to address all Level-I systems.

You should discuss priority in terms of finances, as well as time. Ask yourself the following questions:

- How much money and time can I commit to this resource?
- Which Level-I resources need security the most?

A Level-I system requires significant resources and consideration, whereas a Level-III system might need only virus checking. An unrealistic policy will hurt a company's ability to protect itself and could even damage its ability to communicate efficiently.

If you are conducting electronic customer interaction with credit card or electronic cash transactions, you will require specific security measures for the data and servers used in these systems. You will need both physical and electronic security. If systems are successfully penetrated, your business could be responsible for stolen credit card numbers or other customer information. More important, your reputation is not easily recoverable.

As you construct the security profile for your network, remember that it is helpful to classify your assets into the four resource groups discussed earlier in the section "Protecting Resources."

Assign Risk Factors

Once all of your network's resources have been classified and prioritized, you must assign risk factors. A *risk factor* measures the likelihood of attack. Risk factors should be determined for each resource you have defined.

When assigning risk factors, do the following:

1. Determine the importance of the server to your overall network. Consider what would happen to your business if a particular resource were to be compromised. In some companies, an e-mail server may be more mission-critical than a web server.

2. Determine the system's exposure. Consider, for example, an end-user station used by the company receptionist. This end-user system will likely be exposed to tampering more than an end-user station that is down the hall, behind a secured door.

For example, a company that manufactures paper clips may have a corporate website used only to advertise for the company and provide contact information. The risk factor associated with this website would be much lower than if this company used its site to sell its product to other businesses. Your security infrastructure is the implementation of your security policies at the operations level. It should include multiple levels of defense and varying degrees of protection as determined by each system's classification, as described in Table 1.3.

Define Acceptable and Unacceptable Activities

To design security measures for specific resources, an effective security administrator must differentiate between *acceptable* and *unacceptable* activity. Such activity must be defined in terms of each resource. Your security implementation should specify both acceptable (permitted) and unacceptable (forbidden) activity.

The categories of *acceptable* and *unacceptable activity* will always remain valid when it comes to security. However, organizations will determine acceptable behavior differently, based on their business needs. A policy that might work for one company could have disastrous effects for another. Therefore, while the principles remain the same, the individual applications will differ, sometimes radically.

Acceptable Activities

Acceptable activity will vary from resource to resource. Hypothetically, acceptable activities for your corporate website might include permission for users to browse only the contents of HTML pages in the public folders and submit orders for items. Your policy might give systems administrators additional access to all the directories on the website, allowing proper administration of this service. Finally, your security policy would undoubtedly give your company's webmaster further access that allows him or her to modify the contents of the HTML documents.

Unacceptable Activities and Implementation

Unacceptable activity will also vary from resource to resource. As you face the task of defining what is unacceptable, you can take one of two approaches. You can either state that all activities are unacceptable (i.e., forbidden) unless explicitly allowed, or you can state that all activities are allowed unless explicitly forbidden. Each method has its own advantages and drawbacks. If applied improperly, the approach of forbidding all but a few activities can stifle user activity and impede your organization's ability to function properly. However, allowing everything and then expressly forbidding certain activities could create loopholes that might expose you and your company to unforeseen dangers. Legal problems can arise quickly in both cases. If, for example, you have a policy that allows all activities except for just a few, it can become quite difficult to terminate an employee who has clearly engaged in hacking but who has *technically* not engaged in one of the unacceptable activities you have listed.

Because no two businesses or workplaces are identical, it is your responsibility to define unacceptable activity. The most comprehensive solution, as determined by the writers of the CIW test objectives, is to forbid all activity unless it is expressly allowed. It always helps, however, to then provide examples of unacceptable activity. Be sure to clarify that any activity you list is an example and that the example does not limit the scope of the policy. State that any list of specific activities is simply intended to help employees understand the scope of the security policy. Creating a policy using these guidelines will take considerable time; you might also have to update it frequently. Still, such repetition will allow you to create an effective, current policy that reflects the needs of your business.

Educate All Employees

It is vital you educate each employee according to that employee's job level. Table 1.4 suggests the levels of training you can provide to users of your company's network.

TABLE 1.4 Security Education Levels

Level	Amount of Knowledge
User	Creates sensitivity to security threats and vulnerabilities; produces recognition of the need to protect corporate information and resources.
Executive	Provides the level of organizational security knowledge necessary to make policy decisions on information security programs.
Administrative	Develops the ability to recognize and address threats and vulnerabilities so that security requirements can be set for systems and resources.

An Illicit Server Attack

An *illicit server* is a program that is able to open a port on a network host without the user's or systems administrator's knowledge. Many different types of illicit servers exist, including NetBus, Girlfriend, and BackOrifice. Usually, illicit server applications contain two parts: a server and a client. NetBus, for example, has a client named netbus.exe, shown on the next page.

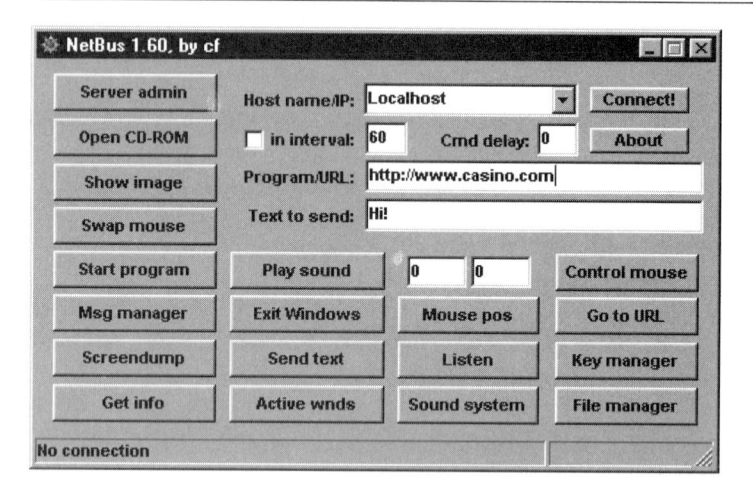

The older NetBus client is designed to attach to port 12345 by default. The NetBus server, called `patch.exe` by default, listens on port 12345 once it is activated. Newer versions of NetBus (e.g., NetBus II) allow the use of any port.

NetBus, like many illicit servers, was often sent via an e-mail message in hopes that an unsuspecting user would run the application, which activated the `patch.exe` program. One of the original ways to distribute NetBus to unsuspecting users was to hide it inside a game called "Whack-a-mole." This game seemed quite fun, until users and systems administrators began to realize that their systems had been taken over. Once a NetBus client attaches to a server, it can download and upload files, as well as take screen captures of the remote system. The client can even delete the server, which helps ensure that the hacker's illicit server will not be detected. More sophomoric uses of NetBus include opening the remote system's CD drive, which was an obvious sign of NetBus infection.

The NetBus exploit is considered passé; it is widely known, and any quality antivirus scanner will discover it. Most network firewalls are configured to block port 12345. However, NetBus represents a classic paradigm: e-mail viruses, which are malicious applications that are activated by double-clicking an attachment. Many e-mail virus attacks have occurred over the past several years, all of which require unsuspecting, naïve users to activate the application.

As you categorize your network's resources and educate employees, do not forget that your network is present to enable your business to function as efficiently as possible. As you categorize your network and create your security policy, make sure that the needs of your employees, the "normal people" in your company, drive the policy and all technological considerations, as suggested in Figure 1.2.

FIGURE 1.2 Policy and technology

People drive policy. → Policy guides technology. → Technology serves people.

Determine Who Will Administer Your Policy

The person ultimately responsible for administering the policy is in upper management. Usually, this person is a vice president of the organization or company. Titles vary, but the person in charge is usually known as a Chief Information Officer (CIO) or Information Security Officer (ISO). This officer is responsible for ensuring that the business is able to communicate quickly and securely. It is important to remember that security is often considered to be a business issue first, and a technical issue second.

The CIW exam does not test on this concept at length, but it is important to understand that there needs to be a direct chain of command and that there must be a division of duties. A direct chain of command ensures that security responsibilities are carried out thoroughly. Division of duties is ensured by making the systems administrators and security managers report to different vice presidents. You have already seen that a security manager reports to a CIO or an ISO. Systems administrators report to a Chief Technology Officer (CTO), whose responsibility is to ensure that all systems are in good technical order. In larger companies, the CTO is not directly responsible for administering the security policy. Division of duties ensures that no conflict of interest occurs, because it ensures that the security manager will not feel the need to ignore a security problem because solving the problem would be too difficult or time consuming. Rather, the security manager will simply contact the systems administrator to ensure that any necessary changes have been made.

Encryption

Encryption is the process of making something readable only to the intended recipients. Encryption has been used for centuries. Julius Caesar, for example, used a wheel (often called "Caesar's Wheel") to encrypt messages for his troops, and 60 years ago, Nazi Germany used the Enigma device to encrypt messages. It is very likely that forms of encryption have existed since the beginning of oral and written communication. All forms of encryption use an *algorithm*, which is a complex mathematical formula designed to scramble information. Encryption can occur at both the network and document levels. At the document level, encryption turns an easily read plain-text file into *cipher text*, which is text that cannot be read unless it is unencrypted. The only way someone can unencrypt cipher text is to gain access to the string of text, called a *key*, that was used to turn the information into cipher text. Because the Internet is an open network, encryption has become important not only for e-mail, but also for network communications.

Encryption Categories

You have probably heard of different ways to encrypt files, including the use of such algorithms as the Data Encryption Standard (DES), RSA (an acronym based on the last names of the people who created the algorithm, Ron Rivest, Adi Shamir, and Leonard Adleman), and Message Digest 5 (MD5). Each of these different methods is an example of the three main encryption categories used in networking:

Symmetric   Encrypts data using one key to both encrypt and decrypt a file.

Asymmetric   Encrypts data using a key pair. Each half of the pair is related to the other, although it is very difficult (if not impossible) to analyze the public key and derive the private key. What one half encrypts, the other half decrypts, and vice versa. This is an important concept to remember. Another name for asymmetric encryption is *public-key cryptography*.

Hash encryption   Encrypts data using a mathematical equation called a "hash function" that (theoretically) scrambles information so it can never be recovered. This form of encryption creates *hash code*, which creates a fixed-length representation of a message. Another name for this type of encryption is *one-way* encryption, because of the fact that data encrypted in this method cannot be decrypted.

> **Note:** Encryption enables the five services shown in Table 1.1.

Encryption Strength

A commonly discussed but frequently misunderstood aspect of cryptography is the strength of encryption. What constitutes strong encryption, which is protected by U.S. export laws? What level of encryption is required for various security needs? How do you determine the effective strength of different types of encryption?

Encryption strength is based on three primary factors. The first is algorithm strength, which includes such factors as the inability to mathematically reverse the information with anything short of trying all possible key combinations. For our purposes, we should rely on industry-standard algorithms that have been tested and tried over time by cryptography experts. Any new or proprietary formula should be viewed with significant distrust until it has been verified commercially.

The second factor is the secrecy of the key, a logical but sometimes overlooked facet. No algorithm can protect you from compromised keys. Thus, the degree of confidentiality that stays with the data is directly tied to how secret the keys remain. Remember to differentiate between the algorithm and the key. The algorithm need not be secret. The data to be encrypted is used in conjunction with the key and then passed through the encryption algorithm.

The third facet, the length of the key, is the best known. In terms of encryption and decryption formula application, the key length is determined in bits. Adding a bit to the length of the key doubles the number of possible keys. In simple terms, the number of possible combinations of bits that can make up a key of any given length can be expressed as $2n$, where n is the length of the key. Thus, a formula with a 40-bit key length would be 2^{40}, or 1,099,511,627,776 possible different keys. Working against this high number is the speed of modern computers.

Although corporations and governments can certainly defeat 40-bit encryption with modern computers, the amount of effort involved typically exceeds the value of the information. Indeed, one factor for deciding the length of key needed is the value of the information being protected. Although 40-bit keys are not always appropriate for financial transactions, they are usually sufficient for individuals' needs.

Authentication

In network operating systems, *authentication* is the ability to verify the identity of a user, system, or system element. A system element can include an internal process, such as an application, or it can include network packets being sent from one computer to another. After authentication has taken place, the authenticated user or system element can then have access to a resource, according to the parameters established by the systems administrator.

If you have used an ATM card, presented a student ID card, or used your driver's license, you have engaged in a form of individual identification. If you have used a password to log your computer on to a network, you have participated in user authentication.

Authentication Methods

Users or systems can prove that they are what they claim to be in one of four ways. When it comes to authentication, this book discusses specific programs based on these four methods. You can prove your identity by:

- Proving what you know
- Showing what you have
- Demonstrating who you are
- Identifying where you are

What You Know

The most common authentication method on the Internet and in the computer world is password authentication. When you log on to a computer network, it usually asks you for a password. This is something you know. The computer bases its authentication on the password. If you give your password to someone else, the computer will grant this other person access because the authentication is based on knowing the password. This is not a failure on the computer's part, but on the part of the user.

> **TIP** Failure also results from the simplistic application of only one mode of authentication. You will find that the most secure networks will discover ways to combine each of the methods discussed in this section.

What You Have: Smart Cards

This method is slightly more advanced, because you need a physical item for authentication. A good example of "what you have" authentication is a building entry card. Anyone who moves the card over the scanner will be granted access to the building. A limitation to this method, however, is that authentication is based on possession of the card. If you were to give the card to someone, he or she could enter the building. Therefore, should you want to create a more sophisticated authentication system for entering your building, you would require not only a card (an authentication method based on what you have), but also a password (a method based on what you know). In the computer industry, the "what you have" method is best exemplified by the use of a *smart card*.

All smart cards contain a microchip. The chip can contain specific information about its owner, including multiple credit card accounts, driver's license information, medical information, and so forth. A smart card can be the size of a standard credit card or larger, depending on the capacity of the embedded chip. Sometimes, the embedded microchips contain read-only information. In this sense, the chips hold more information than the magnetic strip typically found on the back of a credit card. Such limited smart cards can be programmed only once, and they are entirely dependent on a machine called a smart-card reader to operate.

A smart-card reader is an electrical device that scans the card. American Express, for example, provides a reader with its card. Some smart cards do not require additional power to operate. Others contain their own power source, and still others derive power from the smart-card reader before the microchip activates.

The two kinds of smart cards are *contact* and *contactless*. Contact smart cards must directly touch the reader device, whereas contactless cards can communicate with the reader through a wireless electromagnetic connection. A contactless card could, theoretically, authenticate a user.

Smart cards can offer many features. Some allow their persistent memory to be reprogrammed. Others act as minicomputers in the sense that they have input/output devices, persistent memory (e.g., mini-hard drive space), random access memory (RAM), and an active central processing unit (CPU). Smart cards are valuable for authenticating users who want to:

- Enter buildings
- Use cell phones
- Log on to a specific host and participate on a network
- Conduct banking and e-commerce transactions

Who You Are

As far as users are concerned, proving "who you are" is based on some physical, genetic, or otherwise human characteristic that cannot be easily duplicated or stolen. The use of fingerprints and picture IDs is the most common form of "who you are" authentication.

One advanced method of "who you are" authentication is known as biometrics. Until recently, advanced biometric authentication was very expensive and implemented only in highly secure environments. Now, hundreds of companies have produced low-cost biometric solutions. Examples of this method include fingerprints, facial pattern scans, retinal eye scans, and voice analysis. For example, Compaq Corporation provides a fingerprint scanner about the size of a standard serial mouse, which fits on the side of a monitor. You can find more information about this reader at **www.compaq.com/products/options/fit/index.html**.

Veridicom (**www.veridicom.com**) specializes in fingerprint identification that authenticates users with standard equipment and operating systems, including Windows 2000. Some of its products use simple scanners connected via parallel port and/or universal serial bus (USB) connections.

Where You Are

The weakest form of authentication, this strategy determines your identity based on a system's location. For example, the Unix **rlogin** and **rsh** applications authenticate a user, host, or process based partly on the source of its Internet Protocol (IP) address. Reverse DNS lookup is not strictly an authentication practice, but it is related because it at least attempts to determine the origin of a transmission before allowing access to a system. For years, U.S. sites providing software that used strong encryption (e.g., applications that used 128-bit encryption or higher) conducted reverse DNS lookups on all hosts. If a server found that a host belonged to a domain outside the United States, the server would deny the connection if the reverse DNS lookup was not possible. This practice is still quite common in various settings.

However, authentication based on location can be easily fooled, especially on a local network. For example, suppose a server with an IP address of 192.168.2.3 containing valuable information allowed access only from a system that had an IP address of 192.168.2.4. Suppose further that an administrator of a third system with the IP address of 192.168.2.5 existed. This third user would only have to reconfigure his or her system to use the 192.168.2.4 IP address. The server would then grant access to the illicit system, because this server authenticates only by location and no other method. This example is extremely simplified, but it illustrates the dangers of relying on location to authenticate users and systems.

Specific Authentication Techniques

Below are two techniques that augment authentication systems. They combine encryption techniques with additional strategies to verify identity. You do not have to use such programs as Kerberos and one-time password generators, but using such techniques in your authentication methods will help you avoid security breaches. These techniques are specific implementations of the "what you have" and "what you know" authentication methods described in the previous section.

Kerberos

Kerberos (pronounced "Care bear-ose") is a key management scheme that authenticates unknown principals who want to communicate with each other securely. The name Kerberos came from the mythical three-headed dog said to guard the entrance to the underworld (Hades) in ancient Greek tradition. Kerberos is initially defined in RFC 1510. Additional RFCs that discuss Kerberos include 2942, 2712, 2623, 1964, and 1411. As of this writing, version 5 is the most current version of Kerberos.

Essentially, a Kerberos server acts as a trusted third party that knows the identity of the parties who want to communicate. The job of a Kerberos server is to vouch for their identities. It maintains a database of users, as well as network services, such as web, e-mail, and database servers. A single entry in a Kerberos database is called a *principal*. A Kerberos database of principals will have the public and private keys of authorized participants throughout the organization, and a server authenticates these servers for only a certain period of time. Thus, it is vital that all systems in a Kerberos network have the same time. Most Kerberos-enabled networks use the Network Time Protocol (NTP) to ensure this.

Kerberos clients then obtain the public keys from the Kerberos server. A Kerberos client then uses this public key as evidence that a trust relationship exists between this client and the Kerberos server. Next, the client obtains a ticket-granting ticket (TGT), which allows the client to request additional network services. When the client wants to connect to another server on the Kerberos network, the client uses the TGT to obtain a ticket from the Kerberos server. This ticket contains a *session key*, which is a short message that enables authentication for a certain user or process. The session key allows the two Kerberos clients to communicate.

Once the user is authenticated, he or she can then access additional services or daemons. All of these services or daemons must also belong to the Kerberos system. Whenever an application is modified so that it can participate in a Kerberos domain, it is said to be "kerberized." Commonly kerberized services include Telnet, FTP, and various login services.

Kerberos has several advantages:

- Authentication, encryption, and integrity goals are met even with users who do not know each other.

- Kerberos clients need only enter password information locally. Through the use of public-key cryptography, full passwords are never sent across the network, not even in encrypted form.

- Kerberos encrypts packets of information as they traverse the wire, making information more secure.

- Kerberos can limit authentication to a certain time span.

- Kerberos can control access to various resources. Again, using public-key cryptography, Kerberos allows an end user to access a printer through the use of "tickets."

The Kerberos scheme safeguards both the authentication process and all subsequent communication. Once you configure a client, such as an e-mail application, to communicate with Kerberos, it will perform all the authentication automatically.

> **Note:** Kerberos was originally written for the Unix platform. Microsoft has added its proprietary version of Kerberos version 5 to Windows 2000 domains.

A Kerberos server is actually composed of two different services (also called daemons): The first authenticates users, and the second issues special "tickets" that a user can present to various services (e.g., printers, Internet access, file servers, and so forth). Most of the time, these two different servers are incorporated into one host, called a key distribution center (KDC). Table 1.5 explains some of the terminology found in Unix-based Kerberos implementations.

TABLE 1.5 Kerberos Terms

Element	Description
Key distribution center (KDC)	The central server that contains a database storing all users, hosts, and network services for a Kerberos realm. Each entry in the KDC database is called a principal. The KDC contains two services. The first is the ticket-granting server (TGS), which issues ticket-granting tickets and actual service and host tickets. The second is the authentication server (AS), which issues tickets for actual network services.
Ticket-granting ticket (TGT)	A special key granted by the KDC. This ticket does not provide access to any resources. Rather, it authenticates a Kerberos user and determines the network services this person is allowed to use.
Ticket	A session key appended to all subsequent network communication that guarantees the identity of the ticket holder. A ticket is reusable for a certain period of time (8 hours, for example) and provides access to specific services, such as printers, routers, and the login services of remote systems.
Principal	The name given to a user, host, or host service (e.g., a print server, or a system running Telnet).

TABLE 1.5 Kerberos Terms *(continued)*

Element	Description
`kinit`	The Unix command a client issues to receive a ticket from the TGS.
`klist`	The Unix command that allows users to list their cached credentials.
`kdestroy`	The Unix command that erases client tickets so they cannot be reused.

> **NOTE** Some Kerberos implementations, such as that found in Windows 2000, do not use this terminology, nor do they use applications such as `kinit`, `klist`, or `kdestroy`. This is because Windows 2000, for example, uses the term *domain controller* for a KDC. The clients automatically create, manage, and destroy credential caches during logon and logoff.

Kerberos Drawbacks

The main disadvantage of any Kerberos implementation is that if the KDC is compromised, all communication becomes vulnerable. Thus, Kerberos networks are susceptible to a single point of failure. Additionally, the Kerberos server does not ensure that all the client machines are secure; if an unauthorized user gains access to an authorized system terminal (one on which an employee has used `kinit` but not `kdestroy`), he or she will be able to access information, because this terminal is still properly authenticated. Although Kerberos clients can delete the session keys by using the `kdestroy` command, many users fail to use this command.

Additionally, if you implement Kerberos, you must ensure that all network clients and daemons support it. If just one user starts a standard telnet session to one standard telnet server, a malicious user can obtain the network password with a standard network sniffer, such as `tcpdump`.

> **WARNING:** The chief causes of failure in a normally working Kerberos system are incorrect DNS host entries and failed time-clock synchronization between the KDC and the Kerberos clients.

One-Time Passwords (OTP)

One-time passwords (OTP) are meant to help prevent malicious users from capturing and reusing passwords used for authentication. An *OTP* is a way to "harden" an authentication system. This method generates and uses passwords only once, and then discards them after use. In such a system, the server stores or generates a predetermined list of passwords, which a client then uses. Because the passwords are used only once, a hacker who decodes any given password has no advantage in trying to reuse it.

Internet service providers (ISP) often use generated OTPs, as do organizations that employ traveling sales forces and users who work remotely. CompuServe augments a standard "what you know" password method with an OTP. When a user logs on to CompuServe, he or she sends the password that is usually associated with his or her account, but adds the actual minute the connection is made between its server and a user. This combination of the standard password and time is then sent to CompuServe for authentication. If a hacker stole and deciphered this password/time combination, it would be useless, because it was valid for only a moment (the time the user logged on) and could be used only at that time. This method does not replace the "what you know" system of passwords, but it does add another layer of protection.

You can learn more about OTP in RFC 2289. The Onetime Passwords in Everything (OPIE) program is available for Linux systems at `http://inner.net/opie`.

Access Control

Whenever a system ensures that individuals, systems, or processes access only what they are supposed to, it is engaging in *access control*. A network's internal mechanisms ensure that each user and system can access only what the security policy allows. The two general ways to implement such control are *access control lists* and *execution control lists*. The access control step follows user or process authentication. After a system has authenticated you and established that you are who you claim to be, it uses access control schemes to control what you can access in the system. These schemes can be used to grant or deny privileges.

> **Understanding Access Control**
>
> A good analogy to help understand access control is to consider a company building. Most companies have a lobby to which anyone may be admitted. This lobby can be likened to a web server that allows unauthenticated users to access the home page. To enter the company's actual offices, a person would need to present an identification badge. This is a form of security that allows only authenticated employees to access company offices. After employees have entered the building, their identification cards will allow them to access only certain offices. For example, an employee of the marketing department may not be authorized to use his or her identification card to access the CEO's office. This procedure is a form of access control. It limits what authenticated users can access.

All operating systems that support access control differ slightly in how they implement this form of security. Access control mechanisms are essential when securing servers. However, when securing a system, you must limit what certain users can access on a server, as well as the access granted to services and daemons.

Access Control List (ACL)

An *access control list (ACL)* is a list of individual users and/or groups associated with an object, such as a web server directory or a folder on a hard drive. Modern information systems treat all resources, such as directories, users, and groups, as objects. As far as a network is concerned, objects can be devices such as printers, remote systems, and even the disks on remote systems. An ACL determines whether or not a user has access to a particular object. If a user has access to an object, the ACL defines exactly what the user can do to it.

An ACL can also include *access levels*. Common access levels include read-only, write-only, read-write, and delete. Each entity will be granted a level of access for the resource being used. If the entity accessing the resource tries to perform an operation beyond its authorized level of access, the operating system authentication mechanisms will raise an exception or error notification.

> **Web Servers and ACLs**
>
> Web servers, such as Apache (www.apache.org) and Microsoft Internet Information Server 5.0 (www.microsoft.com), allow the use of an ACL. Apache, for example, allows a systems administrator to create an ACL using a file named .htaccess. This file contains instructions that point to a user database created by a program called htpasswd. You will see how this works in the exercise at the end of this chapter.

Execution Control List (ECL)

An *execution control list (ECL)* is a list of the resources and actions that an application can perform while it operates. Both applications and operating systems use ECLs. Any operating system or application that supports an ECL can determine which of the program's or operating system's activities are appropriate and which are not. In essence, the operating system can exert system-level control over a single application. Before ECLs, a user was completely subjected to what the programmer or operating system considered appropriate program behavior.

Examples of ECLs include the following:

- The Windows 2000 Local and Domain Security Policy settings.

- Pluggable Authentication Modules (PAM), found on Linux systems. By editing files in the /etc/pam.d and /etc/security/console.apps directories, you can control application execution.

- Browser *sandboxing*, which ensures that Java and JavaScript applications can be limited. For example, it is possible to configure Microsoft Internet Explorer or Netscape Navigator so that it will not execute JavaScript or VBScript applications. All browsers limit how Java applets can be executed so that a malicious applet cannot easily compromise the entire system.

Auditing

Auditing is an essential aspect of an overall security plan. All modern operating systems, from Windows 2000 to Cisco's Internet Operating System (IOS) to Linux, record all their activity in log files. These logs enable you to determine the effectiveness of your security implementation. Through these activity logs, you can usually determine if and how an unallowable activity occurred.

Two types of auditing exist: passive and active. Let's take a look at each.

Passive Auditing

In *passive auditing*, the computer simply records activity and does nothing about it. Therefore, passive auditing is not a real-time detection mechanism, because someone must review the logs and then act on the information they contain. The principle of passive auditing demands that you take no proactive or preemptive action. Also, when auditing passively, make sure your auditing infrastructure consumes as few system resources as possible.

It is vital that you take the time to check your system logs, however. Audit logs will not help you secure your systems unless you audit them regularly and search for patterns of illegal activity. You will learn more about such patterns in Chapter 14.

Active Auditing

Active auditing involves actively responding to illicit access and intrusions. Responses might include:

- Ending the session
- Blocking access to certain hosts (including websites, FTP servers, and e-mail servers)
- Tracing illicit activity back to the point of origin

Because of the effort required to view and decipher log reports, you must balance your time between auditing and other tasks. Too much auditing places unnecessary stress on system resources. Too little could threaten your security because you will not be able to determine a hacker's activities precisely.

EXERCISE 1.1

Implementing Authentication and Access Control in Apache Server

Not only is Linux an excellent example of the Unix operating system, it also provides the opportunity to implement and examine many security concepts relevant to the CIW Security Professional exam. In this exercise, you will enable access control for an Apache web server

EXERCISE 1.1 (continued)

directory on a Red Hat Linux system. You will use the .htaccess access file and htpasswd program to enable an ACL for a directory. This directory will be called /acltest.

1. Log on to your Linux system as root.

2. Check to see if the web server is installed:

   host# rpm -qa | grep apache
   host# apache-1.3.9-4

3. If any information about Apache Server is returned, you know it is installed. If it is not installed, obtain the Apache Red Hat Package Manager (RPM) file from one of the following sites:

   http://www.rpmfind.net
   http://www.apache.org

4. Open a browser and see if httpd is running, or use the following command: ps aux | grep httpd. Now that you know httpd is running, change to the root directory:

   cd /

5. Create a directory named acltest. This will be the directory to which you will control access.

   mkdir acltest

6. Use chmod so that the directory is owned by the user named apache and the group named apache. Also, allow this directory to be read and executed by the user named apache:

   host# chown apache acltest/
   host# chgrp apache acltest/
   host# chmod 500 acltest/

7. Use cd to change to the acltest directory. Use touch to create a file named index.html in the acltest directory. You need this file, or Apache Server will not allow access to the directory:

   touch index.html

EXERCISE 1.1 *(continued)*

8. Use a text editor such as vi to enter the following code in `index.html`:

   ```
   <HTML>
   <HEAD>
   <TITLE>Creating an ACL
   </TITLE>
   </HEAD>
   <BODY>
   This is a secret page
   </BODY>
   </HTML>
   ```

9. Save the changes to this file and exit by first pressing the Esc key, then entering **ZZ** (be sure to use all capital letters). This series of commands has vi save your changes.

10. You have now created a simple HTML file. Next, you will program Apache Server to recognize this new directory so you can view it in a browser. Change to the `/etc/httpd/conf` directory:

    `cd /etc/httpd/conf/`

    Red Hat Linux uses the `/etc/httpd/conf/` directory. Other versions of Linux and other installations of Apache may store configuration files in a different location, such as `/var/usr/httpd/conf`.

11. Using a text editor, open the `httpd.conf` file:

    `vi httpd.conf`

12. Scroll down to the Aliases section of the file and enter the following code exactly as shown:

    ```
    Alias /acltest    "/acltest"
    <Directory /acltest>
    AllowOverride All
    Order allow,deny
    Allow from all
    </Directory>
    ```

EXERCISE 1.1 *(continued)*

The first line in this entry creates an alias named /acltest. Users will enter this alias into their browsers. The syntax of the alias directive is very specific. First, list the name of the alias (i.e., the text a user enters into the browser), then the name of the directory that exists on the hard drive. The second line starts a directory definition for the /acltest directory on the hard drive. The AllowOverride directive allows you to specify an .htaccess file, which in turn allows you to customize this directory's behavior. The next two lines have Apache Server allow access to all users, except as defined by any entries in the .htaccess file. You must then end the directory definition.

To learn more about Apache Server directives, go to http://httpd.apache.org/docs-2.0/mod/directives.html.

If you include a trailing slash (/) on the URL path, the server will require a trailing slash in order to expand the alias. In other words, if you use Alias /acltest/ /acltest/, then the URL /acltest will not be aliased by Apache Server. You would have to use /acltest/, with the trailing backslash.

13. Once you have correctly entered the new alias and directory definition, exit vi, making sure to save your changes.

14. You have just created a virtual directory. Now, Apache Server needs to reread its configuration files so that the new virtual directory and alias you created earlier will take effect. Completely stop and restart Apache Server:

/etc/rc.d/init.d/httpd restart

Simply issuing a kill -HUP command or an httpd start command will not work as quickly as you want because Apache Server multi-threads various connections. To make sure the exercise works quickly, stop all httpd processes, then restart httpd from root using the /etc/rc.d/rc.local/httpd stop command. You can also use the killall command as follows: killall apache. You can also use the kill command, if you know Apache's process ID (PID). Also, make sure you have fully quit any previous instances of your web browser, in case it is caching old information.

EXERCISE 1.1 *(continued)*

15. Open a browser, such as Netscape Navigator or Lynx (a simple text-based web browser), and test your work. You may wish to use your fully qualified domain name (FQDN). For example, if your FQDN is `myserver.mynetwork.com`, enter the following:

    `lynx myserver.mynetwork.com/acltest`

    If you use only an IP address or just the first name of the server, you may have to enter the password twice because Apache Server assumes that requests will come for its FQDN, and not an IP address or relative (i.e., partial) DNS name. If you really want to change this arrangement, you can change this behavior by entering a `ServerName` directive in `httpd.conf`. If your server's name is `student10`, you would enter the following line:

    `ServerName myserver`

    You must then restart Apache Server. Also, many web browsers cache information. If necessary, exit and restart the browser to ensure that you are reading current output from the daemon.

16. Now that you have verified that this directory works, you are ready to create an ACL for it. Change to the `/acltest` directory:

    `cd /acltest/`

17. Use the `touch` command to create a hidden file named `.htaccess`. This hidden file is the ACL for this resource. To perform this action, use a period in front of the file name:

    `touch .htaccess`

    You must include a period in front of the `htaccess` file. Failure to do so will cause your ACL to fail because a leading dot creates a hidden file.

18. Use a text editor such as vi to open `.htaccess`. Make sure you place a period in front of the file name. Otherwise, you will open a new file named `htaccess`, not the hidden file you actually want to edit (`.htaccess`):

    `vi .htaccess`

EXERCISE 1.1 *(continued)*

19. Enter the following code:

    ```
    AuthUserFile /apachepasswd/.htpasswd
    AuthGroupFile /dev/null/
    AuthName "My secret directory"
    AuthType Basic
    require valid-user
    ```

20. You have just created a file that allows the use of an ACL. The file you have just edited must exist in the directory to which you want to limit access (/acltest). The AuthName entry allows you to specify text to help users know where they are authenticating on your server. Now, exit this file, making sure to save the changes.

21. Next, you will create a new user accounts database that Apache Server recognizes for authenticating users. This database will be the ACL; it is a separate user database from /etc/passwd or /etc/shadow. First, create the directory in which the database will reside:

    ```
    mkdir /apachepasswd
    ```

    You can give this directory any name you want. For this exercise, use /apachepasswd.

22. Make the /apachepasswd directory owned by the user named apache and the group named apache. Also, allow this directory to be read and executed by the user named apache, as shown:

    ```
    host# chown apache apachepasswd/
    host# chgrp apache apachepasswd/
    host# chmod 500 apachepasswd/
    ```

23. To create the user authentication database, enter the command below. You will be asked immediately for the password for the new user named webuser1. Make this password password:

    ```
    htpasswd -c /apachepasswd/.htpasswd webuser1
    New password:
    Re-type new password:
    ```

EXERCISE 1.1 *(continued)*

24. You have now created a file named .htpasswd in the /apachepasswd directory and populated it with a user named webuser1. You have also given this user a new password. Now, populate this database with additional user accounts named webuser2, webuser3, and webuser4. When creating additional users, you cannot use the -c option, as you did above. Make sure you do not use the up arrow key. Each time you issue the htpasswd command, htpasswd will create the account, then immediately ask you to create a new password. Have all accounts use password as the password:

    ```
    host# htpasswd /apachepasswd/.htpasswd webuser2
    New password:
    Re-type new password:
    ```

    Again, do not use the htpasswd command with the −c option, because this action will erase the existing file and re-create a new one.

    You have now created a user accounts database for Apache Server.

25. Now, using a browser such as Lynx or Netscape Navigator from your X-Window System (or a browser from a separate Windows 2000 system), access your /acltest/ directory using the /acltest alias.

26. You should be prompted to give a password. If you are not, make sure that you have properly created the virtual directory and that you have specified the proper location for the .htpasswd file. Check your .htaccess file. It should be hidden (it should have a period in front of it), and it should contain the code found in Step 19. Finally, make sure you are using an FQDN and that your browser is not simply giving you cached information.

27. Now, issue the following command:

    ```
    tail /var/log/httpd/access_log
    ```

    You should see records concerning who has accessed your web server.

Summary

In this chapter, you were introduced to the foundational security concepts covered in the CIW Security Professional exam. You learned about the open nature of the Internet, the types of hackers on the Internet, and the steps you can take to secure your resources. You then learned about security standards and practical ways to secure systems through encryption, authentication, access control lists, and other methods. Specifically, we discussed how to:

- Secure an open network.
- Identify types of hackers.
- List resources that need security.
- Recognize common security standards and organizations.
- Formulate the basics of an effective security policy.
- Explain key user authentication methods.
- Understand access control methods.
- Use access control lists and execution control lists.
- Recognize the need for auditing.

You now have an understanding of the basic concepts involved in the CIW Security Professional exam. In the next chapter, you will use encryption technologies to apply concepts such as data confidentiality and data encryption.

Exam Essentials

Understand the ramifications of trying to conduct secure, private communication over public networks. As corporations have embraced the Internet, the challenge in using it is to find ways to make TCP/IP not only scalable, but also secure and ready for e-commerce.

Be able to identify types of hackers. Be aware that anyone who tries to scan a system to gain information from it is a "black hat" hacker. Two types of black hat hacker exist: casual and determined.

Know common security standards and organizations. From the ISO 7498-2 document to the Common Criteria and BS 7799, it is vital that you understand the terminology and nomenclature the industry uses.

Understand the basics of an effective security policy. Creating a security policy not only involves determining acceptable and unacceptable behavior; it also involves categorizing systems and identifying risks and vulnerabilities.

Know key user authentication methods. Authentication is simply the ability to determine the identity of a user, host, or host element (e.g., a process or a network packet). Make sure that you can readily categorize authentication examples according to the material discussed in this chapter.

Understand access control methods. Access control always takes place after authentication. Access control includes the ability to generate and use an access control list (ACL). It is also important to understand the concept of access control levels, as well as execution control lists.

Understand the need for auditing. Active and passive auditing are essential to a secure network. Make sure that you can readily identify and categorize examples that are given to you.

Key Terms

Before you take the exam, be certain you are familiar with the following terms:

acceptable and unacceptable activity

access control list (ACL)

access levels

algorithm

asset

auditing

black hat hackers

casual hacker

Common Criteria (CC)

connectivity

controls

determined hacker

Key Terms

discretionary access control

execution control list (ECL)

hacker

Health Insurance Portability and Accountability Act (HIPAA)

illicit server

Kerberos

key

one-time password (OTP)

open network

packet sniffer

risk

sandboxing

scalable

security

security levels

security mechanisms

smart card

threat

vulnerability

white hat hackers

Review Questions

1. Don suspects that his server has been attacked and that a hacker has gained illicit access to its user account database. The server is on the Internet, though it is behind a firewall. Which of the following security measures will enable him to identify and eliminate a threat in a web server?

   A. Implementing a network perimeter

   B. Building a firewall

   C. Checking the logs

   D. Implementing a closed network

2. Cindy has entered the cubicle of a fellow employee and has run Windows Explorer and the Search facility on this person's computer. Next, she begins viewing files using Microsoft Word and Adobe Acrobat. What is the name for this type of activity?

   A. Non-repudiation

   B. System snooping

   C. Superzapping

   D. Data tampering

3. Bill is a systems administrator of a network that uses Unix and Windows systems. Many of the users on this network use Telnet and the Network File System (NFS) to communicate back and forth between systems. Bill has become worried that his network is not properly protecting information as it passes along the network wire. What service provides for the protection of data from unauthorized disclosure?

   A. Data confidentiality

   B. Access control

   C. Data integrity

   D. Non-repudiation

4. Jane runs a small business selling antiques over the Web. She discovers that her web servers are no longer responsive on the network, and she begins receiving complaints that no one can reach her site. After analyzing her network, she discovers that her servers are being bombarded by thousands of Internet Control Message Protocol (ICMP) packets a minute. She is able to trace these packets to a particular user and ISP. However, when she contacts the ISP, she is discouraged to find that the user account has been deactivated. What network service makes it impossible to deny participation in all or part of a network transaction?

   A. Data confidentiality

   B. Access control

   C. Data integrity

   D. Non-repudiation

5. Ruth has installed a piece of software designed to enable her operating system to monitor and limit system calls. She hopes that this will improve her server's existing security. What is the name for a mechanism or piece of software that strengthens an existing mechanism?

   A. Trusted functionality

   B. Event detection

   C. Security recovery

   D. An audit trail

6. Which of the following security standards describes the use of security targets, protection profiles, and targets of evaluation?

   A. British Standard 7799

   B. The Common Criteria

   C. The Orange book

   D. A security matrix

7. Randall has been asked to plan a network from scratch. What is the first step he should take when planning a secure network from the ground up?

    A. Enable auditing and administration.

    B. Impose user authentication.

    C. Create a security policy.

    D. Enact encryption.

8. What is the first step in reducing risk?

    A. Determining who will administer the policy

    B. Assigning risk factors

    C. Determining security priorities for each system

    D. Classifying systems

9. Which of the following resources are often used as "jumping-off points" for attacks on additional resources?

    A. Server and network resources

    B. Information storage and network resources

    C. End-user and server resources

    D. End-user resources and storage resources

10. Which of the following is a possible symptom that you do not have a balanced security policy?

    A. An end user has broken into your server and accessed the Human Resources database.

    B. An end user has written down passwords underneath his keyboard.

    C. An end user cannot receive or send e-mail from her workstation.

    D. A server's auditing log becomes full, resulting in a crashed system.

11. What type of encryption scrambles and reassembles data using a key pair?

    A. Symmetric

    B. Asymmetric

    C. Hash

    D. Cipher text

12. Proving what you know, showing what you have, demonstrating who you are, and identifying where you are represent methods of what security element?

    A. Encryption

    B. Authentication

    C. Data integrity

    D. Non-repudiation

13. Abdul needs to log on to a server that uses the Kerberos authentication system. What is the name of the Unix application used to obtain a ticket-granting ticket?

    A. `kinit`

    B. `klist`

    C. `kdestroy`

    D. `tgt`

14. Kristine has found that one of the walls in an easily accessible room can be opened, revealing the network wiring that leads to both the network router and the database servers for the network. Which type of resource has been compromised?

    A. End-user resource

    B. Network resource

    C. Server resource

    D. Information storage resource

15. In regard to the ISO 7498-2 standard, what is the significance of a digital signature mechanism?

    A. It uses public-key encryption to authenticate information.

    B. It encrypts digital signatures as part of the authentication process.

    C. It enables digital signatures to be decrypted for authentication purposes.

    D. It provides a third party for authentication purposes.

16. Julie discovers that the operating system she is using does not use traffic padding. What is the benefit of a padding mechanism in network security?

    A. Padding encrypts authentication packets, making it impossible to reuse them.

    B. Padding makes all authentication packets appear to be the same size.

    C. Padding prohibits the reading of authentication data so that it becomes impossible to use a network sniffer.

    D. Padding makes it more difficult to differentiate important packets from unimportant packets.

17. Davis has been tasked with creating an authentication scheme for his corporate network. The company has three divisions: Accounting, Research and Development, and Human Resources. Only Research and Development needs to access the Internet to send and receive e-mail. What is the most efficient method for ensuring that employees with access to the Internet do not engage in unacceptable activity concerning the World Wide Web, chat, and FTP servers?

    A. Give the members of the Research and Development division only enough Internet access to do their jobs.

    B. Terminate all employees who engage in unacceptable activity, such as downloading software not relevant to their job role.

    C. Enforce your security policy and educate your users.

    D. Audit users carefully and issue warnings concerning unproductive behavior.

18. Joel has just restricted a portion of his website to only 15 executives in his corporation. When authorized users log in, a special Common Gateway Interface (CGI) script will be executed. What access control element has Joel used?

   A. Authentication

   B. An access control list

   C. An execution control list

   D. Access levels

19. Jacob is a systems administrator for a small-sized company (15 users). His company president has decided to outsource all e-mail server services. Clients on his corporate LAN will communicate with a remote e-mail server for both Internet Message Access Protocol (IMAP) and Simple Mail Transport Protocol (SMTP) traffic. Jacob wishes to ensure that network transmissions between his network clients and recipients will be encrypted. What security service is Jacob employing?

   A. Authentication

   B. Data integrity

   C. Data confidentiality

   D. Non-repudiation

20. Sandi has configured an application called eTrust Intrusion Detection to automatically cancel the connection of any network transmission that uses port 12345. This activity will occur without Sandi's knowledge. What type of auditing is Sandi imposing on the system?

   A. Passive auditing

   B. Active auditing

   C. System auditing

   D. Network auditing

Answers to Review Questions

1. **C.** Of the choices given, log checking is the only way to learn about a threat.

2. **B.** Any unauthorized person who is viewing files on a system is engaging in system snooping. Cindy is not tampering with files yet, because she is only viewing them.

3. **A.** Data confidentiality is a mechanism that allows a system to communicate with remote systems with the reasonable assurance that no one can intercept the data packets and read them.

4. **D.** Non-repudiation is the ability to prove beyond a reasonable doubt that a certain user or system in fact did send a network packet. Without any security enhancements, TCP/IP does not provide any mechanisms for non-repudiation. Thus, it is possible for hackers to use TCP/IP in illicit ways.

5. **A.** Trusted functionality describes a piece of software or operating system add-on that strengthens the existing components of an application. An add-on to TCP/IP, for example, uses a technology called IPsec, which encrypts transmissions between hosts. Also, Ipv6, the next generation of IP, uses encryption as a trusted functionality component.

6. **B.** The Common Criteria uses security targets, protection profiles, and targets of evaluation to ensure network security.

7. **C.** A security policy is the first thing Randall should define for his network. Without a security policy, he will not be able to respond to network intrusions as efficiently, nor will he be able to enforce policies on users.

8. **D.** It is vital that you first classify your systems. This process allows you to verify which systems are the most important to your company, and it also helps you determine how vulnerable these systems are to tampering and attacks.

9. **C.** End-user resources are often used as attack platforms. For example, e-mail viruses spread from one end-user system to another. Server platforms, such as web and e-mail servers, can also be used as platforms for attacks.

10. **B.** You must balance the need for security with the ability of your end users to cope with the requirements of your security policy. If your security policy requires too much knowledge, or it requires end users to make too many radical changes, your users will often find ways to cope with it. As a result, the overall effectiveness of your network security will be less than if you had no security policy at all.

11. **B.** Asymmetric, or public-key, cryptography uses a mathematically related key pair. One key remains private, and the other key can be distributed publicly.

12. **B.** Authentication uses various methods to prove identity. These include proving what you know, showing what you have, demonstrating who you are, and identifying where you are.

13. **A.** The `kinit` program resides on a Kerberos client host. It is then used to request a ticket-granting ticket.

14. **B.** Because Kristine has found the network wiring, she is accessing a network resource. It is true that the compromised network wiring leads to a network router (also a network resource) and the database servers (information storage resources). However, the resource that is currently compromised is the network wiring.

15. **D.** The digital signature mechanism is significant because it provides a third party to authenticate transactions.

16. **D.** The true benefit of traffic padding is that it adds ostensibly useless bits of information to important packets, which makes it more difficult to tell the true nature of the packets. Traffic padding applies to more than authentication packets. Furthermore, traffic padding does not make packet sniffing impossible. It simply makes analyzing traffic more difficult.

17. **A.** This question is asking about access control. The most efficient method for ensuring that employees do not engage in unacceptable activity is to limit access as much as possible. According to the scenario, employees do not need access to services such as the Web, chat servers, and FTP. Creating and/or enforcing a security policy is not efficient, because if users cannot access questionable services in the first place, the problem will not arise.

18. B. This question involves the use of the access control list (ACL). Authentication is assumed, because authentication occurs before access control. Because the question is asking specifically about an access control element, choosing authentication is incorrect. Even though a special CGI script is going to be executed, nothing in the scenario involves limiting access of this script. Rather, this script is executed only after the ACL does its job. Finally, all of the 15 executives will be allowed to log in; thus, access levels have not been used.

19. C. The data confidentiality mechanism almost exclusively uses encryption to ensure that data remains secret.

20. B. The practice of active auditing involves activities such as stopping suspicious network activity as it happens. Even though Sandi is not present during the process, the application she is using actively ends a connection it is auditing. Passive auditing involves collecting information. In Sandi's case, information has been collected and acted on.

Chapter 2

Applied Encryption

THE CIW EXAM OBJECTIVE GROUPS COVERED IN THIS CHAPTER:

- ✓ Define encryption and the encryption methods used in internetworking.
- ✓ Use universal guidelines and principles of effective network security to create effective specific solutions.

As you learned in Chapter 1, you can apply encryption for many different reasons. Encryption helps ensure data confidentiality and authenticate users. In addition, it enforces data integrity, because it can be used to verify that information has not been altered in transit. In this chapter, you will apply specific techniques that allow you to use private, public, and one-way encryption to secure communications. Specifically, you will see how it is possible to use encryption to create a *trust relationship*.

Creating Trust Relationships

A *trust relationship* between two hosts means that the hosts can do two things: First, they can verify each other's identity. Second, they can encrypt transmissions between each other. Establishing a trust relationship requires that two or more hosts exchange keys with each other. When a host gives its key to another, this host can encrypt information so that only that remote host can decrypt it. The most powerful trust relationships are those accomplished by using public-key encryption, in concert with symmetric-key and one-way encryption. When establishing a trust relationship, keys can be distributed using two methods:

Manually With manual distribution, you have to trade public keys with a recipient first, then encode messages to the recipient's public key. This method is usually required for encrypting e-mail messages between recipients.

Automatically In automatic distribution, Secure Sockets Layer (SSL) and certain versions of IPsec can exchange information in a reasonably secure manner through a series of data exchanges called *handshakes*. You will learn more about this method later in this chapter.

Creating a trust relationship involves all three types of encryption. Before we move ahead, therefore, it is important to understand all encryption terminology. In a later chapter, you will learn about how *Public Key Cryptography Standards (PKCS)* protocols and servers make it possible to manage trust relationships across the Internet.

Encryption Terminology

You'll recall that symmetric- and asymmetric-key encryption was introduced in Chapter 1. Before we continue with the topic of trust relationships, it is necessary to describe some of the terms used in these types of encryption. First, a *round* is a discrete part of the encryption process. An *algorithm* generally submits information to several rounds. A higher number of rounds is preferable. Most symmetric-key algorithm rounds first process half of the unencrypted data, then process the second half. Then, each half is reprocessed to make the resulting encryption stronger. Separating information into rounds makes symmetric keys faster. In encryption, *parallelization* means the use of multiple processes, processors, or machines to work on cracking one encryption algorithm. Individual hosts can be parallelized using a parallel cluster server. Using such technology allows many different hosts to work together as one system to crack a piece of code. TurboLinux (www.turbolinux.com), for example, sells parallel cluster servers, as well as load-balancing cluster servers. You can also use the Beowulf cluster server, available at www.beowulf.org.

Block and Stream Ciphers

Two types of symmetric-key encryption algorithms exist: *block mode* and *stream-cipher mode*. Block-cipher algorithms encrypt data in discrete blocks. It is the more popular mode, because it is easier to verify the integrity of data before it is encrypted. Generally, the plain text will be padded up to be a multiple of the block size and then encrypted. This process makes the cipher text the size of the plain text, rounded up to the next multiple of 64 or 128 bits. The most common block sizes are 64 and 128 bits.

Stream-cipher modes encrypt data (e.g., messages, network transmissions, and files) bit by bit in real time. Stream-cipher algorithms encrypt information by creating a key stream and then combining this stream with the document being encrypted. This method is much quicker than using block mode, especially when it is used on smaller bits of data. However, it is not considered to be as secure, because it cannot verify data during encryption.

Symmetric-Key Encryption

In symmetric-key encryption, one key is used to encrypt and decrypt messages. Another name for symmetric-key encryption is "single-key" encryption. Figure 2.1 illustrates single-key encryption.

FIGURE 2.1 Symmetric, or single-key, encryption

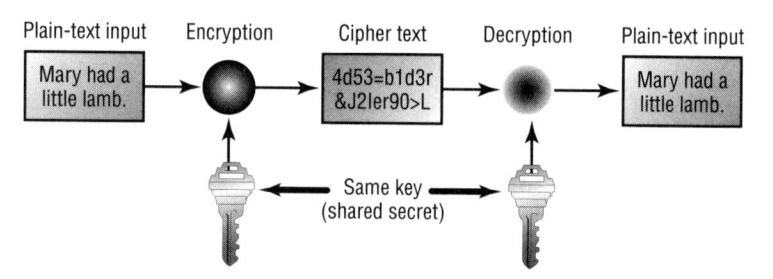

The benefit of symmetric-key encryption is that it is fast, strong, and simple. This type of encryption allows you to encrypt a large amount of information, such as a 4MB Microsoft Word file, in less than a second. Encrypting files and data via a symmetric key is a relatively simple process; many applications, such as Microsoft Word and various archiving applications (including PKZIP) contain utilities that can symmetrically encrypt a document or file.

The chief weakness of symmetric-key encryption is that it can't support an easily implemented, secure distribution method for the key. Because all recipients must possess the same key, all users must have a secure way to send and retrieve the key. If users are going to pass information in a public medium such as the Internet, they need a way to transfer this key among themselves. In some cases, the users could meet and transfer the key physically. However, such physical meetings are not always possible or practical.

One solution might be to send the key by e-mail. However, such a message could be intercepted easily, thereby defeating the purpose of encryption. The users could not encrypt the e-mail containing the key because they would have to share yet another key to encrypt the e-mail that contains the original key. This dilemma raises the question: If the symmetric key has to be encrypted itself, why not use the method that encrypted it in the first place? One solution is to use asymmetric-key encryption, a process that will be discussed later in this chapter. In addition to this concern, hackers can compromise symmetric keys with a *dictionary program*, which uses a relatively large list of common password names that the program repeatedly uses to gain access. *Password-sniffing* attacks can also capture unencrypted information as it passes across the network wire.

It is important to understand that if you enter a password that is, for example, four characters long, this password will only generate a short key. A longer password will generate a longer key. However, if you use a longer key, you will have to recollect a longer password.

Symmetric-Key Algorithms

In spite of the drawbacks to symmetric-key encryption, it is still an essential encryption method. This is because it is often used in tandem with public-key and one-way encryption. Below is a discussion of the more important symmetric-key encryption algorithms.

Data Encryption Standard

In 1977, the U.S. National Institute of Standards and Technology (NIST) formally adopted the Data Encryption Standard (DES) as the de facto symmetric-key encryption standard. DES, also referred to as the Data Encryption Algorithm (DEA), is a block-mode cipher. It encrypts data in 64-bit blocks and uses a technique called "diffusion and confusion." The 64-bit block of data is divided into two halves, and each half is successively passed through the key (called a round, as you'll recall from the section "Encryption Terminology"). DES has 16 rounds, and the key is bitwise-shifted for each round. The bit shifting that occurs takes some data from one round and applies it to the next round, making it (theoretically) more difficult to retrieve the contents of the original without the key. Forty-eight bits of the key are applied to the 32 bits of data for the round.

The advantages of DES are that it is fast and simple to implement. DES has been in production use for more than 25 years, so many hardware and software implementations use the DES algorithm. However, key distribution and management are difficult, again because DES relies on a single-key model.

> **NOTE** You can learn more about NIST at (www.nist.gov). DES and its cousin, triple DES (which we'll describe in the next section), remain the standard form of encryption for many companies and organizations. It is described in the U.S. Federal Information Processing Standard (FIPS) PUB 46-1 (www.nist.gov/itl/div897/pubs/index.htm).

This book provides more than enough information about encryption algorithms to pass the CIW Security Professional exam. If you wish to learn more about encryption, take a look at Bruce Schneier's excellent *Applied Cryptography: Protocols, Algorithms, and Source Code in C, 2nd Edition* (John Wiley & Sons, 1995).

Triple DES

Normal DES uses a 56-bit key. For more sensitive information, triple DES may be the answer. In triple DES, the message is first encrypted using a 56-bit key, then decrypted with another 56-bit key, and finally encrypted again with a third 56-bit key. The triple DES thus effectively has a 168-bit key.

The biggest advantage of triple DES is its ability to use existing DES software and hardware. Companies with large investments in the DES encryption algorithm can easily implement triple DES.

RSA Security Symmetric-Key Algorithms

Ron Rivest, Adi Shamir, and Leonard Adelman invented their public-key encryption system in 1977, and they named it after the first letters in their last names. Since then, they have gone on to invent several different symmetric- and asymmetric-key algorithms. RSA algorithms are used in several commercial operating systems and programs, including Microsoft Windows and Netscape Navigator.

RSA Security (www.rsa.com) is one of the best-known and most effective companies in the field of cryptography. RSA's technologies are included in existing and proposed standards for the Internet and the World Wide Web. The RSA website, whose home page is shown in Figure 2.2, contains substantial information about cryptography and security.

FIGURE 2.2 RSA security home page

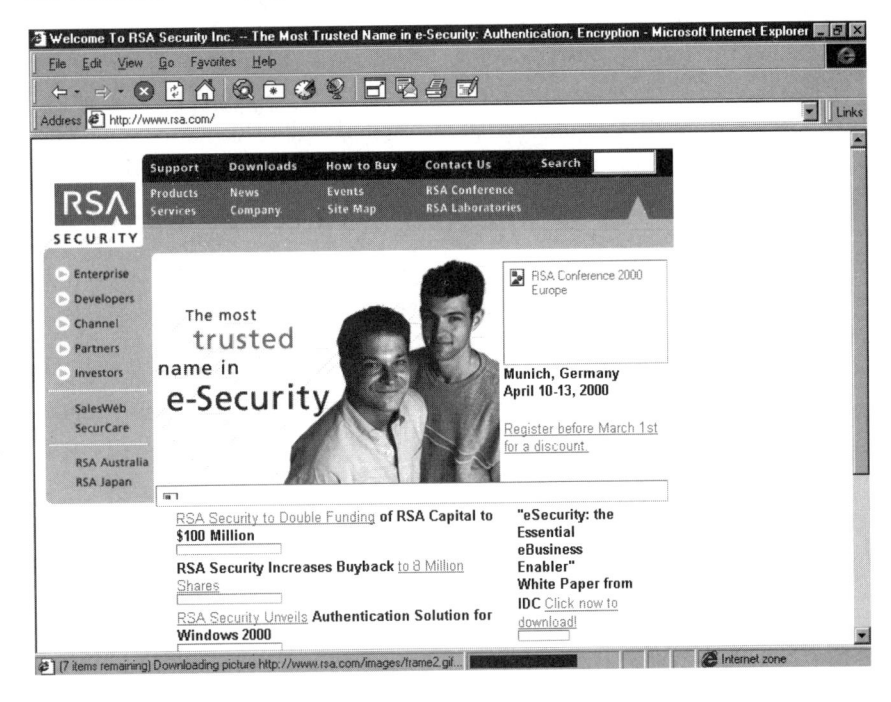

RSA is best known for its asymmetric-key encryption algorithm called RSA. Do not confuse symmetric-key algorithms created by the RSA (e.g., RC2 and RC4) for the asymmetric-key algorithm called RSA.

RC2, RC4, RC5, and RC6

RC2, developed by Ron Rivest, stands for Rivest Cipher No. 2. It is a block cipher that encrypts messages in 64-bit blocks. Because it is a variable-length key, it can work with key lengths from zero to infinity, and the encryption speed is independent of the key size.

RC4, which Rivest developed in 1987, is a stream cipher. The RC4 key length can be varied; the normal key length is 128 bits in the United States and 40 bits for export outside the United States, due to U.S. export restrictions. Lotus Notes, Oracle Secure SQL, and CDPD use the RC4 algorithm.

RC2 and RC4 are commonly used in commercial applications. They can use variable-length keys up to 128 bits in the United States. Internationally, RC2 and RC4 may be freely exported from the United States with up to 40-bit keys.

RC5 is similar to RC2 in the sense that it is a block cipher, but the algorithm accepts variable block size and key size. Also, the number of rounds the data passes through the algorithm can be varied. The general recommendation is to use RC5 with a 128-bit key and 12 to 16 rounds to obtain a secure algorithm.

After RC5 was introduced, researchers noticed a theoretical weakness in how RC5 processed its encryption during specific rounds in the process. The RC6 series, introduced in 1998, is designed to remedy this weakness. RC6 also makes it easier for systems to calculate 128-bit blocks during each round. Unlike many of the other newer encryption algorithms, RC6 consists of an entire family of algorithms. For more information about the RC series of algorithms, go to the RSA home page at www.rsasecurity.com.

IDEA

The International Data Encryption Algorithm (IDEA) was developed in 1990. At that time, it was called the Proposed Encryption Standard (PES), and it evolved into the Improved PES (IPES). Finally, in 1992, it evolved into IDEA. Like RC2 and RC5, IDEA is a block cipher and operates on 64-bit data blocks. The key is 128 bits long. Even though many consider this a stronger algorithm, it has not gained popularity. You can learn more about IDEA by reading RFC 3058, which is available at various sites, including www.rfc-editor.org. This particular RFC discusses ways to incorporate IDEA into S/MIME, but it does contain a helpful discussion of IDEA.

Blowfish and Twofish

Blowfish is a very flexible symmetric algorithm created by Bruce Schneier, who has made significant contributions in the cryptography arena, apart from his contributions as an author. Blowfish is a variable-round block cipher that can use a key of any length up to 448 bits.

Schneier has also created a newer algorithm named Twofish. This algorithm uses a 128-bit block and is much faster than Blowfish. Twofish supports

28-, 192-, and 256-bit keys. Twofish has been seen as a promising candidate for use on smart cards.

Skipjack

Skipjack is an encryption cipher designed by the U.S. National Security Agency (NSA). The actual mathematical formula is top secret but is implemented in such products as the Fortezza and Clipper chips. It uses an 80-bit key and 32 rounds on 64-bit blocks to accomplish its encryption. To learn more about how Skipjack has been used for various purposes, consult the NSA Web site, at www.nsa.gov.

MARS

A block-cipher algorithm, MARS was introduced by IBM. It uses 128-bit blocks and supports keys longer than 400 bits. The MARS algorithm presents better security than DES and it is faster. Like Twofish, it is especially designed to work well on smart cards. To learn more about the MARS algorithm, see www.research.ibm.com/security/mars.html.

Rijndael and Serpent

The Rijndael algorithm allows the creation of 128-, 192-, or 256-bit keys. It is a block cipher. The developers were especially interested in making an algorithm that could perform quickly on various platforms, including ATM networks, Integrated Services Digital Network (ISDN) lines, and even high-definition television (HDTV).

Serpent is designed to have a 128-bit block design, and it supports key sizes up to 256 bits. It is especially optimized for Intel-based chips. Although much more advanced, Serpent is somewhat comparable to DES in the way it processes information. To learn more about Serpent, consult the NEC ResearchIndex site (http://citeseer.nj.nec.com/315610.html).

Additional Symmetric-Key Algorithms

Below is a quick overview of more obscure symmetric-key algorithms. They are not widely used, but you may hear about them.

- MISTY1 and MISTY2: Developed by Mitsubishi Electric, Inc., these are block ciphers that use 64-bit blocks with a 128-bit key. MISTY2 has additional fixes that make it operate faster.

- Gost: First developed by researchers in the former Soviet Union, this algorithm (also known as "Ghost") is 4 bits, and it uses a 256-bit key. It is a block-cipher algorithm.

- Cast 256: This is a block cipher that uses 64-bit blocks but a 256-bit key. The original Cast algorithm uses a 64-bit key.

- HNC: A series of proprietary and undocumented encryption algorithms developed by the HNC Network (www.hack-net.com), HNC is designed to create access codes for software package distributions.

The Advanced Encryption Standard (AES)

Most security experts believe that DES and triple DES no longer meet security requirements. In January 1997, NIST began the process of determining a successor to DES. It was decided that the symmetric-key algorithm chosen would be called the *Advanced Encryption Standard (AES)*. Among other requirements, the symmetric-key algorithm chosen for AES had to allow the creation of 128-bit, 192-bit, and 256-bit keys; provide support for various platforms (smart cards, as well as 8-bit, 32-bit, and 64-bit processors); and be as fast as possible.

Candidate algorithms included:

- MARS
- RC6
- Rijndael
- Serpent
- Twofish

On October 2, 2000, NIST chose *Rijndael* as the official symmetric-key algorithm for AES. You can learn more about Rijndael/AES, as well as the reasons for its adoption, at http://csrc.nist.gov/encryption/aes.

> **NOTE**
> Any of the previously mentioned symmetric-key algorithms have advantages and disadvantages, ranging from susceptibility to defeat to royalty costs for using the algorithm. Regardless of the advantages and disadvantages, it is important to realize that both parties (i.e., the sender and the receiver) involved in an encryption attempt must agree ahead of time on the symmetric-key algorithm they will use.

> Generally, the three primary factors to consider when determining encryption strength are the strength of the algorithm, the secrecy of the key used, and the length of the key.

EXERCISE 2.1

Reviewing Symmetric-Key Encryption Algorithms

In this exercise, you will encrypt a file using the AES.

1. Boot into Windows 2000 as administrator.

2. Using Notepad or any other text editor, create a file named symmetric.txt on your desktop. Enter the following text, substituting your name for the asterisk:
   This was encrypted with Rijndael/aes by *.

3. Obtain the Apocalypso program from the CD that accompanies this book and place it on your desktop. Unzip the file, if necessary, and double-click the binary.

4. The Apocalypso interface will appear, as shown here.

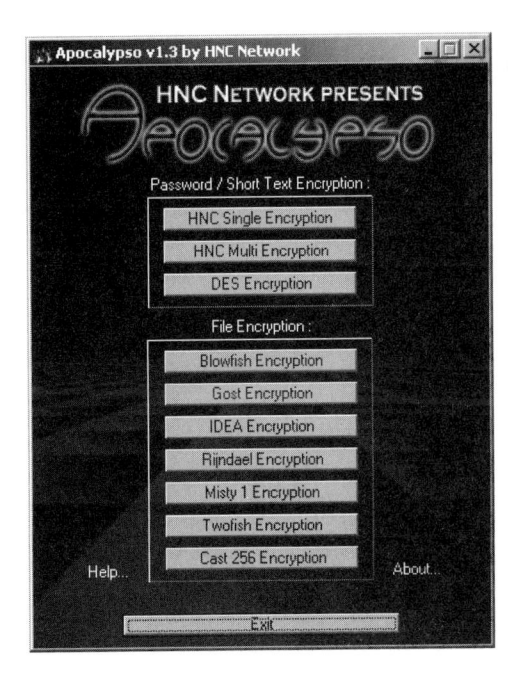

EXERCISE 2.1 *(continued)*

5. Click the Rijndael Encryption button. The Apocalypso — Rijndael Encryption dialog box will appear, as shown here.

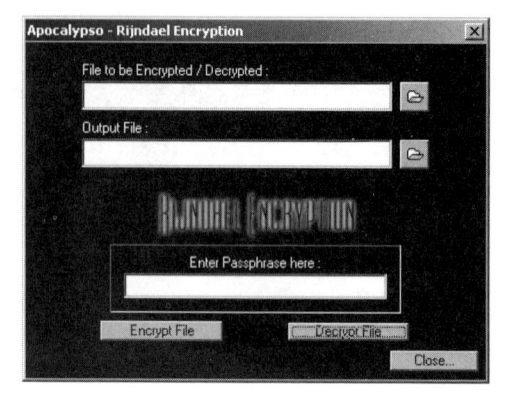

6. Enter the path and filename to symmetric.txt in the File To Be Encrypted / Decrypted text box.

7. In the Output File text box, enter the same path, but enter the following file name, substituting your first name for the asterisk: encryptedsymmetric*.txt

8. Enter a passphrase that you can remember in the Enter Passphrase Here text box, then click the Encrypt File button.

9. The file will be encrypted. Open the encryptedsymmetric.txt file in Notepad. You will see that the contents are unreadable.

10. Now, decrypt the file by opening the Apocalypso — Rijndael Encryption dialog box and entering the path to the encrypted file (encryptedsymmetric*.txt) in the File To Be Encrypted / Decrypted text box. The path should be to your desktop. For the output file name, enter the same path, but enter the following file name: unencryptedsymmetric.txt

11. Now you are ready to decrypt your file to your desktop. Because you are simply unencrypting the file yourself, you only need to figure out how to use the Apocalypso application. However, consider

> **EXERCISE 2.1 (continued)**
>
> what would happen if you sent this encrypted file to a friend who lives across the world. You would experience a key distribution problem. Consider the following questions:
>
> - How could you securely communicate this password to your friend over a long distance?
> - What medium (e.g., the telephone, a web page, or a physical note) is secure enough to carry this password?
> - What if the person were not available to receive the password from you?
> - Where would you and your friend store this password? Would it be safe?
>
> 12. Now enter your password in the Password text box, and click the Decrypt File button.
>
> 13. The file unencryptedsymmetric.txt will appear on your desktop. Open the file to see the contents of the original file.

Asymmetric-Key Encryption

Asymmetric-key encryption uses a *key pair* in the encryption process, rather than the single key used in symmetric-key encryption. A key pair is a mathematically matched key set in which one half of the pair encrypts and the other half decrypts. Although private and public keys are mathematically related to one another, determining the value of the *private key* from the public key is so difficult and time-consuming that it is practically impossible. The public key simplifies Internet-based key management because it can be freely distributed while the private key stays secure with the user.

> **NOTE** It is essential to understand the following principle in public-key encryption: What A encrypts, B decrypts; what B encrypts, A decrypts.

In asymmetric-key encryption, one of the keys in the pair is made public, whereas the other is kept private, as shown in Figure 2.3. The half that you decide to publish is called a public key, and the half that is kept secret is the private key. Initially, it does not matter which half you distribute. However, once one of the key pairs has been distributed, this key can remain public. However, the private key must always remain private. Consistency is critical.

FIGURE 2.3 Encrypting information into cipher text, using a public key

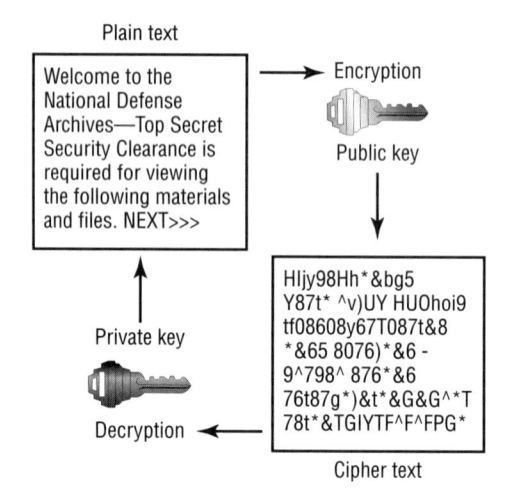

One of the drawbacks of asymmetric-key encryption is that it is quite slow, due to the intensive mathematical calculations asymmetric-key algorithms require. If a user wanted even a rudimentary level of asymmetric-key encryption for a 4MB file, the encryption process could take hours, even on a relatively powerful system.

Using Public Keys

To send a secret file to X using public-key encryption, you encrypt the file with X's public key and then send the encrypted text. When X receives the encrypted text, he or she will decrypt it with his or her private key. Anyone who intercepts the secret file cannot decrypt it without X's private key. Interestingly enough, if you encrypt a file to X's public key, you will no longer be able to read the file. Remember, it has now been encrypted to X's public key; only a user who has X's private key can decrypt it.

Backing Up the Private Key

It is possible to back up your key pair. Doing so allows you to recover from a crashed system. This backup should be stored safely. The private key will be relatively small, so it is possible to store it on a floppy disk. Consider using a more durable medium, such as a CD-R drive. Whichever storage medium you choose, make sure that you place it in a secure place, such as a safe. Should this key become compromised, the person who has obtained it will be able to read your encrypted information.

Asymmetric-Key Encryption Elements

The three most common asymmetric-key encryption elements are *RSA*, the *Digital Signature Algorithm (DSA)*, and *Diffie-Hellman*. As we explained in the section "RSA Security Symmetric Algorithms," the RSA algorithm was created by RSA Security. It has traditionally been the most popular asymmetric algorithm. However, RSA requires a royalty for its use. Because many vendors and independent programmers have not wished to pay this royalty, they have sought alternatives, such as DSA.

The DSA algorithm was introduced by NIST and is available openly. Although it functions differently from RSA, it is not proprietary and has been adopted as the standard signing method in GNU Privacy Guard (GPG), the open-source alternative to Pretty Good Privacy (PGP).

Diffie-Hellman is a protocol that provides a secure exchange of keys; thus, it is known as a key-exchange protocol. It is not an encryption algorithm per se, because it does not scramble text. Diffie-Hellman is an open standard and has been widely adopted by the security community, with only one major change: Because the Diffie-Hellman key-exchange method was at one time especially prone to attacks that stole information during the key exchange process, the Station-to-Station (STS) protocol alters the Diffie-Hellman protocol to include proper authentication. You can read more about the details of the Diffie-Hellman protocol at `ftp://ftp.rsa.com/pub/pkcs/ascii/pkcs-3.asc`. When you download this file, the `.asc` extension may confuse your browser. Choose to read the file using WordPad.

Hash Encryption

Hash encryption (also called *one-way encryption*) converts documents and information of variable length into a scrambled, 128-bit piece of code, called a *hash value*. Hash encryption creates a "hash value" that is unique to the specific piece of data from which it was generated. A hash value is always mathematically unique because hash encryption is extremely dependent on the contents of the message. The slightest change in the message will result in a different hash value, which can help you discover a change in a file. The person who wants to sign the data now only has to encrypt the hash value to ensure that the data originated from the sender. This form of signing provides security mechanisms, authentication, and data integrity.

It may seem illogical that anyone would want to encrypt something permanently. However, many uses exist for encryption that not even the user can decrypt. For example, an ATM does not actually decrypt the personal identification number (PIN) entered by a customer. The magnetic stripe has the customer's code encrypted one way into a hash code. Once the card is inserted, the ATM calculates the hash code on the PIN that the customer enters, which yields a result. This result is then compared with the hash code on the customer's card. When this method is used, the PIN is secure, even from the ATM and those who maintain it. Thus, ATMs compare values from two different entities without revealing the information. Another use for hash encryption is signing files, which we'll look at next.

Hash Encryption and Signing

Signing is often implemented by passing the data you want to sign through a one-way encryption algorithm. During the signing process, authentication of the signature is provided when the sender encrypts the hash value with his or her private key. This authentication assures the receiver that the message originated from the sender. Data integrity is achieved from the one-way encryption. Obtaining the hash value allows the receiver to run the data through the same one-way encryption algorithm to obtain his or her own hash value. The two hash values are then compared. If they are the same, this means that the data was not modified in transit.

Another advantage of using the combination of one-way and asymmetric algorithms is that the asymmetric-key algorithm has to encrypt only a small amount of data. Because hash values are typically only a few kilobytes in size, significant time is not needed to encrypt the hash value using the asymmetric-key algorithm.

MD2, MD4, and MD5

The Message Digest 2 (MD2), MD4, and MD5 hash algorithms belong to a group of one-way hash functions. These functions take any length byte streams and generate a unique fingerprint of a certain length (usually 128 bits). The process is one-way because you cannot generate the message back from the signature, and the fingerprints are unique because no two messages will have the same hash. MD5 is often used in e-mail applications.

In addition to helping create RSA, Ron Rivest developed MD2. The development process for MD2 suggested that several improvements could be made to speed up the algorithm. Research into these improvements led to the creation of MD4. MD4 produces a 128-bit hash and is faster than MD2, which explains why it gained more acceptance. However, MD4 was found to be susceptible to attacks that could break the key. As a result, Rivest developed MD5, and most applications use MD5 now. If you wish to learn more about MD5, consult RFC 1321.

Rivest's design goals for the MD series are security, speed, and simplicity. These algorithms also favor the Intel processors, as opposed to Unix and Reduced Instruction Set Computing (RISC) chips. Because the majority of client systems are Intel-based, the use of MD5 is relatively logical for most client-side applications. Also, many high-end servers use Intel-based chips, and MD5 is suitable in these situations, as well.

Secure Hash Algorithm

Secure Hash Algorithm (SHA-1) is another hash function. Also known as Secure Hash Standard (SHS), it was developed by NIST and NSA and is used in U.S. government processing. It can produce a 160-bit hash value from an arbitrary-length string.

SHA is structurally similar to MD4 and MD5. Although it is about 25 percent slower than MD5, it is much more secure. It produces message digests that are 25 percent longer than those produced by the MD functions, making it more secure against attacks than MD5.

> **NOTE** Although one-way encryption is often used to sign information, symmetric-key encryption can also be used. SSL, for example, uses symmetric-key encryption to sign information.

Implementing Hash Algorithms with the MD5sum Command

MD5 can be applied in Windows 2000 and Linux, and it is often implemented with various encryption utilities, such as those designed to encrypt hard disks. The Linux md5sum utility creates a fixed-length checksum of an individual file. The file being checked can be of any length, but the resulting checksum created by MD5 will always be fixed at 128 bits. This checksum is very useful, because it verifies whether a file has experienced tampering. You would first run MD5sum against a file to obtain its original signature. You would then run MD5sum against it at a later time to determine if the signature has changed.

For example, suppose you have a newly installed Linux system as a DNS server. Further, suppose you want to be able to check whether the /usr/sbin/named file has been changed over time. This file is the executable that starts the DNS service on your system. Because /usr/sbin/named is a binary file, you want to be able to determine whether anyone has altered it or replaced it with a trojan. In this example, we are working from the /var/james directory. Issue the following command:

```
host# md5sum /usr/sbin/named
5we5odble392,eoc97mbmd0003ndodom3xep
```

The text string immediately beneath the md5sum command is the 128-bit hash of the /usr/sbin/named file. You can save this output into a file, in this case, named.md5:

```
host# md5sum named > named.md5
```

The contents of the named.md5 file appear as follows:

```
5we5odble392,eoc97mbmd0003ndodom3xep  /usr/sbin/named
```

Notice that this file maps the 128-bit hash to the /usr/sbin/named file.

To compare the files at a later time, you can use one of the following two strategies:

- Use the cat command to compare the contents of the named.md5 file to the output of the md5sum myfile command.

    ```
    host# cat named.md5
    5we5odble392,eoc97mbmd0003ndodom3xep  /usr/sbin/named
    host# md5sum named
    5we5odble392,eoc97mbmd0003ndodom3xep
    ```

    The above output shows that the named file has not changed.

If the named file had somehow changed since the last time you ran md5sum, you would see a difference when you ran md5sum:

```
host# cat named.md5
5we5odble392,eoc97mbmd0003ndodom3xep /usr/sbin/named
host#/usr/bin/md5sum named
74s60as2djka8sjk48e1d90kdbgsdaiu90dn
```

Notice that the output is now different, showing that the file has indeed been altered since the last time md5sum was run. This change has occurred because algorithms such as MD5 use the contents of the files they encrypt and generate hash values from those contents. If the slightest change occurs, the hash value will be different.

- Use the -c option: host -c named.md5:

```
host#/usr/bin/md5sum -c named.md5
fix: OK
host#
```

The above code shows that no change has occurred. If the named file had somehow changed, you would see the following output:

```
host#/usr/bin/md5sum -c shadow.md5
/etc/shadow: FAILED
/usr/bin/md5sum: WARNING: 1 of 1 computed checksum
did NOT match host#
```

If you know a legitimate change has occurred to the file and want to generate a new hash value, delete the file containing the old hash value and create a new one.

Applied Encryption Processes

Most modern dynamic encryption uses a combination of symmetric-key, asymmetric-key, and hash encryption. This combination capitalizes on the strengths of each type of encryption, while minimizing their weaknesses.

Programs such as Internet Information Server (IIS), Netscape Suite Spot, PGP, Microsoft Exchange Server, and Windows 2000, as well as protocols such as Secure *Multipurpose Internet Mail Extension* (S/MIME), PGP MIME (PGP/MIME), and SSL, all employ a combination of symmetric-key, asymmetric-key, and hash encryption. *Virtual private networks (VPN)*, which are extended local area networks that allow a company to conduct secure, real-time communication, and protocols such as *Secure HTTP (S-HTTP)* also use such combinations. You will learn more about S-HTTP in the section "Secure HTTP."

Encryption and E-Mail

E-mail is the most obvious application for encryption, especially now that business users are relying on it. Popular ways to encrypt e-mail include PGP/MIME and S/MIME. Additional methods exist, such as those used in Microsoft Exchange Server and Lotus Notes. However, these methods are proprietary in nature and are not as universal.

Even though encryption standards differ, the principles remain the same. However, although many encryption programs use a variety of symmetric-key, asymmetric-key, and one-way algorithms as well as changing the order in which the data is encrypted, the overall process is the same.

Following is a step-by-step account of the encryption process that was outlined in Figure 2.3:

1. The sender and receiver need to obtain each other's public keys before an e-mail message is sent.

2. The sender generates a random *session key*, which is a small, disposable piece of information used to encrypt information. In this case, the information is the e-mail message and any attachments. This key is typically generated with respect to time and some randomness, such as file size or date. The algorithms used for the encryption are typically DES, triple DES, IDEA, Blowfish, Skipjack, RC5, and so on.

3. The sender passes the session key and message through a one-way encryption to obtain a hash value. This value provides data integrity so the message is not altered in transit. The algorithms used at this step are MD2, MD4, MD5, and SHA1. MD5 is used with SSL, and SHA-1 is the default with S/MIME.

4. The sender encrypts the hash value (obtained from Step 3) with his or her private key. By using the sender's private key, the receiver is certain that the message originated only from the sender.

5. The sender encrypts the e-mail message and any attachments with the random session key that was generated in Step 2. This encryption provides data confidentiality.

6. The sender encrypts the session key with the receiver's public key, to ensure that the message can be decrypted only with the receiver's corresponding private key. This provision provides authentication.

7. The encrypted message and message digest are sent to the receiver. The decryption process occurs in the reverse order of the encryption process. See Figures 2.4 and 2.5.

FIGURE 2.4 Asymmetric-key encryption

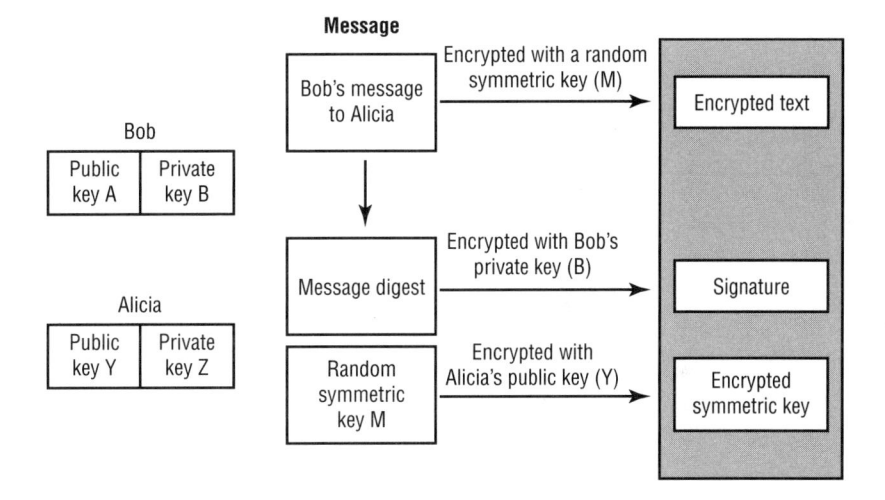

FIGURE 2.5 Asymmetric-key decryption

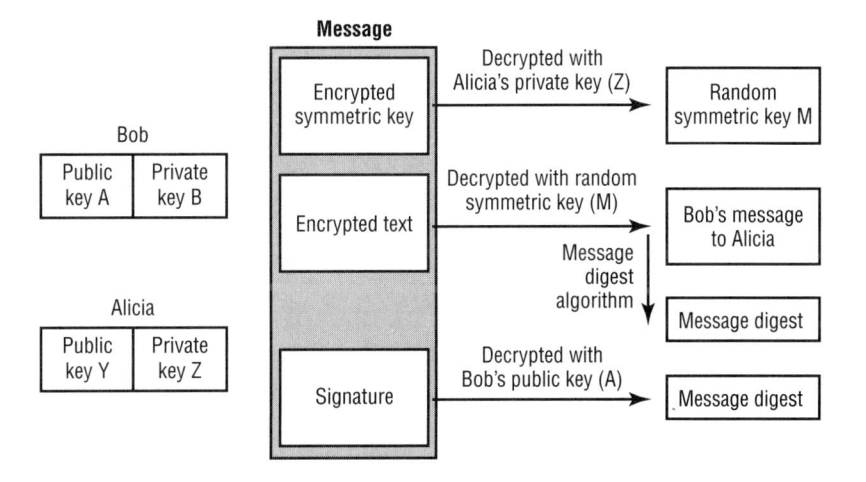

The following section explains a specific implementation of e-mail encryption as used by the methods mentioned above.

Pretty Good Privacy (PGP) and GNU Privacy Guard (GPG)

Perhaps the most popular high-technology encryption programs for e-mail and text files are Pretty Good Privacy (PGP) and GNU Privacy Guard (GPG). They are both successful because they exploit the advantages of symmetric- and asymmetric-key encryption technology, as well as hash encryption. PGP was first developed by Phil Zimmerman, then sold to Network Associates. Network Associates has now discontinued PGP development. Nevertheless, you can access the PGP home page, shown in Figure 2.6, at www.pgp.com.

FIGURE 2.6 PGP home page

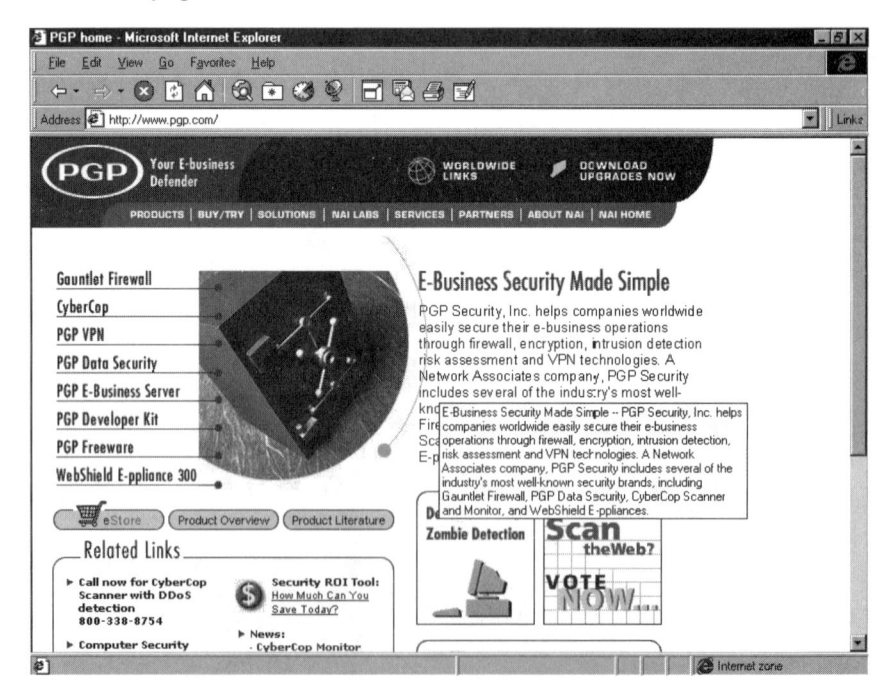

NOTE The International PGP site is www.pgpi.org. As of this writing, the International version of PGP is identical to that found at www.pgp.com.

GNU Privacy Guard is available at www.gnupg.org. The remainder of this discussion applies to both applications.

Applied Encryption Processes   77

Note: Whenever you use PGP or GPG, you are implementing a secure version of the *Multipurpose Internet Mail Extension (MIME)* protocol. MIME allows e-mail clients and servers to exchange different file types easily. Because you are using PGP and GPG, you are using PGP/MIME, which can encrypt all e-mail contents.

Upon installation, PGP and GPG generate a public and private key pair. However, as outlined above, this pair is an asymmetric key and should be considered two halves of one whole. The two halves are, in effect, two sides of the same coin. For example, the following code represents a public key, as generated by PGP 7.0.3:

```
-----BEGIN PGP PUBLIC KEY BLOCK-----
Version: PGP for Personal Privacy 6.5.8
mQGiBDRrg38RBAD1OuD2Pbi5WbIURQYt3RjnKIOouxY7MW+/Bwyp
AaLjCAjeC6T7bVPwpoyNAvzJM9MFQaku7WEOcJZJjdgH8BhdTK6o
buvz13TdVkOnOIGJHNKeE6ul2/FKbyPKN3eA8/n8iuHSmwk3W8Va
LUOdDvnMePSAdFukVYW6vBInOyKCwCg/8deO16e3ZRM6JScakrQx
R8C13UD/1YuDWhhsqYtxYDAeaDcHR5aICEXGo5Gl0ygfucP40yen
4FWBUYswKQkGIo4iDBUfZUc8uCaZ1GnWQktNaT6AyJtu6zLv/+zj
r4B4IvLi8WtvRvJq4rrDqgpoDYWxmROyvgiJG1HyXHSuM+EMEQme
rA2zjRULmogXASAB3LpZB8sA/sHJH7gtr5LrL1nnBOeUozWHtE/R
35uKVR20DL8dgQ1gAKhSgo+n1a4Aa8vmKmIBTQ9LpLv2Hg7erAcp
ghoHiU/8Y4WGodEcntelhaHDlmXVCc4c8NUd6Rryo+AA7KUkZAGt
sIjHEcJgk7u7/jtF7eF+yhmOFVILRvUP7XFK8CSDrQiSmFtZXMgU
3RhbmdlciA8amFtZXNzdEBjc25zeXMuY29tPokASwQQEQIACwUCN
GuDfwQLAwECAAoJEIBvyZAV1wnSqrMAoI++A94aySoJcxdsmyQTa
NQyB+ULAKDZyhnUMXLeiBk8pg9q82fRibqoIbkCDQQ0a4OAEAgA9
kJXtwh/CBdyorrWqULzBej5UxE5T7bxbrlLOCDaAadWoxTpj0BV8
9AHxstDqZSt90xkhkn4DIO9ZekX1KHTUPj1WV/cdlJPPT2N286Z4
VeSWc39uK50T8X8dryDxUcwYc58yWb/Ffm7/ZFexwGq01uejaClc
jrUGvC/RgBYK+X0iP1YTknbzSC0neSRBzZrM2w4DUUdD3yIsxx8W
y209vPJI8BD8KVbGI2Ou1WMuF040zT9fBdXQ6MdGGzeMyEstSr/P
OGxKUAYEY18hKcKctaGxAMZyAcpesqVDNmWn6vQClCbAkbTCD1mp
F1Bn5x8vYlLIhkmuquiXsNV6TILOwACAgf/bqRjodnx9/O7CJtkZ
mAGPwyFvvFfZgoIw/CNht1cnMR/cJmwofpFpeW8ERvY5RpYq1QVW
=VzmN
-----END PGP PUBLIC KEY BLOCK-----
```

This code represents one half of the asymmetric code known as the public and private key pair. The user who created this code can freely disseminate it; it is his or her public key. However, the other half of the code, which is mathematically equivalent to the above example, is not distributed and becomes the private key. Again, because there is one code that is cut in half, and because these two halves work together, this coding process is called asymmetric.

To ensure greater security, PGP and GPG also use a simple symmetric code. Besides generating the public and private keys, it also asks you to create a simple, memorable password that protects the asymmetric key pair, which is a form of symmetric-key encryption. In this way, both PGP and GPG create a powerful encryption system that is easy to use and that operates quickly and efficiently.

The actual message is encrypted with a random symmetric key, which is then encrypted with the recipient's public key. Finally, both PGP and GPG use hash code in that they create a cipher-text signature that can only be compared without divulging the actual information that created the key.

EXERCISE 2.2

Installing PGP 7.0.3 in Windows 2000

In this exercise, you will install PGP 7.03.

Warning: Removing PGP has been known to render your system inoperable. Specifically, removing PGP can cause the system software to not recognize the network interface card. Install and uninstall PGP at your own risk. For more information, consult the PGP documentation at www.pgpi.org.

1. Log on to your system as Administrator. Obtain the International version of PGP from Tucows (www.tucows.com) or the International PGP site (www.pgpi.org). Save this file to your desktop. You may also have to obtain WinZip or another archiving application to unzip the downloaded file.

2. Check to see what e-mail client you are using. You should have Microsoft Outlook Express installed. If you do not, obtain it from www.microsoft.com.

3. Close all programs.

EXERCISE 2.2 *(continued)*

4. Once you have extracted all files, double-click setup.exe.

5. Click Next at the Welcome screen.

6. Accept the software license agreement by clicking Yes.

7. Click Next when you see the Important Product Information screen.

8. Enter your name and company and click Next.

9. Accept the default destination location by clicking Next.

10. Make sure the plug-ins for Microsoft Outlook Express are selected, then click Next.

11. At the Ready To Start Copying Files section, review your settings and click Next. PGP will begin the installation.

12. When asked if you have any existing key rings you want to use, select No.

13. When you see the Setup Complete dialog box, make sure the Launch PGPkeys check box is selected and click Finish. The Key Generation Wizard should appear.

14. The Key Generation Wizard will inform you that you have to create a key pair. Click Next.

    Note: If the wizard does not appear automatically, select Start ➤ Programs ➤ PGP ➤ PGPkeys to start PGPkeys.

15. Enter your full name and e-mail address.

16. If necessary (for some versions of PGP): Choose Diffie-Hellman/DSS Key Pair Type (the default) and click Next.

    Note: Diffie-Hellman/DSS is a key exchange mechanism that provides a safe means of key exchange. It is a near-universal standard.

17. If necessary (for some versions of PGP): Although you can select encryption strength, choose the default (2048 bits) and click Next.

EXERCISE 2.2 *(continued)*

18. If necessary (for some versions of PGP): You will be asked when you want the key pair to expire. Accept the default, which indicates that the key pair never expires. Click Next.

19. You should see a screen that allows you to enter a passphrase, as shown here.

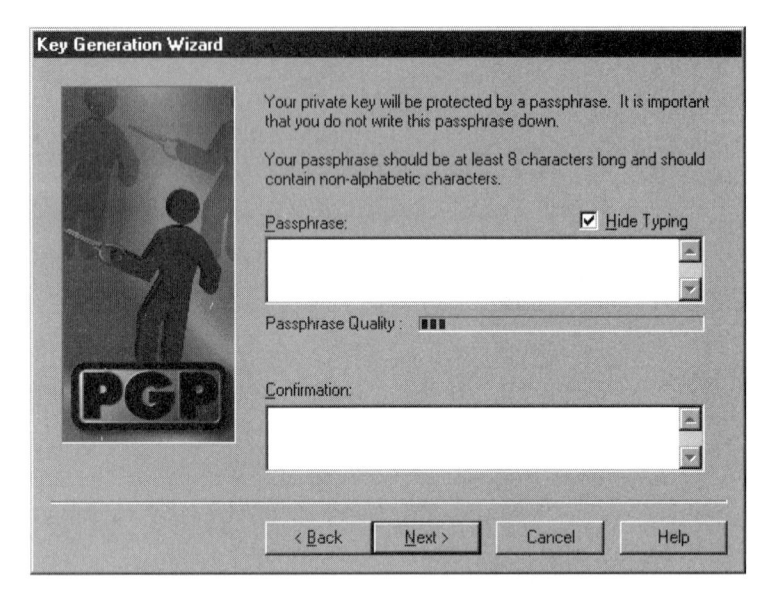

20. Add a password that includes non-alphanumeric and special characters.

21. Confirm this password, then click Next.

22. PGP will generate a new key pair. When it is finished, a message that reads "Complete" will appear on the wizard. Select Next.

23. Leave the Send My Key To The Root Server Now check box blank and click Next.

24. Click Finish to start PGPkeys.

EXERCISE 2.2 (continued)

25. Go to Programs ➢ PGP ➢ PGP Keys. Find and expand your public key, as shown here.

26. Right-click the public key you have generated and select Key Properties. Make sure your key is already fully trusted.

27. Click the Subkeys tab, and see how you can revoke the key. Do not revoke it now, or you will have to generate a new public key.

EXERCISE 2.3

Exporting and Signing Public Keys Using PGP for Windows 2000

In this exercise, you and your friend will export their public keys to each other. By the end of the exercise, you both will have a full trust relationship established using asymmetric-key encryption.

Warning: Removing PGP has been known to render your system inoperable. Specifically, removing PGP can cause the system software to not recognize the network interface card. Install and uninstall PGP at your own risk. For more information, consult the PGP documentation at www.pgpi.org.

1. If it is not already open, open PGPKeys.

2. Right-click the key pair you have just generated and choose the Export option.

EXERCISE 2.3 *(continued)*

3. The Export Key To File dialog box will open, as shown here.

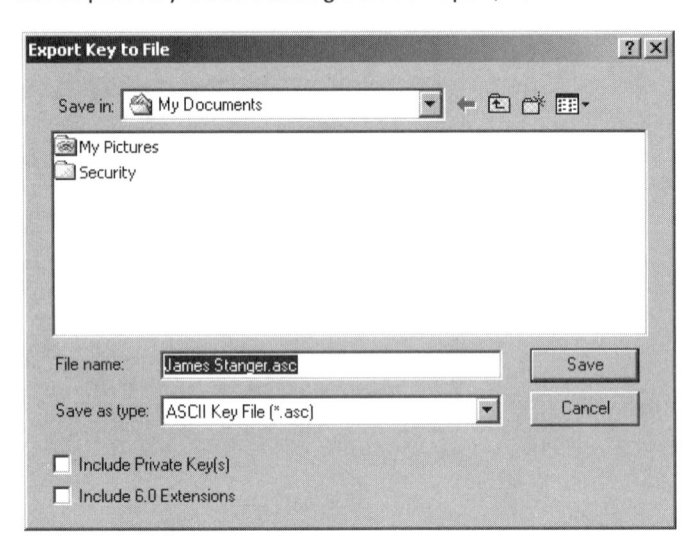

4. Do not include your private key. Because you are going to use this as a signature, you only want to export the public key. Exporting the private key would be for backup purposes only. To export your private key would result in total compromise of your key pair. Use the default name and save the public key to your desktop. You will have to navigate to your desktop and click Save. When you have finished, a file with your name and an .asc extension will appear on your desktop.

5. Open Microsoft Outlook Express.

    Note: You should see a button called Launch PGPkeys on the menu section for Outlook Express. PGP added this section during setup.

6. Configure Outlook Express to become a client to an e-mail server.

7. Once you have configured your e-mail client, send your public key to a friend as an attachment, and have your friend send his or her public key to you.

8. When you receive your friend's public key, save it to your desktop.

9. Once you have saved your friend's public key to your desktop, you can use PGPkeys to add it to your key ring. Use the Outlook Express icon to open PGPkeys. Once in PGPkeys, go to Keys ➢ Import.

EXERCISE 2.3 *(continued)*

Note: If the Open PGPkeys icon is not present, select Start ≻ Programs ≻ PGP ≻ Launch PGPtray. This selection will make the Open PGPkeys icon appear in the Taskbar. It will also ensure that the PGP buttons are found in Outlook Express.

10. The Select File Containing Key dialog box will appear. Map to your desktop and find your friend's key, select it, and click Open.

11. The Select key(s) dialog box will appear. Make sure your friend's key is highlighted and select Import.

12. Your friend's key is now in your key ring. However, it has not yet been signed and is therefore not trusted. You can see that the trust level for your friend's key ring is at 0, because the bar in the Trust field of PGPkeys is dimmed. Change this level by right-clicking your friend's key and selecting the Sign option.

13. When the PGP Sign Key dialog box appears, highlight your key and select the Allow Signature To Be Exported check box. Then click OK.

14. You will be prompted for your own passphrase (see Step 20 in Exercise 2.2). Enter a passphrase that contains non-alphanumeric characters. Write down your passphrase here for future reference: _____. You should understand that this passphrase is for your own private key, not for your friend's key. Enter it now.

15. A green icon should appear next to the key. It is now signed. Notice also that your signature is now on the key.

16. Right-click your friend's key and select Key Properties.

17. At the bottom of the dialog box, you should see that this key is now untrusted. Slide the bar from Untrusted to Trusted and click Close.

Note: If you do not conduct Steps 12 through 17, you will still be able to encrypt messages (i.e., you will be able to perform a data confidentiality service), but you will not be able to authenticate users.

18. You will now see a solid bar, indicating that this signature is trusted. You can now use it to exchange information securely.

EXERCISE 2.4

Exchanging Encrypted Messages Using PGP for Windows 2000

In this exercise, you will use PGP and Outlook Express to send encrypted e-mail.

Warning: Removing PGP has been known to render your system inoperable. Specifically, removing PGP can cause the system software to not recognize the network interface card. Install and uninstall PGP at your own risk. For more information, consult the PGP documentation at www.pgpi.org.

1. Open Outlook Express and prepare an e-mail message to your friend.

2. Before you send the e-mail message, you must encrypt it to your friend's public key. Do this by clicking the PGP Encrypt button, then the PGP Sign button, which are to the far right of the e-mail composition window.

   Note: As you choose your encryption option, make sure you select the PGP encryption buttons, not the ones supplied by Microsoft Outlook Express. If the PGP-specific icons are not present (do not confuse them with the Microsoft-specific icons), go to Start ➢ Programs ➢ PGP ➢ Launch PGP Tray. The PGPTray icon will appear in the Taskbar. It will also ensure that the PGP icons are found in Outlook Express.

3. When you have clicked the PGP Encrypt and PGP Sign buttons, click the Send button.

4. The Recipient Selection dialog box will appear. This dialog box allows you to choose your friend's public key. Add your friend's public key by double-clicking on it.

5. Click OK to encrypt and sign this e-mail message to your friend's public key.

   Note: Simply clicking OK will not choose a key. You must first add the key and then click OK.

6. You will be prompted for the password to your own private key. Enter **ciwcertified** now.

EXERCISE 2.4 *(continued)*

7. When you and your friend receive e-mail messages from each other, you will notice that they are encrypted. Double-click the message so you are reading it in its own window.

8. Click the Decrypt PGP Message button. If you do not see this button, expand the window to occupy the full size of the screen.

9. Because this message was written to your public key, you now must enter the password of your private key to decrypt it. Do so now.

10. You will see that the e-mail message is now decrypted and informs you about a "good" PGP signature status, as well as who the signer is.

EXERCISE 2.5

Generating a Key Pair Using GNU Privacy Guard (GPG) for Red Hat Linux

In this exercise, you will implement public-key cryptography using GPG. This application is included with Red Hat Linux.

1. As root, verify that GPG is installed on your system:

```
host# rpm -qa | grep gpg
gnupg-1.0.4-11
```

2. If it is not available, obtain the GPG RPM from the Red Hat installation disk, www.rpmfind.net or www.gnupg.org. You can install the RPM by using the rpm -ivh command.

3. Once you have verified the installation of GPG, you need to generate a key pair:

```
host# /usr/bin/gpg --gen-key
gpg (GnuPG) 1.0.0; Copyright (C)
1999 Free Software Foundation, Inc.
This program comes
with ABSOLUTELY NO WARRANTY.
This is free software,
and you are welcome to redistribute it
under certain conditions.
```

EXERCISE 2.5 *(continued)*

```
    See the file COPYING for details.
    Please select what kind
    of key you want:
       (1) DSA and ElGamal (default)
       (2) DSA (sign only)
       (4) ElGamal (sign and encrypt)
    Your selection?
```

4. Enter **1**, then press Enter.

5. Select 2048 Bits as the key size.

6. Press Enter to configure the key so it never expires.

7. Confirm your decision by entering *y* and pressing Enter.

8. Enter your real name, then your e-mail address and a comment (such as the passphrase `ciwcertified`).

9. Enter a passphrase (`ciwcertified`). You will have to confirm the passphrase.

10. The GPG program will then generate a new key pair. While it does, type on the keyboard and move the mouse so the computer has some random information to help generate a stronger key pair.

11. After some time, the GPG program will finish. Confirm that GPG has created a private key by entering the following:

    ```
    host# /usr/bin/gpg --list-secret-keys
    /root/.gnupg/secring.gpg
    ------------------------
    sec   1024D/0840A624 2000-02-24
    James Stanger (ciwcertified) <mail@mail.com>
    ssb   1024g/90A6DEB7 2000-02-24
    host#
    ```

12. Verify that you have a public key:

    ```
    host# /usr/bin/gpg --list-keys
    /root/.gnupg/pubring.gpg
    ------------------------
    pub   1024D/0840A624 2000-02-24
    James Stanger (ciwcertified) <mail@mail.com>
    sub   1024g/90A6DEB7 2000-02-24
    host#
    ```

EXERCISE 2.5 (continued)

13. Verify that you have signed your key:

    ```
    host# /usr/bin/gpg -list-sigs
    host# gpg --list-sigs
    /root/.gnupg/pubring.gpg
    -----------------------
    pub   2048D/0840A624 2000-02-24
    James Stanger (ciwcertified) <mail@mail.com>
    sig           0840A624 2000-02-24
    James Stanger (ciwcertified) <mail@mail.com>
    sub   2048g/90A6DEB7 2000-02-24
    sig           0840A624 2000-02-24
    James Stanger (ciwcertified) <mail@mail.com>
    ```

14. You are now ready to trade public keys.

EXERCISE 2.6

Exchanging and Signing Public Keys in Linux

In this exercise, you will exchange public keys with a friend and then sign them.

1. You will now use GPG to export your public key. Specifically, you need to export the key into a file. Name this file after your first name and give it an .asc extension:

   ```
   gpg --export > yourfirstname.asc
   ```

2. Copy this file to your FTP directory:

   ```
   cp name.asc /var/ftp/
   ```

3. Have your friend use anonymous FTP to pick up the public key.

4. You should now have your friend's key. Use GPG to import your friend's key into your own key ring. If your friend's name were Vlad, you would enter the following:

   ```
   /usr/bin/gpg --import vlad.asc
   gpg:/root.gunpg/trustedb/gpg: trusdb created
   gpg:Total number processed: 1
   gpg:                    imported: 1
   ```

EXERCISE 2.6 *(continued)*

5. You have just imported your friend's public key into your database. List all keys again using GPG's `--list-keys` option.

6. You should see that you have added your friend's key. However, this key is untrusted; no one has signed it. If you are reasonably sure that this key did in fact come from your friend, begin the sequence to sign the key. The sequence begins with the `--sign-key` option, followed by the public key name, which can either be the username or the e-mail address. In the example, below, James is signing Sandi's key. You must confirm your choice and then enter your own private key's password to finish the signing:

```
/usr/bin/gpg --sign-key
gpg --sign-key sandi@mail.com
pub  2048D/D324EB6E
created: 2000-02-24 expires: never      trust: -/q
sub  2048g/54FA9880
created: 2000-02-24 expires: never
(1)  Sandi Stanger (ciwcertified) <sandi@mail.com>
pub  2048D/D324EB6E
     created: 2000-02-24 expires
: never     trust: -/q
          Fingerprint:
717F F1B2 3702 BEB7 BBC3  C32F 5157 A02B D324 EB6E
     Sandi Stanger (ciwcertified) <sandi@mail.com>
Are you really sure that you want to sign this key
with your key: "James Stanger"
 (ciwcertified) <james@mail.com>"
Really sign? y
You need a passphrase to unlock the secret key for
user: "James Stanger (ciwcertified) <james@mail.com>"
1024-bit DSA key, ID 0840A624, created 2000-02-24
host#
```

7. List all signatures again using the `--list-sigs` option. You should see that your friend's key is now signed:

```
host# gpg --list-sigs
/root/.gnupg/pubring.gpg
-----------------------
```

EXERCISE 2.6 *(continued)*

```
pub  2048D/0840A624 2000-02-24
  James Stanger (ciwcertified)
<james@mail.com>
sig        0840A624 2000-02-24
  James Stanger (ciwcertified) <james@mail.com>
sub  2048g/90A6DEB7 2000-02-24
sig        0840A624 2000-02-24
  James Stanger (ciwcertified) <james@mail.com>
pub  2048D/D324EB6E 2000-02-24
  Sandi Stanger (ciwcertified) <sandi@mail.com>
sig        D324EB6E 2000-02-24
  Sandi Stanger (ciwcertified) <sandi@mail.com>
sig        0840A624 2000-02-24
  James Stanger (ciwcertified) <james@mail.com
✋sub  1024g/54FA9880 2000-02-24
sig        D324EB6E 2000-02-24
  Sandi Stanger (ciwcertified) <sandi@mail.com>
host#
```

8. You are now ready to encrypt messages and files to your friend using his or her public key.

EXERCISE 2.7

Encrypting and Decrypting Files Using GPG

In this exercise, you will use GPG to encrypt a file to your friend's public key.

1. Write your friend's public key name down on a separate piece of paper for future reference.

2. Create a simple text file named secret:

   host# touch secret

3. Using a text editor such as vi, enter the following text: **This message is secret**. If using vi, enter the following command:

   host# **vi secret**

EXERCISE 2.7 *(continued)*

4. To enter text, put vi into the text insert mode by pressing the I key. When you've finished entering text, exit your text editor and save changes by pressing Esc, then ZZ.

5. Encrypt this file to your friend's secret key:

   gpg --encrypt -r
     public_keyname secret

6. Whenever GPG encrypts a message, it appends the .gpg extension to the file. Use cat to read the secret.gpg file:

   host# cat secret.gpg
   ...__TTú˜_____úœë(_R'L3
   host#

   Note: Issuing this command may corrupt your terminal screen. If it does, log off and log back on. Make sure you log back on to the directory in which you were working.

7. You cannot read this file because it is now encrypted to your friend's key. At this point, copy this file to your FTP directory and have your friend pick up the file.

8. Pick up your friend's file when he or she has finished processing it.

9. Each of you should now have a file encrypted using GPG. Your friend has used your public key to encrypt the file to you. Using GPG, decrypt it using your secret key as follows:

   host# gpg --decrypt secret.gpg

10. Enter your passphrase for your secret key (**ciwcertified**).

11. You should see the message sent by your friend. If you want to create a new file that contains this message, enter the following command:

    host# gpg --decrypt secret.gpg > secret

12. You can then use a text editor (or cat) to read the file.

> ### EXERCISE 2.8
>
> **Creating a Signature File**
>
> In this exercise, you will create a signature file and then give it to your friend.
>
> 1. Use touch to create a file. Name it after your first name.
>
> 2. Create a cleartext signature file. For example, if your file's name is james, you enter the following command:
>
>   `host# gpg --clearsign james`
>
> 3. Enter your passphrase (**ciwcertified**).
>
> 4. If your original file is named jill, GPG will generate a new text file named jill.asc. Use cat to read this file:
>
>    ```
>    -----BEGIN PGP SIGNED MESSAGE-----
>    Hash: SHA1
>    -----BEGIN PGP SIGNATURE-----
>    Version: GnuPG v1.0.0 (GNU/Linux)
>    Comment: For info see www.gnupg.org
>    iD8DBQE4tJ1LqmqRrAhApiQRA
>         jL3AKCJu5DBrDnysa8i/h7XmKGA097JXACcCLBN
>    HcZrsYcShJz7IszVow15taY=
>    =NpP1
>    -----END PGP SIGNATURE-----
>    ```
>
> 5. You can now distribute this file using e-mail, or any server (FTP, HTTP, and so forth). Remember that you must give the file an .asc extension.
>
> 6. Obtain your friend's signature file. You now have cleartext signature files. You can use these files to verify documents signed by your friend.

Proprietary Asymmetric-Key Encryption

Microsoft Exchange, Lotus Notes, and Novell GroupWise can use proprietary algorithms. The actual e-mail servers, not the clients, encrypt and decrypt messages. The advantage of such proprietary encryption systems is that because the encryption is fully integrated at the mail server level, a user need only click a button to encrypt and decrypt. This solution is efficient because its users do not have to generate keys or take steps to decrypt messages. This method can save valuable time.

The disadvantage of such a proprietary asymmetric-key encryption method is that it is compatible only with other servers by the same vendor. Thus, a Lotus Notes user could not send encrypted e-mail to a Microsoft Exchange client. For example, many organizations use Unix for SMTP and POP3 servers. Any communication sent between an Exchange server and a Unix server would not be secure, unless the users employed Secure MIME, PGP, or some other encryption program. This restriction could significantly limit your organization's ability to communicate securely and still conduct business.

Encrypting Drives

In addition to encrypting e-mail, you can encrypt files and entire portions of hard drives, create checksums for files, and create hidden, encrypted drives. The Windows 2000 Encrypting File System (EFS) is an example of a native operating system solution. It can encrypt both files and folders. You can enable EFS on Windows NT File System (NTFS) drives by right-clicking a file or folder. Third-party products that implement file encryption include:

- BestCrypt (www.bestcrypt.com or www.jetico.com)
- Locker (www.locker4u.com)
- EasyCrypt (www.easycrypt.co.uk)

Secure HTTP and Secure Sockets Layer

The Secure Hypertext Transfer Protocol (Secure HTTP) and the Secure Sockets Layer (SSL) each allow automatic encryption. They are often used in web, e-mail, and Network News Transfer Protocol (NNTP) servers to help secure transactions and communications. Additional applications used in the security community also support SSL. Like PGP, both Secure HTTP and SSL use symmetric, asymmetric, and one-way encryption. Specifically, they use an asymmetric key to exchange a symmetric key, and they use one-way encryption to sign all the data packets.

Secure HTTP

As shown in Figure 2.7, Secure HTTP (S-HTTP) uses the asymmetric process to secure online transactions, but as soon as this connection is made, it uses a symmetric key. Most browsers support this protocol, including Netscape Navigator and Microsoft Internet Explorer.

FIGURE 2.7 Asymmetrically encrypted information passed through a network

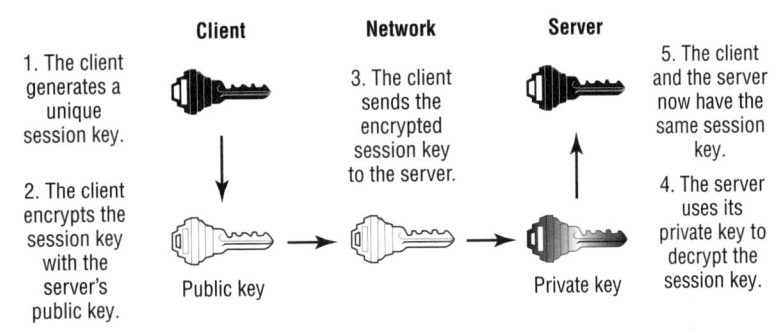

1. The client generates a unique session key.

2. The client encrypts the session key with the server's public key.

3. The client sends the encrypted session key to the server.

4. The server uses its private key to decrypt the session key.

5. The client and the server now have the same session key.

Secure Sockets Layer (SSL) and Digital Certificates

The Secure Sockets Layer (SSL) protocol allows users to configure their applications to privately exchange data over public networks. SSL helps prevent eavesdropping, tampering, and message forgery. SSL 3.0 is an Internet Engineering Task Force (IETF) specification. (The IETF is an organization that determines the standards and protocols for the Internet. You can learn more about the IETF at www.ietf.org.) All major web browsers and many e-mail clients support SSL, as do many additional applications used in the security industry. SSL sessions occur on TCP port 443 by default.

SSL uses a *digital certificate* to enable two applications to authenticate over a network. A digital certificate is created by a *certificate authority*, which is a trusted third party that attempts to determine the validity of a certificate request from person or host. Once a digital certificate is signed by a certificate authority, it enables a server to prove its identity to a client. A digital certificate can also ensure data confidentiality because it encrypts all information between the client and the server. Finally, SSL provides data integrity services, because it uses one-way encryption to ensure that data has not been altered in transit.

Essentially, a digital certificate is a specific form of an asymmetric key, except that digital certificates contain several fields that help a client (e.g., a web browser) determine authentication. Each of these fields is governed by the X.509 standard, as defined by RFC 2459. You will learn more about X.509 in Chapter 6.

SSL encryption occurs above the Transport layer of the Operating Systems Interconnection Reference Model (OSI/RM). SSL uses a six-step handshake process to build a connection between a client and a server. It acts as a thin veneer between the session and transport layer. Fortunately, we need not explain the details here. The top-level sequence of the SSL protocol is as follows:

1. The client generates a random session key using a symmetric-key algorithm.
2. After authentication, all data is encrypted using this session key. The algorithms typically used are DES or RC4.
3. The message authentication hash, or one-way encryption (SHA/MD5), signs all the packets providing data integrity.

> **NOTE** The SSL specification details the data structures, client/server handshake protocol, certificate and key exchange procedures, messages, constants, and so forth. You need not know all the internal details of the SSL to use the protocol.

In some ways, SSL might be more secure than other methods because the encryption process takes place at a lower level of the network, according to the OSI model. Furthermore, SSL can encrypt more activity than S-HTTP because S-HTTP will encrypt only HTTP activity, whereas SSL encrypts the entire packet. The transport level of SSL takes place at a lower level of the stack than S-HTTP. Both protocols require certificates.

> **NOTE** When connecting to a website that uses SSL for encryption, usually only the web server has a digital certificate. Thus, only the web server is authenticated, but not the client or browser. Client authentication does not typically occur because most Internet users do not have digital certificates installed on their machines. However, it is possible for a web server to require client authentication. In such cases, the server's administrator must configure the web server to require client certificates, and must also ensure that each client receives a certificate.

> **NOTE** OpenSSL allows Linux systems to create certificate authorities and create SSL certificates. You can download it at www.openssl.org.

How Do Browsers Use Public-Key Encryption?

You have probably used a web browser to conduct an e-commerce transaction. It has become standard to encrypt such transactions using the Secure Sockets Layer (SSL). Most web browsers already have certificates from trusted certificate authorities, and most websites have had their certificates signed by the same authorities. Once your web browser recognizes that a web server's certificate has been signed by a trusted authority, the SSL session is granted, as long as the browser verifies that:

- The certificate has been signed by a trusted authority.
- The web server has the same name as given in the certificate.
- The certificate is still valid and has not expired.

If any one of these checks fails, most web browsers will warn you and ask if you want to proceed. Usually, failures occur because a certificate has expired, or because a web server's name has been changed.

Common SSL Client Errors

It is important to understand that in an SSL session, the server presents a certificate to the application being used (e.g., a web browser). Below is a short list of the typical errors a web browser will experience when you're using SSL:

Certificate authority not recognized   In many cases, this error suggests that the server's certificate has not been properly signed. In most cases, the SSL session should not be continued. In some instances, the certificate is perfectly valid, and the client simply needs to import the certificate into his or her browser.

Certificate name is not valid for this server   This means that the X.509 Common Name (CN) field in the certificate presented to the web browser is different than the DNS name for the server. This is evidence that a problem exists, and the SSL session should be terminated. Sometimes, the problem is simply a misconfigured server.

Certificate has expired   Digital certificates are valid for only a specific period of time. Time periods ensure against certificate misuse. Whenever a client experiences any of the above errors, he or she can either proceed with the transaction or the session can be ended. It is sometimes necessary to import a certificate permanently into a browser. In most cases, however, users should be encouraged to import certificates only for the current session. Once the user closes the web browser, the certificate will be flushed from the system. When the user accesses the site again, he or she will have to again import the certificate.

Additional Uses for Digital Certificates

Digital certificates are useful in many situations and are not limited to SSL. For example, software developers can use a digital certificate to assign responsibility. Device drivers, as well as ActiveX and Java programs, for example, can be signed to show who created them. It is important to understand, however, that signing applications and drivers only helps trace where they came from. A signed device driver or applet can still contain a dangerous application that can compromise your system's security. However, you would have the benefit of knowing where this driver came from.

The Certificate Revocation List

It is possible to create a certificate revocation list (CRL), a list of certificates that have been manually revoked before their normal expiration date. This list makes it possible to quickly inform all affected parties that a private key currently in use is no longer valid. A CRL may become necessary, for example, when an employee is terminated, and you no longer wish this employee to use signed messages on behalf of the company.

Summary

In this chapter, you have applied encryption principles. You created trust relationships and learned about some of the more powerful encryption options currently available. You have learned about public-key cryptography and hash algorithms, and studied how to use them on Windows 2000 and Linux. Finally, you reviewed certificate principles and the use of SSL on your web server. Now that you understand how to implement encryption, you can learn more about different types of attacks commonly waged against systems.

Important tasks to know include:

- Creating trust relationships using encryption
- Listing specific forms of symmetric-key, asymmetric-key, and hash encryption
- Deploying public-key encryption in Windows 2000 and Linux

In the next chapter, you will learn more about the various attack types discussed in the CIW Security Professional exam. As you read through Chapter 3, try to remember some of the things you have learned about encryption. You will find that encryption helps thwart some of the attacks described in that chapter. For example, man-in-the-middle, spoofing, and many DNS-based attacks can be thwarted by using symmetric-key, public-key, and hash encryption.

Exam Essentials

Know how to establishing trust relationships. Know some of the methods used to create trust relationships. These can include using PGP, SSL, and other methods that enable users to encrypt data and verify identity. You should know how to use a popular application such as PGP or GPG.

Understand encryption terminology. You will need to be familiar with the terms commonly used in cryptography. These include rounds, parallelization, block and key ciphers, as well as the Diffie-Hellman exchange protocol. You must understand how public and private keys are used to encrypt contents.

Be able to list symmetric-key and asymmetric-key algorithms. Be especially familiar with the DEA (Rijndael), DES, and triple DES algorithms. It is also important to understand the benefits and drawbacks of symmetric key and asymmetric algorithms.

Understand Secure HTTP (S-HTTP) and Secure Sockets Layer (SSL). It is vital that you identify how S-HTTP and SSL encrypt transmissions.

Key Terms

Before you take the exam, be certain you are familiar with the following terms:

- Advanced Encryption Standard (AES)
- algorithm
- block mode
- certificate authority
- dictionary program
- Diffie-Hellman
- digital certificate
- Digital Signature Algorithm (DSA)
- handshakes
- hash encryption
- hash value
- key pair
- Multipurpose Internet Mail Extension (MIME)
- one-way encryption
- parallelization
- password sniffing
- private key
- Public Key Cryptography Standards (PKCS)
- Rijndael
- round
- RSA
- Secure HTTP (S-HTTP)
- session key
- signing
- stream-cipher mode
- trust relationship
- virtual private networks (VPN)

Review Questions

1. Jeanne must encrypt an e-mail message to her friend, Pedro. What must Jeanne use to encrypt her e-mail so that only Pedro can read it?

   A. Her private key

   B. Her public key

   C. Pedro's private key

   D. Pedro's public key

2. According to industry standards, what is the minimum key length for strong encryption?

   A. 128 bits

   B. 56 bits

   C. 168 bits

   D. 40 bits

3. Because the Data Encryption Standard (DES) encrypts data in 64-bit blocks, it is considered to be which of the following?

   A. A hash algorithm

   B. A block cipher

   C. A 56-bit key

   D. A dictionary program

4. Mary has become concerned that her home page may be subject to attack. She wants to sign her home page so that she can verify that it has not been changed. Which of the following encryption algorithms will she most likely use?

   A. RC2

   B. RC6

   C. Diffie-Hellman

   D. MD5

5. What type of encryption converts documents and information of variable length into fixed, scrambled, and unique code that are 128-bits in length?

   A. Asymmetric-key encryption

   B. Symmetric key encryption

   C. Hash encryption

   D. Strong encryption

6. It has become necessary to change the IP addresses for your web server farm. During this change, a systems administrator has renamed one of the web servers from www1 to www3. By checking the logs, you note that e-commerce traffic has suddenly dropped on this server. Also, you note that some customers have called, informing you that their web browsers sometimes give messages that this server's name is no longer trusted. What has happened?

   A. The certificate has expired, and you must request a new one.

   B. There is an IP address conflict with another server.

   C. The firewall does not allow the server to communicate on the network.

   D. The certificate is no longer valid for this server.

7. What benefit does the Diffie-Hellman key exchange method provide?

   A. It encrypts public keys between two users and their hosts.

   B. It encrypts private keys between two hosts.

   C. It provides a secure method of transferring keys.

   D. It encrypts transmissions between hosts.

8. William wishes to communicate securely with Mary. Mary has given William her public key. William has distributed his key pair to a public, centralized server. What must be done now in order for William to communicate securely with Mary?

   A. William must create a new key pair.

   B. Mary must obtain William's public key.

   C. Mary must create a new key pair.

   D. William must encrypt messages using his public key.

9. Which of the following services can a digital certificate provide?

    A. Data padding

    B. Server authentication

    C. Physical security

    D. Hash encryption

10. Which of the following algorithms is a symmetric-key algorithm?

    A. Diffie-Hellman

    B. RSA

    C. DSA

    D. RC5

11. Michelle has just received a public key from a friend, Sandi. Sandi has used PGP to generate this public key. Michelle wishes to add this public key to her own PGP key ring. If Sandi used the default extension for her public key name, what would be the name of her public key file?

    A. sandi.txt

    B. sandi.acp

    C. sandi.asc

    D. .sandi.pgp

12. Ruth has just imported James' public key into her key ring. What must she do now in order to use this public key?

    A. Sign the key.

    B. Export it.

    C. Create a cleartext version.

    D. Create a certificate revocation list.

13. Between which layers of the OSI/RM does SSL operate?

    A. Between the Transport and Network layers

    B. Between the Transport and Session layers

    C. Between the Physical and Datalink layers

    D. Between the Application and Presentation layers

14. Margot wishes to purchase an item from an SSL-enabled website. When the SSL session begins, which type of encryption generates and signs the session key?

    A. Asymmetric

    B. Symmetric

    C. Hash (i.e., one-way)

    D. Both symmetric and hash encryption

15. Which of the following Windows 2000 Server elements represents an operating system-level encryption utility?

    A. Windows File Protection (WFP)

    B. Message Digest 5 (MD5)

    C. Encrypting File System (EFS)

    D. The Windows driver signing utility

16. What is the default SSL TCP port for a web server?

    A. 443

    B. 110

    C. 80

    D. 143

17. You have just backed up your private key. Where should it be stored?

    A. On a public server

    B. On a recipient's CRL

    C. On a recipient's key ring

    D. In a secure place

18. Which X.509 field provides the name for a server?

    A. The Server Name (SN) field

    B. The Common Name (CN) field

    C. The Server Authentication (SA) field

    D. The Certificate Authority (CA) field

19. An employee has left the company. You wish to bar this employee from signing messages using your certificate. What tool do you have available to you?

    A. Public-key encryption

    B. A symmetric key

    C. A certificate revocation list (CRL)

    D. A digital certificate

20. What is the purpose of the Station-to-Station protocol?

    A. To secure the Diffie-Hellman protocol

    B. To secure the DSA algorithm

    C. To secure the PGP protocol

    D. To secure the Rijndael algorithm

Answers to Review Questions

1. **D.** Remember the following formula when applying public-key encryption: What A encrypts, B decrypts; what B encrypts, A decrypts. This means that if you wish to encrypt transmissions to someone, you must first obtain that person's public key and encrypt all transmissions to that key. Then, only that person's private key can decrypt the message.

2. **A.** The security industry considers 128-bit keys to be acceptable for strong encryption. Longer keys are preferable.

3. **B.** A block-cipher algorithm encrypts data into discrete blocks during the encryption process. Breaking data into blocks makes it easier to verify the integrity of data before it is encrypted. Most symmetric-key algorithms in use today are block ciphers.

4. **D.** One-way encryption (i.e., hash encryption) is generally used to sign a file in the manner described. MD5 encryption, for example, is often used in the Linux operating system to verify that a file has not been altered.

5. **C.** Hash encryption (i.e., one-way encryption) creates 128-bit values that are highly dependent on the contents of the file it encrypts. Thus, the values are always going to be unique.

6. **D.** SSL certificates are used to verify the authenticity of a server, among other things. If the server's DNS name changes and the certificate is not updated, the certificate is no longer valid for this server and must be replaced.

7. **C.** The Diffie-Hellman key exchange method does not encrypt transmissions. Rather, it provides a method for key exchange.

8. **A.** When using public-key encryption, the private key must remain private. A key pair contains both the private and public keys generated by a user. Because William has published his private key to a public server, his key pair is no longer secure.

9. **B.** Digital certificates can authenticate servers. They can also make it possible to encrypt transmissions between hosts.

10. **D.** RC5 is the only symmetric-key algorithm listed. Diffie-Hellman is a key exchange protocol and is not an algorithm. RSA and DSA are asymmetric-key algorithms.

11. C. By default, PGP gives the extension .asc to all public-key files.

12. A. All keys must be signed by a valid authority before they can be safely used. In regard to PGP, the holder of the private key can sign any public key, or the holder of the private key can ask for a key to be signed by a trusted third party.

13. B. SSL is a thin veneer placed above the Transport layer of the OSI/RM.

14. B. In SSL, the session key is signed using symmetric-key encryption.

15. C. Although the Windows driver signing utility does use hash encryption to sign drivers, the EFS feature in Windows 2000 is the only operating system-level encryption utility listed.

16. A. Although SSL can be conducted on almost any port, the default port for use with web browsers is 443. POP3 uses port 110, and the standard web server port is 80. IMAP servers use port 143.

17. D. A private key must always remain private. It should be stored in a place accessible only by its true owner.

18. B. An X.509 certificate contains many different fields. However, the CN field contains the server name. This name must match the DNS name of the server, or else a client will receive an error message.

19. C. A CRL allows authorized users to determine if a private key has become invalid before its expected expiration date. Whenever a certificate becomes compromised, a CRL should be created or updated.

20. A. The Diffie-Hellman key exchange protocol was once prone to an attack that enabled public keys to be compromised. The STS protocol solved this problem.

Chapter 3

Types of Attacks

THE CIW EXAM OBJECTIVE GROUPS COVERED IN THIS CHAPTER:

- ✓ Apply security principles and identify security attacks.
- ✓ Identify penetration and control strategies and methods, including but not limited to: potential attacks, router security, threat containment, intrusion detection.

The CIW Security Professional exam requires that you understand the types of attacks commonly waged on the Internet. Before drilling down into each attack type, however, it is important to understand that each can be placed into two broad categories: accidental threats and intentional threats. Here is a short summary of each type:

Accidental threat Caused by systems administrators and innocent users without any premeditated thought or plan. For example, a user may remotely access a system and accidentally enter a login session that was not terminated cleanly by the previous user. The second user can potentially access any vital information to which the previous user had access. In Unix, a login shell setting to ignore signals for a phone hang-up action can sometimes cause this problem. Equally possible, a system may shut down due to a sudden outage, and when it is turned on again, inconsistencies in the disk information because of the outage can cause it to boot up in a single-user but privileged mode (sometimes without a password, depending on the Unix machine's configuration).

Intentional threat The result of intentional action, in which a planned action is carried out. Its effects range from a simple examination of files, without alteration of data, to a systematic change in the entire system that causes malicious damage.

Intentional threats can be further divided into the following:

Passive threats This type of threat includes the use of a sniffer on a network to read data packets being sent without altering the contents or changing the destination. Legitimate users of the data would probably not even know about the activity. This type of activity is usually not logged.

Active threats Includes activities such as repeated access attempts and the modifying of information stored on the operating systems. It can also include the creation of multiple packets that flood the network.

The CIW Security Professional exam differentiates between an attack and a vulnerability. An *attack* describes a method used by a hacker to attack your system. A *vulnerability* describes the state of a network host that, in one way or another, invites an attack.

Specific Attacks

Now that you have reviewed the general categories of threats, you can identify the various types of active and passive attacks that are waged on the Internet. Table 3.1 describes the attack types covered on the exam.

TABLE 3.1 Types of Attacks

Type	Description
Spoofing (i.e., masquerade)	An attack in which a host assumes another entity on the network. The entity under a spoofing attack is convinced it is dealing with a trusted host.
Man-in-the-middle	An attack in which applications are used to capture and/or manipulate packets as they pass across the network wire.
Denial-of-service	Any type of attack that brings a system offline or otherwise makes a host's service unavailable.
Insider	An attack perpetrated by employees. This category includes eavesdropping, which involves employees purposefully spying on the network to uncover information. It also includes social engineering, in which employees are duped into divulging sensitive information. Insider activities include, for example, "shoulder surfing," in which a hacker obtains passwords and other information by eavesdropping on an employee as he or she works.

TABLE 3.1 Types of Attacks *(continued)*

Type	Description
Bug-based	An attack that takes advantage of applications, services, and daemons that have been improperly configured or that have problems embedded in their code. As a result of system flaws, the system can be compromised.
Keylogging	An application that is capable of capturing all keystrokes made by a user. Such applications generally store all captured keystrokes in a word readable file that can be accessed remotely. Captured information can include passwords and other sensitive information.
Brute-force	The use of repeated attempts to defeat authentication. These attacks involve the use of a plain-text file containing various words and names. This file is used to guess usernames and passwords, and is often called a "word file" or "dictionary file."
Trojan	An application or daemon that appears to have a legitimate purpose but that has a hidden function designed to defeat security.
Virus	An application designed to spread from system to system. It requires user intervention in order to be activated. A virus often contains a payload, which can alter file contents or even disable the operating system.
Worm	An application that resembles a virus, except that a worm is capable of propagating itself without user intervention.

The attack types discussed in Table 3.1 are explained only in the most general terms. The rest of this chapter will provide specific examples of each.

> **NOTE** Scanning systems to learn about open ports and vulnerabilities is also an attack. Never scan systems that you do not own. You will learn more about legitimately scanning systems in Chapter 11.

Spoofing

Spoofing and masquerading are forms of identity theft. Generally, spoofing is discussed in the CIW Security Professional exam in terms of *IP spoofing*, which is the ability of one machine to imitate another. As you might suspect, IP spoofing exploits the Internet's open network design, as well as traditional trust relationships established between Unix systems. Remember, unless countermeasures are taken, all IP-enabled servers assume that a packet has been generated by a legitimate source. However, various applications exist that enable Windows and Linux systems to forge source and destination IP addresses. Spoofing makes it quite difficult to determine exactly who sent an IP packet to a network host.

Hackers use IP spoofing to great advantage by creating programs that issue forged IP packets. Hackers can use these programs, combined with programs and/or processes that establish TCP connections, to make one system appear to be another. Hackers can then proceed to attack systems at will, because it is very difficult to trace the origin of the attack. Hackers can also use IP spoofing as part of other attacks. For example, as you will see in the section "Connection Hijacking and Combined Attack Strategies," IP spoofing is an integral part of connection hijacking.

IP Spoofing and the Unix R-Series of Commands

The r-series of commands (`rlogin`, `rexec`, and so forth) are designed to make logging on to remote systems more convenient. Most systems administrators strive to ease their administrative burden, and applications such as `rlogin` have been popular administrative tools. `rlogin` is a Telnet-like application that allows a user to log in to a remote system without having to provide a password. To use `rlogin`, the systems administrator must create what are called `rhosts` and `rlogin` entries.

Many Unix systems contain `rhosts` and `rlogin` entries that create trusted connections between hosts over untrusted networks, such as the Internet. It has been traditionally assumed that using `rlogin`'s authentication system provides adequate security because it combines the use of "where you are," address-based authentication with the Unix system's authentication scheme. However, `rlogin`'s "where you are" authentication is too dependent on the initial assumption that an IP address cannot be forged. It is possible to defeat `rlogin` authentication through IP spoofing, and thus the r-series of commands should not be used.

Blind and Non-Blind Spoofing

Two types of spoofing exist:

Non-blind spoofing   Occurs when a hacker manipulates a connection on the same subnet or the same physical line.

Blind spoofing   Occurs when a hacker manipulates a connection that exists on a separate physical line.

The latter is more difficult to execute, though still common.

Spoofing and Traceback

Many applications created by hackers can spoof IP addresses. The ability to falsify this information is useful for a hacker because it thwarts detection. Most security administrators try to trace suspect connections. This activity is called a *traceback*. The victim of an attack that also includes IP spoofing will find it difficult to trace the attack to its true origin. Although a systems administrator may be able to check system log files and packet captures, these checks may not reveal the true source IP address of the attack if the hacker has successfully spoofed the source IP address.

> **NOTE** One of the more powerful examples of spoofing is *Address Resolution Protocol (ARP) cache poisoning*. IP spoofing is the ability to generate falsified information within an IP header. IPv4 is especially prone to this practice, because the IP stack does not contain the innate ability to prove origin of source. IPv6, however, has this ability and improves security considerably. ARP cache poisoning allows a host to insert bogus information into a local or remote host's ARP table. This attack is effective only on networks that are connected to the local network. Thus, ARP poisoning is effective against switches, but not against routed networks.

Many network administrators place DNS, e-mail, and web servers outside the protecting firewall. One popular hacker move against networks that place resources outside the firewall is to spoof the IP addresses of these hosts. Thus, it is best to place all hosts inside the firewall. You can then configure the firewall so that only certain traffic types are allowed in and out of the network.

Man-in-the-Middle Attacks

A *man-in-the-middle attack* is one in which a hacker attempts to act on packets being sent from one network host to another. This category is rather broad because it contains all of the attacks that can occur on network data as it passes across a network. The one thing that unifies all of the attacks in this category is that the hacker must be physically located between the two legitimate hosts being attacked. Here is a list of the most common types of man-in-the-middle attacks.

Packet capturing This type of attack involves sniffing the packets to gain username and password information. Any other information sent in cleartext, such as the contents of e-mail messages, can also be captured. Man-in-the-middle attacks are very common in LANs and on the Internet. However, the advent of switches has lessened the possibility of these attacks, because a switch opens a dedicated connection between two hosts. However, applications like ettercap (`http://ettercap.sourceforge.net`) use such strategies as ARP poisoning to enable sniffing in a switched environment.

Packet alteration It is possible to edit captured packets using various applications. For example, it is possible to alter checksum and header information to make that information useful in a future attack. Editing packets is sometimes referred to as "cooking" them. The NetDude application (`http://sourceforge.net/projects/netdude/`) allows any user to capture and then alter a packet stream captured from a network transmission. A *packet stream* is a series of network transmissions that the hacker has obtained and is acting on.

Packet injection Once a packet stream has been edited, it is possible to send it back out on the network. *Packet-injection attacks* include the replay attack, in which a hacker captures a login session between one remote host and another, then resends (i.e., replays) those packets in an attempt to gain access. Usually, these packets are edited so that the header information, such as the sequence numbers, matches what the victim server expects.

Connection hijacking This type of attack involves intercepting and taking over connections that are in progress. A malicious user can actually monitor a Telnet or IRC chat session and then inject any text he or she wants. It is also possible to make a host impersonate another host with the goal of capturing the contents of the network transaction. We'll discuss connection hijacking used in combination with other attack strategies in the section that follows.

Connection Hijacking and Combining Attack Strategies

It is necessary to engage in three separate attacks when hijacking a connection. You must first begin the hijack, then conduct a denial-of-service attack and spoof IP addresses. The section "Denial-of-Service (DoS) Attacks" provides more information. Before we learn more about these attacks, though, let's take a look at the focus of a connection-hijacking attempt: the *TCP handshake*. To establish the TCP connection, a three-way handshake must be completed. The three-way handshake consists of the following steps (this example uses the client/server model):

1. The client (or requesting end) performs an *active open* by activating the SYN flag in the TCP header. The TCP header also contains:
   - The desired port number for connection.
   - The sequence number field with the *initial sequence number (ISN)*. This number, which is generated randomly, is used to synchronize the client and server when they transfer data on the byte stream.

2. The server performs a *passive open* by sending its own SYN to the client that specifies:
   - The server's ISN
   - An acknowledgment (ACK) of the client's SYN

3. Finally, the client returns an ACK to the server. The client and server can now transfer data using the byte stream, and the connection is established. Figure 3.1 illustrates this entire process.

FIGURE 3.1 Establishing a TCP connection

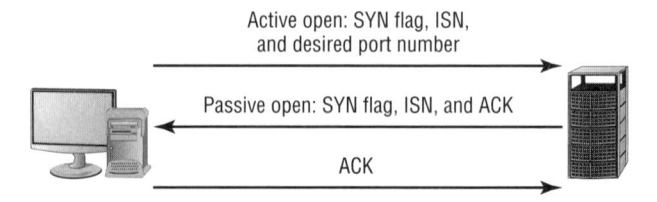

> Generally, strong encryption is the best protection against a man-in-the-middle attack.

Compromise can occur just after the first active open occurs. Suppose you have three hosts: Host A, Host B, and Host C. When Host A begins to communicate with Host B, the attacker, Host C, finds a way to assume Host B's identity. Once this happens, Host C impersonates Host B and begins receiving and transmitting data sent from Host A. In a successful attack, the legitimate hosts believe they are communicating directly with one another, when in reality the hacker is intercepting all traffic and routing it to each host. The hacker can then do anything he or she likes with the data.

The attacker who wants to hijack a connection must conduct a denial-of-service attack against the host he or she is impersonating. For example, if the attacker assumes Host B's identity, the attacker must eliminate this host from the network.

The hacker who conducts an IP spoofing attack requires several programs, among them:

- A packet sniffer.
- An application to kill a TCP connection or crash the entire server.
- An application to generate a TCP connection and spoof an IP packet.

Some applications, such as hunt, can do all three. You can download hunt at various sites, including packetstorm.linuxsecurity.com.

Attacks on DNS Servers

Below are two types of man-in-the-middle attacks that can be waged against a DNS server:

Unauthorized zone transfers By default, many DNS servers allow any host to obtain a *zone transfer*. If a hacker obtains a DNS zone file, he or she will be able to easily identify all of the hosts on the network. Allowing unauthorized users access to such information essentially allows them to obtain a map of your network.

DNS poisoning Even if a DNS server is placed behind a firewall, it usually has to conduct a zone file transfer. A zone transfer between a master and a slave DNS server occurs using TCP port 53. Because TCP is used during such a transfer, it is possible to inject packets into it. Depending on the talent of the hacker, it is possible to populate the secondary DNS server with bogus information. This activity is called *DNS poisoning*.

Denial-of-Service (DoS) Attacks

In a *denial-of-service (DoS) attack*, a hacker prevents a legitimate user from accessing a service. For example, if a hacker creates a malformed packet that crashes your e-mail server, he or she has conducted a DoS attack against your network's ability to provide e-mail. A DoS attack could also focus on an attempt to overload a system. For example, the attacker may try to overburden an FTP server by logging on as many times as possible, or by uploading so much information to the server that its hard drive fills to capacity. Alternatively, the hacker may target the actual network connection and flood it with bogus TCP and UDP packets. In such cases, the entire network is denied service to the Internet.

In some circles, DoS attacks are considered to be rather useless because they don't directly lead to system penetration. This, however, is a mistaken assumption. DoS attacks are often quite useful to a hacker. The three main purposes behind a DoS attack are:

- To crash a server and make it unusable to everyone else.
- To assume the identity of whatever system the hacker is crashing. Hacker strategies, such as connection-hijacking attacks, must often deactivate the true host that they are spoofing. The DoS attack does not enable a hacker to assume an individual's identity, but it does ensure that the legitimate individual cannot reply.
- To install a Trojan or an entire root kit. Windows hosts, for example, often require a restart whenever an application has been installed. A DoS attack can be used to force a restart that, in turn, starts a service or application meant to compromise the system.

In the sections that follow, we'll discuss several popular DoS attacks. Pay careful attention to these descriptions, because a DoS attack may be more than just an annoyance; it may be an indicator of a more serious attack.

SYN Flood

The *SYN flood* is one of the most commonly perpetrated attacks against servers on the Internet. It takes advantage of the otherwise normal activity of establishing a TCP handshake. A hacker can create multiple half-open TCP connections. During the process, the hacker drops a connection with a server while it is engaged in creating a port. The hacker then makes another connection and leaves it, only to make thousands of others, until the target server has opened hundreds or thousands of half-open connections. As a result, the server's performance is severely limited, or the server actually crashes. See Figure 3.2.

FIGURE 3.2 A SYN-flood attack

The attacking host sends active open (SYN) packets, with spoofed source IP addresses.

Attacking host

Victim host

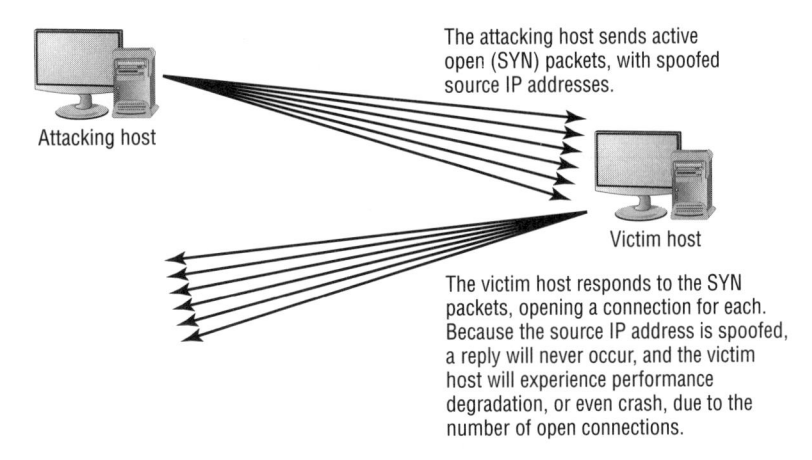

The victim host responds to the SYN packets, opening a connection for each. Because the source IP address is spoofed, a reply will never occur, and the victim host will experience performance degradation, or even crash, due to the number of open connections.

Figure 3.2 shows that a host from one network has attacked a host on another network. Usually, the attacking host spoofs the return IP address, which makes the attack even more powerful. This is because the attacking host will not have to reply to any of the victim host's acknowledgments. Many times, a firewall will not stop such attacks because it has not been configured to detect a SYN flood.

> **NOTE** A packet sniffer and the `netstat` command are perhaps the best two tools to use when trying to identify and recognize SYN floods and other attacks waged from across a network. A packet sniffer allows you to view the details of any packet (ICMP, IP, TCP, UDP, and so forth). The `netstat` command will reveal active TCP and UDP connections on your system.

Smurf and Fraggle Attacks

The *Smurf attack* involves manipulating the Internet Control Message Protocol (ICMP), the protocol invoked by the ping program. As shown in Figure 3.3, a hacker first creates a packet that appears to originate from what will become the victim host. Next, the hacker sends this packet to an unwitting third party, which becomes the intermediary host. This host will quite naturally respond with its own ICMP response packet, thus becoming an unwitting conspirator in the Smurf attack.

FIGURE 3.3 A smurf attack

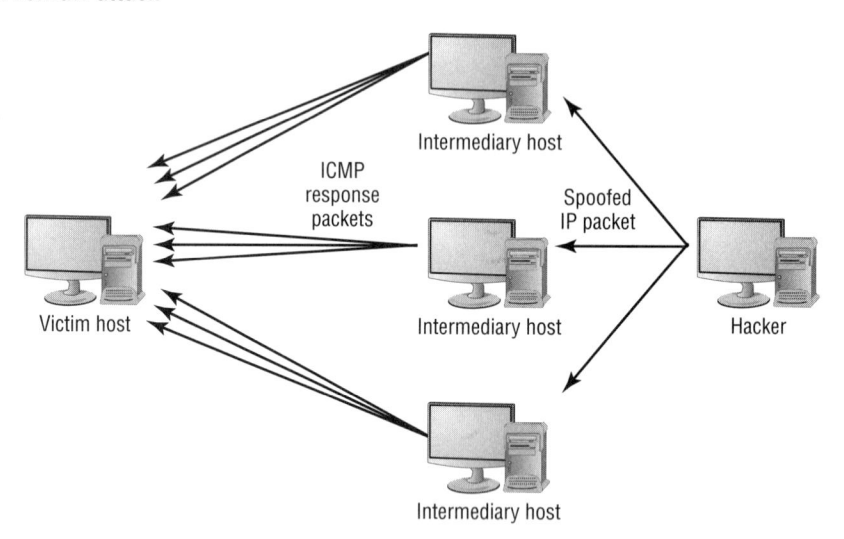

If a hacker sends enough ICMP packets, the replies will overwhelm the victim's computer. Once the system becomes overwhelmed, it will stop responding to network requests. The hacker may then proceed to attack more systems. If you are especially unlucky, the hacker may begin to spoof connections using your now crashed server.

> **NOTE** As you might deduce from this description, many attacks use IP spoofing to avoid detection.

A *Fraggle attack* is similar, except it uses UDP. Although the typical port is 7 (the echo port), most programs that wage Fraggle attacks allow you to specify any port you want.

The best way to protect yourself against Smurf and Fraggle attacks is to filter out ICMP packets at the firewall or to disable pinging on your server. These measures, however, make it rather difficult to test connectivity if a problem occurs.

Smurf, Fraggle, and Broadcast Addresses

Broadcast addresses are those ending in .255. Some routers generate responses to broadcast IP addresses. A broadcast address can be used legitimately as a troubleshooting tool. You can send one ping packet to an entire subnet to see which hosts are responding. On the other hand, these addresses can be used in a Smurf or Fraggle attack. When just one broadcast address is entered, up to hundreds of hosts can participate in an attack.

As a security professional, you should recommend that networks should disable directed broadcasts at their routers. You can learn more about directed broadcasts and Smurf and Fraggle attacks at http://netscan.org.

Teardrop/Teardrop2

The *Teardrop* series of attacks takes advantage of code that does not properly reassemble overlapping UDP packets. It is generally associated with the identification protocol, which ties a TCP connection to a particular user identity. For example, sendmail uses the ident service to authenticate users attempting to access the service. You can learn more about the identity protocol in RFC 1413.

Unpatched Linux and Windows systems (NT/2000, 9*x*, ME) are particularly prone to these attacks, making this a well-known form of attack. Teardrop is a DoS attack resulting in the "blue screen of death," showing the *STOP 0x0000000A* error. Although most systems are now patched against this attack, Teardrop can still be used to consume processor time and host bandwidth.

The key difference between the Teardrop and Teardrop2 attacks is that the latter uses 20 bytes for data padding and also spoofs the UDP packet length, allowing the newer attack to bypass certain service packs and hotfixes. For more information about the Teardrop and Teardrop2 attacks, consult the CERT (www.cert.org) or SANS (www.sans.org) website.

> **Note:** The Teardrop attack is often called the "Boink attack." Teardrop2 is called the "Bonk attack."

Ping of Death and Ping Floods

The *ping-of-death* attack crashes a system by sending an ICMP packet that is larger than 65,536 bytes. Generally, it is impossible to send an IP datagram of 65,536 bytes. However, a packet can be divided into pieces, then reassembled at the victim's address. This process causes a buffer overflow in the victim's system. You will learn more about this in the section titled "Buffer Overflows." Most modern operating systems have been updated to thwart this attack.

A ping flood is created when an application generates thousands of ICMP packets. Linux systems, for example, can use the `ping -f` command to generate many packets. However, dedicated ping-flood applications can generate many more packets. Such attacks are designed to clog network connections or make systems respond slowly to network requests.

Land Attack

The *land attack* occurs when a hacker sends a spoofed IP packet to a target computer that has the same source and destination port and IP address. The land attack is a DoS attack resulting in a system crash or slowdown. Most systems are already patched against this attack.

Distributed Denial-of-Service (DDoS) Attacks

A *distributed denial-of-service (DDoS) attack* is one in which several remote systems work together and generate network traffic meant to crash a remote host. Such attacks can often focus enormous amounts of traffic on one host, causing it to crash under the burden. In other cases, a DDoS attack focuses on the "network pipe" (for example, the T1 or T3 line) and fill it with fraudulent traffic. Your systems may be able to operate, but no one will be able to access their services.

DDoS traffic often consists of false ICMP packets, although UDP and TCP are also used. As shown in Figure 3.4, multiple hosts are combined to create a data stream that cripples the victim host.

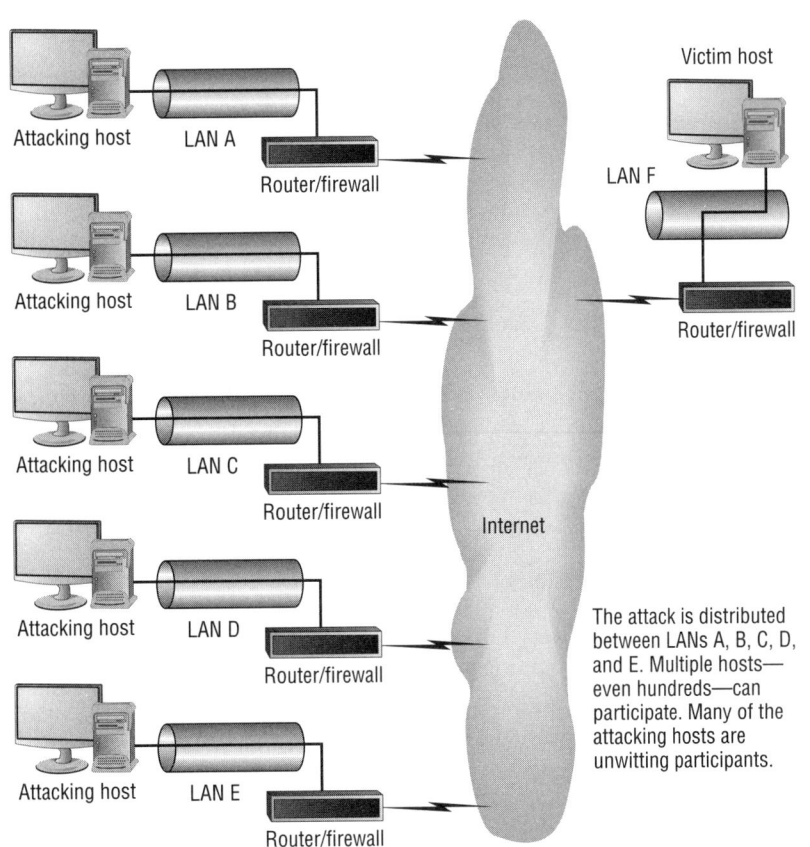

FIGURE 3.4 Understanding a DDoS attack

The attack is distributed between LANs A, B, C, D, and E. Multiple hosts—even hundreds—can participate. Many of the attacking hosts are unwitting participants.

Recovering from DoS and DDoS Attacks

Recovering from a DoS attack may require a simple reboot, if the attack has caused a system crash. However, DDoS attacks often require you to reprogram your switches and routers to drop offending traffic. On Windows 2000 systems, you can invoke IPsec policies that allow you to limit or forbid traffic from certain hosts. On Linux systems, you can use the `ipchains` (for the 2.2 kernel and earlier) or `iptables` (for the 2.3 kernel and later) applications to completely block DDoS traffic.

Preventing DoS and DDoS Attacks

You can reduce the likelihood of DoS and DDoS attacks by doing the following:

Update the operating system. All operating systems require updates. Updates are often called "patches" or "service packs." Install only the latest, stable version of these patches.

Closely observe the code being used. If you have employees creating custom applications, carefully monitor the code-creation process. If possible, have the code audited to ensure that the creator did not accidentally or intentionally insert code that can cause a security breach.

Obtain only stable versions of servers, services, and applications. Never use experimental or "beta" software on a production server. Test any new software or operating systems on an isolated subnet to ensure that they behave as expected.

Insider Attacks

Insider attacks are at least as common as attacks from the outside. The same methods used in external perimeter attacks to gain unauthorized access can also be executed internally, sometimes with greater ease, because many systems and security administrators do not expect attacks from inside the firewall. Eavesdropping on messages between applications and compromising existing control mechanisms are two techniques used in insider attacks. Physical attacks are also common. In a physical attack, the hacker obtains access to the system and steals one of its elements, or otherwise manipulates data on the server.

Social Engineering

In *social engineering*, a hacker uses tricks and disinformation to gain access to sensitive information. In many ways, social engineering can turn legitimate employees into unintentional hackers. For example, suppose a group of high school students want to gain access to a local business's computer network. To this end, they create a form that asks for what appears to be innocuous personal information, such as the names of all of the secretaries and executives and their spouses, as well as the names of children, pets, and so forth. The students-turned-hackers say that this simple survey form is part of a social studies project. Using this form, the students are able to quickly penetrate the system because most of the people on the network are using the names of pets and spouses for their passwords.

Another form of social engineering is a hacker's attempt to imitate a legitimate user by confusing a switchboard operator or guard. For example, a hacker calls a company, posing as the systems manager. He explains that he has accidentally locked himself out of his computer and that the password needs to be changed. Once he has obtained the password from the guard, all the hacker would then have to do is log on to the machine with full administrative access. Many clever variations of this basic strategy have been attempted.

Con artists who dupe people into revealing their credit card numbers often engage in social engineering. The con artist somehow confuses the victim into divulging sensitive information, often by getting the victim to forget that it was he or she who was first approached. Once this error on the victim's part occurs, a hacker can often obtain confidential information. Typical targets of this social-engineering strategy include anyone who has access to information about systems they do not use, including secretaries, janitors, some administrators, and even security staff.

Terminating Employees

Insider attacks often occur immediately after an employee has been terminated. When an employee is terminated, it is not enough to simply remove the user account. It is necessary to end the user's login session, because even if the user account is gone from the domain controller's Security Accounts Manager (SAM) database, the login session is still resident in memory. A systems administrator who forgets this can indirectly cause a security breach.

It is also often necessary to physically escort the employee out of the office to ensure that he or she does not remove equipment, change passwords, or create back doors that will allow him or her to enter the system.

Bug-Based Attacks

A *system bug* is an unintentional flaw in a program that creates an inadvertent opening. For the purposes of the CIW Security Professional exam, a bug is also an unintentional configuration mistake, such as the use of default server settings. Many times, an operating system or program running on the server contains these coding problems. Hackers almost always know about such problems and exploit them. Let's take a look at the various types of bug-based attacks.

Back Doors

A *back door* is an undocumented opening in an operating system or program, generally placed there deliberately by the software developer. Program designers sometimes intentionally place a back door in an operating system or program so they can support the product quickly. In this sense, some back doors are not the products of malicious intent; unlike a bug, a back door is intentionally left by the designer.

However, many systems administrators are not aware of back doors in their operating systems, whereas many hackers are. Therefore, what was intended as an aid to the system quickly becomes a liability.

The lesson to learn regarding back doors is that you should never trust a new service or application without first reading about it and asking trusted colleagues. When you audit a system, take the time to carefully document any applications that have an unknown origin or a questionable history.

Trap Doors

A *trap-door attack* takes place when specified conditions occur. An example of a condition is the time of day in which certain commands are executed. Another example is what may occur when several commands are run at the same time. A common hacker strategy is to install an application, then have it run only at a specified time. The result of a trap-door attack is that the system is left vulnerable.

> **NOTE** Trap-door attacks are also called "logic" attacks.

System Defaults

Thus far, you have learned about some rather exotic attacks. However, the most common and pressing problem in systems security is the fact that most systems use default settings. One way to solve this problem is to ensure that your security policy has administrators ensure that all systems have default settings changed to a custom value.

Information Leakage

Almost all network daemons leak too much information by default. During a connection, each computer must supply potentially sensitive information to create a connection between a server and the Internet. Organizations must determine how to minimize the information they provide to the public, as well as take the proper steps to provide only the necessary legitimate information. The first step is to determine what information is necessary, and what is not.

Take steps to protect the following information:

- Contents of a DNS server
- Routing tables
- User and account names
- Banner information running on any of the servers

Banner information is crucial to hackers so they can identify the type of operating system and Internet service that a host is running. The banner information can sometimes be obtained by telnetting directly to a specific port on a host. Many security administrators are now removing this information so that hackers cannot use it against them.

> **NOTE** Applications such as nmap (www.insecure.org) can identify operating systems by examining how an operating system creates and receives TCP, UDP, and IP packets. Most operating systems implement TCP/IP in slightly different ways. Each implementation leaves behind distinct signs, or "fingerprints," that allow a hacker to deduce the type of operating system that created it. Hiding these fingerprints is very difficult. Still, you can reduce information leakage by reducing the information presented by daemon banners.

Information Leakage in Apache Server

Apache Server, for example, defaults to providing full information concerning its configuration. Default information provided includes:

- Full information about Apache Server, including the version name.
- The type of operating system on which it is installed (e.g., Red Hat Linux or Windows 2000).
- All installed modules (e.g., `mod_ssl/2.6.6 OpenSSL/0.9.5a mod_perl/1.24`).

To solve this problem, Apache Server allows you to edit the `/etc/httpd/conf/httpd.conf` file and enter any of the following:

ServerTokens Full   The default setting, which reveals all information about the daemon and the server.

ServerTokens ProductOnly   The banner contains only the word "Apache." This feature is supported only in later versions of Apache Server 1.3.*x*.

ServerTokens Minimal   Apache's banner sends the following: Apache/1.3.0.

ServerTokens OS   The server's banner contains the name of the web server, as well as the operating system version.

You make these changes in the `httpd.conf` file, which is in the `/etc/httpd/conf/` directory, in Red Hat Linux servers.

Whenever you change the contents of this file, remember to restart Apache Server (using the command `/etc/rc.d/init.d/httpd restart`).

> **NOTE** Telnetting to port 80 and reading the information will not test whether this banner fix is operating. Use a more advanced vulnerability scanner to test the difference between banners. For example, Symantec's NetRecon or Internet Security Systems' Internet Scanner would be ideal for gaining such information. These scanners can also gather much more information, such as weak passwords, low system patch levels, and other vulnerabilities. You will learn more about vulnerability scanners in Chapter 11.

Buffer Overflows

In order to run, all applications, services, and daemons allocate a slice of memory from the operating system. This slice of memory is called a *buffer*. Good coding practice stipulates two things about buffers: First, the receiving buffer should always have enough room to accommodate the information being placed into it. Competent programmers work hard to create routines that verify and size the data before it is placed into a buffer. Second, the type of information should be checked before being passed from one process to another and placed into the receiving buffer. This data must be verified, because sometimes it can crash the application or cause it to behave unexpectedly. Sometimes, however, the validation routines used by programmers cannot anticipate the amount or type of data that is actually placed into a buffer. At other times, conditions not anticipated by the programmer occur, and too much information can be placed into a buffer, even though the information is checked.

When a buffer fails in the manner just described, a *buffer overflow* is said to occur. Another, less popular name for a buffer overflow is *buffer overrun*. Buffer overflows can be perfectly harmless, or they can lead to conditions that cause complete compromise of a server (e.g., a web or database server).

In some cases, when a flood of data or a piece of improperly formatted data overflows a program's storage buffer in memory, it actually overwrites the buffers of other daemons operating on the system. In such catastrophic cases, the result can cause a "shell" (i.e., a space of memory) to be left behind. This shell often has administrative (e.g., root) permissions. Hackers then focus on this shell, because often it will accept any command the hacker wants to issue. In IP-enabled systems, this shell can be linked to a certain port, thus opening the system to a remote attack.

Many hackers then create applications that exploit these conditions. These applications enable hackers to execute code arbitrarily on the system. Such code can include commands that:

- Cause password databases to be sent to a user via e-mail, or copied to a world-readable place on the hard drive, such as the FTP root directory

- Start (or stop) certain services or daemons

- Open additional ports that then request malicious applications to be uploaded and installed on the system

- Write any information (such as HTML and GIF files as directed by the hacker) to places on the hard drive, such as the system's web document root directory (e.g., C:\inetpub\wwwroot\ or /var/www/html)

Although the skill level required to craft these attacks is advanced, the programs to execute them, once designed, are quite simple and are freely distributed across many Internet-based hacking sites. This simplicity and availability pose a significant threat to security professionals, because they allow a relatively inexperienced user to "own" (i.e., compromise) an Internet server by simply clicking a mouse button or entering a few simple commands.

Languages such as C and C++ are especially vulnerable to buffer overflows, mainly because they make direct calls to system memory without checking to see whether that memory exists in the first place. Buffer overflows are arguably the most pressing security concern today. For more information about buffer overflows, go to www-4.ibm.com/software/developer/library/overflows/index.html.

Buffer overflow attacks have occurred for some time, and new ones are being discovered regularly. In May 2001, programmers at Eeye Digital Security (www.eeye.com) discovered a buffer overflow related to IIS 5.0 that allowed a malicious user to execute arbitrary code on the system. Eeye then released code meant to exploit this vulnerability, which left all Windows 2000 systems exposed (even those with the latest service packs and hotfixes). Many site defacements subsequently occurred.

> **NOTE** Eeye has a history of discovering Windows-based buffer overflows. In 1999, for example, Eeye researchers discovered a buffer overflow in IIS 4.0. After contacting Microsoft about the problem, they also released exploit code that many hackers were able to use.

Microsoft IIS and Buffer Overflows

One IIS buffer overflow was discovered when researchers discovered that 420 bytes of information were sent in a simple HTTP GetRequest header meant for the Internet printing services feature. The specific filter was located at \WINNT\System32\msw3prt.dll. This filter was part of the Internet Server Application Program Interface (ISAPI), which is designed to allow programmers to create applications for the IIS 5.0 web server. Because IIS 5.0 resets (i.e., restarts) itself automatically, the shell that is left behind after the initial crash operates indefinitely, allowing hackers to execute arbitrary code. Furthermore, because the attack was designed to use the existing TCP connections between the web server and the client, firewalls did not stop them. Microsoft issued several hotfixes to solve the problem.

Combining Attacks: Sending Fake E-Mail

As you might suspect, it is possible to combine various attack types. For example, using some social-engineering talents and a simple Telnet client, a hacker can trick an end user into revealing information. The Telnet client is especially important, because a hacker can use it to access an improperly configured e-mail server and assume someone else's identity. All a hacker has to do is find an e-mail server that allows relaying. With relaying, the SMTP server does not check its user account database and allows anyone to use its services.

> **NOTE** E-mail servers that do not restrict access to authenticated users are often used by individuals and companies that send bulk e-mail messages to thousands of people. Such unsolicited bulk e-mail is called *spam*.

Once a hacker finds such a server, he or she can use a Telnet client to access port 25 of the e-mail server and create a *fake e-mail* message that appears to originate from a legitimate user. The message created by the hacker looks quite legitimate. Such messages are real in the sense that they have been sent from a legitimate source (the e-mail server) to a legitimate user (the victim). To most e-mail users, the message will seem absolutely authentic.

However, the message sent is fraudulent in the sense that a hacker has generated it by tricking an e-mail server. Many older SMTP servers do not enforce relaying by default, and few companies spend the time or money to add an authentication process to their mail servers. Therefore, hackers can easily assume any identity they want, and then send as many messages as they like. The venerable SMTP daemon used by most Internet providers, sendmail, stopped allowing relaying by default as of version 8.9. Still, many e-mail servers use older sendmail versions and remain vulnerable.

It is possible to configure your e-mail server to automatically reject e-mail from servers that have a history of indiscriminately relaying. Special servers often called "e-mail black holes" keep lists of relaying servers. For more information about this practice, read the home page of the Coalition Against Unsolicited E-mail (CAUCE) at `www.cauce.org`. You can find additional information at the Network Abuse Clearinghouse site (`http://spam.abuse.net`) and the Open Relay Blackhole Zones (ORBZ) site (`www.orbz.org`).

Hackers can use fake e-mail to engage in social engineering. To gain passwords and other sensitive information, a hacker can send an e-mail message that appears to be coming from a legitimate source. Combined with a well-placed telephone call, a hacker can quite easily convince a naive user that he is a legitimate systems administrator. As a result, that user could end up revealing sensitive information, such as usernames and passwords. Or the naive user may be convinced to perform some sort of action that compromises network security.

As the following exercise demonstrates, a hacker can send an e-mail message that appears to be a systems administrator's legitimate request for a username or password. This attack is a combination of social engineering and a bug-based attack.

EXERCISE 3.1

Sending Fake E-Mail

In this exercise, you will send fake e-mail to your partner.

Note: This exercise will work only if the e-mail server allows relaying. Many e-mail servers do not allow this, because it is a security risk.

1. In Windows 2000, go to Start, and enter **telnet** in the window.

2. Enable local echo by entering **set local_echo**.

3. You now will be able to see what you are typing after you connect to the server. Connect to an e-mail server of your own choosing as follows:

   open email.yourserver.com 25

   This command has you open a connection to the server email.yourserver.com at port 25, which is the default SMTP port.

Note: Conduct this exercise on a server that you own. Also, never send fake e-mail to anyone else. Doing so is unethical, and in many cases may be illegal.

4. Enter the following strings and press Enter after each (<CR> indicates a hard return):

   ```
   helo <cr>
   mail from: fake@anydomain.com<cr>
   rcpt to: yourownaccount@e-mailserver.com<cr>
   data <cr>
   Subject: This is fake!<cr>
   <cr>
   <cr>
   enter message (1 or more lines)<cr>
   .<cr> "on a separate line,
      enter a period and <cr>
      to end the data input section"
   quit<cr>
   ```

EXERCISE 3.1 *(continued)*

5. Open an e-mail client and check for an e-mail yourself.

   The following is a sample of a slightly more ambitious fake e-mail session, accompanied by commentary. The commentary appears on or below each line:

   ```
   220 relayserver.company.com
   ESMTP server (Netscape Messaging Server -
   Version 3.
   62) ready Thu, 15 Jun 2000 12:39:10 -0700
   helo mail.anyserver.com <CR>
   *   The "sender's" server
   mail from: hacker@hack.com <CR>
   * The fake e-mail address of the sender
   rcpt to: you@yourserver.com <CR>
   *   The real e-mail address of the recipient
   data <CR>
   *   Begins the e-mail
   From: James Stanger <CR>
   * Creates the "From" line
   Subject: Contract <CR>
   *   Subject line
   <CR> * Note the two hard returns at this point
   <CR>
   Body of Message <CR>
   *   Message body
   .   <CR>
   *   Use a period,
   *   then ENTER to end the e-mail message
   quit <CR>
   *   Close the connection
   ```

6. You have now sent a fake e-mail message. At this point, view all of the message headers. Note that the return address is not legitimate. Also, take a look at how the message was transmitted.

   You should be able to tell that it was sent by a hacker who has been tampering with an e-mail server that allows relaying.

It is possible to secure your e-mail servers from sending fake e-mail. The procedures vary from server to server. If you are using sendmail, for example, study the no-relaying options.

Keylogging

A *keylogger* invisibly records every keystroke on a computer, can store the keystrokes in a file, and can optionally send the file to a predefined e-mail address. A keylogger can:

- Intercept all keystrokes, mouse clicks, captions of active windows, static text, and any other user input
- Run silently and not affect the victim's computer performance
- Intercept passwords and logon names
- Save usernames and logon times
- Save the URLs of websites visited
- Save text from message boxes and windows
- Encrypt the output log file so that only the hacker can read it

Many keylogging applications exist. To download keyloggers for Windows NT/2000, visit www.keyloggers.com. Also, you can download a free evaluation copy of Ghost KeyLogger for Windows 95/98/NT/2000 at www.keylogger.net. To download keyloggers for Linux and Unix, you can visit various sites, including http://packetstorm.linuxsecurity.com.

Keylogging and Securing the Linux Search Path

For the sake of convenience, all flavors of Unix store the location of frequently used commands in the system path. The system path is stored in an environment variable named PATH. The PATH environment variable contains a set of directories. If you are using the Bourne shell (the default shell in Red Hat Linux, for example), you can learn a system's path by typing the following:

```
host# echo $PATH
```

The order in which these directories are listed is important, because when your Linux system searches for a command you have specified (such as when you use the su command), it will stop searching as soon as it finds that command. Suppose, for example, you have two copies of the su command. One is stored in the /tmp/ directory, and the other is stored in the /bin/ directory. If the /tmp/ directory is listed first in the system path, then the copy of the su command in the /tmp/ directory will be run before the one in the /bin/ directory.

Configuring your *search path* in this way can be a problem, especially if the su command stored in the /tmp/ directory is not a legitimate program but is in fact a simple shell script designed to capture your password. It is possible to do this on many Unix systems, because the /tmp/ directory is world-readable. Therefore, make sure you check your system's path to ensure that it does not provide hackers with the opportunity to substitute illegitimate applications easily.

Protecting Yourself Against Keyloggers

Below are ways to protect systems against keylogging applications:

Use antivirus programs. Antivirus applications such as Sophos Anti-Virus (www.sophos.com), Norton AntiVirus (www.norton.com), and AntiVir for Linux (www.hbedv.com) will usually find and delete these applications.

Document the system's state. Applications such as Tripwire (www.tripwire.com) can verify if system files have been altered from their original state. You will learn more about verifying system state in Chapter 7.

Use encryption. Using applications such as the Windows Encrypted File System (EFS), or third-party applications such as BestCrypt and md5sum, you can actually encrypt your hard drive or create digital signatures for certain files and applications to help you detect Trojans and keyloggers.

Physically secure the computer. Make sure that only authorized personnel can approach the system and install applications at will.

Now that we have discussed keyloggers, let's take a look at how hackers defeat authentication.

Brute-Force Attacks

A *brute-force attack* uses random combinations of numbers and letters in order to guess a username and password. A brute-force attack involves repeated access attempts as the application uses the random letter, number, and character combinations. Brute-force applications are designed to grind away at a server or data file by simply guessing usernames and repeatedly accessing a server. A brute-force attack requires the server to respond willingly to repeated attacks. Depending on the speed of the systems involved, thousands of attempts can be made per minute. A brute-force attack is a rather unsophisticated attempt to try everything, including a dictionary file, a sniffer, and repeated logon attempts.

An example of a brute-force attack is a hacker's attempt to break a code using a combination of computers and information. Suppose a hacker responds to a challenge to decrypt a single message that has been encrypted by the RC4 algorithm and an asymmetric key. To defeat this algorithm, the hacker resorts to sophisticated and extensive measures. He uses 120 workstations clustered together, two supercomputers, and information from three major research centers. Even with all this equipment, it takes him eight days to defeat the encryption algorithm. In fact, for breaking encryption, eight days is a rather short time. Applications such as `grinder` and `authforce` are designed to conduct brute-force attacks against Windows 2000 systems and Apache Server, respectively. Many others exist.

Brute-force attacks conducted against secure systems require a great deal of time, and they are often the result of either desperation or great determination. Many systems, however, are prone to exposure from such attacks, mainly because of inadequate security settings and policies. Brute-force attacks are often easy to detect because they involve repeated logon attempts, and account lockout can be enabled as a strategy to defeat such attacks.

> Windows NT and 2000 systems have a feature that allows you to lock out an account after a certain number of failed login attempts. This feature is designed to thwart brute-force and dictionary attacks.

Dictionary Attacks

A *dictionary attack* is a customized, directed version of a brute-force attack. If a potential hacker were to try to obtain a password using a traditional brute-force method, he or she would have to try every possible character, including lowercase, uppercase, numeric, and nonalphanumeric characters. A dictionary attack narrows the potential possibilities by trying only specific passwords. Many users mistakenly use a standard word for a password. A dictionary attack attempts to decipher a password by consulting a file, often called a "dictionary file," that contains a long list of words. Sometimes these dictionary files are very large (more than 10MB), and they can contain words belonging to several different languages.

A *strong password* helps defeat dictionary attacks. Generally, a strong password combines lowercase, uppercase, numeric, and nonalphanumeric characters, and is at least six characters long. Hackers often use such programs as John the Ripper for Unix or Novell PassCrack to obtain illegal access. Such attacks are versions of the brute-force attack and are often used against networks. However, hackers can use dictionary programs in other ways. A dictionary program can allow hackers to work in conjunction with many computers or to defeat passwords on Zip files.

If a hacker has targeted a Windows NT/2000 system, he or she can use the NetBIOS Authentication Tool (NAT) to test for weak passwords. Figure 3.5 shows the NAT graphical user interface. It also has a command-line interface, which is popular because of its small footprint. The command-line program is easy to install and operate.

FIGURE 3.5 NAT interface

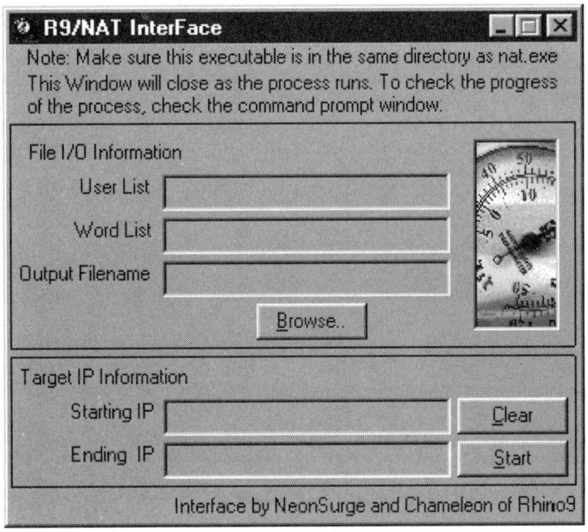

When using NAT, you must specify three text files and a range of IP addresses. You can also specify only one address, if you prefer. NAT uses two of the text files to conduct the attack, and it uses the third to store the results of the attack. The first text file NAT uses contains a list of usernames. You can create this list in a text file. The second file stores a list of likely passwords.

When using the command-line version, you would use this syntax:

```
nat -u username.txt -p passwordlist.txt -o outputfile.txt
```

Even if a server has established password aging and lockout, hackers can still use NAT or repeated logon attempts to harass administrators. By simply locking out all known accounts, they can greatly affect access to a server. This is one reason that some systems administrators do not enforce account lockouts.

Trojan

You have already learned that a *Trojan* is an application, service, or daemon that behaves legitimately on the surface but that in fact has an additional, secret function that is meant to defeat authentication. The word "Trojan" is borrowed from the mythical story of how the ancient Greeks stormed the city of Troy by hiding themselves in a gift shaped like a horse. When the citizens of Troy slept, the Greeks emerged from the Trojan and sacked the city.

> **NOTE** Some networking professionals refer to a Trojan as a "Trojan horse."

Any file that has been altered to contain an illicit file is said to be "Trojanized." Trojanized applications often include files that open ports bound to a root shell or to a command prompt with administrative privileges. Such files can hide their own presence by altering existing files meant to detect running processes. Once installed, a Trojan can relay sensitive information back to a hacker and upload programs that further defeat your system's security measures. Trojanized applications can also contain keylogger applications, worms, or viruses.

> **NOTE** Do not confuse an illicit server with a Trojan. A Trojanized program often contains an illicit server. However, a Trojan can also contain a keylogging program, a worm, or a virus.

Root Kits

A *root kit* is a collection of Trojans designed to compromise the system. Traditionally, root kits were threats only to Unix systems, but versions for Windows NT Server 4 and Windows 2000 have appeared in the past few years. A root kit usually consists of a series of programs that replace legitimate programs with Trojans.

In Unix systems, root kits often replace or modify the following system elements:

/bin/login Many root kits focus on using this file as the Trojan used to open ports that allow hackers to take control of your system. These ports are usually tied to a "root shell," which is a terminal where the hacker can issue commands at will.

/bin/ps This command is responsible for discovering what processes exist on the system. Altered forms of ps are usually written to exclude specific process names associated with Trojans that have opened ports bound to a root shell. Some Linux root kits replace the netstat application with a Trojan that reports false data concerning open ports. Thus, when a systems administrator runs netstat, the open ports will not be listed.

/bin/ls The list files command is used to list a directory's contents. Some root kits replace this command with a Trojanized file. Once activated, the Trojanized file launches a daemon that opens a port on the system. Hackers can then connect to the opened port.

/bin/su Simple Trojans can capture the password a systems administrator enters to become root and place it in a world-readable directory, or actually send the password to the hacker via e-mail.

Of course, any binary on a Unix or Windows 2000 system can become a target. Root kits can also do the following:

Create hidden directories. Many root kits create hidden directories, which can hide additional exploit applications.

Install loadable kernel modules (LKM). Many Linux systems use LKMs to extend the function of the kernel. They are usually legitimate elements, and they are always quite powerful. Much like a device driver, an LKM has the ability to add functionality to the computer. Many root kits designed for Linux systems install an LKM that modifies how the system misreports system information, which helps hide the Trojan's existence.

Launch hidden processes. Most of the time, these processes open a port that allows a hacker to enter the system. This opening is not logged.

Here are two examples of root kits that have been popular in the past:

Adore This root kit installs many of the applications listed earlier, including an LKM. Variations of Adore patch the kernel, which necessitates a reboot for the patch to become functional. Once the system is rebooted, the root kit is fully installed, complete with many of the modified applications listed earlier. Many variations of Adore exist. You can learn more about Adore's behavior at www.team-teso.net.

T0rn   This root kit uses Trojanized versions of SSH to encrypt transmissions going in and out of a compromised server. It even allows the hacker to require authentication for the root shell. The root kit is precompiled for most popular Linux installations, which means that it can be quickly installed. If you decide to visit this web page, make sure you use a zero when spelling "t0rn."

A new root kit will frequently replace different files. Although newer root kits will be developed, they will still behave largely as outlined above. The SANS website has an informative article about T0rn (www.sans.org/y2k/t0rn.htm).

How Root Kits Get Installed on the System

If you have not physically secured your system, hackers can simply uncompress the package, install it, and (if necessary) reboot. However, root kits are most often installed remotely. Root kits such as Adore can be installed by programs that, for example, exploit buffer overflows or another security problem. For instance, many root kits were installed in late 2000 and early 2001 when a common version of the Washington University FTP daemon (wu-FTPD, available at www.rpmfind.net) was found to have a buffer overflow that left a root shell behind. The attack first gained control of the system, then used crond to install the root kit. Thus, if you see that a system has been rebooted for no apparent reason, you may have become the victim of a root kit attack.

Repairing Infected Systems

Detecting root kits is extremely difficult. The following are some tactics to repair your system if it has been infected by a root kit:

Completely erase and reinstall the operating system.   When reinstalling the operating system, make sure you do not reinstall from backups, because they can be infected with the Trojan. The CIW Security Professional exam considers this the best option.

Replace the affected binaries.   This step is somewhat risky, because a root kit can exploit different files than you might expect.

Root kits are often quite thorough in replacing system components. It is best to adopt a strategy that helps you avoid a root-kit installation in the first place. The steps below can greatly decrease the likelihood of a successful root-kit attack:

If using a Linux system, compile a monolithic kernel. A monolithic kernel does not allow modules to be installed, thus eliminating LKM-based root kits. Such a kernel can, however, access all the necessary elements (the NIC, system applications, and so forth) to allow your server to fulfill its role in your business.

Install an application such as Tripwire or the Windows File Protection (WPF) utility. You will have to install Tripwire for Unix yourself. You can obtain it at www.tripwire.org. However, the WPF utility is activated by default. It will inform you of any changes to files such as SYS, DLL, OCX, TTF, FON, and EXE files. WPF will discover and reverse any illicit changes made by any installation application other than authorized Windows 2000 Service Packs, hotfixes, Windows Update, or operating system upgrades.

Use antivirus applications. Enterprise-grade antivirus applications, such as Sophos AntiVirus (www.sophos.com) and AntiVir (www.antivir.com), can help proactively detect root kits and other viruses.

Install applications only from trusted resources. When downloading files, obtain the MD5 hashes or PGP keys from the individual or company offering the download. Carefully compare these values to ensure that they have not been Trojanized. If using a PGP key, you will first have to add the key to your key ring, then test the file's PGP signature with the key you have installed. Comparing MD5 hashes is much simpler, especially if you have access to the md5sum command.

Viruses

A computer *virus* is a malicious program designed to damage network equipment, including stand-alone computers. A virus has two parts: the application that activates and spreads the virus, and the "payload," which is what the virus does to the operating system or file. Table 3.2 describes the types of viruses found in modern systems.

TABLE 3.2 Virus Types and Descriptions

Virus type	Description
Boot sector/Master Boot Record (MBR)	This type of virus infects the first sector of a floppy disk or a hard drive. The boot sector is the part of a floppy that enables it to be read and written to. If infected with a virus, the floppy can then act as a transport mechanism for the virus. The MBR on most IBM-compatible systems is a similar place on the hard drive. Once a virus writes itself to the MBR, it can then generate activity that is either annoying (e.g., your system will play sounds at certain times of the day) or destructive (e.g., it will erase your hard drive).
File infecting	Some viruses attach themselves to legitimate programs. Launching the application activates the virus.
E-mail/Macro/Script	This type of virus is often found in e-mail attachments. Viruses such as Melissa and "I Love You" are all based on the VBScript computing language and exploit the trust relationships between Microsoft Office applications and the operating system. An end user must double-click on an e-mail attachment to activate the virus.

Virus Behavior

Some viruses will replicate or activate simply when an application or hard drive is activated, or when an icon is double-clicked. A virus can also act as a "time bomb," activating only after a certain number of days have elapsed. Some time-bomb viruses activate only on certain days of the year. Other viruses can conduct a logic attack, which means they will activate only under certain conditions. For example, a virus may replicate itself or deliver its payload only if a certain application is running on a certain day.

Antivirus applications eliminate most, if not all, known viruses. Antivirus companies use the word "signature" to describe the known behavior of a virus. However, some viruses can alter their configuration (i.e., their signature) to escape detection. These types of viruses are known as *polymorphic* viruses. The best way to counter threats from polymorphic viruses is to update your antivirus applications often. For servers connected to the Internet, weekly or even daily updates may be appropriate.

Most viruses are destructive in nature. They can, for example, erase files, or even format entire parts of the hard drive. A virus generally does not defeat authentication.

Worms

A *worm* is much like a virus, except that a worm can spread from system to system without user intervention. The Nimda worm, which was released on September 18, 2001, was a particularly powerful worm that infected all unpatched IIS servers. It also spread to any Windows-based share. As a result, this worm had the ability to spread itself throughout a company LAN in seconds. This worm was able to spread so quickly because once it compromised a Web server, it then used that server to spread itself. As a result of this attack, Gartner Group, a respected consulting company, encouraged its customers to abandon Microsoft's IIS in favor of other web servers while Microsoft worked to shore up IIS's security against the Nimda worm.

All worm-based attacks follow the same pattern as the worm created by Robert Morris Jr., a graduate student in the Cornell University department of computer science. According to Morris, his program was designed to demonstrate that the Internet was vulnerable and contained many security holes. On November 2, 1988, the worm was released on the Internet.

The worm ended up propagating itself on approximately 7,000 hosts. Each of these hosts continued propagating the worm. The worm exhausted each affected system's CPU and memory resources, causing the system to no longer be responsive. Systems administrators had to spend considerable time verifying that no other problems had been introduced. The incident effectively crashed the Internet as it was known at the time.

In today's Unix world, worms are somewhat rare. Although Unix e-mail servers can spread e-mail viruses and worms, most modern worms have focused on the Microsoft Windows operating system. Worms are relatively rare on Unix systems because those systems use different hardware architectures. For a true Unix virus to exist, it must be capable of recognizing every known Unix version and hardware platform known or developed since January 1, 1970. When such Unix viruses do exist, they are usually confined to a few specific hardware models and a specific Unix flavor peculiar to that hardware (e.g., BSD 4.3 or Solaris 8).

Unix/Linux systems remain much less popular than Windows systems for client, desktop-based use. Usually, most hackers who create viruses want to affect as many systems as possible. Thus, Windows systems are a much more attractive target.

> **NOTE** The popular term *in the wild* describes a virus or worm that has been released and is currently found on the Internet.

Summary

In this chapter, we described specific attacks that hackers perpetrate against target systems. You learned about IP spoofing, as well as how a hacker can wage various man-in-the-middle attacks. These attacks are designed to either obtain or manipulate data as it passes across the network wire. Man-in-the-middle attacks can be quite insidious and powerful, because they involve the ability to capture usernames and passwords, as well as the ability to hijack connections between two legitimate systems.

Over the years, various denial-of-service attacks have been waged against Internet servers. These attacks have usually been waged by inexperienced hackers, but the results have been devastating nevertheless. In this chapter, you learned about additional attacks, including how it is possible to obtain valuable information from insiders through the practice of "social engineering," and how a keylogger can be used to obtain information as it is entered through a keyboard. You saw how brute-force and dictionary attacks are used to break into servers. Finally, we examined Trojans, viruses, and worms, all of which have received high-profile coverage through the years.

Now that you are familiar with these methods, the next chapter will show you how to begin protecting your operating systems by placing them behind a firewall.

Exam Essentials

Be able to recognize specific attack incidents. Demonstrate the ability to identify an attack from symptoms given in a scenario.

Understand specific types of security attacks. You must be able to describe the various attack types discussed in this chapter. For example, you should be able to discuss what a SYN flood looks like, or the specific behavior of an e-mail worm. This is different from identifying the symptoms of an attack.

Know how to categorize passive and active threats. Once you have been provided with an attack type, you need to be able to categorize it as a passive or an active threat. Although you may already be familiar with the attacks described in this chapter, be able to show how any one attack is passive or active. An active attack involves making a person or operating system actively respond to your activities (e.g., conducting a brute-force attack until the operating system recognizes a valid password). A passive attack involves activities such as "shoulder surfing" and network data sniffing.

Understand the importance of IP spoofing. IP spoofing is often used as a strategy in various attacks. For example, most DDoS applications are capable of spoofing source addresses, which makes it difficult to conduct tracebacks. As you study for the exam, make sure that you are able to identify how spoofing affects the length and accuracy of a traceback.

Know the different types of man-in-the-middle attacks. Many different types of man-in-the-middle attacks exist. Some of these attacks are active in nature, while some are passive. For example, an active man-in-the-middle attack includes connection hijacking. It is also possible to inject packets into a data stream. Usually, such attacks are simply annoying to those engaged in IRC chat rooms or in Telnet sessions. However, it is possible to inject packets into more sensitive transmissions.

Understand the significance of insider attacks. It is possible for a "hacker" to be an employee of your company. An insider can be duped into revealing information through social engineering, or can actively take part in strategies meant to defeat company security. Even though the CIW Security Professional certification is meant to discuss Internet-based servers (e.g., web, DNS, and e-commerce servers), the creators are aware of the fact that company insiders can cause security breaches.

Be able to identify common system bugs and how they affect host security. Hackers exploit system bugs more than any other strategy. Make sure that you understand what a buffer overflow is. Be able to describe what a buffer is, and some of the ways in which an overflow condition results.

Know why default settings are a problem. Hackers regularly take advantage of default settings and passwords. Be able to identify common default settings for the CIW Security Professional exam. Later chapters will identify various default settings that you will need to identify and fix. Be able to describe how to stop system services and daemons from leaking information. It is important to stop systems from providing information to hackers, because once a hacker knows what daemon or service you are running, it is then possible to research the targeted system for common weaknesses.

Be able to describe a root kit. Although you do not need to describe the intimate details of a root kit, you will need to know that it replaces legitimate operating system elements. Be able to explain how a root kit is a collection of Trojans, how a kit can create such things as hidden directories, or how it can open ports on your system. You do not need to be able to identify different root kits (e.g., Adore or T0rn), but you do need to consider ways that they are placed onto a system. Finally, be able to explain how to protect systems from Trojans, and how to recover if a root kit has been installed on a system.

Key Terms

Before you take the exam, be certain you are familiar with the following terms:

active open	buffer
Address Resolution Protocol (ARP) cache poisoning	buffer overflow
attack	denial-of-service (DoS) attack
back door	dictionary attack
banner information	distributed denial-of-service (DDoS) attack
blind spoofing	DNS poisoning
broadcast addresses	Fraggle attack
brute-force attack	in the wild

Key Terms

initial sequence number (ISN)
insider attacks
IP spoofing
keylogger
land attack
man-in-the-middle attack
non-blind spoofing
packet-injection attacks
packet stream
passive open
ping of death
root kit
search path
Smurf attack
spam

strong password
SYN flood
system bug
TCP handshake
Teardrop
threat
traceback
trap-door attack
Trojan
unpatched
virus
vulnerability
worm
zone transfer

Review Questions

1. In what type of attack does a fraudulent host access the system disguised as a legitimate host?

    A. A brute-force attack

    B. A social-engineering attack

    C. A spoofing attack

    D. A dictionary attack

2. What is the name for an undocumented opening placed in an operating system or program?

    A. A logic attack

    B. A bug

    C. A social engineering attack

    D. A back door

3. How does a denial-of-service attack work?

    A. A hacker prevents a legitimate user (or group of users) from accessing a service.

    B. A hacker tries to decipher a password by using a system, which subsequently crashes the network.

    C. A hacker uses every character, word, or letter he or she can think of to defeat authentication.

    D. A hacker attempts to imitate a legitimate user by confusing a computer or even another person.

4. Sarah has installed a custom antivirus application meant to clean up a virus that has infected her computer. This is a simple application that contains one executable. However, she discovers that her system has been compromised again, this time through a different means. When she checks her server logs, she discovers that this new attack occurred immediately after she installed her custom antivirus application. What type of attack has she fallen victim to?

A. A virus attack

B. A man-in-the-middle attack

C. A root kit attack

D. A Trojan

5. Which of the following attack types does not involve an attempt to defeat authentication on the victim server?

A. Brute force

B. Denial-of-service

C. Dictionary

D. A back door

6. Robert has used his packet sniffer to listen in on network transmissions. He has gathered several passwords. Which of the following attacks has Robert waged on his network?

A. A man-in-the-middle attack

B. A hijacking attack

C. An illicit server attack

D. An active attack

7. What type of attack involves using a program capable of replicating itself with little user intervention and then depositing a payload?

A. A hijacking attack

B. An illicit server

C. A virus

D. A man-in-the-middle attack

8. What is the best defense against man-in-the-middle attacks?

A. Strong passwords

B. A firewall

C. Strong encryption

D. Traceback

9. Stacy notices that her system has become unresponsive. She receives several phone calls from customers who complain that they cannot access any of the servers on her LAN. She opens up her packet sniffer and discovers that one system is being bombarded by ICMP packets that are originating from multiple hosts. What type of attack is she observing?

   A. A SYN flood

   B. A denial-of-service attack

   C. A distributed denial-of-service attack

   D. A Teardrop attack

10. Which of the following is the primary objective of a root kit?

    A. It creates a buffer overflow.

    B. It opens a port to provide an unauthorized service.

    C. It replaces legitimate programs.

    D. It provides an undocumented opening in a program.

11. Paul receives an e-mail from a friend. After reading the body of the text, he double-clicks the attachment. After about 15 minutes, Paul receives phone calls from several of his business associates, asking him why he has sent them a message. What type of attack has Paul experienced?

    A. A fake e-mail attack

    B. An e-mail virus attack

    C. A worm attack

    D. A buffer overflow attack

12. What does a Smurf attack do?

    A. It takes advantage of establishing a TCP handshake.

    B. It attempts to defeat authentication.

    C. It tests for weak passwords.

    D. It manipulates ICMP.

13. What occurs in a ping-of-death attack?

    A. It takes advantage of the process of establishing a TCP handshake.

    B. It sends an ICMP packet that is larger than 65,536 bytes.

    C. It sends a spoofed IP packet to a target computer with the same source and destination port and IP address.

    D. It takes advantage of code that does not properly reassemble overlapping UDP packets.

14. What type of attack changes its signature and/or payload to thwart detection by antivirus programs?

    A. Macro

    B. File infecting

    C. Boot sector

    D. Polymorphic

15. Three days ago, Julie installed a peer-to-peer application named Grokster on her workstation. She is using the Grokster application to share MP3 files on the Internet. For two days now, at 10:10 A.M., her computer begins beeping for 5 minutes straight. Nothing else happens, and no files appear to be altered or damaged. What type of attack is Julie experiencing?

    A. A spoofing attack

    B. A trapdoor attack

    C. A replay attack

    D. A denial-of-service attack

16. After reading his log files, Davis discovers that several users have logged in to his system using his administrative account. He also notices that several files now reside in a world-readable directory, and that his log files show this directory has been accessed from a remote host. Which of the following allowed these users to obtain his account information?

A. A keylogger program

B. A denial-of-service program

C. The Unix `rlogin` command

D. An e-mail virus

17. Jacob wishes to install a new application onto his Windows 2000 server. He wants to ensure that any application he uses has not been Trojanized. What can he do to help ensure this?

A. Obtain the application via SSL.

B. Obtain the application from a CD-ROM disc.

C. Compare the file's MD5 signature with the one published on the distribution media.

D. Compare the file's virus signature with the one published on the distribution media.

18. Steven has obtained several packets and has decided to send them back out onto the network in an attempt to log on to a server. He does not have an account for this server but hopes to use these packets to log on. What type of attack is Steven considering?

A. A logic attack

B. A buffer overflow attack

C. A hijacking attack

D. A replay attack

19. You have just logged on to a Linux operating system using the Bourne shell (i.e., the bash shell). What command would you use to check the path for this account?

A. echo PATH

B. echo $PATH

C. SET PATH

D. SET=PATH

20. Joel has discovered that his IIS 5.0 web server has crashed. He suspects his ISAPI applications have caused a problem. Which of the following describes an attack that occurs when a daemon such as a web server receives too much information from a helper application and then crashes?

   A. A buffer-overflow attack

   B. A denial-of-service attack

   C. A trap-door attack

   D. A root kit attack

Answers to Review Questions

1. **C.** A spoofing attack is, in many ways, an attempt to defeat authentication. It involves one host trying to appear as another.

2. **D.** A back door is an undocumented opening in a system. A bug can cause an unintentional security vulnerability, but it is important to differentiate between an opening placed in an operating system or application and an unintentional bug.

3. **A.** A denial-of-service attack involves trying to keep legitimate users from using a service or daemon.

4. **D.** The scenario has described an incident where Sarah has unwittingly installed a Trojan on her computer. The custom antivirus application is the Trojan. Sarah has not installed a root kit, because a root kit is a rather complex set of applications, not just one application.

5. **B.** A denial-of-service attack does not in and of itself attempt to defeat authentication. Although it can be used as part of an overall strategy to defeat authentication, a denial-of-service attack does not directly attack authentication, as do brute-force, dictionary, and back-door attacks. Each of these three attacks involves defeating authentication and gaining access to the system.

6. **A.** A sniffing attack is a man-in-the-middle attack. So, too, is a hijacking attack, except that hijacking does not simply involve a packet sniffer; it involves additional applications. Robert has not used an illicit server at all, and the use of packet sniffers is categorized as a passive attack.

7. **C.** A virus can replicate itself, but it does require some user intervention. A virus also carries a payload. An illicit server is not capable of replicating itself, whereas man-in-the-middle and hijacking attacks do not deposit payloads on a server.

8. **C.** Strong encryption provides the best protection because it scrambles information so that it cannot be readily obtained. Although it is possible to decrypt such information, doing so takes a great deal of time. Decrypting strongly encrypted information also takes considerable computing power that individuals do not have. Most large companies do not even have such resources. A firewall cannot protect you

against a man-in-the-middle attack if it is conducted inside a LAN. In fact, a firewall will not protect you against an unencrypted transaction as it passes across the Internet. Even if a firewall is involved, unencrypted traffic can still be captured and acted on by a hacker. Traceback is the ability to learn the true origin of an attack, but it does not defend against a man-in-the-middle attack.

9. C. A distributed denial-of-service attack consists of attacks from multiple hosts. This type of attack usually uses ICMP. A SYN flood is TCP-based, whereas a Teardrop attack is UDP-based.

10. C. The primary objective of a root kit is to replace legitimate programs. The new illegitimate programs can do many things, including creating buffer overflows, opening ports, and creating other openings. However, these functions occur after legitimate programs are replaced.

11. B. An e-mail virus attack best describes the scenario given. E-mail viruses have the ability to spread to many different users, as long as one user activates the virus so that it can read the e-mail client's address book and send itself to other unsuspecting recipients. Because the e-mail was sent from a legitimate client, it is not a fake e-mail message. Because the e-mail attachment had to be double-clicked, this particular attack is not worm-based. Finally, the above scenario does not provide any information suggesting that this attack involved a buffer overflow.

12. D. The Smurf attack manipulates ICMP and does not take advantage of TCP. Because it is a denial-of-service attack, it does not attempt to defeat authentication, nor does it test for weak passwords.

13. B. The ping-of-death attack is effective on older systems, because it sends an ICMP packet so large that some systems crash before they can process all of the information. It mainly affects older Unix and Linux systems. These systems have been updated and patched to solve this problem.

14. D. A polymorphic virus has the ability to change itself in subtle ways. The reason for this behavior is that virus creators wish to avoid detection by antivirus applications.

15. B. A trapdoor (i.e., logic) attack describes events that occur only when certain conditions are present. It is fairly clear from the scenario that the Grokster application that Julie downloaded contained a virus that activates itself at 10:10 A.M. each day.

16. **A.** The above scenario describes a classic keylogging attack, mainly because it mentions the existence of a world-readable file and because authentication has been defeated. Neither a denial-of-service program nor an e-mail virus application can cause this type of behavior. Although the Unix `rlogin` application poses a security hazard in many instances, it does not use or create world-readable files or directories.

17. **C.** Many vendors and software developers use MD5 signatures to verify contents, regardless of how the application is distributed.

18. **D.** Replay attacks always involve obtaining packets, then sending them back out on the network again.

19. **B.** The $ sign in Linux/Unix systems allows you to inquire for a variable value. The SET command is used to change the system path. If you were to type **echo PATH**, you would simply see the word "PATH" repeated.

20. **A.** Whenever a system element crashes after receiving information from a helper application, it is highly likely that this has occurred due to a buffer-overflow attack. Trap-door attacks occur only when a certain condition occurs. Although this attack did likely result in a denial of service, the immediate cause is a buffer overflow. Finally, root kits may be able to cause a buffer overflow, but it is more accurate to choose the most specific term.

Chapter 4

General Security Principles

THE CIW EXAM OBJECTIVE GROUPS COVERED IN THIS CHAPTER:

- ✓ Apply security principles and identify security attacks.
- ✓ Use universal guidelines and principles of effective network security to create effective, specific solutions.

In this chapter, we will discuss some of the general security principles covered by the CIW Security Professional exam. Although specific security implementations are always unique, 10 easily identified principles are common to all networks and situations:

- Be suspicious of all network activity.
- You must have a security policy.
- No system or technique stands alone.
- Minimize damage when possible.
- Deploy companywide enforcement.
- Provide training.
- Use an integrated security strategy.
- Place equipment according to needs.
- Identify business issues.
- Consider physical security.

If you learn about these principles now, you will be able to implement effective security at your company.

TIP The CIW Security Professional exam may not explicitly test you on these concepts, but they are often implied. If you remain ignorant about any of these principles, you may misread a question or remain unaware of some of the options available to you.

The first step in approaching security is to remain on the lookout for trouble.

Be Suspicious of All Network Activity

Most people expect a security administrator to be, well, a little touchy, so why not justify their expectations? Although the word "paranoid" might seem to be an overstatement, if you are not suspicious to the point of paranoia, you will probably not follow your security policy as diligently as you should.

As you design and enforce your security system, always assume that a hacker will circumvent it. This assumption will ensure that you apply as many techniques as possible on several levels. Put backups in place so that if a hacker breaches one area, another area will be able to contain the hacker's activity. This security principle is simple, but it can save your entire network.

Minimizing Vulnerabilities

You have the ability to manage vulnerabilities. Configure your systems so that, after an attack, the hacker cannot easily manipulate them. Vulnerability minimization is a result of using security principles properly, even if they seem too cautious at first. Two additional methods of minimizing vulnerabilities are:

Enforce stringent user access control. Defining user responsibilities and access is a key element of threat minimization. A hacker who has stolen a legitimate user's identity will be able to access only what that user can access. In other words, if a hacker can assume the identity of a member of your organization, he or she will be able to access the same files and systems as that legitimate user.

Isolate operating system elements. When installing an operating system, do not use the default system paths. For example, do not place system files in the `C:\winnt` directory; specify an alternate one. Doing so can thwart hackers who expect files to be in default locations. If, for example, you protect your FTP files separately from your web files, penetration of web security will not automatically mean that your FTP security has been breached. You will learn more about sectioning off your operating system files from data files in Chapter 9.

TIP
> The above strategy of changing directory names is not a particularly strong one. It is an example of "security through obscurity," which means that although a vulnerability might exist, you have tried to hide it so that only determined hackers can find and exploit it. However, such minor alterations can still help improve your network's security.

Murphy's Law Applies to Networks, Too

The chief motive for using the techniques described in this section is the expectation that if something can go wrong it probably will. And, yes, someone probably is "out there" trying to make things go wrong for you. Few things motivate people more than fear, so do not underrate this perspective when securing your system and creating your security policy.

You Must Have a Security Policy

A security policy is the foundation on which all security decisions are made. If you do not have an effective security policy, your actual implementation will be inconsistent, providing points of access to hackers. A hacker generally searches a site for a "weak link" from which to penetrate. Whether these weak links are overlooked defaults or bugs in the operating system, they exist because the security policy did not remind the systems administrator of the essential steps to take when upgrading an operating system, adding a user, or adding a new program.

A thorough security policy helps you correct such oversights and enables you to make consistent decisions as you secure your network. A security policy defines each rule to be followed and includes clear explanations of its purpose. An obscure or imprecise security policy may not convey the core security values, roles, and responsibilities to the organization.

As far as the CIW Security Professional exam is concerned, keep in mind the following points:

- A well-enforced security policy provides continuity throughout any organization.

- Your security policy is the first resource to consider when responding to an attack.

- The security policy should be subject to change. At times, your policy will be updated to reflect current business concerns. It may also be updated to reflect changes and improvements in technology.

- When a change in a security policy occurs, it is vital that all employees know about the change. They must also acknowledge that they understand the nature of these changes and that they agree to abide by them. Usually, this acknowledgement should be in writing.

> **NOTE**
> A question on the CIW Security Professional exam may appear as if it is quizzing you about a particular procedure, such as securing an e-mail server, configuring a firewall, or responding to an attack. However, the question may actually be testing your ability to follow procedures as outlined by a security policy.

A security policy also ensures that all elements of an organization work together. For example, it is vital to ensure that all servers and related network equipment work together as closely as possible.

No System or Technique Stands Alone

A successful security system is a *matrix*, or combination of individual methods, techniques, and subsystems. Whenever possible, you should use as many security principles and techniques as you can to protect each resource. For instance, a network that relies solely on authentication is not nearly as secure as one that combines authentication, access control, and encryption. Similarly, your site is better protected by packet filtering at the router combined with a firewall backed up by user authentication and intrusion detection.

Use of multiple techniques and technologies at every point allows you to protect against the weaknesses of each individual technique while improving overall effective security. As your security system develops, you will base these choices on the overall balance of security. A balance must be obtained because you can implement too many methods, again resulting in less effective security. The most critical factor is to analyze each method of protection for weakness and determine whether you can reduce that weakness by using an additional method or two while not going too far.

Maintaining security requires more than just installing operating systems and applications. Improving network security requires that you use multiple techniques and approaches. Using multiple techniques at every device (e.g., at both the router and the web server) and at every level, you can limit damage perpetrated by a hacker. No universal product, technology, or solution offers full protection against all threats. Security threats are evolving and growing quickly. You need dedicated staff and resources to perform the security function well.

Minimize Damage When Possible

Security threats can range from a *simple intrusion* to a *catastrophic event*. A simple intrusion may involve a disgruntled former employee who reenters a system and reconfigures the server. A catastrophic event involves the massive loss of data, or the loss of an entire server. More drastically, the former employee may want to "trash" the system, making it unusable. The former employee may also have just enough permissions to enter a file or database server and erase valuable information.

The best way to ensure that data is protected is to properly back it up. For all the talk about data padding, encryption, and other strategies, data that has been backed up using steady, even tedious, procedures is most often a security administrator's salvation.

Finally, catastrophic events can cause data to be lost permanently, even if is backed up. Consider offsite storage as an option.

Verifying Backups

An unverified backup is potentially as useless as having no backup at all. Take special measures to confirm that all backups have properly stored data. If you do not, you may be in for a nasty surprise when you discover that the data you thought was safe is now, in fact, lost forever. It is vital that you verify your data backups. Table 4.1 provides some of the best ways to ensure *secure data backup and storage*.

TABLE 4.1 Backup and Storage Procedures

Procedure	Description
Data verification	Confirm with all management and middle-management personnel that the correct data is being backed up. Also, take a sample of the backed-up data and restore it. This way, you have at least some idea that the backup process has, in fact, worked. In addition, consider using encryption, which can be useful in two ways. First, you can use MD5 hashes to verify data integrity; when it comes time to restore data, you can compare hashes to ensure that data has not been tampered with. Second, you can password-protect data to further ensure that stored information cannot be used if it falls into the wrong hands.
Media verification	Make sure that the media you are using to back up data is reliable. Backup tapes, for example, have a limited lifetime. The closer they come to their limit, the greater the possibility of complete failure. Also, verify that you have enough storage available for all data; the last thing you want to do is run out of tapes or CDs when backing up.
Storage site security verification	Ensure that all data being stored is placed in a secure location. When a small company conducts backups, it might simply designate an employee to take the CDs or tapes home. Larger companies generally have a much more involved backup structure. In any case, it is a security administrator's job to verify that data is secured, preferably in a locked, permanent location, such as a safe.
Process verification	Many times, backups are conducted remotely. If a backup occurs over a WAN link, or even over the Internet, take steps to ensure that the backup is using encryption. Using a VPN connection, for example, may be a solution. If the data needs to be physically transported from one site to another, take steps to ensure that the data actually does make it to the new location.

Once you are reasonably sure that you have secured your data-backup procedures, you can then focus on ensuring that all of your organization's members are helping to implement your security policy.

Deploy Companywide Enforcement

Too often, organizations develop security policies and then the administrators do not enforce the rules on themselves. System and security administrators will give their everyday user accounts *root*, or administrative, access. They do not realize that allowing this type of access could create problems: while administrators know how to avoid accidentally damaging or compromising a system, end users might not be as sophisticated. Hackers will try to locate such accounts and concentrate on penetrating them instead of highly secured accounts.

Some people think that even the most unobtrusive security measures are a waste of time, and will ignore them or create shortcuts around them. Company executives in particular tend to defeat security measures; those measures can seem inconvenient to someone who must access information as quickly as possible. In smaller companies, many owners want root permissions simply because they are "the boss." A good rule is to have as few administrative accounts as possible.

The innocent and seemingly necessary activity we've described creates a security breach that hackers can discover and use. Therefore, a company plan must make *everyone* at every level accountable for security.

> Hackers are adept at discovering weaknesses in the application of a security system, especially when those weaknesses result from incomplete implementation.

Provide Training

It bears repeating that all employees need to be trained in security procedures. Proper training is one of the most effective and easiest security measures you can put in place. A companywide, one-hour user training session on such topics as proper password selection can dramatically increase security levels.

Here is a list of recommended training steps for each of the three user levels discussed in Chapter 1:

End users   Users must be informed of new viruses that are introduced on the web. You can notify them via a companywide e-mail message, voicemail, or even via conference call.

Administrators   Security administrators must remain informed about the latest threats and countermeasures. A good idea is to assign each security administrator a topic or area. For example, one security administrator can keep current with the latest viruses, and another can keep up with the latest hacker tools and techniques.

Executives   Executives need to be kept aware of the latest tools that can be used to keep a site's security up to date. A useful technique is to tell your executives about a successful break-in at a related site.

Use an Integrated Security Strategy

Find out how each department implements the security strategy. Guard against allowing each department to interpret the policy separately or even have its own policy, thereby defeating the overall effect of the security strategy and creating security holes. Again, ensure that all levels of your organization, including your executives, are following this strategy.

Security and systems administrators should always keep a close watch on all components of their network. A site's security can be easily defeated by a poorly secured system, especially if the security administrator is not aware of it.

Deploying New Systems

Even if an organization's security administrators have done a good job securing all their network resources, it is still possible for their measures to be undermined by a simple change in the network. Let's consider one example.

As you probably know, operating system upgrades have become more common, on both client workstations and higher-end servers. In its rush to obtain and test new operating systems, ABC Company's research-and-development (R&D) department obtained a beta version of the Windows 2000 Advanced Server product.

The department manager installed the beta on a test machine to experiment with the new features, but he decided to attach it to the live network. He rationalized that because the server wasn't meant for production use, it would not cause a problem. After all, the server would not be used to house any content, and he believed that just one more server on the network system wouldn't cause a problem. The manager configured the server with a static IP address and began testing. Before long, however, several problems arose.

Right away, the security managers noticed a new system was occupying an IP address that was normally not allocated to a server, and they set about scanning this new system. They began tracing all connections and dispatched two of their security staff to determine where the server was physically located. After about two hours, the problem was cleared up, the server was placed onto an isolated subnet, and everyone was happy again. Still, think about the cost of this very small event. First, at least three members of the security staff spent two hours on this minor problem. Consider the monetary cost. Second, the incident likely caused some frayed nerves, as well as some increased suspicion between the security managers and the R&D department. If the security managers had conveyed more clearly how one system can affect the entire network, the R&D manager would not have deployed the system on a live network.

Finally, imagine what could have occurred. Most beta operating systems contain significant security flaws. Very possibly, a hacker could have compromised this one system. He or she could have then used it to attack other systems on the network. An old cliche applies here: in many ways, a network is only as secure as its weakest link.

By forcing all departments to adhere to your company's security policy, you can easily prevent problems like the one described here.

Place Equipment According to Needs

It is easy to get caught up in your desire to purchase the latest equipment and software. You should, however, always consider how any technology addresses specific business needs. To do this, conduct a *needs assessment audit*. This audit is the primary tool in helping you determine whether a particular piece of equipment or software is necessary.

Conducting a Needs Assessment Audit

A needs assessment audit involves the steps shown in Figure 4.1.

FIGURE 4.1 The elements of a needs assessment audit

Consult with management to determine specific needs.	Determine how a new technology will affect the daily routines of end users at all levels.	Work with management to secure funding.	Conduct research to determine the proper product for your organization.	Study your network to ensure that the new solution is implemented in the right place at the right time.

Your first goal is to obtain management approval. This involves meeting with your managers so you can present the problem and then offer your proposed solution. Keep any and all proposals in simple terms. Then, if pressed, you can explain the technical details. Always be prepared to describe the ramifications of decisions and problems using simple examples. Once you have done this, you can consider how this new technology will affect the way your company does business.

When meeting with management about this issue, be careful to explain the impact of any addition or change to end users. If possible, try to create a demonstration of the change, and ask management to participate. This way, they can take a "test-drive" of the new system before they buy into your solution.

As you work with management to secure funding, you will have to justify the cost in terms of enhanced security and (you hope) the amount of increased end-user productivity. Usually, trying to scare management into adopting a solution will not work. However, it is vital that you carefully explain the ramifications of inaction, as well as the benefits of having a properly secured network.

Once you have obtained preliminary approval, carefully research your solution. In other words, shop around. Find out the best solution for you and your company. When purchasing a product, consider elements such as performance, scalability, ease of use, and licensing issues. Carefully research both open-source and proprietary solutions. Open-source solutions—such as those available at sites like www.sourceforge.net and www.freshmeat.net—may suit your needs. In other situations, a vendor product from a company such as Symantec or Network Associates may be best.

Scalability, which is the ability to cope with increased size and capacity, is particularly important when researching a security product. Most products will perform well in small-scale networks. However, few have the ability to truly manage large-scale networks.

Correctly Placing the Product

When you finally obtain the equipment, your job is not over. You must then determine where and when you will implement the item you have bought. It is important to remember that even if you purchase the correct product at the right price, if you place it on the wrong network segment or on the wrong system, it probably won't increase your network's security level. In fact, improper placement could *reduce* your network's overall security level, because having it would give you a false sense of security.

When placing equipment, you must take the following steps:

Test the system on an isolated subnet. Even if you are familiar with the newly installed system and network daemon/service, you need to ensure that the server and daemon operate in the manner you expect.

Run a vulnerability scanner against the system as part of your test. A vulnerability scanner is able to determine whether any problems exist on the system. You will learn more about these scanners in Chapter 11.

Update any schematics and documents on the production servers you have. Make sure that you keep current on the servers you have in production. This way, you will avoid any surprises.

After you have properly placed the equipment, make sure that you address any concerns management may have about how this product will affect the way the company does business.

Identify Business Issues

Security has become a central business issue, mainly because of the costs involved. Investors and customers want to make sure that companies have done all they can to ensure security. IT management and company presidents, therefore, are now very interested in proving that they have shown due diligence when securing their networks. Doing so helps the business secure funding and maintain a positive company image.

Chargeback

Chargeback is the ability to accurately determine the costs of using various networking security services. Among these services are the following:

- Tasks performed by IT professionals, including system installation, network engineering, and security consulting
- The use of a firewall, server, or additional network resources

Departments and divisions within the same large company often conduct a *chargeback*. Suppose that James was sent from the IT department's help desk to consult with the editing department about a particular security issue. The IT department could charge the editing department for James's time. Large companies have identified ways to manage and justify most security costs. Table 4.2 provides and defines additional terminology used when managing security costs and resources. The CIW Security Professional exam expects you to understand these terms.

TABLE 4.2 Security Management Terminology

Term	Definition
Amortization	*Amortization* is an accounting term used to accurately determine the cost of a particular implementation over time. Amortization also includes accounting for depreciation of software or hardware.
Capacity forecasting	*Capacity forecasting* is the ability to plan the amount of bandwidth required to provide services for future customers. Forecasting becomes increasingly important in security, because many security applications require additional licensing when traffic increases.
Trend analysis	*Trend analysis* is the ability to differentiate between legitimate and illegitimate traffic (e.g., HTTP, login, POP3, versus evidence of repeated logins, or SYN floods and scanning activity). During a trend analysis, you create a *baseline* of activity, which involves identifying patterns of activity that are "normal" to your network. If login activity, for example, deviates significantly from this baseline, you can begin to suspect that a security problem exists. By analyzing trends in network activity, you can help reduce false alarms, as well as determine the type of network traffic that employees are generating. Once you understand the type of traffic on the network, you can purchase additional equipment more intelligently. You can also approach management and employees with evidence of acceptable and unacceptable traffic. You can then begin to act on this traffic, either by using software to end it or by correcting employee behavior.
Performance management	*Performance management* involves determining the existing workload of systems on the network. This type of management involves local and remote monitoring of a server through the use of such applications as Windows Performance Monitor or a Unix application named top.

Business Issues and Network Latency

In the narrowest technical terms, *latency* is the measurement of time needed for a request to be processed between a client and a server on a network. In security, however, latency has a broader meaning. It involves complexities and issues that you may introduce when you implement a particular security solution. It is important to understand that each security solution you implement could have a significant impact on a network's ability to support the business. You might have to train users to deal with this impact.

Enhancing security in your network can increase network latency in a number of ways; for example, consider the extra time needed to encrypt packets. Installing an e-mail virus scanner on your SMTP server can significantly increase the time required for messages to be processed. Security measures can also affect businesses and users in the following ways:

Increased cost Many security solutions are very costly. Firewall licenses for one site can cost between $5,000 and $20,000 or more. Even organizations that are comfortable spending large amounts of money will need to justify these expenses.

Inconvenience New programs and procedures may inconvenience users, especially users who travel often and those who work remotely. Remember to make users aware that even though they will be slightly inconvenienced in the beginning, the long-term benefits will save them time and secure the company.

E-Mail Servers and the Concept of Latency

E-mail has quickly become an essential business tool. Not surprisingly, e-mail servers have also become targets for increasingly sophisticated attacks. The security industry has responded to these attacks by adopting such strategies as stripping e-mail attachments and scanning e-mails for viruses. However, these practices can have a major impact on your business. If you implement a policy forbidding all attachments (usually a bad idea), you may find that this will harm your business. Also, scanning all e-mail attachments can significantly slow e-mail delivery.

> It is possible to strip only those attachments that have certain extensions (e.g., files ending in .exe). However, most employees know how to bypass such measures by simply changing the file extension to another ending that the e-mail server does not scan or eliminate. It is important to realize that if employees can figure out how to defeat this strategy, hackers will, too. When you implement a policy, you may want to exempt some accounts from scanning. For example, you may not have the time to scan the accounts of all systems on your network, or company executives may not want their accounts to be scanned by systems because they do not want them to be cracked.

Consider Physical Security

It is possible for equipment to just "walk away." Equipment is especially liable to disappear in these days of hot-swappable drives and easy-open server cases. You should keep in mind that the loss of equipment is often less important than the loss of the information stored on it.

Many organizations have implemented sophisticated security software, only to have their systems defeated because the actual machine was not physically secured. Perhaps a company places its firewall and network in a public area, exposing it to tampering. Another neglects to restrict access to otherwise secure rooms by simply leaving the door to the server room open and unattended.

Often, a hacker will use a non-Internet security breach to open an Internet security hole through which to enter your systems. Such breaches might include:

- An employee who removes or introduces information manually.
- An employee who accidentally gives the network a virus. Most viruses are the result of otherwise benign user activity, such as an unsuspecting employee bringing in an infected disk from home.

Questions to ask yourself concerning physical security might include:

- Is the corporate firewall in a locked room? How about all of the corporate servers?

- Are the network machines (e.g., the router, the web server, the FTP server, and so forth) fastened and monitored?
- Are any employees working alone in sensitive areas?

Maintenance Personnel

Maintenance personnel present special issues for you to take into account. Many companies hire third-party cleaning crews to clean their offices. Consider what might occur if one of these cleaning crew members were a talented hacker. It would be possible for this person to have full physical access to the corporation, including offices that would normally be off-limits to all but the most trusted company officials.

Even if maintenance personnel are employees of the company, you may want to closely monitor the hiring and firing practices. Ask the following questions:

- Are all maintenance workers relieved of keys, passes, and other tools that would allow them to enter the system?
- Does the company have a policy that allows staff to monitor maintenance personnel as they work?

These simple steps are part of a proactive strategy. Enabling automatic surveillance is another option, if hiring additional employees is not a possibility.

Surveillance Methods

Options for improving physical security include:

- Replacing standard key locks with number pads
- Placing the servers behind a locked door
- Installing video surveillance equipment

Home Solutions (www.x10.com) provides video cameras as a way to increase physical security. More sophisticated solutions are available, but this site provides a helpful example. Cameras can be configured to act as a sort of "trip wire." Whenever anyone walks past the camera, it takes a snapshot, then transmits the image via e-mail or by other means. This strategy can prove quite useful in highly sensitive settings. The Home Solutions web page is shown in Figure 4.2.

FIGURE 4.2 The Home Solutions web page

Physical Attack Strategies

Many different ways exist to physically attack a system. Some methods are quite subtle, whereas others are quite obvious. A hacker's primary goal is to obtain information secretly, without leaving behind evidence that an attack has occurred. Let's discuss the two most common approaches.

Superzapping *Superzapping* involves the use of an application or operating system to mount, read, and even write values to elements of another operating system. Using a superzapping application, it is possible to alter user account information, read files, or create files and directories. All superzapping applications require that the operating system be dormant (i.e., turned off). Some applications, for example, run off a simple floppy disk. All you have to do is reboot the system, load the application into memory from the floppy, and you can, for example, add a new root account or change the password of an existing administrative account. Because these changes occur when the operating system is not running, they are not logged.

Superzapping gets its name from an old mainframe application called "superzap." This program was used to access systems that were having problems. Very quickly, however, hackers began to misuse this application. A simple example of superzapping involves using one file system to mount another. Many systems administrators like to dual-boot between, say, Windows and Linux systems. It is possible to use a Linux system to mount and read the FAT32 and NTFS drives. Linux support for mounting NTFS drives is somewhat limited, but FreeBSD systems have been able to read and write NTFS drives for years. More advanced superzapping methods include the ability to change passwords and alter other values that the operating system will honor when it is rebooted.

Structure infiltration A server or workstation is not necessarily secure just because it is turned off and sitting behind a locked door. You have already seen how it is possible to infiltrate a room through social engineering (cleaning crews and so forth). However, if this form of social engineering is not available, it is always possible to engage in the following types of *structure infiltration*:

- Removing locked doors from their hinges and entering the room
- Obtaining a key to the room, either by stealing a key or creating a new one
- Crawling through false ceilings and entering the room

Sometimes, the ceiling of a server room has only acoustical tile, which a hacker can easily remove. The hacker can then simply crawl over the wall to bypass a locked door. You will find that the most successful hackers prefer to avoid imposing obstacles; they would rather go around, over, or even under them. Examples of such obstacles include putting in place well-configured firewalls and locking doors with keypads rather than standard keys.

The following exercises are meant to show how effective physical attacks can be.

EXERCISE 4.1

Exploiting and Protecting Red Hat Linux Single-Boot Mode Using LILO

In this exercise, you will conduct a physical attack against Red Hat Linux 7. This exercise assumes that your Linux system is using a default Linux Loader (LILO) installation, not the Grand Unified Boot Loader (GRUB) installer.

1. Restart your computer and enter the following at the LILO prompt:

   `linux single`

   If a graphical LILO screen appears, press Ctrl+X to open a text screen, which will allow you to enter this command.

2. Linux will launch into single mode, which is much like Windows 2000 safe mode. This mode automatically provides you (or any other user) with a root prompt. Using the `passwd` command, change the root password to any password you like. Note that if you enter a password that is too short, you will get this message: "BAD PASSWORD: it is based on a dictionary word." You can ignore this message for now, because you are root.

   ```
   bash# passwd
   New UNIX password:
   Retype new UNIX password:
   passwd: all authentication tokens updated successfully
   ```

3. Now, restart your system:

   `bash# shutdown -r now`

4. Boot normally into Linux and enter either **init** 3 (command-line mode) or **init** 5 and log on using your new password.

5. Change your password back to the original (password):

   ```
   host# passwd root
   New UNIX password:
   Retype new UNIX password:
   passwd: all authentication tokens updated successfully
   ```

6. You have now seen how anyone with physical access to your system can gain control of it. To solve this problem, as root open /etc/lilo.conf in a text editor. This file controls how your system boots.

EXERCISE 4.1 *(continued)*

7. Scroll to the end of the first section of the file, just above the `image=` line.

8. You will see that `lilo.conf` has two sections. We will concentrate on the first section. Add the last two lines of the following code to the first section:

   boot=/dev/hda
   map=/boot/map
   install=/boot/boot.b
   prompt
   timeout=50
   default=linux
   <u>restricted</u>
   <u>password=password</u>

   Note: For this exercise, use password as the password. For a production system, you will probably want to impose a stronger password. Do not change the text in the second section.

9. Notice the `restricted` and `password=` lines. The `restricted` line tells Linux to check for a password whenever entering single mode. If you leave out this word, Linux will prompt you every time a reboot occurs, even if the system is not booted into single mode. This prompting could be a problem, because networking support is not enabled in Linux single mode (i.e., at the LILO prompt). Should you need to reboot the system remotely, the system will wait at LILO until you enter a password. This means that if you are trying to control the system remotely, you will never be able to gain access to it again, unless someone physically enters the password. Once you have added the `password=` line, exit /etc/lilo.conf; be sure to save your changes.

10. Issue the following command, exactly as shown:

    host# lilo
    host#

11. The previous command re-creates the /boot/boot.b file. After you have run the `lilo` command, restart Linux.

EXERCISE 4.1 (continued)

12. When the system reboots, you will be prompted with the LILO prompt. Enter `linux single` at the LILO prompt and press Enter. You will be prompted for a password. You have now enabled a measure of physical security for your system.

13. Reboot your system again as soon as you can and then allow it to enter Linux normally (i.e., do not make it go into Linux single mode). You will see that it boots directly into Linux. Now, only single mode is password-protected.

14. If necessary, disable the password protection you have enabled by reediting /etc/lilo.conf, erasing the password= line, and rerunning the lilo command.

EXERCISE 4.2

Conducting a Physical Attack Against a Windows 2000 Server

In this exercise, you will use the freeware Windows NT Change Password utility to gain administrative access to a Windows 2000 server. This application is an example of superzapping.

To achieve expected results, this procedure should be conducted on a stand-alone server, not on a domain controller. Also, because this exercise uses experimental software, you should not conduct this exercise on a production server. Use an experimental one instead.

Note: You can obtain this application at http://home.eunet.no/~pnordahl/ntpasswd/bootdisk.html.

1. Open the Computer Management snap-in and create a new account named physicaltest. Choose a password for physicaltest that is at least eight characters long, incorporating as many characters as possible. Do not reveal this password to anyone.

2. Add this account to the Administrators group.

3. Obtain the bd011022.bin file (or whatever the latest file name is) and unzip it. Note that if your network has systems that use SCSI adapters, you will have to download these, as well.

EXERCISE 4.2 (continued)

4. Use the `rawrite2.exe` program to copy the image from your desktop to a floppy disk in the A: drive, as shown here:

   ```
   C:\DOCUME~1\James\Desktop\NTBOOT~1>rawrite2
   RaWrite 2.0 - Write disk file to raw floppy diskette
   Enter disk image source file name: bd010114.bin
   Enter target diskette drive: a:
   Please insert a formatted diskette
   into drive A: and press -ENTER- :
   Number of sectors per track
   for this disk is 18
   ```

   Note: The `rawrite2.exe` program is also available at http://home.eunet.no/~pnordahl/ntpasswd/bootdisk.html.

5. Place the boot disk you have just created into the A: drive.

6. Shut down and restart the computer.

Note: Your system must be configured to read your floppy drive first at boot time. Enter the system's CMOS and make sure the A:\ drive is selected to be read first.

7. When the boot disk begins, you will see that it is a specialized form of Linux. At the Press Return/Enter To Continue prompt, press Enter.

8. You will be asked if the program should probe for SCSI drivers. Type the appropriate answer for your system (usually **N** for no). Linux will take some time to load. As it loads, view the partition check. You will eventually search one of these partitions for the Windows 2000 Security Accounts Manager (SAM) database.

9. The program will ask you for a partition that contains the Windows 2000 installation. For example, it might offer /dev/hda1 or dev/hda5. Enter the correct partition through trial and error. Sometimes, the program will have already discovered the correct partition. If it does, press Enter.

   You must specify the partition that contains your Windows 2000 server. Systems may vary, depending upon how you have installed Windows 2000. For example, you may want to enter **/dev/hda1** or **/dev/hda5**.

EXERCISE 4.2 *(continued)*

Note: Do not be discouraged or fooled by all failure messages. They often refer to FAT and FAT32 file systems, rather than NTFS (what your system should be using). Check the messages carefully for any text that reads "Partitions found on the disk(s)."

10. The ntchangepass program will give you two options. The first allows you to enter password-changing mode and edit any account. The second allows you to edit the Registry. Select 1 to enter password-changing mode.

11. The ntchangepass program will ask you to enter the full path to the SAM file. By default, ntchangepass knows the Registry directory (winnt/system32/config). This should be correct, so press Enter.

    Note: If, for some reason, the SAM is in a different directory, enter the correct path.

12. You should see a list of files in the directory. They should include AppEvent.Evt, default, SAM, and SECURITY, among others.

13. The Windows 2000 Registry contains groups of settings, called hives. You will be asked which Registry hives you want to edit. Leave the default entry (sam system security) to change passwords and press Enter.

14. You will be informed that it is unwise to disable Syskey. Press N to choose not to disable Syskey and then press Enter.

    Syskey is one of the tools used by Windows 2000 to protect passwords. It is responsible for using strong encryption on the passwords stored in the SAM. Using ntchangepass does not require deactivating Syskey, nor should it. Instead of trying to decrypt passwords, ntchangepass directly writes information to the SAM, bypassing the need for decryption. If you deactivate Syskey, you will reset all passwords, thus alerting the systems administrator that a hack has occurred. Using this attack, you alert only one user, but by then, a hacker would probably add a new user with administrative privileges.

EXERCISE 4.2 *(continued)*

15. `ntchangepass` will automatically present the administrator account to be changed. Rather than changing this account, enter a dot to list all users in the SAM. You will see a list of accounts similar to those shown below:

    ```
    RID: 0194 Username: <administrator>
    RID: 03f6 Username: <guest> *BLANK password*
    RID: 03f9 Username: <IUSR_system>
    ```

16. List several additional accounts in the spaces provided.

    Note: The RID (Relative ID) number is the unique end value given to each user in the SAM. It is necessary to ensure that all usernames remain unique.

17. Enter the name of the `physicaltest` account.

18. Type in a new password, then press Enter. Record the new password in the space provided. Be sure to record your password accurately.

19. Enter Y to indicate that you want to change the password.

20. Enter ! to quit the password-writing portion of the program.

21. Enter Y to write to the hive files.

22. Enter Y again and press Enter to write to the SAM.

23. Remove the floppy disk from the A: drive and press Ctrl+Alt+Del to restart your system.

24. Using your new password, log on as `physicaltest` using the password you have just entered. You will be able to log in using the password you set.

The best way to secure yourself from this type of attack is to carefully control your server room. You will have to monitor it carefully, as well. Stating in your security policy that no one is allowed to approach the security room during certain times is a good idea. Although physical attacks require access to the server, this process is not difficult for a determined hacker who knows how to defeat locks and improperly constructed rooms.

Creating Effective Solutions

When you take the CIW Security Professional exam, you must have an understanding of the 10 principles listed in this chapter. Here are specific ways you can implement those principles:

Update the system often. Expect a hacker to find a buffer overflow or other system bug. Make sure that you obtain and install the latest, stable system patches. Regardless of the operating system you use, updates are freely available.

Check system logs. The truly paranoid systems administrator checks system logs often. They are the primary means of determining what has happened on your system.

Survey your network. Regularly patrolling all elements of your network makes it easier to find and eliminate simple problems. Thoroughly enforcing your security policy involves various surveillance activities. It is important to physically visit employee areas and determine how well employees are adhering to the security policy. This way, you can identify and solve small problems, such as improper password storage. As far as servers are concerned, the most common security problem is the presence of old user login accounts that have not been properly deactivated. It is also possible to use packet sniffers, systems scanners, and other tools to survey what is happening on your network.

Keep current. Technology has a way of advancing quickly, and it is in your best interest to keep abreast of any changes. For example, wireless networks have become quite common. Securing them is quite a challenge. First of all, 802.11b wireless networks use a relatively powerful encryption scheme, but few activate the feature. Thus, it is possible for a malicious user to sniff packets on these networks. Wireless networks often have difficulty excluding unauthorized users. As a result, the practice of *war driving* has become popular. In war driving, a user with a wireless system literally drives from area to area in a city and taps into multiple wireless networks. Once the hacker has been able to attach to a wireless network, he or she can then begin to attack servers in the network. This activity is made possible by systems administrators and security professionals who have not properly isolated their wireless networks. If a business implements a wireless network without first encrypting and authenticating network transmissions, a hacker can easily obtain information.

Summary

In this chapter, you learned about the key principles to consider when implementing security at your site. If you adhere to these principles, you will be able to create a security infrastructure that is both efficient and easily understood and followed by everyone in your organization. Security entails a balance among security requirements, company needs, and political issues. Such issues include training upper management, long-term employees, and so forth.

Now that you have completed this chapter, you should be able to:

- Describe the universal guidelines and principles for effective network security.

- Use the universal guidelines and security principles to create effective solutions.

You now know the guidelines and practices covered by the CIW Security Professional exam. In the next chapter, we will learn how to apply some of these guidelines in firewalls. Specifically, you will learn about packet filters and proxy servers, and how they help you protect your network.

Exam Essentials

Be able to implement security principles.   You have learned 10 security principles. To feel completely comfortable taking the CIW Security Professional exam, you should be in a job role that gives you experience implementing at least two or three of these principles.

Be able to ensure that all systems work together to create maximum security.   One of the goals of any systems administrator is to ensure that there is no single point of failure on a network. Security administrators should also have this goal. Whenever possible, coordinate systems so that they work together to achieve maximum network security.

Be able to conduct and verify backups.   Although creating backups is not the most exciting task, it is one of the most important. In addition to verifying that backups are properly created, you must verify that the backup process is valid.

Understand how to minimize the impact of a security incident. Minimizing threats involves making sure that various system and network elements are well coordinated. In this chapter, for example, you learned the importance of ensuring that a valid user account has just enough permissions to fulfill a job. This way, if a hacker compromises the account, the hacker will not have full run of the entire system or network. You also learned the importance of isolating operating system elements.

Understand the impact of valid security measures on business practices. Be prepared to identify the ramifications of various security measures. Most systems administrators can determine when it is time to secure e-mail transactions or deny a certain traffic type at the firewall. A true security professional is able to explain what impact such steps can have on a business.

Be able to ensure physical security. Physical security is essential. All network elements must be properly secured.

Key Terms

Before you take the exam, be certain you are familiar with the following terms:

amortization	root
baseline	scalability
capacity forecasting	secure data backup and storage
catastrophic event	simple intrusion
chargeback	structure infiltration
latency	superzapping
matrix	trend analysis
needs assessment audit	war driving
performance management	

Review Questions

1. What is the best way to consistently minimize threats to your system?

   A. Disable all unencrypted network services.

   B. Implement an effective security policy.

   C. Install a firewall.

   D. Centralize user passwords.

2. Which group should have the most detailed training and information about threats and security measures?

   A. End users

   B. Administrators

   C. Managers

   D. Stockholders

3. What is the name for the measurement of time needed for a request to be processed between a client and server?

   A. Trend

   B. Chargeback

   C. Amortization

   D. Latency

4. What is the foundation for effective network security?

   A. Strong encryption

   B. Frequently changed passwords

   C. An effective security policy

   D. Tight physical security

5. When considering where to place equipment, what first step should a systems administrator or security manager take?

   A. Work to secure funding.

   B. Conduct a needs assessment.

   C. Conduct research to determine the proper product.

   D. Determine how the technology selected will affect users' jobs.

6. Todd has used a floppy disk to load a mini-version of Linux from a floppy disk. Using this floppy disk, he has been able to mount a Windows NTFS drive and make changes to the operating system. What name has the security community given to this activity?

   A. Superzapping

   B. Physical attack

   C. Mounting

   D. NT keying

7. Ruth suspects that her system is experiencing a SYN flood. Which tool should she first use when responding to this threat?

   A. `netstat`

   B. A packet sniffer

   C. The security policy

   D. The network firewall

8. Cindy wishes to infiltrate a network server, even though it is behind a locked door. No one else is on the floor, and she needs to enter the system quickly and secretly. What would her next step be?

   A. Engage in social engineering.

   B. Break down the door.

   C. Make an opening in the wall.

   D. Study the building's infrastructure.

9. To increase her company's ability to recover from catastrophic data loss in case of a natural disaster, Elizabeth has had her backup tapes transported to a remote location. Which of the following will ensure the integrity of her backups after transportation?

   A. Storing them in a locked place

   B. Encrypting the backup

   C. Signing the backup using MD5 encryption

   D. Sampling the backup

10. Management has approved your request for a Symantec VelociRaptor™ firewall. You have convinced them that you need it to help secure the accounts payable database server. You have been asked to determine this network element's cost over a period of five years. What is the name for this activity?

    A. Amortization

    B. Chargeback

    C. Latency

    D. Financing

11. Regan normally logs in from 8:00 A.M. to 5:30 P.M., Monday through Friday. In the last few days, however, she has had to alter her login hours. She now logs in from 10:00 A.M. to 7:30 P.M. Her hours have changed because another department requires her services. The security administrator notices her login hours have changed and contacts Regan's manager to ask about the change. What security principle has this security administrator implemented?

    A. Chargeback

    B. Trend analysis

    C. Amortization

    D. Performance management

12. Regan has been asked to act as a consultant for the Research and Development (R&D) department. She normally works for the IT department. The IT department has billed the (R&D) department for her services. What principle is being employed in this case?

    A. Capacity planning

    B. Chargeback

    C. Amortization

    D. Performance management

13. Shirley has installed personal firewall software on all workstations for the Accounting department. Soon, she receives a call from the Accounting department manager, who complains that her employees can no longer access certain websites. Shirley then instructs the end users on how to customize parts of their personal firewalls. What security principle has Shirley confronted in this scenario?

    A. Chargeback

    B. Amortization

    C. Performance management

    D. Latency

14. Which of these mechanisms can help Davis secure his backups?

    A. Encipherment

    B. Traffic padding

    C. Audit trails

    D. Security labels

15. Which of the following additions to the security policy can help ensure that physical security is implemented?

    A. Encrypt all data transmissions.

    B. Verify all tape backups.

    C. Forbid employees from using floppy disks.

    D. Educate end users about social engineering.

16. Which of the following describes root access?

    A. The ability to generate network packets from a system

    B. The ability to access a system and attack a network

    C. The ability to hack into a system

    D. The ability to administer and control a system

17. Which of the following concepts ensures that all network elements work together to ensure maximum security?

    A. Security matrix

    B. Performance analysis

    C. Physical security

    D. Needs assessment

18. After installing an application meant to increase the security on a host, Alan notices that this host no longer responds to requests as quickly. Which of the following security management concepts applies in this case?

    A. Chargeback

    B. Needs analysis

    C. Performance management

    D. Capacity forecasting

19. Joel has been asked to replace standard key locks with numeric keypads. He has also placed his servers behind a locked door and installed video surveillance equipment for these servers. What security principle is he implementing?

    A. Physical security

    B. Server security

    C. Room security

    D. Employee surveillance

20. Jacob has spent considerable time determining his network's ability to sustain company growth. He has focused specifically on his company's router and its ability to accommodate the need for increased bandwidth. Which of the following best describes his activities?

   A. Needs analysis

   B. Amortization

   C. Chargeback

   D. Capacity forecasting

Answers to Review Questions

1. **B.** Threat minimization is the result of using proper security principles as defined by a security policy. You will not be able to consistently minimize threats unless you first define a policy. Disabling all unencrypted network services, implementing a firewall, and centralizing user passwords are all effective security practices. However, each of these activities will not be consistently applied unless you have a well-considered security policy.

2. **B.** Security concepts and practices should be provided on a need-to-know basis. Administrators should learn the most about threats and countermeasures. To stay out of trouble, users only need to know about the most common threats, as well as some basic procedures. Carefully manage information, or user activities could have an adverse effect on your system's security.

3. **D.** Latency is a classic concept that involves calculating the time it takes for a network request to be fulfilled. Implementing security measures can increase system and network latency.

4. **C.** A security policy governs all security practices, including encryption, authentication, and physical security.

5. **B.** Before you place equipment, it is vital that you conduct a needs assessment. This assessment includes conducting research, securing funding, and determining how the new security measure will affect employee performance.

6. **A.** Superzapping is a physical attack. It involves the use of applications or operating systems to mount a dormant operating system.

7. **C.** The primary tool in responding to an attack is the security policy. The use of any application or network host is predicated on the security policy.

8. **D.** The next step for Cindy to take is to study the building's infrastructure. Because no one else is present, social engineering will not work. Breaking down the door or creating an opening in the wall will leave behind evidence of the attack, making it no longer secret. By studying her building's infrastructure, she may find a way into the server room that will keep her infiltration secret. As a security administrator, it is your job to ensure that the server room is as secure as possible, and that false ceilings and heating ducts will not allow easy access.

9. **D.** Sampling the backup ensures that all data was properly transported and that no data is missing. Storing data in a locked place will do little good if the data is incomplete or if it has been tampered with. Encryption should be conducted before the data is moved, not afterwards.

10. **A.** Amortization is a key principle to use when you're purchasing expensive equipment. Many times, a company's ability to properly amortize a product will determine whether or not you can purchase and implement it.

11. **B.** The security manager has noticed a difference in a login trend and has inquired about it. Because no funds have changed hands, this scenario is not describing chargeback. Amortization involves calculating finances over time, and performance management does not address employee performance.

12. **B.** Chargeback involves the ability for one department to charge another for services rendered.

13. **D.** In security, latency describes the impact that a security application has on the operations of a business. Because Shirley has not been assigned to another department, chargeback issues do not apply. Performance management is not an issue, because the personal firewall did not slow down the systems. Rather, it affected the business practices of the Accounting department. Finally, financing was not involved, so amortization is not an issue.

14. **A.** Encipherment, or encryption, can allow Davis to verify data, as well as to password-protect it. The other security mechanisms have little relevance in securing backups.

15. **C.** Although forbidding employees from using floppy disks may not be the best security policy entry, it can help ensure that employees are not engaging in superzapping or the spreading of Trojans or viruses. Encrypting data transmissions is effective but does not directly protect data against physical attacks. Verifying tape backups is a backup and storage procedure, whereas educating users concerning social engineering is part of the process of user education and does not directly affect physical security.

16. **D.** The ability to administer a system is often called "root" access, because in Unix systems, the root account is the most powerful. It is similar to the Windows NT/2000 administrator account.

17. A. The creation of a security matrix ensures that no system stands alone in the case of attack. Once an effective security matrix has been created, no single point of failure exists.

18. C. Performance management is the ability to determine how much a security solution has affected the ability for a system to function. Performance management, which involves the use of diagnostic applications, is different from the concept of latency, which describes the overall impact of a security solution on a network or business.

19. A. Although Joel is placing equipment according to needs, he is more specifically implementing physical security. When taking the CIW Security Professional exam, it is generally best to choose the more specific solution, as opposed to a more general solution that seems related.

20. D. Capacity forecasting is the ability to determine increased bandwidth. Needs analysis focuses on purchasing new hardware and software, whereas amortization involves determining ways to finance purchases. Chargeback involves one department charging another for its services.

Chapter 5

Firewalls Roles and Types

THE CIW EXAM OBJECTIVE GROUPS COVERED IN THIS CHAPTER:

- ✓ Identify firewall types and define common firewall topology.
- ✓ Plan a firewall system that incorporates multiple levels of protection, including but not limited to: firewall system design, proactive detection, setting traps, security breach response, security alerting organizations.

When a building is physically secured from break-ins, the highest protection is placed on access points to the facility. The goal is to prevent any unauthorized person from gaining access to the building so that the company's assets will remain safe. The concept of network security is the same: The security administrator's goal is to restrict access to and from the company's network. Restricting access to a network is accomplished with a *firewall*.

Many references maintain that the term *firewall* comes from a safety technique applied in building construction. Whenever a wall separates sections of a building, such as different businesses or apartments, it is made as fireproof as possible. This measure protects the rest of the occupants in case one unit catches fire. Most firewalls, however, have a heavy door built in them, allowing people to enter or leave that section of the building. So, even though the wall protects people on each side, its door still allows necessary access while affording increased safety from a fire.

In computer networking, a network firewall acts as a barrier against potential malicious activity, while still allowing a "door" for people to communicate between your secured network and the open, unsecured network. A firewall protects a network's boundaries, or *network perimeter*.

A firewall can consist of a single machine, or "box," that sits between a private network and the Internet. This type of firewall is ideal for small business and home networks. Medium-sized and large businesses often need more than just the "firewall box"; they require multiple hosts residing in a subnet that exists between your internal network and the Internet. This area, called a *demilitarized zone (DMZ)*, often consists of a series of network hosts, surrounded by firewall equipment on both sides. The DMZ often contains the company web, DNS, and e-mail servers.

By the time you are ready to implement your firewall, you should know what services your company requires, and what services will be available to both internal and external users. The need for services on both sides of the firewall largely determines what firewall functions you will use. This chapter discusses the simple and complex mechanisms used to shield your internal network from unwanted activity.

The Role of a Firewall

A firewall is the most critical component of any security implementation because it authoritatively defines the difference between the internal network and all other networks. A firewall strategy should meet four goals:

Implement a company's security policy. A firewall is the primary means of enforcing your security policy. In Chapter 4, you were introduced to security policies and learned how important they are for proper network security. For example, your security policy might state that only the Internet mail server will transmit SMTP traffic. You would enforce this policy feature directly at the firewall. A firewall can also work together with network routes to help implement *Type of Service (ToS)* policies. A ToS policy helps prioritize specified types of traffic. ToS-enabled routers can mark IP packets with certain ToS bits. For example, you can set ToS bits for all HTTP traffic so that it is processed before any other traffic type.

Create a choke point. A firewall creates a *choke point* between your company's private network and a *public network*. Proper implementation requires that all traffic be funneled through these choke points. Once these points have been clearly established, the firewall devices can monitor, filter, and verify all inbound and outbound traffic. By forcing all inbound and outbound traffic through these choke points, you can focus your security efforts in just a few places. Without such a point for monitoring and controlling information, you would have too many places to monitor.

> **NOTE** Sometimes security professionals refer to the choke point as the *network perimeter*. However, a choke point is usually just one element of a firewall, which provides perimeter security.

Log Internet activity. A firewall also enforces logging, and it provides alarm capacities as well. By placing logging services at the firewalls, you can monitor all access to and from the external network or Internet. Good logging strategies are one of the most effective tools for proper network security. Firewalls will provide the most information for your log archive.

Firewalls can also account for traffic so that Internet service providers (ISPs) and corporate departments can accurately bill customers for usage. Counting traffic and billing according to the volume of network use is another form of chargeback.

Limit network host exposure. A firewall creates a protected perimeter, or border, around your network. It enhances privacy by "hiding" your internal systems and information from the public. When remote nodes probe your network, they will see only the firewalls, not all of the individual hosts in the network. Whenever a remote host is able to determine the nature of all hosts, it is said to have obtained a *network map*, or the network's *topology*. On the CIW Security Professional exam, a network's topology, in this sense, refers to how your network is laid out.

A firewall limits network exposure by enhancing authentication and providing network-to-network encryption. By making incoming traffic pass through various source checks, a firewall helps limit the attacks that can be waged from the outside.

Now that you have identified what a firewall does, it is time to learn more about the specific tools used.

Firewall Terminology

Firewalls are usually composed of several different elements, including *packet filters*, *proxies*, and *hosts*. You will need to understand each of these elements as well as other firewall concepts, including network address translation and operating system hardening. You should also know how to use screening, choke routers, and demilitarized zones. Not only will having these terms and concepts in your knowledge bank help you pass the CIW Security Professional exam, but it will also ensure that you'll be able to shore up any firewall you build in the future.

Packet Filter

Packet filters are devices that process network traffic on a packet-by-packet basis. They operate only at the Network layer of the OSI/RM, so they allow or block IP addresses and ports, and can be implemented through standard routers (e.g., a Cisco 2501 router) as well as dedicated firewall devices (e.g., a Check Point Firewall-1 device). A pure packet filter looks only at the following information:

Source IP address   Where the packet comes from.

Destination IP address   Where the packet is going.

Source port   The port used by the originating host.

Destination port   The port to which the packet is directed.

Packet type   The type (such as ICMP or EGP).

Packet-filtering firewall supplements, such as *stateful multilayer inspection*, can help extend this basic capacity. You will learn more about this in the section "Stateful Multilayer Inspection."

Proxy Server

A *proxy* is an entity that stands for, or acts for and on behalf of, another person or thing. A simple example is you attending a meeting for an absent colleague. During that meeting, you represent that person, and you receive and convey information for him or her. You relate the contents of that meeting to your colleague, and sometimes you act on things said in that meeting as if you were that person. A *proxy server* does much the same thing: It acts for and in behalf of network clients that need to access outside networks. The two types of proxy servers are:

- *Application-layer proxies* (also called application-layer gateways)
- *Circuit-level proxies* (also called circuit-level gateways)

Application-Layer Proxy

By far the most popular types of proxy servers are those that proxy application-level traffic. Squid, freely available at www.squid-cache.org, can process only certain protocols, including HTTP, HTTPS, FTP, IRC, DNS, and SNMP. This behavior is different from that of packet filters, which do not concern themselves at all with individual applications; they care only about source and destination ports and IP addresses. A proxy server receives requests from an internal *network client* (e.g., client workstations and servers that reside on the internal network). Then, if the client is authorized, the proxy server communicates with external servers on behalf of the client.

> **NOTE** Many companies market proxy servers as multifunctional. Do not confuse how companies market a product with its actual function.

Websites such as www-106.ibm.com/developerworks/security/library/s-fire2.html can help you learn more about proxy servers and firewalls in general.

Circuit-Level Proxy

A *circuit-level proxy* operates at the Transport layer of the OSI/RM. Another name for a circuit-level proxy is a *circuit-level gateway*. This type of firewall monitors the source and destination of TCP and UDP packets; it does not inspect application-layer traffic, nor does it inspect the traffic as thoroughly as does an application-level proxy. Often, a circuit-level proxy consists of two hosts. An encrypted connection exists between the first firewall host and the second, and both work together to process traffic. The benefit of such an arrangement is that it provides fault tolerance in case one host fails. This arrangement also allows the processing load to be shared between hosts.

Circuit-level proxy servers often provide *network address translation (NAT)*, in which a network host alters the packets of internal network hosts so they can be sent out across the Internet. You will learn more in the section "Network Address Translation."

> **NOTE** A packet-filtering firewall can accomplish NAT as well; not every instance of NAT implies a circuit-level gateway. For example, the WinRoute application in Windows 2000 uses a special feature of packet filtering called *masquerading* to enable NAT.

The most popular circuit-level proxy is the type that uses the *SOCKS protocol*. This protocol, invented by David Koblas, filters specific TCP sockets made between systems. As far as the CIW Security Professional exam is concerned, circuit-level proxy firewalls that use the SOCKS protocol are called

SOCKS servers. Many companies, including IBM and Microsoft, support this type of gateway. Two versions of the SOCKS protocol exist: SOCKS version 4 and SOCKS version 5. The latter is used most often, and it provides support for additional protocols. You can learn more about the SOCKS version 5 protocol by reading RFCs 1928, 1929, 1961, and 3089.

The SOCKS home page is at www.socks.nec.com. You can learn more about circuit-level proxies by reading D. Brent Chapman and Elizabeth Zwicky's *Building Internet Firewalls*, *2nd Edition* (O'Reilly & Associates, 2000).

Advantages and Disadvantages of Circuit-Level Proxies

The primary advantage of using a circuit-level proxy server is that it provides NAT. NAT allows security and network administrators great flexibility when developing an internal IP addressing scheme.

To work with a circuit-level proxy firewall, however, an application must be specifically written to provide all connection information to the SOCKS server. Most web browsers, for example, contain native support for SOCKS servers. But because not all applications are written to cooperate with a circuit-level proxy, using this type of firewall may severely limit users' ability to use custom, mission-critical applications. This means users must alter their practices to accommodate the firewall. Additional weaknesses include the fact that a circuit-level proxy cannot discriminate between bad and good packets; also, it is susceptible to IP spoofing.

Bastion Host

A *bastion* is a secure computer system placed directly between a trusted network and an untrusted one, such as the Internet. You can have a single-homed bastion host. Most often, however, a bastion host uses two network interface cards (NIC). Each card acts as an interface to a separate network. On one card is the production network that you supervise, control, and protect. The other card interfaces with another network, usually a public one, such as the Internet.

Network Address Translation

Network address translation (NAT) is the practice of hiding internal IP addresses from the external network. Another name for NAT is IP *address hiding*. Three ways to provide true NAT are:

- Configure masquerading on a packet-filtering firewall, such as a Linux system. *Masquerading* is the ability for a firewall to rewrite IP headers so that, for example, packets originating from an internal host appear to originate from the firewall's outer NIC.

- Configure a circuit-level proxy server.

- Use a proxy server to conduct requests on behalf of internal hosts.

When a firewall or router is configured to provide NAT, all internal addresses are translated to public IP addresses when connecting to an external host. When packets return from an external host, they are translated back so the internal network host receives them.

RFC 1918 outlines the addresses that the Internet Assigned Numbers Authority (IANA) recommends using for internal address schemes. The internal network address ranges are as follows:

10.0.0.0/8
172.16.0.0/12
192.168.0.0/16

> **NOTE**
> The values appended to the IP addresses denote subnet masks using *Classless Internet Domain Routing (CIDR)* notation. A CIDR notation value of /8 denotes the subnet mask 255.0.0.0. The CIDR notation values of /12 and /16 denote the 255.240.0.0 and 255.255.0.0 subnet masks, respectively.

Notice that the 172.16.0.0/12 and 192.168.0.0/16 networks do not have standard class B and class C subnet masks. If you choose to implement one of the listed network addresses, you need not register the addresses with any Internet authority. The advantage to using one of the listed addresses is that these addresses will never be routed over the Internet. All routers on the Internet are programmed to automatically discard any address that has a source or destination of the aforementioned private network IDs. Not routing these addresses is beneficial if one of the nodes on your network is misconfigured and becomes exposed to the Internet. If the machine is configured with a private address, it still cannot be accessed remotely because no routes are available to it.

Masquerading

Masquerading is the process of altering the IP header. Specifically, a packet filter that masquerades can alter the IP header so that it appears to originate from the firewall rather than from the original host. Masquerading is useful with NAT because it allows hosts using private network IP addresses to communicate with hosts on the Internet. Masquerading is commonly referred to as *packet mangling*.

In Figure 5.1, two networks (192.168.37.0/16 and 10.5.7.0/8) are able to communicate with each other, because each network has firewalls that translate the host IP addresses into Internet-addressable IP addresses (34.09.45.1/8 and 207.19.199.1/24, respectively).

FIGURE 5.1 Implementing NAT in a network

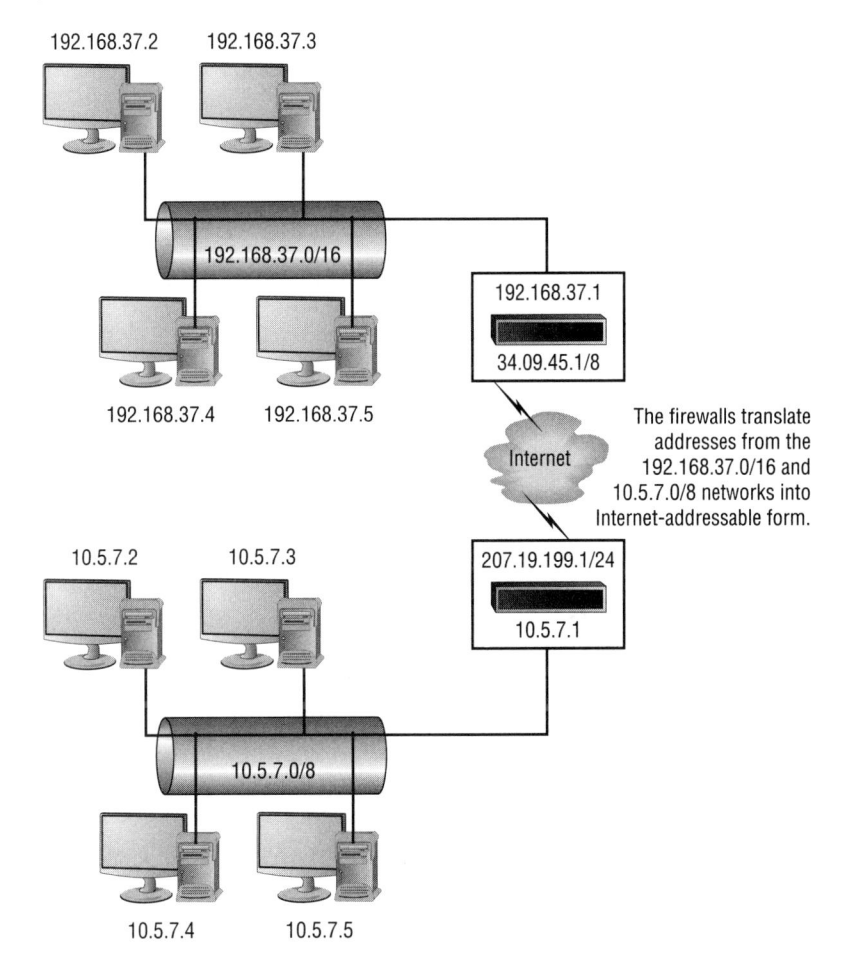

The firewalls translate addresses from the 192.168.37.0/16 and 10.5.7.0/8 networks into Internet-addressable form.

NAT Considerations

When deploying NAT on any multihomed device (such as a router), you will have to determine which NICs are public and which are private. A firewall or bastion host usually has two or more NICs. The inner NIC is often called the *private NIC*, because it faces the internal network. The outer NIC is often called the *public NIC*, because it interfaces with the Internet. Only the public NIC should be used to provide NAT. Many firewalls are configured so that if you perform NAT on the public NIC, no traffic originating from the public network will be forwarded to the other networks. However, traffic originating from the private network can still pass through to the public (i.e., external) network. In this situation, you must create specific rules to prevent traffic passing from the internal network to the external network.

NAT and Vendor Terminology

Each firewall product uses its own terminology. For example, Microsoft Proxy Server 2 uses the terms *trusting* and *trusted* to describe a proxy server's defensive stance in a multihomed situation:

Trusting The proxy server allows traffic from the internal network interface to enter the proxy server's system.

Trusted This term is used to describe the network and/or host that is allowed access to the network.

Trust can occur in one of two ways. For example, you can implement a full one-way trust in which the internal network can cross the proxy server and access external resources. A full two-way trust allows all traffic, regardless of source, to traverse the proxy server. Except for the fact the firewall would still log activity, this stance would defeat the purpose of having a firewall.

Operating System Hardening

A firewall requires only a limited number of services. In operating system hardening, the firewall's installation program disables or removes all unnecessary services.

Most firewall packages, including Symantec Raptor (www.symantec.com), Check Point Firewall-1 (www.checkpoint.com) and Network Associates' Gauntlet firewall (www.networkassociates.com), operate on top of popular operating system platforms. These products work even if the firewall includes a dedicated *network appliance*, which is a single machine dedicated for one purpose. Instead of installing firewall software on a standard computer, you can obtain a specialized system meant only to house firewall software.

Generally, a system designated as a firewall is not suitable for any other network application because the firewall software will prohibit installation and execution of all programs that it does not specifically recognize. The Raptor firewall, for example, includes a special service called Vulture that automatically disables applications and services that you may try to run. You should consider dedicating your firewall system solely to firewall duties, for this reason alone.

The logic behind operating system hardening is that once you strip an operating system to its foundation, it is much more difficult to compromise the host by exploiting system bugs.

Screening and Choke Routers

A *screening router* is another term for a packet-filtering router that has at least one interface exposed to a public network, such as the Internet. A screening router is different from a bastion host in that it does not use additional services to thoroughly screen packets. A screening router is configured to examine inbound and outbound packets based on filter rules.

Another name for a screening router is the outside router, because it presents interfaces to the Internet, not to the internal network.

Choke Router

When two routers are used in a firewall configuration, the internal router (i.e., the router that presents an interface to the internal network) is often called a *choke router*.

A choke router defines the point at which a public network can access your internal network. It also defines the point at which your internal network users can access the public network. Security administrators use choke points to limit external access to their networks. Using a firewall strategy creates choke points, because all traffic must flow through the firewalls.

Demilitarized Zone (DMZ)

A DMZ is a mini-network that resides between a company's internal network and the external network. The network is created by a screening router and, sometimes, a choke router. A DMZ is used as an additional buffer to further separate the public network from your internal private network. A DMZ is sometimes referred to as a *service network*.

Many systems administrators place web and DNS servers in a DMZ, because it is more convenient. The benefit of this practice is that the screening router provides some protection. The drawback is that any server in a DMZ is not as protected as it would be if it resided behind the actual choke router.

Firewall Configuration Defaults

By default, a firewall can be configured to use either of the following stances:

Deny all traffic   In this case, you would specify certain types of traffic that you want to allow in and out of your network.

Allow all traffic   In this case, you would specify certain types of traffic that you want to deny.

Usually, the most secure option is to have the firewall deny all traffic by default. Once you install the firewall, you will need to open the necessary ports so users inside the firewall can access the systems they are authorized to use. In other words, if you want your employees to send and receive e-mail, you will have to create rules and/or start daemons that allow POP3 and SMTP to pass through the firewall.

Remember, a firewall works both ways: It controls access to traffic entering *and* leaving the network. Therefore, you need to take special measures to ensure that all necessary ports have been opened at the firewall. If you do not do this, clients will not be able to complete connections.

Perhaps it will be helpful to review how ports are assigned in IP-aware systems. Any port below 1024 is referred to as a *well-known port*. The CIW Security Professional exam requires you to understand that the ports from 1024 to 65535 will need to be opened in order for client connections to occur. The exam refers to ports from 1024 and higher as *ephemeral ports*. It does not require you to know how to name ports between 1024 and 65535. However, ports above 1023 can be broken into additional categories. The "registered" ports range from 1024 to 49151. Ports that range from

49152 to 65535 are called dynamic, or private, ports. If you have any questions, consult the IANA website at www.iana.org/assignments/port-numbers.

If you have a firewall that allows all traffic by default, you will then have to take measures to create rules and use various services (i.e., daemons) to deny unwanted traffic.

Creating Packet Filter Rules

Because a packet filter is a device that inspects each packet for predefined content, you must define rules that tell the packet filter what to block or allow. Although it does not provide error-proof protection, it is almost always the first line of defense. Many firewall configurations have multiple routers or firewalls, and security engineers often begin filtering packets at the external (i.e., screening) router, which discards certain types of activity entirely. The choke router then filters out additional traffic. This method is very useful for implementing broad restrictions; it also ensures that no single point of failure exists. When packets are filtered at a router, it is usually called a *screening router*, which is another term for a packet-filtering firewall. Also, it is often useful to use two screening routers in parallel. This way, if one router fails, traffic can still pass through the second, which helps eliminate a single point of failure.

The Packet Filter Process

Packet-filtering firewalls work at the Network layer of the OSI/RM. Packet filters use text files that have been created by a security administrator. The text files are composed of rules that are sequentially read line by line. Each rule contains specific entries to help determine how incoming packets will be handled.

Rules can be applied based on source and destination IP addresses or source and destination network addresses. Packet filters also can enforce rules based on TCP and UDP ports. All Internet services are based on specific TCP and UDP ports, and can therefore be subject to examination. Packet filters are read and then acted upon on a rule-by-rule basis.

Once a packet has failed any portion of a filter, the subsequent rules will not be read. Remember to consider the order of rules within a filter. A packet filter will provide two actions: allow or block. The allow action routes the packet as normal if all conditions within the rule are met. The block action will discard all packets if the conditions in the rule are not met. Packet filters will discard any packet unless it has specifically been allowed within a rule.

> **TIP**
>
> Microsoft Networking uses many different ports. However, one of the primary ways to ensure security at the firewall is to forbid outside connections to ports used by Microsoft Networking. These ports include UDP ports 137 and 138, and TCP ports 135 and 139.

Rules and Fields

Packet filters use rules to determine what packets are allowed to traverse the firewall. A rule is composed of several fields. Specific implementation involves telling the router to filter the content of IP packets based on the information found in each field.

Packet filters work best for restricting certain IP addresses and TCP and UDP applications from entering or leaving your network. For example, to disable the ability to telnet into internal devices from the Internet, you could create a packet filter rule. Telnet, for example, uses TCP port 23. In a packet filter that allows all access by default, a packet filter rule that stops Telnet would look similar to the values in Table 5.1.

TABLE 5.1 Telnet Packet Filter

Rule Number	Action	SRC IP	DST IP	SRC Port	DST Port	Protocol
1	Discard	*	*	23	*	TCP
2	Discard	*	*	*	23	TCP

The information listed in Table 5.1 tells the router to discard any packet going to or coming from TCP port 23. An asterisk indicates any value in a particular field. If a packet that has a source port of 23 is passed through rule 1, it will immediately be discarded. If a packet with a destination port of 23 is passed through this rule, it will be discarded only after rule 2 has been applied.

> **Note:** Our examples are meant to describe the concept of packet filter rules. Actual implementations of the rules will vary widely. For example, Cisco routers require you to format a particular rule much differently than does Check Point's FireWall-1.

Standard FTP Clients and Creating Packet Filter Rules

Standard FTP clients make data connections to two ports on an FTP server: ports 20 and 21. Port 20 on the server is the data channel (i.e., the port that sends the actual information). Port 21 on the server is the control channel, which the server uses to listen for connections and issue commands.

A standard FTP client builds a connection with a server by first opening a port above 1023 (e.g., port 4998) that is directed to port 21 on the server. Once the client has connected to port 21, it issues a PORT command to the server. This command has the server open its own port 20 and initiate a connection back to the same ephemeral port on the client (port 4998 in this case). The client then acknowledges this connection by opening a second ephemeral port (e.g., port 4999), this time directed to port 20 on the server. Once these transactions occur, data transfer can begin between the client and the server. Thus, in a firewall that disallows all access by default, the rules shown in Table 5.2 will allow an internal standard FTP client to connect to outside FTP servers.

TABLE 5.2 Packet Filter for Internal Standard FTP Clients

Rule Number	Action	SRC IP	DST IP	SRC Port	DST Port	Protocol
1	Allow	192.168.10.0/24	*	>1023	21	TCP
2	Allow	*	192.168.10.0/24	21	>1023	TCP
3	Allow	*	192.168.10.0/24	20	>1023	TCP
4	Allow	192.168.10.0/24	*	>1023	20	TCP

Rule 1 allows internal systems (e.g., systems on the 192.168.10.0/24 network) to make a connection to port 21. Rule 2 allows servers to make connections back to ephemeral ports in the 192.168.10.0/24 network. Rule 3 allows outside FTP servers to open port 20 and make a connection back to ports 1024 or higher. Rule 4 may seem similar to rule 1; however, you'll notice that rule 4 is allowing clients on the 192.168.10.0/24 network to acknowledge connections to port 20, not port 21.

Passive FTP Clients and Packet Filter Rules

Most modern Web browsers and FTP clients do not use standard FTP. Rather, they use passive FTP. Like standard FTP, the server listens for connections on port 21, and clients use a port above 1023 to make a connection to this server port. However, when a passive FTP client begins the data connection, it does not use the PORT command. Rather, the client uses the PASV command, which tells the server to open up one of its own ports above 1023, rather than port 20, to build a data channel. In passive mode FTP, a server never uses port 20.

Table 5.3 contains a set of packet filter rules that allows internal passive FTP clients to connect to outside FTP servers. These rules assume a firewall stance that all connections are blocked unless explicitly allowed.

TABLE 5.3 Packet Filter for Internal Passive FTP Clients

Rule Number	Action	SRC IP	DST IP	SRC Port	DST Port	Protocol
1	Allow	192.168.10.0/24	*	>1023	21	TCP*
2	Allow	*	192.168.10.0/24	21	>1023	TCP
3	Allow	192.168.10.0/24	*	>1023	>1023	TCP
4	Allow	*	192.168.10.0/24	>1023	>1023	TCP

The first rule allows all clients inside the 192.168.10.0/24 network to open ports above 1023 to a destination port of 21 (where the server is listening for connections). At this time, the client makes a PASV request. The second rule allows the server to respond to the PASV request. The third rule allows the client to open a second port back to the server to begin the data channel. The fourth rule allows the server to acknowledge the data connection, so that files can be transported.

Passive FTP is often called "firewall friendly" FTP. This is because in a passive FTP session, the server does not initiate a new connection with a client using a well-known port (e.g., port 20), as it does in a standard FTP session. Although passive FTP sessions do require a server to use port 21 to connect to a client, this connection takes place as an acknowledgment to a connection first made by the client. Thus, many firewalls recognize that this connection is part of a previous session. In the case of standard FTP, the server initiates the connection between port 20 and the client, and many firewalls are configured to automatically drop such connections.

It should be understood that the above rules will now allow an unknown external system to make an initial connection to an internal system on a port greater than 1023. As a result, your internal systems may begin to use illicit programs that accept initial connections from outside clients and servers. For example, the above rules may allow file-sharing programs similar to KaZaA, Morpheus, or Napster. Most (if not all) firewalls allow you to create special rules to avoid this problem. In short, it is possible for any firewall to control connections by making sure that packets requesting services from the outside are part of an acknowledgment of an existing session.

For example, you can create a rule that blocks all initial connections to an ephemeral port. Remember, initial connections have the SYN bit set. (See Figure 3.1 in Chapter 3 for an illustration of the TCP handshake.) In `iptables`, for example, you can use the `--syn` option to block SYN-based connections to ports above 1023, but you would allow only in-progress connections from an outside server.

Packet Filter Advantages and Disadvantages

The main advantage to using a packet filter is that the devices and software needed are probably already in place, because most routers natively support packet filtering. Since all the devices are already in place, you will have to spend little or no money on new equipment. After you learn how to format the rules, you can begin controlling access.

Packet filters used as screening routers are normally the first line of defense for a firewall system. Packet filters can screen entire applications or network IDs. For example, a packet filter could restrict all inbound traffic to a specific host. This restriction would prevent a hacker from being able to contact any other host within the internal network.

> The biggest problem with packet filters or screening routers is that they cannot discriminate between good and bad packets. If a packet passes all the rules, it will be routed to the destination. Packet filters cannot tell whether the routed packet contains good or malicious data. Packet filters are susceptible to embedded code within a standard packet. Using our first FTP example, a hacker could embed a program that scanned all IP addresses on the 192.168.10.0 network to create a map of the internal network. As long as the hacker initiated the packet with a source port of 20, the packet filter would pass all the packets.
>
> Another weakness ties directly to the one mentioned above. Creating packet filters requires extensive knowledge of TCP/IP. Most TCP/IP applications are client/server-based, so the filters will need multiple rules to deal with the client/server communication. Generalizing rules is difficult because most TCP/IP applications have special TCP/UDP port requirements.
>
> Another problem with packet filters is that you usually have to create more than 100 rules to limit and permit network access. Creating all these rules can be time-consuming. Yet another significant weakness of packet filters is their susceptibility to spoofing. Spoofing is similar to the first weakness, the inability to discriminate between good and malicious data. If a hacker spoofs his or her source address with a source address that is specifically allowed by a rule within the filter, the firewall will pass or route the packet.
>
> Finally, because packet filters work at the Network layer, less processing power is needed. As a result, many high-volume sites, such as Yahoo!, eBay, and others, use packet-filtering firewalls, because many proxy-oriented firewalls cannot quickly process high volumes of traffic.

Stateful Multilayer Inspection

Introduced by Check Point, *stateful multilayer inspection* allows packet filters to overcome weaknesses inherent in packet filtering. Packet filters that engage in stateful multilayer inspection can examine packets in context because the firewall can maintain a database of past connections. By analyzing and comparing connections, the firewall can understand the nature of a series of connections. Stateful multilayer inspection allows you to detect and thwart ping and port scans, and help determine whether a packet has been spoofed.

Another benefit of stateful multilayer inspection is that it allows packet filters to inspect packets at all layers of the OSI/RM, not just the Network layer. Many companies now use stateful multilayer inspection in their packet-filtering firewalls.

> **Note:** Some of the more popular packet-filtering firewall and router products are Check Point FireWall-1 (www.checkpoint.com), Cisco PIX (www.cisco.com), and WinRoute (www.winroute.com or www.tinysoftware.com).

EXERCISE 5.1

Configuring Packet-Filtering Rules

In this exercise, you will install WinRoute onto your Windows 2000 system. It is possible, and even recommended, to install WinRoute on a dual-NIC system. This way, it can act as a true firewall. In these exercises, however, a system with only one NIC is assumed. Working with only one NIC should nevertheless teach you the concepts and principles necessary to pass the CIW Security Professional exam. You will use WinRoute to restrict access to ICMP packets and certain TCP and UDP ports, and then forbid certain IP addresses to access your server. This exercise assumes that you have two systems. One will house the firewall software, and the other will act as a client to the firewall.

1. Obtain the WinRoute software from www.winroute.com and place it on your desktop. As Administrator, install the application. Once it is installed, go to Start ➢ Programs ➢ WinRoute Pro ➢ WinRoute Administration to launch WinRoute.

2. You will be asked to authenticate. Because this is the first time you have used WinRoute, click OK to enter. You can specify a user password later.

EXERCISE 5.1 *(continued)*

3. After clicking OK, go to Settings ➢ Advanced ➢ Packet Filter. The Packet Filter dialog box will appear. Your NIC will be automatically detected and will appear in this dialog box. For example, here is the dialog box on a system using a 3Com NIC:

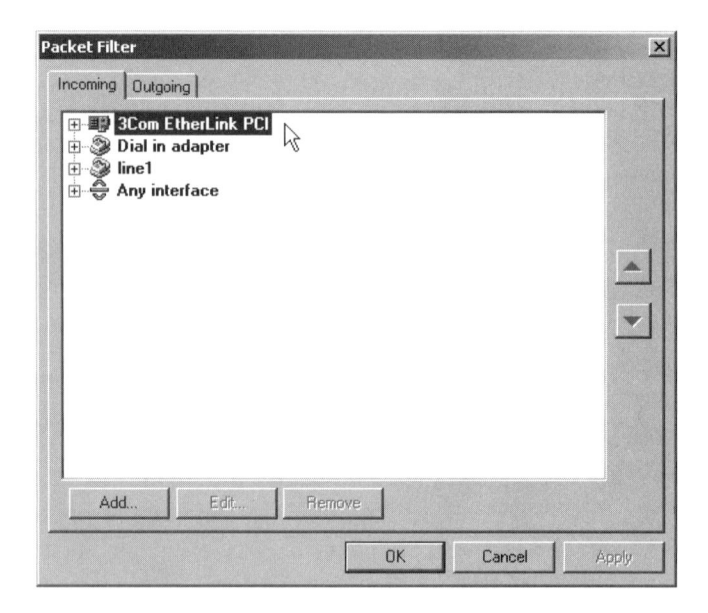

4. System 1: Once you have reviewed your interface, click Cancel.

5. System 1: Highlight and expand the icon that represents your NIC by clicking the plus sign (+) sign next to it. You will see that no packet-filtering rules have been associated with this NIC.

Creating Packet Filter Rules 213

EXERCISE 5.1 *(continued)*

6. System 1: With your NIC's icon highlighted, click the Add button. The Add Item dialog box will appear, as shown here:

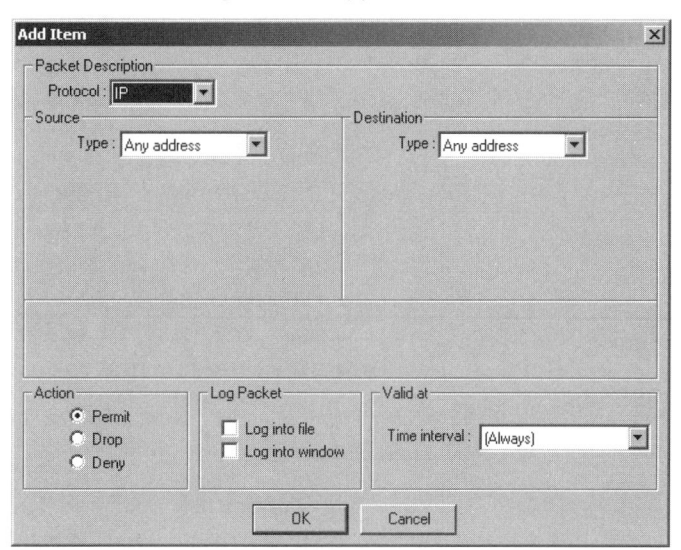

7. System 1: From here, you can add packet filters for any protocol at the Network layer of the OSI/RM. Begin with ICMP. In the Protocol drop-down box, select ICMP. Once you select ICMP, a new dialog box will open, as shown here:

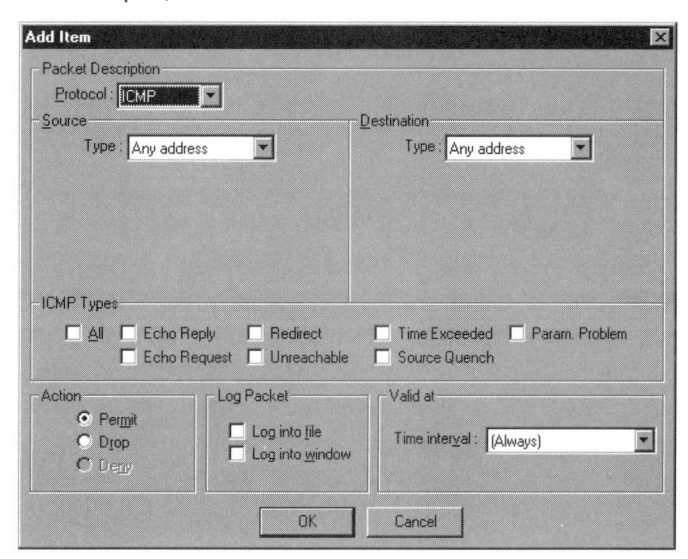

EXERCISE 5.1 *(continued)*

8. System 1: In the ICMP Types section, select All. In the Action section, select the Drop radio button and then click OK. You will see that you have created an ICMP rule. You must now click the Apply button to make this rule take effect.

9. System 2: When System 1 has finished, ping System 1. You will not receive any replies.

10. System 1: Now, create a rule that blocks all traffic from your neighbor's host to TCP port 80. In the Add Item drop-down box, select the TCP protocol. Under Source, select Host from the Type drop-down box and enter your System 2's IP address. Under Destination, make sure Any Address is selected, and in the Port drop-down box, select the Equal to (=) option and enter **80** as the port number.

11. In the Action section, select the Drop radio button. Click OK and then click Apply.

    Note: The difference between specifying the Deny radio button and specifying the Drop radio button is that Deny causes your host to reply with a UDP packet informing the host that the request was dropped, whereas Drop sends back no message at all.

12. System 2: Use your web browser to test System 1's HTTP packet-filtering rule.

13. System 1: Create filtering rules for FTP as well, and then have System 2 test these rules.

Using *ipchains* and *iptables*

The Linux operating system natively supports packet-filtering rules. Kernel versions 2.2 and earlier support the `ipchains` command. Beginning with the experimental 2.3 kernel and continuing with the 2.4 kernel, the `iptables` command is generally used. `ipchains` and `iptables` are mutually exclusive; you cannot use both on one system. Nevertheless, both of these commands are used to access the Linux kernel *Netfilter* feature, which is also supported as a series of modules. Using Netfilter, you can create a personal firewall for a Linux workstation, or you can create an actual firewall used to create a network perimeter.

> **NOTE** All operating systems have a core set of functions, which is called a *kernel*. In many systems, this core can be upgraded to obtain the latest features and the functionality you need. Some operating systems, such as Linux, allow administrators to compile new kernels. For example, some kernels don't include the Netfilter function. In such cases, you will have to recompile the kernel. In still other cases, you may have to load modules to augment the kernel. Such modules exist for both ipchains and iptables.

The ipchains and iptables commands have similar syntax, but Netfilter contains several features that require additions. Using either of these commands, you can create packet-filtering rules that accept, drop, or masquerade traffic.

These commands allow you to control packets by manipulating *chains*, which are specially defined areas of the packet filter designed to hold different rules. Let's take a look at the elements manipulated in both commands.

Creating Rules

Regardless of whether you are using ipchains or iptables, you must first specify the protocol you wish to block. Because ipchains and iptables are packet-filtering applications, the protocols you specify are limited to ICMP, TCP, and UDP. You can specify individual ports, as well as port ranges. Next, you need to specify a target. ipchains and iptables use similar target names, such as ACCEPT and DENY. Still, each application does use slightly different terminology.

> **NOTE** Usually, ipchains and iptables are not set by default. However, recent versions of Red Hat Linux (versions 7.1 and higher), for example, allow you to choose various "firewall" levels during system installation.

Now let's discuss how you can use both ipchains and iptables to control packets on your host. Study the differences and similarities carefully; you will likely encounter systems that use one or the other.

ipchains

The `ipchains` application uses three built-in chains, often called *special chains*. They are as follows:

input Used to control packets entering the interface.

output Used to control packets leaving the interface.

forward Used to control packets being masqueraded, or sent to remote hosts.

You must specify a target using the -j option. Allowed target built-in values are ACCEPT, DENY, REJECT, MASQUERADE, REDIRECT, and RETURN. The MASQUERADE target allows you to establish NAT on a firewall. Case is important for both the chains and the targets. In `ipchains`, all chains are in lowercase letters, and all targets are in uppercase. It is possible to create custom chains that can be used as targets. Usually, built-in chains are adequate.

Examples of *ipchains*

Suppose, for example, that you have a host with the IP address of 192.168.2.0/24 and that you want to create a simple personal firewall that blocks all incoming ICMP traffic sent from remote hosts to your own host. To do so, you issue the following command:

```
ipchains -A input -p icmp -s 0/0 -d 0/0 -j REJECT
```

This command tells the input chain to forbid any ICMP traffic from any host. If you want to block ICMP traffic from only, say, the 10.100.100.0/24 network, you flush the above rule and replace it with one that specifies only that subnet. The commands to do so are as follows:

```
ipchains -F
ipchains -A input -p icmp -s 10.100.100.0/24 -d 0/0
↳ -j REJECT
```

The host can no longer receive packets, but it can still send them. This is because you have only blocked the input chain. To prohibit this host from sending packets to the 10.100.100.0/24 network, you use the following command to add an entry to the output chain:

```
ipchains -A output -p icmp -s 192.168.2.0/24 -d
↳ 10.100.100.0/24 -j REJECT
```

Now, this host can no longer receive or send ICMP traffic. You are not, of course, limited to controlling just ICMP traffic. If you want to block incoming POP3 traffic from all hosts, you issue the following command:

```
ipchains -A input -p tcp -s 0/0 -d 0/0 110 -j REJECT
```

If you want to deny all traffic by default and then specifically allow only, say, POP3 traffic, you could use the -P option, which sets a policy for the chain you specify. You could then begin to allow the POP3 traffic, as well the DNS service and the ephemeral ports necessary for your system to connect to a POP3 server:

```
ipchains -P output DENY
ipchains -P forward DENY
ipchains -P input DENY
ipchains -A input -p tcp -s 0/0 -d 0/0 110 -j ACCEPT
ipchains -A input -p tcp -s 0/0 -d 0/0 1024: -j ACCEPT
ipchains -A input -p udp -s 0/0 -d 0/0 1024: -j ACCEPT
ipchains -A output -p tcp -s 0/0 -d 0/0 1024:
    ↳ -j ACCEPT
ipchains -A output -p udp -s 0/0 -d 0/0 1024:
    ↳ -j ACCEPT
ipchains -A output -p udp -s 0/0 -d 0/0 53 -j ACCEPT
```

Notice that the last rule allows the system to generate a packet to any host on port 53. This rule allows the use of any DNS server. You could be more specific, if you knew the IP address of your DNS server.

You don't have to create a full masquerading firewall to understand how `ipchains` and `iptables` work. These examples should be enough to get you started creating firewalls. Still, another short example may be helpful. Suppose that you have an internal NIC (named `eth0`), with the IP address of 192.168.2.1/24, and an external NIC (named `eth1`), with the IP address of 45.9.2.23/24. The following entry would enable all systems that are using the internal NIC as a default gateway to use the Internet:

```
ipchains -A forward -i eth0 -s 192.168.2.0/24
    ↳ -d 0/0 -j MASQ
```

The above entry adds an entry to the forward chain, which is designed to allow masquerading. The -i option specifies the `eth0` interface, which is the internal interface. The -j ACCEPT target means that this interface will accept masquerading for the 192.168.2.0/24 network. You can then begin to deny or accept traffic as you see fit.

218 Chapter 5 · Firewalls Roles and Types

> Linux names the first NIC in a system eth0. The second NIC is eth1, the third eth2, and so forth.

Before you can masquerade a connection, you must enable IP forwarding and IP defragmentation on the system, whether you are using `ipchains` or `iptables`. On a Linux system, you do this by issuing the following commands:

```
echo "1" > /proc/sys/net/ipv4/ip_forward
echo "1" > /proc/sys/net/ipv4/always_defrag
```

You can do this manually, or you can enter the commands at the bottom of the `/etc/rc.d/rc.local` file if you want these settings to be made automatically. To learn more about how to use `ipchains` to create a full-blown firewall, consult the IPCHAINS-HOWTO at **www.linuxdoc.org**.

Using *iptables*

The `iptables` command is used to manipulate Netfilter. The CIW Security Professional exam does not delve into all of Netfilter's functionality. However, you will be required to understand some of the basic syntax, much like that in `iptables`. Some significant differences exist between `ipchains` and `iptables`. First, in `iptables`, all built-in chains are in uppercase letters. Second, `iptables` has several different tables, each of which contains various chains. `ipchains` has only one table—`filter`. `iptables` keeps the `filter` table, then adds two more (which explains why the command name is now `iptables` instead of `ipchains`):

filter Contains the INPUT, OUTPUT, and FORWARD chains. This is the default table, and it will report its contents when you list chains using the `iptables -L` command.

nat Used for creating NAT tables. Contains the PREROUTING, OUTPUT, and POSTROUTING tables. The PREROUTING table alters packets as soon as they enter (used when masquerading connections), the OUTPUT table alters locally generated packets, and POSTROUTING alters packets before they are about to be sent on the network. If you are using a Linux kernel that supports modules, you must have the `iptables_nat` module installed to use this table.

mangle Alters the packets. Generally, you do not use this for establishing NAT. This table has two chains: PREROUTING (which alters packets that have entered the system) and OUTPUT (which is used for altering packets that have been generated by the local operating system). If you are using a Linux kernel that supports modules, you must have the iptable_mangle module installed to use this table.

> **NOTE** You can read the filter, nat, and mangle entries by using the iptables -t command. Do not uppercase these entries. For example, to list the nat table, you would use the following command: iptables -t nat -L. The -L option allows you to list various tables and chains.

Allowed target values in iptables are DROP, ACCEPT, QUEUE, and RETURN. iptables also allows the creation of user-defined chains.

Examples of *iptables*

Because iptables has three tables to read instead of one, you need to know how to list and manipulate them. The filter table is listed by default. You use these two commands to list the nat and mangle tables:

```
iptables -t nat -L
iptables -t mangle -L
```

When creating a personal firewall, however, you do not have to use the nat or mangle tables. To create a simple personal firewall that blocks all incoming ICMP traffic, you issue the following command:

```
iptables -A INPUT -p icmp -s 0/0 -d 0/0 -j DROP
```

To block ICMP traffic from only the 10.100.100.0/24 network, you issue this command:

```
iptables -A INPUT -p icmp -s 10.100.100.0/24
↳ -d 0/0 -j DROP
```

To deny all but POP3 traffic, you issue the following commands, after flushing any existing rules:

```
iptables -P INPUT DROP
iptables -P FORWARD DROP
iptables -P OUTPUT DROP
iptables -A INPUT -p tcp -s 0/0 -d 0/0
↳ --dport 1024: -j ACCEPT
```

```
iptables -A INPUT -p udp -s 0/0 -d 0/0
↳ --dport 1024: -j ACCEPT
iptables -A OUTPUT -p udp -s 0/0 -d 0/0
↳ --dport 53 -j ACCEPT
iptables -A OUTPUT -p tcp -s 0/0 -d 0/0
↳ --dport 110 -j ACCEPT
```

The first three entries automatically configure the personal firewall to drop any and all connections. Lines 4 through 6 then allow any server on the Internet to connect to your workstation's ephemeral ports (i.e., ports 1024 and higher). If you know the IP addresses of your DNS and e-mail servers, you could restrict all of the entries to a specific IP address, rather than the entire Internet. If, for example, the IP address of the DNS server was 10.100.100.100/8 and the e-mail server were at the address of 203.54.23.3/24, you would enter the following:

```
iptables -A INPUT -p tcp -s 10.100.100.100/8 -d 0/0
↳ --dport 1024: -j ACCEPT
iptables -A INPUT -p udp -s 10.100.100.100/8 -d 0/0
↳ --dport 1024: -j ACCEPT
iptables -A OUTPUT -p udp -s 0/0 -d 203.54.23.3/24
↳ --dport 53 -j ACCEPT
iptables -A OUTPUT -p tcp -s 0/0 -d 203.54.23.3/24
↳ --dport 110 -j ACCEPT
```

WARNING Make sure that you flush any existing rules. An old rule that you may have forgotten about could be causing you a problem.

If you want to masquerade a connection using `iptables`, you would use the `nat` table. Using the same scenario as the `ipchains` command, you would masquerade your internal network so that it could connect to the Internet as follows:

```
iptables -t nat -A POSTROUTING -o eth1 -j MASQUERADE
```

For more information on using `iptables`, read the IPTABLES-HOWTO at http://netfilter.samba.org/unreliable-guides/packet-
↳ filtering-HOWTO/packet-filtering-HOWTO.linuxdoc.html
and other locations on the Internet. If you want to learn more about masquerading using a Linux system, consult the following URL:

www.linuxdoc.org/HOWTO/IP-Masquerade-HOWTO.html

> **Obtaining More Information About Linux**
>
> The CIW Security Professional exam requires knowledge of Linux. You can read the Linux Network Administrators Guide at the following URL:
>
> www.linuxdoc.org/LDP/nag2/index.html
>
> Internet search sites such as www.altavista.com and www.google.com are also very helpful when researching information about open-source products such as Linux.

Logging with *iptables* and *ipchains*

Both the `filter` and `mangle` tables contain additional chains. The `iptables` command also allows additional logging options. For example, the `ipchains -l` option causes a rule to log any match and send a message to the /var/log/messages file. The `iptables` command, however, requires that you use the `-j` option and specify the target LOG for any rule. You can learn more about `ipchains` and `iptables` by consulting their respective man pages.

> **Switching a Linux System between *ipchains* and *iptables***
>
> Because most Linux systems use modules to extend the functionality of the kernel, use the `lsmod` command to verify what modules are installed. Look for entries such as `ipchains`, `ip_tables`, or `iptable_filter`. If you have kernel 2.4 and later but the `ipchains` module is installed, issue the following command:
>
> ```
> modprobe -r ipchains
> ```
>
> This command removes all `ipchains` modules. You can then load all of the `iptables` modules, if they are present:
>
> ```
> modprobe ip_tables
> ```
>
> In many systems, simply issuing the `ipchains` or `iptables` command will automatically load the necessary modules. If the `iptables` modules are not present, then install them from www.rpmfind.net. If these modules will not install, you need to recompile your kernel to use Netfilter. Most systems, however, ship with kernels that support Netfilter.

> To remove `iptables`, you can issue the following commands:
>
> `modprobe -r iptables`
>
> `modprobe -r iptable_filter`
>
> You can then use the `modprobe ipchains` command to reinstall `ipchains`, if you wish. It is wise to use `lsmod` often to determine what else you need to install or uninstall. Remember that some systems use monolithic kernels, which means that they will not allow the use of modules. In such cases, you will have to recompile the kernel to include Netfilter, or to allow modules.

> **NOTE**
>
> You do not have to configure `ipchains` and `iptables` manually. Linux applications such as `firewall-config` and Mason are available. For more information, consult your installation disks or sites such as SourceForge (www.sourceforge.net) and FreshMeat (www.freshmeat.net).

EXERCISE 5.2

Using the *ipchains* Command to Create a Personal Firewall in Linux (for Kernels 2.2 and Lower, or for Systems Running the *ipchains* Module)

In this exercise, you will use the `ipchains` command to create packet-filtering rules for your system. This exercise implies the use of two systems, which are helpful for testing purposes.

Note: If you have a kernel of 2.2 or earlier, `ipchains` is generally used. Use the `uname -a` command to verify your kernel version before continuing with this exercise. Also, use the `/sbin/lsmod` command to determine which module is currently installed.

1. Boot into Linux and log on as root. Verify that each of your systems can connect with each other.

2. System 1: Verify that the `ipchains` module and command are installed:

```
host# rpm -qa | grep ipch
ipchains-1.3.9-1
```

EXERCISE 5.2 (continued)

If the `ipchains` RPM is not installed, obtain it from www.rpmfind.net.

3. System 1: To block ICMP to all hosts, issue the following command:

   `ipchains -I input -i eth0 -p icmp -s 0/0 -d 0/0`
   ↳ `-l -j REJECT`

   This command causes `ipchains` to add a rule to the input chain that rejects all ICMP packets from all sources (-s 0/0) to all destinations (-d 0/0). The -i option specifies an interface (e.g., eth0, eth1, eth2, and so forth). The -l option sends a log entry to the /var/log/messages file for every ICMP packet received.

4. System 2: Ping your system. You will not receive any echo reply messages, and you will see error messages. Do not press Ctrl+C to stop pinging the host; just let the error messages continue on your screen.

5. System 1: List all your chains:

   `host# ipchains --line-numbers -nL`

   You will see that the input chain contains the ICMP rule you created, complete with a line number. The -n option disables DNS lookups, which is helpful in case no DNS resolution is available. Otherwise, the listing will "hang" indefinitely waiting for resolution to occur. This option is helpful when you have a long list of rules.

6. System 1: When System 2 is ready, issue the following command to flush all rules from the input chain:

   `host# ipchains -F`

7. System 2: Notice that when you flush the rules for this system, it is possible to ping it. Ping the system to verify that you have flushed your `ipchains` rules.

8. System 1: Verify that your web server is running, and verify that it is serving web pages. To block all traffic to your web server, issue the following command:

   `ipchains -I input -i eth0 -p tcp -s 0/0 -d 0/0 80`
   ↳ `-l -j REJECT`

EXERCISE 5.2 (continued)

9. System 2: Use a web browser, such as Lynx, to access your web server.

10. System 1: Add the following rule for FTP traffic:

    ```
    ipchains -I input -i eth0 -p tcp -s 0/0 -d 0/0 21
    ↳ -l -j REJECT
    ```

11. System 1: Issue the following command to view your kernel output file:

    ```
    host# tail -f /var/log/messages
    ```

12. System 2: Use an FTP client to test this rule.

13. System 1: You will see information concerning each packet that is received. Test whether your system can log ICMP and TCP packets sent to port 80.

14. System 1: List the rules that you have established. Now, delete the FTP rule. If, for example, the FTP rule is the third rule, you would issue the following command:

    ```
    host# ipchains -D input 3
    ```

15. System 1: Before you flush all these rules, use the following command to save your existing rules to a text file:

    ```
    host# ipchains-save > iptablesrules.txt
    ```

16. Both systems: When you have finished, use `ipchains -F` to erase all chains. Failure to perform this step will cause problems in the future.

EXERCISE 5.3

Using the *iptables* Command to Create a Personal Firewall in Linux (for Kernels 2.3 and Higher)

In this exercise, you will use the `iptables` command to create packet-filtering rules for your system. Although you do not have two NICs, you can create a personal firewall for your system.

EXERCISE 5.3 (continued)

Note: Systems using kernels 2.3 or later often use `iptables`. Use the `uname -a` command to verify your kernel version before continuing with this exercise. Also, use the `/sbin/lsmod` command to determine which module is currently installed.

1. Boot into Linux and log on as root. Verify that this system can connect with others on the network.

2. Verify that the `iptables` module and command are installed:

   ```
   host# rpm -qa | grep iptab
   ipchains-1.2.1a-1
   ```

   If the iptables RPM is not installed, obtain it from www.rpmfind.net. Make sure that you are using kernel 2.3 or higher.

3. To block ICMP to all hosts, issue the following command:

   ```
   iptables -I INPUT -i eth0 -p icmp -s 0/0 -d 0/0
   ↳ -j DROP
   ```

   Note: This command causes `iptables` to add a rule to the INPUT chain that rejects all ICMP packets from all sources (`-s 0/0`) to all destinations (`-d 0/0`). In `iptables`, the `-i` option specifies the input device. Notice that you must specify the INPUT chain, not the `input` chain; case is important.

4. Now, log this rejection:

   ```
   host# iptables -I INPUT -i eth0 -p icmp -s 0/0
   ↳ -d 0/0 -j LOG
   ```

5. Go to a separate system and ping the first system. You will not receive any echo reply messages, and you will see error messages. Do not press Ctrl+C to stop pinging the host; just let the error messages continue on your screen.

6. List all your chains on both systems:

   ```
   host# iptables --line-numbers -nL
   ```

   You will see that the INPUT chain contains the ICMP rule you created, complete with a line number. This option is helpful when you have a long list of rules.

EXERCISE 5.3 (continued)

7. On the separate system, issue the following command to flush all rules from the INPUT chain:

    ```
    host# iptables -F
    ```

8. After flushing the chains on the second system, you will be able to ping your host again. Do this, now, to verify that you have flushed all `iptables` tables and chains.

9. Verify that your web server is running on the first system, and verify that it is serving web pages using your second system. Then, on the second server, block and log all traffic to your web server using the following commands:

    ```
    iptables -I INPUT -i eth0 -p tcp -s 0/0 -d 0/0
    ↳ --dport 80 -j DROP
    iptables -I INPUT -i eth0 -p tcp -s 0/0 -d 0/0
    ↳ --dport 80 -j LOG
    ```

10. Use a web browser, such as Lynx, to access the second web server.

11. On any system, add the following rule for FTP traffic:

    ```
    iptables -I INPUT -i eth0 -p tcp -s 0/0 -d 0/0
    ↳ --dport 21 -j DROP
    iptables -I INPUT -i eth0 -p tcp -s 0/0 -d 0/0
    ↳ --dport 21 -j LOG
    ```

12. After adding the above rule, issue the following command to view your kernel output file:

    ```
    host# tail -f /var/log/messages
    ```

13. Now, use an FTP client to test this rule.

14. You will see information concerning each packet that is received. Work with the remote system to test whether your system can log ICMP and TCP packets sent to port 80.

15. List all of the rules that you have established. Now, delete the FTP rule. If, for example, the FTP rule is the third rule, you would issue the following command:

    ```
    host# iptables -D INPUT 3
    ```

> **EXERCISE 5.3 *(continued)***
>
> 16. Before you flush all these rules, use the following command to save your existing rules to a text file:
>
>   `host# iptables-save > iptablesrules.txt`
>
> 17. When you have finished, use `iptables -F` to erase all chains in each system. Failure to perform this step will cause problems in the future.

Configuring Proxy Servers

When any type of proxy acts for and in behalf of a client host, it uses its own IP address in place of the original that belongs to the client host. In this sense, the host's effective IP address is contingent on the proxy server itself. This process effectively hides the actual IP address from the rest of the Internet, because all clients must access the Internet through a specific port, as shown in Figure 5.2.

FIGURE 5.2 Proxy server configuration

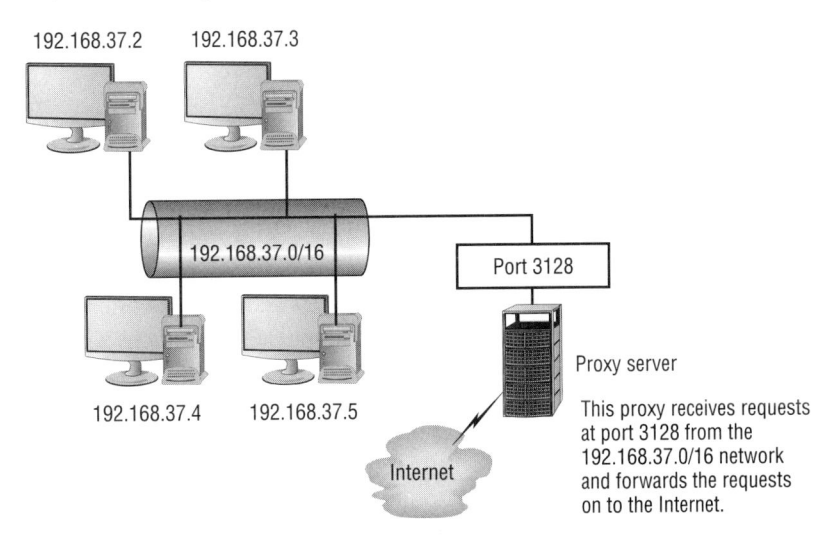

Figure 5.2 shows that the network is protected by a proxy server, which requires all clients to connect at a specific port, in this case 3128 (the standard port for the WinRoute and Squid proxy servers).

> **Proxy-Oriented Firewall Products**
>
> Proxy-oriented firewall products include:
>
> - Symantec Raptor Firewall (www.symantec.com).
> - Microsoft ISA Server (www.microsoft.com).
> - Squid Proxy Server (www.squid-cache.org).
>
> Symantec Raptor Firewall is a highly respected proxy-oriented firewall. Microsoft ISA Server is also commonly used. Most professionals agree that large enterprises require a product more robust than Microsoft Proxy Server. Many organizations use a product such as Raptor for the bastion host, but then use Proxy Server to handle web traffic. When they are used in tandem, proxy servers can divide traffic, thereby providing some load balancing and fault tolerance. Squid Proxy Server has become a popular open-source proxy server for Linux systems. It supports many protocols, and is reliable and highly configurable.

Proxy Server Advantages and Features

The main advantage of a proxy server is its ability to provide NAT. Shielding your internal network from the public is paramount. Here are some additional benefits:

Authentication   Most proxy servers can be configured to first require a client to authenticate before being allowed access to Internet services (HTTP, FTP, e-mail, and so forth). Once a user authenticates and receives an access token, the proxy server can then determine exactly which resources that user can use.

Logging and alarming   The logging and alarming features provided are often much more robust than those in packet filters and circuit-level gateways. Proxy servers analyze much more information than the other two types of firewalls, so they can log nearly every portion of a TCP/IP session, from the network frame up to the Application layer.

> **NOTE** In regard to logging, using a SCSI-based system is advisable. Proxy-oriented servers can generate vast amounts of log entries, and the logging process can tie up a system. If a system's I/O is slow, and if the disks themselves are not capable of keeping up with logging, the performance of the firewall will be adversely affected.

Caching Because proxy servers need to analyze a TCP/IP packet at every layer of TCP/IP, the proxy server will often cache this information to disk. Any subsequent request for the same data will then be accessed from the proxy server's hard disk instead of the remote server. Retrieving the data from disk is much faster than retrieving it from the remote server. Many rules can be applied to the proxy server to configure how often it will check the remote sites for updated content.

Fewer rules A proxy-oriented firewall generally requires fewer rules than a packet filter. In addition, creating the rules generally takes less time. Remember, a general rule concerning firewalls is to keep the design as simple as possible. Because proxy servers require fewer rules, they can be less complex to administer.

Reverse Proxies and Proxy Arrays (Cascading Proxies)

Another advantage of using application gateways is their ability to provide reverse proxy services. These services work similarly to standard ones, except that they proxy inbound requests. *Reverse proxy servers* are located at the edge of a firewall configuration and have an IP address on the external NIC that can be accessed from the Internet. The reverse proxy server then maps this external IP address to one or more internal IP addresses. When public users access the external IP address, the users may think that they are accessing the web server, but in fact they are accessing the reverse proxy server. The reverse proxy server will then forward the client request to the web server. When public users access the web server, they are actually connecting to the proxy server. This setup prevents public users from contacting the web server directly. If a hacker tries to break into the web server, he or she will only be breaking into the proxy server. The proxy server does not contain the actual data on the web server, so breaking into the proxy server does not yield any usable information.

A *proxy array* is several proxy servers configured as one. Proxy arrays, also known as *proxy clusters* or *cascading proxies*, are useful for load balancing. When several reverse proxy servers are used together, the total amount that the servers can cache is increased. The group also provides fault tolerance in case one of the proxies fails. Certain proxy arrays can also act as a single unit. For example, depending on how the proxy servers in the array are configured, changing a setting of one will change the settings on all. Proxy arrays are often used in a reverse proxy environment as well. When proxy arrays are used with a reverse proxy solution, public users can access several web servers simultaneously.

Proxy Server Drawbacks

Clients that use a proxy server for remote TCP/IP connectivity must be configured to use a proxy and have all the correct parameters specified. If the internal users use different client applications for each Internet application (for example, browsers, mail clients, news clients, FTP clients, and chat programs), each application must be configured to use the proxy server for remote access. Often the Internet applications will not interface correctly (or at all) with a proxy server. As a result, your company may have difficulty accessing a vital Internet service. Most Internet-based applications are aware of proxy server issues. However, if a company has to create custom applications, the presence of a proxy server will have to be taken into account.

Speed and Hardware Considerations

Remember that proxy-oriented firewalls delve deeply into the IP packet. They do not stop at the Network layer of the OSI/RM. They are capable of reading strings of text at the Application layer, and they are also capable of authenticating users. Because proxy servers provide more features, they generally require additional system resources. Thus, running a proxy server on your network may require more expensive hardware.

Also, at extremely busy sites, a proxy-based firewall can become a liability, because it can cause unacceptable latency. The general rule when recommending proxy-oriented firewalls is that they will suit T3 speeds. Any company that requires a faster connection speed needs a packet-filtering product, such as Check Point's FireWall-1.

Summary

In this chapter, we discussed the basics of configuring packet filters and proxy servers. You learned how a firewall establishes perimeter security by differentiating between a public network, such as the Internet, and a private network, such as your corporate intranet. A firewall is of critical importance to your overall security policy, mainly because it is where you can enforce authentication on all users and monitor all inbound and outbound traffic. A properly placed firewall can increase security and still enable a business to function well.

We examined packet-filtering firewalls, which are the most common type of firewall used on the Internet today. This type of firewall, which includes

Linux Netfilter (iptables and ipchains), operates at the Network layer of the OSI/RM. You learned about proxy servers, including application-layer and circuit-level gateways. We also described the relative strengths and weaknesses of the various firewall types.

Now that you understand how to create packet-filter and proxy-oriented firewall rules, it is time to learn more about the hardware configurations referred to in the CIW Security Professional exam. In the next chapter, we will discuss actual firewall topologies. You will learn more about the DMZ, bastion hosts, and common firewall designs. Once you understand the various topologies involved, you will be able to implement a secure perimeter for your network.

Exam Essentials

Know what a firewall does. A firewall implements perimeter security and enables you to enact the policies in your security policy. It also provides access control and, in the case of proxy servers, authentication services. A firewall acts as a choke point between the internal network and the external network.

Understand that a firewall is bidirectional. Do not forget that whenever you want to allow an internal client to access an external service, you will have to consider how the client on the internal network communicates with the server on the external network. Remember, for example, that if a firewall blocks all traffic and you want to allow a client to access a POP3 server, you will have to allow internal systems to open ports above 1023 to access an external destination at destination port 110. You will also have to allow the POP3 server to access your clients.

Understand default firewall stances. A firewall can have only one stance. Two defaults are available. A firewall can either deny all traffic at first, then allow exceptions, or it can allow all traffic at first, then lock down certain ports that are not wanted. IT administrators too often concentrate on what a firewall limits, rather than what it allows. In other words, consider what happens when a firewall is too restrictive. While you do want to create an effective perimeter that blocks traffic, you also need to ensure that the firewall allows an organization or business to function properly.

Understand firewall terms. Make sure that you are familiar with terms such as DMZ, screening router, choke router, rules, and operating system hardening. Also, it is important to understand the differences between a packet filter and a proxy-oriented firewall. For example, a packet filter operates at the Network layer of the OSI/RM, whereas a proxy server can operate at the Application or Transport layer.

Be able to identify when to choose a packet-filtering firewall and a proxy-filtering firewall. Packet-filtering firewalls are very popular in high-traffic situations. Proxy servers are typically placed in low-traffic areas where user authentication is an issue. Because proxy servers are capable of authenticating users, they are sometimes believed to offer more security. However, they often are not able to handle as much traffic as packet filters.

Be able to create firewall rules. Be able to show how a rule can allow or deny certain types of traffic. You should know the commonly used ports, such as POP3 (110), SMTP (25), HTTP (80), and SSL-enabled HTTP (443). It is also important that you understand how a firewall is bidirectional. You should, for example, remember that you must allow clients to use their ephemeral ports to access remote systems.

Know the drawbacks of different firewall types. No firewall type is "better" than another. A proxy-oriented firewall is ideal in low- to medium-traffic situations, where user authentication is important, or where you want to limit traffic to just a few Application-layer protocols. A packet-filtering firewall is ideal in higher traffic situations. Although a proxy-oriented firewall requires fewer rules, it is not best suited for high-volume traffic. Packet-filtering firewalls are often challenging to configure, because they assume extensive knowledge of TCP/IP.

Key Terms

Before you take the exam, be certain you are familiar with the following terms:

address hiding	chains
application-layer proxy	choke point
bastion	choke router
cascading proxies	circuit-level proxy

Key Terms

Classless Internet Domain Routing (CIDR)

demilitarized zone (DMZ)

destination IP address

destination port

firewall

host

ipchains

iptables

masquerading

Netfilter

network address translation (NAT)

network appliance

network client

network map

network perimeter

packet filter

packet type

private NIC

proxy

proxy array

proxy clusters

proxy server

public network

public NIC

reverse proxy servers

rules

screening router

SOCKS

source IP address

source port

special chains

stateful multilayer inspection

topology

trusted

trusting

Type of Service (ToS)

Review Questions

1. What is another common name for a system placed directly between a trusted network and an untrusted one?

    A. An FTP server

    B. A choke point

    C. A bastion host

    D. A gateway

2. What is the name for a device that processes network traffic solely by IP address and source/destination port?

    A. A proxy server

    B. A packet filter

    C. A bastion host

    D. A choke point

3. A firewall is the primary tool for establishing which of the following?

    A. Internal security

    B. Internet security

    C. Perimeter security

    D. Effective security

4. Samuel has configured a Windows 2000 workstation on a network that uses proxy servers. He has installed TCP/IP, and the network DHCP server has given this system a valid IP address. Samuel can ping the default gateway, and he can ping hosts outside his network. He can also read his e-mail, and the e-mail server is on a remote site across the Internet. However, when Samuel opens his web browser, he cannot access the World Wide Web. What can he do to solve this problem?

A. Configure the web browser to access the packet filter.

B. Reconfigure the workstation to use the correct default gateway.

C. Contact the systems administrator and ask for a new entry to be placed in the firewall.

D. Configure the web browser to access the proxy server.

5. What security does network address translation (NAT) provide?

   A. It acts as a proxy server between two networks.

   B. It deploys gateway services.

   C. It hides internal IP addresses from the external network.

   D. It creates a check point, or "funnel," for network traffic.

6. Jacob has created a small subnet that contains a router at one end and a proxy-oriented firewall at the other. Inside this subnet are several hosts, including the company web, e-mail, and DNS servers. On the other side of the router is a public network. On the other side of the proxy-oriented firewall is the private network. What is a common name for the subnet Jacob is creating?

   A. A bastion

   B. A DMZ

   C. A firewall

   D. A circuit-level proxy

7. Serena has created a bastion host with three NICs. The first NIC (eth0) faces the internal network. The second NIC (eth1) is attached to the network DMZ. The third NIC (eth2) is attached directly to the Internet via a switch and a T1 line. Which of the following interfaces should have NAT enabled?

   A. The first NIC

   B. The second NIC

   C. The third NIC

   D. All NICs

8. Davis needs a firewall that allows him to authenticate users. Which type of firewall should he research and obtain?

   A. A packet-filtering firewall

   B. A bastion host firewall

   C. An `iptables` firewall

   D. A proxy-oriented firewall

9. What type of firewall is a SOCKS server?

   A. A proxy-oriented firewall

   B. A packet-filtering firewall

   C. A circuit-level gateway

   D. A Linux firewall

10. Julie is using the IP address block 192.168.0.0/24. Which of the following would allow her clients to access web servers on the Internet?

    A. A bastion host

    B. A proxy server

    C. A choke router

    D. A screening router

11. You want to block all web access to the Internet. Which source and destination ports could you block so that internal hosts cannot access web servers on the Internet?

    A. Connections to outside hosts that have a destination port lower than 1024

    B. Connections to outside hosts that have the source port of 80

    C. Connections to inside hosts that have a destination port higher than 1023

    D. Connections to outside hosts that have the destination port of 80

12. Which of the following is a registered port number?

    A. 443

    B. 110

    C. 80

    D. 4001

13. Which of the following applications would you likely use to create a packet-filter rule, or chain, in a Linux system with a 2.4.2 kernel?

    A. Squid

    B. iptables

    C. ipchains

    D. Netfilter

14. You have a Windows 2000 system that you want to use as a bastion host firewall. Which of the following applications could you use?

    A. ISA Server

    B. ipchains

    C. iptables

    D. Squid

15. You are using iptables to create a packet filter on a Linux system. Which of the following is a legitimate special value target in iptables?

    A. drop

    B. DROP

    C. DENY

    D. deny

16. Which of the following does NAT accomplish?

    A. It hides a network's topology.

    B. It defeats all hacking attempts.

    C. It allows you to use a router.

    D. It allows you to use a firewall.

17. Which of the following generally requires fewer rules when creating a network perimeter?

    A. A proxy-oriented firewall

    B. A packet-filtering firewall

    C. A router

    D. A switch

18. A user on the Internet thinks that he has connected to a web server, but in fact has connected to a dedicated system on the Internet that forwards his web connection to a host inside the Internet. What type of firewall has he used?

    A. A forwarding server

    B. A reverse proxy

    C. A packet filter

    D. A proxy server

19. What is the path that an SMTP packet takes when it reaches a firewall that drops all packets by default, yet is configured to allow packets originating from port 110?

    A. The packet is dropped.

    B. The packet is accepted.

    C. The firewall forwards the packet.

    D. The firewall logs the packet.

20. Which of the following terms describes the removal of unnecessary services on your bastion host?

    A. Perimeter creation

    B. Network address translation

    C. Operating system hardening

    D. Bastioning

Answers to Review Questions

1. **C.** A bastion host is usually your first line of protection against outside attack. It can be a packet-filtering router, or it can be a proxy server.

2. **B.** A packet filter operates at the network layer of the OSI/RM, and does not read traffic such as HTTP, FTP, or POP3.

3. **C.** A network perimeter exists at the outer edge of the network. A firewall is the chief way of defining the difference between the inner and outer network. By using a firewall, you are essentially creating a network perimeter.

4. **D.** Nothing is wrong with the workstation. It can access all relevant services, including other systems in the WAN, as well as the e-mail server. In this scenario, the most likely answer is that the web browser needs to be configured to use the network's proxy server.

5. **C.** NAT is not necessarily a security concept, but it is one that is often associated with firewalls. The chief benefit of NAT is that it hides internal hosts. It also allows you to use private IP addresses for your network's internal systems, which can save your company considerable money.

6. **B.** A DMZ (demilitarized zone) is usually defined as a subnet that contains hosts. This subnet is usually partially isolated from the Internet by a screening router.

7. **C.** Network address translation (NAT) is often accomplished by the network firewall. It must always be enabled on the public NIC. Otherwise, outside systems would be able to easily enter your network, thus defeating the reason for having a firewall.

8. **D.** A proxy-oriented firewall is capable of authenticating users. True packet-filtering firewalls do not have this feature; thus, `iptables` is not an option in this case.

9. **C.** A SOCKS server is the most popular example of a circuit-level gateway. A SOCKS server is often used to provide NAT.

10. **B.** A proxy server can allow a workstation to access the Internet, even if the workstation is using private IP addresses. The 192.168.0.0/24 block of IP addresses is part of the private IP address block, and

packets with these source or destination addresses will automatically be dropped by all Internet routers. However, if Julie configures a proxy server, end users can configure their applications to access the proxy server and access the web.

11. D. When you create a packet filter, you need to consider the source IP address(es) and ports, as well as the destination IP address(es) and ports. When a host on your internal network connects with a remote web server, for example, it must open an ephemeral port (i.e., a port above 1023). This source port then connects to the remote web server at port 80, the default TCP port for web servers. Answer D describes one of the required packet-filtering rules. You would also need a rule that allows internal connections with the source port greater than 1023 to allow hosts to originate the connection.

12. D. Registered port numbers are those that include ports 1024 through 49151. The CIW Security Professional exam will lump together the registered and dynamic/private IP ports and call them "ephemeral ports."

13. B. Although it is possible for a Linux system running the Linux 2.4.2 kernel to use either `ipchains` or `iptables`, most Linux systems using anything higher than the 2.3 kernel will use `iptables`. You can use `ipchains` on systems using a kernel lower than 2.2. Netfilter is the general technology that allows Linux systems to engage in packet filtering. The Squid application does not enforce packet filtering.

14. A. Microsoft ISA Server allows you to create packet-filtering rules. Although it is possible to compile the Squid proxy server on a Windows 2000 system, it is not a packet-filtering firewall. `ipchains` and `iptables` are commands used on Unix/Linux systems.

15. B. `iptables` requires that all targets are in uppercase, and does not allow the target name of DENY, even if it is in uppercase. It is also possible to create custom chains that can be used as targets. Custom chains can be in upper or lower case. However, the question has asked for the name of a special, built-in value, not a user-defined chain.

16. A. NAT allows you to hide the topology of a network. Although a firewall does allow you to establish a network perimeter, it does not completely protect you from intrusion. For example, a firewall cannot protect you from internal attacks. Many different technologies allow you to use routers and firewalls; NAT is not required for you to use them.

17. A. A proxy-oriented firewall generally requires fewer rules to allow network access. Packet-filtering firewalls often require multiple rules. Although routers and switches can engage in packet filtering, they are not the proper choices here, because they generally do not enable proxy services.

18. B. Reverse proxy servers are designed to first field requests and then forward them to the web server. A forwarding server is a common name for a DNS server that forwards requests to other DNS servers. A packet filter works at only the Network layer and generally does not cache requests. A reverse proxy server is in fact a proxy server, but choosing "proxy server" in this case is incorrect, because it is a more general term.

19. A. An SMTP packet originates from port 25, so the packet will be dropped. Port 110 is the POP3 port. Because the firewall is configured to drop all packets by default, the packet will be dropped, because it does not match the rule accepting POP3 packets. The firewall will not forward the packet, due to its default stance. Although firewalls have the ability to log packets, not enough information is given as to whether the firewall is configured to log them.

20. C. Operating system hardening is the practice of "locking down" the system as much as possible. This usually involves removing all extraneous services so that the firewall becomes a less promising target. The more services (i.e., daemons) that the firewall opens, the greater the chance that one of the services may introduce a security problem.

Chapter 6

Firewall Topologies and Virtual Private Networks

THE CIW EXAM OBJECTIVE GROUPS COVERED IN THIS CHAPTER:

- ✓ Define encryption and the encryption methods used in internetworking.
- ✓ Identify firewall types and define common firewall topology.
- ✓ Plan a firewall system that incorporates multiple levels of protection, including but not limited to: firewall system design, proactive detection, setting traps, security breach response, security alerting organizations.

Your firewall strategy is the most critical aspect of your company's network security. Building a firewall device with the proper hardware and software configuration is the first step in developing such a strategy. To design and configure a firewall that best suits your company's needs, you need to be familiar with some basic concepts.

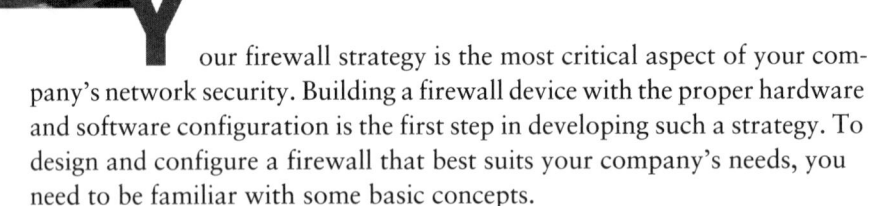

Take great care when preparing and building your firewall device. You should be especially careful when purchasing and constructing your bastion host, which can be an element in any one of the three types of firewalls: packet filter, circuit-level gateway, or application-level gateway. By definition, a bastion host is a publicly accessible device. When Internet users attempt to access resources on your network, the first machine they will encounter is the bastion host. This high level of exposure will dictate the hardware and software configurations.

You can think of the bastion host as a guard at a military base. The guard must check your credentials to determine if you may enter the base and what areas of the base you can access. Guards are often armed to prevent entry by force. Similarly, bastion hosts must check all incoming and outgoing traffic. They have to be prepared for attacks from external and possibly internal sources. Bastion hosts must be armed with logging and alarming features to prevent attacks. Some can even take action when a threat is detected.

Design Principles

When building a firewall device, you should keep the following in mind to ensure that your firewall does its job:

Keep the design simple. The most common way a hacker will penetrate a system is to take advantage of overlooked components installed on a host. Build your bastion host with the fewest possible components, both hardware and software. The bastion host should be configured to provide only firewall services. Do not install application services, such as web servers, and you should remove all unnecessary services or daemons. Having only a few running services on the bastion host gives a potential hacker fewer opportunities to overcome the firewall.

Make contingency plans. If your firewall design is set up properly, the only public access to your network will be through your firewalls. When designing firewalls, you must create a *contingency plan* to follow in case the firewall host crashes or is compromised. If you have only one firewall device separating the Internet and your internal network, and hackers penetrate your firewall, they will have full access to your internal network. To prevent this penetration, design several levels of firewall devices; do not rely on a single firewall device to protect your network. (Firewall designs will be covered in the section "Common Firewall Designs" later in this chapter.) Your security policy should state what to do in the event your security is compromised.

Specific steps to take include:

> **Make an identical copy of the software used in the installation.** Sign it to ensure it has not been altered or Trojanized.
>
> **Configure an identical system.** Keep this system in safe storage.
>
> **Ensure that all software necessary to install the firewall is handy.** This step includes making sure you have rescue disks.

Carefully consider resource placement. *Resource placement* has a tremendous effect on your ability to protect your assets. The most important aspect of firewall placement is creating choke points. The fewer physical points of access to your resources from the Internet, the easier it is to control them. Internet site security is in many ways easier than internal network security because it allows you to create fewer choke points.

> **WARNING** As you place resources, ensure that you properly check your modem banks. Hackers would much rather dial in to your network than try to defeat a firewall. In fact, a modem is the most popular means of defeating a firewall. Tools called *war dialers* enable hackers to scan large banks of telephone numbers to learn about the location of modem banks. Patrol your modem connections carefully. If at all possible, find ways to coordinate your modem bank with the firewall so that you do not create an attractive target.

Concentrate mechanisms and ease site administration requirements.
By funneling the incoming and outgoing information into the smallest number of points, you can concentrate your protection mechanisms. This focus will allow you to get the most security for the least amount of effort. Another benefit to using choke points is easier site administration, because you will know exactly where information enters and leaves your system. The most comprehensive and extensive monitoring tools should be configured on the choke points.

Placement is, in many ways, a resource issue, mainly because if you do not place your firewall system correctly, you will need more hardware to achieve the required level of protection, or you will never be able to truly protect your network.

Types of Bastion Hosts

When you're creating a bastion host, remember its function in your firewall strategy. Determining the bastion host's role will help you decide what is needed and how to configure the device. There are three common types of bastion hosts; they are not the only types that exist, but most firewalls fall into one of these three categories:

Single-homed bastion hosts A *singled-homed bastion host* is a firewall device with only one network interface. Single-homed bastion hosts are used for application-level gateway firewalls. The external router is configured to send all incoming data to the bastion host, and all internal clients are configured to send all outgoing data to the host. The bastion host will then test the data against the security guidelines and act accordingly. The main disadvantage of this type of firewall is that the router can be reconfigured to pass information directly to the internal network, completely bypassing the bastion host. Also, users can reconfigure their machines to bypass the bastion host and send their outgoing information directly to the router.

Multihomed bastion hosts *Multihomed bastion hosts* function identically to single-homed bastion hosts except that they have at least two network interfaces. Multihomed bastion hosts serve as application gateways, and as packet filters and circuit gateways as well. The advantage of using multihomed bastion hosts is that they create a complete break between the external network and the internal network. This break forces all incoming and outgoing traffic to pass through the bastion host. For a hacker to access internal devices, he or she must compromise the multihomed bastion host, giving you more time to react and prevent a security break-in.

Single-purpose bastion hosts A *single-purpose bastion host* can be either a single- or multihomed bastion host. Often, as an organization's needs change, new applications and technologies will be required. Many times the new technologies call for a dedicated host. Using a single-purpose bastion host allows you to enforce stricter security mechanisms.

For example, your company may decide to implement a new type of streaming application. Assuming that your security policy requires all inbound and outbound traffic to be sent through a proxy server, you should create a new proxy server solely for the new streaming application. On this new single-purpose bastion host acting as a proxy server, you would implement user authentication as well as restricted IP access. By using a separate proxy server, you do not jeopardize your current security configuration and you can implement strict security mechanisms such as authentication. Furthermore, because streaming video is bandwidth intensive, creating a separate proxy server will reduce the risk of performance degradation.

Internal bastion hosts *Internal bastion hosts* are standard single- or multihomed bastion hosts, but reside inside your company's internal network. Thus, they are not bastion hosts in the classic sense, because they are not directly placed between a trusted network and an untrusted one. They are normally used as application-level gateways that receive all incoming traffic from external bastion hosts. They provide an additional level of security in case the external firewall devices are compromised. All the internal network devices are configured to communicate only with the internal bastion host, and should not be affected by the compromised external bastion hosts.

Hardware Issues

The most common mistake administrators make when deciding what hardware to use for their firewall is to buy the biggest and fastest machine on the market. The idea is that a faster machine will be able to process the incoming and outgoing traffic quickly, and thus improve network performance. It is often wrong to make this assumption, however. The functions provided by bastion hosts are not complex and do not require powerful machines. Using a less powerful machine is sufficient for most firewall implementations, and doing so can save you money. You can install a bastion host on a simple hardware configuration. The operating system on which the bastion host runs will typically dictate the minimum hardware requirements. When choosing hardware, use only common hardware components that have been tested, not cutting-edge technologies. Often, after these new technologies have been subjected to testing in a production environment, security holes are discovered.

The decision about how fast a processor or how much RAM to purchase will be influenced by the role of the bastion host. For example, if the bastion host is going to run an application gateway service, you should install a larger hard disk for the application gateway's caching feature. All bastion hosts will benefit from a sizable amount of RAM.

You must also back up your bastion host; it should be configured with its own tape backup device. If your company has a networked backup strategy, it will probably require accounts and direct access from the tape backup server to the bastion host. These accounts can compromise the security of either the bastion host or the backup server. Performing local backups on the bastion host will eliminate this problem.

> **NOTE** When logging locally on a firewall, consider using SCSI disks. They generally use a faster I/O card and are capable of writing information faster than standard IDE disks. If you use a SCSI disk, performance slowdowns will not occur as easily. If a slowdown does occur, it will be less severe.

Operating System

Often, packet filtering is implemented on routers, which have their own proprietary operating systems that you must use. Using routers in this fashion is a good first line of defense, and most of the configuration process involves creating the proper filters and configuring the routers to implement them. However, if you plan to install a firewall application on a computer, you need to determine the operating system that the firewall application will use. Select an operating system that will help reduce the time required to familiarize yourself with the new firewall product. Doing so will help diminish possible configuration errors.

Another factor in deciding on an operating system is the services needed for your company's network. If your company requires an application server that can filter NNTP, HTTP, and SMTP traffic, the operating system must be able to facilitate these services. The operating system should provide multitasking and support multiple simultaneous connections easily.

If you are building a bastion host and do not have a preferred operating system, Unix is a logical choice, because it has been tried and tested for the past 25 years and is widely supported. Determining which version of Unix to use is also a consideration. Select a version that has been tested on the Internet and is commonly used. Do not choose a version that is new or that has not been thoroughly tested.

> **NOTE** You can create a firewall on a simple floppy disk. Such firewall implementations generally use a version of Linux.

Services and Daemons

You should secure each bastion host individually and at every level. For example, secure the firewall application, operating system, and other services, such as Telnet and FTP. Each of these systems has specific vulnerabilities that must be addressed separately. When you install an operating system, many services or daemons are installed by default. For instance, many versions of Unix install the Telnet daemon by default. All unnecessary services should be disabled and removed from the bastion host. Simply disabling the devices does not ensure that they cannot later be reenabled.

You should also remove as many programs on the operating system as possible. For example, on a Unix system, you should remove many of the programs used for system administration, including rm, chmod, and so forth. These programs can allow a hacker to gain root-level access to the host that is configured as your firewall and cause significant damage.

Another important configuration of firewall devices, especially application gateways, is to remove IP routing. If IP routing is enabled, the bastion host may automatically route packets without first checking to see whether they adhere to the security definitions. If you remove IP routing, the bastion host must use the firewall component to route or proxy the incoming and outgoing traffic.

Removing any unnecessary service, daemon, or application is the most essential step in creating a secure bastion host. Unfortunately, this step is often the most overlooked. Removing applications may seem excessive, but remember that the bastion host will be the first device a hacker tries to penetrate when breaking into a network. By removing all these components, you make the hacker's job more difficult.

Common Firewall Designs

Now that you have a good knowledge of how to create secure firewalls, you should learn to implement a firewall strategy. The first step in designing a secure firewall strategy is to physically secure the firewalls themselves. This point may seem obvious, but if you do not keep your firewalls and production servers in a secure location, any device can be compromised. Entire networks have been brought down because a cleaning person turned off a server in the middle of the night to save power. Most devices allow for administrative or root-level access by physical means—for example, booting a server from a special floppy disk or connecting to a router through a standard serial port. Most of these threats cannot be completely removed from the device, so the answer is to secure the location in which the devices are kept.

The four common firewall designs each provide a certain level of security. Here's a simple rule of thumb: the more sensitive the data, the more extensive the firewall strategy should be. Each of the four common firewall implementations is designed to create a matrix of filters and points that can process and secure information. The four options are:

- The screening router
- A single-homed bastion host
- A multihomed bastion host
- A screened subnet

The screening router option is the simplest and, consequently, the most common. Most organizations use at least a screening router solution largely because all the necessary hardware is already in place. The two options for creating a screened host firewall are a single- or dual-homed bastion host. Both configurations require all traffic to pass through a bastion host.

Another commonly used method is the screened subnet firewall, which uses an additional packet-filtering router to achieve another level of security.

Screening Routers

The *screening router* is considered an excellent first line of defense. Because screening routers are nothing more than routers that implement filters, all the needed hardware is already in place. You learned in Chapter 5 that screening routers can be configured to reject all inbound and outbound traffic based on IP address and TCP and UDP ports. A screening router should be configured to route traffic that is acceptable under the security policy. Screening routers are effective at denying entire ranges of IP addresses or network addresses, as well as filtering unwanted TCP/IP applications. It is also possible to filter out additional protocols, including ICMP.

Figure 6.1 shows a diagram of a packet-filtering router. This approach is inexpensive but still provides significant protection.

FIGURE 6.1 Packet filter configuration

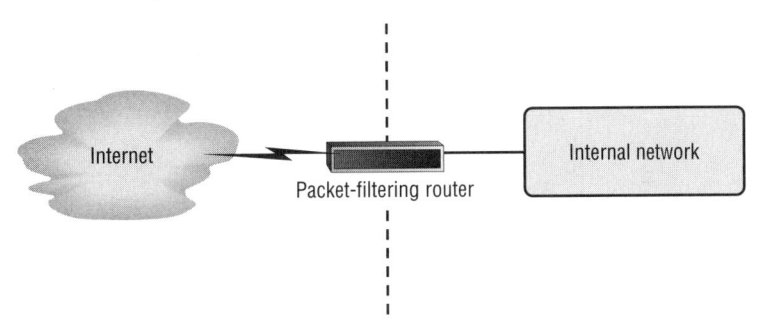

Several drawbacks may result from using only a screening router solution. The main one is that a high degree of TCP/IP knowledge is required to create proper filters. Screening routers rely solely on the use of these filters, and any configuration errors within a filter may allow unwanted traffic to pass or deny acceptable traffic.

Another disadvantage is that only a single device is used to protect the network. If a hacker were able to compromise the screening router, he or she could access any resource on your network. In addition, the screening router does not hide your internal network configuration. Anyone accessing your screening router can see your network layout and architecture with relative ease.

Screening routers also do not typically have high-quality monitoring or logging features. If a screening router receives traffic that violates its filters, it will not provide good information about the violation. Also, screening routers usually do not offer alarm capabilities. If a security violation occurs, screening routers cannot inform the security administrator of the potential threat.

Screened Host Firewall (Single-Homed Bastion)

The second prevalent type of firewall is a screened host that uses a single-homed bastion host in addition to a screening router. Single-homed bastion hosts can be configured as either circuit-level or application-level gateways. When using either of these two types, each of which is a proxy server, the bastion host can hide the configuration of the internal network. The single-homed bastion host provides this functionality by using network address translation (NAT). Using NAT allows the network administrator to use any internal IP address scheme.

The *screened host firewall* is designed so that all incoming and outgoing information is passed through the bastion host. The screening router is configured to route all incoming traffic directly to the bastion host. This routing allows the bastion host to analyze all traffic before it proxies the data to the internal network. The screening router is also configured to route outgoing traffic only if it originates from the bastion host. Configuring the router in this manner does not allow the internal nodes to reconfigure their machines to bypass the bastion host. By accepting outgoing traffic only from the bastion host, internal hosts must conform to the restrictions set at the proxy server. The bastion host is configured to restrict unacceptable traffic and proxy acceptable traffic. A single-homed bastion host is shown in Figure 6.2.

FIGURE 6.2 Single-homed bastion configuration

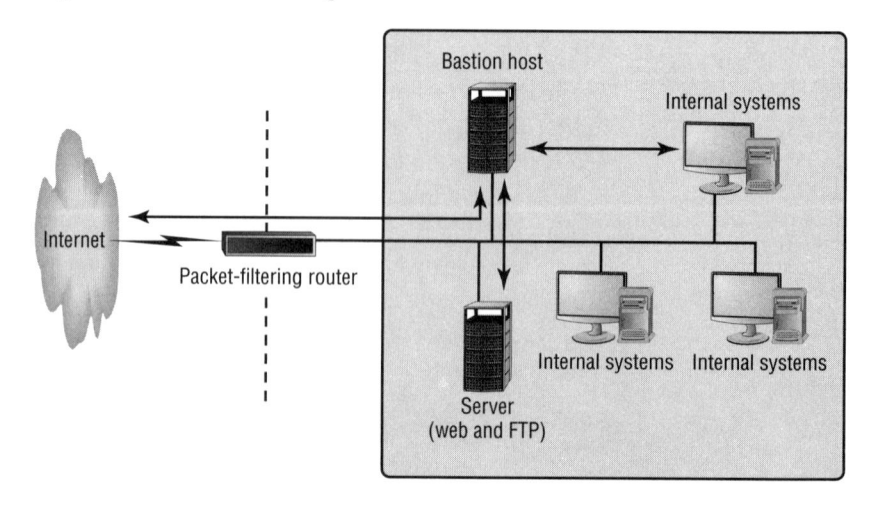

This implementation is superior to the packet-filtering firewall in several respects. First, it adds a bastion host as well as circuit- and application-level gateways. Also, the bastion itself constitutes a second security device. This second device is significantly more difficult for a hacker to subvert than a router. Now, the hacker must subvert not only the router, but also a separate computer that is not designed to accept login requests. With a screened host firewall, the hacker's task becomes doubly difficult.

The disadvantages of this method, compared to packet filtering, are increased cost and the possibility of reduced performance. Because the bastion host processes information, the network often needs more time to respond to user requests. Certain types of bastion hosts can also make user access to the Internet more difficult. If the bastion host functions only as a circuit-level gateway, the internal hosts will be unaffected. If, however, the bastion host serves as an application-level gateway, the internal client must be configured to use the application gateway's services. Also, not all TCP/IP applications will work through an application-level gateway.

Screened Host Firewall (Multihomed Bastion)

This variation of the screened-host firewall adds significant security to the previous method by using a multihomed bastion host. You can have as many NICs in a multihomed bastion host as you wish. Common configurations use two and three NICs. Figure 6.3 shows a dual-homed bastion (e.g., a system that uses two network interfaces).

FIGURE 6.3 Dual-homed bastion configuration

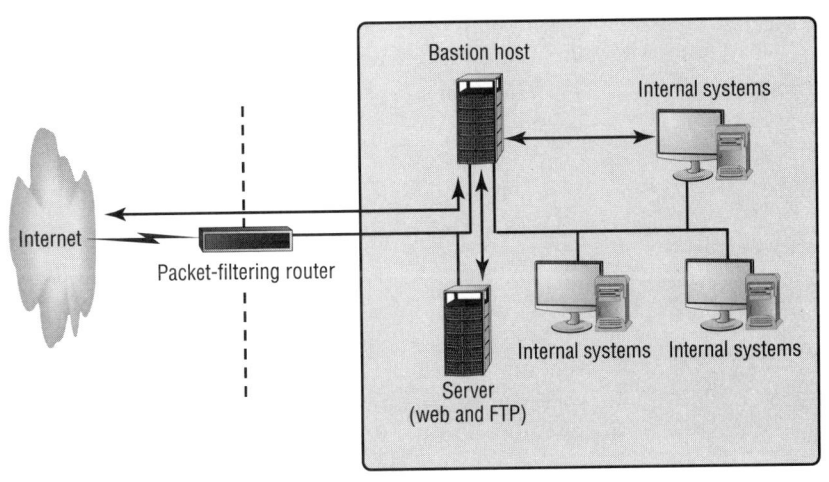

This firewall implementation is secure because it creates a complete physical break between your network and any external one, such as the Internet. As with the single-homed bastion, all external traffic is forwarded directly to the bastion host for processing. In this implementation, however, a hacker must subvert the bastion host and the router to bypass the protection mechanisms.

A single-homed implementation still might allow a hacker to modify the router to not forward packets to the bastion host. This action would bypass the bastion and allow the hacker directly into the network. Such a bypass usually does not happen, however, because a network using a single-homed bastion is typically configured to send packets only to the bastion host and not directly to the Internet. For a hacker to bypass a network properly configured for a single-homed bastion firewall, he or she must reconfigure the entire network to bypass the firewall.

A dual-homed bastion removes even this possibility, however. Furthermore, even if a hacker could defeat either the screening router or the dual-homed bastion host, he or she would still have to penetrate the other firewall implementation type, greatly slowing progress. Dual-homed bastion hosts also allow network administrators to implement NAT.

Screened Subnet Firewall, with Demilitarized Zone

The most common method for implementing a firewall is the *screened subnet*. It is also known as a *demilitarized zone (DMZ)* because it creates a fairly secure space, or subnetwork, between the Internet and your network. It is the most secure of the four general implementations, mainly because it uses a bastion host to support both circuit- and application-level gateways while defining a DMZ. In this configuration, all publicly accessible devices, including modem pools and other such resources, are placed inside this zone. The DMZ then functions as a small isolated network positioned between the Internet and the internal network. See Figure 6.4.

As Figure 6.4 shows, this configuration uses external and internal screening routers. Each is configured so that its traffic flows only to or from the bastion host. This arrangement prevents any traffic from directly traversing the subnetwork, or DMZ. The external screening router uses standard filtering to restrict external access to the bastion host, and rejects any traffic that does not come from the bastion host. This router also uses filters to prevent attacks, such as IP spoofing and source routing. The internal screening router serves as a third line of defense, also using rules to prevent spoofing and source routing. Like its external counterpart, this router rejects incoming packets that do not originate from the bastion host and sends only outgoing packets to the bastion host.

FIGURE 6.4 Screened subnet firewall

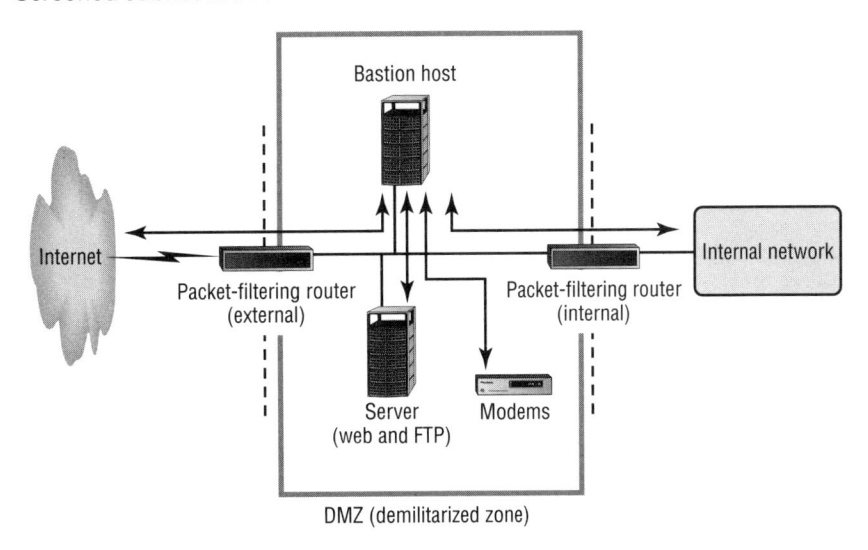

Chief among the benefits of this method is the fact that a hacker wanting to access your network must subvert three separate devices without being detected. A second benefit is that the internal network is effectively invisible to the Internet, because all packets going out and coming in go directly to the DMZ, not to your network. This arrangement makes it impossible for a hacker to gain information about your internal systems. Only the DMZ is advertised in the routing tables. Third, because this routing information is contained within the network, internal users cannot access the Internet without going through the bastion host.

Any packets sent directly from the internal network cannot receive replies from the Internet, because no routing tables exist for the Internet and, thus, no way exists to get the packet back to the internal network. This configuration prevents internal users from bypassing your security measures. You need not employ a dual-homed bastion host in this scenario because the routers ensure the traffic can flow only through the bastion host.

ICMP and Firewalls

The Internet Control Message Protocol (ICMP) communicates errors or other conditions at the IP layer. ICMP is an extremely useful tool for troubleshooting networks. However, ICMP packets can very easily be manipulated. Hackers use ICMP in two ways. First, it is possible to use ICMP packets to gain more information about systems. Applications such as nmap have been able to use ICMP packets to determine the type of remote operating system that is in use. The second way a hacker uses ICMP is to attack systems.

It is tempting to simply block all ICMP packets, and many networks do, especially for web and e-mail servers. However, totally deactivating ICMP on your network can complicate troubleshooting network connectivity. Most firewalls, however, allow you to block specific ICMP types.

Regardless of the topology you are using, it is often necessary to block ICMP packets. An ICMP message is an extension to the IP header and also consists of several levels. Normally ICMP messages are quite useful. For example, when you ping a host to see if it is operational, you are generating an ICMP message. The remote host will respond to the ping with an ICMP message of its own. This process is typically not a problem with most networks. However, there are more ICMP message types than those used by the common ping program.

ICMP Message Types

Each ICMP message contains three fields that define its purpose and provide a checksum: Type, Code, and Checksum. The Type field identifies the ICMP message, the Code field provides further information about the associated Type field, and the Checksum field provides a method for determining the integrity of the message. Table 6.1 contains a list of the ICMP types.

TABLE 6.1 ICMP Message Types

ICMP Type	Name	Description
0	Echo Reply	The packets that are sent back whenever you use the standard ping command to send echo request packets.
3	Destination Unreachable	The message sent by a router whenever a host, network, or port is unreachable. This type contains arguments that have 15 additional values, including: 0: Network unreachable 1: Host unreachable 3: Port unreachable 7: Destination host unknown

ICMP and Firewalls 257

TABLE 6.1 ICMP Message Types *(continued)*

ICMP Type	Name	Description
4	Source Quench	Sent whenever the destination cannot handle the amount of traffic being received.
5	Redirect Message	Used by an intermediate router if it knows of a better route for a packet than the one originally found in the packet. This message supports these additional arguments: 0: Redirect datagrams for the network 1: Redirect datagrams for the host 2: Redirect datagrams for the type of service and network 3: Redirect datagrams for the type of service and host
8	Echo Request	The ICMP message issued when you use the `ping` command.
11	Time Exceeded	Sent by a host whenever a packet's time to live (TTL) has expired and delivery or reply has not been received in time.
12	Parameter Problem	Issued by a host that drops a packet because it was malformed. Messages with the value of 1 indicate that a required element of the packet was missing. Messages with the value of 0 explain where the packet experienced the problem.
13 and 14	Timestamp Request and Reply	Used to synchronize time between two hosts.
15 and 16	Information Request and Reply (Obsoleted)	At one time used by systems to obtain IP addresses.
17 and 18	Address Mask Request and Reply	Used at boot time by computers that need to learn the subnet mask used in a network. Hosts reply with type 18.

A firewall can block any one or all of these message types. Sometimes, network administrators choose to block only certain types; others, once the network has been configured and tested, will block all traffic.

> **TIP** Screened subnet firewalls are often the best firewall type for coping with attacks that use ICMP.

Remote Access and Virtual Private Networks (VPNs)

A *virtual private network (VPN)* is an encrypted tunnel that provides secure access between two hosts across an unsecured network. As suggested in Figure 6.5, two hosts can communicate securely across the Internet using public-key encryption. Most firewalls provide VPN services. In order for the encryption to occur, the firewalls must first exchange public keys.

VPNs extend a company's network over a public medium such as the Internet. The VPN encapsulates all the encrypted data within an IP packet. Because the packet contains valid IP and TCP information, it is routed normally over the Internet. This use of firewalls to communicate with each other forms a *virtual network perimeter*, which is an outer corporate network created using the VPN technologies, thus extending the corporate network to suppliers and customers. Such perimeters are important because the network of firewalls can enable remote employees to connect securely. It can also allow two different companies to expand their perimeters, enabling them to share information quickly and securely. One advantage of virtual network perimeters is that they support remote users with full security. The enhanced security increases freedom for remote users to use corporate applications and resources anywhere in the world.

All VPNs use *tunneling protocols*, because they encapsulate, or tunnel, packets or payloads as they pass between hosts. A tunneling protocol encapsulates data packets into another packet. The types of tunneling protocols include Point-to-Point, IPsec, and the Layer 2 Tunneling Protocol (L2TP). Encryption occurs at the source, and decryption occurs at the destination. Sending packets in this manner has another advantage besides encryption. Because the entire packet is encrypted and then placed within a typical

TCP/IP packet, other networking protocols can be transmitted this way. For example, the IPX/SPX protocol can be tunneled through an IP-enabled VPN.

FIGURE 6.5 Understanding VPN connection

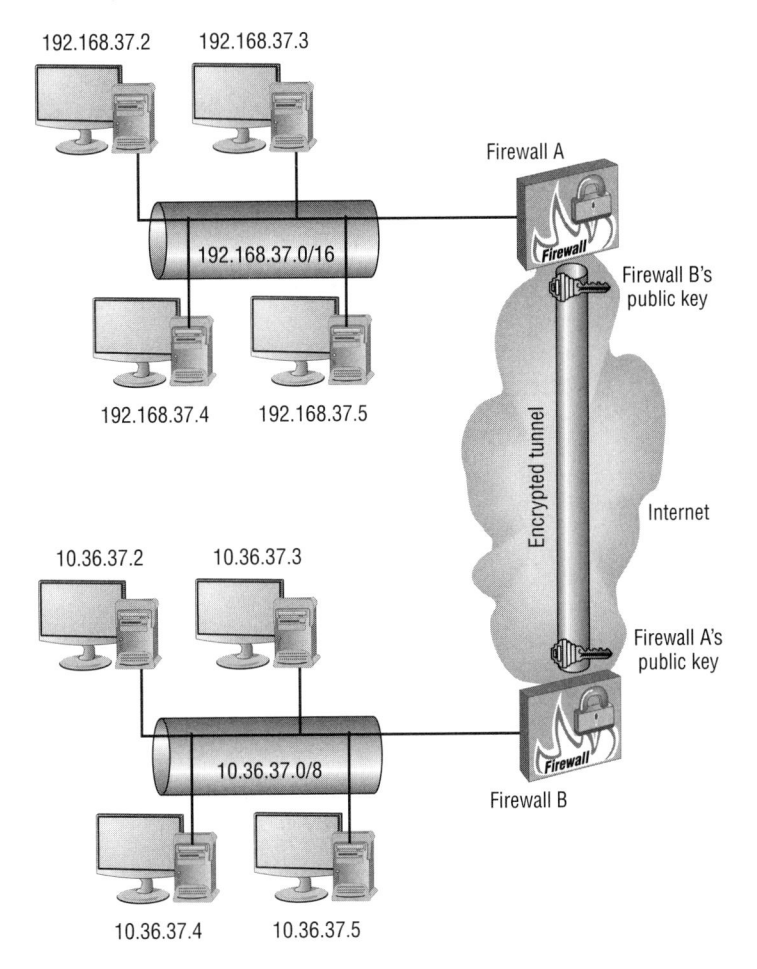

All the security fundamentals (e.g., authentication, message integrity, and encryption) are very important to implementing a VPN. Without such authentication procedures, a hacker could impersonate anyone and gain access to the network. Message integrity is required because the packets can be altered as they travel through the public network. Without encryption, the information may become truly public.

Internet Protocol Security (IPsec)

IPsec is an IETF standard that provides packet-level encryption, authentication, and integrity between firewalls, or between hosts in a LAN. IPsec can use an *authentication header (AH)* and the *Encapsulating Security Payload (ESP)* service to authenticate and encrypt the data payload, or only an authentication header to provide simple authentication. Most IPsec implementations use both.

> **NOTE** It is important to remember that IPsec is implemented as an add-on to IPv4. In this way, IPsec counts as an operating system add-on, because it extends the system's ability to communicate securely. These security features are implemented natively in IPv6.

Security Associations (SA) and Internet Key Exchange (IKE)

A *security association (SA)* is the exchange of data meant to uniquely identify a particular host. Generally, an SA requires the use of public-key cryptography. If you want to use IPsec to communicate securely with another host, you must first create an SA. An SA is evidence that encryption is working and that a trust relationship has occurred.

The *Internet Key Exchange (IKE)* process allows two hosts to establish a trust relationship. IKE enables two hosts to negotiate the exact nature of the connection. Elements of the negotiation include:

- The encryption type
- How long the SA will be valid (for example, 8 hours)
- The authentication method

In most forms of IPsec, IKE occurs in two phases. In the first phase (often called "main mode"), the *Internet Security Association and Key Management Protocol (ISAKMP)* negotiates the encryption type, the authentication method, and so forth. It also maintains SAs and is responsible for removing the keys associated with an SA. You can learn more about ISAKMP by reading RFC 2408.

The *OAKLEY protocol*, discussed in RFC 2412, generates the actual keys. It then issues messages via UDP to help hosts exchange the strongest keys possible. OAKLEY is used as a subset of ISAKMP. Keys generated at the end of the main mode phase then encrypt the actual traffic that passes between network hosts. This second phase of IPsec is called *phase 2*, or *quick mode*.

Most IPsec-compliant software and devices allow you to monitor active SAs. Microsoft Windows 2000, for example, provides the IPsecMon application.

> **NOTE**
> To implement IPsec, you need only one of the following to help provide authentication: a host that automatically issues tokens and certificates (e.g., a Windows 2000 domain controller), a digital certificate recognized by all hosts, or a "shared secret" key, which is a simple string of text to which all hosts refer when decrypting packets.

Here are the two most common protocols used in VPNs today:

The Point-to-Point Tunneling Protocol (PPTP) The Point-to-Point Tunneling Protocol (PPTP) is used to create VPN connections. The chief benefit of PPTP is that it is capable of tunneling and encrypting connections across multiple networks. The Point-to-Point Protocol (PPP) cannot do this. PPP allows encryption to occur only between the client and the ISP's dial-up server.

PPTP works at the Datalink layer (Layer 2 of the OSI/RM), and is capable of using PPP to tunnel various protocols (e.g., TCP/IP, IPX/SPX, and NetBEUI). Although PPTP does require a client to first create a connection to an ISP, the subsequent encrypted connection does not have to be made to the ISP. The VPN connection can be made across many networks to any remote server on any remote network. Thus, with PPTP, the use of encryption is no longer tied to the ISP.

PPTP uses the Challenge Handshake Authentication Protocol (CHAP), which uses hash encryption to ensure passwords are not easily stolen. You can learn more about PPTP by reading RFC 2637.

The Layer 2 Tunneling Protocol (L2TP) L2TP incorporates elements of PPP and another protocol called the Layer 2 Forwarding (L2F) protocol, which was introduced by Cisco Systems. Like PPTP, standard L2TP uses PPP to allow the tunneling of various network protocols. L2TP also supports CHAP.

Unlike PPTP, L2TP borrows its ability to forward connections from the L2F protocol. As a result, L2TP is supported by virtually every vendor of VPN hardware and software. L2TP also uses enhanced compression techniques, which creates faster connections. In addition, standard L2TP supports various network types, including ATM, frame relay, and X.25. You can learn more about L2TP by reading RFC 2661.

Public-Key Infrastructure (PKI)

Modern *Public Key Infrastructure (PKI)* networks have been created to enable the automatic transfer of public keys to trusted users with little effort. Whenever a user, host, or process uses a certificate to prove identity, it is said to be strongly authenticated. This is because the certificate is a powerful form of "what you have" authentication. It is considered a powerful form because it is signed by a third party.

PKI servers are repositories for managing public keys, certificates, and signatures. In addition to authenticating the identity of the entity owning a key pair, PKI provides the ability to revoke a key if it is no longer valid. A key becomes invalid if, for example, a private key is cracked or made public. The primary goal of PKI is to allow certificates to be generated and revoked as quickly as possible. Corporations are especially interested in the ability to establish quick, secure communication methods, and PKI is a promising solution.

PKI Standards

PKI is based on the X.509 standard, with which you are already familiar. A standard for PKI is currently being developed. As of this writing, the latest RFCs include the following:

RFC 2510   Identifies the terminology and protocols used in PKI.

RFC 2560   Provides a discussion of the Online Certificate Status Protocol (OCSP), which enables Internet-aware applications to quickly determine a certificate's validity.

RFC 2585   Describes the architecture and protocols used in PKI.

RFC 2587   Explains how LDAP2 is used to allow access to PKI servers (i.e., repositories).

RFC 2527   An informational document explaining the purpose of PKI.

> **NOTE** In general terms, the X.509 standard is meant to standardize the format of certificates and how they are accessed.

PKI Terminology

You were introduced to certificates, certificate authorities, and certificate revocation lists in Chapter 2. You learned these terms when you learned how SSL uses certificates to authenticate hosts. Here are some additional terms used in full-blown PKI environments:

End entity   An *end entity* is the end user or person listed in the subject field of an X.509 certificate.

Certificate policy statement   This is a public document containing rules and procedures agreed on by the CA and the end entity. This document specifies the certification path and the technologies that enable authentication.

Certification path   A *certification path* is the traceable history of the parties who have vouched for the certificate. Certificates depend highly on the integrity of the party who vouches for them. If a problem exists in a certificate's certification path, the certificate may be deemed invalid and should be revoked.

Registration authority (RA)   A *registration authority (RA)* is responsible for verifying the identify of a person or host interested in participating in a PKI scheme. The RA is a trusted body that is able to verify the authenticity of the person or host. A person who wants to become registered, however, must supply credentials concerning identity. Otherwise, the RA will not issue a certificate.

Certificate repository   This is where clients and CAs store certificates. A *certificate repository* can be managed so that only the most current certificates are listed. A network or series of distributed networks that allow access to certificates.

> **NOTE** PKI refers to the servers, repositories, and other elements controlled by Public Key Cryptography Standards (PKCS).

Creating Certificates

Certificates authenticate users and hosts. A certificate is essentially a public key that has been verified by a trusted third party, which ensures that this certificate authenticates a particular host, company, or person. A number of companies, called *certificate authorities (CAs)*, issue authentication certificates and sign them with their signatures to indicate a program's validity. Two such companies are VeriSign (www.verisign.com) and Entrust (www.entrust.com). You can also act as your own CA, provided you have the software that allows you to generate certificates. Windows 2000 has its own native CA software, and you can use OpenSSL (www.openssl.org) in Linux and Unix systems. The four types of certificates are:

Certificate authority certificate   Used by CAs to validate another CA as a trusted issuer. Only a few CAs are automatically trusted by web browsers.

Server certificate   Used to verify a company's web server. A company applies for a server certificate and sends the request to one of several CAs. The CA will verify that the company is legitimate, and then send the company a digital certificate. Specialized server certificates exist. For example, an IPsec client can obtain a certificate that allows a host to participate in an IPsec-enabled network.

Personal certificate   Used by individuals, usually to encrypt e-mail or authenticate with a web server. The individual contacts a CA to request a personal certificate. The only verification the CA performs is by e-mail address. The CA sends the certificate to the e-mail address specified by the individual. In theory, only that person would have access to the e-mail account, and would therefore be the only one who could retrieve and use the certificate.

Software or publisher certificate   Used to validate software code. For example, if a user accesses a website that is trying to download a Java applet or an ActiveX control, a security warning usually appears. The publisher certificate is used to validate the code to assure the user that the code does not contain malicious programming.

Configuring Microsoft Windows 2000 to Use IPsec

Windows 2000 supports IPsec natively. You can configure IPsec by using the Local Security Policy MMC snap-in (Start ≻ Programs ≻ Administrative Tools ≻ Local Security Policy). Three default security policies are installed by default, though none is marked as active. Before you activate a security policy, make sure it is suitable for your situation. All the security policies, for example, require that you authenticate in one of three ways:

- Systems can authenticate and encrypt by consulting a domain controller. This option is the default. Authentication is accomplished via the modified Kerberos server.

- All hosts can obtain and use certificates to authenticate and encrypt. For example, a central system can create a CA and the client hosts can obtain a special IPsec certificate. This option is often preferable when you want to establish IPsec but do not want to use the proprietary version of Kerberos used in Windows 2000.

- You can use a "shared secret," which is a simple text string that all systems consult to encrypt and decrypt information. This option is the easiest, but it is also the least secure.

Once you configure your policy to use any of the three methods above, you can then apply it to your system. If you apply strict settings, your hosts will be able to communicate only with other IPsec-enabled hosts.

EXERCISE 6.1

Obtaining an IPsec Certificate from a CA

In this exercise, you will request a certificate from a CA and then install it on your system.

1. On your Windows 2000 system, install a stand-alone CA that will process IPsec certificate requests from all clients in your network. You need only one CA, and you need to place it on only one system.

Note: All clients should follow the remaining steps.

2. When you have finished establishing a CA, open a web browser and enter the following URL:

   http://certificate_authority_server/certsrv

   where certificate_authority_server is the DNS name of your CA.

3. The Advanced Certificate Request form will appear. From here, you can generate requests for various certificate types, including those for e-mail, SSL, and IPsec. The Request A Certificate radio button should be selected by default. Click the Next button.

4. Select the Advanced Request radio button and click Next.

5. The Submit A Certificate Request To This CA Using A Form radio button will be selected by default. Click Next. You will be required to enter information about your system.

6. In the Identifying Information section, enter the name of your server in the Name text box, and enter any e-mail address. The additional information should already be present.

EXERCISE 6.1 *(continued)*

7. In the Intended Purpose section, select IPsec Certificate from the drop-down menu.

8. In the Key Options section, make sure that Microsoft Base Cryptographic Provider v1.0 is selected (this is the default) in the drop-down box. Make sure that the Both radio button is selected for Key Usage (this is the default) and that 1024 appears in the Key Size box. All systems must use the same key size.

9. Finally, you must select the Use Local Machine Store check box. If you do not make this selection, you will not be able to specify your IPsec certificate when you need to modify the default system IPsec policy. Your certificate form should look like this:

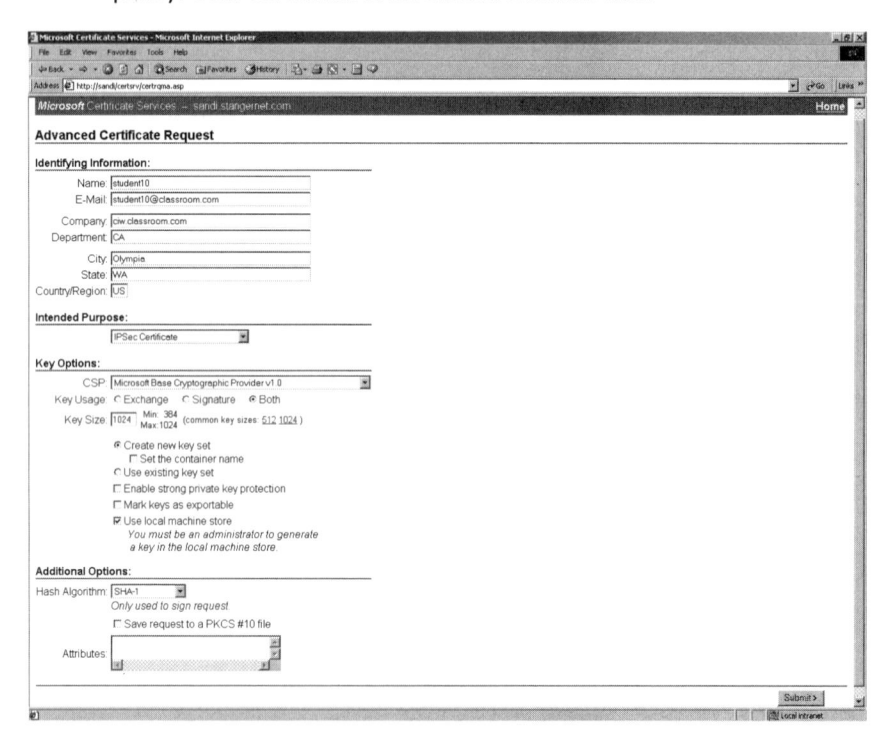

10. At this point, click the Submit button at the far right.

11. Now process this request. You do this by using the administrator account. First, open the Certificate Authority snap-in (Start ➢ Programs ➢ Administrative Tools ➢ Certificate Authority). Next, expand your CA server's name and click the Pending Requests icon. Then, right-click the pending certificate and click Issue.

EXERCISE 6.1 *(continued)*

12. When you have processed the request, use your Web browser to access your CA again (http://certificate_authority_system/certsrv) and click the Check On A Pending Certificate radio button to obtain the certificate from your CA.

13. Follow the web pages and click the Install This Certificate radio button to install the certificate on your server.

EXERCISE 6.2

Configuring a Windows 2000 System for IPsec

In this exercise, you will use the Local Security Policy snap-in to modify and enable the Secure Server (Require Security) built-in IPsec policy.

1. Select Start ➤ Programs ➤ Administrative Tools ➤ Local Security Policy to open the Local Security Policy snap-in, and then click the IP security Policies Local Machine icon.

2. Double-click the Secure Server (Require Security) icon. The Secure Server (Require Security) Properties dialog box will appear, as shown here:

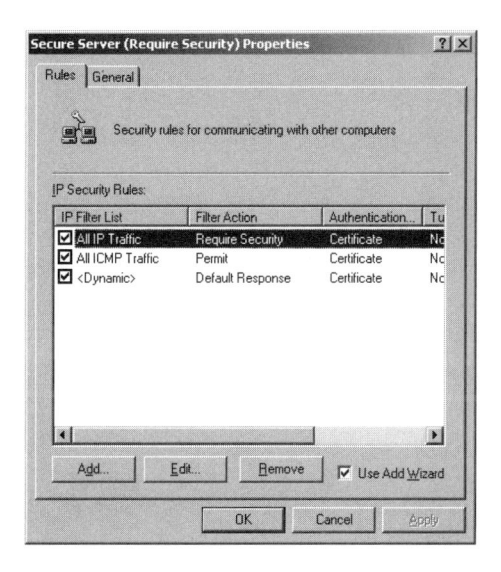

EXERCISE 6.2 *(continued)*

3. Select All IP Traffic and then click the Edit button. Select the Authentication Methods tab and click the Edit button.

4. Select the Use A Certificate From This Certificate Authority (CA) radio button, and click the Browse button to search for the certificate you obtained in the previous exercise. Click OK until you reach the Local Security Policy snap-in.

5. Edit the All ICMP Traffic and Dynamic IP filters to use the certificate you obtained in the last exercise.

6. Right-click the Secure Server (Require Security) icon in the Local Security Policy snap-in and select Assign.

7. When all systems on the network have chosen the correct certificate and assigned the correct policy, use a web browser or FTP client to connect to your remote system. To verify that IPsec is working correctly, select Start ➢ Run and enter the following:

   IpsecMon

   You will then be able to monitor the security associations as they occur. Here are two security associations for the systems named Keats and James:

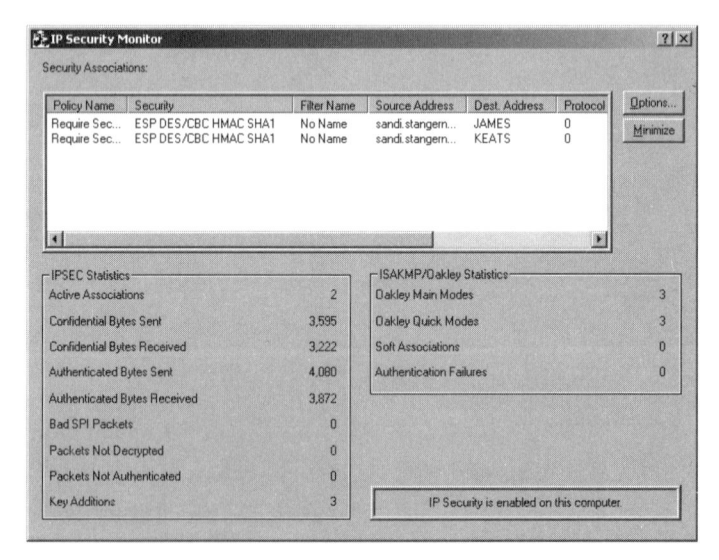

Policy Name	Security	Filter Name	Source Address	Dest. Address	Protocol
Require Sec...	ESP DES/CBC HMAC SHA1	No Name	sandi.stangern...	JAMES	0
Require Sec...	ESP DES/CBC HMAC SHA1	No Name	sandi.stangern...	KEATS	0

   IPSEC Statistics

Active Associations	2
Confidential Bytes Sent	3,595
Confidential Bytes Received	3,222
Authenticated Bytes Sent	4,080
Authenticated Bytes Received	3,872
Bad SPI Packets	0
Packets Not Decrypted	0
Packets Not Authenticated	0
Key Additions	3

   ISAKMP/Oakley Statistics

Oakley Main Modes	3
Oakley Quick Modes	3
Soft Associations	0
Authentication Failures	0

   IP Security is enabled on this computer.

8. If you have difficulty using certificates, a quick and easy way to implement IPsec is to use a shared secret. Double-click the Secure

EXERCISE 6.2 *(continued)*

Server (Require Security) icon. Once the Secure Server (Require Security) Properties dialog box appears, click the Edit button to open the Edit Rule Properties dialog box. Then, click the Authentication Methods tab. Once there, click the Edit button to view the Edit Authentication Method Properties dialog box. Select the Use This String To Protect The Key Exchange (Preshared Key) radio button. Then, enter the following text:

Ciwcertified

9. Click OK and reassign your policy. As long as all clients are using the same shared secret, IPsec encryption will occur.

10. Now disable the Require Security policy to ensure that your computer can communicate with others.

Unix and IPsec

The standard IPsec software for Unix and Linux systems is FreeS/WAN (www.freeswan.org). You can download it from the FreeS/WAN home page, shown in Figure 6.6. The FreeS/WAN project has taken pains to follow the IPsec RFCs and is widely considered to be a truly universal implementation.

FIGURE 6.6 The FreeS/WAN home page

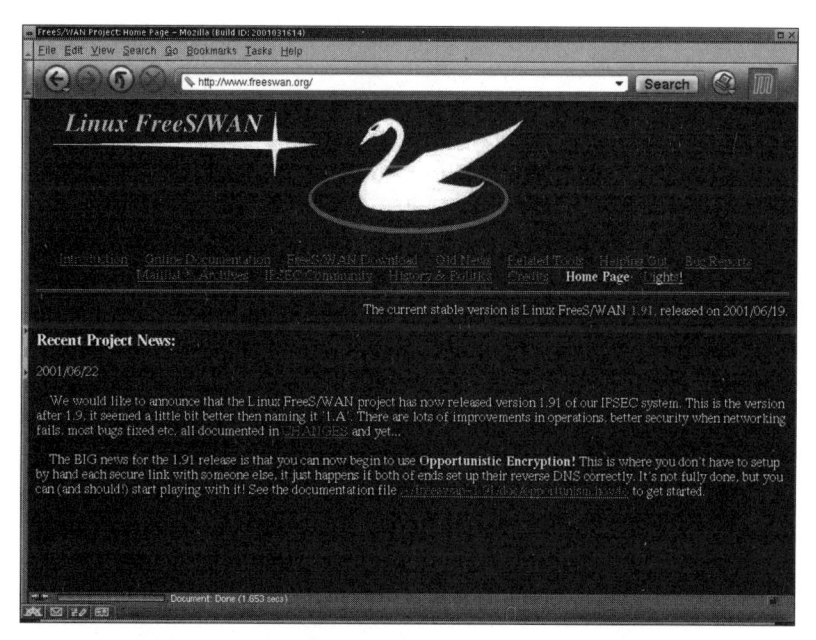

The Linux and Windows 2000 IPsec software can be configured to work together. Go to www.freeswan.org/freeswan_trees for more information about the latest distribution and interoperability documents.

Summary

From firewall placement to removing unnecessary services, you must understand the steps needed to apply an effective firewall strategy. In this chapter, you learned how to create and configure a secure bastion host, and you were introduced to some firewall strategies. You also learned about various ICMP types, and why it is so important to filter ICMP properly at the firewall. Some companies have blocked all ICMP packets, whereas others are more selective. The CIW Security Professional exam will not ask you to make this type of choice, but it will expect you to identify ICMP types, in addition to firewall types.

Many firewalls are capable of establishing VPN connections between two enterprise networks, which allows them to exchange information in a relatively secure manner. As you learned in this chapter, VPN uses public-key encryption. It is important to understand that VPNs use certificates in order to authenticate information before encryption occurs. You also learned more about PKI and strong authentication, as well as how to encrypt IPv4 using IPsec. IPsec has become a primary means of protecting Internet-based communication from sniffing attacks.

Now that you have the knowledge necessary to implement perimeter security in a network, it is important to understand that a firewall is not the only tool you can use to protect your hosts. In the next chapter, you will implement proactive-detection methods. These methods include creating dummy accounts and login scripts, and using automated checksum utilities.

Exam Essentials

Understand the importance of proper firewall design. Firewalls must be placed properly, or hackers and employees will find ways around them. As you place your firewall, consider the existing network topology. Make sure that the firewall design is as simple as possible. Also, ensure that you have properly backed up all firewall software and that you can easily access and manage your equipment.

Be able to identify historical and current firewall designs.   Make sure you understand the concept of single- and multihomed bastion hosts. A firewall must be powerful enough to ensure that it will not create a bottleneck. You should be comfortable describing various firewall configurations, including ways to create a DMZ.

Understand firewall terminology.   Be familiar with such terms as choke router, bastion host, and modem bank. The exam may ask you to define these terms, or it may include questions that assume you already know these terms.

Know the ways that firewalls can be defeated.   One of the primary means of defeating a firewall is simply going around it. You should know that hackers often target modem banks, because traditionally they have not been required to work with the firewall.

Understand the purpose of a VPN.   You can create a VPN in several ways. First, a VPN can involve two firewalls that create an encrypted tunnel over a public network. A VPN can also consist of a single host that connects with an individual system or firewall. Third, a VPN can be composed of individual systems in a LAN or WAN that use IPsec to guarantee secure communications.

Be able to list VPN and IPsec technologies and terms.   Make sure you understand such terms as virtual network perimeter, CHAP, IKE, ESP, and security association. Also, make sure that you understand how to monitor VPN connections. Given a scenario, you should be able to recommend a VPN as a relevant solution.

Know PKI terminology and use certificates.   You have already learned about certificates and certificate authorities. This chapter has discussed additional PKI elements that you need to understand. These elements include certificate repositories and registration authorities. It is vital that you understand that certificates are important tools for creating trust relationships across untrusted networks.

Key Terms

Before you take the exam, be certain you are familiar with the following terms:

- authentication header (AH)
- certificate repository
- certification path
- Challenge Handshake Authentication Protocol (CHAP)
- contingency plan
- dual-homed bastion hosts
- Encapsulating Security Payload (ESP)
- end entity
- internal bastion hosts
- Internet Key Exchange (IKE)
- Internet Security Association and Key Management Protocol (ISAKMP)
- IPsec
- Layer 2 Forwarding (L2F)
- Layer 2 Tunneling Protocol (L2TP)
- multihomed bastion hosts
- OAKLEY protocol
- Point-to-Point Tunneling Protocol (PPTP)
- Public-Key Infrastructure (PKI)
- registration authority (RA)
- resource placement
- screened host firewall
- screened subnet
- screening router
- security association (SA)
- single-homed bastion host
- single-purpose bastion hosts
- tunneling protocols
- virtual network perimeter
- virtual private network (VPN)
- war dialers

Review Questions

1. What is a single-homed bastion host?

    A. A firewall device with only one network interface

    B. A firewall device with at least two network interfaces

    C. A standard bastion host residing inside an internal network

    D. A firewall device that works as a proxy server

2. What is an internal bastion host?

    A. A firewall device with only one network interface

    B. A single- or multihomed bastion host residing outside the network

    C. A single- or mutlihomed bastion host residing inside the network

    D. A firewall device that acts as a proxy server

3. What is a screening router?

    A. A firewall device with only one network interface and that has two interfaces exposed to a public network

    B. A router that implements filters and that has one interface exposed to a public network

    C. A screened host that uses a single-homed bastion host and that engages in NAT

    D. A dual-homed bastion host residing inside the network and that engages in NAT

4. What is the most secure of the four general firewall implementations?

    A. A screening router

    B. A single-homed bastion host

    C. A dual-homed bastion host

    D. A screened subnet

5. What is the simplest, and consequently the most common, firewall design?

   A. A screened subnet

   B. A screening router

   C. A dual-homed bastion host

   D. A single-homed bastion host

6. You want to encrypt traffic between firewalls (i.e., you want to create a VPN). What is the first step you will need to take to enable the VPN connection?

   A. Sign the key with a certificate.

   B. Exchange a shared secret.

   C. Exchange a key.

   D. Create a DMZ.

7. You are using IPsec. What element of an IPsec-enabled IP packet verifies the identity of a host?

   A. The Encapsulating Security Payload (ESP)

   B. The Internet Key Exchange (IKE)

   C. The authentication header (AH)

   D. The Layer 2 Tunneling Protocol (L2TP)

8. Which of the following elements of IPsec is responsible for establishing a trust relationship?

   A. The security association (SA)

   B. The Internet Security Association and Key Management Protocol (ISAKMP)

   C. The OAKLEY protocol

   D. The Internet Key Exchange (IKE)

9. Which of the following is an extension of PPTP and includes elements of a proprietary protocol that enables encryption to cross over multiple intervening networks?

    A. LPT2

    B. L2TP

    C. MS-CHAP

    D. LPT1

10. Jane wishes to create a VPN. She wants to use Ethernet adapters to house the VPN, but dial-up clients will be connecting to it. Which of the following VPN protocols should she use?

    A. ISAKMP

    B. PPTP

    C. L2TP

    D. CHAP

11. What is the numerical equivalent of an ICMP echo request packet?

    A. 8

    B. 9

    C. 10

    D. 11

12. Which of the following firewall types requires that the hacker defeat at least three different systems?

    A. Dual-homed bastion host

    B. Triple-homed bastion host

    C. Screened subnet firewall

    D. Circuit-level gateway

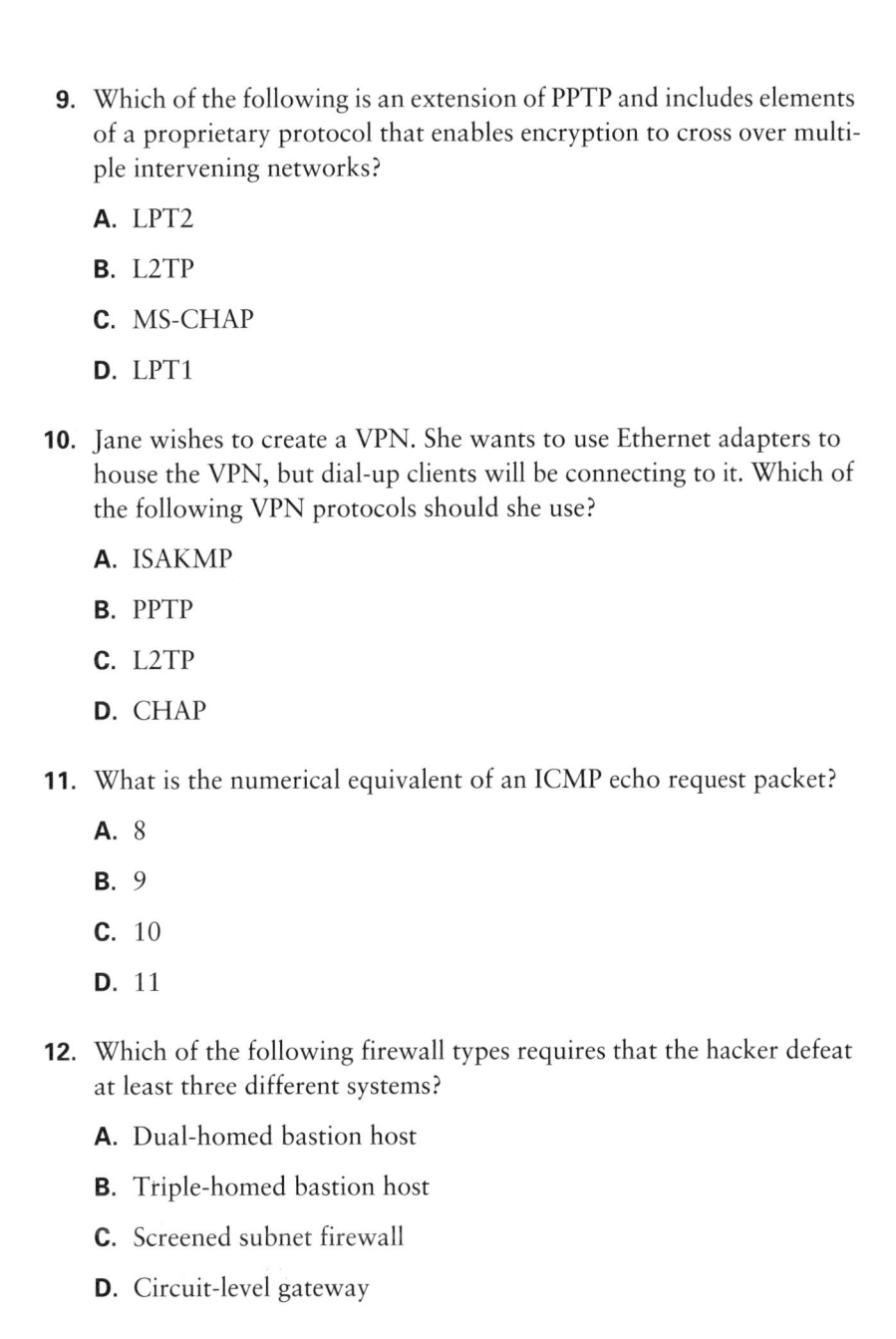

13. Which of the following involves a contingency plan?

    A. Placing resources properly to ensure traffic cannot avoid the firewall

    B. Ensuring that end users are trained

    C. Making administration as easy as possible

    D. Configuring an identical system and keeping it in safe storage

14. Jacob has configured a screening router, a bastion host, and a choke router. However, he still suspects that a remote user has been able to enter his network and snoop around. Which of the following provides one of the easiest ways for a remote user to defeat a firewall?

    A. A circuit-level gateway

    B. A packet filter

    C. A modem

    D. A choke router

15. William is using three Linux systems that are clustered together to provide web services for a medium-sized e-commerce business. He is using Apache Server for all three systems. William wants to secure communications between these three servers. What product could he choose?

    A. PPTP

    B. L2TP

    C. IPsec

    D. FreeS/WAN

16. Joel has been able to compromise a firewall by using a piece of software to mount the firewall's operating system and implant an illicit server. What type of attack has Joel been able to wage against this firewall?

    A. Denial of service

    B. Physical

    C. Illicit server

    D. Hijacking

17. Which of the following elements generates the actual keys used to create a security association in an IPsec-enabled host?

    A. ISAKMP

    B. L2TP

    C. OAKLEY

    D. IPsecMon

18. Susan has obtained a certificate, which she will use to create IPsec security associations. Where will she place this certificate?

    A. Onto her system

    B. Onto a remote system

    C. Into a certificate repository

    D. On an end entity

19. Aaron has purchased a certificate from VeriSign. Which of the following is used to ensure the authenticity of the certificate given to Aaron?

    A. A server identification certificate

    B. A personal authority certificate

    C. A software authority certificate

    D. A certificate authority certificate

20. Aaron has used VeriSign to obtain a certificate. He will use this certificate to assure recipients that his e-mail is in fact from him and not another person. With PKI, what role has VeriSign played in verifying Aaron's identity?

    A. It has provided a certificate policy statement.

    B. It has acted as an end entity.

    C. It has acted as a registration authority.

    D. It is the certificate repository.

Answers to Review Questions

1. **A.** Single-homed bastion hosts are less common today, but the CIW Security Professional exam may still ask for such knowledge. Single-homed bastion hosts were common in low-traffic networks. Often, these hosts used one NIC and a dial-up connection. Many small companies use this type of firewall to connect to public networks via a proxy server.

2. **C.** A firewall does not necessarily have to create a perimeter between the entire network and the entire Internet. Sometimes, it is necessary to use a firewall within a company to isolate certain departments and/or divisions that use sensitive information.

3. **B.** A screening router is often the first line of defense, and it is used to eliminate (i.e., screen out) the most common attacks. Using a screened router along with a choke router helps ensure that you do not have one single point of failure. Such redundancy may be more expensive, but it does tend to provide a more secure environment.

4. **D.** A screened subnet contains more equipment, which can actually cause more configuration problems. However, when configured correctly, a screened subnet allows you to monitor traffic more closely. It also provides a physical break between you and the hacker.

5. **B.** A screening router is essentially a router that has packet filtering turned on. Many small companies use nothing but a screening router as their firewall. The drawback of such a solution is that it provides a single point of failure.

6. **A.** A certificate is necessary before you can create a VPN. You need a certificate to sign public and private keys so that a trust relationship is created. Once you have obtained a certificate, you must then exchange keys. You must first sign the key with a certificate, and you can then exchange keys. A DMZ is not necessary with a VPN, although it is a desirable feature of a firewall.

7. **C.** The authentication header ensures that the host is properly identified. If the AH is not verified, the connection will be dropped.

8. **D.** IKE is responsible for exchanging keys; whenever keys are exchanged, a trust relationship exists. The security association, ISAKMP, and OAKLEY protocols are all elements of IPsec, but are not responsible for key exchange.

9. **B.** The L2TP protocol extends Microsoft's PPTP and includes elements of the L2F protocol, which was developed by Cisco Systems. L2TP, unlike PPTP, is capable of encrypting packets over multiple intervening networks. Many vendors have embraced L2TP as a tunneling protocol. LPT1 and LPT2 are names of parallel port interfaces. MS-CHAP is a proprietary version of the Challenge Handshake Authentication Protocol (CHAP), which is a replacement for the Password Authentication Procedure (PAP). PAP simplified the process of dialing into an ISP, and CHAP improved on this process by using one-way encryption. CHAP issues a challenge to a client in the form of a text string; the client then issues a response. The server uses one-way encryption to compare hash values. If the client has responded with the correct hash value, authentication is allowed to proceed. If the hash values do not compare, the authentication process is terminated.

10. **C.** The primary benefit of L2TP is that it supports connections between different adapters. PPTP, for example, only supports connections between dial-up adapters.

11. **A.** ICMP messages come in various types. Echo request packets are type 8. Echo replies are type 0.

12. **C.** A screened subnet firewall uses screening and choke routers, as well as a bastion host. These three systems, when working together properly, can prove difficult to defeat.

13. **D.** A firewall is a network device like any other. It has an operating system and hardware. Although its hardware and software may be more specialized, these elements are just as prone to failure as any other. Create a backup that enables you to recover quickly from a problem, or you may be responsible for denying service to your entire company.

14. **C.** Modems and modem banks are the primary means of defeating a firewall. Take great care when configuring your network and your firewall; a careless connection on the part of an employee can seriously reduce your network's security level.

15. **D.** The product commonly used to enable IPsec on Linux systems is FreeS/WAN. It allows Linux systems to implement IPsec. Because the question asks for the product William would choose, the correct answer is FreeS/WAN, not IPsec.

16. B. Using a piece of software to mount the firewall's operating system and implanting an illicit server is a description of superzapping, which is a physical attack. Even though an illicit server was involved, the illicit server was implanted due to lax physical security. As you plan and audit your firewall system, ensure that it is physically secured.

17. C. The OAKLEY protocol is responsible for generating the actual keys used in IPsec. The ISAKMP protocol helps negotiate the type of encryption between the two hosts beginning an IPsec connection. L2TP is not an IPsec protocol, although it is used to create VPN connections. The IPsecMon application is used in Windows 2000 systems to monitor security associations and other IPsec elements.

18. C. PKI-enabled systems use certificate repositories to house their certificates. These repositories can be on the local host or on remote systems. Make sure that you can identify the terminology used with PKI.

19. D. Even certificate authorities need someone to vouch for them. The certificate used to do so is in fact called a certificate authority certificate.

20. C. Whenever a person or host wants to participate in a PKI scheme, a registration authority must be involved. The registration authority is a trusted body that is able to verify the authenticity of the person, who must supply credentials concerning identity.

Chapter 7

Detecting and Distracting Hackers

THE CIW EXAM OBJECTIVE GROUPS COVERED IN THIS CHAPTER:

- ✓ Plan a firewall system that incorporates multiple levels of protection, including but not limited to: firewall system design, proactive detection, setting traps, security breach response, security alerting organizations.

- ✓ Identify penetration and control strategies and methods, including but not limited to: potential attacks, router security, threat containment, intrusion detection.

Despite the sophistication of your firewall equipment and security techniques, it is very likely that your network's security will be scanned and tested, and a compromise might occur. Whether the intrusion comes from a determined hacker, a careless employee, or someone bent on industrial espionage or a good time, you should prepare for a security threat. This chapter will show you specific ways to detect, distract, and even punish hacker activity. It will also discuss some of the steps that the CIW Security Professional exam expects you to take when a break-in occurs.

Proactive Detection

Proactive-detection techniques are often the only way to repel potential hackers. An effective detection policy always includes auditing, but you must also make it as easy as possible for your system to detect problems and present solutions automatically.

> Hacking activity tends to increase at night (between 7:00 P.M. and 6:00 A.M.). Most of the time, systems administrators and security professionals are not present to counter this increased threat. Consider these times when you're configuring the proactive-detection tools. If you enhance your proactive-scanning activities during these times, you might improve your chances of stopping or containing a security breach. Your scans will also be less inclined to interfere with standard activity created by company employees.

In Chapter 15, you will learn how to impose intrusion detection, which is arguably the most powerful form of proactive detection. For now, let's look at specific ways that you can remain proactive in the face of subtle, repeated attacks.

Automated Security Scans

Automated security scans are important, because your systems are especially tempting targets during off hours. Consider using such programs as the Windows 2000 Task Scheduler or the cron daemon in Linux (if you have not already disabled them) to execute applications. You should run such a program during off hours, when the traffic load is light, so that you can detect hackers and avoid inconveniencing users.

> **NOTE** If your company's activity level does not drop at night, find another time when the network is not as busy. As with other methods, be flexible when implementing your security scans.

Alternatively, you can use batch scripts to log current connections and resources in use, or to perform numerous other security tasks. Again, you should run a batch script after hours, or you can execute the script on the target machine from an internal machine running the scheduler service. Either way, it is another technique in your arsenal to fight system intruders.

> **TIP** You can save time by having an automated log check specific items within a system, thereby directing your security techniques. Event logs are especially useful if you are suspicious of certain system activity. They can yield more pertinent information than poring over several pages of detailed logs.

Login Scripts

You can use a *login script* for several purposes. Normally, a login script is used to customize a user's environment when he or she logs on. The script is executed upon a successful logon. You can also use login scripts to enhance your network's security. As you know, most hackers ultimately will try to obtain privileged user access to a system by compromising the Unix root account and/or the Windows 2000 administrator account. Security administrators can modify the login scripts executed by these accounts to activate various auditing features. For example, you could create a login script to be executed when the root account logs on; such a script would record the hostname and IP address of the system that is attempting to log on. You could then compare this information to previously recorded information to identify any suspicious logon attempts using the root account.

Using login scripts in this way is not limited to only the privileged accounts. Hackers will not usually attempt to access a privileged account directly for fear that they might trigger alarms. Consider using login scripts with the *system accounts* used by services and daemons. Normally, these accounts are not used to log on as typical user accounts, but to authenticate the daemons and services with the operating system. You should be concerned when one of these system accounts is used for logging on. The login scripts associated with these accounts can run paging applications that alert the security administrators as soon as the account is used in a logon attempt.

Login scripts can be used in almost unlimited ways. A login script can use anything that can be issued from a command line or executed from within a script. Using login scripts is also a very inexpensive solution because they are a feature of nearly every type of server operating system.

Personal Firewalls

A *personal firewall* is a software agent that resides on a network host. Usually, personal firewalls are placed onto employee workstations, and not onto network servers or actual firewalls. They can help block connections, as well as ensure that certain viruses and Trojans cannot be loaded onto the system. They are an important operating system add-on that can do the following:

- Log all attempted network connections and port openings.

- Block access of system elements to e-mail viruses. Many operating systems, such as those created by Microsoft, contain legitimate operating system elements that make it easier for end users to manage information. However, these elements can also be used by a hacker to have the system automatically e-mail the virus to another computer. Personal firewall software can block such connections.

- Send alert messages to a system or network administrator.

Many personal firewalls are available, including the Zone Labs ZoneAlarm product at www.zonelabs.com, and Network ICE's BlackICE personal firewall (www.networkice.com).

Automated Audit Analysis

You should always enable auditing on your servers. Auditing enhances the default log entries provided by many operating systems, such as Windows NT/2000 servers. Log files provide you with useful information to help prevent security break-ins.

One of the challenges of logging is deciding exactly what to log. In general, two types of information can be logged: successful and unsuccessful actions. You can also monitor information at a variety of locations, such as at the router or with a specific application service. When determining what to log, you should err on the side of logging too much rather than too little.

Scan log files on a regular basis. The amount of information in them is often overwhelming, but you can write scripts that will scan your network and automatically analyze activity and parse logs so that you receive only relevant information. Such automation frees up your time, reduces administrative costs, and enhances security. If you have an area of special concern, you can use a script to search for specific patterns in the logs.

It is important to understand that auditing applications are not foolproof. They are subject to two major problems: false positives and false negatives. A *false positive* occurs when the auditing application reports a problem where none exists. False positives can spell trouble for two reasons:

- They distract you and cause you to spend time on problems that do not, in fact, exist.
- They can cause log files to grow too large and can affect system performance.

False positives occur for many reasons. The chief reason is the fact that it is easy for an application to mistake various text strings and commands as being threatening. As sophisticated as applications have become, they still have difficulty differentiating benign commands from those that are threatening.

A *false negative*, on the other hand, occurs when the logging or auditing application does not report a problem, even though you are sure that one exists. False negatives occur for many reasons. For example, you may not have configured your logging application to search for the correct event. Even if you are using a scanning program, you may be using an older auditing application that needs to be updated to find the latest problems. Also, firewalls can drop connections, causing certain scanners to fail to report a host that has experienced a problem.

False positives and false negatives can occur in various applications and daemons, including antivirus applications, firewalls, and intrusion-detection applications. Chapter 13 will discuss false positives and false negatives in intrusion detection.

Distracting the Hacker

Besides simply identifying hacker activity, there are many ways to distract hackers. One reason to do this is to keep them on the network long enough for you to trace them. For instance, you can set a firewall rule so that the source IP address directs the hacker to a dummy system. Many large companies have created an entire system within their network full of disinformation meant to preoccupy hackers and keep them online until they can be caught.

From fictional accounts to dummy files, tripwires, and jails, if your company has the resources and incentive, you should carefully consider these techniques. Using these methods is not without risk, however, and many companies choose to simply end the connection.

First, let's take a look at providing the hacker with bogus information.

Dummy Accounts

By now, you know that system defaults are one of a hacker's first targets. However, you can use system defaults against hackers by creating *dummy accounts*, which are false accounts that look real but that have alarming mechanisms attached to them.

For instance, the Windows 2000 administrator account is called *administrator*. Windows NT and Windows 2000 allow you to rename the administrator account. You can then go one step further by creating a new account called administrator and giving it no access to your system while simultaneously setting heavy auditing and alarms. For instance, you could use the account's login script to alert you when an attempt to log on occurs.

It is possible, for example, to create a second root-level account and then alter some of the original root account's access permissions. For example, you can deny the root account a login shell by replacing its standard shell (e.g., `/bing/bash`) with `/dev/null` or `/bin/false`. This way, hacker applications that search for a root account by default may not be successful when attacking your system. You are not limited to creating dummy accounts, however.

Dummy Files

You can create intentionally misleading files to either misinform an information seeker or simply distract a thrill seeker. These are called *dummy files*. You can use dummy files to supply false financial spreadsheets, as well as other files, to a corporate spy. You are limited only by your imagination.

Once you have created the dummy files, you should take additional measures to provide better security. For example, you could create a Microsoft Excel file called `salaries.xls` and place the file on a server that would be a potential target. An additional security measure may be to configure an alarm whenever that file is accessed.

Dummy Password Files

One way to use a dummy file is to create a false password file. In this file, you supply false names and passwords, making sure that they are plausible, but of course not in use. A false password file can significantly distract the hacker.

It is also important to document your system's original state, as well as configure alerts. Next, we'll take a look at how you can determine whether a system has changed its state, as well as how to create a login script that alerts you about attacks on your system.

Checksums and Tripwires

Hackers often break into a computer to plant a Trojan or illicit server. The hacker hopes that the file will eventually be executed either automatically or when the system is restarted. A very common hacker technique is to create a Trojan with the same name as a frequently used operating system file. The hacker then breaks into a server and replaces the original operating system file with the Trojan.

To thwart such attacks, consider signing your files to verify system state. You might need to analyze the size of key operating programs to ensure that a hacker has not tampered with them. Several programs, such as MD5SUM and Tripwire (found in Linux and other Unix flavors), will automatically scan files and generate information. The information they generate will include a *time stamp*, which indicates when the file was last read or altered. MD5SUM can create hash signatures, whereas the *Tripwire* application creates detailed reports on changes that it discovers. MD5SUM and Tripwire can then provide dates and exact times of the change. Whenever such applications conduct these scans to create signatures or time stamps, they are said to be conducting a *checksum analysis*. A checksum analysis is helpful in determining a system's state.

> **NOTE** Like the CIW Security Professional exam, this chapter uses the word *tripwire* in a generic sense. The Tripwire application, discussed in the section "Tripwire Concerns," is actually a specific example of the tripwire concept.

When checking a system's state, you compare the results of a current checksum analysis against a previous analysis. If a file has been modified or the time stamps and size do not match, you know that the file has probably been replaced with a Trojan. If you find a Trojan or virus, immediately replace it with a known good file and determine where the hacker broke into your system to place the Trojan.

Tripwires

A *tripwire* is simply an alerting tool. A tripwire in network security is based on the tripwire concept used in military applications. The idea behind a tripwire is that when a potential hacker attacks a system, he or she will either fall into a trap that you have placed or leave behind unequivocal evidence of tampering.

A tripwire can do a variety of things, such as documenting the server's original state and then storing it in a database. The tripwire application can then inform you of any change that has occurred. Alternatively, a tripwire can consist of a simple alert, such as an e-mail or a Windows pop-up message, or it can be configured to send a message to a pager. You can create more sophisticated tripwires that automatically drop the offending connection. Once again, when creating and deploying tripwires you are limited only by your skill and imagination.

Tripwire Concerns

Take great care when placing tripwires. They must not be accidentally activated by an internal user or by another network administrator, or a false alarm will result, especially when logon tripwires are used.

Also, remember that hackers can manipulate tripwire scripts and applications. For example, consider the Linux application Tripwire, which is designed to inform you when a directory or file has been altered or removed. Once the Tripwire application becomes operational, it creates a database of system files. When files are then altered, Tripwire will notice these changes and alert you. However, if the Tripwire database has been eliminated or altered, subsequent scans will not detect any problems. Therefore, consider using read-only drives and media to store sensitive databases and files.

The following exercise will demonstrate how to send a network message to a host in the case of an unauthorized login attempt. In essence, this script establishes a "tripwire" that alerts the systems administrator.

EXERCISE 7.1

Setting a Logon Tripwire Script in Windows 2000

This exercise assumes that the network security policy would stipulate that no one ever use the administrator account interactively. Instead, systems administrators should use the training account because the steps below create a tripwire for the administrator account that alerts a designated host every time an interactive logon occurs.

1. Create a new user named `training` and make it a member of the Administrators group. Make the password `Tr$ining1`. This will be your new administrator account.

2. Create a new text file with the following lines:

    ```
    @echo off
    net send DESTINATION_SYSTEM_NAME
    ↳"Break-in in progress!"
    ```

    Note: In place of *DESTINATION_SYSTEM_NAME*, enter the name of the system to which you want this message to be sent.

3. Save the file as `script.bat` in the `C:\winnt\system32\repl\import\scripts` directory. Create and share this directory, if necessary.

EXERCISE 7.1 *(continued)*

4. Open the Local Users and Groups utility in the Computer Management snap-in.

5. Double-click the Administrator account.

6. Select the Profile tab.

7. Add `script.bat` as the Logon Script Name, as shown here:

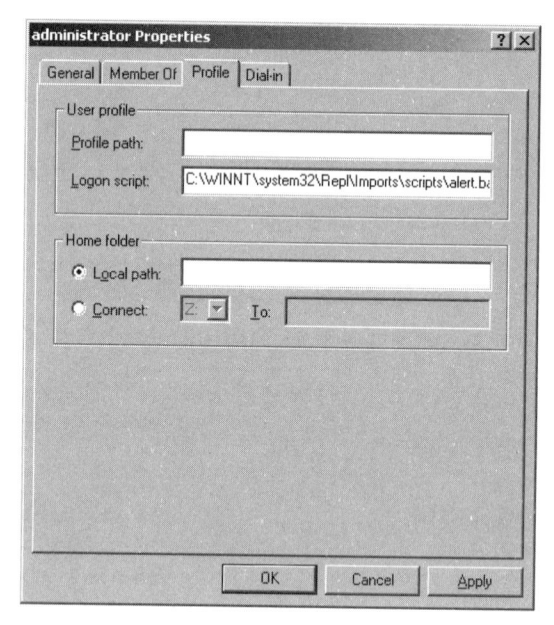

8. Save all of your changes, then log off and back on interactively as `Administrator`. An alert message will be displayed on the computer you designated in Step 2.

Jails

A *jail* is a separate system you can create to delay or distract a hacker. A jail, also known as a *honey pot*, looks just like a series of actual network hosts, when in fact it is a series of tripwires designed to issue alerts to the systems administrator. A jail is usually a single *sacrificial system* that appears to be several network hosts. Jails commonly supply deliberately inaccurate information that allows an administrator time to detect and catch the hacker.

Jails can be a dangerous way to contain hacker activity, mainly because of the potential for a hacker to "break out" of your jail and into your real system. Also, if you plan to use jails, make sure that your security policy allows them. Systems administrators have sometimes created a jail, only to learn later that their company forbids such activity. The decision to create a jail or other such device should be made by managers who fully understand the benefits and drawbacks of such techniques.

A jail might be advisable for several reasons, especially if the network is particularly large. A determined hacker is going to relay through several sites before penetrating your system. To locate a hacker's origin, you usually need to obtain packet traces and physical-line traces. Both will track the hacker to his or her source.

Packet and Physical-Line Tracing

A *packet trace* is the activity of learning where a packet of information has come from. Because any information sent across the Internet has probably passed between at least five or six computers, it is often necessary to learn the route by which that information came. Packet traces can occur in real time, in which case the hacker must remain online. It is also possible to conduct a packet trace by reading log files. In this case, you can conduct a *forensic analysis* on the log files either during or after the attack. A forensic analysis of a log file can include the following:

- Determining the source IP and port of the attacking host
- Identifying various hosts that the attacker spoofed during the attack
- Classifying the attack type
- Determining if this is a known attack or a new one

NOTE Make sure that you conduct a forensic analysis at the correct time; if you have good log files, you do not necessarily need to analyze them during an attack. Your time may be better spent warning other systems administrators and finding ways to actively respond to the attack.

A forensic analysis also includes reviewing the file system of the machine that has been attacked. For example, it is possible to use tools such as the Forensic Toolkit (http://packetstorm.linuxsecurity.com) to analyze the hard drive of a Windows system. It is also possible to undelete (i.e., "resurrect") files. In Unix systems, the Coroner's Toolkit (www.porcupine.org/forensics/) is capable of resurrecting files using its "lazarus" tool. Many times, you will simply want to recover deleted data because it is important to your business. At other times, however, you will want to recover deleted data because it can help you discover an attacker's methods. If you are lucky, you may be able to find the person who attacked your system.

A *physical-line trace* is an attempt to determine the port or telephone line a hacker has used. To accomplish this type of tracking, you must keep the hacker online. Talented hackers use a system for only a few minutes at a time, even when they are gaining control of it. In fact, most hackers usually work with several systems at a time, going back and forth between them. This practice makes hacker activity seem intermittent, and therefore non-threatening. The result is that it is quite difficult to detect even the most malicious activity until it is too late.

A good hacker, like a good administrator, is paranoid. Sometimes, the only way to catch a hacker is to take a proactive stance. Such proactive methods may include making the hacker stumble across a tripwire.

Punishing the Hacker

Often, simply cutting off a hacker is insufficient, because he or she will return. The difference between punishing hackers and distracting them is that punishing hackers extends past catching them; it drops the connection (sometimes permanently), or ensures that the hacker will be contained.

Methods

When detecting and deterring a hacker, you are limited only by your knowledge of available resources and your understanding of your network. The following methods are available:

Log traffic and send e-mail messages. Check your system logs and determine the origin of the attack. You can also try to trace an existing connection by using a *port listener*. A port listener is able to log connections and, in some cases, drop them. A port listener can even add the names of hosts to a database. Once a host is entered into this database, it will not be allowed to connect to this system. If you are reasonably sure that your logs' connection trace has given you the true identity of an attacker, you can then send the systems administrator or ISP an e-mail message requesting an explanation.

> **NOTE** A port listener is much like a personal firewall. However, many port listeners are especially designed to be deployed on firewalls and production network servers. A personal firewall is mostly meant for use on client workstations.

Conduct reverse scans. If you can identify an attacker, consider scanning the system to learn more about the origin of the attack. This is known as a *reverse scan*. Reverse scans will not prove useful if the attacker has spoofed an IP address. Still, if you spend enough time studying the log files and obtaining information from any system that appears to be a source, you may be successful. Understand, however, that conducting a reverse scan is a highly controversial practice. Consider reverse scans only if you have been given specific permission to do so, and if conducting the scan can actually provide you with any helpful information. Even then, keep in mind that scanning is viewed as an attack and that your reverse scan may be construed as an attack by your ISP or by law enforcement.

> **NOTE** It might be somewhat comforting to note that most of the devastating denial-of-service e-mail attacks waged in the past few years were rather easily traced.

Drop the connection. You can configure your system to automatically drop the connection. You can also enter the host's IP address into a database so that the host cannot connect to your system again in any way.

Tools

Many security tools are available for responding to hackers. Responses range from notifying the administrators to hardening the firewall so that it closes the connection. As shown in Table 7.1, security tools at your disposal range from simple packet sniffers to personal firewall applications and individual applications.

TABLE 7.1 Tools for Responding to Attacks

Tool	Description
Sniffers	Sniffers include Sniffer Basic (www.networkassociates.com), tcpdump (www.tcpdump.org), and Ethereal (www.ethereal.com).
Personal firewalls	Tools such as ZoneAlarm (www.zonelabs.com) and BlackICE (www.networkice.com) can detect and respond to attacks on Windows systems.

TABLE 7.1 Tools for Responding to Attacks *(continued)*

Tool	Description
The route command	The route command is generally used to configure a Linux system's routing tables. However, it can also be used to drop connections.
ipchains/ iptables	Both of these commands allow you to create entries that will permanently drop all connections from a host.
PortSentry	This tool can identify port scan attacks and take several actions, including automatically dropping all connections to a system. You can learn more about PortSentry at www.psionic.com/abacus/portsentry.
Port Scan Attack Detector (PSAD)	A tool similar to PortSentry, PSAD is designed to work more closely with ipchains and iptables. For more information, go to www.cipherdyne.com/psad.

> **TIP** When implementing security tools, do not automatically assume that your network is protected. Often, security tools are created based on current hacker techniques and tools. Hackers are constantly updating their tools and techniques to penetrate systems. Your security tools might not detect or respond to a new hacker tool.

You can find additional tools at the following locations:

www.packetstormsecurity.com   A site devoted to both white hat and black hat hackers. A faster mirror of this site is at packetstorm.linuxsecurity.com.

www.sourceforge.net   Although not a site devoted specifically to security, it contains many valuable security tools.

Problems with Retaliation

Carefully consider the use of *retaliatory measures*. A retaliatory measure is any response that involves connecting to the hacker's system. Thus, a reverse port scan would count as a retaliatory measure. You can also use the `iptables`, `ipchains`, or `route` commands to drop connections. Although they will stop many hackers, such strategies could also lead to negative consequences for your company. Remember, hackers often spoof IP addresses, so you might end up retaliating against the wrong host.

Also, a hacker can spoof IP addresses that are important to the proper function of your network. For example, consider what would happen if you use the `iptables` command to automatically block all scanning hosts, and a hacker spoofs your own DNS servers or the IP addresses of legitimate customers. Also, some hackers might interpret your measures as an insult or a challenge, thus increasing their resolve to compromise your network. In such cases, retaliatory measures can cause more problems than they solve.

Suppose, now, that you actually detect a break-in. In the next section, you will learn more about what the creators of the CIW Security Professional exam feel are necessary steps to take.

Creating an Attack-Response Plan

When a security breach does occur, you need a strategy to deal with the hacker. You should have a well-planned policy that explains how and when to report a problem, and it should also detail the proper organizations and people to inform.

Consider the steps described in this section and then customize them to conform to your own situation. You must write down these steps, because they will form your *response policy*, a simple but effective document that explains the proper steps to take. Keep this policy in view of all IT professionals at all times. See the section "Execute the Response Policy" for more information.

Decide Ahead of Time

You need to make policy decisions well before a crisis happens. Research has repeatedly proven that people in crisis situations make poor decisions unless a clearly defined policy exists. For example, your policy could stipulate that systems administrators should contact the president of operations before contacting law enforcement. Such requirements will help everyone make sound decisions without embarrassing the company and creating unnecessary attention.

For example, in 1995, workers at AT&T discovered that hackers had penetrated its network. The systems administrators, trying to solve the problem, decided to create an electronic jail. Although this action seemed prudent to help the company locate the perpetrators, the administrators were reprimanded because management deemed that their solution had endangered the company's network.

The confusion at AT&T was the result of miscommunication between management and the systems administrators. This confusion could have been avoided if everyone had known and followed the same written plan. Acting prudently is easy if you have a well-organized, written policy to follow.

When considering what to do if a hacker attacks your network, decide what steps you will take and then record those decisions. Itemize a detailed list of procedures, and include it in your written policy. Then, make sure all concerned employees have a copy. Your security plan should stipulate when to end a hacker's session and when to keep the hacker busy.

Do Not Panic

It is easy to tell someone not to panic during an emergency or a security breach, but actually remaining calm at such a time is difficult. However, with a prewritten policy, your plan of action will be mapped out for you, allowing you to think clearly and respond more efficiently.

> It might be a good idea to create a detailed list of steps and place the list in an obvious place. When an attack occurs, all the systems administrator has to do is follow the list, which will be in plain view.

Document Everything

System and server logs are, of course, essential to documentation. Auditing logs are often proof that a hacker has infiltrated the system. However, if a security breach occurs, you should also document the responding moves that you make. Audit logs are only half of what you need.

Create an Attack Report

An example of a detailed *attack report* account might look something like this: "On September 13, 2001, at 8:00 A.M. Pacific Standard Time,

I noticed that certain administrative permissions had been reset by account ty2, which was still active. I then called my supervisor, Bill Evans, who ordered me to conduct a trace route, which I did at 8:10. As I was waiting for the program to finish, I also began looking through the auditing logs." Your plan should indicate which systems were affected, where the hacker entered (if possible), and any peculiar or interesting moves the hacker made.

If you are careful to record your own activities, as well as what you can learn about the hacker's, your chances of avoiding further problems improve significantly.

> An accurate attack report helps you retrace the steps you took in response to an attack. It also helps you fix damaged systems, changed permissions, and so forth.

Assess the Situation

Determine whether an actual security breach has occurred. Often, the activities of an inept user can resemble hacker activity. The suspicious activity might have been the work of someone with administrative access.

Even the best policy can fail if you make a hasty conclusion and begin the incident-response process. However, once you have identified a problem, you should be vigilant and thorough.

Determine the Scope of the Breach

Once you have confirmed that a hacker has entered your system, analyze the situation. Your first task in the determination process is to find out if the hacker is at Stage 1 (discovery), Stage 2 (penetration), or Stage 3 (control). Other steps to take include:

- Determining the accounts affected
- Identifying which files have been read, altered, or substituted
- Tracing the hacker's activities in your system
- Consulting audit logs
- Determining whether any permissions have been reset

A security group or department should determine the scope of the damage to your system. During this activity, systems administrators should stop all their activities because even routine activity will generally destroy evidence that the hacker has left behind. If the hacker has erased files, for instance, administrators can reclaim them only if the space on the hard drive has not been rewritten. Normal activity will rewrite the hard drive space, thereby causing the files to be lost forever.

Stop or Contain Activity

In the same way that a hacker penetrates a system and attempts control, the next step you should take to defeat a hacker involves *containing activity*. You should either break the link or contain the activity, as directed by your security policy. Just remember that containment is often dangerous. In spite of a sound policy, such decisions still depend on the situation.

The previous steps are universal to most organizations. Stopping and containing activity, as well as executing a response plan, should be determined solely by your organization's policy and the nature of the security breach.

Execute the Response Policy

You must have a response policy. Most of the time, responding is a matter of doing what your policy says. Such steps include:

- Notifying management
- Breaking the link or creating a jail
- Calling law enforcement
- Contacting the hacker
- Conducting trace routes and other activities to further map the hacker's activity
- Reconfiguring the firewall

Notify Affected Individuals

If a hacker has compromised a legitimate user account, you will probably need to direct that user to change his or her password. In addition, you must thoroughly check the files on that computer to see whether anyone has tampered with them.

Notify the Service Provider

Three reasons exist for notifying your Internet service provider (ISP):

- The Internet is composed of many different backbone network switches and routers. This equipment provides basic connectivity between large networks run by ISPs. ISPs have access to these backbone routers and switches. This access can enable them to block and allow traffic to and from various networks. You can have the ISP terminate the connection so that the attack can be stopped.

- The ISP can help you trace the attack, because it can access backbone Internet network equipment.

- In many cases, insurance companies and law firms have decided that all parties must be informed of an attack. An ISP is designed to service many different organizations and companies. Although an attack might appear to be against you only, it might still affect other parties. If you keep this attack secret, and the attack is affecting others, you might be liable for their damages, unless you make a good-faith effort to inform all affected parties.

In the case of several denial-of-service attacks waged against Yahoo!, Microsoft, and Amazon in early February 2000, the most effective course of action was to reconfigure routers so that traffic could not be passed to the victim hosts. Once Yahoo!, Microsoft, and the other companies reconfigured their routers, they were able to at least partially mitigate the attack since ICMP packets were not passed on. Some of these companies had to contact their ISP to solve this problem, because the ISP was able to stop the ICMP traffic from addressing their firewalls.

If possible, consider notifying the ISP of the person or group you believe has executed the attack.

Notify CERT

The Computer Emergency Response Team (CERT) receives thousands of e-mail messages and hotline calls every year. CERT is widely respected, and it has been issuing security alerts longer than any other agency. CERT staff investigates many of these reports and then issues alerts. If you suspect that a hacker has broken into your system, confirm that the attack has actually occurred, then take steps to react to the connection, as defined by your security policy. Once the activity is contained, you should notify CERT immediately. Explain the nature of the break-in, including the type of operating system, the service attacked, and the results of the attack. You do not have to reveal sensitive information about your server or network, but if you supply useful information, CERT can use it to provide help to others. CERT's service is not mandatory. However, taking time to supply information helps strengthen the security community.

> **TIP** CERT has been criticized for being rather slow to issue alerts. To remain current about attacks, work closely with other systems administrators and join lists such as those supplied by CERT, as well as the list at www.ntbugtraq.com.

Reconfigure the network

You may have to alter network settings to make sure that the attack never happens again. You can, for example, install personal firewall software, or reconfigure the network firewall to ensure that the attack cannot be waged as easily.

Analyze and Learn

The final and, in many ways most important, step in the response process is to learn from the incident. To best analyze your response, ask the following questions of everyone involved:

- How did the hacker(s) bypass the security? By compromising an employee? Through social engineering? By using a brute-force attack? By modifying the routing tables? Through an inadequate firewall? Ask specific questions and write down the answers.

- What were the strengths of the actual response effort? What could have been improved? What should be done differently in the future?

- What is it about the network security policy that could have caused an employee to try and defeat it? You have already learned that a security breach can occur because the policy requires too much of end users, or because it fails to take their jobs into account. You might have to reconsider your security policy, or even reconfigure your network to accommodate user and management needs. Whenever you decide to reevaluate your network's configuration, always conduct a needs analysis and carefully study the ramifications of any change.

- Finally, record the specific lessons you have learned, and then update or modify your security policy and implementation, taking into account what you have learned from your experience.

> **Security Mailing Lists**
>
> Many organizations exist that can help you remain informed about common attacks. Follow these steps to subscribe to respected security mailing lists.
>
> 1. Browse to the CERT web page at www.cert.org and subscribe to the mailing list. Notice also that CERT provides an alerting service.
>
> 2. Go to www.ntbugtraq.com. This site has gained much respect because it provides quick, unbiased information about the security problems faced by Microsoft Windows applications. Subscribe to the ntbugtraq mailing list by selecting the appropriate links.
>
> 3. Go to www.securityfocus.com. Subscribe to the newsletter by clicking on the appropriate links. While at this site, note that several non-English language security sites are available.
>
> 4. Observe the contents of the packetstorm.linuxsecurity.com link. Although it does not provide a monthly newsletter or messaging service, this site nevertheless contains useful information about some of the latest attacks and security tools.
>
> 5. Visit the following sites specific to the U.S. government:
>
>   - The Computer Incident Advisory Capability home page (www.ciac.org/ciac)
>
>   - The Center for Internet Security (www.cisecurity.org/home.html)

> - The National Infrastructure Protection Center (www.nipc.gov)
> - The National Security Agency (www.nsa.gov)
>
> Although these sites are specific to the United States, they can still provide important information about worldwide security incidents. As far as the CIW Security Professional exam is concerned, you may want to spend most of your time at the CERT web page.

Summary

A hacker's best friend is a security staff that thinks its job was finished when protective services and programs were installed. Proactive security detection in the form of scripts and automated programs can help busy systems administrators. Find ways to protect your system, which may involve detecting, distracting, and even punishing hackers.

In many ways, responding to an incident is as important as implementing sound hardware and software security. Unless you itemize proper solutions and follow them exactly, you might panic and become further victimized by a hacker. In this chapter, you learned how to respond appropriately to hacker activity. You also learned about the necessity of keeping accurate, written accounts of all activity, when breaking a hacker's connection might be appropriate, and what to learn from hacker activity.

Now that you have completed this chapter, you should be able to:

- Customize your network to manage hacker activity.
- Implement proactive detection.
- Distract hackers and contain their activity.
- Set traps and deploy various types of tripwires.
- Identify steps to take when responding to a security breach.

In the next chapter, you will learn more about operating system security. Specifically, you will learn how Windows and Linux systems authenticate users. The chapter also discusses specific ways to secure Windows 2000 and Linux systems from attacks.

Exam Essentials

Know examples of proactive detection.   Proactive detection can include conducting automated security scans, using login and batch scripts, and running checksum analysis programs. Proactive detection means that you find ways to identify problems before they occur. If you are able to configure simple tripwire scripts, as well as more sophisticated checksum analysis applications such as Tripwire, you will be able to identify break-ins easily.

Know the importance of jails and honey pots.   Jails and honey pots distract a hacker while they alert you to his or her presence. It is possible to create false account entries, as well as configure applications that make a single sacrificial system appear to be an entire network. As a hacker attacks these supposed network resources, you can begin to trace the attacker.

Be able to differentiate between packet and physical-line traces.   As you conduct traces, you either read log entries or attempt to trace the physical connection. If you engage in physical-line traces, you have to ensure that the hacker is still physically connected. Many times, you do not have this luxury, which means you have to conduct a forensic analysis using log files.

Understand issues involved in punishing hacker activity.   It might be tempting to punish a hacker who has entered your system. You can, for example, conduct a denial-of-service attack against the hacker. Doing so, however, might not be the best option. For example, if the hacker has spoofed all of the connections, you could be attacking the wrong person. More important, punishing a hacker can very easily turn you into a hacker. It would be quite embarrassing if you were terminated for breaking your company's security policy because you engaged in hacker activity. You could become subject to civil action, as well.

Know the steps to take when reacting to an attack.   Outlining the steps to take in case of an attack, and then publishing the steps so that everyone knows what to do, is critical. Although it is sometimes easy to panic in the face of an attack, if you provide enough training and information to your employees, you can help ensure that they will make good decisions.

Be able to explain the function of the Linux Tripwire application. The CIW Security Professional exam uses the word *tripwire* to describe any tool that helps detect hacker activity. However, it will also refer to the Tripwire application, found at `www.tripwire.org`. Make sure that you are familiar with how that application works. You must, for example, run an initial scan to determine a system's original state. It is important, therefore, to run Tripwire on a system when it is in its optimal, original state. Then, if any changes occur, you can begin to investigate the nature of the change.

Key Terms

Before you take the exam, be certain you are familiar with the following terms:

- attack report
- checksum analysis
- dummy accounts
- dummy files
- forensic analysis
- honey pot
- jail
- login script
- packet trace
- personal firewall
- physical-line trace
- port listener
- proactive detection
- response policy
- retaliatory measures
- reverse scan
- sacrificial system
- system accounts
- time stamp
- tripwire

Review Questions

1. When a security breach has occurred, what is the first task for a security administrator?

   A. Trap the hacker and punish him or her if at all possible, using industry-standard tools.

   B. Determine how many systems the hacker has attacked and whether the connection is still active.

   C. Notify corporate management and, if possible, law enforcement authorities.

   D. Execute the predetermined response plan, including breaking the link, creating a jail, or notifying authorities.

2. What security tool helps you prove that a hacker has infiltrated your network, enables you to fix problems in your security system, and helps you retrace your own steps after a crisis?

   A. System logs

   B. Network jails

   C. File tripwires

   D. Dummy accounts

3. After a security breach or attack has been detected, why is it sometimes a good idea to stop all system activity (including normal usage)?

   A. Because the presumed attack could actually be the result of inept user activity.

   B. Because continued activity on the network can destroy evidence that the hacker has left behind.

   C. Because the attack might have been waged by company employees.

   D. Because executive management should be on hand to lead and coordinate the recovery effort.

4. What can a security administrator create to mislead or disinform hackers?

   A. A checksum

   B. A tripwire

   C. A packet-filtering rule

   D. A dummy file

5. Joel has detected a distributed denial-of-service attack against his web servers. Following his security policy, he has notified management and taken his servers offline. He has also contacted his ISP about the attack. Why is it important for Joel to notify his ISP?

   A. It helps him reduce traffic.

   B. It enables other companies to trace attacks to his servers.

   C. The ISP can help Joel trace the attack.

   D. The ISP can bill him for the attack.

6. What can you use to locate a hacker's origin?

   A. A packet trace or physical-line trace

   B. A tripwire or checksum

   C. A dummy file

   D. A jail

7. Aaron has been asked to ensure that all attempted network connections to end-user workstations are logged. He has decided to install an agent on each of the workstations. What is the name for the type of agent Aaron is installing?

   A. An SNMP agent

   B. A network scanner

   C. An antivirus application

   D. A personal firewall

8. Ruth has decided that she needs to read through her system logs and trace some connections that have occurred in the past. She has obtained log files from her ISP that she feels are relevant to several attacks that have occurred on her server. What is one name for what Ruth is doing?

   A. A logical line trace

   B. A physical-line trace

   C. Forensic analysis

   D. Proactive detection

9. Cindy has just edited the /etc/tripwire/twpol.txt file to ensure that her critical operating system files are protected. Which of the following does the Linux Tripwire application enable?

   A. Personal firewall

   B. Packet tracing

   C. Physical-line tracing

   D. Checksum analysis

10. Which of the following controversial activities can be used to punish a hacker yet result in the least amount of damage or impact to the hacker's system?

    A. Reverse scanning

    B. Ping flood

    C. SYN flood

    D. Distributed denial-of-service attack

11. Rick has used his Linux firewall to drop a suspicious connection. Which of the following tools could he have used to drop the connection?

    A. lsof

    B. tcpdump

    C. A personal firewall

    D. iptables

12. Someone has attacked Randy's FTP server. Randy has followed his security policy and informed management and other related parties. He has also conducted a forensic analysis, and he has brought the FTP server offline to ensure that normal end-user activity does not erase important information. What is the final step that Randy should take after he has recovered from this attack?

    A. Document the attack to ensure all information is recorded.

    B. Determine the effectiveness of the response.

    C. Reconfigure the firewall to ensure the attack will not occur again.

    D. Install a personal firewall on the FTP server.

13. Which of the following contains information summarizing a security event?

    A. A packet trace

    B. A physical-line trace

    C. An attack report

    D. A log entry

14. Mia has decided that she needs to install an agent onto her web server to detect and, if possible, block attacks. What type of agent should she install?

    A. SNMP

    B. Port listener

    C. Personal firewall

    D. Logging

15. Mia has just noticed that an attack is in progress. What should she do first?

    A. Consult the security policy.

    B. Create a honey pot.

    C. Create a tripwire.

    D. Contact the manager of the IT department.

16. Which of the following strategies can help thwart a hacker who is attacking the network from an internal host?

    A. Contacting the hacker

    B. Reconfiguring the firewall

    C. Encrypting transmissions

    D. Creating an attack report

17. You have discovered that an employee has attached a modem to his telephone line and workstation. He has used this modem to dial in to his workstation, thereby bypassing your firewall. A security breach has occurred as a direct result of this activity. The employee explains that he used the modem because he had to download software for a department project. What can you do to solve this problem?

    A. Reconfigure the firewall.

    B. Conduct a needs analysis.

    C. Block all modem use.

    D. Enforce your security policy.

18. Which of the following most consistently specifies the need to drop a connection if it is deemed suspicious?

    A. The security policy

    B. The security manager

    C. A network scanner

    D. The IT manager

19. Glen has renamed the default administrative account on his database server. What does this single action enable on his server?

    A. A tripwire

    B. A checksum

    C. A honey pot

    D. Punishment

20. Glen has just enabled auditing for all "in" boxes (e.g., drop directories that contain incoming e-mail) on his e-mail server. What must he do now in order to properly audit his server?

    A. Nothing. Auditing is enabled.

    B. Review log files.

    C. Enable NTFS.

    D. Audit the operating system files instead.

Answers to Review Questions

1. **D.** Even during an attack, the security policy remains the most important tool. It governs various actions, including your response, as well as management and/or law enforcement notification.

2. **A.** Never underestimate the importance of system logs. They can be used both during and after an attack. Logs can be used as proof that an attack has occurred, and they can also be used to identify host and network weaknesses.

3. **B.** Stopping activity on the server that has been hacked can help you stop the flow of information into the system's logs. This way, you can focus on the attack without being distracted by additional activity. Legitimate activity could erase evidence on the hard drive that is crucial to your forensic effort.

4. **D.** A dummy file is a simple example of a "honey pot." Honey pots are designed to fool the hacker into thinking that he or she has compromised a system and obtained valuable information, when in fact the hacker has found nothing and has instead tripped off alarms. A tripwire is part of a honey pot but in and of itself does not mislead or disinform hackers. Packet-filtering rules are part of firewall and perimeter security, whereas a checksum is a vital tool in creating tripwires.

5. **C.** Among other benefits, the ISP can help Joel trace the attack. Informing the ISP of the attack does not necessarily help him reduce traffic. The ISP would first have to block connections. Informing the ISP would not allow the ISP to bill Joel for the attack, because he did not initiate the attack. Because Joel is a victim of these attacks and did not initiate them, other companies would not be able to trace the attacks to his servers, either.

6. **A.** Packet traces and physical-line traces allow you to determine where a connection has originated. Because hackers might use IP spoofing, however, such traces can be time consuming and provide false information, at least at first.

7. **D.** A personal firewall is the generic term for an agent that allows you to log and even block network connections. Simple Network Management Protocol (SNMP) agents are not meant to provide security data,

such as login information. Rather, they collect network-based statistics and do not provide specific information about security break-ins. A network scanner is also not designed to provide login information, nor is an antivirus application.

8. C. Because Ruth is reading logs from packets, she is not doing real-time network analysis. A physical-line trace must take place before the connection is terminated. As far as security is concerned, the term "logical line trace" is not relevant. Also, because Ruth is reading these packets after an attack has occurred, she is not engaging in proactive-attack detection.

9. D. The Tripwire application creates signatures of each file that it has been configured to analyze. It then compares new signatures to existing signatures. If Tripwire identifies a difference in the signature, or checksum, it generates an alert.

10. A. Reverse scanning allows a host being attacked to automatically run a port scan against the attacking system. Such scans will generally not crash a system. Ping and SYN floods, as well as distributed denial-of-service attacks, can crash systems and clog existing bandwidth. Conducting a reverse scan can easily be construed as an attack, and is generally not a good idea unless you have specific jurisdiction for doing so.

11. D. The `iptables` command can be used to create a packet-filtering firewall, and Rick could have used `iptables` to drop the connection. The `lsof` command can be used in conjunction with `kill` to drop connections, but it cannot drop connections by itself. `tcpdump` is a network sniffer that, in and of itself, cannot drop a connection. Personal firewalls can do this, but they are not installed on a network firewall.

12. B. The final step for Randy to take should be to analyze the response to see if he could have taken any additional steps. Randy should take this step after he has altered the network to ensure that the attack never happens again. Administrators need to document an attack as soon as they become aware of it. Reconfiguring the firewall might be a step toward ensuring proactive detection, and personal firewall software should be installed only on employee workstations.

13. **C.** An attack report contains a detailed report on a security event. Packet and physical-line traces can supply information that you can include in the attack report. A log entry might contain information about an event, but it does not provide a summarized analysis.

14. **B.** A port listener is especially designed to be installed on production servers (e.g., web, FTP, and/or e-mail servers). SNMP agents are capable of collecting statistics, but they do not collect information about port scans. A personal firewall is designed to be installed on client workstations. Logging agents do exist, but generally they are capable only of collecting information about attacks and are not able to respond to them.

15. **A.** The first step to take is to consult the security policy. The security policy may then direct Mia to contact a systems administrator, create a tripwire or honey pot, or take another course of action.

16. **C.** Encrypting transmissions is the best choice for thwarting an attack. For example, many sniffing attacks are conducted by employees, and encrypting transmissions can help thwart such attacks. Contacting the hacker, reconfiguring a firewall, and creating an attack report are generally activities to pursue after an attack has occurred.

17. **B.** A needs analysis is the best choice here, because it helps determine what caused the employee to use a modem in the way described. If it is a legitimate reason, then you will have to modify some of your networking procedures to ensure employees can do their job. Reconfiguring the firewall would be premature, and useless because the modem completely bypasses the firewall. Blocking all modem use may not be the proper measure, especially if remote employees use modems to connect to the network legitimately. As far as enforcing your security policy is concerned, not enough information has been given about its contents, so enforcing it at this point would not be appropriate.

18. **A.** The security policy is the most consistent resource in directing behavior. As long as it has been read and understood, it will provide useful instructions and advice concerning what to do during a security breach. It is always the first resource to consult when you detect a suspicious connection.

19. C. Renaming the administrative account on the server allows you to create a honey pot. By itself, the account does not constitute a tripwire, because no login script has been assigned. The account is not a checksum, because it does not enable the systems or security administrator to verify the system's original state. The account is not a way to punish the hacker, because it does not conduct a reverse scan or drop the connection. The account is, basically, bait for the trap. Glen now must find a suitable trap to configure.

20. B. Auditing will do little good unless you regularly check your log files.

Chapter 8

Operating System Security

THE CIW EXAM OBJECTIVE GROUPS COVERED IN THIS CHAPTER:

- ✓ Identify key principles for securing an operating system, including but not limited to: industry evaluation criteria, Unix and Windows servers, security management, default settings.
- ✓ Identify the mechanisms, security parameters, and techniques necessary for securing Windows and Unix accounts.

Regardless of the particular daemon or service you want to use, it requires some sort of an operating system in order to run. The designers of the CIW Security Professional exam understand this concept. Thus, the exam assumes knowledge of Windows 2000 and Linux. It also assumes that a security professional understands that a problem with the underlying operating system can compromise the e-mail, web, or FTP daemon that is operating on top of it.

The key areas of vulnerability in any operating system are:

- Users and groups
- The file system
- The use of system defaults
- Uncorrected system bugs
- Improper or nonexistent auditing procedures

Default installations of almost any operating system are not configured for optimal security. Operating systems default to low security settings for two main reasons. First, most organizations generally have their own policies and procedures for configuring the operating system. Strict default security settings can cause these organizations too much trouble. Second, operating system manufacturers tend to assume that the person installing the operating system is aware of security principles. In this chapter, we will discuss issues specific to Windows 2000 and to the Linux operating system.

Windows 2000 Security Components

Below is a list of the Windows 2000 security components that apply to the C2 certification, which you learned about in Chapter 1.

Discretionary access control   Windows 2000 supports *discretionary access control* as defined in the TCSEC C2 requirements. Those requirements include allowing the owner of an object to control who can access the object and how that access occurs. An *object* is any resource in Windows 2000 (e.g., a share, a user account, or a file).

Object reuse   Windows 2000 provides *object reuse* protection. It specifically prevents all system applications from accessing information contained in any resource (such as memory or disk) that another application is using.

Mandatory logon   Unlike in Windows for Workgroups, Windows 95, and Windows 98, all Windows 2000 users must log on to authenticate themselves before they can have access to any of its resources. This is called *mandatory logon*. The lack of this necessary enforcement for network connectivity is another primary reason that networking had to be disabled3 for earlier Windows products to achieve a C2 rating. Strangely enough, Windows NT 3.51 was C2-compliant only if you removed it from the network.

Auditing   Because Windows 2000 uses a single mechanism to control access to everything, that mechanism can also centrally record all accesses.

Control of access to objects   Windows 2000 disallows direct access to any resource in the system. As we mentioned earlier, a resource is called an *object*. This lack of direct access is the key mechanism that allows access control. Before access is granted, the rights of the user or application to access that resource are first verified. Windows 2000 can also invoke encryption as an access-control strategy.

> Because the CIW Security Professional exam focuses on using Windows 2000 as an Internet and/or intranet server, issues associated with Active Directory are not within its scope.

Windows 2000 Objects

To implement its security features, Windows 2000 is designed to handle all resources of any type in the system as specific objects. These objects contain the resource itself, as well as the mechanisms and programs necessary to access it. By encapsulating everything as objects and developing a single mechanism to use them, Microsoft created a single avenue for controlling access to those objects. Because of this fundamental methodology, Windows 2000 is commonly called an object-based operating system.

Microsoft security is based on the following object principles:

- Objects represent all resources.
- Only Windows 2000 can directly access those objects.
- Objects can contain both data and functions.
- All access to objects is first verified by the Windows 2000 security subsystem.
- Several types of objects exist. Each object type determines what that object can do.

The primary object types in Windows 2000 are:

- Files
- Folders
- Printers
- I/O devices
- Windows
- Threads
- Processes
- Memory

The key goal of this architecture is consistency. The design, which requires all access to be authorized in the same way, diminishes the chances that the security mechanism can be bypassed.

> **NOTE** These concepts also apply to Windows NT 4 Server.

Security Components

The local Windows 2000 security subsystem consists of the following key components: security identifiers, access tokens, security descriptors, access control lists, and access control entries. The use and interaction of these components control user actions.

Security Identifiers

A *security identifier (SID)* is a statistically unique number assigned to all users, groups, and computers. A SID is statistically unique because it is created in a way that reduces the likelihood that any two SID values will be the same. Every time a new user or group is created, it receives a unique SID. Each time Windows 2000 is installed and set up, a new SID is assigned to that computer. The SID uniquely identifies the user, group, or machine, not just on that particular computer but also during interaction with other computers.

To ensure that SIDs are unique, they are created with a formula that combines the computer name, current time, and the amount of time the current user mode thread has spent using CPU time. A SID looks like this:

S-1-5-21-1649288664-1549824960-1244863647-500

SIDs are a cornerstone of the Windows 2000 security infrastructure, so it is important that you understand what one looks like.

Access Tokens

Part of the key purpose of the logon process is to give all users *access tokens* after they have been validated. The access token consists of the user's SID, the SIDs for any groups to which the user belongs, and the user's name.

This access token is the user's "ticket" to access system resources. Whenever the user attempts to access something, the access token is presented to Windows 2000. The system then checks the access token against the access control list of the object being requested. If the user is authorized to use the object, access is granted in the appropriate way.

The access token is issued only during the logon process, so any changes to the user's access rights require the user to log off and then log back on to receive an updated access token.

Security Descriptors

Every object within Windows 2000 has a *security descriptor* as part of its properties. The security descriptor holds that object's security settings. The descriptor consists of the object owner SID, a group SID for use by the POSIX subsystem, a discretionary access control list, and a system access control list. See Figure 8.1.

FIGURE 8.1 A security descriptor

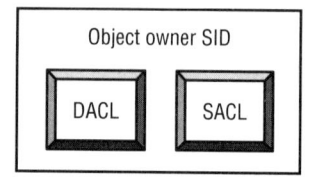

Access Control Lists

The two types of *access control lists (ACL)* are discretionary and system, as shown in Figure 8.2. A discretionary ACL holds a list of users and groups, and their appropriate permissions, either allowed or denied. Each user or group with specific permissions is listed in the discretionary ACL.

FIGURE 8.2 Access control lists

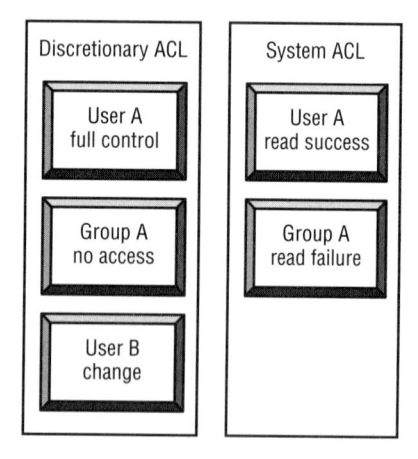

The system ACL contains a list of events that are audited for the object. When the type of ACL is not specified, it is usually a discretionary ACL. In this book, we will assume this is the case for any mention of Windows 2000 ACLs.

Access Control Entries

Each *access control entry (ACE)* contains the user's or group's SID and permission to the object. An ACE exists for each permission assigned to an object.

Access control entries are one of two types: AccessAllowed or AccessDenied. AccessDenied ACEs precede AccessAllowed ACEs in the ACL. When authorization for a user is being checked, the process stops as soon as an appropriate AccessDenied ACE or the end of the ACL is reached, whichever comes first. Therefore, No Access takes precedence over all other permissions.

When the administrative tools list the access rights for an object, they list them in alphabetical order by user, then by group. Therefore, administrator access appears first in the list unless a user occurs alphabetically before "administrator."

> **TIP** The CIW Security Professional exam spends little time discussing domains.

The Windows 2000 Security Subsystem

Now that you understand the general Windows 2000 security components, we will discuss the software within Windows 2000 that allows the security measures to work. This software is collectively referred to as the *security subsystem*.

The security subsystem consists of several parts:

- Winlogon
- Graphical Identification and Authentication DLL (GINA)
- Local Security Authority (LSA)
- Security Support Provider Interface (SSPI)
- Authentication packages
- Security support providers
- The Netlogon service
- Security Account Manager (SAM)

Figure 8.3 shows the parts of the security subsystem.

FIGURE 8.3 The security subsystem

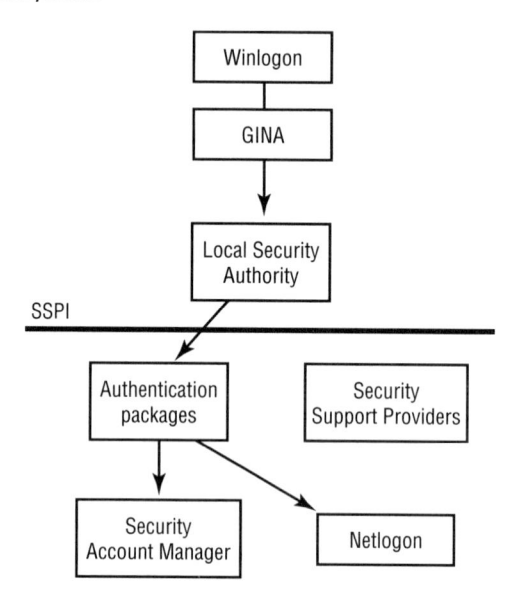

```
                    ┌──────────┐
                    │ Winlogon │
                    └────┬─────┘
                         ↓
                    ┌──────────┐
                    │   GINA   │
                    └────┬─────┘
                         ↓
                    ┌──────────┐
                    │  Local Security  │
                    │    Authority     │
         SSPI       └────┬─────┘
    ─────────────────────┼──────────────────────
                         ↓
         ┌──────────────┐      ┌──────────────┐
         │Authentication│      │   Security   │
         │  packages    │      │Support Providers│
         └──────┬───────┘      └──────────────┘
                ↓      ↘
         ┌──────────────┐      ┌──────────┐
         │   Security   │      │ Netlogon │
         │Account Manager│     └──────────┘
         └──────────────┘
```

The Winlogon, Local Security Authority, and the Netlogon service can be seen as processes in the Windows Task Manager. The other pieces all consist of DLLs that are called and loaded by those processes.

Local Security Authority

The *Local Security Authority (LSA)* is a protected subsystem that is responsible for several tasks:

- Loading all authentication packages, which includes checking for the existence of an `AuthenticationPackages` value in the Registry under `\HKLM\System\CurrentControlSet\Control\LSA`. Beginning with version 4, Windows NT, and continuing through Windows 2000, the system also looks for the existence of the `SecurityPackages` value in the Registry under `\HKLM\System\CurrentControlSet\Control\LSA`. If either of these values exists, the DLLs stored in them are loaded.

- Retrieving any local group SIDs and user rights for the user.

- Creating the user's access token.

- Managing the service accounts used by locally installed services.

- Storing and mapping user rights.
- Managing the audit policy and settings.
- Managing trust relationships.

Security Support Provider Interface

The Microsoft Security Support Provider Interface (SSPI) is very similar to the Generic Security Services API as defined in RFC 2743 and RFC 2744. The Security Support Provider API provides a way for applications and services to request secure authenticated connections.

Authentication Packages

The *authentication package* is the component that provides the user with authentication. The authentication package verifies the credentials supplied through GINA. When a user's credentials are verified, the authentication package returns the SIDs to the LSA so they can be included in the user's access token.

Security Support Providers

Security support providers are installable drivers that support any additional security mechanisms. At least three are included with the default installation of Windows 2000:

Msnsspc.dll The Microsoft Network (MSN) challenge/response authentication scheme.

Msapsspc.dll The Distributed Password Authentication (DPA) challenge/response scheme, which is also used by MSN.

Schannel.dll The authentication scheme that uses certificates issued by certificate authorities such as VeriSign. This authentication is used during Secure Sockets Layer (SSL) and Private Communication Technology (PCT) protocol communications.

Netlogon

The *Netlogon service* must establish a secure channel for pass-through authentication. To do so, it locates a domain controller with which to establish the secure channel. Finally, it passes the user's credentials through the secure channel and then retrieves the domain controller's response in the form of the user's SIDs and user rights.

Security Account Manager

The *Security Account Manager (SAM)* is the database that holds the users and their credentials. It is stored in a portion of the Windows 2000 Registry itself. In Windows NT 4, each domain has a different SAM, which is part of the replication that takes place between domain controllers. A Windows 2000 domain uses Active Directory instead of the SAM.

Linux Security Architecture

In Linux, the equivalent of the Windows 2000 security architecture (i.e., the Windows 2000 Registry, GINA, and the SAM) is a combination of text files and applications running in memory. Some of these text files are the /etc/passwd, /etc/shadow, and /etc/groups files. Additional files include the *Pluggable Authentication Module (PAM)* configuration files.

Depending on their configuration and purpose, Linux systems are generally susceptible to the same vulnerabilities as Windows systems. The following problems are especially important to understand when configuring Linux systems:

Misconfigured authentication settings Many times, user accounts are allowed to exist on systems, even after the user has stopped using them.

Unnecessary services Consider the purpose of your system. The general rule for establishing a secure server is to dedicate each server to only one purpose. For example, if you want to configure an FTP server, you should lock down all other daemons; if you are reasonably sure that you will not need to access your Linux server remotely, you can disable Telnet access.

Default account policies Although Linux systems audit by default, you should consider reviewing and defining user account policies.

Non-root user access to sensitive commands By default, many Linux distributions allow non-root users to use the halt, reboot, and poweroff commands. It is good practice to limit access to these commands only to the root user.

Before you learn more about the Linux security architecture, let's view some of the default Linux settings.

Pluggable Authentication Modules (PAMs)

This section will discuss PAM configuration files. No centralized program, such as the Windows 2000 RegEdt32 application, modifies Linux PAM files and applications. You must configure PAMs using their configuration files, which reside in both the `/etc/pam.d/` and `/etc/security/` directories. Table 8.1 shows the relevant PAM directories and their purposes.

TABLE 8.1 PAM Directories

PAM Directory	Description
/etc/pam.d/	Contains files that allow you to determine what must occur before a user can be logged in.
/etc/security/	Contains files that allow you to set limits concerning users and daemons once they have logged onto the system.
/lib/security/	Contains the PAM modules.

The benefit of PAM is that developers and systems administrators can create additional authentication parameters without affecting existing authentication systems.

PAM Entry Format

The syntax for configuring PAM services in the `/etc/pam.d/` directory files is as follows:

```
module type    flags    path    args
```

Table 8.2 explains the four module types.

TABLE 8.2 Module Types

Module type	Description
auth	Specifies ways in which the user will authenticate with the system (usually via a password).
password	Allows the system to update a user's account information (username and password).

TABLE 8.2 Module Types *(continued)*

Module type	Description
account	Allows you to control when a user can access the system, and which resources he or she can access. Also allows you to choose specific locations and terminals from which a user can authenticate.
session	Provides limits on applications and daemons that a user invokes after authentication.

Flag types determine module type priority. The four flag types are:

required   Indicates that the module must be loaded for authentication to succeed. If this module fails, additional modules will still be checked.

requisite   A stricter flag than `required`. If the module is not invoked, the system will not look for any other modules.

sufficient   If this module is invoked, authentication will occur immediately.

optional   Tells the system that this module is not required for authentication.

> **NOTE** The order of entries in the /etc/pam.d/login file is important. Imagine what would happen if a system read a module flagged `sufficient` before reading all other modules.

After specifying a module type and a flag, you can specify the path of the actual PAM module. Specific arguments are not absolutely necessary. The following three lines are taken from a typical /etc/pam.d/login file:

```
auth       required    
↳ /lib/security/pam_securetty.so
auth       required      /lib/security/pam_pwdb.so
↳ shadow nullok
auth       required    
↳ /lib/security/pam_nologin.so
```

The first line of this code requires that the system check the `/etc/securetty` file to restrict direct root login from a remote system. The part of the line that reads `/lib/security/pam_securetty.so` is the path to the actual module. Note that the line has two arguments, `shadow` and `nullok`. These arguments tell the operating system to use its own password database and to check for the presence of the shadow passwords package. The next line requires that the system load the `/lib/security/pam_nologin.so` module, which checks for the presence of the `/etc/nologin` file.

Arguments (args) are often not necessary. When used, they customize PAM behavior.

The /etc/security Directory

Table 8.3 describes the purpose of each file in the `/etc/security/` directory. The last column describes the entry that must be entered into the `/etc/pam.d/login` file for the module to be properly configured.

TABLE 8.3 Files in the /etc/security Directory

File	Description	/etc/pam.d/login entry
access.conf	Determines users who can access the machine, and from where.	account required /lib/security/pam_access.so
group.conf	Controls login at a group level.	account required /lib/security/pam_group.so
time.conf	Sets times when specific accounts can log on.	account required /lib/security/pam_time.so
limits.conf	Specifies limits based on percentage of processor usage, as well as the number of processes that a user can run simultaneously.	session required /lib/security/pam_limits.so

Restricting Access to the *poweroff* Command

To restrict access to the `poweroff` command, enter the following into the `/etc/security/console.apps/poweroff` file using any text editor:

```
USER=root
SESSION=true
```

Once you enter these entries into the file, only root will be able to use the `poweroff` command. You can also use the same entries for the `halt` command, as well as others. The `USER=` value denotes the user that can use the command. The `SESSION=true` value specifies the session PAM element.

Telnet Access and the Root Account

The `/etc/securetty` file contains the entries of any terminal that allows direct access to a terminal. It affects Telnet users, as well as those who log in interactively (i.e., those who log in using the system's keyboard). Any terminal definition, such as tty1 or tty2, that is not present in this file will not support direct root login. By default, the `securetty` file does not contain terminals for remote clients. Linux systems use the `pts/1` entry to refer to the first virtual terminal. Thus, you must first log in as a standard user and then use the `su` command to become root. However, if you were to enter **pts/1** into this file, you would be able to directly log in as root to the system.

> **TIP** It is always advisable to work as a non-root user. Assume root privileges only when necessary. Most Unix administrators can spot a "newbie" user when that user always works as root.

Using the *su* Command

The su command does not mean "super user"—it means "substitute user." Used without arguments, the su command allows a user to become root. It is possible, however, for the su command to take arguments. For example, suppose that you were a user named sandi. The command would allow you to become the user named james: su james. Additional arguments to su exist. For example, if you wanted to become root to issue only one command, you could use the -c option. The following command allows a non-root user to assume root permissions and start Apache Server:

```
su -c "/etc/rc.d./init.d/httpd start"
```

The quotation marks are important, because they inform the su command that one command is being issued. The user james will be required to enter root's password. Once the command is executed, root permissions will immediately be surrendered.

EXERCISE 8.1

Understanding the /etc/securetty File

In this exercise, you will examine a PAM component, the /etc/securetty file.

1. Boot into Linux as root. Open a Telnet client and attempt to log on to your remote system as root. This attempt should fail, because the /etc/securetty file disallows it.

2. Make a copy of the /etc/securetty file:
   host# cp /etc/securetty /etc/securetty.orig

3. Now, move the /etc/securetty file to the /root directory:
   host# mv /etc/securetty /root/securetty

4. Make sure that the /etc/securetty file no longer exists.

5. From a remote system, log on directly to your reconfigured system directly as root. The root user will now be able to log on directly to the system.

6. Now, move the /root/securetty file back to /etc/securetty.

Instantly Denying Telnet Login with PAM

By using the /etc/nologin file, you can deny Telnet access to all local and remote users. The mere presence of the file will deny login to all users except root. By default, Linux systems do not allow direct login using the root account; therefore, the only way to log on to a system with the /etc/nologin file is to log on interactively as root. This file is useful during an emergency or for systems that require only interactive root login.

You can populate the /etc/nologin file with any text you choose. Its contents will be displayed upon login failure. Figure 8.4 shows a typical entry.

FIGURE 8.4 Denying access with the /etc/nologin file

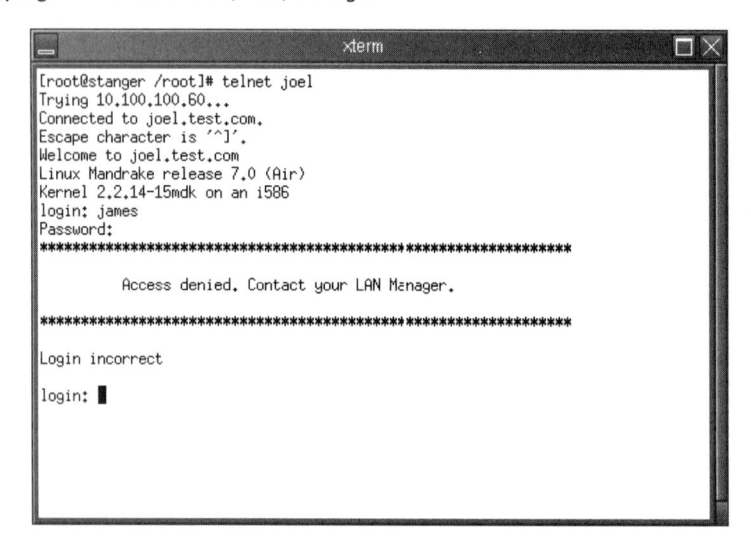

```
[root@stanger /root]# telnet joel
Trying 10.100.100.60...
Connected to joel.test.com.
Escape character is '^]'.
Welcome to joel.test.com
Linux Mandrake release 7.0 (Air)
Kernel 2.2.14-15mdk on an i586
login: james
Password:
****************************************************************
              Access denied. Contact your LAN Manager.
****************************************************************
Login incorrect
login:
```

> The /etc/nologin file will have no effect on FTP and HTTP sessions. Similarly, the file does not support authentication via SSH.

Account Security in Windows 2000 and Linux

Improperly secured user accounts are a primary source by which attackers enter systems. Many potential problems can be prevented by careful user account management, including good password selection, effective policies enforcing sound user habits, and the proper assigning of permissions. All these requirements must be met to achieve a good measure of security. Complicating the whole process is the fact that all these tasks must be completed for many users, while minimal intrusion is maintained to avoid inconveniencing the users.

Local account security is an important part of overall system security. In this section, we will explore various methods of securing a local account. The individual topics will help you form an overall strategy for securing your system.

Passwords

Passwords are one of the core strengths of basic Linux and Windows 2000 security. If the password is compromised, the basic security scheme or model is affected. To enforce good password selection, you need to do more than just select the appropriate values in account policies. You also need to help users choose a *strong password*.

Because so many different operating systems are available, no universal standard exists for the ideal strong password. However, strong passwords generally contain at least three of the following four types of content:

- Uppercase letters
- Lowercase letters
- Numbers
- Nonalphanumeric characters, such as punctuation

Users should also obey these rules when creating passwords:

- Do not use common names or nicknames.
- Do not use common personal information; for example, date of birth.
- Do repeat letters or digits in the password.
- Think like a hacker and avoid schemes that might expose the password to being guessed or found (such as writing it on notepaper and placing it in a drawer near the computer).

Windows 2000 and Strong Passwords

In most cases, fostering good password habits among end users is not adequate. You must also encourage good password choice. A good password choice is one that cannot be easily guessed and that is resistant to even brute-force attacks, such as dictionary attacks. The best way to ensure that these characteristics are present is to require strong passwords.

Windows 2000 supports passwords of up to 127 characters. Windows NT had a limit of 14 characters. However, consider that it would be impossible to expect users to remember 127-character passwords, though it is recommended by Microsoft that passwords should not exceed 14 characters in Windows 2000 and XP, due to backward compatibility.

Even 14-character passwords would be extremely difficult to remember. A practical, strong Windows 2000 password generally uses at least seven characters, does not contain any part of the user's name, and uses at least three of the following four character sets: uppercase letters; lowercase letters; numerals; and nonalphanumeric characters, such as punctuation.

Most password-cracking applications, such as L0phtCrack, can defeat an eight-character password as easily as they can a seven-character password. The next level of password strength in Windows 2000 is 14 characters. For more information about Windows 2000 and XP password security, consult the following URL:

www.microsoft.com/technet/treeview/default.asp?url=/TechNet/prodtechnol/winxppro/proddocs/windows_password_tips.asp

> **NOTE** When any remote Windows systems other than Windows 2000 connect to your Windows 2000 system, they can use only 14-character passwords. To be downward compatible with previous Windows systems, Windows 2000 uses the same password hashes. Therefore, the cracking programs, such as L0phtCrack, pwdump, and John the Ripper, work for Windows NT and 2000 networks.

Enforcing Strong Passwords in Windows 2000

You can enforce strong passwords by opening the Local Security Policy snap-in, choosing Account Policies ➢ Password Policy, and then selecting the option Passwords Must Meet Complexity Requirements. Once you select the Enabled radio button and click OK, users must then use passwords that are at least seven characters long and that have the following: uppercase and lowercase characters, a number, and a symbol.

> **TIP** Windows NT servers require a different approach than Windows 2000. You must first install at least Service Pack 2, and modify the operating system to use the passfilt.dll file. For more information about this, consult the following URL: http://support.microsoft.com/support/kb/articles/Q161/9/90.asp.

Linux and Strong Passwords

Red Hat Linux systems default to using six-character passwords. By default, Linux systems also reject any password that resembles a *dictionary password*, which is any text string that appears too much like a name you would find in a standard dictionary file. As a result, you would have to use a password such as bigmo$ney instead of bigmoney. You can, however, enforce more stringent passwords. For example, many Linux systems administrators prefer a password of eight characters, and require two nonalphanumeric characters.

A Note About Shadow Passwords

Some years ago, the `/etc/passwd` file on all Unix systems contained all username and password information. The `/etc/passwd` file was world-readable, because users needed to access this file to log on and/or change their passwords. It was quickly discovered that including all this information was a problem. Using any password-cracking application such as John the Ripper or L0phtCrack, hackers could obtain the passwords from this file.

The *shadow password* package removes the encrypted passwords from the `/etc/passwd` file and places them into the `/etc/shadow` file, which is readable and writeable only by root (i.e., its permissions are -rw-------, or 600).

Users can still change their passwords, because the shadow package allows users to initiate a password change. The accompanying shadow package files (e.g., `useradd`, `pwconv`, and `groupadd`) can be run by any user, but they are the only files that can write to the `/etc/shadow` file. This way, non-root users can update their passwords without having to involve the root user.

Understanding the Root Account

The root account is not necessarily unique. A privileged user is simply any user who has the user identifier (UID) of 0 (zero). You can specify multiple privileged users, if you prefer. Remember, Linux, like all Unix systems, differentiates among users in the following way: At account creation time, a number is assigned to the UID. This numbering begins at zero, and in most Unix systems (including Linux), the lowest number (or highest privilege) is assigned to the login account called root. Root can execute any program, open any directory, examine any file, change the attributes of any object in the system, and perform many other functions with little or no restriction.

Windows 2000 Account Policies

In addition to keeping the user database clean, you need to help enforce good user habits and make it more difficult for attackers to perpetrate a brute-force attack on your accounts. These tasks are accomplished primarily through the use of the policy setting in Windows 2000.

> **NOTE** Policies are not just technical in nature. They should stem directly from a corporate security policy; thus, administrators' activities should be governed by reliable policies as well. By deciding ahead of time exactly how you want activities to occur, you can reduce the possibility of security gaps.

After selecting the appropriate controls, you need to implement them. A good place to start is on the password controls. You can set account aging and lockout policies by modifying the values in the Account Policies ➢ Password Policy and Account Lockout Policy sections of the Local Security Policy snap-in.

Password Aging

Password aging controls how often users must change their passwords. The following are password-aging subcomponents found in most operating systems:

Maximum Password Age Specifies the amount of time a user can keep an existing password.

Minimum Password Age Specifies the amount of time a user must keep a password before changing it.

Password History Determines the number of passwords the operating system will remember. If a user chooses a password that resides in the password history database, the operating system will force the user to choose another password.

Minimum Password Length Contains the lowest acceptable number of characters for a user password.

Password Complexity Requires users to use nonalphanumeric characters and/or uppercase letters in a password. If complexity settings are set too low, the resulting security gain can be rather small, because many users will resort to using password01, password02, and password03 to get around this restriction. Although password complexity by itself does not offer optimal security, using it wisely is better than allowing users to use the same password continuously.

Encryption Options It is also possible to encrypt locally stored passwords so that they cannot be easily obtained and used. For example, Red Hat Linux allows the use of MD5 (theoretically nonrecoverable) or 3DES passwords. Windows 2000 offers similar options through the Syskey tool, which was discussed in Chapter 4. Encryption options are technically not related to password-aging parameters. However, they are important options that you should consider.

Password age is an important parameter to implement because it can make password cracking with brute-force and dictionary attacks more difficult. When setting the Maximum Password Age value, most organizations assign a value between 30 and 90 days. Requiring more frequent changes leads to user activities such as writing down passwords because they cannot remember them.

> You have already learned how password-aging parameters can cause some security problems if the settings are too strict. A quick rule of thumb when determining password-aging elements is to compare the estimated security gain against the increase in difficulty to users. When the burden on users exceeds the additional security, you should consider very carefully whether the cost is worthwhile.

Password Lockout

Password lockout is the primary tool used to thwart password guessing. It works by disabling accounts after a given number of invalid passwords have been entered. This technique is especially useful for preventing remote brute-force or dictionary-based password attacks. A good number for lockout is three to five invalid logon attempts.

Account Reset

Account reset options allow you to choose whether you want the account to reset automatically after a given interval. Enabling the account reset option is often a good idea, because valid users can forget their passwords, especially near the times when password changes are required. Large organizations in particular must often allow accounts to reset automatically after a given interval. Even a period as short as 15 minutes will generally prevent the effective use of a brute-force password attack. One drawback to requiring manual account reset is that it allows for a possible denial-of-service attack. An attacker can disable users' accounts by launching a large password-guessing program against them.

> As far as the CIW Security Professional exam is concerned, setting password-lockout parameters is not the same as setting password-aging parameters.

Password Aging in Linux

On Linux systems, *password aging* is managed by the chage command. chage options are described in Table 8.4.

TABLE 8.4 Linux Command Options

Option	Meaning
-m	Specifies the minimum number of days between password changes. A value of 0 means the user may change a password at any time.
-M	Specifies the maximum number of days between password changes.
-W	Specifies the number of days before the user gets a warning message that his or her password will be rendered invalid.
-E	Specifies the expiration date. After this date, the account will not be usable. Specified either as a number of days since the Unix epoch (January 1, 1970) or in MM/DD/YY form.
-I (upper case I)	Specifies the number of days a password can be inactive before the account will be automatically disabled.
-l (lower case L)	Lists current settings. Used by unprivileged users to determine when their passwords or accounts will expire.

Here is an example of using chage to learn current password-aging settings for the user james:

```
% chage -l james
Minimum:           0
Maximum:           99999
Warning:           7
Inactive:          -1
Last Change:                 Jan 13, 2000
Password Expires:            Never
Password Inactive:           Never
Account Expires:             Never
```

Timing Out Users

To further enhance security, some organizations encourage the use of secure practices at the grassroots level. It is possible, for example, to configure systems to automatically log off users after a certain period of time, or when a certain time of day (or night) arrives. In Linux systems, the clobberd daemon, available at www.rpmfind.net, allows you to track and control the amount of time users spend on your system. You can also configure clobberd to automatically log off users when their login time expires. Alternatively, publicly available programs such as autologout can watch for inactivity and force a session termination (with some advance notice).

> **TIP** You have learned about rather complex account security options. Users who leave their screens unattended or idle for too long may risk inviting someone to access confidential data or files on their workstations. A simple password-protected screensaver can increase account security.

Removing Accounts

One of the chief indicators of a poorly secured system is the presence of old login accounts. Disgruntled employees can use these accounts to log back into the system and delete or alter critical files. Remove or deactivate all old accounts as soon as possible.

WARNING In Windows 2000 and Linux, if a user has already logged in and you delete the account or change the password, that user will still be able to use that account until he or she logs out. You must end the user's session in order to lock the person out of the network. Thus, if an employee is going to be terminated, it is important that you forcibly log that person out of the system and then remove the account.

To remove an account in a Windows 2000 stand-alone server (for example, a non-domain controller), use the Local Users and Groups utility, found in the Computer Management snap-in. You can also use the Local Users and Groups utility to change passwords and alter group memberships. To change passwords, simply right-click the account and select Reset Password. A dialog box will open that allows you to change the password.

In Linux, using the `userdel` command is most often the best way. You can also manually delete entries from the `/etc/passwd`, `/etc/shadow`, and `/etc/group` files. However, it is best to use the `userdel` command. The `-r` option to `userdel` is quite handy. It not only removes the user account information from the system, but it also removes the user's login directory (e.g., `/home/james/`).

TIP When an employee is terminated, investigate the accounts and passwords that this employee knows. Usually, removing the user's account information will ensure that this user can no longer access network resources. However, in some networks, the password database is not centralized in a Network Information Services (NIS) server, Kerberos server, or domain controller. Passwords and accounts may exist on several servers. You may want to change this account information to ensure maximum security.

Renaming Default Accounts

Windows 2000 Professional and 2000 Server systems ship with default accounts, such as Administrator and Guest. Using the Local Security Policy snap-in, you can rename these accounts to help deter certain hackers. Once in the Local Security Policy snap-in, select Security Settings ≻ Local

Policies ➢ Security Options, and then double-click the Rename Administrator Account icon. You can enter any value you want. You can also rename the Guest account.

Linux systems also have default account names, including root, operator, daemon, and adm. Although it is not at all wise to rename these accounts, it is possible to limit the default root account's login shell, as discussed in Chapter 7. It is also possible to use the Sudo package to control access to the root account. Sudo is not specifically addressed in the CIW Security Professional objectives, but you can learn more about it at the Sudo home page (www.courtesan.com/sudo/).

> As in other cases, altering these default settings as described only provides "security through obscurity." They are not definitive fixes. For example, an application called Red Button can find the default administrator account, even if the account has been renamed. By using Red Button to get the newly named default account name, the hacker can obtain everything but the password. The hacker can then resort to a brute-force or dictionary attack to obtain the password. However, attacks via Red Button can be thwarted if you disable the server service.

Summary

In this chapter, you examined several aspects of Windows 2000 and Linux security. You learned about guidelines for determining general security levels, the security mechanisms used to implement security systems, and different areas of security management. You experimented with Windows 2000 "out-of-the-box" security and discovered that most components work internally on this operating system. This chapter also discussed how to enable strong passwords on Windows 2000 and Linux systems, and how to enable account policies and remove accounts on both operating systems.

Now that you have completed this chapter, you should be able to:

- Identify the mechanisms, security parameters, and techniques necessary for securing Windows and Linux accounts.

- Investigate default Windows 2000 and Linux settings and lock down services and daemons.
- Discuss key security settings in Windows 2000 and Linux.
- Explain the security architectures found in Windows 2000 and Linux.
- Secure accounts in Windows 2000 and Linux.

Exam Essentials

Understand the security architecture for Windows 2000. The security subsystem is a particularly vital component of Windows 2000 security, so make sure that you understand it. You should also be familiar with the concept of objects, as well as access tokens, security descriptors, and the function of the Graphical Identification and Authentication DLL (GINA).

Be able to explain the contents of the Security Account Manager (SAM) in Windows 2000. Make sure that you are familiar with the function of the Security Account Manager (SAM). Study how a SID is created in Windows 2000, including the information used in calculating it.

Know the security architecture for Linux. To understand Linux security, be familiar with the shadow password package and the use of Pluggable Authentication Modules (PAM). Make sure that you understand how to create the /etc/shadow file from the /etc/passwd file. It is also important to know how to modify PAM settings. Understand the purpose of files in the /etc/security/ directory, as well as the function of the /etc/securetty and /etc/nologin files.

Understand password-aging and lockout parameters. Both Windows 2000 and Linux allow you to age passwords. Parameters include the minimum password age, the maximum password age, the password history, and the length and complexity of the password. Password-lockout parameters enable you lock out a user's account in case of multiple login failures. While it is always possible to manually unlock accounts that have been disabled, it is also possible to have the account automatically reset itself after a certain period of time. Be prepared to explain how to do this in Windows 2000 systems, and be prepared to explain why it is advisable to enable account lockout and reset settings.

Know ways to secure accounts in Windows 2000. Make sure that you understand how to establish and create lockout settings, and that you can also have the system reset an account after it has been locked out automatically. Be familiar with the Local Security Policy snap-in, as well as the Computer Management snap-in. Also, study the ways in which you can create what Windows 2000 considers to be strong passwords. It is also important to know some of the limitations imposed when Windows 2000 and Windows XP systems have to work with older clients, such as Windows NT, 98, and 95. In addition, be able to explain how to use the Syskey command in Windows 2000.

Understand ways to secure accounts in Linux. Study the arguments to the `passwd` and `chage` commands, and be able to describe what Linux considers to be strong accounts. Also be prepared to explain how it is possible to time out users in Linux. It is also important to understand how to monitor accounts in both Linux and Windows 2000. Usually, monitoring involves reading log files. You will learn about checking log files in Chapter 14.

Be able to control access to applications in Linux using PAM. Several Linux applications allow all users to access them. For example, the `halt` and `poweroff` commands allow non-root users to shut down and restart the system. To secure these commands, you must place entries in the `/etc/security/console.apps/poweroff` file that allow only root to access this command.

Understand strong password usage patterns common to Windows 2000 and Linux. Windows 2000 and Linux have very similar default password requirements. Make sure that you understand the common elements of a strong password.

Key Terms

Before you take the exam, be certain you are familiar with the following terms:

access control entries (ACE)	Netlogon service
access control lists (ACL)	object
access tokens	object reuse
account reset	password aging
authentication package	password lockout
default installations	Pluggable Authentication Module (PAM)
dictionary password	Security Account Manager (SAM)
discretionary access control	security descriptor
/etc/nologin	security identifier (SID)
/etc/securetty	security subsystem
Local Security Authority (LSA)	shadow password
mandatory logon	strong password

Review Questions

1. What is the name of a statistically unique number assigned to all users on a Windows 2000 system?

    A. A user access token (AT)

    B. A security account descriptor (SAD)

    C. An access control list (ACL)

    D. A security identifier (SID)

2. What is the function of the /etc/pam.d/ directory?

    A. It determines what console applications are allowed to be run by non-root users.

    B. It holds configuration files for individual applications.

    C. It contains the Linux Registry.

    D. It contains the passwd and shadow files.

3. You are using Telnet to log into a system. You fail to authenticate, and then see a message informing you that Telnet access is forbidden. Which of these files has been configured to do this?

    A. /etc/nologin

    B. /etc/pam.d/telnet

    C. /etc/security/telnet

    D. /etc/security/access.conf

4. Which of the following consists of the user's SID, the SIDs for any groups to which the user belongs, and the user's name?

    A. A Linux account name

    B. A Windows 2000 access token

    C. A Windows 2000 name

    D. A Linux access token

5. On a secure Linux system, who owns the /etc/shadow file?

    A. The administrator account

    B. The wheel group

    C. The root account

    D. All superuser accounts

6. What should you do regularly to help secure your user accounts database?

    A. Set accounts to become disabled after two weeks.

    B. Disable all accounts that remain inactive for two weeks.

    C. Regularly scan the accounts database and disable old user accounts.

    D. Regularly scan the accounts database and delete old user accounts.

7. What Windows 2000 feature can you use to rename default accounts?

    A. The Computer Management snap-in

    B. The Connection Manager Administration Kit

    C. The passfile.dll file

    D. The Local Security Policy snap-in

8. What is password aging?

    A. The practice of requiring users to change their passwords after a specified interval

    B. The length of time a system login manager will hold a password after a user logs on and changes his or her password

    C. The practice of requiring an account to lock out after a certain number of invalid login attempts

    D. The number of times in a calendar year that a user may select the same password when renewing a password

9. In Linux systems, what is the purpose of the GID field in the password file?

   A. It contains a list of all group names on the server.

   B. It contains the group identification descriptor.

   C. It contains the system's GINA identification descriptor.

   D. It contains the user's group identification number.

10. On Linux systems, how is password aging managed?

    A. With the page command

    B. With the chage command

    C. With the change command

    D. With the age command

11. On Linux systems, how can root logins be restricted?

    A. With the .profile file

    B. With the /etc/default/login file

    C. With the /etc/default/useradd file

    D. With the /etc/securetty file

12. Which of the following Windows 2000 elements is responsible for creating a user's access token?

    A. The Local Security Authority (LSA)

    B. GINA

    C. The Netlogon service

    D. The Netlogin service

13. Which of the following components hosts the user account information for all users on a stand-alone Windows 2000 system?

    A. The SID

    B. The SAM

    C. GINA

    D. GID

14. Which of the following entries in a file off the `/etc/pam.d/` directory is used to invoke checks on applications and daemons that a user runs after authentication?

    A. `auth`

    B. `password`

    C. `account`

    D. `session`

15. Paul is a systems administrator of a small network. The clients use Windows ME and 98 systems to connect to his Windows 2000 system. What is the limit of passwords that he should impose on these clients?

    A. 6

    B. 8

    C. 12

    D. 14

16. Eric finds password information in the `/etc/passwd` file of a Linux server. What can he do to solve this problem?

    A. Remove the password information.

    B. Enable shadow passwords.

    C. Run the `passwd` command.

    D. Run the `enable` command.

17. What is a password history?

    A. The ability for a system to age passwords

    B. The ability for a system to remember usernames

    C. The ability for a system to remember passwords

    D. The ability for a system to disallow repeated login entries

18. Serena issues the command `chage -l james` as root. What has Serena done to the james account?

    A. She has renamed it.

    B. She has disabled it.

    C. She has listed it.

    D. She has required a password change.

19. How can you change a password for a local account in a Windows 2000 system?

    A. In the User Manager snap-in, right-click the account.

    B. In the Local Security snap-in, right-click the account.

    C. In the Local Security Policy snap-in, right-click the account.

    D. In the Local Users and Groups utility, right-click the account.

20. What is an access control entry in Windows 2000?

    A. It contains a user's or group's SID and object permission settings.

    B. It contains an access control list for each user.

    C. It contains an access control list of resources that can be used by the account.

    D. It contains a list of group permissions used by the default administrator account.

Answers to Review Questions

1. **D.** A security identifier represents a user, group, or computer in a Windows 2000 system.

2. **B.** The `/etc/pam.d/` directory contains individual files that include entries for specific PAM modules. Modules can be marked as `required` or `optional`, and are applied in the order found in the file. Some of the modules govern the actual login process, whereas others control parameters concerning the login session.

3. **A.** The `/etc/nologin` file is designed to instantly deny remote access via Telnet. Other ways exist to deny login, such as closing down the `telnetd` daemon through `inetd` or `xinetd`, depending on what your Unix/Linux daemon uses. The `/etc/nologin` file can also contain a text message that is presented to a user who fails to log in.

4. **B.** Windows 2000 is the only system mentioned that uses the term SID. A Windows 2000 access token, in fact, contains the user's SID, the groups to which the user belongs, and the user's name. An access token is then used to ensure that the user can access only those resources that are explicitly granted.

5. **C.** The root account owns the `/etc/shadow` file, and the file's permissions are 600, so only root can read and write to the file. This is important, because the `/etc/passwd` file is world-readable. If shadow passwords are not enabled, it would be possible for any user to obtain and crack the passwords inside it.

6. **D.** One of the chief signs of lax security in a network is the existence of old login accounts that have not yet been removed. Although it is a rather simple process to remove accounts, many systems administrators omit this step.

7. **D.** The Local Security Policy snap-in allows you to rename the Administrator and Guest accounts. The Local Users and Groups utility can also be used on a non-domain controller. Active Directory is used to rename domain accounts. The Computer Management snap-in allows you to change passwords, as well as group information, login scripts, and other settings specific to the user account. There is no such thing as the Connection Manager Administration kit or the `passfile.dll` file in Windows 2000.

8. **A.** Password aging is an effective technique that forces users to change passwords after a certain interval. It is available on both Windows 2000 and Linux servers. Make sure, however, that you know the individual applications used in each operating system. In a stand-alone Windows 2000 system (e.g., one that is not connected to a domain), you would use the Local Security Policy snap-in. In Linux, you would use commands such as `chage` and `passwd`.

9. **D.** The `/etc/passwd` file contains various values, including information about the group to which the user belongs. Familiarize yourself with these settings, including the GID, the UID, and the value that determines the user's shell and login directory.

10. **B.** The `chage` command is used to determine when a password will expire.

11. **D.** The `/etc/securetty` file contains the terminals that the root account can directly log on to. If a terminal is not listed, you must first log in as a non-root user, and then use the `su` command to assume root privileges. By default, this file does not contain any remote terminal names.

12. **A.** The LSA has several responsibilities, including creating the access token. It also stores user rights and manages auditing.

13. **B.** In a non-domain controller, the Security Account Manager (SAM) stores all local user account information. It is, in many ways, the equivalent of the Linux `/etc/passwd`, `/etc/shadow`, and `/etc/group` files. A SID is an individual identifier for a user, whereas GINA supplies authentication credentials to the authentication package. A GID is an often-used abbreviation for a group user ID in Linux.

14. **D.** The `session` entry is used to regulate and limit commands that can be issued using the command in question. PAM usually regulates the login process, but it can also be used to regulate commands after login occurs.

15. **D.** It is possible for Windows 2000 systems to support extremely long passwords (up to 127 characters). However, some Microsoft clients can only support up to 14 characters, so in the interests of backward compatibility, Paul should limit the number of characters to 14 or less.

16. B. The shadow passwords package moves password information out of the /etc/passwd file and into the /etc/shadow file. Security is enhanced, because the shadow file is not world-readable, as is the /etc/passwd file.

17. C. Password-history settings are used to ensure password uniqueness. It is possible, for example, to configure a system so that it remembers the last three passwords used. If configured in this way, the system will not allow the end user to choose any of these passwords.

18. C. The chage command can do many things. However, the -l option simply lists the account settings for an account.

19. D. All you have to do to change a password in a Windows 2000 system is to access the Computer Management snap-in and right-click the account. You can then select Reset Password, and you will see a dialog box that lets you change the password.

20. A. Each access control entry (ACE) contains the user's or group's SID and permission to the object. An ACE exists for each permission assigned to an object.

Chapter 9

File System Security

THE CIW EXAM OBJECTIVE GROUPS COVERED IN THIS CHAPTER:

- ✓ Identify the mechanisms, security parameters, and techniques necessary for securing Windows and Unix accounts.
- ✓ Identify, assign, and use file system permissions for Windows and Unix servers.

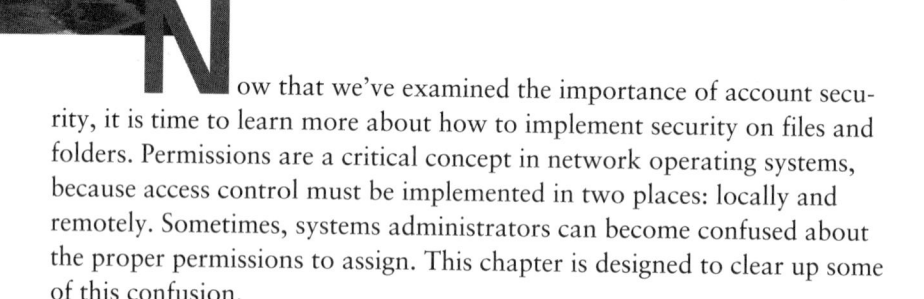

Now that we've examined the importance of account security, it is time to learn more about how to implement security on files and folders. Permissions are a critical concept in network operating systems, because access control must be implemented in two places: locally and remotely. Sometimes, systems administrators can become confused about the proper permissions to assign. This chapter is designed to clear up some of this confusion.

Windows 2000 File System Security

When establishing file permissions, you must first implement the *New Technology File System (NTFS)* in Windows 2000. The alternative, based on the use of *file allocation tables (FAT)*, supports no direct file permissions. A newer standard, FAT32, is equally problematic. FAT/FAT32 is often appropriate for lower security operating systems.

NTFS provides the following security benefits:

- Auditing
- User-level security
- File encryption
- File compression
- The ability to create a single volume from local and remote drives

> **TIP** In Windows 2000 and Windows NT, it is possible to convert FAT/FAT32 drives to NTFS using the command `convert c: /FS:NTFS`.

Once you have implemented NTFS, you can use Windows Explorer to set user-level permissions on files and folders. You need to understand what permissions you can assign, along with a few rules on how permissions are handled during daily activities.

> **Note:** Once you change from FAT or FAT32 to NTFS, you cannot change back to FAT or FAT32 unless you reformat the entire partition.

Before we move on to discuss Windows permissions, let's take the time to review standard, generic permissions found in most operating systems that invoke user-level security. Most secure network operating systems allow you to assign specific permissions for files and folders. The terms shown in Table 9.1 below are meant as a generic review of these permissions, and are not specific to any one operating system.

TABLE 9.1 Basic Permissions Review

Permission	On a folder/directory, allows you to...	On a file, allows you to...
Read (R)	Display the folder/directory name, attributes, owner, and permissions.	Display file data, attributes, owner, and permissions. In the Windows operating system, often combined with Execute, as you will see in Table 9.2, below.
Write (W)	Add files and folders/directories, change a folder's attributes, and display owner and permissions.	Display owner and permissions; change file attributes; create data in and append data to a file.
Execute (X)	Display folder/directory attributes and display owner and permissions.	Display file attributes, owner, and permissions. Run a file if it is executable.
Delete (D)	Delete a folder/directory.	Delete a file.
No Access	Generic term used to deny access to a folder. As you will see in Table 9.2, Windows 2000 uses the word "Deny," instead of No Access.	Generic term used to deny access to a file.

The Windows 2000 operating system allows you to establish complex file and folder permissions. You can view them by opening the Properties sheet for a file or folder, clicking the Advanced button on the Security tab, and then clicking the View/Edit button. To simplify file and folder security management, Windows 2000 offers several standard sets of permissions, shown in Table 9.2. In most cases, you can use these sets rather than assigning individual permissions.

TABLE 9.2 Standard Windows 2000 Permissions

Standard permission	Permissions on folders	Permissions on files
Deny	None	None. This permission overrides all others. This permission was known as "No Access" in Windows NT.
Read	Provides the ability to view files and subfolders, as well as ownership and permissions information.	Allows the file to be read.
Write	Provides the ability for a user to add new files and subfolders with the folder. Can also view ownership and permissions, and alter attributes of the folder. Contents cannot be deleted.	Similar to the -a option of the chattr command, because a file can be written to, but not deleted.
List Folder Contents	Allows viewing of file names and subfolders.	N/A
Read and Execute	Allows users to "traverse" folders, which means that they can access files and folders in subdirectories.	Allows a file to be read and executed.

TABLE 9.2 Standard Windows 2000 Permissions *(continued)*

Standard permission	Permissions on folders	Permissions on files
Modify (M)	The user has the ability to delete the folder, as well as write, read, and execute files. Modify includes the Delete (D) privilege for folders. Users also have the ability to change a folder's permissions.	Users also have the ability to change a file's permissions.
Full Control (RWXM)	Control all elements of a file. Includes the ability to take ownership of a folder.	Control all elements of a directory. Includes the ability to take ownership of a file.
Take Owner-ship (O)	Take ownership of a folder/directory. This is not a standard permission, but it is worth noting, because it is often necessary to take ownership of a folder before modifying it further.	Take ownership of a file. This is not a standard permission, but it is worth noting, because it is often necessary to take ownership of a file before modifying it further.

> **NOTE** Windows NT uses the phrase "No Access," whereas Windows 2000 uses the word "Deny." When taking the CIW Security Professional exam, do not become confused if you see a reference to "No Access." The exam often uses this term because it is more vendor-neutral.

By assigning these permissions on a minimal basis, you can achieve the necessary access control. But determining what you need for minimal permissions can be difficult. The Everyone group has full control of new NTFS partitions by default. The Everyone group includes all users—not just those defined on the particular system. Allowing any user on your local area network (LAN) or the Internet is not a very good idea, given that even unauthenticated users belong to the Everyone group. If you indiscriminately remove the Everyone group from all areas or assign the Deny permission to the Everyone group, you can cripple your Windows 2000 installation. The Everyone group must have access to certain system folders (such as the logon folder) so users can connect and log on to the server. Because users have not yet authenticated when they begin the logon process, you must use the Everyone group to provide access so they can authenticate.

Assigning Deny to the Everyone group on the system presents even more risk. Because Access Denied precedes and thus overrides Access Granted, and because all users always belong to the Everyone group, you would completely disable access to the file system.

Folder permissions are assigned in the same way as files. Keep in mind that folder permissions affect new files created in that folder. In other words, any newly created file starts with the same permissions as the folder. Any time you set or change permissions on a folder, you can reset the permissions on any existing files in that folder.

> **TIP**
>
> Windows 2000 strictly enforces *inheritance* in NTFS. Inheritance means that all subfolders and files have, or "inherit," the permissions of the parent folder. Thus, if you are working in a subfolder and want to change permissions, you will have to deselect the Allow Inheritable Permissions From Parent To Propagate To This Object check box. Remember this when, for example, you want to alter permissions in the C:\inetpub\wwwroot\ folder, or in a folder that resides off your desktop folder (e.g., C:\Documents and Settings\Administrator\Desktop).

EXERCISE 9.1

Assigning Advanced NTFS Permissions

In this exercise, you will assign advanced NTFS permissions so that you will be able to identify key concepts addressed by the CIW Security Professional exam.

1. As Administrator, check the C: drive (or whatever drive you are using), and make sure that it is an NTFS drive. See the earlier tip on converting a drive to NTFS, if your system is still using FAT.

2. Create the user named **test**. Make the password for the test account **Tr$ning1**. This password is necessary if you are using strong passwords in Windows 2000. Once you have created this user, log off the system and log on as test.

EXERCISE 9.1 *(continued)*

Note: Make sure that this user has a password and the permission to log on locally. Otherwise, this part of the exercise will fail.

3. Open Windows Explorer and create a folder named `C:\test\`. Create a file in this folder named `ntfs.txt`. Enter some text into the file. Notice that you can make these changes. You can save the changes, because Windows 2000 defaults to assigning full control permissions to the Everyone group for any new file and folder.

   Note: Make sure that you create a folder off the C: partition. If you create a folder in your desktop folder (e.g., `C:\Documents and Settings\Administrator\Desktop`), the folder you create will inherit permissions from its parent folder.

4. In Windows Explorer, right-click `ntfs.txt` and choose Properties, and then click the Security tab.

5. You will see that the Everyone group has full control access to this file, as shown here. Notice that full control access implies the Modify permission, which was known as the Change permission in Windows NT Server 4.

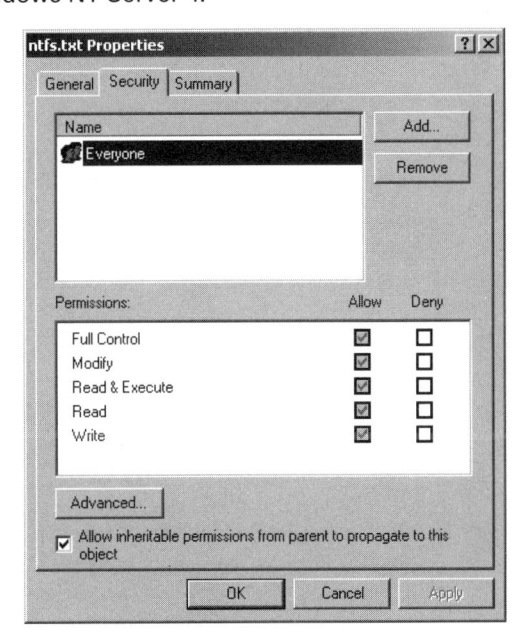

EXERCISE 9.1 *(continued)*

6. Click the Advanced button. The Access Control Settings dialog box will appear, as shown here:

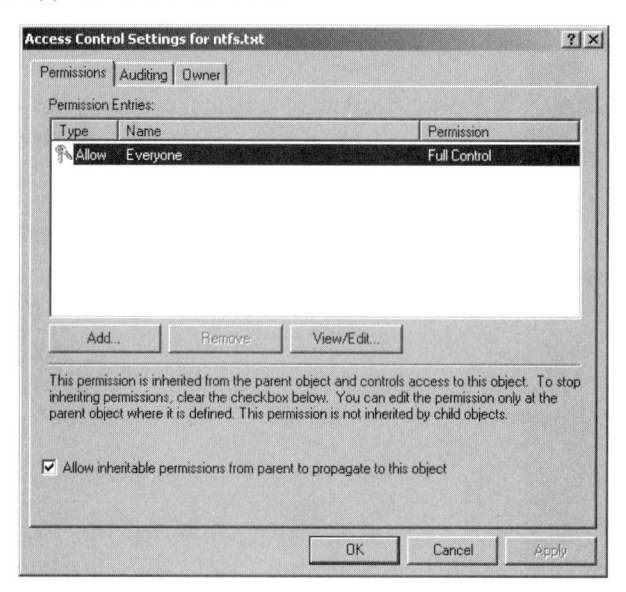

7. On the Permissions tab, select the Everyone group, and then click the View/Edit button. You will see the Permission Entry dialog box shown here:

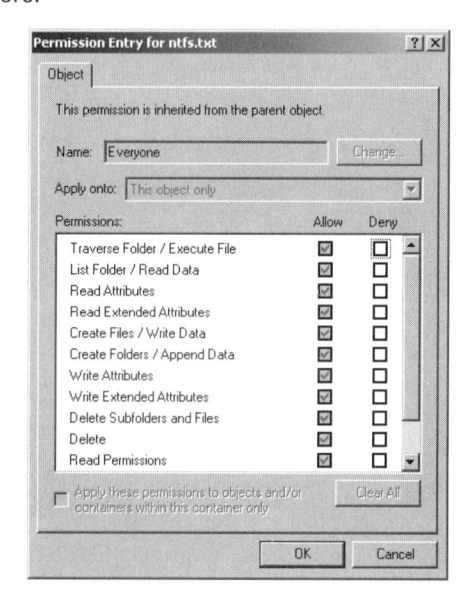

EXERCISE 9.1 *(continued)*

8. You are viewing all permissions for this particular file. Notice that the Everyone group has full access. You can modify the settings in this dialog box, but for now do not change any settings. Click Cancel until you return to Windows Explorer, and then log out of this system.

9. Log on as Administrator.

   Note: If you have renamed the Administrator account, use the appropriate name.

10. Open the Permission Entry dialog box for the Everyone group for the `C:\labs\ntfs.txt` file.

11. Alter the permissions on the file, as shown here:

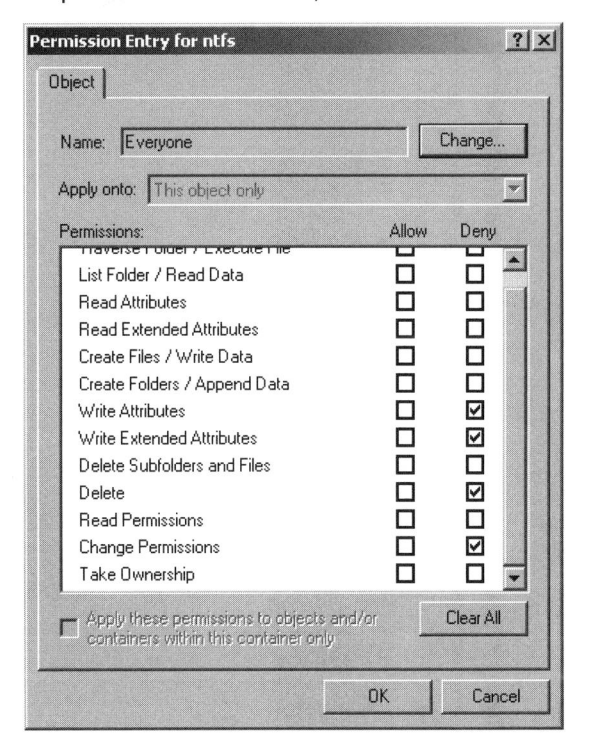

    ![Permission Entry for ntfs dialog box showing Everyone selected, Apply onto: This object only. Deny checkboxes are checked for: Write Attributes, Write Extended Attributes, Delete, Change Permissions.]

12. Click OK until you see a message informing you that Deny entries take precedence over Allow entries. Click Yes, and then click OK until you return to Windows Explorer.

EXERCISE 9.1 *(continued)*

13. Log off the system, and then log on as test and use Notepad to open `C:\labs\ntfs.txt`. Note that you can still open the file.

14. Add the line **NTFS allows you to assign detailed file and folder permissions**.

15. Select File ➢ Save to open the Save dialog box. If you proceed to save this file as **ntfs.txt**, you will receive the error shown here, due to your lack of write privileges:

    > **Notepad**
    > Cannot create the C:\Labs\NTFS.Txt file.
    > Make sure that the path and filename are correct.
    > [OK]

16. Exit Notepad and then log off the system. Log on as Administrator.

17. Open the Permission Entry dialog box for the Everyone group for the `C:\labs\ntfs.txt` file.

18. Alter the file's permissions so the Administrator can change these permissions. When you select the Security tab, you will be informed that you only have permission to view the current information about `ntfs.txt`. This is because the Administrator account is part of the Everyone group, which no longer has write-level access to this file. Click OK, and then click the Advanced button.

19. Click the Owner tab and take ownership of the file by highlighting the Administrator account and clicking Apply. Then click OK until you return to Windows Explorer.

20. Access the properties for this file again and select the Security tab. You will not see a warning message this time, because you now own this file. You can now modify this file at will. Click the Add button.

21. The Select Users, Computers, Or Groups dialog box will appear. Add the test user by highlighting the user account and clicking the Add button.

EXERCISE 9.1 *(continued)*

22. Click OK.

23. Make sure the test user account is highlighted, and then modify its access permissions by selecting the Deny check box, as shown here:

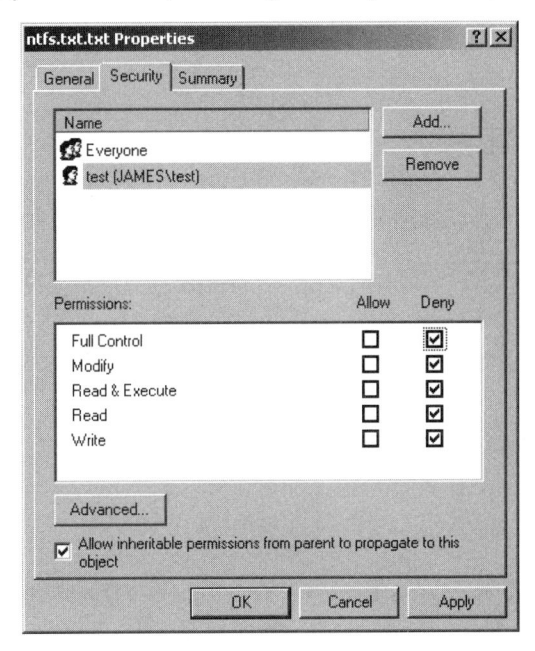

24. Click Apply, then click OK.

25. Log off as Administrator and log on as test.

26. As the test user, try to access the C:\labs\ntfs.txt file. You will receive an Access Is Denied message. Log on as any other user to see if other users can access the file.

Drive Partitioning in Windows 2000

To help minimize damage in case of a hacking attack, it is often a good idea to place the actual operating system files for Windows 2000 on their own partition. This way, a problem involving the operating system might not spread as easily to additional partitions that contain data, such as shared files or the files used for the corporate website. Installing just Windows 2000 on this partition also makes the administrative task much easier. A potential drive partitioning might resemble Figure 9.1.

FIGURE 9.1 Potential drive partitioning

Windows 2000 files	Program files	Data

Although this separate partitioning requires extra planning, it yields several advantages, most notably easier administration of directory permissions. The data directories can be segmented down as far as necessary. If you are running a device such as a web server, you might consider placing your HTML, graphic, and other static files on one partition and your scripts on another. You can set the scripts to execute-only and the static files to read-only. Doing so at the very least makes a hacker's attempt at web graffiti a little more difficult.

Copying and Moving Files

Finally, you should understand what happens when files are copied and moved from one location to another. Whenever a file is copied to a new folder, the new file inherits the target folder's permissions. When you create a file, new file-creation rules apply. When files are moved, the process is more complicated. If a file is moved from one folder to another on the same partition, the file permissions are retained. When a file is moved on the same partition, Windows 2000 updates the directory allocation table to the new folder location. When a file is moved between two different partitions, Windows 2000 first copies the file to the new location. Upon successful completion of the copy, Windows 2000 deletes the original file. A new file is being created, so the rules for new file creation apply and the target folder's permissions are inherited.

Remote File Access Control

Remote access to files and directories is provided through share permissions. A *share* is a network access point through which remote users can access files. When configuring these shares, you set the permissions. The application of permissions on shares works similarly to the application of permissions on NTFS. The primary difference is the lack of finely granulated permissions. See Table 9.3.

TABLE 9.3 Remote Access Permissions

Permission	Allows you to...
Full Control	Change file permissions. Take ownership of files on NTFS volumes. Perform all tasks allowed by the Change permission.
Modify	Create folders and add files. Change data in, and append data to, files. Change file attributes. Delete folders and files. Perform all tasks permitted by the Read permission.
Read & Execute	Display folder and file names. Display file data and attributes. Run program files. Make changes to folders within a folder.

Share permissions and *share points* must be assigned carefully. Because permissions are assigned only to the share points, any files or folders accessible under that share point are accessed with the same permissions as the share point itself. This problem is illustrated in Figure 9.2.

As you create shares on your network, do not assume that simply creating a more restrictive share point necessarily denies access to the directory you are sharing. The simple principle concerning shares is as follows: Share permissions are always cumulative. However, remember the difference between a share point and the contents of a folder and its subfolders. Except in the case of NTFS permissions, the access token Windows 2000 grants to a user regarding a share allows that user access to all subfolders of the shared folder. This fact can lead to some access security problems if it is not properly understood.

FIGURE 9.2 Share permissions

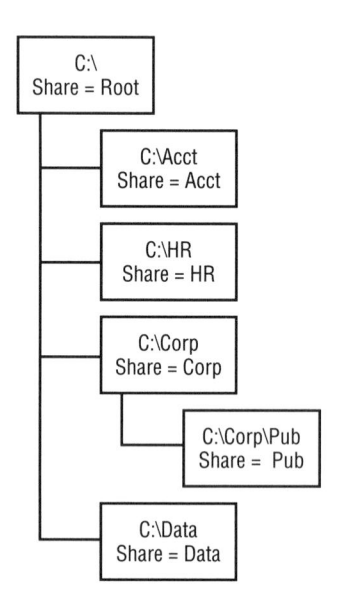

```
C:\
Share = Root
├── C:\Acct
│   Share = Acct
├── C:\HR
│   Share = HR
├── C:\Corp
│   Share = Corp
│   └── C:\Corp\Pub
│       Share = Pub
└── C:\Data
    Share = Data
```

Consider how the `C:\Corp\Pub` folders are shared in Figure 9.2. Suppose that the `\Corp` share allows Everyone access. This share allows access to a subfolder named `\Pub`. However, notice also that this subfolder has been given its own share name of Pub.

Suppose that, contrary to its name, the Pub share allows access only to a user named Sandi. As expected, only the user named Sandi could directly access this share by using its Universal Naming Convention (UNC) or by clicking its share icon. If James tries to directly access the Pub share (e.g., `\\machine\Corp\Pub`), he will be denied access. However, he (or anyone else) can still view the restricted folder by connecting to the `\Corp\` share and then using the Network Neighborhood or My Network Places applet to move down to the `\Pub` subfolder. Remember that the Corp share point gives all access to anything beneath the shared directory. James would be able to access additional subdirectories of `C:\Corp\` even if they are not shared. This access is possible because share-level access tokens apply to all subfolders.

Combined Local and Remote Permissions

Windows 2000 permissions are designed with the intention of combining NTFS and share permissions together. Because Windows 2000 is designed as a server, users will rarely access the files directly. Certainly, share security is insufficient for most security needs, so both need to be used.

When you combine share and NTFS permissions, the more restrictive of the two sets of rights is used. The result is the ability to use share permissions for broad user permissions when connecting to a share point. The NTFS permissions can then be used to further tighten permissions on a much more granular basis.

Linux File System Security

Remember, in all Unix systems, information—even network connections and directories—is always stored as a file. This file has a name associated with it. The remainder of this chapter focuses on how permissions are handled in a standard Unix file system. These permissions control what users may access and how they may access it. The file system is the basic manner in which Linux security is enforced.

Reviewing Files Permissions

Linux reads and writes data to files, which are maintained in a tree-like structure. Since the beginning, Linux systems have allowed long file and directory names. All files have an *inode*, which contains all the statistical and logistical information about a file or directory. Some of the data an inode contains includes:

- File type (sometimes called the magic number).
- Size (in bytes).
- Reference count, usually greater than one if several different filenames appear that are actually the same file (called *links* or *linked files*).
- Pointer to a list of block addresses, where the contents actually reside.
- Several time stamps; e.g., when the file was last accessed (`atime`), when the file's contents were last modified (`mtime`), and when this inode was last updated (`ctime`).
- Security-related fields: the user identifier (UID) and the group identifier (GID) to which the file belongs.

366 Chapter 9 ▪ File System Security

- File access permissions or bits, which are also called mode bits. We will examine these bits in detail.

We can now take a look at a typical listing to further examine the data and its meanings. The ls command is the most commonly used Unix command, and is used to look at file and directory permissions. Figure 9.3 shows four ls commands.

FIGURE 9.3 Typical listing of files in a home directory

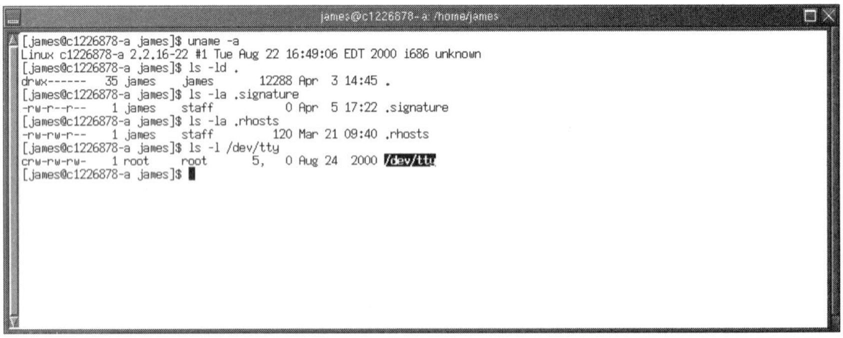

```
[james@c1226878-a james]$ uname -a
Linux c1226878-a 2.2.16-22 #1 Tue Aug 22 16:49:06 EDT 2000 i686 unknown
[james@c1226878-a james]$ ls -ld .
drwx------   35 james    james       12288 Apr  3 14:45 .
[james@c1226878-a james]$ ls -la .signature
-rw-r--r--    1 james    staff           0 Apr  5 17:22 .signature
[james@c1226878-a james]$ ls -la .rhosts
-rw-rw----    1 james    staff         120 Mar 21 09:40 .rhosts
[james@c1226878-a james]$ ls -l /dev/tty
crw-rw-rw-    1 root     root        5,   0 Aug 24  2000 /dev/tty
[james@c1226878-a james]$
```

You can ignore the uname -a command, which simply shows the version of the operating system, including the kernel. The first relevant command (ls -ld .) tells the system to list the contents of the file called "." (dot), which is usually the current directory; in this case, the user was automatically sent or logged on to his or her home directory. The system should also list (in long form) the file/directory permissions and treat the "." filename as a directory.

The output line shows the elements explained in Table 9.4.

TABLE 9.4 *ls* Command Output

Output symbol	Meaning
d	Indicates the directory.
r	Specifies that the owner (whose login name is james) has Read access.
w	Specifies that the owner has Write access.

TABLE 9.4 *ls* Command Output *(continued)*

Output symbol	Meaning
x	For a directory, implies that Execute access or capability is granted to the owner.
-	Indicates that Read access is not available to the group (in this case, staff).
-	Specifies that no Write permission is granted to the group.
-	Specifies that the Execute permission for this directory is not granted to the group.
-	Specifies that the Read permission is denied to all others (i.e., everybody).
-	Specifies that no Write permission exists for all others.
-	Specifies that the Execute permission in this directory is not available to all others.
james	Indicates the owner's login name.
james	Specifies the group to which this user belongs. Linux assigns users to their own group to help simplify group administration. With groups named after users, it is possible to know exactly which groups you can work with; as long as you know a user's name, you know a group name, as well.
12288	Indicates the size (in bytes) of this directory.
Time Stamp	Indicates the date on which the size was last changed.
14:45	Indicates the time at which that change occurred.
.	Specifies the filename to which all this information pertains.

368 Chapter 9 • File System Security

The second command (`ls -la .signature`) displays the output of the instruction to list the information about a single file (in this case, `.signature`). Its components are listed in Table 9.5.

TABLE 9.5 File Information—Command Output

Field value	Meaning
-	Indicates a plain file.
r	Specifies that Read access is granted to the owner.
w	Specifies that Write access is granted to the owner.
-	Usually indicates plain file; i.e., not executable.
r	Specifies that Read access is granted to the group.
-	Specifies that no Write permission is granted to the group.
-	Specifies that no Execute permission is granted to any members of the group.
r	Specifies that Read access is available to all others (everybody).
-	Specifies that no Write permission is granted to the world.
-	Specifies that no Execute permission is granted to the world.
0	Indicates the file size.
Time Stamp	Indicates the date on which the file was created. When the time stamp exceeds six months, a file-listing program or utility will convert it to a year display.

The third command (`ls -la .rhosts`) illustrates the result of the `list` command on a file that is associated with network-based access permissions. The file here is called `.rhosts`. Most of the fields have same meaning; what is notable is that this file allows access to the staff group. This is something of a mistake, actually, because the directory does not allow access to any other group. Thus, even though the .rhosts file is marked to allow access by the staff group, the directory's permissions will forbid access to the file.

The fourth command (ls -1 /dev/tty) illustrates the typical permissions on a system file called /dev/tty. This file is where all screen typing is echoed, and where the messages sent by another program are written to (or your screen). Table 9.6 explains the permissions.

TABLE 9.6 Permissions

File value	Meaning
c	Indicates a character device. Character devices are often video monitors (as in this case), or printers.
rw	Specifies that Read and Write access is granted to the owner.
rw-	Specifies that Read and Write access is granted to the group.
rw-	Specifies that Read and Write access is available to all others.
1	Represents the reference count (which indicates a unique file).
root	Specifies the actual owner of this file.
root	Specifies the group to which the file belongs.
26	Indicates the file size (in bytes).
Time Stamp	Indicates the date on which the file was first created (in this case, the actual file pointed to).
->	Indicates the link or symbol used to indicate the real file.
../devices/pseudo/sy@0:tty	Specifies the physical location of the file symbolically known to the Linux kernel as /dev/tty.

Now that you understand some of the various mode bits for a file (or directory) in Linux, we can look at the various ways in which these bits can be changed.

The *umask* Command

The umask command is used widely in all Unix systems to set subsequent file-creation mode bits. It is also used often in login profiles to set up default permissions. Entering this command displays the current values. To change them, the user can enter the umask command with various combinations to alter the default creation mode bits.

The mode value bits are summarized in Table 9.7.

TABLE 9.7 Mode Value Bits

Mode values (octal form)	Meaning of octal mode bits (additive in nature)
7	Read, write, and execute.
6	Read and write. This permission is a combination of 4 plus 2. It is also known as rw.
5	Read and execute (e.g., 4 plus 1, or rx).
4	Read only (e.g., 4, or r).
3	Write and execute (e.g., 2 plus 1, or wx).
2	Write (e.g., just 2, or w).
1	Execute (e.g., just 1, or x).
0	No mode bits (i.e., access absent).

The umask command subtracts from the value 666 (i.e., read and write to owner, group, and others) for plain files. Each bit pattern (or octal value) is assigned to each component of the file's three values (owner, group, and others). For directories, the umask value is subtracted from 777 (i.e., read, write, and execute for owner, group, and others).

The `umask` command is set to "mask away" a certain pattern of bits from the default pattern for files, directories, and executables, thereby giving the final (or resultant) remaining access permission bits. This practice is referred to as *"AND"-ing* the default permission bits with the complementary values of the user mask bits. These bits determine the bits that need to be *"mask"-ed*, or hidden. For example, the `umask` value 022 gives us:

	0666	Default file permissions bits (owner, group, others)
AND	0022	`umask` values for the owner, group, and others
Final	0644	mode bits

The information given above specifies read and write permissions for the owner, and read-only access for the group and others. See Figure 9.4.

FIGURE 9.4 umask's role in file creation

At sites where users expect to protect their data by default from inspection by other users, all users should have a `umask` value of 077. For users working on group projects, a `umask` value of 037, which permits group access to files by default, may be a better choice.

The *chmod* Command

The `chmod` command is used to manipulate file permissions. This command may be applied in two ways:

Absolute mode   When `chmod` is used in *absolute mode*, the command looks like `chmod 666 filename`. Here, the permission mode bits are being absolutely applied to a filename (or to many, if necessary). Variations are based on the mode bits outlined in Table 9.7, with bits applied to each component (the owner, group, and others).

Symbolic mode When chmod is used in *symbolic mode*, the command looks like `chmod a+rwx filename`. Here, the permission bits are Read, Write, and Execute granted to all components (the owner, group, and others) for the filename (or filenames). Because the symbols correspond to those displayed by the ls command, this mode helps decipher (and decide what those bits should be). Here is an example of this type of usage:

```
uname -a
Linux james 2.2.16-22 #1 Tue
    Aug 22 16:49:06 EDT 2000 i6868 unknown
host# umask
022
host# ls -l chmodtest
ls: chmodtest: No such file or directory
host# touch chmodtest
host# ls -l chmodtest
-rw-r--r--   1  james    james   0 Apr 5:18:42 chmodtest
host# chmod ugo+wx chmodtest
-rwxrwxrwx   1  james    james   0 Apr 5:18:42 chmodtest
host#
```

The chmod command can be inadvertently used to impart "stumbling permissions" too:

```
uname -a
Linux james 2.2.16-22 #1 Tue Aug 22
    16:49:06 EDT 2000 i6868 unknown
host# umask
022
host# ls -l chmodtest
ls: chmodtest: No such file or directory
host# touch chmodtest
host# ls -l chmodtest
-rw-r--r--   1  james    james   0 Apr 5:18:42 chmodtest
host# chmod ugo+wx chmodtest
-rwxrwxrwx   1  james    james   0 Apr 6:32:05 chmodtest
```

```
host# chmod a-rwx chmodtest
ls -1 chmodtest
----------  1  james    james   0 Apr 6:34:48 chmodtest
host#
```
Notice that halfway through the sequence given here, the `chmodtest` file first receives 644 permissions, but then, as a result of the `chmod ugo+wx` command, receives more permissions than just Read and Write. Be very careful when using symbolic permissions, because you can assign more permissions to the file than you wanted to. Table 9.8 summarizes all the symbols used in the `chmod` command.

TABLE 9.8 *chmod* Command Symbols

Symbol	Meaning
u	Specifies the user or owner.
g	Specifies the group.
o	Specifies others.
a	Specifies all user, group, and other components.
+	Adds the permissions that follow.
-	Takes away the permissions that follow.
=	Sets the file to equal only the exact permissions that follow.

> **NOTE** When using `chmod` against a directory, use the -R option to set permissions for all files and subdirectories.

UIDs and GIDs

All the file permission bits and controls we have described apply in a discretionary manner toward all objects. These objects are files, directories, and executables (such as programs). This information is kept in the inode portion of the file system where the objects are located. As we mentioned earlier, an inode in Linux is the descriptor containing all the statistical and logical information about a file. A certain portion of each file's inode (depending on the actual vendor implementation) is set aside for these bits. Usually this portion is 16 bits and is handled collectively as an entity. Nine bits are used for the file modes (read, write, execute, and none bits). Three additional bits describe or state how these bits may work with certain *user identifiers (UIDs)* and *group identifiers (GIDs)* that are also associated with a file.

UIDs are uniquely indicated in the system's `/etc/passwd` file, while the GIDs are uniquely described in the system's `/etc/group` file. When an application is used on the system, a process is started for each invocation. This process is tracked by the kernel and is then assigned to a resource such as memory, CPU, I/O, and so forth. To help the kernel track this information, each process must have a process identifier (PID). Each PID has in its table four other numbers. Two are the familiar UID and GID. An extra pair of UID and GID numbers is also assigned, called the *effective UIDs and GIDs*. The process may occasionally need to acquire an identity different from its primary UID and GID (such as becoming another user or boosting its privilege level to change that user's password). In such an instance, the effective UID and GID are different from the initial set of values. These effective values are evaluated by the Linux kernel to grant security access.

The *chown* and *chgrp* Commands

The `chown` command is used to change ownership of a file or directory. If you are using `chown` or `chgrp` against a directory, the -R option will change all files and subdirectories. The `chgrp` command is similar to the `chown` command, except that it changes the group ownership of a file or directory.

The Set Bits: Setuid, Setgid, and Sticky Bits

Unix allows programs to assume another UID or GID when running. A program that changes its UID is called an *SUID* (set-UID or *setuid*) program; similarly, when a program changes its GID, it is called an *SGID* (set-GID or *setgid*) program. One situation in which a program changes its UID or GID is when the SUID or SGID permission bit is set in the file permissions. A program can have both of these bits set at the same time.

When a setuid program is executed, its effective UID becomes that of the user who owns the file containing that program. This UID may differ from the UID of the person (or user) who is running it.

Table 9.9 illustrates the extra set bits that may be used for changing effective UIDs or GIDS.

TABLE 9.9 Extra Set Bits

Permission bit	Meaning
S	When set in file's owner section and the execute bit is not set, indicates to the Linux kernel that if executed, its effective UID should be set to that of the owner.
s	When set in the file's owner section, indicates that setuid is on, but the execution bit (x) is also set.
S	When set in the file's group component, indicates to the Linux kernel that upon execution, the effective GID should be set to that group.
s	Indicates that setgid is on, but the group execution bit (x) is also set.
T	If set on a file, indicates that the system, upon program termination, will not immediately remove the program from the Linux swap/paging area. This option is obsolete. Modern Unix systems ignore this bit when set on files.
t	When set on a directory, indicates that a user can delete a file in that directory only if he or she has Write permission for that file. Normally, only Write permission on the directory is needed.

The setuid bit is the twelfth bit, the setgid bit is the eleventh bit, and the sticky bit is usually the remaining tenth bit in the inode 16-bit word.

Programs that need extra permissions use the SUID/SGID features. For example, the `passwd` program, which must write to the system password file, needs to run with root permissions to perform that task. Because the SUID/SGID mechanism temporarily grants a user more permissions than he or she is normally entitled to, all programs in a system that have these bits set must be monitored and examined for changes.

> **Setuid**
>
> The setuid bit is a legitimate, helpful tool. Many applications, such as the /usr/bin/passwd command, have legitimate setuid permissions. The /usr/bin/passwd file must be setuid root so that it can obtain access to root permissions and write to the /etc/passwd and /etc/shadow files to change passwords for specific users. Sometimes, however, applications can mistakenly be given setuid root permissions. As a result, security can be compromised, because the application might be able to damage the system or issue additional commands that can defeat security. For example, it is possible for an illicit setuid application to copy the /etc/shadow file to a world-readable directory.

EXERCISE 9.2

Finding Setuid and Setgid Programs in Your Linux System

In this exercise, you will search for Setuid and Setgid programs on your Linux system.

1. Try the following command and search for setuid/setgid commands available on your system:

   host# find / \(-perm +4000 \) -exec ls -l {} \;

2. If you want to discover both setuid/setgid and files that have at least read permission bits set in the Other field, you would enter the following command:

   host# find / \(-perm +4000 -o -perm +2000 \)
   ↳-exec ls -l {} \;

   Note: The arrow on the second line is a continuation arrow. Make sure you enter the entire command as one line.

3. Graphical Linux tools exist to help you issue some simplified find commands. One is called kfind, and is part of the K Desktop

EXERCISE 9.2 *(continued)*

Environment (KDE). If you have the KDE desktop installed, open a terminal in the X Window environment and issue the following command:

kfind &

4. When the kfind GUI appears, have kfind search all files on the system. Make sure the Name & Location tab is selected, enter an asterisk in the Named field, and enter a forward slash in the Look In field, as shown here:

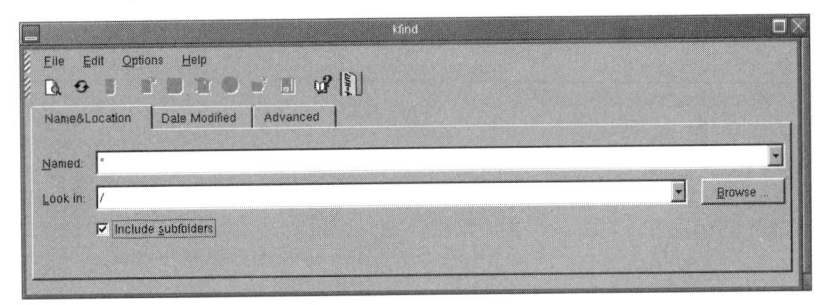

5. Select the Advanced tab and select the SUID Executable Files option.

6. Click the Start button.

7. After the search is complete, you will see a list of SUID executable files, as shown here:

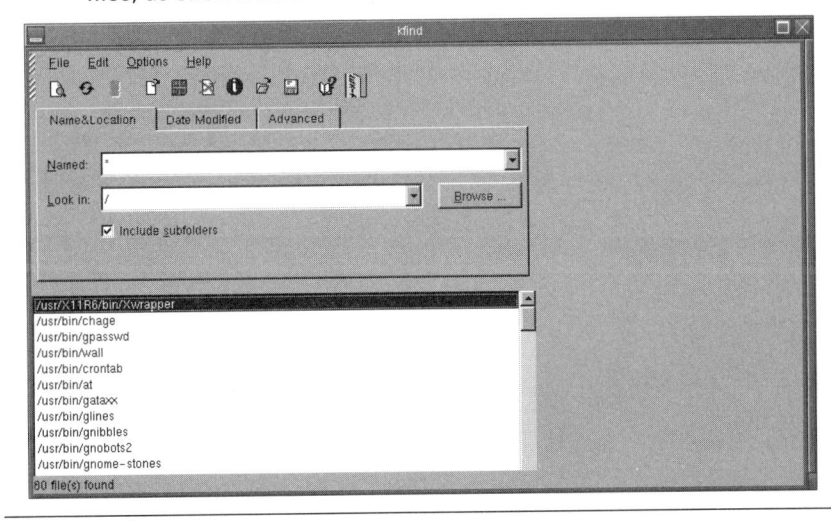

EXERCISE 9.3

Testing the *umask* Command in Linux

In this exercise, you will study how to alter the umask value on a Linux system.

1. The default umask value is 022 for Linux systems. This default is generally acceptable, but you may want to use a stricter setting. Assume root permissions using the su command.

2. As root, try the following umask commands. As you issue each command, create text files to see how different umask values change the default file and folder settings:

    umask 222

    umask 333

    umask 066

3. Reboot your system using the reboot command. You can also use the command shutdown -r now.

4. As the system reboots, notice that the umask value returns to its default. To configure your system to use a custom umask value each time it boots, you can edit the /etc/bashrc file using a text editor, as you will do in the next few steps.

5. Make a copy of the /etc/bashrc file, in case a problem occurs. Name the file /etc/bashrc.orig:

    cp /etc/bashrc /etc/bashrc.orig

6. Once you have made a copy of the /etc/bashrc file, open it in a text editor such as vi, Emacs, or pico. Once the /etc/bashrc file is open, scroll down to very end of the file. Enter the umask 066 line so that the last three lines of the /etc/bashrc file appear as follows:

    fi

    umask 066

    fi

    Note: Many Linux configuration files use if statements. They often describe the following logic: "If x takes place, then do y." The letters "fi" simply represent the end of an if statement.

EXERCISE 9.3 *(continued)*

7. Exit the file, making sure to save your changes, and then reboot your system again.

8. Log on as root again and test your new umask value. You will see that the custom umask value is in effect.

Note: If a problem occurs, it is probably because the /etc/bashrc file was not edited correctly. Enter Linux single mode, and then copy the /etc/bashrc.orig file to /etc/bashrc and reboot your system again.

Summary

In this chapter, you examined file permissions available for implementing access control in Windows 2000 and Linux. In Windows 2000, you identified and assigned file-level permissions and learned how partitioning drives and copying and moving files affects security. When securing a system, you must be able to quickly identify suspicious permissions. Doing so will help you avoid attacks waged due to server misconfiguration.

You also identified remote file access control permissions, assigned and used share permissions, and combined local NTFS and remote share permissions. In Linux, you learned about file system security concepts and discovered the function of the umask command. You also learned how to use chmod to set the setuid, setgid, and sticky bits.

Now that you have completed this chapter, you should be able to:

- Secure Windows 2000 files and directories using NTFS.
- Control access to local and remote files.
- Identify file permissions and storage concepts in Linux.
- Set permissions in Linux systems.
- Explain the function of the umask command in Linux.
- Use the setuid, setgid, and sticky bits to ensure security in Linux systems.

Now you are now ready to learn more about what the CIW Security Professional exam expects you to know when assessing and reducing risk to your individual servers.

Exam Essentials

Know how to assign Windows 2000 NTFS permissions. NTFS lies at the heart of security settings for Windows 2000 and other Microsoft operating systems that enforce user-level security. Be able to identify what happens when files are copied and moved between folders and partitions. Also, make sure you understand the ramifications of the Deny permission, which is primarily that it overrides all other settings. Also, be able to identify the commands that you can issue to convert a FAT drive to NTFS.

Understand partitioning strategies in regard to security. To minimize damage in case of an attack, separate the operating system files from the data files. Doing so makes it easier to administer the system, and it also helps secure the system.

Understand permissions for local and remote resources. Be able to identify what happens when a resource is made available remotely. In Windows 2000, be able to identify what happens when share and NTFS permissions are combined. Also, make sure that you can identify the issues that might arise when a folder is shared beneath another share point.

Be able to assign Linux permissions. Become familiar with the chmod, chown, and chgrp commands. When using chmod, make sure that you can assign symbolic and absolute permissions. Be prepared to view a readout of file permissions and interpret the results. For example, you should be able to read an entry such as r--rw--rwx and provide the numeric equivalent.

Know how to use the umask command. Be able to identify the purpose of the umask command, as well as the ramifications of changing the value. For example, be able to calculate the default permissions of a file if the umask value is changed from 022 (the default) to 111.

Be able to set setuid, sgid and sticky bits. Understand what happens when a sticky bit is set on a directory (any file created in that directory will inherit the permissions of that directory, and not the permissions possessed by the user). The setuid permission is especially important to understand, because some applications that have improper setuid permissions can cause security problems. Be able to identify these special permission bits in both symbolic and absolute notation.

Key Terms

Before you take the exam, be certain you are familiar with the following terms:

- absolute mode
- file allocation table (FAT)
- group identifiers (GIDs)
- inheritance
- inode
- New Technology File System (NTFS)
- setgid
- setuid
- SGID
- share points
- SUID
- symbolic mode
- umask
- user identifiers (UIDs)

Review Questions

1. What must be implemented in Windows 2000 to establish user-based local file permissions?

    A. The file allocation table (FAT)

    B. The Windows *New Technology File System* (NTFS)

    C. The owner identifier (UID)

    D. The group identifier (GID)

2. What does Write (W) permission allow the user to do at the file level in Windows 2000?

    A. Change a file's permissions, delete a file, and display file data and attributes.

    B. Display owner and permissions, change file attributes, and create data in and append data to a file.

    C. Display file data, attributes, owner, and permissions, and delete a file.

    D. Change a file's permissions, run a file if it is executable, and take ownership of a file.

3. What does Read (R) permission allow the user to do at the file level in Windows 2000?

    A. Change a file's permissions, delete a file, and display file data and attributes.

    B. Display file data, attributes, owner, and permissions, and take ownership of a file.

    C. Display file attributes, owner, and permissions. Run a file if it is executable.

    D. Display file data, attributes, owner, and permissions.

4. What is the purpose of the standard sets of permissions in Windows 2000?

- A. To allow the Everyone group to assign all permissions
- B. To simplify permissions management
- C. To lock out all non-system-privileged users
- D. To assign Read or higher permission to all users

5. Why is drive partitioning important for Windows 2000 security?
   - A. Because it makes administration of folder permissions easier.
   - B. Because it allows easy copying and moving of files.
   - C. Because it assigns permissions to everyone in all groups.
   - D. Because it gives access to the logon directory to the Everyone group.

6. What happens when a file is copied to a new folder in Windows 2000?
   - A. The new file inherits the target folder's permissions.
   - B. The original file permissions are retained.
   - C. The directory allocation table is updated.
   - D. The original file is deleted after the copy is completed.

7. You want to make a file available to all users. You place it in the public FTP folder, but users still cannot read the file, which is located in the same directory with several other files that users can read. What is the most likely cause of the problem?
   - A. The file has SGID permissions.
   - B. The file is not owned by the FTP server.
   - C. The file is marked with the Executable permission.
   - D. The file does not have the read bit set.

8. Which rights are used when share and NTFS permissions are combined, and the share is accessed from a remote host?
   - A. The more granular permissions
   - B. The less restrictive permissions
   - C. The more restrictive permissions
   - D. The share permissions provided

9. What Linux command is used to set subsequent file-creation mode bits?

   A. umask

   B. mask

   C. cmask

   D. chmask

10. What would the command `chmod 007 filename.txt` accomplish?

    A. It would make the file named `filename.txt` completely inaccessible to all users.

    B. It would give the owner full permissions to the file, but forbid access to the other and group members.

    C. It would make the file a secret file for use only in an inode.

    D. It would make the file accessible by all users.

11. Which of the following bits allows an application to run with the permissions of a different user?

    A. setuid

    B. sticky

    C. umask

    D. GID

12. John is a systems administrator of several Linux servers. He receives an error message that essentially informs him that the inode for the `/etc/shadow` file is no longer present. What has occurred?

    A. The file has been modified.

    B. The file has been deleted.

    C. The file has been moved.

    D. The file has been copied.

13. Robert wants to enable the Encrypting File System (EFS) on a Windows 2000 drive. Currently, this system does not allow user-level permissions. What must he do first?

    A. He must right-click on the file or folder he wants to encrypt.

    B. He must first enable encryption on the partition.

    C. He must first generate a key pair.

    D. He must first convert the drive to NTFS.

14. A shared file named `readme.txt` has been allowed full access to Everyone through NTFS and has been given read-only share-level access to Everyone. What are the effective permissions of this file if accessed locally?

    A. No Access or Deny

    B. Full Control Access

    C. Read

    D. Write

15. A file named `secret.txt` already has the permission value of 700. You issue the command `chmod ug+x secret.txt`. What permissions does the file now have?

    A. 710

    B. 716

    C. 710

    D. 610

16. What does the Write permission allow you do to a folder on an NTFS drive?

    A. Add files and folders.

    B. Delete a folder.

    C. Take ownership of a folder.

    D. Change permissions.

17. James is in the Webusers and Database User groups. Through NTFS, he has full access to the C:\web\ folder because he belongs to the Webusers group. However, he has been given No Access to the C:\web folder as a member of the Database User group. What are his effective permissions to access the C:\web\ folder?

    A. Full Access

    B. No Access or Deny

    C. Read

    D. He can only access the file locally.

18. Which of the following applications or snap-ins is used to assign NTFS permissions?

    A. Windows Explorer

    B. Computer Manager

    C. Disk Management

    D. Local Security Policy

19. You have just converted a FAT32 drive to NTFS. What permissions does a newly created NTFS-enabled directory give to the Everyone group?

    A. Read

    B. No Access or Deny

    C. Full Control Access

    D. Write

20. Joel has just enabled NTFS on his system. Which of the following can he now do?

    A. Logging

    B. Undeleting files

    C. Auditing

    D. Establishing user-level shares

Answers to Review Questions

1. B. You must implement NTFS in order to set user-based local file permissions.

2. B. It is important to realize that the Write permission in Windows 2000 implies other permissions, including Read.

3. D. As with the Write permission, there is more than meets the eye with the Read permission.

4. B. The standard permission sets make it possible to assign permissions to files and folders quickly, without having to worry about improperly combining permissions.

5. A. Drive partitioning eases administration. It also secures the system from some attacks, because they cannot spread easily across partitions. If, for example, a hacker uploads too many files to an FTP server, the partition containing user-based FTP files may crash, but the operating system partition may still be intact and operating properly.

6. A. Files copied to new folders in Windows 2000 always inherit the attributes of the target folder.

7. D. The read bit is essential; without it, the file would not be listed properly.

8. C. When NTFS and share-level permissions are combined in a resource accessed from a remote host, the more restrictive setting applies. Remember, however, that this setting applies only to users accessing the resource remotely.

9. A. The `umask` command sets the default permissions for newly created files.

10. D. The 007 permission would give no permissions to the owner or the group, but would allow all users (i.e., everyone, or "the world") full access. This is because 7 is in the "everyone" section, and 7 is a combination of Read (4), Write (2), and Execute (1).

11. A. The setuid bit allows an application to be run by various users. However, its effective permissions will be those of the owner. Many applications, such as the `/usr/bin/passwd` command, are properly configured as setuid root. Sometimes, however, applications can mistakenly be given setuid root permissions.

12. **B.** In Unix systems, an inode represents a file or directory. If an inode is missing, the file has been deleted. As a result, John will have to restore the /etc/shadow file from a backup. He should also take steps to track down the cause of this deletion, because it can constitute evidence that an attack has occurred.

13. **D.** The Encrypting File System (EFS) requires NTFS. You must use the Convert command to convert a drive without damaging existing information.

14. **B.** Share-level permissions apply only to remote users logging in to the server. NTFS permissions apply to both local and remote users. Because the file gives Full Control Access permissions to Everyone, and because the file is being accessed locally, there are no restrictions.

15. **C.** The ug+x adds the user execute permissions to the user and group, but not to everyone. Whenever you use chmod in symbolic mode, you run the risk of inadvertently adding permissions to existing permissions.

16. **A.** The Write permission does not allow a user to delete the folder or take ownership of it. The ability to change ownership is given only to the systems administrator, and you need ownership of a file or directory to change permissions on a folder.

17. **B.** The No Access or Deny permission overrides all other permissions.

18. **A.** Windows Explorer is the tool that allows you to assign NTFS permissions. You do this by right-clicking a file or folder and then assigning permissions and ownership privileges through the GUI.

19. **C.** By default, Windows NT/2000 systems are "wide open," meaning that everyone has access to the partition. Certain files and folders are more restricted, but it is important to understand that newly created directories are given full control access to all users by default.

20. **C.** You cannot enable auditing without NTFS. Auditing is a chief reason why you would enable NTFS on a partition. The rest of the activities listed were possible before Joel enabled NTFS.

Chapter 10

Assessing and Reducing Risk

THE CIW EXAM OBJECTIVE GROUPS COVERED IN THIS CHAPTER:

- ✓ Assess common risks associated with Windows and Unix servers, including but not limited to: operating system attacks, system scanning, NIS, NFS, Trojans.
- ✓ Reduce risk by modifying system parameters and locking down services.

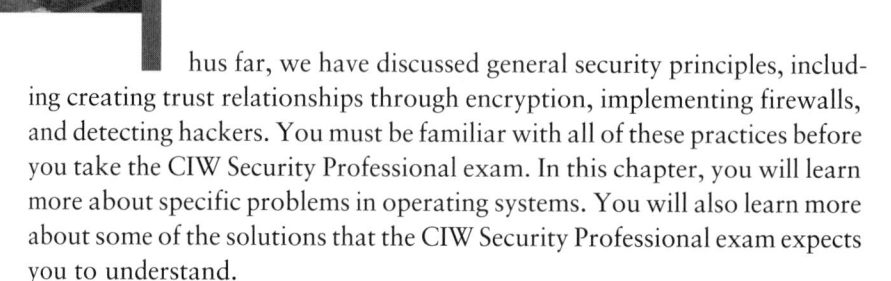

Thus far, we have discussed general security principles, including creating trust relationships through encryption, implementing firewalls, and detecting hackers. You must be familiar with all of these practices before you take the CIW Security Professional exam. In this chapter, you will learn more about specific problems in operating systems. You will also learn more about some of the solutions that the CIW Security Professional exam expects you to understand.

This chapter mostly discusses the Windows 2000 operating systems, as well as Linux. Although the exam does not favor any one operating system over the other, the Windows and Linux operating systems are relatively easy to obtain and install, and it is possible to implement the concepts necessary to succeed as a security administrator. Although this chapter may not describe all of the concepts necessary to secure your operating system, it will provide you with the material necessary to answer questions on the exam.

Reducing Risks in Windows 2000

Windows 2000, like every other significant network operating system, contains numerous *default settings* and options, which are accepted by most administrators. These system defaults are well known to experienced attackers and are used to penetrate systems. While some default values cannot be changed, many can. Such changes can offer significant security gains. Here is a short list of common default settings in Windows 2000:

- Default file locations
- Buffer overflows

- Unquestioned intra-operating system trust relationships
- Default shares
- No protection on the Windows Registry
- Server Message Block (SMB) connectivity (Windows 2000 servers can be tricked into negotiating an SMB dialect that has a low level of encryption)
- Easily revealed last logon name
- Default accounts

You should consider changing many of the default file locations during the initial installation of Windows 2000. For instance, the Windows 2000 operating system is installed by default in the \WINNT directory of the primary drive. Using a different directory causes no problems for legitimate users, but it does create difficulties for attackers attempting to remotely access files through a medium such as a web server.

Windows 2000 automatically creates *default shares* for administrative purposes. They include C$, D$, and any other root volumes in the system. ADMIN$ is a share set to the \SYSTEMROOT directory, which would be C:\WINNT if you accepted default settings when installing Windows onto a C:\ drive. Although these shares are configured for administrative use only, they still pose an unnecessary risk. You can remove these default shares by right-clicking the appropriate drive and then clicking the Sharing tab on the Properties sheet. You can then identify the default share and remove it.

> **TIP** Disabling the Server service will also remove all default shares. However, it will also disable all sharing, which might not be desirable in certain situations.

Windows NT/2000/XP systems have long been susceptible to buffer overflow attacks. As you will see later, the best way to protect yourself against buffer overflow exploits is to update the patch level of your operating systems.

In addition, Windows systems often fall prey to the fact that one part of the operating system trusts the other unquestionably. This phenomenon is called automatic intra-operating system trust. It occurs when information processed by one element of the operating system is allowed to pass to another without question. As a result, Windows systems have been used as platforms to wage attacks against other network systems. E-mail viruses such as Melissa, "I Love You," and others, for example, have been able to take advantage of the conveniences offered by Windows systems. The best way to solve such problems is to use antivirus software and personal firewalls, and engage in e-mail-attachment scanning.

In the next section, we will learn more about securing the Windows Registry.

Windows 2000 Registry Security

Ultimately, all the configuration settings and controls for modern Windows systems reside in the *Registry*. Thus, if the Registry is not secure, the Windows 2000 installation is not secure. Many of the changes we've discussed in this book so far have required Registry modifications. Just as the file system has to be secured, access to the Registry must be secured as well.

Most of the vulnerabilities discovered by hackers have centered on accessing portions of the Registry to which only read-level access is granted. Like the default permissions for NTFS, the default security on various portions of the Registry is inadequate for protecting systems.

Unfortunately, knowing that the Registry needs to be secured and knowing what contents to secure and how to secure them are separate issues. Microsoft has never released a comprehensive document explaining the permissions required for various portions of the Registry. Most of the recommended settings we will examine have been determined through research and experimentation outside Microsoft.

WARNING Given the critical nature of the Registry in Windows 2000, you must proceed cautiously with changes to the Registry permissions. If changes are made incorrectly, you can reduce security and render the entire system inoperable.

Registry Structure

The Registry in Windows 2000 is a series of database engine data files typically stored in the \WINNT\System32\Config directory (if your Windows 2000 installation uses the \WINNT directory and not another one you specified during startup). The Windows 2000 operating system stores part of the Registry exclusively in RAM. Backups of some or all of these files are also stored in the \WINNT\Repair directory. You should use NTFS security to properly protect the physical files and backups. Only the system account needs access to these files.

Although you can use either the Regedit or the Regedt32 application to edit the Registry, the Regedt32 program allows you to implement security settings for the Registry. Because no icon exists for Regedt32, you need to call it up by selecting Run ➢ Start and typing **regedt32**, as shown in Figure 10.1.

FIGURE 10.1 The Run dialog box

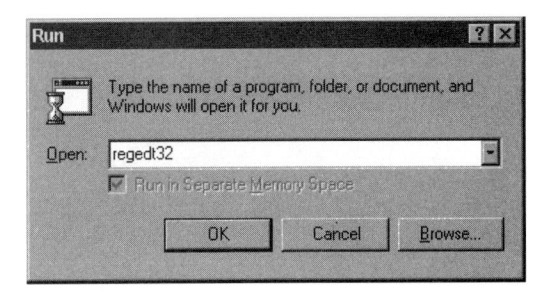

Immediately upon bringing up Regedt32, you will see the five main portions of the Registry. The five main portions of the registry are normally referred to as keys, and everything below them as *subtrees*. The *Registry subtrees* together comprise all system configuration in Windows 2000. Table 10.1 identifies the subtrees and their uses.

TABLE 10.1 Subtrees and Their Uses

Subtree	Description
HKEY_LOCAL_MACHINE	Contains all operating system configuration data related to the local computer. Information such as which device drivers to load is stored here. The subtree is constant regardless of the user logged on locally. The key is often referred to as HKLM.
HKEY_USERS	Contains two subtrees: Default, which contains the system default settings used when the Ctrl+Alt+Delete logon screen is displayed. The security identifier (SID) of the current user. This key is often referred to as HKU.

TABLE 10.1 Subtrees and Their Uses *(continued)*

Subtree	Description
HKEY_CURRENT_USER	Contains interactive data about the current user. Any user account that has ever logged in locally has a copy of this subtree stored in the \WINNT\Profiles\username directory in a file called NTUser.dat. If any keys are duplicated between this subtree and HKLM, the values in this subtree take precedence. This subtree is actually a pointer to the HKU\SID subtree, and is often referred to as HKCU.
HKEY_CLASSES_ROOT	Contains software configuration data, such as file extension mappings. It is actually a pointer to \HKLM\Software\Classes.
HKEY_CURRENT_CONFIG	Contains data about the active hardware profile. This data comes from the Software and System portions of HKLM. This key is often referred to as HKCC.

As you can see, most of the Registry derives from the HKLM subtree. Equally important is to protect the HKCU subtree, because an attacker could use its precedence over HKLM to override settings there.

HKLM contains several distinct subtrees of its own, as shown in Table 10.2.

TABLE 10.2 HKLM Subtrees

Subtree	Description
Hardware	Re-created every time Windows 2000 starts up, it contains information about the physical devices attached to the computer.
SAM	Contains the actual user accounts and passwords. The Security Account Manager (SAM) is not accessed directly but rather through APIs in the Windows 2000 operating system.

TABLE 10.2 HKLM Subtrees *(continued)*

Subtree	Description
Security	Contains all security information for the local computer. Like the SAM subkey, it cannot be accessed directly either.
Software	Contains application configuration information that is independent of the current user.
System	Stores configuration information for services and devices in the computer.

Auditing the Registry

You can audit changes to the Registry. As shown in Figure 10.2, you can select the relevant part of the Registry and then select the users to audit. You can choose to audit the entire Registry, or you can audit sections.

FIGURE 10.2 Registry subtrees

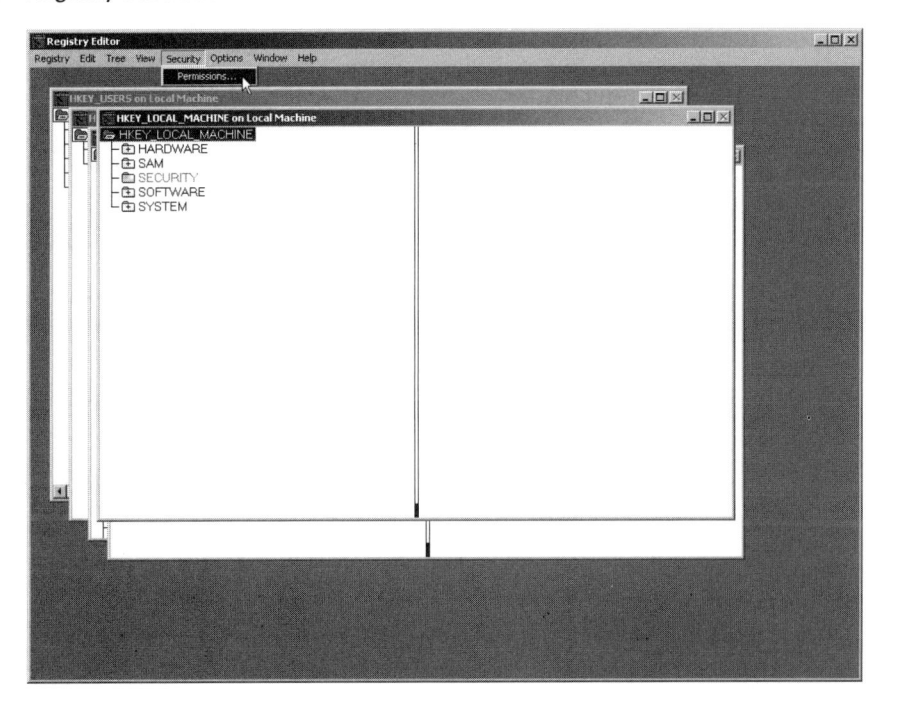

Once you have determined what part of the Registry you want to protect, you can select it and then add the users you want to audit. If you add the Everyone group, for example, any changes to the Registry will be logged.

Still in Regedt32, you can select Security ➢ Permissions, then click the Advanced button and select the Auditing tab. You can add the users or groups you want to audit by clicking the Add button, as shown in Figure 10.3.

FIGURE 10.3 The Access Control Settings dialog box

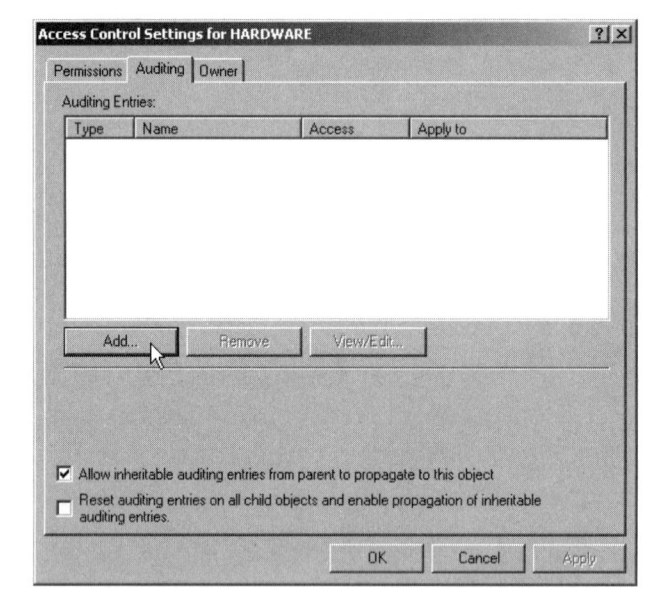

The Everyone group is sometimes a good choice to audit as long as your system has enough hard drive space, RAM, and CPU power to record all the information that might be generated. Carefully choosing what you want to audit in the Registry is critical, however. The Registry is accessed hundreds or thousands of times per second. If you enable too much auditing, the burden on the system will become too great, and the system could become unstable.

Backing Up the Registry

Because the Registry is so important, the first step in securing it is to back it up to a secure media. This way, if an attack compromises your Registry, you can restore a secure version of the Registry to your system.

Setting Registry Permissions

Two broad security permissions and several granular ones are available. The broad permissions are Read and Full Control. The specific control permissions are shown in Table 10.3.

TABLE 10.3 Specific Control Permissions

Permission	Description
Query Value	Allows a user or group to read a value entry from a Registry key.
Set Value	Allows a user or group to set value entries in a Registry key.
Create Subkey	Allows a user or group to create subkeys from a given Registry key.
Enumerate Subkeys	Allows a user or group to identify a Registry key's subkeys.
Notify	Allows a user or group to audit notification events from a key in the Registry.
Create Link	Gives a user or group the right to create a symbolic link in a particular key.
Delete	Allows a user or group to delete a selected key.
Write DAC	Allows a user or group to gain access to a key for the purpose of writing a discretionary ACL to the key. This is effectively a change-permission right.
Write Owner	Allows a user or group to gain access to a key for purposes of taking ownership of the key.
Read Control	Allows a user or group to gain access to the security information on a selected key.

The process for auditing the Registry is similar to setting auditing on any resource. Select the appropriate group and choose the permission type you want, as Figure 10.4 shows.

FIGURE 10.4 Special Registry access permissions

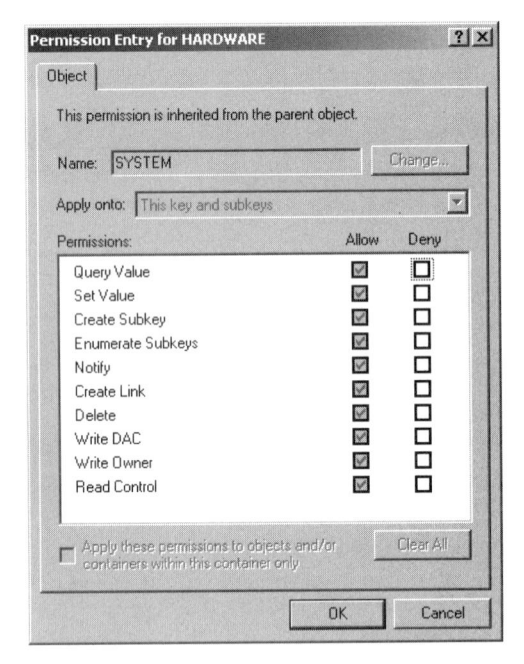

> Improper Registry permissions can cause your system to become unstable. Edit Registry permissions at your own risk, and be extremely careful.

EXERCISE 10.1

Auditing the Windows 2000 Registry

In this exercise, you will enable auditing on events specific to the HKLM key.

1. Open the Regedt32 application.

> **EXERCISE 10.1 *(continued)***
>
> 2. Once Regedt32 opens, select Security ➢ Permissions to open the Permissions dialog box.
> 3. Make sure that the HKLM key is selected.
> 4. Click the Advanced button and then select the Auditing tab.
> 5. Add the Everyone group by clicking Everyone and then clicking OK.
> 6. The Auditing Entry dialog box will appear. Choose all items and then click OK.
> 7. Click Apply, then click OK until you return to Regedt32. You have now enabled auditing for the Everyone group on your system's HKLM key.

Disabling and Removing Unnecessary Services in Windows 2000

Because Windows 2000 is designed as a robust network operating system, it includes numerous services and networking protocols. Generally, a typical implementation does not need to use them all. It is always a good idea to configure your Windows 2000 system for a specific purpose by removing *unnecessary services*. By removing any services not needed for a particular purpose, you can remove some of the risk factors.

Some services cannot be easily removed without damaging Windows 2000; thus, they must be disabled. The *Server service* (which handles incoming *NetBIOS* network requests) is typical. When using Windows 2000 as an Internet/intranet server, you do not need NetBIOS support. In fact, leaving NetBIOS support running when it is unnecessary introduces numerous vulnerabilities. By disabling it, you can stop a great many of the exploit tools used to break into Windows 2000.

> **TIP** If you want to stop or disable a Windows 2000 service, you do so through the Services snap-in.

EXERCISE 10.2

Removing Unnecessary Services and Protocols in Windows 2000

In this exercise, we will disable unnecessary services and protocols on your Windows 2000 system.

1. Go to Start ➤ Programs ➤ Administrative Tools ➤ Services and open the Services snap-in.

2. The Services menu displays a list of services in the system and their current settings. The Task Scheduler service is often useful, but it is also a popular target for attackers. Although one default service (the Remote Storage Engine) is dependent on the Task Scheduler, you can disable both services without crippling Windows 2000. First, highlight the Task Scheduler icon, and then stop the service.

3. You will see a prompt telling you that the Remote Storage Engine service is dependent on the Task Scheduler. If you are not going to use the Remote Storage Engine, choose to stop this service by clicking Yes.

4. Right-click the Task Scheduler icon, select properties, and then change the Startup Type field to Disabled.

5. Click Apply and then click OK.

6. Right-click the Remote Storage Engine icon, select properties, and disable this service. Disabling differs from stopping because it prevents the service from starting at the next boot.

7. You have now disabled services in Windows 2000. If you need these services in the future, you can change their settings so they will start automatically.

Note: To completely remove the Task Scheduler service, you can delete the entire file, which is in the C:\winnt\system32\ directory (e.g., \WINNT\system32\MSTask.exe, if your system is installed on the C: drive).

8. Assuming that your server is Internet based, you do not need the File And Print Services for Macintosh and the Appletalk protocol. First, remove the File Services for Macintosh and Print Services for Macintosh by opening Control Panel and then double-clicking the Add/Remove Programs icon.

EXERCISE 10.2 (continued)

9. Click the Add/Remove Windows Components icon. At the Windows Components window, scroll down to the Other Network And Print Services icon, and click the Details button. Deselect both check boxes referring to the Macintosh services and then click OK.

10. Click Next and complete your task of removing these unnecessary services.

11. Now, you can remove the Appletalk protocol. Right-click the My Network Places icon to access the Local Area Connection Properties dialog box, and right-click the Local Area Connection icon; select properties.

12. Highlight and uninstall the Appletalk protocol.

13. To remove NetBIOS support from your system, open the Local Area Connection Properties dialog box, highlight the Internet Protocol (TCP/IP) icon, and click the Properties button.

14. Click the Advanced button and then select the WINS tab. Modify settings so that the tab appears exactly as shown here:

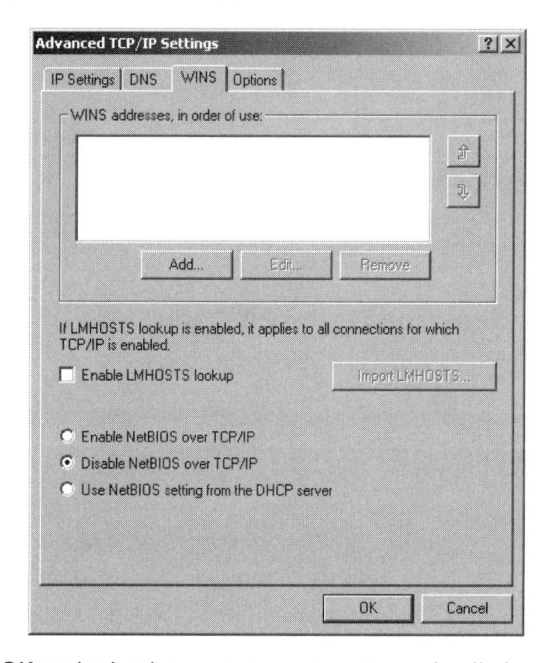

15. Click OK and take the necessary steps to apply all changes.

Sometimes you cannot disable services internally because you must provide connectivity for those services to internal users while still blocking them for external users. This method of disabling services is the least desirable, but is better than leaving them directly accessible.

Table 10.4 shows some of the common Windows 2000 services you might want to block externally and which ports they listen on so you can implement filters at the router or firewall to insulate them.

TABLE 10.4 Common Windows 2000 Services and Corresponding Ports

Service	TCP/IP Ports Used
DNS Zone Transfers	TCP 53
Microsoft Networking	UDP 137 and 138; TCP 139
MS RPC	TCP 135; UDP 135
MS RPC (Secondary)	UDP 1028
MS SQL Server	TCP 1433
SNMP	UDP 161 and 162

> Make sure that you are able to identify the ports used in Microsoft Networking, both in configuring a firewall and identifying internal network traffic.

Securing Network Connectivity

Once you have disabled or blocked services, you need to take other measures to protect your network. Windows 2000 networking is based on a protocol called *Server Message Block (SMB)*, which Microsoft often refers to as the *Common Internet File System (CIFS)*. Windows 2000 systems use SMB to communicate, and SMB is at the heart of Microsoft Networking. By default, all Windows NT/2000/XP systems encrypt SMB packets that travel across the network. Figure 10.5 shows an overview of the SMB connection process.

FIGURE 10.5 SMB connection process

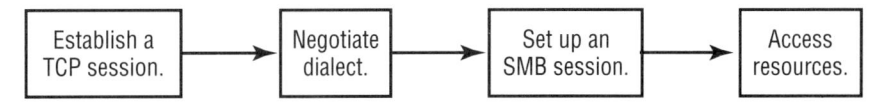

```
Establish a  →  Negotiate  →  Set up an    →  Access
TCP session.    dialect.       SMB session.    resources.
```

Windows 2000 supports seven kinds of *SMB dialects*. In ascending order of encryption strength, they are:

1. PC Network Program 1.0
2. Microsoft Networks 1.03
3. LanMan 1.0
4. LM 1.2X002
5. LanMan 2.1
6. Windows NT LM 0.12
7. NTLM version 2.0 (NTLMv2, for Windows 2000)

Microsoft-compatible clients and servers must negotiate the dialect they want to use. The negotiation process is designed to find the highest version of SMB that can be used between the server and the client. The biggest problem in this scenario is that the strength of the authentication depends on the client and not the server. Obsolete encryption can be forced from the client end by configuring the client to support only the lowest possible SMB client.

If authentication fails during the SMB process, one of two things occurs: Either access is denied or a *null SMB session* is created. The latter result is dangerous because, by default, the null session is still a member of the Everyone group, and anything accessible to the Everyone group is accessible to the unauthenticated user. Hackers can use applications that take advantage of this connection to gain information about your system accounts and services.

To prevent null sessions, you can alter the Registry using the Local Security Policy snap-in, or you can alter the following key using any Registry editor:

HKLM\System\CurrentControlSet\Control\Lsa\restrictanonymous

The value of 0 is the default setting, whereas the value of 1 restricts the listing of accounts and shares. A value of 2 has the system restrict all anonymous access, unless a service, such as FTP, explicitly allows it.

> **Additional Choices for Null Sessions**
>
> In some cases, adding HKLM\System\CurrentControlSet\Control\Lsa\ restrictanonymous might cause problems with some network-based services that read remote Registry entries. If your system needs to provide parts of the Registry to remote systems, first try running the Server service with a named domain account. If that is not possible or does not solve the problem, add **winreg** to the NullPipeSessions value in HKLM\System\ CurrentControlSet\Services\Lanmanserver\parameters.
>
> The above change keeps accounts hidden, but reopens the rest of your Registry. Also, if you have a trust relationship, RestrictAnonymous will prevent the trusting domain from retrieving the user list in permission dialog boxes. Group and usernames from the trusted domain will have to be entered manually.

SMB Encryption Issues

If your clients are Windows 2000 Professional workstations only, you can also disable LAN Manager authentication. Windows 95/98/ME, Windows for Workgroups, and Samba all use LAN Manager authentication, so this action will disable access of those clients as well and is therefore not usually feasible. However, if your server is acting as a standard e-mail, FTP, or web server, you can safely change this setting.

Another option with the same control is to configure the server to authoritatively determine which type of client authentication it allows, rather than allowing the client to make the determination. This option is not extremely effective, because the server will still send all of its dialects to the client as possibilities. What it primarily does is stop a specific attack called the SMB downgrade attack. That particular attack uses a variant of a packet sniffer to listen for the SMB authentication process. When the server detects the process, it sends a message claiming to be from the client. The message indicates that only the low-end, plain-text-only authentication is available. The server accepts this message and establishes the session in that manner. The client then passes the password in plain text, which the attacking system then captures and stores.

To control LAN Manager authentication, you need to make changes to the `HKLM\System\CurrentControlSet\Control\LSA\LMCompatibilityLevel` key. The Local Security Policy snap-in allows you to control these settings precisely.

Another effective option is to enable SMB signatures, which make Windows 2000 use cryptographic signatures on all the packets (MD5) to prevent spoofing. This method helps to eliminate the possibility of forged packets. However, it can have adverse effects on Windows 95/98/ME and Windows for Workgroups client connectivity, so it should be tested before being used. To enable a server to accept only signed packets, you need to change the value of `HKLM\System\CurrentControlSet\Services\LanManServer\Parameters\RequireSecuritySignature` from 0 to 1. If you enable this setting, all clients must also be configured to generate and respond only to signed packets. On the clients, you need to change `HKLM\System\CurrentControlSet\Services\Rdr\Parameters\RequireSecuritySignatures` from 0 to 1.

You can use the Local Security Policy snap-in to perform this configuration. In fact, this snap-in gives you a choice of always encrypting the data channel or encrypting the channel only if the client can support this feature. Because you are establishing an Internet server, consider always encrypting the data channel.

EXERCISE 10.3

Controlling SMB Connectivity in Windows 2000

In this exercise, you will configure your system to use the strongest encryption possible for SMB connectivity.

1. Open the Local Security Policy snap-in.

2. Choose Security Settings ➢ Local Policies ➢ Security Options to open the Security Options dialog box.

3. Double-click the Additional Restrictions For Anonymous Connections icon. Once the Local Security Policy Setting dialog box appears, select the strongest setting from the drop-down box, which is No Access Without Explicit Anonymous Permissions. Click OK.

> **EXERCISE 10.3 *(continued)***
>
> 4. Next, you will strengthen the client SMB authentication by moving SMB negotiation control from the client to the server. Still in the Security Options dialog box, double-click LanManager Authentication Level.
>
> 5. Set the level to the strictest setting, which is Send NTLMv2 Response Only\Refuse LM & NTLM, and then click OK.
>
>   Note: If you want your systems to remain compatible with Linux systems running Samba, the strictest setting you can choose is Send LM & NTLM–Use NTLMv2 Session Security If Negotiated.
>
> 6. Now, enable the Secure Channel: Digitally Encrypt Or Sign Secure Channel Data (Always) value. This step will reduce the likelihood of spoofed IP connections.
>
> 7. Next, enable the Digitally Sign Client Communication (Always) value.
>
> 8. Now, enable the Secure Channel: Require Strong (Windows 2000 Or Later) Session value.
>
>   Note: Samba is compatible with all the settings established in Steps 6 through 8.
>
> 9. If you want to test your SMB connectivity, start the Server service and connect to another system. Sometimes web servers use SMB when creating virtual directories between systems.

Miscellaneous Windows 2000 Configuration Changes

You should consider numerous additional changes that do not reside in any specific category. For example, if you do not need the Task Scheduler service, disable it. Also, you can make these changes in the Local Computer Policies snap-in:

Securing printer drivers   To restrict installation of *printer drivers* to administrators and print operators only, make sure that the Prevent Users From Installing Printer Drivers value in the Local Security Policy snap-in is enabled.

Hiding the last username   A small precaution that can prevent an illegitimate user who has physical access to the computer from knowing a legitimate username involves modifying a key called `DontDisplayLastUserName` of type `REG_SZ` so that it has the value of 1. The key you need to modify is at `HKLM\Software\Microsoft\Windows NT\CurrentVersions\Winlogon`. The Local Security Policy snap-in allows you to alter this feature by enabling the Do Not Display Last User Name In Logon Screen option.

This precaution is not foolproof because anyone with direct access to the computer can compromise the system quickly anyway. Anyone with access to the network, even a standard user, can easily access the list of user accounts as well. However, this step is worthwhile because a quick and simple change that causes undue problems might delay a potential attacker.

Clearing the page file on shutdown   The page file in Windows 2000 is used as memory while Windows 2000 is operating. Someone with direct access to the computer can copy the page file by booting from a floppy disk or using a similar tactic. The page file will hold any sensitive information that was paged and not overwritten during usage. Applications can be created to obtain this information. The Clear Virtual Memory Pagefile When System Shuts Down value in the Local Security Policy snap-in allows you to instruct Windows 2000 to overwrite the entire page file with random information during shutdown.

This clearing occurs only during a clean shutdown, so if someone has access to the computer's power switch, it can be made ineffective.

Disabling caching of logon credentials   Windows 2000 normally caches a user's logon credentials locally so that if a domain controller fails or cannot be contacted, the user can still log on and work locally.

Credential caching can cause a vulnerability. For example, suppose that Joe Smith is being fired from your company after he returns from lunch. Joe's account in the domain has been disabled during lunch to prevent him from logging on and destroying data when he returns to collect his personal belongings. But because Windows 2000 cached his credentials locally, Joe could still return to his office, disconnect his machine from the network, and then log on. When his machine could not authenticate with the domain controllers due to lack of connectivity, it would return to his cached credentials, which do not reflect that his account was disabled. Joe could still access his local computer and copy or destroy local data.

Although caching is not a significant threat, if you want to disable Windows 2000 caching credentials locally, open the Local Security Policy snap-in and set the Number Of Previous Logons To Cache setting to 0.

Creating an interactive login message You can configure your system to present messages to any user who logs on interactively (i.e., any user who logs in at the system console). An interactive login message will not thwart a determined hacker, but it can help you prove to insurance companies that you have taken measures to secure your systems. The Security Options section of the Local Security Policy snap-in contains two settings that can help you do this. They are:

Message Text For Users Attempting To Log In The text that users will see as soon as they press Ctrl+Alt+Delete to begin the login process.

Message Title For Users Attempting To Log In Changes the title of the dialog box that contains the message text.

Interactive login messages can provide visible evidence that you have worked to increase security settings. Such evidence may be important to show compliance to security standards as well as to recommendations made by internal auditors.

Securing removable and mass storage media Normally, *removable media* such as floppy disk drives and CD-ROM drives are accessible across a network if they have been shared. You can restrict access to the removable media drives to interactive users only. Thus, the disk and CD-ROM drives are not allocated unless a user is logged on physically at the machine, and then only to that user. To enable this security, open the Local Security Policy snap-in and enable the following values:

- Restrict CD-ROM Access To Locally Logged-On User Only
- Restrict Floppy Access To Locally Logged-On User Only

Establishing default account names It is worth emphasizing the need to rename default accounts, such as Administrator and Guest. Use the Local Security Policy snap-in to do so. An unchanged default account can make a hacker's job all that much easier when it comes to defeating authentication.

Microsoft Service Packs

Any software as complex as the Windows 2000 operating system will necessarily have system bugs of various sorts. Most do not endanger systems.

Unfortunately, the few bugs that present security risks often pose complex problems that can be easily manipulated by a malicious user. To combat buffer overflows and other problems, Microsoft releases occasional major operating system updates in the form of *service packs*. Between service pack releases, Microsoft releases repairs called *hot fixes*. These are specific problem patches meant to correct a particular bug.

It is very important that you install these when you are reasonably sure that they are stable. Indiscriminately installing the latest service pack can actually cause problems for you, especially if it makes changes to the system that you don't know about. Be sure that you understand all changes made by the service pack, and that it will not inadvertently cause any problems for you and your system.

Microsoft service packs include the patches and fixes for Windows 2000. Service packs are located at www.microsoft.com, and the most current service pack for Windows 2000 is available there. It is important, however, that you ensure that the hot fix or service pack you install is stable and useful for your system. Just because a hot fix or service pack has been made available does not necessarily mean that you should download and install it.

Reducing Risks in Unix Systems

The CIW Security Professional exam focuses on the following Unix security risks:

- The `rlogin` command
- Network Information System (NIS)
- Network File System (NFS)

Although these are useful daemons, they are generally not appropriate in an Internet setting. The exam also expects you to find ways to secure your systems. In the sections that follow, you will learn more about how to mitigate and countermand risks.

Disabling *rlogin*

Most modern systems ship with `rlogin` disabled. If you find that a system has `rlogin` enabled, you can disable it by editing either the /etc/xinetd.d/

rlogin file or the /etc/inetd.conf file. You will learn more about xinetd and inetd later in this chapter.

If you require the convenience that rlogin provides, you still have hope. It has become common for systems administrators to replace daemons such as Telnet, rlogin, rsh, and others with Secure Shell (SSH), which encrypts authentication and transmissions.

> **WARNING** Before disabling any daemon or service, make sure that your actions do not cause problems for coworkers. When you see a problem, identify it and then propose a solution. You can then either disable the daemon or replace it with a more secure one. For example, it is possible to replace rlogin and Telnet-based applications with Secure Shell (SSH). As you will see in Chapter 15, SSH encrypts transmissions and allows strong authentication to occur.

The *hosts.equiv* File and *rlogin*

On systems that support rlogin, the /etc/hosts.equiv file extends the actions of this command by placing the remote (incoming) host's name in its contents, allowing any user on the incoming host to have the same trust on the remote host if a login exists on the destination host. The rlogind begins checking the /etc/hosts.equiv file from the top down, until it finds a host that matches the name of the incoming system. A few options exist for how the contents of the hosts.equiv file may be specified. For example:

```
spam.com

-@devils

+@angels
```

These options indicate to the rlogind that the users on the host "spam.com" may log on to the destination host with their customary login names without a password. Spam.com is therefore a trusted host.

The entry -@devils, used for netgroups, should not be trusted or allowed to log on to the destination system. However, the netgroup +@angels is completely trusted and allowed access, provided that its members have login names on the destination system.

NIS Security Concerns

The Network Information System (NIS) is one way to create a distributed computing environment on a local network. NIS was invented by Sun Microsystems, but it has been adopted by the Unix community. It provides a network database of user accounts, and makes it possible for an organization to store user accounts in a single server, called a primary server. NIS clients can then access the primary server in order to authenticate. Once authenticated, these clients can use only one password in order to log into multiple servers. The main NIS server can then replicate its user database to a backup NIS server called a slave server.

To understand the need for a system such as NIS, imagine a network of Unix machines used by a group of people. For a user to log on to the various machines in the network, he or she would need separate accounts, with separate passwords, on each machine. This type of arrangement is awkward. Long ago, it was determined by most systems administrators that users should be able to log on to any machine in the network using a single, centrally administered network password. One of the principal purposes of NIS is to provide a central password database that allows users to have a single account valid on all machines in the network.

Administering a large local network of Unix machines raises other problems besides keeping a central password database. One problem is maintaining the many configuration files necessary to keep the machines in the system operating properly. Without a system like NIS, changing the configuration of machines in the network forces the administrator to log on to each machine individually and make the necessary modifications. NIS allows the relevant configuration files to be distributed from a central location, so changes can be made in a single place and propagated throughout the network.

Although NIS is still widely used by Linux, AIX, and HP-UX networks, Sun provides the NIS+ system, which is far more secure. It uses public-key encryption to secure effective trust relationships. Administering NIS+ is similar to NIS, but it is also a proprietary technology; it is possible for non-Solaris systems to become NIS+ clients, but you must use a Solaris server to create an NIS+ domain. You can learn more about NIS+ by consulting the Sun Microsystems website (www.sun.com). The exam doesn't cover NIS+ in depth, so there is no need to study it any further.

Here is a short overview of standard NIS shortcomings:

The Portmapper Remote Procedure Call (RPC) Daemon The *Portmapper* daemon in Linux is responsible for accepting a *remote procedure call*

(RPC). An RPC allows an application on a local host to make requests of applications or daemons on remote hosts. The portmapper daemon fields remote requests and then maps the request to a local service. This mapping is accomplished by allocating an ephemeral (i.e., registered) port. Two of the Unix-based network daemons that use the Portmapper are NIS and the Network File System (NFS). The problem with allowing RPCs on an Internet-based server is that the RPC protocol does not require authentication. Partial solutions to this lack of security include the following:

- Use a wrapper program, such as *TCP Wrappers*, that enables you to restrict Portmapper access to hosts with certain IP addresses or domain names. (You will learn more in the section "TCPWrappers," later in this chapter.) Still, even with the use of wrappers, the Portmapper is vulnerable to "spoofing."

- Use the RPC protocol behind strong firewalls, and trust any host inside the firewall.

- Use the *Secure RPC* protocol. This enhancement addresses the authentication problem to a certain extent by introducing a public key–based host and user-authentication scheme. Unfortunately, the underlying encryption scheme is based on a 90-digit RSA key that was broken (and the results published) several years ago. As a result, Secure RPC does provide more security, but it does not solve all of the problems presented by the Portmapper service. It is best to just disable NIS and the Portmapper.

Server contact by broadcast   The primary NIS server contacts the master NIS server by broadcast. Therefore, anyone with access to the local network can set up another server and distribute forged NIS maps. Some more recent versions of NIS, such as those distributed with Linux, allow you to specify the NIS server's IP address when you configure an NIS client, which improves security. This feature does not solve the more fundamental authentication problems discussed previously, however.

Plain-text distribution   NIS maps are distributed in plain text. In particular, the NIS password map can be read by anyone with network access using the `ypcat` program, and therefore the encrypted passwords can be seen. Some versions of NIS allow distribution of a shadow password map, which slightly improves security. However, a packet sniffer can still catch the shadow map on the wire, revealing the encrypted passwords. These passwords can then be attacked with a dictionary program.

Encryption and authentication   By default, the NIS does not encrypt its transactions authentication. Thus the plain-text, unencrypted passwords cross the network when a user changes his or her password.

Improving NIS Security: The *securenets* File

One significant improvement in NIS security can be obtained from the securenets file, available on Sun NIS servers and the Linux server. This file allows you to restrict your NIS server so that only certain hosts on particular networks or subnetworks can access it. The securenets file controls access to the NIS server only.

In the securenets file, the subnet mask value is used to compare the IP addresses of incoming requests against the listed network addresses. If the addresses match, the request is honored. To make these steps clearer, here is a sample securenets file:

```
# Always allow access for localhost
255.0.0.0      127.0.0.0
# This line gives access to everybody. PLEASE ADJUST!
0.0.0.0        0.0.0.0
# This line allows access to anyone on the 198.153.142.0
# subnetwork:
198.153.142.0
```

Using securenets improves NIS security somewhat, but does not resolve all NIS security problems.

The Network File System (NFS)

The *Network File System (NFS)* is a system for distributing file systems across a network. Under this system, some machines, called NFS clients, can mount file systems that are physically located on other machines, called NFS servers. An NFS server that makes file systems available for remote mounting is said to export or share those file systems. NFS servers use the /etc/exports directory to list directories that they will share with clients.

The NFS was developed by Sun Microsystems and subsequently adopted by the Unix community. It has many applications in a Unix environment, including:

Distributed home directories   If a user's home directory resides on a file system that is exported by an NFS server and then mounted by a community of computers on a network, that user can access his or her files regardless of which computer he or she logs on to. In conjunction with NIS network passwords, NFS can thus make a large collection of computers interchangeable from the user's point of view.

Centralized administration of software packages Using NTFS, you can place a large software package on a server and then have clients install it. Administrative changes need only be made to the single copy on the exported partition, and the client hosts will immediately be able to use the updated package.

Conservation of disk space You can share infrequently changed, large sets of files among several computers by installing the files on a shared NFS partition. For example, you could share a single copy of the complete Unix manual pages among many computers by exporting one copy of the manual pages over NFS.

NFS is widely used in LANs, but is also used by web servers. Many systems administrators use NFS to enable a web server to serve up content from remote drives. Doing so enables a web server to provide more content without having to update its hard drive. Thus, using NFS reduces downtime, while improving service to customers.

NFS Security Concerns

You have already learned that NFS uses the Portmapper daemon, which can cause problems with authentication. For example, suppose that you use the /etc/exports file to restrict access to the /psycho partition to a certain list of hosts. A host claiming to be one of these allowed hosts is taken at its word. Similarly, a user claiming to be the user with UID 1001 does not have to prove his or her identity.

Here are two additional concerns:

User and group ID confusion NFS tends to assume the use of a properly functioning central login server daemon, such as NIS or Kerberos. If an NIS or Kerberos daemon is not available to coordinate authentication information, local and remote user and group IDs can become confused. As a result, it is possible for a remote user to log in and obtain the privileges of another user.

Unencrypted NFS file transfers Even when Secure RPC is used, the bulk data transfer across the network during NFS transactions is not encrypted. Programs such as `tcpdump` can see the contents of all files transferred across an NFS mount.

For all of the reasons we have outlined, NFS should be used only on trusted networks behind adequate firewall protection. Even then, however, NFS and NIS are still prone to attack from insiders.

Updating Linux Binaries

Thus far, you have learned about some of the security concerns related to the NIS and NFS protocols. However, it is possible for the actual daemon binaries to develop problems due to bugs that have been inadvertently coded into them. The primary way to solve this problem is to update the code to its latest, stable version.

Many types of Linux exist, so you can find support at the appropriate websites and through various commands found in the operating systems. For instance, Red Hat Linux offers updates on its website. Errata lists are located on the web at http://bugzilla.redhat.com/bugzilla. Using the `rhn_register` script, you can create a profile for your system, including one that will automatically send you e-mail updates concerning the latest errata. Once you register, you can then run the `up2date` script, which enables you to:

1. Add the Red Hat public key to your key ring. This enables you to ensure that packages you download are actually from Red Hat and that they have not been tampered with.

2. Select packages that can be updated.

WARNING Because they replace core system files, these patches often can be uninstalled. You should always choose the option to accept this feature. Without a backup of replaced files, the system might be unrecoverable if the patch renders it unstable.

Regardless of the patch's function, you should perform a full backup of production systems before applying patches. If possible, apply updated RPM files on a trial system that duplicates the production system before using it on the production system.

To register for updates using the graphical version of up2date, follow these steps:

1. Issue the command rhn_register.

2. Fill out the relevant information to obtain a username and password.

3. Once you have registered, you can either issue the command up2date from a terminal, or you can go to www.redhat.com/network, read the errata, and choose to update the packages you want.

> **NOTE** To use the graphical version of up2date, you will need the latest versions of python-xmlrpc, usermode, and up2date-gnome. You can also use the up2date-config script to update how up2date retrieves content. For example, you can enable it to authenticate with a proxy server, and to automatically retrieve and omit certain packages.

EXERCISE 10.4

Updating Red Hat Linux and Disabling the *cron* and *at* Services

In this exercise, you will use the Red Hat up2date application to ensure that you have the latest patch level on your system.

1. Connect to the Internet, open a command prompt, and issue the following command:

   rhn_register

2. Register your current system on the network.

3. Issue the command up2date from a terminal. (To use the graphical version of this utility, you must have the proper packages installed. See the discussion of up2date earlier in this chapter.) Or, go to www.redhat.com/network and choose to update the packages you want.

4. Earlier in this chapter, you disabled the Windows 2000 Task Scheduler service. The Linux version of this service is called crond. Stopping this daemon can cause problems for your system. However, if you want to stop it, kill its PID using the following command:

   host# /etc/rc.d/init.d/crond stop

> **EXERCISE 10.4 (continued)**
>
> 5. You can then use the `ntsysv` command to ensure that `crond` does not start the next time your system reboots. Make sure that you have `ntsysv` disable running the script in run levels 3 and 5. Linux also uses the `atd` daemon, which schedules jobs to run one time in the future. You can disable this daemon the same way as `crond`.

xinetd and inetd

The `xinetd` and `inetd` daemons are often called the Internet daemon, *or the super daemon*, because they are used to launch additional daemons. The `xinetd` daemon is used on newer Linux implementations, such as any Red Hat Linux system from 7.0 and up. The `inetd` daemon is now considered a legacy daemon and is found in older systems, such as Red Hat Linux 6.2 and lower. Both `inetd` and `xinetd` control various daemons, including:

- FTP
- Telnet
- Finger
- SWAT (Used to configure Samba)
- TFTP
- Chargen
- Daytime
- POP3
- BOOTP
- Echo

Configuring Daemons Launched by xinetd

Because `xinetd` is used to launch additional daemons, the creators decided to use individual text files to configure each daemon. These individual text files are stored in the `/etc/xinetd.d/` directory, shown in Figure 10.6. If you want to configure a daemon launched by `inetd`, you must search for its file in this directory.

FIGURE 10.6 The contents of the `/etc/xinetd.d/` directory

```
[root@albion /root]# ls /etc/xinetd.d/
chargen       daytime      echo-udp        ntalk    rsh     swat.orig  time
chargen-udp   daytime-udp  finger          rexec    rsync   talk       time-udp
cvspserver    echo         linuxconf-web   rlogin   swat    telnet     wu-ftpd
[root@albion /root]#
```

Usually, the files stored in the `/etc/xinetd.d/` directory are named after the daemon they configure. For example, the Wu-FTPD daemon is one of the more common FTP daemons. Its file is named `wu-ftpd`. The contents of this file are shown here:

1. service ftp
2. {
3. disable = no
4. socket_type = stream
5. wait = no
6. user = root
7. server = /usr/sbin/in.ftpd
8. server_args = -l -a
9. log_on_success += DURATION USERID
10. log_on_failure += USERID
11. nice = 10
12. # only_from = 10.100.100.50
13. }

The lines of this file have been numbered for the sake of convenience. For the purposes of the CIW Security Professional exam, lines 3 and 12 are important. Line 3 allows you to either enable or disable the service. The `disable = no` line means that `xinetd` will enable FTP connections. To disable connections, change the file to read `disable = yes`.

Line 12 shows you the syntax to use when limiting FTP connections only from one host or network. The particular example in line 12 prohibits access from all hosts, except for ones with the IP address of 10.100.100.50. All others will be denied access. This limitation is effective, but it does rely on "where you are" authentication, which means that it is still susceptible to IP spoofing. As a result, the FTP daemon will allow connections to a host that has reconfigured its IP address to 10.100.100.50. The hacker would have to know a username and a password, but he or she would still be able to defeat one of your defense strategies. Finally, notice that line 12 is commented out using the # character. Because it is commented out, the line will not be read by xinetd, and all connections will be allowed.

> **TIP** The /etc/xinetd.conf file is used to configure the xinetd daemon. It is not used to configure the daemons launched by inetd.

Configuring Daemons Launched by *inetd*

You control all daemons launched by inetd by using the /etc/inetd.conf file, shown in Figure 10.7.

FIGURE 10.7 The /etc/inetd.conf file

```
# To re-read this file after changes, just do a 'killall -HUP inetd'
#
#echo    stream  tcp     nowait  root    internal
#echo    dgram   udp     wait    root    internal
#discard stream  tcp     nowait  root    internal
#discard dgram   udp     wait    root    internal
#daytime stream  tcp     nowait  root    internal
#daytime dgram   udp     wait    root    internal
#chargen stream  tcp     nowait  root    internal
#chargen dgram   udp     wait    root    internal
#time    stream  tcp     nowait  root    internal
#time    dgram   udp     wait    root    internal
#
# These are standard services.
#
ftp      stream  tcp     nowait  root    /usr/sbin/tcpd  in.ftpd -l -a
telnet   stream  tcp     nowait  root    /usr/sbin/tcpd  in.telnetd
##
# Shell, login, exec, comsat and talk are BSD protocols.
#
#shell   stream  tcp     nowait  root    /usr/sbin/tcpd  in.rshd -h
#login   stream  tcp     nowait  root    /usr/sbin/tcpd  in.rlogind -h
#exec    stream  tcp     nowait  root    /usr/sbin/tcpd  in.rexecd
#comsat  dgram   udp     wait    root    /usr/sbin/tcpd  in.comsat
talk     dgram   udp     wait    nobody.tty  /usr/sbin/tcpd  in.talkd
ntalk    dgram   udp     wait    nobody.tty  /usr/sbin/tcpd  in.ntalkd
#dtalk   stream  tcp     wait    nobody.tty  /usr/sbin/tcpd  in.dtalkd
#
# Pop and imap mail services et al
#
#pop-2   stream  tcp     nowait  root    /usr/sbin/tcpd  ipop2d
pop-3    stream  tcp     nowait  root    /usr/sbin/tcpd  ipop3d
imap     stream  tcp     nowait  root    /usr/sbin/tcpd  imapd
swat     stream  tcp     nowait.400 root  /usr/sbin/swat  swat
# The Internet UUCP service.
```

It is important to realize that inetd is an older daemon and that it does not use separate text files for each daemon. All entries are found in the single /etc/inetd.conf file.

> **NOTE** Sometimes, both inetd and xinetd are found on the same systems. This is often the case when a system has been upgraded.

Restarting the Daemon

Regardless of whether you are configuring `xinetd` or `inetd`, you must restart the daemon whenever you change a text file. Restarting forces a reread of the configuration files. Only then will any changes you make become active.

The `xinetd` and `inetd` daemons can launch daemons directly, but most often, they launch daemons in a special way so that it is possible to secure them further using a special collection of applications called TCPWrappers. In the next section, we will take a look at these applications.

> **Note:** If you create an improper entry in any of the configuration files, you will find that both `xinetd` and `inetd` will fail to start. Carefully reconsider each entry to determine the cause of a problem.

TCPWrappers

All modern versions of Unix (e.g., FreeBSD, Solaris, and Linux) can use TCP-Wrappers. The primary usefulness of TCPWrappers is that it is able to block access to the certain daemons controlled by `xinetd` and/or `inetd`. The chief components of TCPWrappers are as follows:

TCPD   This daemon is the first service that `xinetd` or `inetd` refers to when running a daemon such as `ftpd`, `telnetd`, the login shell, and others.

/etc/hosts.allow   This text file contains all hosts that are allowed to access a specific daemon. This file is considered first. Thus, if this file contains a host that is in `hosts.deny`, the host will be allowed.

/etc/hosts.deny   This text file contains the names of all hosts that are forbidden to access a specific daemon. This file is considered after `/etc/hosts.allow`.

Syntax for *hosts.allow* and *hosts.deny*

The syntax for the `hosts.allow` and `hosts.deny` files can get quite involved. Here are some simple examples from the `/etc/hosts.deny` file:

```
in.ftpd: ALL EXCEPT myserver.mynetwork.com
in.telnetd: ALL
```

The first line specifies `ftpd` and then denies access to any and all hosts except for ones with the DNS name of `myserver.mynetwork.com`. The second line specifies `telnetd` and then denies all hosts access to that daemon.

A simple example of an access control policy would be to create the file /etc/hosts.deny and place in it a single line such as ALL: ALL. This line would state that all external clients are refused access unless an explicit grant is made via the /etc/hosts.allow file. To grant Telnet access to a trusted host, create the file /etc/hosts.allow and place `in.telnetd: trusted.host.com` in it.

> **TIP** It is also possible to use IP addresses in both hosts.allow and hosts.deny. If, for example, you are planning to add lines concerning the Portmapper daemon, you must specify IP addresses, not hostnames, to prevent deadlocks that may occur due to DNS resolution problems.

When a change is made to either of these files, a restart of `xinetd` or `inetd` is not necessary. This is because both `xinetd` and `inetd` read these `files` upon each connection.

Stand-Alone Services

Not all daemons are started through `xinetd` or `inetd`. Some, called *stand-alone services*, are started directly by the kernel. For example, `xinetd` and `inetd` are stand-alone daemons; this is out of necessity, because they must first run in order to run the other daemons for which they are responsible. Additional stand-alone services include:

- Apache Server (called `httpd`)
- sendmail
- The Network Time Protocol (`ntpd`)
- Scripts to start load modules for `ipchains` and `iptables`, as well as scripts to create personal firewalls
- Network File System (`nfsd`)
- Portmapper (`portmap`)
- Domain Name Server (`named`)
- The system logger (`syslogd`)

- SNMP agents (`snmpd`)
- Database servers, such as MySQL and PostgreSQL

Many systems use a special directory to store scripts used to start stand-alone services. For example, Red Hat Linux servers store these scripts in the `/etc/rc.d/init.d/` directory.

Summary

In this chapter, we identified the potential vulnerabilities inherent to Linux and Windows 2000, and examined methods for eliminating them. We explained how to secure the Windows 2000 Registry, as well as how to further secure a Windows 2000 server communicating on a network.

We also described how to alter default settings in Windows 2000 and Linux systems. For example, we showed you how to secure the Registry, eliminate the threat of an SMB downgrade attack, and ensure greater physical security.

In addition, you learned about commonly exploited daemons and applications in Linux. We discussed the `rlogin` command, as well as how NIS and NFS can cause problems. We also talked about the `xinetd` and `inetd` daemons, and you learned how to secure them using TCPWrappers. It is vital that you understand how TCPWrappers work, and how to formulate entries in the `/etc/hosts.allow` and `hosts.deny` files.

Now that you are familiar with reducing vulnerabilities, the next chapter takes a closer look at the auditing process.

Exam Essentials

Be able to change default settings in Windows 2000 and Linux. For Windows 2000, understand that you do not have to accept default file locations during installation. Be able to use applications such as the Local Security Policy snap-in and the Services snap-in, and make sure that you can identify what happens in a default server during SMB encryption. For Linux, be able to identify the purpose of the TCPWrappers package, including `hosts.allow` and `hosts.deny`. For example, remember that TCPWrappers considers the `/etc/hosts.allow` file before `hosts.deny`.

Know how to remove unnecessary services and daemons. For Windows 2000 systems, know how to disable such services as the Task Scheduler, as well as how to reduce physical attack risk. For Linux systems, make sure that you understand how to stop stand-alone and `xinetd`/`inetd` servers.

Understand the importance of system patch levels. Understand that bug-based attacks occur because of low patch levels. Also, be able to recognize the phrases "patch level" and "service pack," and identify when it is time to obtain a patch or service pack.

Know ways to secure the Windows 2000 Registry. You know the importance of auditing the Registry. However, it is also vital that you understand that auditing all changes might cause the log files to fill up. When log files fill up in Windows systems, the system can become unstable. Thus, choose to audit changes based on your system's ability to log a great deal of information. A memory or hard disk upgrade, for example, might be necessary.

Understand what happens when two Windows systems negotiate an SMB connection. Be aware that Windows 2000 servers can be tricked into negotiating an SMB dialect that has a low level of encryption. Hackers will try to imitate an older server in the hopes of cracking the encryption between the two. If the hacker is successful, he or she will be able to either sniff data as it passes across the wire or obtain a password that allows access to the system.

Be able to identify areas of the Local Security Policies snap-in. Know how to use the Local Security Policy snap-in to improve security. Options include securing printer drivers, hiding the last username, and clearing the page file on shutdown.

Understand security issues presented by `rlogin`, NIS, and NFS. Be aware that many Unix daemons do not encrypt transmissions, which makes them susceptible to sniffing attacks. The `rlogin` account is dangerous for two reasons: First, it uses IP-based authentication that can be duped with relative ease. Second, these applications do not encrypt transmissions after authentication. Because NIS and NFS use the Portmapper daemon, authentication becomes a problem. The use of NFS without NIS, for example, can cause a conflict between local and remote user IDs. It is also important to understand how to secure NIS using the `/etc/secrenets` file.

Be able to identify weaknesses concerning the Portmapper daemon, as well as ways to begin to secure its use. Know that the Portmapper daemon (`portmapd`) uses a weak authentication structure and that it is usually best to disable this daemon on Internet systems. However, if you require NFS or NIS, you will need to activate `portmapd`. To secure it in newer systems, you can use the TCPWrappers files `/etc/hosts.allow` and `/etc/hosts.deny`.

Know how to create entries in the `hosts.allow` and `hosts.deny` files. In order to secure `inetd`- and `xinetd`-related commands, it is vital that you understand how to make entries in the `/etc/hosts.allow` and `hosts.deny` files. It is also important to remember that these files will not secure stand-alone servers, such as Apache Server or sendmail.

Key Terms

Before you take the exam, be certain you are familiar with the following terms:

Common Internet File System (CIFS)	removable media
credential caching	`rlogin`
default shares	`securenets`
NetBIOS	Secure RPC
Network File System (NFS)	Server Message Block (SMB)
Network Information System (NIS)	Server service
null SMB session	SMB dialects
Portmapper	stand-alone services
printer drivers	super daemon
Registry	TCPWrappers
Registry subtrees	unnecessary services
remote procedure call (RPC)	

Review Questions

1. Michelle is installing a Windows 2000 system. She needs to decide where to install her system files. During the installation process, which of the following directories will the installation program provide by default?

    A. \etc\

    B. \winnt

    C. \win32\

    D. \localhost\

2. Which of the following can you do to learn about changes to the Windows 2000 Registry?

    A. Enable auditing on the /winnt directory.

    B. Remove the Everyone group from the Registry.

    C. Enable auditing on the Registry.

    D. Enable auditing on the SAM.

3. Which of the following is a chief means of securing the Registry in case of a successful attack?

    A. Enabling auditing

    B. Removing the Everyone group

    C. Moving the Registry

    D. Backing up the Registry

4. Which of these protocols allow unencrypted authentication and data transfer?

    A. NFS, NIS+, and Telnet

    B. RSH, Telnet, and SSH

    C. NFS, NIS, and Telnet

    D. SMB, RSH, and Telnet

5. What protocol attempts to add strong authentication to requests for NFS processes?

   A. TCP/IP

   B. HTTP/S

   C. S/MIME

   D. Secure RPC

6. Serena wishes to disable a protocol that is commonly attacked on Windows systems. She has been told that it is the source of a majority of attacks against her Windows 2000 system. What protocol should she disable?

   A. NetBIOS

   B. IPX/SPX

   C. NetBEUI

   D. TCP/IP

7. Where are the configuration settings and controls for Windows 2000 located?

   A. In the Server service

   B. In the encryption subsystem

   C. In the PAM subsystem

   D. In the Registry

8. Which of the following applications can Sarah use to disable a default Windows share?

   A. Windows Explorer

   B. Local Security Policy

   C. Server Manager

   D. Component Services

9. Which of the following is created after an application fails to authenticate once it has connected to a Windows 2000 system with default SMB settings?

   A. An authenticated session

   B. A plain-text session

   C. A null session

   D. An SMB session

10. What is contained in the SAM subtree of the HKLM subtree in Windows 2000?

    A. Application configuration information that is independent of the current use

    B. Actual user accounts and passwords

    C. All security information for the local computer

    D. Configuration information for services and devices in the computer

11. In Windows 2000, what specific control permission allows a user or group to gain access to the security information on a selected key?

    A. Create Subkey

    B. Write Owner

    C. Read Control

    D. Create Link

12. Davis has discovered that his IIS server has been attacked by an application that takes advantage of a system bug. He remembers reading about this bug some time ago. What should Davis have done before this attack?

    A. Stopped the IIS service; his server did not need it.

    B. Installed a service patch.

    C. Upgraded his encryption level.

    D. Used a different web server.

13. Your Windows 2000 server is at its default SMB encryption setting. What will your server do when another system connects to it and makes an SMB request?

   A. It will respond with an NTLMv2 encryption request.

   B. It will allow only NTLM encryption.

   C. It will allow only LM encryption.

   D. It will negotiate the appropriate encryption level.

14. Which of the following changes to an interactive login session can help you show compliance to security standards?

   A. Backing up the Registry

   B. Upgrading SMB encryption settings in the Registry

   C. Creating a login banner

   D. Disabling login banners

15. William has been fired during his lunch hour. His logon session has been terminated, and his account has been removed. However, William has still been able to log into the Windows domain, and he has copied and deleted sensitive files and information. How has this been possible?

   A. The password to the file server was not changed.

   B. William found a system bug.

   C. William used a cracking application.

   D. William used cached logon credentials.

16. Which of the following text files allows a user to log into a remote host without first providing a password?

   A. /etc/hosts.allow

   B. /etc/rlogin.allow

   C. /etc/hosts.equiv

   D. /etc/securenets

17. Which of the following files does TCPWrappers consider first when a remote user logs in using an FTP client to a system?

   A. `/etc/hosts.allow`

   B. `/etc/hosts.deny`

   C. `/etc/securenets`

   D. `/etc/xinetd.d/wu-ftp`

18. Which of the following Unix daemons is responsible for connecting a remote procedure call (RPC) to a local port?

   A. `xinetd`

   B. `inetd`

   C. NetBIOS

   D. Portmapper

19. Consider the code `in.ftpd: ALL`. Which of the following files would this code be found in?

   A. `/etc/rc.d/init.d/xinetd`

   B. `/etc/securenets`

   C. `/etc/hosts.deny`

   D. `/etc/rc.d/init.d/inetd`

20. Julie has changed the `/etc/xinetd.d/finger` file so that it contains the entry `disable = yes`. Remote users are still able to connect to the `finger` daemon and gain information. What is the problem?

   A. Julie must restart `inetd`.

   B. Julie must use the `/etc/hosts.allow` file.

   C. Julie must use the `/etc/hosts.deny` file.

   D. Julie must restart `xinetd`.

Answers to Review Questions

1. **B.** It is important to be aware of default settings during system installation. You can change these defaults. Doing so helps obscure the workings of the operating system from some intruder attacks.

2. **C.** Auditing is one of the more effective means of securing the Registry. By enabling auditing on the Registry, you will be able to learn more about changes made to it. Enabling auditing on the /winnt directory will not give you direct information concerning the Registry. Removing the Everyone group from the Registry would likely have disastrous results on the server. Enabling auditing on the SAM would provide information about only one part of the Registry. When enabling auditing, make sure that your settings are reasonable, or you will be given too much information.

3. **D.** In case of a successful attack, having a backup copy of the Registry is the best way to secure your system.

4. **C.** NFS, NIS, and Telnet do not encrypt transmissions, both during and after authentication. SSH and NIS+ encrypt transmissions and enable strong authentication. SMB also enables encryption, although it has been subject to cracking attacks. RSH is an rlogin-style application, and is thus also subject to spoofing and sniffing attacks.

5. **D.** The Secure RPC protocol adds more authentication support to RPC. However, it still causes problems on Internet-based systems.

6. **A.** The NetBIOS protocol is often attacked. Windows 2000 allows you to disable NetBIOS support.

7. **D.** The Registry holds configuration settings for all modern Windows systems. Any application that you use to modify system parameters and lock down services will change settings in the Registry. An application might even add subkeys to the Registry in order to further secure the system.

8. **A.** Default shares can be disabled by using Windows Explorer.

9. **C.** When the Server service is still running and authentication fails, a null session is still established. A hacker can gain valuable information, such as user account names, through null sessions. Disabling the Server service can solve this problem.

10. B. The SAM subtree of the Windows Registry HKLM subtree contains user account information. Cracking applications go after this subtree in order to learn user account and password information.

11. C. If it is possible to read the Registry, then it is generally possible to use that information against the system.

12. B. A service patch usually solves such system bugs. Generally, when a vulnerability is reported in a service or daemon, systems administrators work to install a service patch as soon as possible. Davis should have updated the patch level of his system. You do not have enough information to determine whether he should have deactivated the IIS service. Upgrading the encryption level on this system would not have solved the problem, because the hacker did not attack the encryption subsystem on the server. Davis does not have to use a different web server; he should instead ensure that it is as safe as possible, and that involves updating his system using the latest stable service pack.

13. D. Whenever a default Windows 2000 system begins using SMB, it chooses the SMB dialect appropriate to the connecting host. It is possible for the connecting host to wage an attack against this behavior by having the Windows 2000 system downgrade its SMB encryption level to cleartext.

14. C. Creating a login banner that pops up for each user can help prove that you are taking steps to increase security. Although such banners do not stop a determined hacker, they do allow you to demonstrate good-faith efforts that you have begun to change settings.

15. D. Even if you take steps to terminate a user's logon session and change passwords, that user still may be able to use cached logon information to gain access to sensitive information. To solve this problem, either ensure that the user is physically escorted off the premises or disable logon account caching on all systems used by this end user.

16. C. The /etc/hosts.equiv file contains the information that allows the session to occur. The /etc/hosts.allow file is not a part of the r-series of applications. Rather, it is part of TCPWrappers. Although the rlogin binary does allow a user to attempt a login without using a password, there is no such thing as the /etc/rlogin.allow file. The /etc/securenets file is not directly used by NFS.

17. A. TCPWrappers always considers the `hosts.allow` file when logging into a system. The `hosts.deny` file is considered next. The `/etc/securenets` file is used by NIS, and the `wu-ftp` file is used by `xinetd`, which considers the connection before TCPWrappers.

18. D. The Portmapper service allocates local ports and allows remote connections. The Portmapper service is often the target of attacks because it does not strongly authenticate users. The `xinetd` and `inetd` daemons are used to launch additional daemons, whereas NetBIOS is a protocol used in Microsoft Networking.

19. C. The `/etc/hosts.deny` file is used by TCPWrappers to deny access to various `xinetd`/`inetd` services. The `/etc/securenets` file is used by NIS only. Scripts residing in the `/etc/rc.d/init.d/` directory are used to start stand-alone servers.

20. D. After making changes to `xinetd`'s configuration files, Julie must restart `xinetd`. A restart forces the daemon to reread all of the files. Julie is configuring `xinetd`, not `inetd`. The `/etc/hosts.allow` and `/etc/hosts.deny` files are used by TCPWrappers and are not directly related to the issue Julie is having.

Chapter 11

The Auditing Process

THE CIW EXAM OBJECTIVE GROUPS COVERED IN THIS CHAPTER:

- ✓ Identify security auditing principles, including but not limited to: security auditor's duties, network risk factor analysis, audit steps.

- ✓ Define the security auditing and discovery processes, plan an audit, and install and configure network-based and host-based discovery software.

In this chapter, you will learn the steps involved in conducting a successful network security audit. You will learn more about the role of an auditor, and how an auditor assumes different roles and adopts several perspectives to increase a network's security level. This chapter also discusses the auditing process, as well as how to conduct a risk assessment.

You will also learn about the standard system applications, port scanners, and vulnerability scanners that you can use to conduct an audit. Finally, this chapter will delve into the tools and techniques necessary for discovering network resources, the first step in the auditing process. However, before you begin using any applications, it is important to define exactly what an auditor does.

What Is an Auditor?

An *auditor* is an individual who is entrusted with assessing risk. As an auditor, your job is to determine the effective security of your network. On the CIW Security Professional exam, the phrase effective security refers to the amount of measurable compliance to a company's information security policy.

Generally, you measure compliance to a security policy by conducting internal audits. As you will see in this section, an internal audit consists of the following:

- Discovering vulnerabilities
- Determining if these vulnerabilities lead to system penetration
- Identifying systems that are controlled by hackers
- Learning if existing system vulnerabilities allow hackers to spread from system to system

When auditing systems, the most effective security professionals approach the network from two perspectives:

- They think like hackers so they can protect company systems from illicit activity.
- They think like employees and managers to determine how proposed security measures might affect the ability of a business to function properly.

What Does an Auditor Do?

An auditor interested in achieving a high level of effective security engages in two specific activities: determining compliance and engaging in a *risk analysis*.

The Compliance Analysis

Any well-managed network has a list of procedures and policies addressing compliance. However, a network administrator or security manager will often implement a sound policy, only to have users defeat it. Sometimes, employees unwittingly avoid compliance; however, at other times, they do so deliberately.

To determine compliance, an auditor must conduct a compliance audit. Sometimes, this audit is called a *gap analysis*, because the audit is designed to reveal any gap between what the security policy mandates and what is actually occurring.

Here is a list of general tasks you should consider when planning a compliance analysis:

Determine the nature of the business you are auditing. You will not be able to successfully audit a network or network resource unless you understand its business role. Too often, an auditor considers only the technical nature of a network's problem. Doing so can cause serious problems. For example, if you do not understand the function of a business, you may recommend that a certain service be shut down, only to find that this recommendation is impractical for that particular business.

When provided with a scenario on the CIW Security Professional exam, always take into account how a suggested change will affect the company's way of doing business. The best way to understand the role of a network resource is to first read the network security policy.

Check what is written in the information security policy. No network can have effective security without a written security policy in place. Most security professionals refer to a written security policy as a *security road map* or a "framework" because it enables a network to remain secure as it scales for growth. As an auditor, read this policy carefully, and then determine exactly how well employees are following it.

An effective policy is one that is as simple as possible. Although your policy may have one goal, namely improved network and host-level security, an organization's security policy will probably consist of several sub-documents. Some documents will define standard user and network policies, including:

Employee behavior Includes acceptable Internet use and supported software installations.

Procedure Includes detailed documents that outline how to react to unauthorized network use, damage to files due to equipment failure and hacker intrusion, and other unplanned occurrences.

Design Includes documents and maps that explain the network's topology and protocols. They also discuss how the company plans to deploy its perimeter and internal security devices.

> **NOTE** In many organizations, the standard procedure is for the Human Resources department to identify acceptable Internet use. Many times, IT professionals are asked to write, or at least approve, such documentation.

Work with management and employees to determine past and potential problems. When conducting a gap analysis, ensure that you understand how management works. Determine the proper chain of command, and learn how well employees are able to interpret and implement directives. Once you do this, you are ready to survey employees and determine ways that their behavior may be compromising the network. Chapters 3 and 4 of this book have already discussed the problems that a network can encounter, and the security principles involved in countermanding them.

In addition to conducting a gap analysis, it is possible to conduct a risk analysis audit.

Understanding the Risk Analysis

Risk analysis is the ability to locate resources and determine the likelihood of attack. Let's examine the steps you should take when planning a risk analysis.

Check for a Written Security Policy

You have probably noticed that this is the second time we have recommended you check for a written security policy. Checking for a policy is vital to both a compliance analysis (i.e., a gap analysis) and a risk analysis audit. During a gap analysis, the auditor will use the security policy to determine the ideal practices for a network. During a risk analysis, the auditor will consult the written security policy to see if any omissions have been made that might have helped create the condition for a security breach to occur. Problem areas can include:

- Improper firewall configuration
- Inadequate mandates for user training
- Insufficient intrusion-detection steps
- Places in the policy that do not emphasize systematic upgrades, including server patch levels and antivirus application updates

In short, carefully read the security policy to determine whether anything is missing. As an auditor, you will be expected to identify any lapses. You can then report those lapses when you have finished conducting the audit.

Analyze, Categorize, and Prioritize Resources

After you have checked your company's security policy, you can then work to discover the most important resources on the network. Hackers often prey on less important systems, hoping to use them as platforms to attack more valuable network resources. Table 11.1 describes some of the questions you should ask as you conduct a risk analysis.

> **NOTE** Some problems cannot be prevented, including extended power outages, natural disasters, and fire. You must determine what is possibly at risk, what is probably at risk, and your ability to countermand such risks.

438 Chapter 11 · The Auditing Process

TABLE 11.1 Key Questions to Determine Risk

Question	Determination
What is the target?	If the target is a general-user local system, the risk is low. However, if the target is a human resources system, for example, the risk factor is higher.
How serious is the adverse result?	If the threat is carried out, what are the ramifications? Could it affect the entire organization or just isolated individuals? Generally, you should quantify results in terms of estimated dollar losses due to a realized threat, such as nonfunctional time.
What is the likelihood of occurrence?	How likely is the threat to actually take place? Is it an unlikely occurrence or something extremely probable?

One reason your data can become vulnerable is that it is distributed among several different operating systems, web servers, and database applications. Such distribution enables security holes to be opened accidentally. From a technical standpoint, you will naturally want to categorize resources according to type, as shown in Figure 11.1.

FIGURE 11.1 Categorizing network resources by type

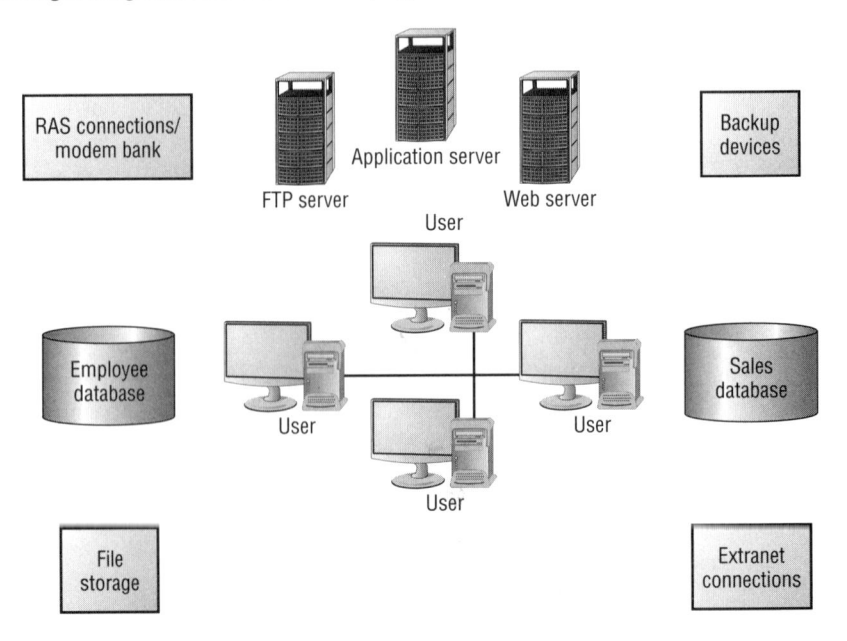

Table 11.2 lists some of the more commonly attacked resources, often called hot spots.

TABLE 11.2 Hot Spots and Potential Threats

Hot Spot	Potential Threat
Network resources	Routers and switches
	Firewalls
	Network hosts
Server resources	Security account databases
	Information databases
	SMTP servers
	HTTP servers
	FTP servers

Prioritizing by type is often a wise strategy. Doing so allows you to easily determine weaknesses particular to a specific category. However, you might not have the luxury of categorizing a resource according to its technical function. In many cases, you might have to consider how a particular host's function relates to the company's organizational structure, as shown in Figure 11.2.

FIGURE 11.2 Prioritizing network resources by department

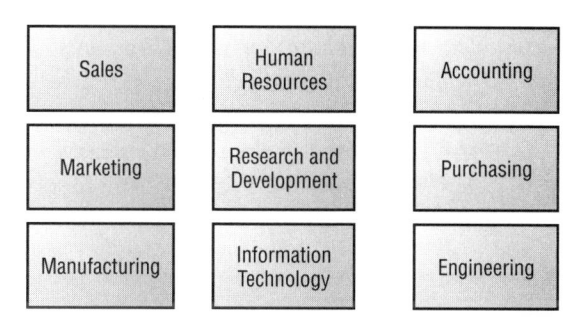

Sales	Human Resources	Accounting
Marketing	Research and Development	Purchasing
Manufacturing	Information Technology	Engineering

Determining resource priority often demands that you consider the company's organizational structure, because one department database could contain more sensitive information than another. For example, each of the departments listed in Figure 11.2 might have its own database. However, the Human Resources, Accounting, and Research and Development databases might be more sensitive resources than others.

Consider Business Concerns

Customize your security policy to your organization's needs. Implementing a security policy can be quite expensive. You will have to consult with management to ensure that they are inclined to adopt your proposed solution. Parties you may have to work closely with include:

- Upper management
- Legal counsel
- Department heads
- Human resources
- Public relations
- Research and development

Each of these parties may not support your recommendations unless your policy accounts for their concerns and enables them to work efficiently.

Emphasize that you will probably be able to improve the workings of most departments and make their data more secure.

Evaluate Existing Perimeter and Internal Security

First, you need to discover what kind of security is already in place. This step involves learning about the company's perimeter and internal security, as well as the management control architecture, logging, access-control mechanisms, and other elements. A company's management control architecture includes any software that allows you to monitor the company's ability to authenticate and log users. Elements of a management control architecture include vulnerability scanners, firewalls, and intrusion-detection system (IDS) software. You will learn about IDSs in Chapter 13.

Perimeter security refers to a network's ability to differentiate itself from other networks. A firewall is the first line of defense in defining perimeter security. As an auditor, you will want to ensure that your network can recover from the following external attacks:

Bandwidth consumption An attacker sends fraudulent data meant to clog a connection to the network and thus deny services.

Faulty firewall configuration Improperly created proxy and packet-filter rules can create holes in the network.

Systems placed outside the firewall Try to place as many systems as possible inside the firewall.

However, a firewall is not the only line of defense. IDS software can help you discover and thwart internal attacks, and antivirus software can help you ensure that information is secure.

Although you will learn more about intrusion detection in Chapter 13, for now keep in mind that as an auditor, you also need to detect and countermand unauthorized activity. Internal security is often neglected. However, the 2001 CSI/FBI Computer Crime and Security Survey, available at the Computer Security Institute home page (www.gocsi.com), shows that threats perpetrated by insiders have become a true concern. Although attacks from outside are still of paramount importance, do not underestimate the potential for internal employees to cause security problems.

Use Existing Management and Control Architecture

Administrators can choose several different ways to manage network security. Sometimes, a network will have such elements in place. If so, you must understand how these systems work. More often, however, you will need to recommend appropriate security solutions.

As shown in Figure 11.3, the *network-based management model* deploys security software on one server, which then issues queries on the network wire. The system that issues the queries is generally called a *manager*. The manager then scans the network wire for any suspect activities.

FIGURE 11.3 A simple query architecture

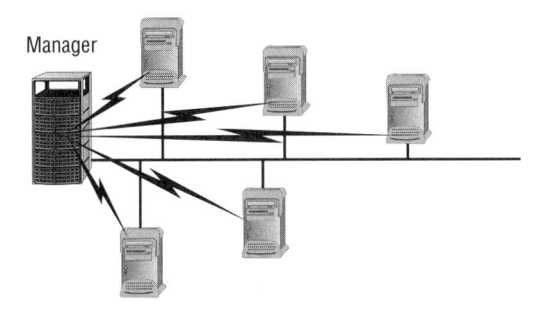

In this particular model, each computer that is queried responds passively to the agent queries. Network-based security software, such as eTrust Intrusion Detection (www.cai.com), Snort (www.snort.org), Network Flight

Recorder (www.nfr.com), and Symantec NetProwler (www.symantec.com), follow this model.

One benefit of this model is that the individual hosts do not know they are being monitored. You need not install software on the hosts you want to manage. However, one of the drawbacks of this management structure is that you have to take special measures to make it work in switched networks, because a switched network will open a dedicated connection between hosts. Additionally, network-based scanning software generally cannot pass across a router.

The *host-based management model* uses the standard three-tier management structure shown in Figure 11.4. The first tier of the structure involves a simple graphical user interface (GUI) whose only function is to communicate with managers and display information. The second tier of the management structure, often called the manager, issues queries to agents, receives information from agents, and returns information to the GUI. An *agent* is the small piece of software installed on each host.

FIGURE 11.4 A user/agent architecture

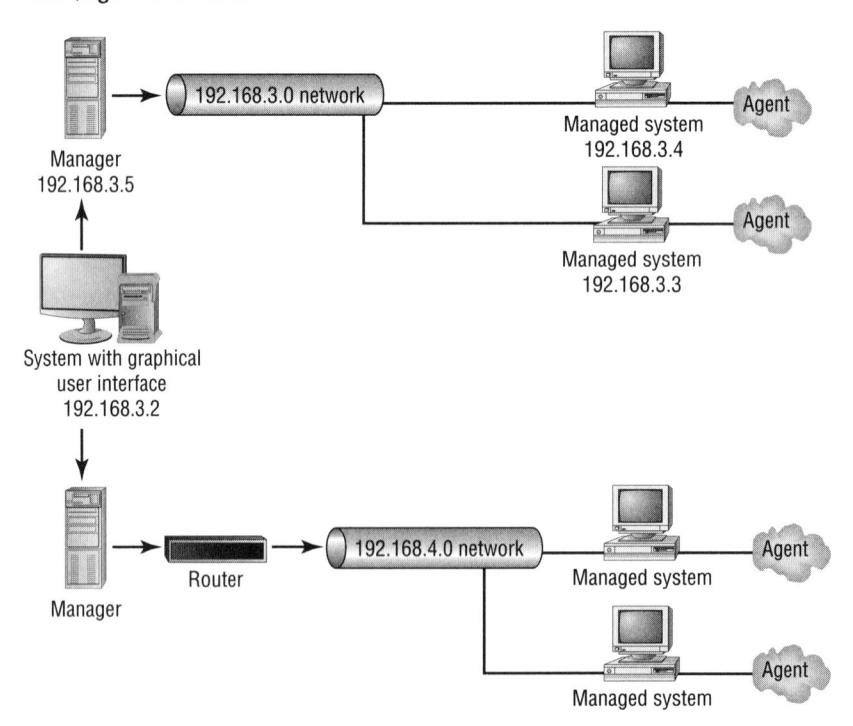

This model is more ambitious because it requires you to install software on each node you want to manage. The agents must first be registered with the manager. The manager can then issue queries directly to these agents. Sometimes, the agents can then issue queries to non-managed hosts. This architecture can report network activities much more accurately.

A *host-based scanner* is efficient in switched networks and can query agents across a router, as long as that router does not filter out the ports used by the manager. Host-based scanners can also delve more deeply into the inner workings of the operating system. They can identify weaknesses in areas of the operating system that are not directly related to networking but that can still cause potential problems should certain conditions occur. For example, a host-based scanner may discover problems in a database that has not yet been put online.

Still, neither of these architectures is inherently better than the other. Each is appropriate for specific tasks. You may recommend a different strategy for using the management architecture that is already in place. You may also suggest that the company deploy an additional management strategy.

Writing and Delivering Reports

An auditor does not just find problems and then talk about them. An auditor must present an *audit report* about what has been found. An audit report often consists of several documents. In fact, reports will often fall into three categories:

Executive report An executive report tells upper management what the audit has found. Of course, this report must be accurate, but of a general nature that summarizes how the company's security level has increased or decreased. It should be as brief as possible (under a page, if at all possible).

This document should contain as little technical language as possible. Most of the time, management will consider such language to be unintelligible or unimportant jargon. This document should be designed to enable executives to make decisions regarding money and other resources to allocate when solving a problem.

Procedural report This report describes how you went about the audit. Upper management sometimes reads this document, but it is not designed to enable executives to make decisions. Rather, it is intended to allow all parties to verify that your auditing methods are sound.

IT report This report contains detailed information about the nature of the problems that have been discovered. It also includes advice on how to correct problems. This report is designed for IT professionals, and so technical language is expected.

In some situations, this report will be combined into one. However, this one report should contain all of the three elements discussed here. The information contained in these reports is highly confidential. Once you create these reports, make sure that you deliver them in a secure way. For example, if you send a report via e-mail, you should consider using an application such as Pretty Good Privacy (PGP) to encrypt the results. You will learn more about creating assessment reports in Chapter 14.

Auditor Roles and Perspectives

As an auditor, you must be willing to approach a network from at least two perspectives: that of a security manager, and that of a consultant posing as a talented, curious, but thus-far uninformed hacker.

As a security manager, you know how the network is configured and you want to probe it for possible weaknesses. In a sense, you act as an informed, skilled hacker because you are searching systems that you already understand. Another term for this perspective is *administrative auditing*. In essence, the security manager will test the firewall to see if it can be penetrated, and will then move on to controlling network hosts. This perspective requires you to understand how to audit firewall logs and analyze typical firewall configurations.

> **NOTE** As an auditor, you will find that many systems administrators place sensitive equipment outside the firewall. For example, many systems administrators place web, DNS, and FTP servers outside the firewall for the sake of convenience. Pay special attention to these systems and recommend placing them behind the firewall whenever possible.

Consultants conduct many of the same activities as security managers. However, the auditor operating as a consultant/hacker has (at first) little or no knowledge of the network's topology, servers, protocols, or operations. As this type of auditor, your task is to discover, penetrate, and demonstrate how you could control the network.

This type of auditor is often called an *ethical hacker* or *white hat hacker*. The IBM ethical hacking division (i.e., its "white hat hackers") and the Symantec Tiger Team provide examples of this type of auditor. The benefit of this approach is that you are able to investigate your network's resilience to strategies adopted by most talented hackers.

> **NOTE** Third-party consultants are highly effective tools. However, you should be aware that many "reformed hackers" might not be the best auditors. If you consider using a third party, take great care to legitimatize the party's claims. Ask for recommendations and security clearances, and perform in-depth background checks before bringing that third party into your network.

Auditor as Insider

Many times, an auditor will combine both perspectives to provide a more thorough audit. Thus, an auditor should also operate as an insider. If you operate from this perspective, you will first meet with the IT manager and other relevant employees, such as IT assistants and managers from other departments. You might even want to meet with several other employees. You will then conduct an on-site analysis, learning all the network's resources and methods. As you operate in this mode, you are a third party who evaluates the network's existing security. The benefit of this approach is that you can identify which former employees may be able to attack, should they want to.

> **NOTE** Hackers themselves use many of the tools, techniques, and principles you will use as a legitimate auditor. Thus, a security auditing tool can be used in an illegitimate way. Both security managers and hackers have used the Security Administrator Tool for Analyzing Networks (SATAN) programs to test networks.

Regardless of the role you adopt as an auditor, you will have to probe systems from behind the firewall, as shown in Figure 11.5.

FIGURE 11.5 Auditing from behind the firewall

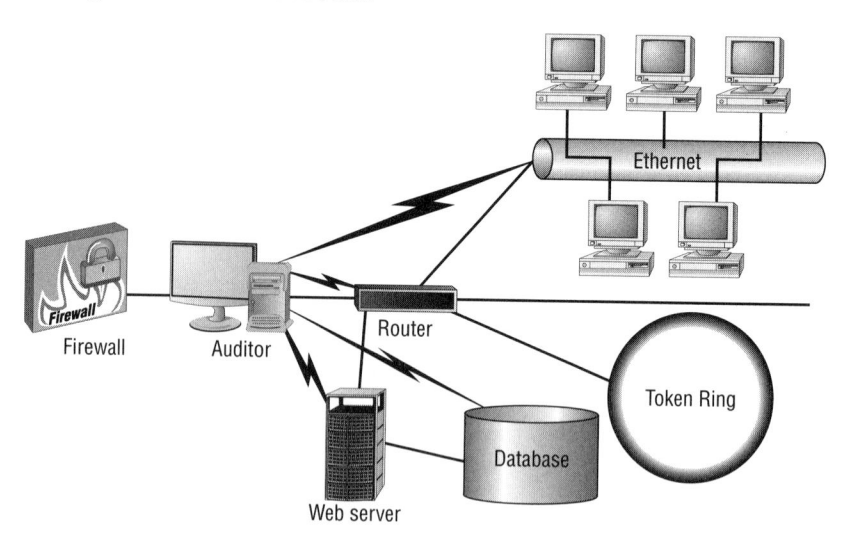

This perspective allows you to test your network for possible employee-based snooping. Such audits focus more on individual hosts and servers, rather than on the firewall. However, it is always necessary to conduct tests from outside the firewall.

Such tests are essential in determining just how easily a hacker can avoid your firewall. For example, you have to determine if the firewall is allowing spoofed IP packets to pass through, or if firewall rules should be implemented to help control access to internal systems.

Auditing Steps and Stages

As you conduct your audit, you will attempt some hacker activities: You will try to discover, penetrate, and control network systems. You will also perform certain analyses that will help you improve the network's effective security. This ability to analyze and then report is the main difference between a hacker and an auditor.

Discovery

During the *discovery stage*, you will scan and test the systems for effective security. Discovering the network involves mapping it out and determining the location of each resource, including IP addresses (in an IP network), open ports, topology, and so forth. This analysis is usually the most time-consuming and the one you will perform most often. The end result of an implementation analysis should be firm conclusions about the effectiveness and overall security achieved. This analysis will often use automated scanners, as well as techniques that the hackers use.

Implementation analysis calls for a system-by-system examination. Some of the areas reviewed and tested on each system are:

- Known vulnerable services
- Default installations
- Unsecured network management
- Trivial passwords
- Improperly configured services
- Topology flaws
- Information leakage
- Unauthorized devices or servers
- Manageable devices
- Unauthorized services
- Cryptography implementation
- Excessive user rights
- Known vulnerable software versions

Once you have identified the hosts on the network, you can then determine whether they can be illegally accessed.

Penetration

The *penetration stage* is where an auditor (or, for that matter, a hacker) has been able to bypass access-control mechanisms, such as login accounts and passwords. You will also attempt to compromise data confidentiality and integrity by defeating encryption schemes, as well as deny access to services provided by the network.

In this phase of the auditing process, you inspect various systems for weaknesses, attempting to defeat the following elements:

- Encryption
- Passwords
- Access lists

Control

The *control stage* is where an auditor or hacker has been able to effectively administer the server or network at will. An auditor never attempts to control a network host, but does demonstrate that he or she could have begun the control phase and could have taken over the host. As you will see, control means that a hacker can become something like an administrator because he or she can access resources, create accounts, and manipulate logs. As you prepare your written report, you must show how you can prevent hackers from gaining control of the network or system.

Control also implies the ability for a hacker to spread to other systems. Most of the time, a hacker will not stop with just one penetrated system. Rather, the hacker will try to use trust relationships between the compromised system and others. As an auditor, your job is to determine how easily a hacker can spread from system to system.

Now that you are familiar with each stage of the auditing process, let's take a closer look at the discovery process.

> **NOTE** You will learn about the penetration and control stages in Chapter 12.

Discovery Tools and Methods

As you learned earlier, the first step a security auditor or a hacker takes is to discover the network. Discovery is accomplished by scanning and researching systems. Security scans come in many varieties. As you will see, you can use `ping` and port scanners to discover a network. You can also use existing applications, such as Telnet and SNMP, to determine where a network is leaking valuable information.

You must use several tools to learn about the nature of your systems. Some tools are modest, focused applications that you can install and use quickly. However, auditors and hackers often create their own tools, using programming languages such as Perl, C, C++, and Java. Such activity is usually a result of their realization that no tool exists for the particular weakness they want to expose or exploit.

Other tools are more sophisticated and require configuration before you can use them. Also, once you use them, you will have to spend considerable time analyzing and interpreting the reports. Before you learn about such "hacker-in-a-box" solutions, however, you should study the individual techniques used by hackers to date.

DNS Tools

DNS is a foundational Internet service. All systems rely on it. As an auditor, take advantage of DNS to learn more about the network. The Whois service allows you to query the domain name service authority. You can access this service by using an application such as Ping Pro, or through a website such as Network Solutions (www.networksolutions.com). You can gain valuable information about administrators, additional domains, physical locations, and domain name servers used by an organization. Once you obtain Whois information, you can then learn about the primary and secondary domain servers.

Using Nslookup, a DNS troubleshooting tool, you can use the information gained from your Whois query to learn more about the network. For example, you can configure Nslookup on your system to imitate secondary (i.e., slave) servers. If you are successful in your imitation, you can ask a DNS server to conduct a zone transfer to your system. Once you obtain a zone transfer of a master DNS server, you will have gained a great deal of information, including:

- The names and IP addresses of all systems that use this DNS server for name resolution.

- The networks and/or subnets the company uses.

- The nature of the server's role on the network. Many organizations provide descriptive DNS names, such as mail.companya.com, www.companyb.com, and print.companyc.com.

> **NOTE:** If the site uses Host Information (HINFO) records, you can determine the CPU and operating system of each network host.

The process of using Nslookup to conduct a zone transfer is:

1. Issue a Whois query about the target network. For example, from a Linux prompt, you would enter **whois targetnet.com**.

2. Determine the DNS server(s) for a company. For this example, suppose that the primary DNS server is dns1.targetnet.com.

3. Open the Nslookup client. By default, Nslookup will use the default name server for your domain. Change the default server by entering the following command: **server dns1.targetnet.com**. This command allows Nslookup to connect to the primary DNS server.

4. Now issue the following command: **ls ?d dns1.targetnet.com > target file**. The DNS server will then transfer its database to you. However, the server administrator of the particular name server you are targeting may have instructed the DNS server to deny zone transfers. Also, many organizations place their DNS servers inside the firewall and allow zone transfers only to certain hosts.

Once you have gained information from a zone transfer, you can conduct port scans on each host to learn more about the services each offers. If you are not able to conduct a zone transfer, you can resort to ping and port scans as well as additional tools, such as traceroute.

> **NOTE:** Note that in some operating systems, the Nslookup program has become deprecated in favor of applications such as host and dig.

Most Unix systems provide the host command to help find information about hosts on the network. It converts hostnames to IP addresses and vice versa. You can use host to:

- Conduct zone transfers.
- Obtain name server information.
- Learn about the mail servers for a domain.

The -v option is useful because it displays more information. The -l option conducts zone transfers. The -t option allows you to query specific

DNS server records. For example, to query for the MX record for the `ciwcertified.com` domain, you would enter the following command:

```
host -t mx ciwcertified.com
```

Consult the Unix manual entry for more information.

> **NOTE** The `dig` command in Linux is quite powerful. Consult the `dig` man page for more details.

Ping Scanning

Ping scanning involves using ICMP to learn the entire IP address range used by that organization. Once you learn the HTTP server's IP address, you can use a ping scanner to ping an entire range of addresses on that same subnet. This knowledge helps you create a map of the network.

As shown in Figure 11.6, you can use a ping-scanning application such as Rhino9's Pinger to learn the physical topology of a network.

FIGURE 11.6 Rhino9 Pinger ping scan application

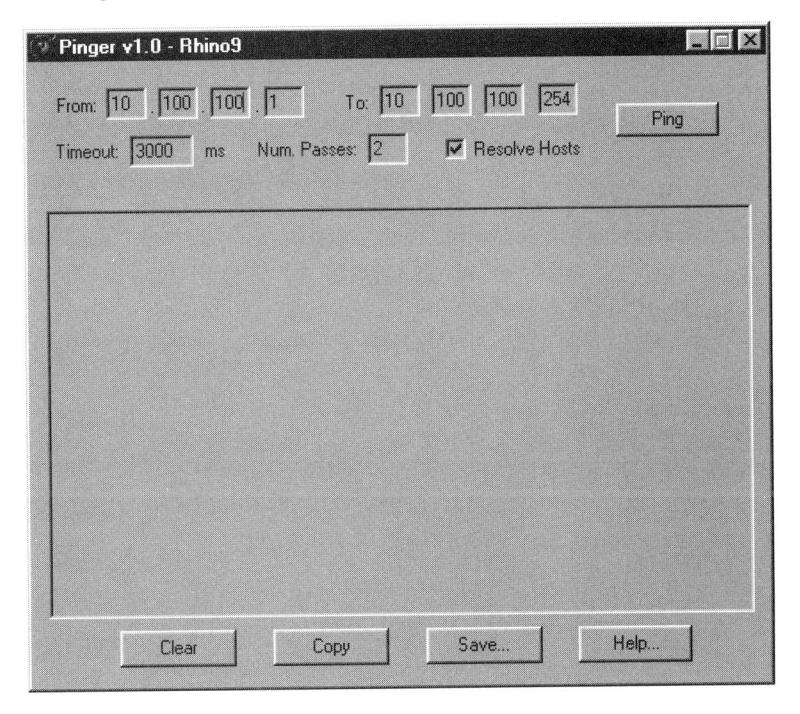

A ping scan program will automatically query IP addresses in a range that you specify.

Port Scanning

A *port scan* is similar to a ping scan, except that instead of simply reporting back the IP addresses, the port scanner also discovers any active UDP and TCP ports present on the system. Figure 11.7 shows a port scan discovering various services.

FIGURE 11.7 Port scan anatomy

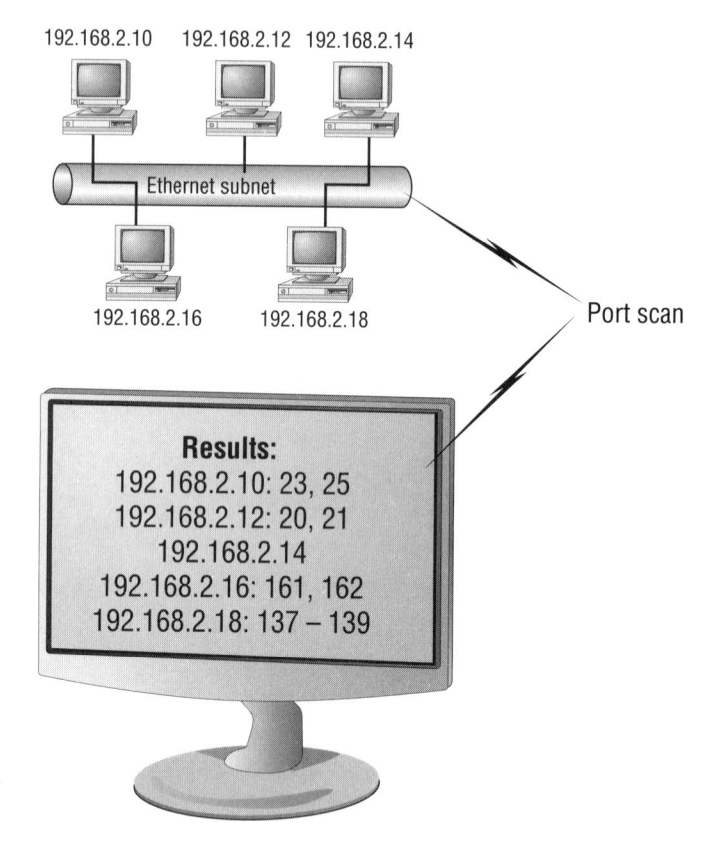

In this example, the 192.168.2.10 address is running SMTP and Telnet servers, whereas the host using IP address 192.168.2.12 is running an FTP server. The host at 192.168.2.14 is not running any identifiable port, and the host at 192.168.2.16 is running SNMP. Finally, you can tell that 192.168.2.18 belongs to a Microsoft network, because Microsoft networks use UDP ports 137 and 138, and TCP port 139.

Port Scan Software

Port scanners are among the most commonly available hacker tools. Some port scanners are stand-alone tools such as Port Scanner 1.1, shown in Figure 11.8.

FIGURE 11.8 A common port scanner set to scan a range of IP addresses

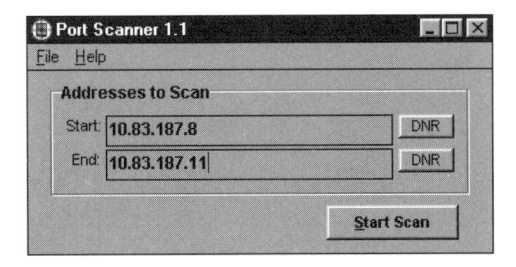

After entering the IP address and declaring which port you want to scan, you can conduct a scan. The results will resemble those shown in Figure 11.9.

FIGURE 11.9 Results from a port scan utility

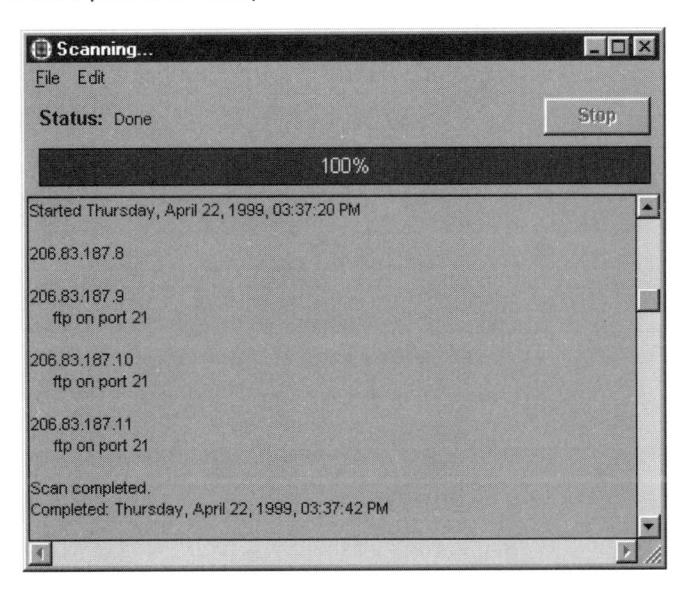

Many stand-alone port-scanning applications exist, including UltraScan. Like ping scans, many applications lump this service together with other related services. NetScanTool, Ping Pro, and other applications attempt to combine as many tools as possible. As you will see, many enterprise-grade

network probes incorporate ping and port scanning into their security analysis regimen.

Network-Discovery and Server-Discovery Applications

Using a simple program such as Ping Pro, shown in Figure 11.10, you can discover Microsoft network ports open on the physical wire. Ping Pro is designed to search for TCP and UDP ports 135 (the Remote Procedure Call service), as well as UDP ports 137, 138, and 139. Other network-discovery applications allow you to discover Unix Network Information Service–based, Novell, and AppleTalk networks as well.

FIGURE 11.10 Scanning Microsoft Network

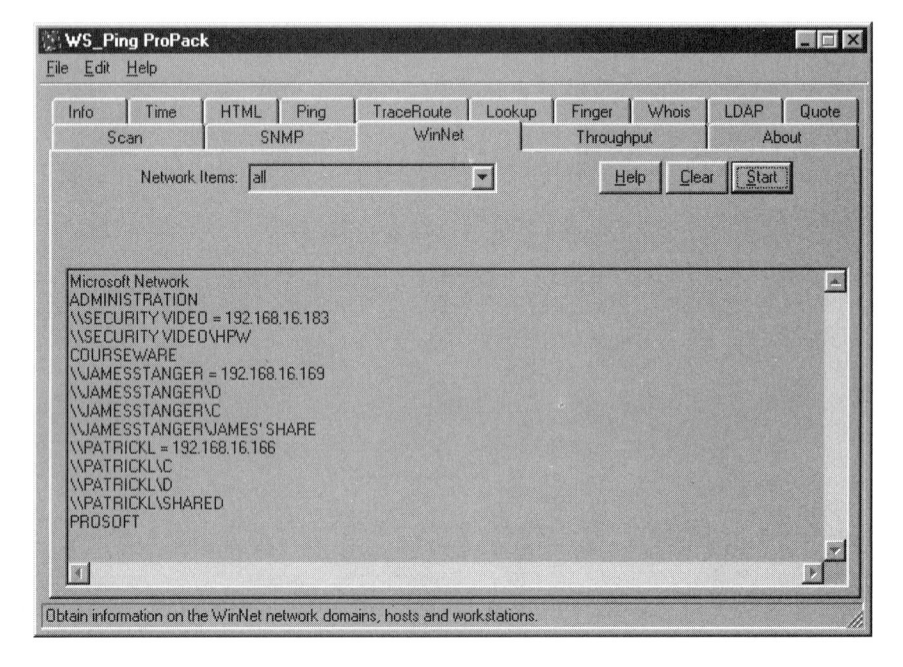

Although Ping Pro will work only with the particular subnet on which it is installed, more sophisticated programs exist. More powerful applications are generally not network specific, because their designers are interested in identifying as many network and server types as possible.

For example, nmap is a Unix tool that allows you to track the subtle differences in how a particular operating system implements TCP/IP. You can obtain nmap at www.insecure.org. Additional programs include checkos, queso, and the older SATAN program.

> **Note:** Most of these applications run on various flavors of Unix.

Stack Fingerprinting and Operating System Detection

Many of the applications discussed in this chapter use *stack fingerprinting*, a technique that allows you to use TCP/IP to help identify specific operating systems and servers. This process is often necessary because most systems administrators address information leakage whenever possible and disable information banners. However, each server and vendor has its own behaviors regarding TCP/IP—behaviors that are difficult or impossible for a systems administrator to control. Many auditors and hackers work to document these subtle differences in TCP/IP implementation, thereby creating a sort of fingerprint for each operating system.

The key to learning how one operating system uses TCP/IP differently from another is to generate idiosyncratic TCP/IP packets and direct them to IP addresses and ports. Certain operating systems will respond to these packets in different ways, allowing you to deduce which type of system the host is running. For example, you can send a FIN packet (or any packet without an ACK or SYN flag) to a host's open port. By doing so, you can elicit a response from the following systems:

- Microsoft Windows 2000, NT, 98, 95, and 3.11
- FreeBSD
- Cisco
- HP/UX

Most other systems will not respond. Although you have narrowed the field only slightly, you have at least begun to investigate the nature of the host you are targeting.

If you generate a TCP packet with an undefined flag in the header, versions of Linux before 2.0.35 tend to include this undefined flag in their responses. This behavior is unique to this version of Linux, allowing you to determine the operating system running at that host.

In Unix systems, you can download files from `/bin/ls`. The files you might find could reveal important information about the flavor of Unix on the host.

The following is a partial list of checks made by fingerprinting programs. Many operating systems implement these activities differently, allowing the program to learn more information.

- ICMP Error Message Quenching
- Type of Service (TOS) value
- TCP/IP options
- SYN flood resistance
- TCP initial window: Whenever TCP begins its three-way handshake, it starts with an initial SYN packet. A program such as nmap sends initial SYN packets that trick the operating system into a response. A fingerprinting application can deduce several things from the way this packet is formed, then arrive at an educated guess concerning the operating system.

nmap

nmap is popular because it is relatively powerful, constantly updated, and free. It is an effective network discovery program for two reasons. First, it deploys a fairly sophisticated series of TCP/IP fingerprinting engines. Its creator, who is known as Fyodor at www.insecure.org, is also actively updating these engines so they can arrive at as many educated guesses as possible. nmap can accurately scan server operating systems (including Novell, Unix, Linux, and NT), routers (including Cisco, 3COM, and HP), and dial-up devices. Second, it is effective because it is designed to defeat perimeter security applications, such as firewalls.

> **NOTE** A version of nmap for Windows NT and Windows 2000 is available at the following locations on the Internet: www.eeye.com/html/Research/Tools/nmapnt.html or from www.packetstorm.linuxsecurity.com.

One of the ways nmap defeats firewalls is through its ability to fragment scans, primarily via the stealth option. You can send stealth FIN packets (-sF), stealth Xmas tree packets (sX), or stealth NULL packets (sN). These options allow you to fragment TCP queries to bypass most firewall rules. Such strategies have been effective on even the most popular of software companies, as well as many other organizations. Figure 11.11 shows the results of a scan.

The -O option causes nmap to use stack fingerprinting to identify an operating system. In Figure 11.12, for example, nmap has been used to identify a Windows 2000 system.

FIGURE 11.11 A sample nmap query of firewall-protected server

```
# Log of: nmap -sF -o www.firewallprotectedcompany.com
Interesting ports on  (218.57.234.210):
Port     State         Protocol    Service
1        open          tcp         tcpmux
2        open          tcp         compressnet
3        open          tcp         compressnet
4        open          tcp         unknown
5        open          tcp         rje
6        open          tcp         unknown
7        open          tcp         echo
8        open          tcp         unknown
9        open          tcp         discard
10       open          tcp         unknown
11       open          tcp         systat
12       open          tcp         unknown
13       open          tcp         daytime
14       open          tcp         unknown
15       open          tcp         netstat
16       open          tcp         unknown
```

FIGURE 11.12 Identifying a Windows 2000 operating system with nmap

```
[root@keats /root]# nmap -O sandi

Starting nmap V. 2.53 by fyodor@insecure.org ( www.insecure.org/nmap/ )
Insufficient responses for TCP sequencing (3), OS detection will be MUCH less re
liable
Interesting ports on sandi.stangernet.com (192.168.2.4):
(The 1503 ports scanned but not shown below are in state: closed)
Port       State       Service
7/tcp      open        echo
9/tcp      open        discard
13/tcp     open        daytime
17/tcp     open        qotd
19/tcp     open        chargen
23/tcp     open        telnet
53/tcp     open        domain
135/tcp    open        loc-srv
139/tcp    open        netbios-ssn
445/tcp    open        microsoft-ds
515/tcp    open        printer
554/tcp    open        rtsp
1025/tcp   open        listen
5050/tcp   open        mmcc
6666/tcp   open        irc-serv
7007/tcp   open        afs3-bos
8080/tcp   open        http-proxy
9090/tcp   open        zeus-admin
12345/tcp  open        NetBus
12346/tcp  open        NetBus

Remote OS guesses: Windows NT 5 Beta2 or Beta3, Windows 2000 RC1 through final r
elease, MS Windows2000 Professional RC1/W2K Advance Server Beta3

Nmap run completed -- 1 IP address (1 host up) scanned in 3 seconds
[root@keats /root]#
```

You can also conduct long-term scans using nmap. The -T option accepts several different arguments, including the following:

Paranoid   Waits 5 minutes between sending packets to a host it wants to scan.

Sneaky   Waits 15 seconds between sending packets.

Polite   Waits 0.4 seconds between sending packets.

You can also spoof source IP addresses, so auditors can evade traceback during a scan. Issuing the nmap -h command will display a list of helpful commands. Consult the nmap manual page (man nmap) for more information.

Using Telnet

Telnet is a program designed to allow a user to work with a remote computer as if he or she were sitting at the remote computer's terminal. By default, Telnet uses TCP port 23. However, you can use any Telnet client application to connect to different ports.

For example, you can connect to an HTTP port with Telnet. If you press Enter a few times, the server will usually disconnect you from the system because it will not recognize the request. However, you will generally receive some sort of message from the HTTP server. Many times, you can use this message to learn the server vendor, the version (such as Apache Web Server 1.36 or IIS 5), and so forth. Other messages might not be as informative, but you can often deduce the server type from the error message it delivers. As shown in Figure 11.13, you will probably be disconnected from the web server port but part of the error message will include the HTTP server version.

FIGURE 11.13   Scanning port 80 for web server

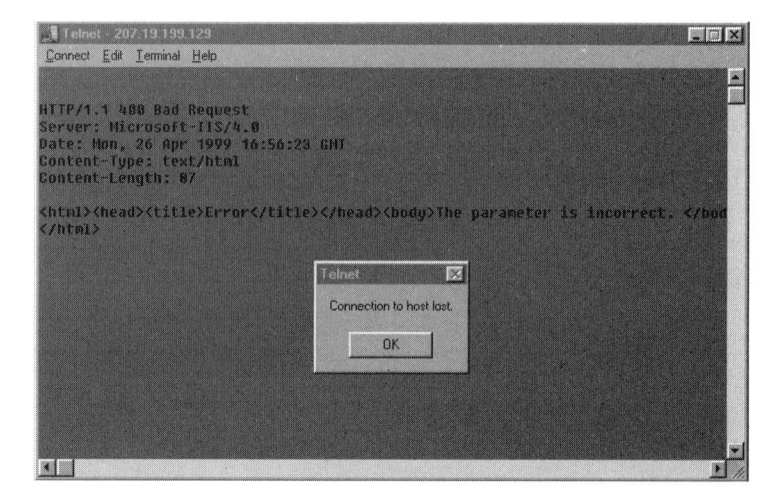

You can also use Telnet to attach to a system and use the SYST command. Many TCP/IP stacks will reveal important information.

Finger, SNMP, and Trivial TCP/IP Services

The `finger` command, available on both Windows 2000 and Unix systems, allows you to access user information from remote servers. Using `finger`, you can learn information about a user account, including whether or not the user is currently logged in. If you find a Finger service or daemon running, consider disabling it unless a compelling reason exists for using it.

The Simple Network Management Protocol (SNMP) is an effective tool used for obtaining network statistics. Implementation of this protocol usually implies the use of a manager and at least one agent. Agents can be placed on various hosts on the network. SNMP has three major versions: SNMPv1, SNMPv2, and SNMPv3. SNMPv1, the most commonly used version, uses UDP ports 161 and 162. It has two chief weaknesses:

- Communication between agents and managers is not encrypted.

- Managers and agents use a simple unencrypted text string to authenticate users. Furthermore, this unencrypted text string, called a *community name*, is often left at its default, which is "public."

If you encounter SNMPv1 as an auditor, consider the following options:

- Make sure that the community name is not left at "public."

- Upgrade SNMPv1 to SNMPv3, which allows you to encrypt transmissions and use more elaborate authentication schemes. Upgrading is not always possible, due to the increased complexity and cost that SNMPv3 implies.

Trivial TCP/IP services include the "Quote of the Day" service (`quotd`), which provides a simple quote, usually from a famous historical figure, each time the port is queried. The `quotd` service operates at TCP and UDP port 17. Additional trivial services are shown in Table 11.3.

Trivial IP services can provide too much information, and can even contain system bugs. To an auditor, they can be helpful when determining the type of operating system. However, disable them if possible.

TABLE 11.3 Trivial IP Services

Service	Description
TFTP	Allows file transfer without authentication at UDP port 69.
Character Generator	Provides continuous output on TCP/UDP port 19.
Daytime	Provides the time of day at port TCP/UDP port 13.
echo	Echoes any input at TCP/UDP port 7.

Vulnerability Scanners

Thus far, you have learned about some of the simple tools available for an auditor's use. These tools are useful because they are easy to install and use. They can give you a great deal of information about a network. They also help you to assess risk in a particular system.

The main weakness of the applications already discussed is that they only report services that are open. They generally do not test these services to see if they exhibit specific vulnerabilities. These applications are also not capable of issuing multiple queries against a single host. They are not configured to conduct a coordinated discovery of multiple systems and services.

To successfully test weaknesses and coordinate scans, an auditor needs a *vulnerability scanner*. Enterprise-grade auditing applications such as vulnerability scanners attempt to beat hackers at their own game. These programs subject a network to a barrage of coordinated attacks, allowing you to detect specific problems in a real-time, practical setting.

Common Vulnerability Scanners

Below is a very short list of popular vulnerability scanners.

- ISS Internet Scanner (www.iss.net)
- Symantec NetRecon (www.symantec.com)

- Network Flight Recorder (www.nfr.com)
- eEye Retina Scanner (www.eeye.com)

Many open-source scanners exist. These scanners are not sold but are updated often, and represent an effective alternative for auditors on a tight budget. Highly regarded network scanners include:

- Nessus (www.nessus.org)
- Saint (www.wwdsi.com/saint)

Network Scanning Issues

Most enterprise-grade applications allow you to determine the extent of the security scan. A light network scan generally searches the well-known ports (0 through 1023) as well as standard security weaknesses, including poor password protection, low patch levels, and extraneous services. If you scan a small subnet, the scan might take up to 30 minutes. Medium and heavy scans can take several days, depending on the speed of the network, the clock speed of the processor running the network probe, and so forth. Figure 11.14 shows the scan-level selector in the ISS Internet Scanner application.

FIGURE 11.14 Selecting a scan level in ISS Internet Scanner

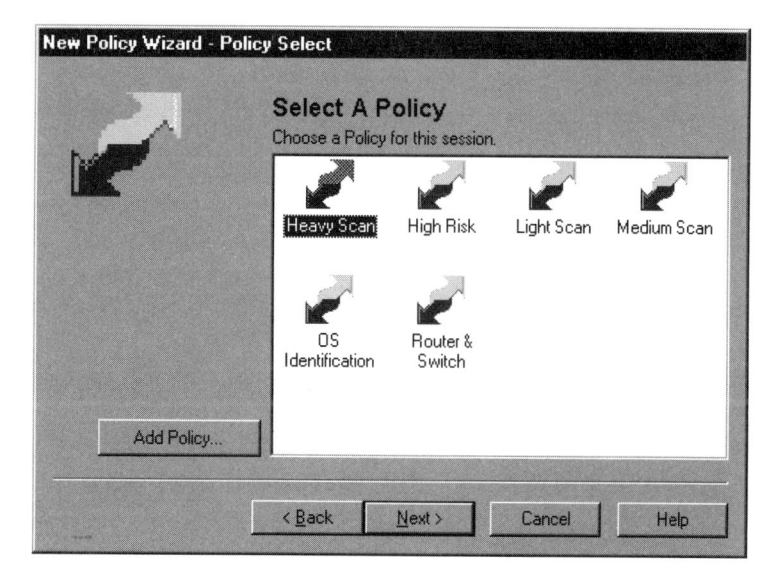

A heavy scan policy allows the application to conduct a barrage of attacks, some of which can actually crash a host. If you set a scanning application to scan all 65,535 ports, as well as attempt to defeat passwords and conduct a detailed analysis of every service from administrative accounts to Unix subsystems, your scan could take days to complete. Such scans can also clog network connections and overwhelm the target host. Therefore, time your scans so they do not interfere with the business you are auditing. Thus, consider network latency when conducting a scan.

An auditor does not want to be held liable for employee downtime. To avoid inconveniencing employees and customers, conduct your network scans after hours, for example. As far as vulnerability scanners are concerned, most of the problems you will discover will be present, even if employees are not accessing the network. As long as you have ensured that all network hosts are participating on the network, your scan will be successful without inconveniencing anyone.

Some scanners require you to configure additional hosts to help conduct an effective scan. This is because some tests conducted by network scanners applications cannot cross subnets. As a result, you will have to install some scanners on various subnets in order to obtain the most revealing results.

What Information Can You Obtain?

As a security auditor, you can categorize the information you receive into network-level and host-level information. Table 11.4 discusses some of the more valuable network-level information you can obtain.

TABLE 11.4 Network-Level Information

Information	Description
Network topology	A security auditor should learn the network types (Ethernet, Token Ring, and so forth) as well as IP address ranges, subnets, and other network information. Location of access panels and wiring closets can also be valuable. As a security manager, your goal is to keep such information away from hackers through the use of firewalls, proxy servers, and so forth.

TABLE 11.4 Network-Level Information *(continued)*

Information	Description
Routers and switches	Learning the types of routers and/or switches is extremely valuable for analyzing security. You can cause routers to leak information.
Firewall type	Most networks have a firewall. If you can gain access to the specific type of firewall, you can then study it and learn about possible weaknesses.
IP services	The most essential services include DHCP, BOOTP, WINS, Samba, and DNS. DNS services are especially prone to buffer overflow attacks.
Modem banks	Perhaps the most popular way to get around a firewall is to exploit modem connections, by conducting a man-in-the-middle attack and packet sniffing. War dialers, which are programs that speed-dial numbers across the Internet to find network connections, are important auditor tools.

Table 11.5 describes some of the more valuable host-level information you can learn.

TABLE 11.5 Host-Level Information

Information	Description
Active ports	You can find ports for each of the servers you run. More important, vulnerability scanners query the daemon or service that is listening on that port.
Databases	The database type (e.g., Oracle, Microsoft SQL Server, IBM DB2) as well as the physical location and connecting protocol can be valuable.

TABLE 11.5 Host-Level Information *(continued)*

Information	Description
Servers	The server type is very useful information. Once you determine whether a server is Microsoft or Unix, you can then exploit system defaults and patches, as well as discover login account names (if not the passwords), weak passwords, and low patch levels.

Vulnerability Scanners and Reporting

Any enterprise-grade scanning application will provide detailed reporting mechanisms. You should be able to export this information into several formats, including:

- Simple ASCII text
- HTML
- Word-processing document formats, such as Rich Text Format (RTF), or proprietary formats, such as Adobe's Portable Document Format (PDF) or Microsoft Word (DOC)
- A spreadsheet, such as Microsoft Excel
- A database, readable by any application capable of issuing SQL commands
- Graphics for inclusion in a slide presentation, such as Microsoft PowerPoint or IBM Freelance

As an auditor, pay close attention to the quality of your scanner's reporting mechanism, because many customers will rely on these reports to secure their networks and network hosts. Although many applications generate reports in a proprietary format, they increasingly have turned to generating HTML-based reports, which anyone can view with a common web browser.

Figure 11.15, for example, shows a report generated by Symantec's NetRecon.

FIGURE 11.15 Excerpt from a NetRecon report

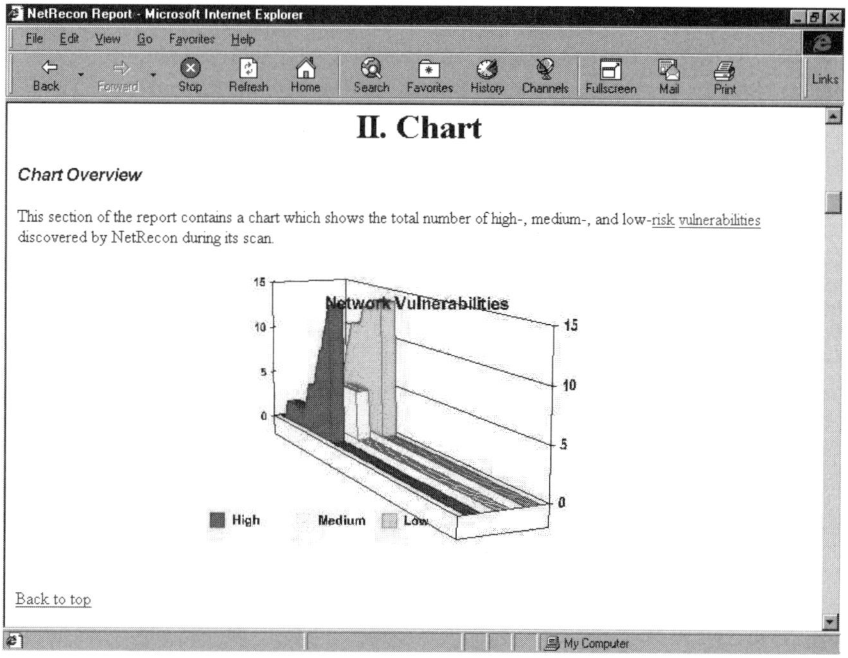

Most network scanners categorize threats into low, medium, and high risk. You will see how various network scanners report what they have found.

Additional Auditing Strategies

You have now been introduced to several discovery programs, some of which are quite sophisticated and comprehensive. However, consider the convenience of having someone else discover network elements for you. A good auditor will find ways to learn information about the network from human sources. Although it is possible to use social engineering to penetrate and control a network, it is also quite helpful when a hacker is attempting to learn more about network devices. As a security manager, do not underestimate this threat. When conducting security audits, you should not omit social engineering from your list of tools and techniques. Consider the social engineering strategies discussed in Chapter 3.

Education and Social Engineering

For the security manager, the best way to ensure that network users do not become discovery tools is to provide end-user education. If you raise people's understanding of the equipment they use and give them a sense of responsibility, they will be more difficult to manipulate.

The Next Step: Research

In recent years, most successful hackers have been people with a lot of spare time. Hackers devote much of this time to reading manuals and learning about system defaults and built-in weaknesses. Regardless of whether you are a security manager or a security auditor, you should learn as much as possible about system weaknesses. Research can take many different forms, including the following:

- Live testing, in which auditors test popular network daemons and services for weaknesses.

- Searching recognized security sites for reports about bugs relevant to a particular daemon, operating system or combination thereof. For example, you can study the TCP/IP RFCs to learn more about how vendors implement TCP/IP.

- Networking with known auditors and hackers to learn more about ways common daemons are attacked.

- Studying the source code of the daemon in question. Although obtaining code for commercial applications is very difficult, it is possible to study the source code of open-source operating systems and applications.

> ### "Legitimate" vs. "Illegitimate" Auditing Tools
>
> A hacker can use any tool, regardless of its sophistication. In other words, no difference exists between a hacker tool and an auditing tool. Some of the tools discussed in this chapter, such as Symantec's NetRecon, broadcast the name of the host issuing the query. This information can help a systems administrator or security manager determine the source of a scan more readily. Nevertheless, the use of such programs is not limited to legitimate systems administrators.

> Hackers can use any of the tools mentioned in this chapter. Using enterprise-grade tools usually occupies a tremendous amount of bandwidth, and is therefore not a stealthy discovery method. This means that any systems administrator, security auditor, or hacker interested in using a network-scanning application runs the risk of either drawing attention or bringing down an entire network segment. It is highly recommended that you use your security policy to help ensure that employees know what types of applications, services, and daemons they can install on their networks.

eEye Retina

Retina is developed by the eEye team (www.eeye.com). The eEye team is proficient at finding buffer overflows, which are occurrences of an application writing data onto an area of memory that the operating system has not actually allocated to it. Buffer overflows also tend to focus on web servers. Thus, Retina reflects these strengths.

The Retina scanner, shown in Figure 11.16, is easy to use and has numerous reporting capabilities.

FIGURE 11.16 Retina scanner

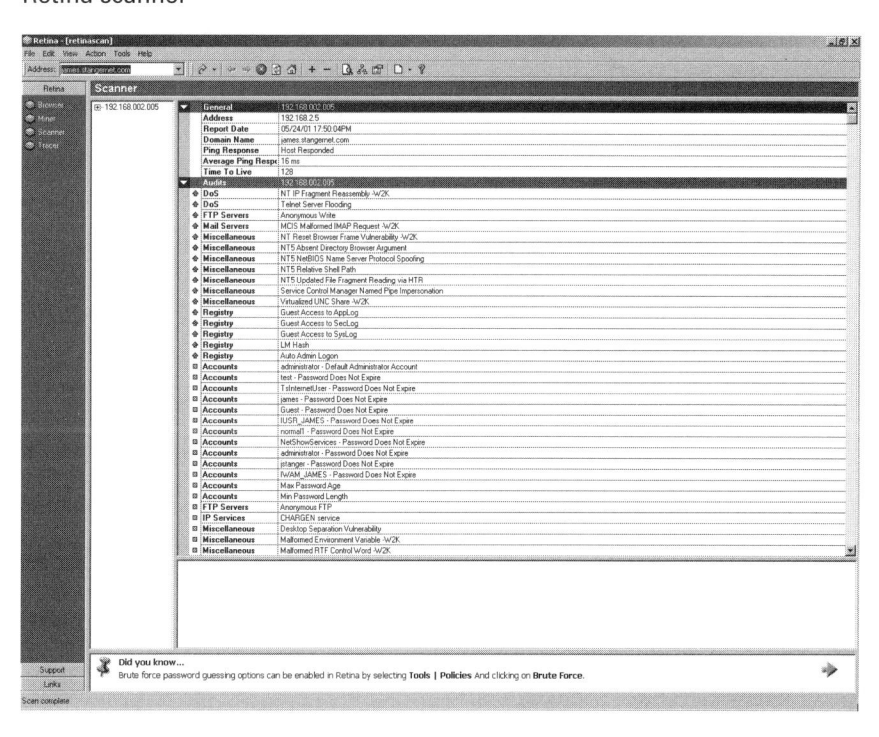

Retina has the following strengths:

- It can be configured to conduct brute-force attacks against remote hosts, in various IP ranges. Thus, the scanner can be used to audit hosts from across the Internet.

- It offers the ability to imitate hacker behavior through the Common Hacking Attack Methods (CHAM) feature, which conducts quick scans against web servers (including CGI- and script-based attacks).

EXERCISE 11.1

Deploying eEye Retina 3.0

In this exercise, you will install eEye Retina on your Windows 2000 system and then scan hosts on your network. Please note that it is never ethical, and sometimes illegal, to scan hosts that you do not administer.

1. Obtain an evaluation copy of eEye Retina from www.eeye.com.

2. Double-click the installation file (retina3.exe) and follow the installation instructions.

3. Go to Start ➤ Programs ➤ Retina ➤ Retina and open the application.

4. The Retina main interface will appear.

5. Select File ➤ Save and save the current session under your name.

6. Choose Edit ➤ IP Range and enter the IP addresses of your network.

7. Click the Scanner button. "Scanner" will appear on the Taskbar. Now, click the Start button, which is on the right side of the screen. The scan will begin.

8. When the scan finishes, your screen will appear significantly similar to that shown here.

Additional Auditing Strategies 469

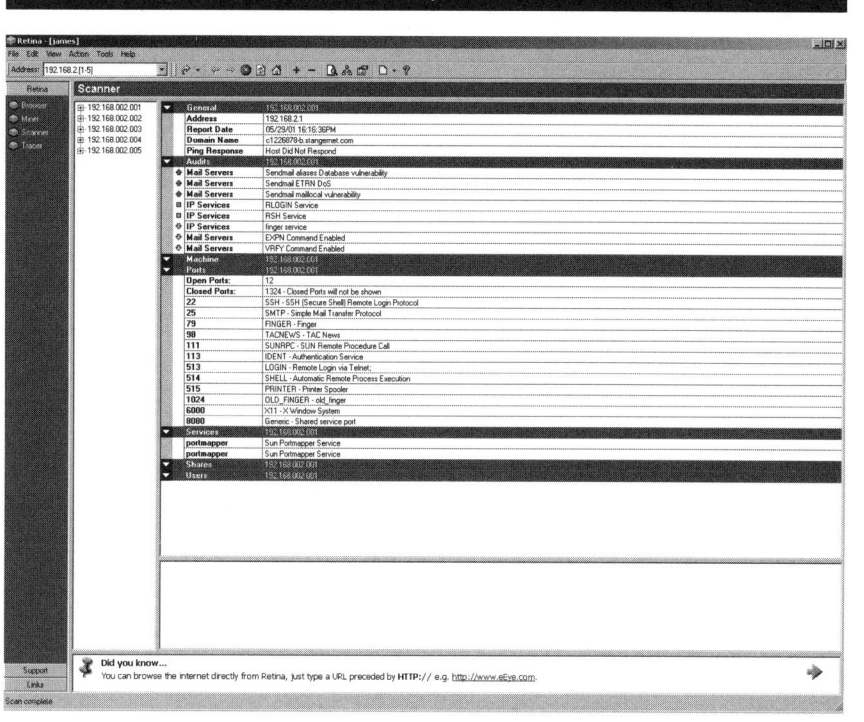

EXERCISE 11.1 *(continued)*

[Screenshot of Retina scanner showing scan results for 192.168.002.001, including General info, Audits (Mail Servers, IP Services), Machine ports, Services, Shares, and Users.]

9. By default, the first system scanned will be reported. Click on the icons to view individual weaknesses. Note that weaknesses are presented by IP address. You can then drill down into each IP address and learn about specific weaknesses. Retina will give you general information about the remote server, then about specific "audits," which show system weaknesses. You will then be shown open ports and services, as well as users defined on the system. When you have finished viewing the first system, click the next IP address in the left-hand panel. View all the systems that Retina was able to discover.

10. Now, identify a remote Linux system that you own, and then rerun Retina against it. Note how the vulnerabilities have changed from one operating system to another.

> **EXERCISE 11.1 *(continued)***
>
> 11. Go to Tools ≻ Policies and select Brute Force. Now, Retina is configured to conduct a brute-force attack against your remote Linux system. Rescan this remote host to see what Retina discovers.
>
> 12. Retina's Miner feature allows you to scan web servers for weaknesses. It is designed to be a feature that mimics actions of a potential hacker. This feature can take considerable time, because it conducts various brute-force attacks. Select one system and then use the Miner feature against it.
>
> 13. Finally, use the Tracer feature, which conducts a `traceroute` between you and a remote system. The browser feature is simply a web browser, much like Internet Explorer.

Summary

In this chapter, you learned about an auditor's specific role in analyzing risk and end-user compliance. As an auditor, you must learn how to view a network from a hacker's perspective. To this end, you have learned about various applications such as port scanners and vulnerability detectors. You can use these applications to help you understand your network's risk level. You also learned about the various duties of an auditor, including finding ways to test firewalls and network hosts for compliance problems.

You have also learned about specific techniques such as stack fingerprinting, ping scanning, and the use of DNS to gain information about specific hosts. Now that you have a clear understanding of an auditor's duties and understand the hacker's "discovery" stage, it is time to learn about the next steps: penetration and control.

Exam Essentials

Know the steps necessary for conducting compliance and risk audits. While it is not important to differentiate between compliance and risk audits, make sure that you are able to explain the importance of checking the corporate information security policy. Also, it is important to understand the concept of effective security, which includes understanding how a gap can occur between actual practice and what is proposed by the security policy.

When prioritizing resources and determining what is at risk, make sure that you understand how a technical change can affect business concerns. When generating reports, direct them toward the correct audience.

Be able to identify the tools needed to discover network host and host vulnerabilities.   Understand the usefulness of both network-based and host-based scanners. The former is effective when scanning hosts in a large network. Host-based scanners can delve more deeply into a host's weaknesses, but will sometimes be less revealing about vulnerabilities presented by network daemons.

Know the difference between a port scanner and a vulnerability scanner.   A port scanner is a tool that checks to see if ports are open or not. Usually, these scanners do not test the daemon listening behind the open port. A vulnerability scanner is generally more sophisticated and conducts tests on the daemon to see if it is vulnerable to a pre-chosen list of vulnerabilities.

Understand the importance of working inside the firewall and outside the firewall.   An auditor must be able to work inside the firewall, as well as outside it. Auditing from within the firewall, the auditor can identify systems that are susceptible to employee tampering. From outside the firewall, the auditor can test the firewall's configuration to determine if it is properly configured.

Understand auditor roles and perspectives.   The auditor can take various perspectives. The auditor can act as an uninformed hacker who must discover, penetrate, and control systems. Or the auditor can act as an informed insider who is able to conduct more in-depth investigations. The benefits of the uninformed hacker approach include the ability to test the network's ability to hide its resources. The benefits of the insider view include being able to show how to secure the network from skilled hackers.

Know the difference between executive, procedural, and IT-level reports.   As an auditor, you will have to create reports. However, these reports will not always be for the same audience. Be able to identify the hallmarks of executive, procedural, and IT-level reports. For example, an executive report is nontechnical in its language, and is as brief as possible. A procedural report, on the other hand, is used to explain the steps you took during the audit.

Understand the impact an audit can have on the network. Auditing applications allow you to conduct light, medium, and heavy scans on network hosts. A heavy scan can overburden or even crash an individual host. Multiple heavy scans can consume bandwidth and significantly affect the network's overall performance. Be aware that vulnerability software can interrupt business operations if run during business hours.

Key Terms

Before you take the exam, be certain you are familiar with the following terms:

audit report	network-based management model
auditor	penetration stage
community name	ping scanning
control stage	port scan
discovery stage	risk analysis
ethical hacker	security road map
gap analysis	stack fingerprinting
host-based management model	vulnerability scanner
host-based scanner	white hat hacker
manager	

Review Questions

1. During an audit, what is an auditor's chief purpose?
   A. To provide security services
   B. To assess risk
   C. To provide security products
   D. To encrypt data and create passwords

2. From what two perspectives must an auditor approach a network?
   A. Hacker and security manager
   B. Hacker and consultant
   C. Security manager and consultant
   D. Systems administrator and hacker

3. What is the first recommended step in conducting a risk analysis?
   A. Analyze, categorize, and prioritize resources.
   B. Evaluate existing perimeter and internal security.
   C. Consider business concerns.
   D. Check for a written security policy.

4. At what stage of an audit would an auditor inspect systems for weaknesses, attempting to defeat the encryption, passwords, and access lists?
   A. Penetration
   B. Control
   C. Audit planning
   D. Discovery

5. At what stage of an audit would an auditor scan and test the systems for effective security?

   A. Penetration

   B. Control

   C. Audit planning

   D. Discovery

6. What does the Whois service do?

   A. It allows you to conduct a ping scan.

   B. It allows you to query the domain name service authority.

   C. It tells you the number of routers or hops a packet must travel.

   D. It discovers any active UDP and TCP ports present on a system.

7. What does a ping scan do?

   A. It allows you to query the domain name service authority.

   B. It helps you learn the entire IP address range used by an organization.

   C. It discovers any active UDP and TCP ports present on a system.

   D. It offers a fingerprinting program to help identify specific operating systems.

8. What frequently used Simple Network Management Protocol (SNMP) community name do hackers first try when attempting to gain access to SNMP?

   A. guest

   B. community

   C. password

   D. public

9. Ruth knows the user account name of a user, and she wants to learn more about this user. What TCP/IP service allows her to access user information without authenticating with the server containing the account?

   A. The `finger` command

   B. The `setRequest` command

   C. Telnet

   D. Share scan software

10. Cindy has been asked to conduct a heavy scan of web and e-mail servers for her corporate network. She has decided to use a vulnerability scanner. What will a heavy scan policy provide?

    A. The categorization of threats into low, medium, and high

    B. The ability for the application to conduct numerous attacks

    C. A scan of the well-known ports and standard security weaknesses

    D. Detailed reporting mechanisms in several formats

11. Why is it important to audit behind the firewall?

    A. The firewall acts as a network perimeter.

    B. It is expected of auditors.

    C. Auditors can identify external vulnerabilities.

    D. Auditors can determine internal vulnerabilities.

12. Why is it important to audit outside the firewall?

    A. The firewall acts as a network perimeter.

    B. Auditors can obtain evidence of employee accountability.

    C. Auditors can identify external vulnerabilities.

    D. Auditors can determine internal vulnerabilities.

13. Jason has begun analyzing and categorizing resources. What type of audit is he conducting?

    A. A security audit

    B. A risk analysis

    C. The network security policy

    D. Upper and middle management

14. Mia is categorizing network resources. Which two categories could she use?

    A. Technical function or organizational structure

    B. Operating system or server role

    C. Foundational or mission-critical service

    D. Corporate employees or management

15. Which of the following is a common external attack directed at a network's bandwidth?

    A. An "out-of-band" attack

    B. A SYN flood

    C. Bandwidth consumption

    D. Connection hijacking

16. Beth has created an audit report. She wants to distribute this report via e-mail. What should she do before sending it?

    A. Confirm that she has generated the correct report.

    B. Confirm that she has distributed the report to the appropriate individuals.

    C. Encrypt the presentation.

    D. Ensure that it contains an executive summary.

17. Sandi has created a one-page report indicating that the security level has decreased in the network during the past quarter. Which of the following terms describes this report?

    A. An IT audit report

    B. An audit report

    C. A management report

    D. An executive report

18. Kim wishes to learn more about a remote host. She uses the nmap application. Even though no daemons are running on this host, she is able to determine that this host is running kernel 2.4.2 and that it is most likely a Red Hat Linux system. How was she able to determine this information?

    A. Social engineering

    B. A system bug

    C. Stack fingerprinting

    D. Trivial IP services

19. Which of the following is best suited for determining whether a specific tool is a legitimate or a hacker tool?

    A. The company president and chief information officer

    B. Company employees

    C. Company auditors, as approved by the chief information officer

    D. The company security policy

20. Which of the following ports does quotd use?

    A. 17

    B. 19

    C. 13

    D. 7

Answers to Review Questions

1. **B.** A security auditor should be prepared to determine risk, as well as the level of compliance. Providing products or security services such as encryption is an activity that comes after the risk and compliance assessment stages.

2. **C.** The terms used by the CIW Security Professional exam are *security manager* and *consultant*. Although a consultant can impersonate, as it were, a hacker, make sure that you understand the nomenclature used on the exam.

3. **D.** Checking for a written security policy is the first step of a risk analysis as well as a compliance analysis. Knowing the security policy ensures that you are approaching your audit with an understanding of both the technical and business concerns.

4. **A.** The penetration stage involves trying to defeat access lists and encryption.

5. **D.** The discovery stage enables the auditor to determine the hosts that are present. It also involves determining and researching any known weaknesses, and then making recommendations about those weaknesses.

6. **B.** The Whois service is a logical starting place when discovering hosts; using it, you can discover the network administrator's name and the DNS servers used by the corporation. Using just this information, you can engage in social engineering and can begin identifying the network's infrastructure.

7. **B.** Ping scanning is used to determine which hosts are participating on a network. Firewalls make it possible to block ping scans, because they distinguish between public and private networks.

8. **D.** In SNMPv1, the community name is a simple text string that controls authentication. It is not stored encrypted, nor is it encrypted during the authentication phase. Thus, it is possible to sniff these passwords, even if you have changed the default community name from public to another name.

9. **A.** The `finger` command is used to provide information about users. It does not require an auditor to authenticate before divulging information about a server's authorized users. The auditor does, however,

require the name of the account that is to be fingered. Still, the Finger service does not require the auditor to first log on and provide proof of identity.

10. **B.** A heavy vulnerability scan policy allows you to determine the maximum amount of vulnerabilities exhibited by a network host (e.g., a workstation, a firewall, or an e-mail server).

11. **D.** When you audit behind the firewall, you are auditing the internal network. Doing so means that you are looking for vulnerabilities in the internal network.

12. **C.** Whenever you audit outside the firewall, you are essentially trying to identify problems that reside at the firewall. You are also trying to find network design flaws that might allow hackers to bypass the firewall and enter the network.

13. **B.** A risk analysis involves categorizing and prioritizing resources. This step is essential, because it helps you determine which resources are worth protecting.

14. **A.** Most auditors approach categorizing a network resource in terms of its technical function, or according to the company's organizational structure. It is tempting to always approach the network as a technical resource, but it is often essential to consider the business function of the resource.

15. **C.** A bandwidth-consumption attack is a form of denial-of-service and distributed denial-of-service attack. An "out-of-band" attack involves opening up a second connection to attack a host. A SYN flood bogs down a specific host and does not necessarily occupy too much bandwidth. Connection-hijacking attacks are designed to interrupt the TCP connection process and are not explicitly designed to attack a network's bandwidth.

16. **C.** When distributing a presentation, you should take great measures to ensure that only certain people can read it. Encrypt the presentation using an application such as Pretty Good Privacy (PGP). Although it is important to create the proper type of report for your audience, your first concern is to take reasonable steps to ensure that only authorized parties can receive it. You should confirm that you are giving this report to the proper party before sending it. In other words, if the design is meant for executives, make sure that you are not delivering it to an IT worker, and vice versa.

17. **D.** An executive report should be concise, though accurate. It should quickly explain increases and decreases in security levels, and aid the executive in making a decision on resource allocation.

18. **C.** Stack fingerprinting is the practice of identifying the operating system by the way it responds to various queries. Even though developers are supposed to follow standards when writing network applications, differences inevitably occur. Social engineering is one strategy for gaining information, but nothing in the scenario suggests it. System bugs can also lead to the revelation of too much information, but do not provide as direct an explanation as stack fingerprinting. Trivial IP services are also effective, but the question indicated that this system is not running any daemons at all.

19. **D.** The company security policy, which is maintained by upper management, is the final authority. Whenever a change is needed, the security policy must be updated.

20. **A.** The `quotd` daemon, which provides a different quote upon each connection, uses port 17.

Chapter 12

Auditing Penetration and Control Strategies

THE CIW EXAM OBJECTIVE GROUPS COVERED IN THIS CHAPTER:

- ✓ Identify penetration and control strategies and methods, including but not limited to: potential attacks, router security, threat containment, intrusion detection.

Once the hacker has determined the scope of your systems, he or she chooses a specific target for penetration. Usually, this target is the one with the weakest security or for which the hacker has the most tools. Several general methods of illicit entry exist. As a security auditor or security manager, you should be aware of these methods. In this chapter, you will review penetration strategies and learn more about how servers are controlled. When auditing any Internet system, you have various options available when trying to penetrate them. These can include:

- Crack the password database of the machine using a dictionary and/or brute-force attack.

- Obtain encrypted or unencrypted passwords as they pass across the network.

- Ignore the password database and find a vulnerability through a system bug, such as a buffer overflow.

- Engage in social engineering.

In this chapter, we will investigate some of the methods that have been adopted for auditing systems. We will not investigate each of these, because some, such as social engineering, have already been discussed in sufficient detail. This chapter will start with how network elements are commonly compromised, and then investigate how it is possible to crack network hosts using applications such as L0phtCrack 3 (LC3) and John the Ripper. You will then learn about common events that occur after a host has been compromised.

Compromising Network Elements

A router is always exposed, especially when connected to the Internet. Many routers use SNMPv1, making them possible targets. It is, of course, necessary to program routers and switches, but once programming is finished, it is important to secure remote access. Failure to do so increases the potential for a hacker to access and reconfigure the router. Physical security must also be considered. Most routers and switches allow themselves to be programmed via a local serial port. As an auditor, check the routers to ensure that a person cannot physically attach to the router and conduct a terminal session.

To avoid unauthorized router programming, use your firewall to filter out Telnet (port 23) on the external router port, just as you programmed your router to ignore ports 161 and 162 (the SNMP ports). Work to secure additional protocols, such as Secure Shell (port 22), as well.

> **NOTE** Many network administrators prefer to disable remote access after initial configuration because most routers do not require much maintenance. If the router should need further configuration, you can establish a physical connection.

Firewalls

You have already learned how to configure a firewall. When auditing the firewall, you need to consider several issues, many of which are similar to those you encounter when auditing routers:

Is it possible to defeat the firewall? Review all firewall logs to learn about the nature of traffic through the firewall. Firewalls can log large amounts of traffic. As a result, the log files can grow quite large, and it can be somewhat difficult to find anything useful. Some firewalls ship with log-analysis software. WebTrends (www.webtrends.com) sells a product called WebTrends Firewall Suite, which is designed to scan log files and identify suspicious traffic.

Auditing a firewall is often called "penetration testing." When testing a firewall, consider the following items:

- Determine if the firewall's configuration allows spoofed packets to enter the network. Most current firewalls automatically disallow an IP packet if it has an originating address that is the same as the internal network. However, you should never assume that all of these rules are properly configured. Applications such as firewalk (www.packetfactory.net/Projects/Firewalk) allow you to forge packets that can help you analyze and defeat misconfigured firewalls.

- Determine if the firewall itself has accepted any logins. Review login logs to discover any evidence of tampering. Evidence can include actual log entries that the hacker forgot to erase, or anomalies in dates or login times. An entry that appears strange might be the result of an awkward attempt at altering log files. It is important to understand, however, that simply checking firewall logs does not increase the level of security; it simply allows you to learn more about the firewall's history.

- Make sure that the firewall is physically secure. Keep your firewall behind a locked door, and further secure it by removing any keyboards or other input devices. They can be added later when you need to configure the firewall.

Is it possible to avoid the firewall? Check the *modem bank* to see if it is offering a way around the firewall. If improperly configured, the modem bank may allow a hacker to easily authenticate and enter your network. Check all log entries, as well as authentication settings. Look for any dual-homed systems on the network that allow direct connections between your private network and the Internet. Sometimes, naive systems administrators will make such connections, which can allow a hacker to simply "walk around" the firewall.

For more information on how to penetrate a system, read Chapter 3, which discusses the types of attacks used during the penetration phase. Now, it's time to learn more about what happens during the control stage.

Control Phase

So far, we have discussed how to discover and penetrate systems. As an auditor, you are also obligated to inform your client about ways a person can establish control over a server or network. To do this efficiently, you must be familiar with the principles, tools, and methods available to those who successfully gain network control. In Chapter 1, you examined a classic method of control when you learned about NetBus and the "Whack-a-mole" exploit. Knowledge of such exploits can help you recognize more current attacks. Once a hacker successfully penetrates your system, he or she will immediately attempt to establish control of it. Typical goals in this stage include the ability to:

- Gain root access
- Gather information
- Open new security holes
- Erase evidence of penetration
- Spread to other systems

If the hacker is successful at even a few of these attempts, it will be quite difficult to detect—let alone terminate—the penetration.

Gaining Root Access

The primary goal of any hacker is to gain administrative access. The CIW exam will often refer to administrative access as *root access*. Root access is the ultimate achievement because it provides the ability to create more accounts and manipulate services, ensuring continued control over the system. Many times, a hacker will first gain non-administrative access to a server, and then try to *escalate privileges* by exploiting a system bug, social engineering, or other strategies, including those discussed in the preceding chapters. Illicit servers, such as BackOrifice and NetBus, are all examples of well-known tools that have allowed a hacker to obtain and keep root access. Unix systems are particularly prone to root kits and buffer overflows.

> **Tracing Root Kits**
>
> Root kits are especially difficult to detect. You can, for example, test common applications such as `ls`, `su`, and `chmod` to see if they work properly. If they do not, then this is one sign that a root kit is installed. Additional methods exist to audit for the presence of a root kit. For instance, you can obtain applications such as Chkrootkit, which is currently available at `ftp://ftp.pangeia.com.br/pub/seg/pac/`. You can also search for Chkrootkit on sites such as `http://packetstorm.linuxsecurity.com`. Alternatively, you can use the `strace` command in Linux, which allows you examine the system calls that an application makes. This command is found in Red Hat Linux by default. If you do not have the `strace` command, you can download it from `www.liacs.nl/~wichert/strace`. To use `strace` to check the calls the `ls` command makes, you would issue the following command as root:
>
> ```
> strace ls
> ```
>
> You will then see output that helps you determine exactly what this command is doing. If you find references to ports, or if you see no output at all, you can begin to suspect a root kit. However, if the creators of a root kit have customized the root kit so it behaves differently, or if they have trojanized the `strace` application, these methods of detection will fail.

Illicit services and trap doors can enable a hacker to use a legitimate account as a tool to upgrade access permissions. If a hacker can obtain a legitimate user account, it is much easier to upgrade and obtain an administrative account. Access, however, is not all that a hacker wants to do with accounts.

Creating Additional Accounts

To minimize the possibility of being removed from the system, a hacker generally creates many accounts after obtaining root access. By using several different accounts, hackers can also spread the unusual activity around, thereby minimizing the chances of detection.

Multiple accounts also give hackers additional doors back inside in case they are detected. Some larger companies, for example, have been so thoroughly penetrated that they are unsure which accounts are valid and which are not. The hacker's goal is to create and exploit this type of uncertainty.

One way to create additional accounts is through a *batch file*, which is a simple text file that contains commands. When the batch file is run, these commands instruct an operating system to run specified applications and processes. For example, you can create a text file in Windows Notepad similar to the one shown in Figure 12.1.

FIGURE 12.1 Batch file text

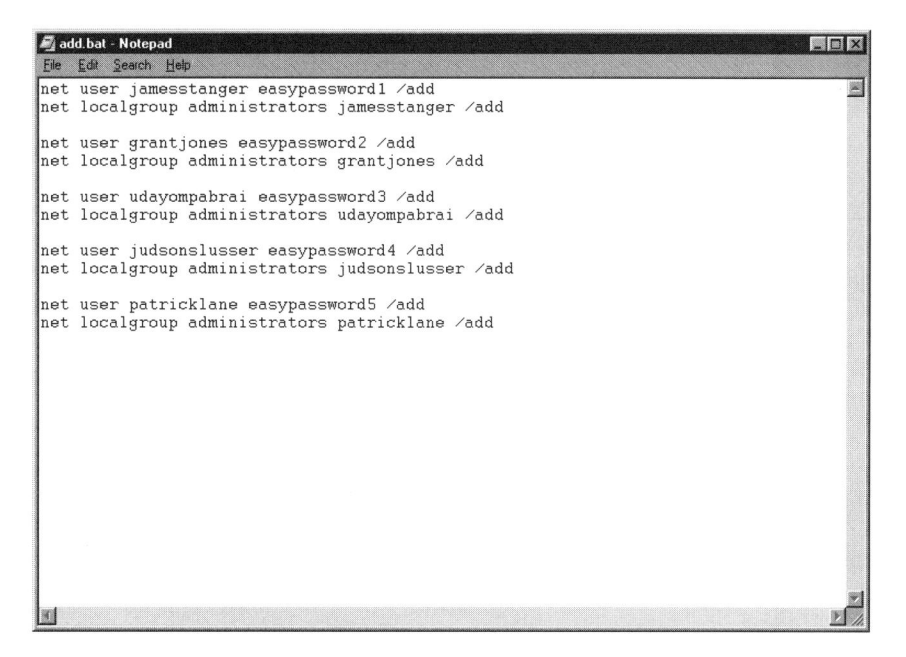

```
net user jamesstanger easypassword1 /add
net localgroup administrators jamesstanger /add

net user grantjones easypassword2 /add
net localgroup administrators grantjones /add

net user udayompabrai easypassword3 /add
net localgroup administrators udayompabrai /add

net user judsonslusser easypassword4 /add
net localgroup administrators judsonslusser /add

net user patricklane easypassword5 /add
net localgroup administrators patricklane /add
```

You can name the file whatever you like, as long as it has the .bat filename extension. This particular batch file adds several users to a Windows 2000 accounts database with the `net user` or `net localuser` command. You can even add a password, if you want. All you have to do is place the text string `/add` after the command. As shown here, this batch file also uses a similar string text to add the newly created users to the Administrators group. If the group does not exist, the batch file will create it. You can also add administrative users with no password at all. It is possible to create similar exploits in Unix and Novell systems.

One way to audit such exploits is to search for user accounts that are incompletely filled out. For example, the batch file in Figure 12.1 does not create any descriptions in the Users section of Local Users and Groups, in the Computer Management Snap-in.

> The use of a batch file implies administrative access. Otherwise, a system bug would have to exist that would allow non-administrative users to run batch files that create administrative users.

Obtaining Additional Information

Once a hacker has obtained root access, he or she will immediately scan the server's information stores. Examples might include files and programs in the human resources database, the accounts payable database, and end-user systems that belong to upper management. A hacker who reaches this phase already has a goal in mind. This type of information gathering is much more specific than the discovery process; this information can lead to the loss of sensitive files and leakage of sensitive information. It can also allow the hacker to control the system.

> This step might seem more like a discovery activity, but it is actually part of penetration. The type of information gathered here centers on what lies inside the server or host, rather than focusing on how that host operates or communicates with the network.

One way hackers can obtain information is to manipulate a remote user's web browser. Most companies allow web use of some kind and generally do not consider HTTP traffic to be inherently dangerous. However, a web browser can open up a serious security problem. Such problems include the *cross-frame browsing bug*, as well as *window spoofing*. The cross-frame browsing bug appeared in the 4.x versions of Netscape Navigator and Windows Explorer. The bug makes it possible for a malicious website to imitate a legitimate site. Many times, the goal of the site operator is to trick a user into revealing sensitive information, such as credit card numbers.

The cross-frame browsing bug allows a malicious website operator (or any of the site's employees) to create a web page that can obtain information from a user's computer. It exploits the 4.x and 5.x versions of Netscape and Microsoft browsers. This browser-based problem can help hackers gain access to files only if they know the locations of the files and folders beforehand. This limitation might seem debilitating, but in fact it is not. Consider, for example, that any hacker would know the default installation path for sensitive Unix files (\etc), Windows NT/2000 files (\winnt), IIS (\inetpub\wwwroot), and so forth. If, for example, a department manager is using a Windows 9*x*/Me system and Microsoft Word, Excel, or Access, he or she is probably using the \desktop\My Documents folder. The hacker might know very little about the person who owns the system or its actual file and folder layout. By guessing where spreadsheet, database, and word processing programs store files by default, the hacker can obtain valuable information.

Window spoofing is the ability for a malicious site owner to imitate a legitimate website. Thus, although the unwitting user thinks the content is legitimate, he or she is actually viewing content that has been created by the malicious user. If the malicious site owner is clever enough, he or she would be able to trick an end user into revealing sensitive information, such as credit card numbers.

Browsers are also prone to buffer overflows, allowing a hacker to conduct a denial-of-service attack against a host running a browser. Once hackers are able to crash a system partially, they can execute scripts that allow them to penetrate and control it.

> Although Unix systems are by far the most common enterprise-grade servers, it is important to realize that most end users operate from Windows-based systems. Such systems have traditionally become platforms for future hacker activity.

Although hackers cannot control a system by manipulating a browser, this manipulation is certainly the first step in establishing control. The type of information obtained from a cross-frame browsing bug is much more detailed than that found in the network discovery or penetration stage. The ability to read the contents of files often allows a hacker to gain enough server information that a systems administrator can foil the hacker only by radically reconfiguring the server.

L0phtCrack 3 and Auditing

L0phtCrack 3 (LC3) is an effective tool for both attacking and defending systems, and it allows the user to conduct dictionary and brute-force attacks. It is quick, and it will generally defeat most password schemes that do not use any alternative characters, such as !@#$%^ *()&. LC3 is available from @stake at www.atstake.com/research/lc3/download.html.

LC3 first uses a dictionary attack that tries passwords from a word list. If the dictionary attack fails, it resorts to a brute-force attack. This combination of attacks allows LC3 to obtain a password quickly. It works in a variety of ways. First, you can run LC3 against a local *Security Account Manager* (SAM) database. Second, you can run it against a remote Windows NT/2000 computer just by specifying an IP address or hostname. However, this method requires the computer running LC3 to first log on to the target machines. Also, if the remote Windows NT/2000 system is running a utility called Syskey (discussed in the section "LC3 and the Syskey Utility" later in this chapter), the attempt to capture the remote SAM database will fail.

The third way LC3 can be used to ascertain passwords involves configuring the computer on which LC3 resides. You configure the computer as a password sniffer, and it can listen for passwords as they travel across the network. You can then use LC3 to capture any password that is passed along the wire.

> LC3 can take from 24 to 30 days to determine a single strong password. The time needed to crack a password depends greatly on the complexity of each password. Given enough time, however, LC3 will eventually find almost all of your passwords.

EXERCISE 12.1

Using L0phtCrack 3 (LC3) to Crack a Local Windows 2000 SAM Database

In this exercise, you will use LC3 to audit your local SAM database.

Note: The following exercise is designed to show you ways you can control systems. This information is for demonstration purposes only. You should not conduct such control activities during an audit or at any other time.

1. Create a user account using Local Users and Groups in the Computer Management snap-in, and assign the account a dictionary-based word. Select a word that would appear in a typical dictionary. If you have enabled password complexity, disable this feature.

EXERCISE 12.1 *(continued)*

2. Obtain a trial version of L0phtCrack 3.0 from www.atstake.com/research/lc3/download.html.

3. Unzip the archive and install the program.

4. Open LC3 by selecting Start ➢ Programs ➢ LC3 ➢ LC3 to launch the LC3 Wizard, shown here.

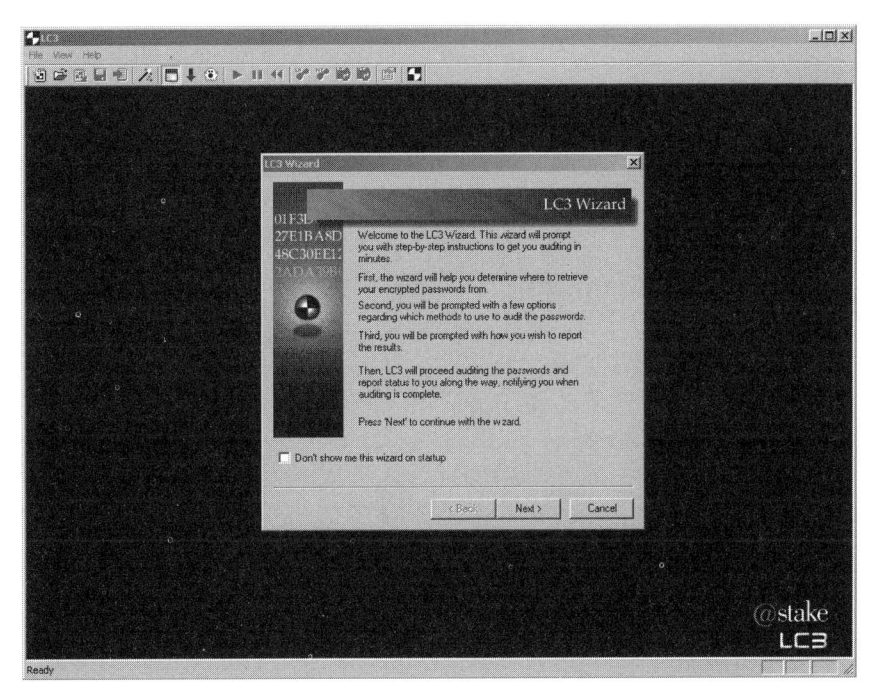

5. As soon as you see the LC3 Wizard, click Next.

6. Make sure the Retrieve From The Local Machine radio button is selected, and click Next.

7. Select the Strong Password Audit radio button and click Next.

8. When the Pick Reporting Style screen appears, leave the settings at their defaults, and click Next.

9. Click Finish. Your local SAM database will appear, and LC3 will begin cracking the passwords immediately.

10. Stop the process after a few minutes by choosing Session ➢ Pause Audit.

> **EXERCISE 12.1 *(continued)***
>
> 11. As we mentioned earlier, LC3 first uses a dictionary file, and then resorts to a brute-force attack. Go to File ➢ Preferences to see the dictionary file used; you'll find it at `C:\Program Files\@stake\LC3\words-english`. Use a text editor to open the file and view the words listed. Is the password you use for the Administrator account listed in this file? If so, LC3 will have discovered the password immediately. If the password for the Administrator account is not listed, LC3 will have to resort to its brute-force mode. Enter the password you are currently using, and then restart the cracking process. You will see that the Administrator account's password will be cracked immediately. You can, of course, specify an alternative dictionary file.

LC3 and the Syskey Utility

LC3 can find and use the password database of many remote Windows NT systems. However, if an NT or 2000 system has the *Syskey* utility enabled, LC3 will not be able to read remote SAM databases. Windows 2000 has Syskey enabled by default.

Syskey represents Microsoft's attempt to add another layer of encryption to the SAM database. The utility, shown in Figure 12.2, uses MD5 encryption. Syskey also protects user accounts so they cannot be easily transferred to a remote system. You can configure Syskey to prevent your system from completing a reboot if one has been requested under suspicious circumstances.

FIGURE 12.2 The Windows 2000 Syskey utility

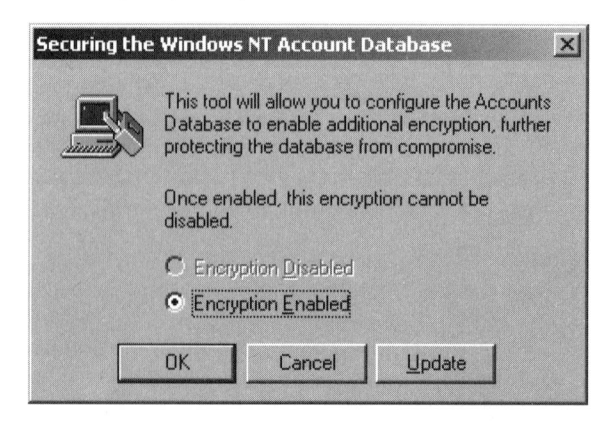

In Windows NT Server 4, Syskey is available in Service Pack 3 and later. You need to run Syskey manually on a Windows NT Server 4 system. For more information about Syskey, see the following URL: http://support.microsoft.com/support/kb/articles/q143/4/75.asp

> **TIP** If you are enabling Syskey for the first time on a Windows NT system, you should first back up the system.

As you might expect, the auditing community has found a way to defeat Syskey. The Pwdump3 utility is available at
http://www.ebiz-tech.com/html/pwdump.html

EXERCISE 12.2

Using Pwdump3 to Access Remote SAM Databases

As an auditor, your job is to do more than obtain the administrator's password. Your job is to test the strength of all passwords on systems found on the network. As a result, you will have to examine password databases on both local and remote systems. Sometimes, you will already have administrative access to a system but will have to test all of the databases. In this exercise, you will use the Pwdump3 utility to access your remote system's Windows 2000 SAM database.

1. Obtain the file named `pwdump3v2.zip` from http://www.ebiz-tech.com/html/pwdump.html. Uncompress the file into a directory named lc3.

2. Once you have unzipped the files, open a command prompt and map to the lc3 directory.

3. Ping your remote system to ensure that you have network connectivity.

4. The syntax for the `pwdump3` command is `PWDUMP3 machineName [outputFile] [userName]`. Issue the following command:

   pwdump3 remote_host samdump.txt administrator

   where *remote_host* is the name of your remote host and *administrator* is the name of the Administrator account. If you have renamed the Administrator account, use that account name instead. The file `samdump.txt` will contain your remote host's SAM database.

EXERCISE 12.2 (continued)

5. You will be asked for the password to the remote system. Provide it when prompted. Below is a slightly edited example of a Pwdump3 session:

```
C:\lc3\pwdump3>pwdump3 james hi.txt administrator
pwdump3 (rev 2) by Phil Staubs, e-business
    technology, 23 Feb 2001 Copyright 2001
    e-business technology, Inc.
This program is free software based on pwpump2
    by Todd Sabin under the GNU General Public
    License Version 2 (GNU GPL)
Please enter the password >********
Completed.
E:\lc3\pwdump3>
```

6. Once you have used Pwdump3, open the samdump.txt file using any text editor. You will see the usernames and encrypted passwords for all users defined on your remote system.

EXERCISE 12.3

Using L0phtCrack 3 to Crack a Remote SAM Database

In this exercise, you will use LC3 to crack passwords on a remote system that you administer. Note that this exercise requires you to first use the Pwdump3 application.

1. Open LC3. When the wizard appears, click Next. Then select the Retrieve From A Remote Machine radio button and click Next.

2. Select the Strong Password Audit radio button and click Next twice.

3. Click Finish.

4. A dialog box will appear, and you will be asked to supply the name of your remote system. If your remote system is named remote1, you would enter the following:

   \\remote1

EXERCISE 12.3 (continued)

5. The import will fail, because Syskey is enabled on your Windows 2000 system. Now, select Import ➢ Import from Pwdump3 to open the Import PWDUMP File dialog box. Map to the directory that has the `samdump.txt` file and open the file into LC3. When you have finished, you will see that the database has been dumped into LC3 and is ready to be cracked, as shown here:

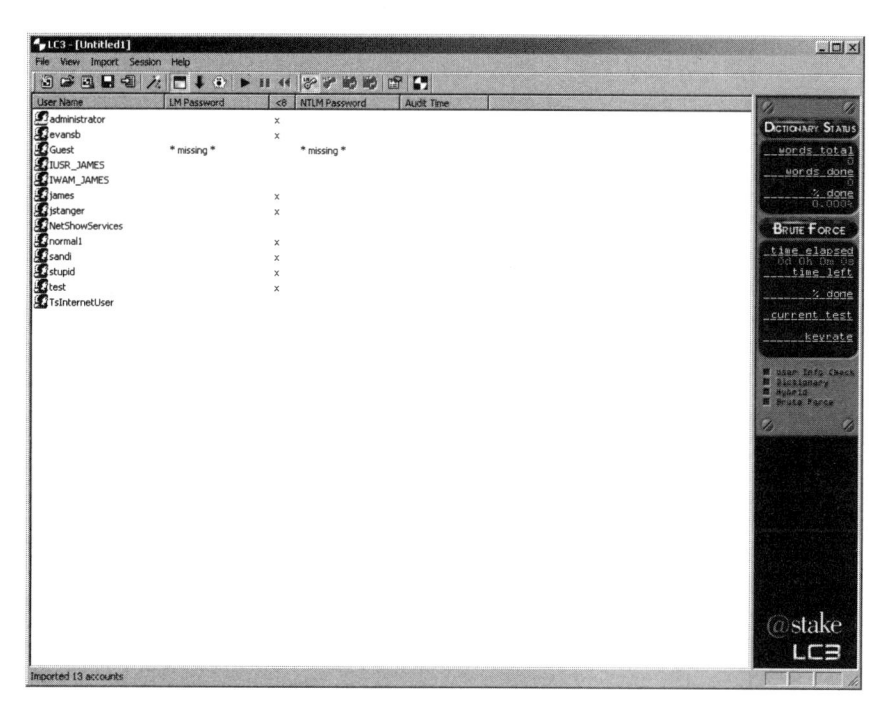

6. To begin cracking passwords, go to Session ➢ Audit. If you have a password such as `password`, LC3 will find it immediately. LC3 will take considerably longer for complex passwords. As you know, LC3 first uses a dictionary-mode attack and then resorts to a brute-force attack.

7. On each system, choose new, more complex passwords. Start by adding numbers to the beginning or end of each password. End with a strong password. Given time (or a comprehensive dictionary file), LC3 will be able to crack even these.

EXERCISE 12.4

Using L0phtCrack 3 to Sniff Passwords

In this chapter, you have learned about security auditing and the control phase. In this exercise, you will use LC3 to sniff *Server Message Block (SMB)*–based passwords as they cross the network wire.

1. Open LC3. In the wizard's Get Encrypted Passwords window, choose Retrieve By Sniffing The Local Network, as shown here. Then, click Next to see a list of options.

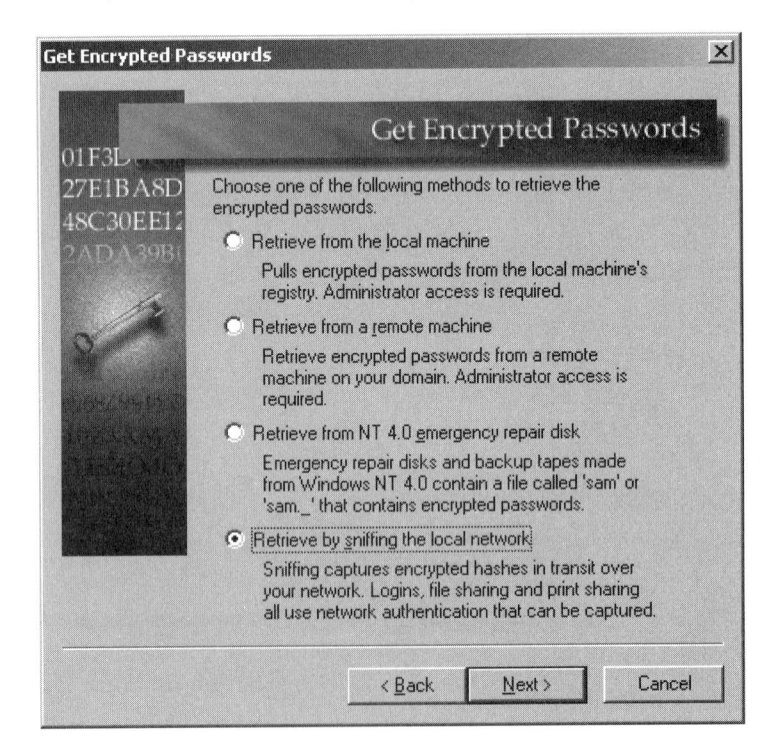

2. Choose Strong Password Audit, and then click through the rest of the options until you are asked to select a network interface. Select the adapter that is listed first, and then click OK. You will then see the SMB Packet Capture Output window, shown next.

EXERCISE 12.4 *(continued)*

[Screenshot: SMB Packet Capture Output window with columns Source IP, Destination IP, Domain\Username, Challenge; buttons Start Sniffing, Stop Sniffing, Clear Capture, Import, Cancel. Selected device: \Device\Packet_{987B33D1-D0F8-4ECE-...]

3. You can then click the Start Sniffing button and have another system on the network make connections to other remote hosts. Your Windows 2000 systems might have already authenticated with each other, and might not send passwords across the network. You might have to restart your remote Windows 2000 systems in order to require their servers to authenticate with each other. The window will begin to fill with passwords. After you have captured some passwords, click the Stop Sniffing button, and then click the Import button. Once you have done this, you can begin cracking the passwords by selecting Session ➢ Begin Audit.

4. Eventually, you will begin to see how LC3 is able to learn at least part of the password.

John the Ripper and Crack

A popular brute-force attack on Unix-based machines involves the use of applications called John the Ripper and Crack. Both are designed to obtain passwords from Unix systems. All versions of Unix keep the user account database in a file called `/etc/passwd` or `/etc/shadow`. The file resides in the same location on all Unix machines. For Unix to function properly, every user must have read rights to this file.

John the Ripper and Crack are the most common programs used to obtain passwords from the shadow or passwd files. These tools try all password combinations and compare the results to the encrypted value in the passwd or shadow file. Once the program finds a match, it has determined the password.

When you audit Unix systems, consider how you can look for problems such as these. Although many scanning applications, such as NetRecon and ISS Internet Scanner, can simulate these attacks, many security professionals use applications such as LC3 and John the Ripper to supplement their audits.

EXERCISE 12.5

Using John the Ripper in Linux

In this exercise, you will install and deploy John the Ripper in Linux.

1. Log on as root.

2. Using `linuxconf`, adduser, or useradd, create the following username/password pairs:

   wordsworth/prelude
   blake/jerusalem
   keats/ode

   When you have finished, the user named wordsworth should have the password prelude, the user named blake should have the password of jerusalem, and so forth.

   To create the user account for wordsworth, enter the following command:

   ```
   host# useradd wordsworth
   host#
   ```

   You would then set the password for the wordsworth account as follows:

   ```
   host# passwd wordsworth
   Changing password for user wordsworth
   ```

EXERCISE 12.5 *(continued)*

```
New UNIX password:
BAD PASSWORD: it's WAY too short
Retype new UNIX password:
passwd: all authentication tokens updated successfully
```

Note: Ignore the error messages you receive when creating the passwords for these user accounts. As root, you can assign any password you want.

3. Issue the following command to create a file named crackfile:

   `host# touch crackfile`

4. Using a text editor such as pico or vi, populate the file named crackfile with the passwords given in Step 2. Be sure to enter the words exactly as shown in that step. Also, enter the word **password**, which should be the password for the root account.

5. You have just created a simple dictionary file you will use with John the Ripper. Now, obtain John the Ripper from the Packetstorm web site (http://packetstorm.linuxsecurity.com or http://packetstorm.deceptions.org). Once you have accessed the Packetstorm site, enter **John the Ripper** in the search field.

6. Once you obtain the file, use gunzip to unzip it:

   ```
   host# gunzip john-1_6_tar.gz
   host#
   ```

7. Use tar to untar the file:

   `host# tar -xvf john-1_6_tar`

8. Change directories into the directory created when you untarred the files:

   `host# cd john-1.6`

9. Change to the src directory:

   `host# cd src`

EXERCISE 12.5 *(continued)*

10. Issue the make command, saving it in a text file named type:

    host# make > type

11. Use a text editor such as vi or pico to open the type file:

    host# vi type

12. Write down the entry that suits your particular system. The first entry, linux-x86-any-elf, should be sufficient.

13. Exit vi. You do this by first entering **ESC**, then by pressing ZZ.

14. Given that linux-x86-any-elf is the proper entry, issue the following command:

    host# make linux-x86-any-elf

    Note: If no entry seems sufficient, issue the command make generic.

15. When the program has successfully compiled, change to the john-1.6/run directory:

    host# cd ../run

16. Once in the run directory, issue the following command:

    host#./john -wordfile:crackfile /etc/shadow

17. The program should immediately discover the user passwords you created earlier.

18. Issue the following command:

    ./john /passwd/shadow -show

    The program keeps a list of passwords it has cracked from the file.

19. Use John the Ripper in brute-force mode:

    host#./john /etc/shadow

20. Press the spacebar to check on the program's progress.

21. After you have waited a sufficient period of time, press Ctrl+C to stop the program. You have now used John the Ripper in both dictionary and brute-force modes.

What Happens After Control Is Established?

As an auditor, it is important for you to identify what a hacker will do after he or she has penetrated and controlled your system. Each of the strategies here are conducted by hackers. You need to be aware of these strategies so that you can identify them in your written report.

Redirecting information   Once a hacker gains control of a system, he or she can engage in *port redirection*. After a hacker has redirected a port, he or she can manipulate connections and gain valuable information. For example, some hackers will disable a service such as FTP and then redirect the FTP port to another computer. This computer can then receive all connections and files from the original computer.

Similar goals might include redirecting the SMTP port, which would allow a hacker to gain access to sensitive information. Consider, for example, what could happen if a hacker obtained all information from an e-commerce server that was using SMTP to transfer e-mail accounts. Even if these transactions were encrypted, the hacker could obtain the transmissions and run a dictionary attack against them.

Creating new access points   You have already learned how a hacker attempts to create as many openings to the system as possible by manipulating or creating new accounts. By installing additional software and modifying system parameters, a hacker can create new *access points* (i.e., back doors) as well. Hackers generally assume that a systems administrator will close the original point of penetration, so they often open others.

Like good systems administrators, hackers always have a contingency plan, so you must be on the lookout for the hacker's alternative methods of control. Another common method of implementing back doors is by depositing Trojans.

Creating accounts automatically   It might seem that any good systems administrator will scan the user accounts database to search for altered permissions, new accounts, and any suspicious changes to system policies. However, old accounts are the hacker's primary means of entry.

Even if an administrator regularly checks the user accounts database, hackers attempt to foil this process by using automated processes, such as scheduling services, to add accounts. By using a scheduling service to automatically create new accounts or reset permissions, hackers can bypass even the most fastidious network administrator.

Erasing evidence of penetration   If you have implemented auditing, you will usually have sufficient records of the hacker's actions. Often, hackers enter a system after repeated attempts that are easily read. One of the best ways for hackers to destroy such evidence is to learn where the system logs are kept. By destroying these logs, the hacker can remain anonymous to systems administrators and security auditors.

Such log files include those in these areas:

- Firewalls and routers
- Web, SMTP, HTTP and FTP servers
- Database servers

> **NOTE** As an auditor, you will not erase evidence of penetration. Rather, you will provide convincing evidence of your penetration that you can place in your audit report(s).

Creating a connection chain   Hackers often use multiple Telnet or FTP sessions to hide evidence of their activities. They create a *connection chain*, which increases the amount of time it takes to trace a connection. Port redirection, as we explained earlier, is the practice of mapping the output of an original port (say, port 80) to another port on a local system, or even to another port on a remote system. Hackers sometimes redirect ports to make it more difficult to accurately trace a connection. When a hacker compromises a legitimate server, he or she can redirect this legitimate server's output to another system. Any client that connects to your server might think that it has connected to a legitimate server, but it has in fact connected to one configured by a hacker. As a result, the hacker might be able to gain valuable information from naive clients.

Spreading to other systems   Often, hackers want to penetrate your system because it enables them to spread to other systems or networks to which you have access. For example, the U.S. National Aeronautics and Space Administration (NASA) servers once were popular targets for hackers, not necessarily because NASA had desired information but because the organization had established trust relationships to other organizations, such as the Department of Defense.

Auditing and the Control Phase

An auditor makes good use of scanning programs, log files, and other tools. However, you must understand what suspicious traffic looks like. This traffic might be packets sent by the usual suspects, such as NetBus and BackOrifice 2000, or from applications you have never heard of or seen. Other suspicious traffic includes unauthorized nmap and SATAN usage.

The key difference between an auditor and a hacker is that the auditor never truly enters the control phase. During this phase, remember to only document what you find as you engage your protocol analyzer and other tools. You should develop detailed reports about what you *could* have done. An auditing professional should never place a file on a server as evidence that he or she was there. This type of activity might seem clever and might be used in movies and television shows, but it crosses the line between auditing and hacking, and could be easily misunderstood.

Many alternative means of reporting potential control problems are available. Each is a far more professional solution that allows you to prove that you could have obtained control over the system. Such methods include:

- Presenting information from automated scanning programs, such as eEye Retina, NetRecon, or ISS Internet Scanner.
- Generating network traffic that produces a log entry. Document the time, and then use the log to show your activity.
- Showing packet captures as samples. These packet captures can reveal port numbers, IP addresses, and other information.
- Taking screen shots of resources that you have penetrated.

Summary

In this chapter, you learned about the specific steps taken during the control phase. Auditing this phase can be quite difficult, because it requires that you obtain proof of control without attempting to control the network yourself. You were reminded of specific ways to report suspicious activities, including the use of NetBus, a classic method of control that can still teach you much about how Trojans work.

You then conducted several control techniques, including the addition of illicit accounts, the stopping and starting of services, port redirection, and the use of batch files to create new accounts. In the next chapter, you will learn how to automate intrusion detection. At this point, you are prepared to explain ways that hackers can begin to penetrate system and network elements, and you can identify how hackers control Windows 2000 and Linux hosts.

In Chapter 13, you will learn how to configure software that helps you identify, track, and even stop attacks that are waged within your network by creating an intrusion-detection system (IDS).

Exam Essentials

Know steps of the control phase. Be able to recognize typical steps of the control phase, including gaining root access, obtaining and cracking the password database, and reconfiguring network hosts. Make sure that you understand various strategies for doing this, including the use of seemingly innocuous batch files and other scripts.

Be able to explain how to audit routers and firewalls. Auditing routers and firewalls enables you to determine if hackers have been able to defeat your network perimeter. It is important to establish whether any of your routers or firewalls are using protocols that can defeat security. Consider physical security as well, and check for modem banks that may inadvertently defeat your firewall.

Understand a hacker's ultimate goal. A hacker's ultimate goal is administrative access. This can be accomplished through a number of means, including password sniffing, social engineering, the exploiting of system bugs, and brute-force/dictionary attacks. Often, a hacker will try to escalate permissions, which means that he or she will use a legitimate account to exploit a system bug that gives this user administrative access.

Know common password database cracking tools, such as LC3 and John the Ripper. LC3 and John the Ripper provide excellent examples of auditing applications that can be used to determine password strength. They can, of course, be used unethically, but in the right hands, they provide you with valuable tools to help test a network's security.

Understand what hackers can do once they gain control of your system.
A hacker will rarely just penetrate and control one server. He or she will work to redirect information, create new access points, establish back doors, and, most important, spread to other systems. The CIW Security Professional exam expects you to be aware of such strategies as you audit systems.

Be able to prove that you, as a legitimate auditor, can control a server.
An auditor should be able to show how vulnerable a server really is. Sometimes, it is necessary for you to prove that a system is vulnerable to attack. Ways to prove that a server has been compromised and controlled include presenting evidence from vulnerability scanners, showing packet captures, and showing copies of files that are unique to the server. You should not alter or create files, unless you have explicit, written permission from the party who owns the server.

Key Terms

Before you take the exam, be certain you are familiar with the following terms:

access points	port redirection
batch file	root access
connection chain	Syskey
cross-frame browsing bug	window spoofing
modem bank	

Review Questions

1. What would a hacker want to do first so that he or she could create new accounts and manipulate services?

   A. Open new security holes.

   B. Erase evidence of penetration.

   C. Gain root access.

   D. Spread to other systems.

2. What is the ability for a malicious website to imitate a legitimate site called?

   A. The cross-frame browsing bug

   B. Window spoofing

   C. John the Ripper

   D. Port redirection

3. What is a useful way to audit for the presence of a root kit on a Unix system?

   A. Determining whether the ls, su, and ps functions work properly

   B. Deleting the ls, su, and ps functions

   C. Creating alternatives to the ls, su, and ps functions

   D. Updating the operating system regularly

4. Joel is auditing a Linux system. He has used information from the Secure Shell (SSH) application to begin searching for ways a hacker can attack remote systems. Which stage has Joel entered?

   A. The discovery stage

   B. The penetration stage

   C. The control stage

   D. The evaluation stage

5. What is the name of the file that contains encrypted hashes of passwords on a Linux system?

   A. /etc/passwd

   B. /etc/shadow

   C. /.secure/.htaccess

   D. /etc/.passwd

6. What is the purpose of the John the Ripper application?

   A. To obtain passwords from Unix systems

   B. To conduct a dictionary attack

   C. To replace legitimate ls, su, and ps programs

   D. To conduct a brute-force attack

7. What does the Syskey utility do to reduce the vulnerability of a Windows 2000 system?

   A. It encrypts the /etc/shadow file.

   B. It encrypts the SAM database.

   C. It hides the SAM database.

   D. It hides the /etc/shadow file.

8. How do you install Syskey on Windows 2000?

   A. By installing Service Pack 3.

   B. By installing Service Pack 1.

   C. By downloading it from the Microsoft website.

   D. It is already installed.

9. Don has obtained a username and password pair from a network and is preparing to log on to a server. What stage has he entered?

   A. Discovery

   B. Penetration

   C. Control

   D. Evaluation

10. Jason has learned about a new system bug. This bug allows him to take advantage of a bug in the way an IIS server processes a certain text standard called Unicode. What step of the auditing process has Jason entered?

    A. Discovery

    B. Penetration

    C. Control

    D. Evaluation

11. Sandi has just exploited a buffer overflow in a Linux print daemon. What stage has she entered?

    A. Discovery

    B. Penetration

    C. Control

    D. Evaluation

12. Bob is auditing a firewall and wants to determine whether a hacker has obtained illegitimate access. What can he do to check if this access has occurred?

    A. Shut down the Telnet daemon.

    B. Shut down the SSH daemon.

    C. Check log-file entries.

    D. Check the modem bank.

13. Which of the following strategies can make a firewall host more secure?

    A. Check the modem bank.

    B. Improve the firewall host's physical security.

    C. Check log files.

    D. Educate end users about the security policy.

14. Which of the following presents a classic case of firewall avoidance?

    A. Unsecured modem banks

    B. Password sniffing

    C. System bugs

    D. Buffer overflow

15. Bob is a systems administrator, but he has only limited access to his network servers. However, he has just used an application downloaded from a hacker site to add himself to the root group on a Linux machine. What is the term for Bob's activity?

    A. Hacking

    B. Auditing

    C. Privilege escalation

    D. System penetration

16. Vern has just created an additional privileged account on a system that he does not administer. What hacking/auditing stage has he entered?

    A. Discovery

    B. Penetration

    C. Control

    D. Evaluation

17. Michelle has tried to use LC3 to obtain the SAM database of a remote system. However, her efforts are repeatedly denied. Why has this happened?

    A. Michelle is using an older version of the application.

    B. Michelle is using the application improperly.

    C. Michelle does not have administrative access to the remote system.

    D. Michelle does not have administrative access to the local system.

18. While auditing his firewall, Robert has noticed that an entire day of log entries is not present. What do these missing entries suggest?

    A. A system bug is present.

    B. A social engineering attack has been waged.

    C. No logins occurred that day.

    D. A possible attack has occurred.

19. Victoria notices that an entry has been made to the root account so that a batch file is run every time she logs in. She does not remember adding this entry. Upon further investigation, she notices that the batch file adds several accounts to the system. What stage of the hacker process does this batch file represent?

    A. Discovery

    B. Penetration

    C. Control

    D. Evaluation

20. During the control stage, what settings does a hacker attempt to exploit when trying to spread to other systems?

    A. System bugs

    B. Trust relationships

    C. Buffer overflows

    D. Password settings

Answers to Review Questions

1. **C.** Gaining root access is the ultimate goal of the hacker. Once a hacker gains administrative (i.e., root) privileges, he or she can then begin other activities.

2. **B.** A malicious website imitates a legitimate site in what is known as window spoofing. This activity is made possible by the cross-frame browsing bug, which existed on older browsers (Netscape and Internet Explorer 4.x).

3. **A.** You can test for a root kit in many different ways. However, one way to start is to use common system applications to see if they work properly. Deleting applications before testing them is rarely a good idea, and creating alternatives to applications by, say, deleting the originals and replacing them with new versions often does not eliminate all root kit elements.

4. **C.** From the scenario given above, Joel has already penetrated a Linux system during his audit, so he has already gone through the discovery and penetration stages. He has, in fact, identified some SSH settings that might enable him to move from one system to another. Because he is considering how to spread to another system, he has entered the control stage.

5. **B.** As an auditor, it is vital that you can identify the most valuable resources in a system. In Linux systems, one of the valuable resources is the `/etc/shadow` file.

6. **A.** The John the Ripper application uses both brute-force and dictionary attacks as methods in its goal to obtain passwords.

7. **B.** The Syskey utility is used to encrypt the SAM database, and is a way of decreasing a Windows 2000 system's vulnerability. It can also be used on Windows NT.

8. **D.** Windows 2000 ships with Syskey already installed. The utility ships with Service Pack 3 for Windows NT 4.

9. **B.** The penetration stage involves actively trying to defeat or bypass authentication. Because Don has obtained a username and password pair and is now using it, he has entered the penetration stage.

10. A. Because Jason has only learned about the system bug, he is still at the discovery stage. Once he obtains or scripts an application that takes advantage of this bug, he will be entering another stage.

11. B. By actually entering a system through a buffer overflow, Sandi has entered the penetration phase.

12. C. The only way to determine whether illicit access has occurred is by checking log files.

13. B. To improve the security of the firewall itself, you need to address any problems that it might be having. Of the choices above, only improving the firewall host's physical security actually makes it more secure. Checking the modem bank does not make the firewall host more secure; rather, it helps you ensure that hackers cannot find a way to get around the firewall. While checking logs can inform you about problems, doing so does not reduce the likelihood of an attack, nor does it solve any particular problem. Finally, educating users about the security policy will help improve network security, but it does not improve the security of the actual firewall host.

14. A. Unsecured modem banks have traditionally presented a means for hackers to avoid a firewall. Password sniffing, system bugs, and buffer overflows can be exploited by hackers. Although it is possible for a firewall to contain a system bug, such as a buffer overflow, an unsecured modem bank presents a much more likely problem.

15. C. Bob already has privileges to enter the system. By using the illicit application to add himself to the root group, he has escalated his permissions and reached the ultimate goal of obtaining administrative access. Hacking and auditing are general terms, and are not appropriate choices, because they do not describe Bob's specific actions. Furthermore, Bob has already had access to this system.

16. C. Whenever an auditor or hacker has been able to add another privileged user account, the control stage has been achieved. Most of the time, a hacker will add a second account to ensure that he or she can reenter the system, even after the systems administrator changes the password.

17. **C.** In order to obtain the SAM database of a remote system, Michelle must first obtain administrative access to that local system. Applications such as LC3 do not enable an auditor to automatically defeat a Windows NT or 2000 system. Rather, they can be used by auditors to test the passwords. The purpose of cracking the rest of the SAM database is so that the auditor can determine if all accounts on the system are using strong passwords.

18. **D.** Although missing log entries are not definitive proof of an attack, they certainly can be grounds for suspicion. System bugs and log daemon failures can also lead to missing log entries, but the truly cautious auditor will begin to suspect tampering.

19. **C.** Whenever a hacker has been able to modify account settings, the control stage is implied.

20. **B.** During the control stage, a hacker attempts to exploit trust relationships in order to spread to other systems.

Chapter 13

Intrusion Detection

THE CIW EXAM OBJECTIVE GROUPS COVERED IN THIS CHAPTER:

- ✓ Identify penetration and control strategies and methods, including but not limited to: potential attacks, router security, threat containment, intrusion detection.
- ✓ Implement intrusion-detection systems in an enterprise environment.

It might seem that a firewall can accomplish everything a systems administrator needs to secure a network. After all, it helps protect against outside attacks by establishing a perimeter around a network. Once a firewall is in place and properly configured, attacks from the outside become much less likely. However, attacks waged by a company's own employees are often as devastating as those waged by outside parties. Attacks waged by internal employees are also quite common. Because employees are already "behind" the firewall, this particular piece of equipment will do little good preventing an internal attack. Furthermore, as formidable as they are, firewalls are not always impenetrable. If somehow a hacker is able to defeat your firewall, your network will be largely unprotected.

Attacks from internal employees and hackers who have been able to defeat a firewall represent very real challenges to a company. The security community has risen to this challenge with the development of various applications that create a solution called an *intrusion-detection system (IDS)*. An IDS is increasingly necessary because it helps security managers detect and respond to illicit activity that occurs behind the firewall. The concept of the IDS has become very popular because it ensures that a firewall is not the only piece of equipment that detects and deters activity; an IDS can act as a backup to the firewall, so no single point of failure exists in terms of security. If, for example, the firewall fails to detect illicit activity that passes across the firewall, an IDS may help detect this activity.

In this chapter, you will learn about the components of an IDS. For example, you will learn about the different types of applications used to comprise an IDS, as well as how an IDS is able to identify and then act on traffic. You will also learn about how to configure IDS applications, and you will see how a properly configured IDS can be a tremendous benefit to your company. Finally, you will learn all of the concepts necessary to answer any of the questions posed by the CIW Security Professional exam.

Understanding Intrusion Detection

Intrusion detection is the real-time monitoring of network activity behind the firewall. An IDS listens to network data streams (i.e., network traffic) and helps security managers with the following responsibilities:

Traffic detection   It is vital that you understand that an IDS usually has two methods for detecting traffic. First, the IDS can place the NIC into promiscuous mode and then listen for traffic. The IDS that uses this method is called a *network-based IDS*. Second, an IDS can continuously read a log file to detect a problem. This type of IDS is called a *host-based IDS*. You will learn more about these two types as you read through this chapter.

Incident identification   All IDSs use some sort of database to identify the traffic that they detect. It is important to understand that identifying traffic is different than simply detecting it; a simple network sniffer such as Ethereal or Sniffer Basic can detect traffic. The key is being able to identify its type and then act on it.

Response   An IDS application has the ability to take action. It can generate responses to traffic when that traffic is deemed objectionable. This response is determined by specific instructions, or rules, created by the security manager.

Logging   All IDSs store traffic into log files for later analysis.

IDS Terminology

The CIW Security Professional exam often uses the term *IDS application*, because an IDS can consist of several different applications that work in concert to detect activity. IDS applications and services help ensure that your network hosts are actively monitored for various events, including:

- Repeated login attempts on a particular host
- Ping scans across a subnet or across the entire network
- Port scans on a specific host
- The use of protocols that you deem to be inappropriate on a network

Signatures and Attack Signature Databases

In terms of an IDS, any activity that is identified as an attack is often called a *signature*. Only when an IDS encounters a signature will it, for example, send an e-mail message or reconfigure your firewall. For instance, the IDS can add a rule to the firewall so that the firewall can block the traffic that has been deemed offensive. Although an IDS can be configured to cooperate with a firewall, it usually works independently of the firewall.

An IDS is quite different in most respects from a vulnerability scanner. First, an IDS works in real time to discover actual attacks on the network. Even if a vulnerability scanner were operating on a host during an attack, it would never discover or report an attack. An IDS focuses on network activity entering into or passing out of the host or across the network wire. It does not try to discover specific configuration weaknesses, as does a vulnerability scanner.

An IDS has one similarity to a vulnerability scanner: it uses an *attack signature database* to identify attacks. However, whereas a network scanner searches for predefined weaknesses in a host, an IDS application monitors and logs network traffic. Perhaps an example will help: If an IDS were operating on a host, and you were to run a scanner against that host, a well-configured IDS application would detect that scan and issue multiple alerts, warning you that the system was being attacked. In some situations, this IDS would not have to be installed on the host being scanned, because the IDS could listen to all of the network transmissions and then react to packets that it deemed suspicious.

IDS Applications and Rules

Much like a firewall, an IDS uses a *rule*, which is an entry that allows the IDS to target and act on a specific type of network communication. These rules determine what the IDS will look for and how it will react once it detects traffic that matches a rule. Each rule consists of fields that, as you might expect, allow the IDS to look for the following items in a network packet:

- Source and destination IP addresses
- Source and destination ports
- Type of network traffic (e.g., a TCP SYN packet, or a UDP packet that has been sent to a port on 30 different machines)

One of the most important rules that IDS applications use is one that allows it to listen for SYN floods, port scans, ping scans, and other attacks discussed in Chapter 3. Most of these rules allow the IDS to detect ranges of IP addresses and ports being used over a short period of time. If the IDS application notices that a range of IP addresses and/or ports is being used over a short period of time, it will detect and log this traffic, and then (under many circumstances) issue an alert.

Taking Action

It is very important to understand that an IDS rule includes some sort of *action*. The action is contained in a *response field*, found in the rule. This field can contain various types of instructions, which we discuss in the next section.

What Can an IDS Application Do?

You can configure an IDS to block network traffic or send messages to inform you of an attack. An IDS application will demand that you create a rule and then assign certain actions to it. As you define a rule, you generally must consider how and when that rule will apply to the network.

Actions to take in response to the event include:

- Activation of logging mechanisms, including SNMP traps
- Launching of a program to countermand the attack or block the attacking host
- Reconfiguration of the firewall
- Issuing of sound, e-mail, fax, pager, and phone notifications
- Connection tracing

In order for the IDS to take action, the response field should contain the following elements:

- A description of the action to take.
- The host(s) that needs protecting or reconfiguration. You can specify an individual host or a range of hosts.
- The host(s) that needs to be logged or forbidden. You can specify an individual host or a range of hosts.
- The time period for which the action will occur.

A description of the event.

IDS Applications and Logging

One of the most important functions of an IDS application is that it enables *redundant logging*, which involves multiple systems generating and processing log files. Experienced hackers know that they should remove all evidence of an attack, and they alter the log files of the systems so that they no longer contain evidence of a connection. However, an IDS can generate an independent set of logs that can help trace hacker activity. So, as you read through this chapter, consider the usefulness of an IDS in a network that already has an effective firewall.

The most sophisticated IDS applications can reconstitute network traffic so that the security manager can view it. For example, Computer Associates' eTrust Intrusion Detection (formerly SessionWall), Snort, Symantec Intruder Alert, and ISS RealSecure allow you to view detailed information about the type of traffic occurring on a network. Generally, these applications allow you to monitor the behavior of a specific host or group of hosts. Figure 13.1 shows how you can use eTrust Intrusion Detection to read the latest web page accessed by the user on a specific network host.

FIGURE 13.1 Using SessionWall/eTrust to obtain HTML traffic information

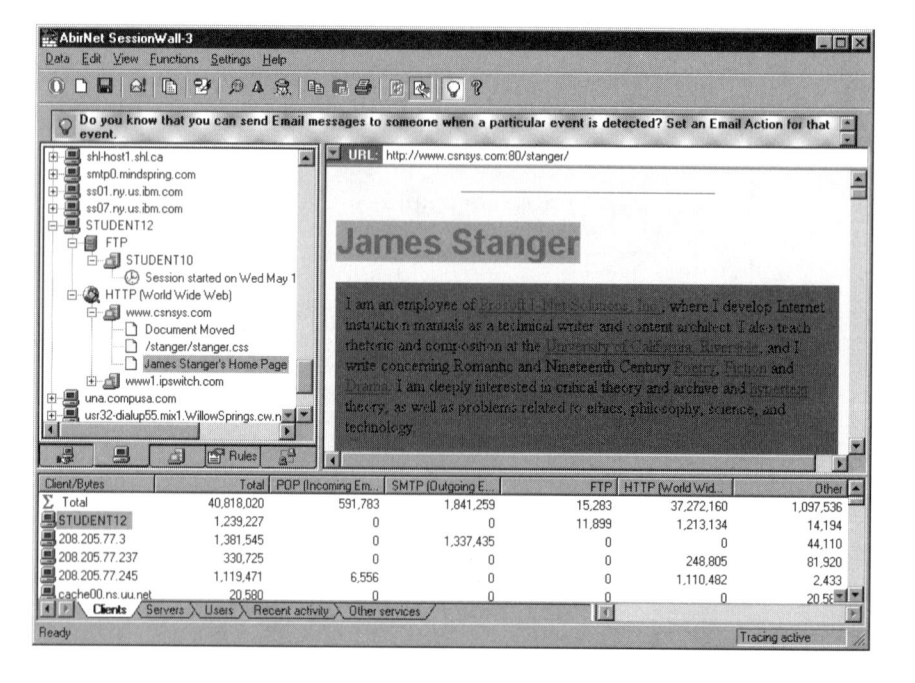

In this figure, you see that the system named "Student12" has conducted FTP and HTTP transactions on the network. The left window lists each computer found on the subnet. The right window provides details about the connection, including the last web page visited by the current user logged onto Student12.

It is possible to obtain similarly detailed information for FTP, SMTP, telnet, and any other traffic you want to capture. In many cases, all you have to do is configure your application to look for a certain traffic type, and you will be able to read it in your IDS application.

> **Additional Capabilities of an IDS Application**
>
> Some IDS applications, such as eTrust Intrusion Detection, can even "sniff" the network wire for offensive traffic and then block it. As it sniffs network traffic, the application searches the actual connections that contain certain text strings. For example, if your security policy blocks access to all pornographic sites, it is possible to configure your IDS to block certain key words and phrases that it finds in HTTP content.

IDS Applications and the Incident Response Team

As we mentioned earlier, an IDS is capable of issuing alerts to an individual or a group of people. It is important to understand that an IDS is incomplete without a team of analysts who can review and respond to traffic. This team, often called the *incident response team (IRT)*, is responsible for:

- Installing and configuring IDS applications.

- Analyzing reports and traffic monitored.

- Ensuring that the IDS application remains operational.

- Confirming that the IDS application is secure from tampering, and that only authorized employees can monitor traffic.

- Cooperating with additional security managers and IT workers to ensure that threats are properly handled.

- Differentiating between false positives and actual attacks. For example, if an attack is suspected, IRT members can use additional network sniffing applications to verify that the attack is, in fact occurring, or they can log on to the system that has reported a problem and confirm it.

- Analyzing systems after they have been broken into in order to learn more about the attack and (it is hoped) the attacker. This activity is often referred to as *forensic analysis*. Conducting a forensic analysis is different than responding to a real-time attack and entails studying damage done by the attacker to determine how to respond to future attacks.

- Reporting incidents to appropriate company members to ensure that the proper response is made.

The IRT is responsible for handling problems in *real time*. In other words, whereas an auditor with a vulnerability scanner searches for configuration problems—such as a Windows 2000 operating system that does not use a current service pack—an IRT actively monitors the network to see if various attacks are occurring or have already occurred. For example, the IRT might ask individuals responsible for the company routers and switches to reconfigure them so that an attack is dropped or contained. Or the IRT might work closely with auditors to analyze an attack to ensure that it will not occur again. Finally, an IRT must often coordinate its efforts with other parties so that they do not waste time chasing false positives. For example, consider what might happen when an auditor forgets to inform the IRT that he or she is going to scan a system. If the IRT does not have any previous knowledge, the team could mistake a legitimate scan for an attack.

> **NOTE** Many companies outsource their intrusion-detection responsibilities. For example, companies such as Symantec (www.symantec.com) and Internet Threat Management Technology (www.itmtech.com) have teams that are capable of monitoring and responding to intrusions. The CIW Security Professional exam does not contain any scenarios or information that require you to recommend outsourcing intrusion detection, however.

IDS Application Strategies

All IDS applications rely on one of two strategies to detect attacks:

Signature detection   With *signature detection*, the IDS application relies on predefined rules in order to act. It is up to the IDS application administrator to make sure the rules are current and relevant to the network being monitored. IDS applications such as eTrust, Snort, and Intruder Alert have adopted this strategy.

Anomaly detection   With *anomaly detection*, the IDS application can create a baseline of normative activity. Then, whenever network traffic alters significantly from the baseline, an alert is issued. This strategy is used less frequently because it relies on the IDS application's ability to accurately determine what constitutes "normal" network activity.

Most IDS applications can perform extremely detailed analyses of network traffic, and they can monitor any traffic you define. Many programs have "out-of-the-box" settings for FTP, HTTP, and telnet traffic, as well as for additional traffic such as NetBus and failed local and remote logons. Most IDS applications can also detect a SYN flood or ping flood by default. You can create your own policies, as well. Learning this information is the only way you can determine "normal" activity on your network. By identifying the types of activities that occur when employees are present, you can catch employees interested in espionage or other security violations.

> **NOTE**
> You should understand both signature-based intrusion detection and anomaly-based intrusion detection. However, the CIW Security Professional exam focuses on signature-based intrusion detection, the more popular of the two strategies. Accordingly, the remainder of this chapter will focus on IDS applications that use signature-detection strategies.

Intrusion-Detection Architectures

You can choose from two intrusion-detection types:

Host-based IDS   A *host-based IDS* is an architecture that queries *agents* installed on individual hosts. These agents read the host's log files and issue alerts.

Network-based IDS A *network-based IDS* is a system that places an NIC into promiscuous mode and "listens" for attacks as they cross the network wire.

Each type has its own advantages. Although host-based intrusion detection is more ambitious and provides more information, it is not always the best choice.

Network-Based IDS Applications

Network-based programs such as Snort and eTrust Intrusion Detection require installation on only one computer. The application (or service) scans all transmissions on a subnet to determine real-time network activity. This type of application acts as both a manager and an agent. The network acts passively, and the host on which the IDS is installed does all the work.

> **WARNING** A network-based IDS application is often required to capture massive amounts of traffic. As a result, the system running the application can become overburdened. Make sure that you carefully consider system requirements before installing a network-based IDS application. Host-based IDS applications generally do not face the same problems. In fact, they are designed to affect standard system performance as little as possible. The chief reason why host-based IDS applications generally do not affect system performance is because they do not listen for all network events. Rather, they listen only to events relevant to the system they reside on.

Benefits and Drawbacks

Network-based IDS applications are easy to install and configure. They often require the installation of only one program onto one host. However, it is also possible for a network-based IDS application to use the manager/agent architecture discussed in Chapter 11. Whether it is a stand-alone application or part of a manager/agent structure, a network-based IDS is especially suited for thwarting scanning attacks and denial-of-service attacks. These type of attacks include:

- SYN floods
- Tribe Flood Network (TFN) and Tribe Flood Network 2000 (TFN2K)

- Ping floods
- Fast network scans, including standard port scans that attack systems in short periods of time, such as a matter of seconds

However, it is important to understand that traditionally network-based IDS applications do not work well in switched and Asynchronous Transfer Mode (ATM) networks. This is because a network-based IDS application relies on network broadcasts, as found in hub-based systems, and a switch does not use broadcasts. Rather, it uses a system's Address Resolution Protocol (ARP) address and opens a dedicated, directed connection to a specific host. Thus, other systems on the network have a difficult time "sniffing" packets.

> **NOTE** Applications such as ettercap (`ettercap.sourceforge.net`) are capable of sniffing connections on switch-based networks. It is very likely that vendors of network-based IDS applications will develop similar capabilities. However, the CIW Security Professional exam reflects traditional network-based IDS application behavior in regard to switches.

Further, this type of IDS is not particularly efficient in dealing with host-specific attacks, such as illicit logons, illegitimate account upgrades, policy tampering, and log-file manipulation. These types of attacks take place after an illicit user has logged on. To detect and counter such attacks, you need a host-based IDS application.

Host-Based IDS Applications

Host-based IDS applications carefully monitor a network host's log files, and then issue alerts when an attack is detected. Host-based IDS applications are ideally suited for detecting the following activities:

- Port scans directed at the local host
- Repeated failed login attempts
- Creation and modification of key user accounts
- Change in file permissions
- Account privilege escalation (e.g., when a user becomes root)
- Services that are started or stopped
- System reboots

> In most cases, a host-based IDS is capable of reporting incidents on that local system, and not on remote systems.

Host-based applications, such as Symantec's Intruder Alert, often use three applications: a reporting system, a manager, and numerous agents. This architecture works as follows: The manager issues queries to agents, which then inform the manager about the network transmissions made by that host. As shown in Figure 13.2, agents and managers communicate directly with each other, solving many connectivity problems in more complex networks.

FIGURE 13.2 Manager-to-agent communication

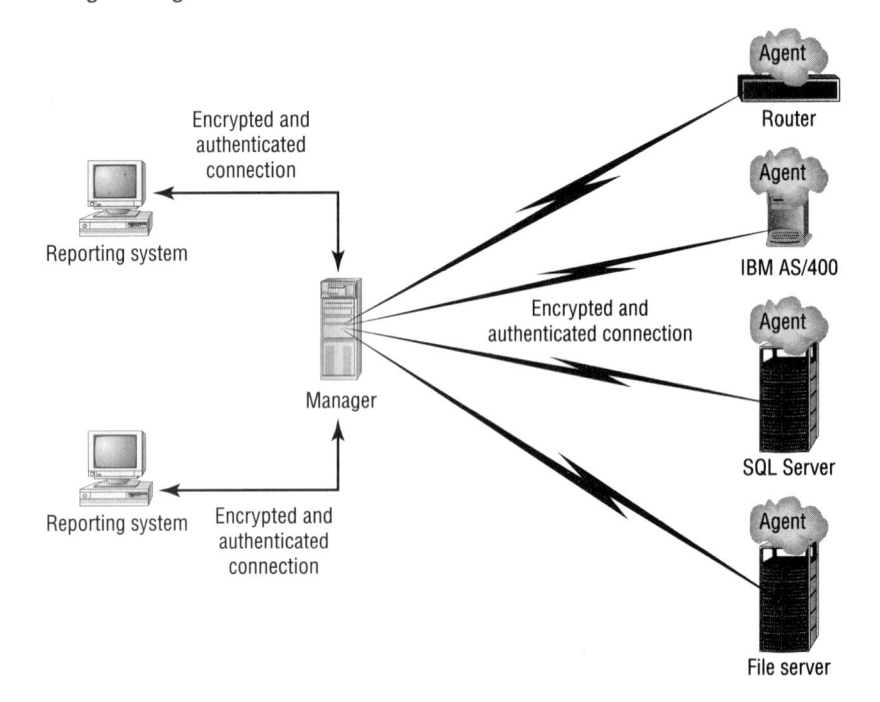

Most IDS implementations allow you to install an agent on any host that will accept configuration. Before purchasing a product, you should make sure that it works well with the hosts on your network. Most products come with agents ready to work with Unix, Microsoft, and Novell networks. Some vendors supply agents for more specialized network environments, such as DECnet, mainframes, and others. Nevertheless, you should test various products to learn which is best suited to your network. Some agents operate in promiscuous mode and capture packets from the network, while others monitor system log files and then log packets or issue alerts depending on what they find.

Optimal Agent Placement

IDS applications and their individual components (e.g., the agents and managers) are often quite costly. Accordingly, consider placing agents only on the most sensitive resources, such as database, web, DNS, and file servers. A network-based IDS application, such as eTrust Intrusion Detection, might be most appropriate for scanning individual hosts at certain times. This tool ensures that you can monitor activity but keep bandwidth use to a minimum.

The following is a partial list of resources that are ideal for agent placement:

- Accounting, human resources, and research databases
- LAN and WAN backbones, including routers and switches
- Temporary worker hosts
- SMTP, HTTP, and FTP servers
- Modem bank servers and/or switches/routers/hubs
- File servers

Organizing Agents

When configuring a host-based IDS network, you will have to organize your agents so that they can be administered easily. If you have 200 agents, you will not want to view information from all of them at the same time. You may want to view information from only certain agents that reside in a specific department, or from agents that reside on a particular operating system type that has experienced more attacks. As you create an *organizational structure*, place agents in a way that allows you to prioritize your resources. Doing so will enable you to monitor your network in the most efficient manner possible. Consider the following organizational structures:

- The servers that have been attacked most frequently
- Department or division
- Operating system type
- Geographical location

The CIW Security Professional exam does not require you to memorize an organizational structure, nor does it require you to state which organizational structure is better than the other. After all, an organizational structure that is ideal in one situation might not make sense in another. However, you might have to understand this concept when reading a scenario and making a choice about different types of IDS applications.

Regardless of how you categorize and organize agents, you should always plan the scheme carefully and then document it. As an auditor, if your client company has a poorly planned or documented architecture, you should take steps to remedy it.

Manager-to-Agent Communication

Generally, managers and agents communicate using a form of public-key encryption. For example, Symantec's Intruder Alert uses a proprietary form of public-key encryption that uses a 400-bit key. Most Secure Sockets Layer (SSL) sessions use only a 40-bit or 128-bit key, so manager/agent communication in this product is quite secure.

However, some older and open-source host-based IDS applications use weak encryption, or do not even bother to encrypt their communication at all. This is rather ironic, because cleartext transmissions of this nature can allow a hacker to obtain authentication information (e.g., usernames and passwords) and other information.

If the IDS application you are using does not natively support encryption and you are using Microsoft Windows 2000, you can implement IPsec to encrypt transmissions between hosts. Similarly, Linux systems administrators can download FreeS/WAN (www.freeswan.org) to enable IPsec on your Linux systems. Once IPsec is enabled, all network transmissions will be encrypted, and you will no longer have to worry about unencrypted manager-to-agent communication.

Creating Rules for an IDS Application

Most IDS applications ship with their own rules, because most IDS vendors are already aware of various attack signatures. These built-in rules are very helpful, because they ensure that the IDS application is ready to detect the most common attacks.

However, all IDS application distributors allow you to create your own rules. This capability is important because it is very unlikely that an IDS application will support all of your needs "out of the box." Furthermore, new attacks constantly appear, and it is vital that you take steps to configure your IDS application to recognize them. An enterprise-grade network- or host-based IDS application usually enforces hundreds of rules. You can add and delete rules according to your own requirements and preferences.

> **NOTE**
> Vendors use auditing terms differently. For example, eTrust Intrusion Detection uses the term *rule* when referring to an instruction that tells the IDS what to look for. Symantec's Intruder Alert uses the term *policies* for the same function. Do not worry about understanding terminology specific to one product. As far as the CIW Security Professional exam is concerned, make sure that you understand the concept of rules, and how it is possible to add and modify them to address an attack. For example, you should be able to read a scenario and recommend that a rule be created to listen for an attack on a specific port, from a specific IP address.

IDS Applications and Slow Scanning Attacks

Most talented individuals interested in attacking a network will work slowly and carefully to first map out the network. Network mapping does not have to be done over a period of seconds or minutes. Over a month or longer, a hacker can surreptitiously send packets to the ports of various network systems, and then save information obtained from system responses in a database. Over time, the attacker will obtain a complete network map, and most systems administrators will never know that their systems have been mapped over time. Such an attack is called a *slow scanning attack*.

Certain IDS applications are capable of detecting scanning attacks that occur over a long period of time. It is possible to use an IDS application to listen for such long-range scans. The IDS application first listens for each packet, and then stores an entry in its database. The security manager or systems administrator can then query the database to see if seemingly random, innocuous packets are in fact a part of a slow scanning attack. One IDS application that is capable of detecting slow scanning attacks is Shadow, available at the Naval Surface Warfare Center–Dahlgren Lab web page at www.nswc.navy.mil/ISSEC/CID/. This particular IDS application uses applications and daemons such as SSH, tcpdump, Perl, and Apache Server to detect and analyze traffic.

IDS Concerns

As long as it is configured properly and supported by a talented team, a well-implemented IDS will help you improve your network's security. However, an IDS application does not provide a magic bullet solution; you will be faced with various challenges. Here is a list of concerns that you should be aware of as you take the CIW Security Professional exam:

Interference with legitimate business traffic An IDS application should not interfere with standard, legitimate network traffic (e.g., authorized IMAP and SMTP traffic generated by employees). Configure your rules carefully so that you do not affect normal business operations.

System and network latency *System latency* can be increased when too many services are installed on a system and these services consume too many CPU cycles and available system RAM. It is important to consider any effect that a host-based IDS application might have on the system it is monitoring. Hackers can coordinate attacks to overburden an IDS. The result could be that the IDS becomes an unwitting participant in a denial-of-service attack.

> **NOTE** Hackers have been known to coordinate attacks so that the IDS cannot track activity on the network.

As far as *network latency* is concerned, make sure that any traffic generated by the IDS application will not consume too much bandwidth. Although IDS applications do not generate much network traffic, it is possible that a slow WAN link could cause connectivity problems.

For example, suppose that you want to use a manager to communicate with several agents across a 56K connection. If you time this communication incorrectly, your management of the agents could cause an unacceptable slowdown for users who are conducting business over the same link. As a security professional, the last thing you want to do is negatively affect legitimate end-user activity.

IDS application testing The first step you should take when configuring an IDS application is to test it on an isolated subnet. IDS testing will help you determine whether your manager-to-agent communications are secure and how such communications will affect network bandwidth. As you test the application, establish how much it is affecting the performance of the server it is residing on. Network-based IDS applications in particular can consume an enormous amount of system resources. You might have to upgrade the server's hardware in order to allow it to function properly. Make sure that your system NIC is supported by the IDS application and that it is a high-quality card. Some IDS applications require you to use a specialized NIC to ensure that it can capture information quickly. You must also make sure that system I/O is fast enough. Many network-based IDS applications require SCSI hardware, because SCSI has faster I/O speeds. Furthermore, you might consider upgrading system RAM and enhancing processing speed (e.g., an upgraded or additional processor).

IDS connectivity and firewalls Firewalls pose another connectivity concern. Many firewalls block all connections unless they are explicitly allowed. Thus, if you attempt to connect to an agent that resides behind a firewall, your attempt could be blocked. To solve this problem, define a firewall rule for all manager/agent communication. Also, it is possible to install an IDS application on a firewall, especially if you want to monitor that firewall carefully.

However, if you do install an IDS application on a firewall, remember that this agent will have to listen on a port. Therefore, you will have to change that application's default port. If you do not change the default port, the agent will use that port on the firewall to listen for connections.

As a result, the firewall will not forward connections from managers to other agents on that port, and no communication will be possible to other agents on the network.

IDS applications and naming services IDS applications often encounter issues with DNS names. Most IDS applications require a fully operational DNS structure. A full structure includes proper forward and reverse lookup zones. Because well-configured DNS structures are hard to come by, you likely will have to reconfigure a network's DNS. Generally, you cannot simply use IP addresses. The use of hosts files or Windows Internet Naming Service (WINS) can work in certain situations, but a fully functional DNS structure is standard. This structure is necessary for two reasons:

- It allows the agents to communicate with the central IDS application.
- It allows the IDS application to properly log activity and report the source of an attack.

> **NOTE** If you have problems with an agent reading a manager, determine whether the services are running. You can also conduct a port scan to see if they are announcing themselves on the network. If you are running DNS and have not created a reverse zone, you could have a problem getting the manager and agent(s) to recognize each other, even if they are operating on the same system.

Problems to solve in regard to DNS include:

- Adding reverse DNS lookup zones
- Adding and changing A and CNAME records to ensure that a system is properly recognized by the IDS application

False positives and false negatives You have already learned about *false positives* and *false negatives* in Chapter 7. The same concepts apply in IDS applications. Both host- and network-based IDS applications are especially prone to mistaking legitimate traffic for an attack. IDS applications, for example, often mistake DNS traffic (e.g., zone transfers) for illicit traffic. Those responsible for maintaining IDS applications must carefully configure them to ensure that they do not mistake legitimate traffic for illegitimate traffic.

Even if you have carefully configured an IDS application, false positives are likely to occur because IDS applications are still relatively new, and because busy networks can generate enormous amounts of traffic that can confuse them. Solutions to this problem include creating more specific rules and segmenting networks so that traffic is reduced.

> **TIP** Network-based IDS applications tend to generate more false positives than host-based ones, mainly because network-based IDS applications are required to interpret different types of information than host-based IDS applications. After all, a host-based IDS application is usually configured to suit a particular operating system. As it searches log files of that operating system, a well-configured host-based IDS application will not likely find log entries that it does not understand.

A false negative is an instance where an IDS application fails to report a problem where one exists. False negatives can occur for various reasons, including the fact that network-based IDS applications cannot work on switched networks. Furthermore, remember that a network-based IDS application cannot detect and react to traffic that is on the other side of a router.

System security Physical security is of utmost importance for network-based IDS applications. You do not want unauthorized individuals to gain access to the information that these applications can discover. Make sure that the IDS is physically secure. Furthermore, make sure that your network-based IDS application is a dedicated host. In other words, you do not want to run the application on a system that is also acting as a web or e-mail server. In fact, you might want to harden the operating system by stopping as many network services as possible.

> **WARNING** Although an IDS is an invaluable tool for a security manager or auditor, a company employee can load a product such as eTrust Intrusion Detection or Snort on your network and gain access to sensitive information. Not only can a hacker read any unencrypted e-mail sent on the system, but he or she could also sniff passwords and gather sensitive protocol information. Therefore, one of your first tasks might be to search for the presence of such programs on your network.

Ways to defeat an IDS *Tunneling* is the practice of embedding one data stream inside of another. Many networks use tunneling to secure traffic. Chapter 6, for example, described the use of the Point-to-Point Tunneling Protocol (PPTP) and the Layer 2 Tunneling Protocol (L2TP). Tunneling is used properly every day to help increase network security. However, tunneling can also be used illicitly. Most IDS applications cannot decrypt traffic. If, for example, HTTP traffic has been encrypted in any way, the IDS application will not be able to read the text string. As a result, many employees have begun embedding, or "tunneling," traffic inside encrypted data streams in order to fool IDS applications and firewalls.

Traditionally, IDS applications have also had problems detecting traffic that has been tunneled inside a legitimate data stream. The Stunnel application, available at http://packetstorm.linuxsecurity.com, is capable of tunneling various protocols (e.g., POP3, IMAP, and FTP) inside HTTP traffic. The Stunnel application pumps the POP3, IMAP, or FTP traffic into one end of an HTTP tunnel, and then translates it on the other end of the tunnel. Usually, one end of this tunnel is "inside" the corporate firewall, and the other end is outside the corporate firewall. Thus, a user is able to avoid detection by the firewall and IDS application by tunneling illicit traffic inside a seemingly legitimate data stream.

The best way to solve this problem is to regularly check employee systems to see if they are using tunneling software. Another way to detect the use of tunneling is to carefully monitor the volume of HTTP traffic coming in and out of your firewall. If traffic suddenly rises and you cannot account for it, consider the possibility that employees could be tunneling.

Purchasing an IDS

When researching your choices, focus on specific issues. Consider the issues and questions outlined in Table 13.1.

TABLE 13.1 Issues and Questions in IDS Purchase Decisions

Issue	Question(s)
Product support	Who are the regional contacts, and when are they available? What is the vendor's complaints policy? When is technical support available? How much does it cost? Is a toll-free support number available?
Product training	What type of training is available? Is it included with the product? How much does it cost?
Update policy	What is the frequency of manager/agent updates? What is the cost of such updates, if any? Are updates free for the first year? How will you learn about upgrades? Does the vendor have a process for suggesting improvements?
Company or organization reputation	What other companies use the product?
IDS capacity	How much traffic can the IDS handle before it becomes saturated? How does the IDS inform you about problems?
Product scalability	How complex can policies be? How many signatures/policies can the IDS search for? How granular are these policies? Can you create your own? How long will the product conduct searches?
Network support	Which network systems does the IDS support most effectively? What weaknesses does it have specific to Unix, Novell, and NT? Which sendmail bugs does the product search for by default? Which operating system or equipment item (e.g., a router) has the product supported the longest?
Encryption	Do the managers and agents use public-key encryption? Which type?

Some IDS vendors might be unwilling to reveal many details about their products. However, be prepared to discern between a company representative who is unwilling to reveal sensitive information and a representative who does not understand the product.

IDS Application Vendors

As you choose a product, consider which is most suitable for you and the company with which you are working. Some products have attractive GUIs, making them easy to use. Others might be more scalable. Other products are less easy to use but offer powerful features. The following is a partial list of vendors:

- Computer Associates' eTrust Intrusion Detection (formerly SessionWall 3)
- Snort (www.snort.org)
- Intruder Alert and NetRecon (www.symantec.com)
- ISS RealSecure (www.iss.net)
- Computer Misuse and Intrusion Detection System (www.cmds.net)
- NFR Security (www.nfr.com)
- Network Associates' CyberCop Monitor (www.networkassociates.com)
- Cisco Secure IDS, formerly NetRanger (www.cisco.com)

EXERCISE 13.1

Installing Computer Associates' eTrust Intrusion Detection

In this exercise, you will install eTrust Intrusion Detection on your system.

Note: If you have a different version of eTrust Intrusion Detection, or an earlier version of eTrust called SessionWall, you might need to alter certain steps of the following exercises. The GUI and functionality of these earlier versions are essentially the same, however.

1. Log on as Administrator.
2. Download eTrust Intrusion Detection Release 1.5 from www.ca.com.

EXERCISE 13.1 *(continued)*

3. Install the application, following the steps suggested by the installation wizard.

   Note: eTrust might require you to uninstall a Windows 2000 service before it will install. For example, if your Windows 2000 server has Terminal Services installed, you will first need to uninstall this feature. Go to Start ≻ Settings ≻ Control Panel ≻ Add/Remove Programs, and then select Add/Remove Windows Components to remove Terminal Services. You will then need to reboot your system before performing Step 3.

4. Setup will ask you whether you want to start the program as a service. Select No, unless you want this application to start automatically each time you boot your system. Selecting No makes eTrust operate as an application. Continue to install eTrust.

5. When prompted, make sure you have selected the Yes radio button to restart your computer. The program will restart your computer.

6. When the system reboots, log on as Administrator.

EXERCISE 13.2

Becoming Familiar with eTrust Intrusion Detection

In this exercise, you will conduct a simple scan to become familiar with the eTrust Intrusion Detection interface.

1. As Administrator, go to Start ≻ Programs ≻ eTrust Intrusion Detection ≻ Intrusion Detection to open the interface.

2. You will see the Logon eTrust Intrusion Detection login dialog box. Click OK.

3. The main interface will appear.

4. View any existing alerts by going to View ≻ Alert Messages, or by clicking the yellow bell icon near the upper-left part of the screen.

5. Clear any alerts you see by clicking the Clear button. When you have finished, exit the Alert Messages window.

6. Open the Show Security Violations window by choosing View ≻ Security Violations, or by clicking the icon that resembles a green man wearing a hat. Clear any alerts you see here as well.

538 Chapter 13 • Intrusion Detection

EXERCISE 13.2 *(continued)*

7. When you have finished clearing all alerts (they are probably all false positives), close all alert dialog boxes and minimize eTrust Intrusion Detection.

8. Obtain Ping Pro from www.ipswitch.com. Install it, then open Ping Pro using the Start ➢ Programs menu, and select the Scan tab.

9. Still at the second system, configure Ping Pro to scan a remote system that is not acting as an IDS application and begin your scan.

10. Check eTrust. It will log and trace this scanning attack. It will also alert you. Note the flashing hat in the button bar and the increased client activity in the lower window. Open the Alert Messages and Detected Security Violations dialog boxes and position them as shown below.

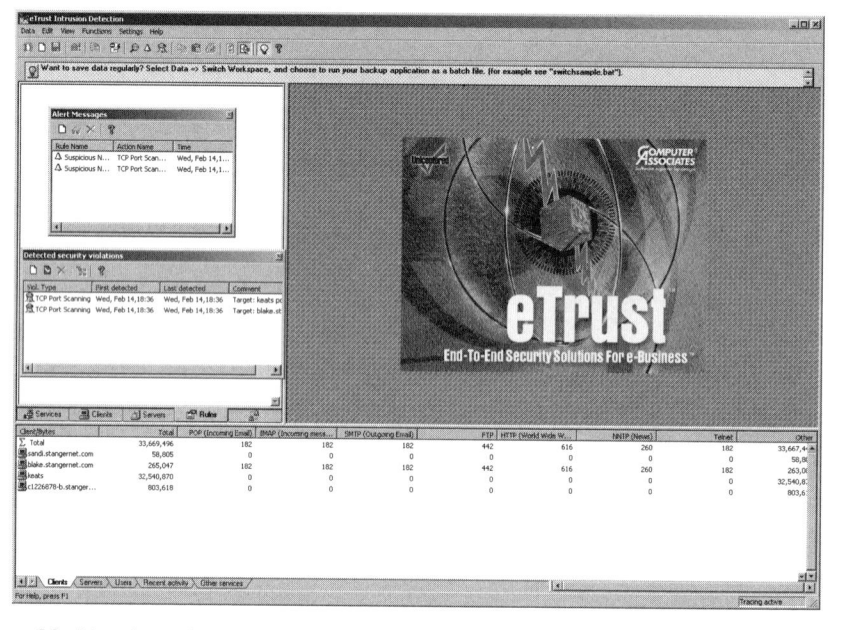

11. You have just viewed messages informing you of a scanning attack. Clear all messages and close the Alert Messages and Detected Security Violations dialog boxes.

12. To gain an overall perspective of the protocols used on your network, go to the bottom of the eTrust Intrusion Detection interface, right-click the Total icon, and select Protocol Distribution as shown next.

EXERCISE 13.2 *(continued)*

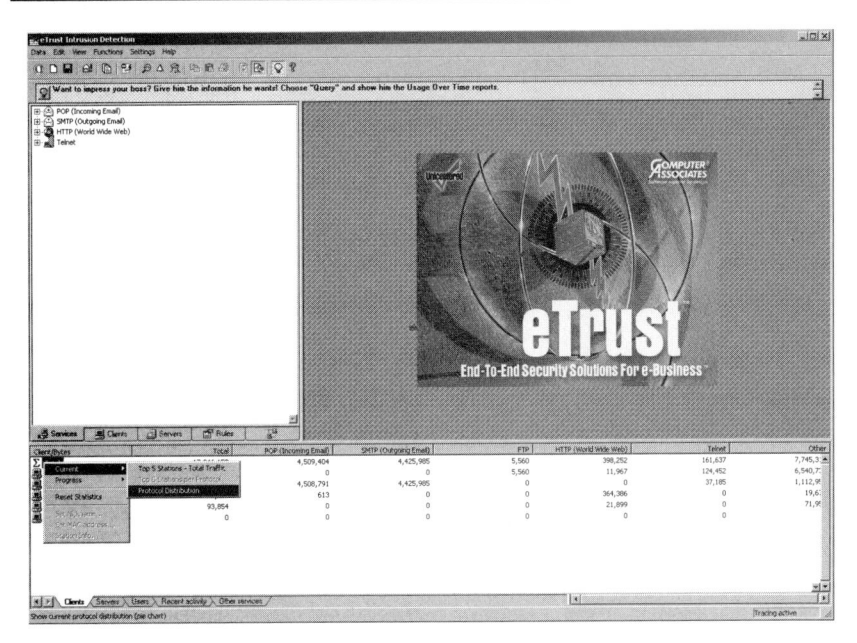

13. Your screen should now show the current protocol distribution on the network, similar to this:

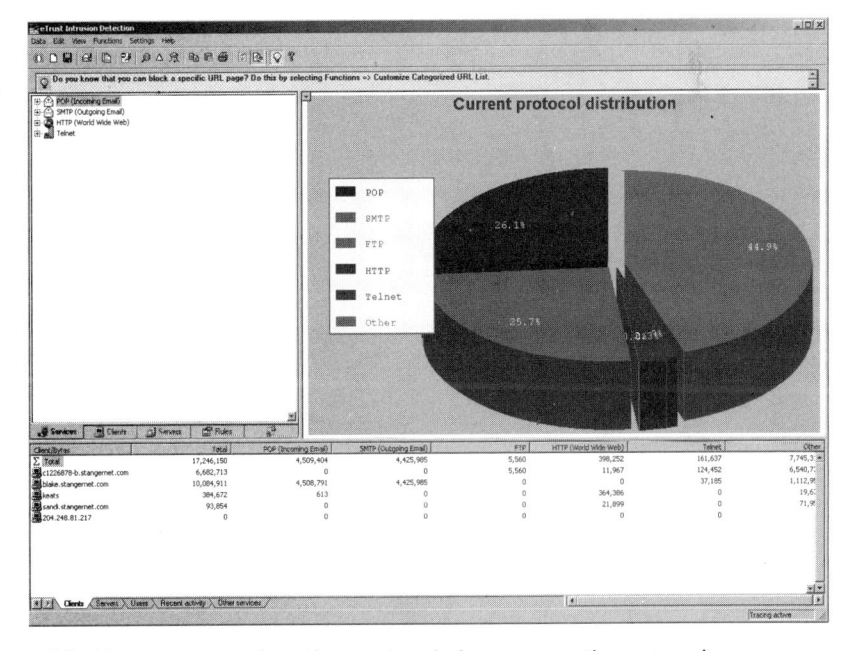

14. You can now view the protocols in use over the network.

EXERCISE 13.3

Viewing Host Network Activity in eTrust Intrusion Detection

In this exercise, you will generate and log traffic using eTrust Intrusion Detection. You will first view the information first in static format and then in dynamic format.

1. Generate additional network traffic, including HTTP and FTP connections. If possible, open other connections such as Telnet or e-mail (SMTP and POP3).

2. Select the Services icon on the far left of the interface.

3. View the left window in the eTrust main interface.

4. Drill down into an HTTP (World Wide Web) icon by clicking the plus sign (+) sign next to it and click the icon representing a remote host on the network.

5. Expand this icon. You should see the page(s) that the user on the remote system has visited. View the contents of the page, as shown here:

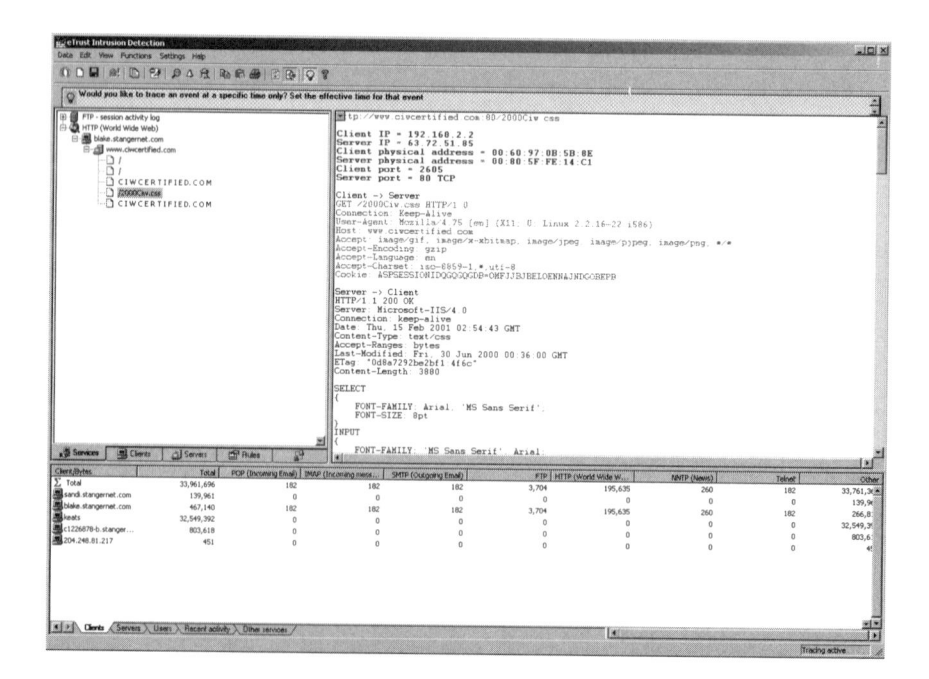

Purchasing an IDS 541

EXERCISE 13.3 *(continued)*

6. View the additional connections made on the network (e.g., FTP, Telnet, SMTP, POP3, and so forth).

   Note: If you are using a demonstration version of the product, you will not be able to read e-mail messages or view passwords from POP3, telnet, FTP, and HTTP sessions. Only the complete version will perform these tasks. However, you should be able to reconstitute entire websites scanned by systems on the network.

7. Go to the bottom of the eTrust screen to the Client/Bytes section. Right-click the Total icon and select Reset Statistics.

8. Right-click the icon that represents a particular computer, and then select Progress ≻ Station Traffic Over Time.

9. Make sure that at least one other system on the network opens several FTP and HTTP sessions to other systems.

10. View the results in eTrust. Depending on the protocols used, your screen should look like this:

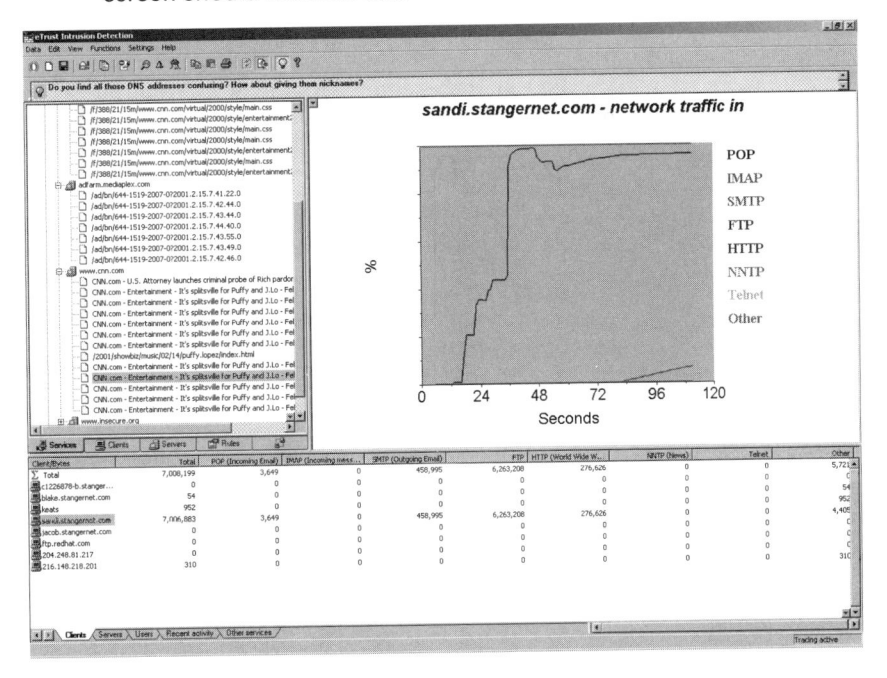

EXERCISE 13.3 (continued)

11. The previous screen shows eTrust monitoring the traffic emanating from a system named sandi. View current statistics for additional systems on the network.

12. Go to the bottom of the screen and right-click the Total network traffic icon again. Select Current ➢ Top 5 Stations – Total Traffic and view the top five most talkative stations on your network. The top system on the list is the busiest. You have now conducted a detailed trace of network activity.

EXERCISE 13.4

Scanning for eTrust Intrusion Detection Activity on Your Network and Generating a Report

In this exercise, you will use eTrust Intrusion Detection to scan for separate instances of eTrust on your network.

1. Begin a report of all network activity by choosing Functions ➢ Reports and selecting the Start Reporter option.

2. When presented with the Start Reporter dialog box, select the Update Statistics and Take Snapshot check boxes.

3. When the Save Snapshot Database As dialog box appears, leave the default name and click the Save button. When you are informed that the database file already exists, overwrite the file by clicking Yes.

4. The eTrust Intrusion Detection Reporter will appear.

5. Select the Summary ➢ Protocol Distribution icon.

6. Click the Preview Report button.

7. You will see the Protocols Distribution window, which enables you to report the types of protocols used on the network. Maximize this window to gain the best view of the protocols used on the network.

8. When you have finished viewing the report, close this window.

9. Select the Top 10 Active Clients Summary icon and click the Preview Report button again. You should see a graphical display of the most active clients on your system.

EXERCISE 13.4 *(continued)*

10. When you have finished reading the protocol distribution, close the Top 10 Active Clients report window. Close this window when you have finished.

11. Close the eTrust Intrusion Detection Reporter dialog box.

    When time permits, investigate eTrust further by going to Functions ≻ Intrusion Detection Rules and investigating the rules that eTrust already has created. Then, create some new rules and test them on the network.

Summary

In this chapter, you learned about the practice of intrusion detection. You learned about network-based and host-based scanners, and experimented with Computer Associates' eTrust Intrusion Detection, which is a network-based IDS application. You studied the use of managers and agents in host-based IDS applications, and you learned how to place them to ensure cost efficiency.

You also learned about the strengths and weaknesses of host- and network-based IDS applications. Finally, you reviewed some of the fundamental concerns that you will have to address when installing and maintaining an IDS application. In many ways, an IDS application augments a network operating system's native logging ability. In the next chapter, you will learn more about what the CIW Security Professional exam requires you to know about checking standard system log files in various network operating systems, including Windows 2000 and Linux.

Exam Essentials

Understand the use and importance of intrusion detection in a network. Be able to determine when an IDS will help detect a problem in a network. For example, given a scenario, make sure that you can identify when a firewall is an appropriate choice, and when an IDS or IDS application will solve the problem. Remember, an IDS does not address problems that exist outside the firewall, and a firewall cannot directly address activity that exists on the internal network.

Know the difference between signature-based and anomaly-based approaches to intrusion detection. The most common type of IDS application is signature based. These IDS applications require you (or the vendor) to configure rules to detect problems on the network. Anomaly-based IDS applications, on the other hand, process traffic and store patterns in databases. Once the database is occupied, the IDS application can then respond to traffic that exceeds established thresholds.

Be able to recommend host-based and network-based IDS applications, given a specific situation. It is important for you to know when you should recommend a host-based IDS application and when a network-based IDS application would be appropriate. For example, if a network administrator is concerned about detecting a distributed denial-of-service (DDoS) attack immediately, you would likely choose a network-based IDS application, because it can search for common DDoS attack traffic as it passes across the network.

If, on the other hand, a systems administrator is concerned about repeated login attempts on the web server, you would choose to install a host-based IDS application, because it can read log files and is thus suited to address that particular threat. Take care to understand the benefits and drawbacks of host- and network-based IDS applications.

Know the importance of accurate rules and responses in IDS applications. An IDS application cannot identify and respond to traffic that it does not recognize. Know when it is time to update or alter the signature database of a particular application.

Be able to identify the duties of an incident response team (IRT). An IRT is responsible for maintaining IDS applications and responding to events. IDS applications are simply tools used by the IRT; they do not replace employees or make decisions by themselves. Make sure that you can identify specific IRT duties.

Understand the importance of agent placement. Remember that network-based IDS applications do not traditionally perform well in switched networks. Furthermore, make sure that you understand that due to their cost, agents should be placed only on the most important servers. Given a particular scenario, be able to identify the server that should receive an agent.

Be able to identify concerns relevant to IDS applications. Like any other tool, IDS applications must be used properly. They also present their own challenges. Make sure that you have created a proper naming structure, and that system and network latency issues are considered. If using a manager/agent architecture, make sure that an intervening firewall does not break the connection between the two. Also, make sure that you properly test your IDS implementation, or you might find that it will not report relevant information to you. Furthermore, as you might suspect, new ways are being devised to avoid and trick IDS applications. Tunneling, for example, is a concern, because users can either encrypt traffic or embed one type of traffic into another.

Key Terms

Before you take the exam, be certain you are familiar with the following terms:

action	network latency
agents	organizational structure
anomaly detection	real time
attack signature database	redundant logging
false negatives	response field
false positives	rule
forensic analysis	signature
host-based IDS	signature detection
IDS application	slow scanning attack
incident response team (IRT)	system latency
intrusion-detection system (IDS)	tunneling
network-based IDS	

Review Questions

1. You cannot connect to an IDS agent that is on the same subnet as your manager. The agent that is experiencing the problem is on a system named www2.company.com. However, you can use the same manager to communicate with an agent on a remote subnet. The system containing this agent is named smtp.company.com. You have confirmed that the agent on www2.company.com is running on the server and listening for connections. You have checked the agent's log file, and it does not record any connection attempts. Which of the following is the most plausible reason for the connection failure?

    A. A firewall is blocking the connection.

    B. The agent resides on a switched network.

    C. The agent resides on a hub-based network.

    D. DNS resolution is causing the problem.

2. You have installed a host-based IDS application on your web server. Which of the following attacks can this host-based IDS application best address?

    A. Failed login attempts

    B. When IIS starts its FTP service

    C. DDoS attacks

    D. Repeated port scans at the firewall

3. Mary wants to install an IDS application that uses a manager/agent architecture. Which of the following is a primary concern about this product?

    A. Encryption between managers and agents

    B. The agent's ability to pass through the firewall

    C. Proper placement of the manager

    D. Proper placement of the agent

4. What does a signature-based IDS application use to respond to an attack?

   A. Properly configured DNS

   B. A rule

   C. A signature database

   D. Log files

5. What does a network-based IDS application use to detect an attack?

   A. An attack profile

   B. Properly configured DNS

   C. A signature database

   D. A packet sniffer

6. Which of the following is not found in an IDS application rule?

   A. A source port

   B. A destination port

   C. A log file entry

   D. A response type

7. Which of the following best describes the practice of intrusion detection?

   A. The defining of granular control at all levels of a network

   B. The applications of actions to rules (i.e., policies)

   C. The real-time monitoring of networks

   D. The logging of activity on a network's servers

8. What is the name for the activity that eliminates unnecessary services and functions on a host to increase its security?

   A. System maintenance

   B. System hardening

   C. System management

   D. Physical security

9. You have been informed of a new type of attack. Your IDS application does not yet have a rule designed to detect and respond to this attack. What can you do in this cases?

   A. Purchase a new signature database.

   B. Reconfigure the firewall.

   C. Shut down your systems until you obtain a new IDS application.

   D. Define a new rule that detects the attack.

10. For what is a network-based IDS especially suited?

    A. Thwarting dictionary attacks and Trojans

    B. Thwarting dictionary attacks and denial-of-service attacks

    C. Thwarting network scans and denial-of-service attacks

    D. Thwarting denial-of-service attacks and Trojans

11. What is a rule in intrusion detection?

    A. An entry in an IDS application that determines the action it will take

    B. The database of parameters that define the elements for which an IDS application will search

    C. The term used in a security policy that determines IDS configuration

    D. An IDS application that determines how the IDS application will behave

12. What is a false positive in regard to an IDS application?

    A. The result of misconfiguration of a particular rule in an IDS application

    B. An instance where the IDS has mistaken illegitimate traffic for legitimate traffic

    C. An instance where the IDS has mistaken legitimate traffic for illegitimate traffic

    D. A hasty response made by the security manager during an attack

13. You want to enable an IDS application to take action against a particular entry in a log file. Where would you place this action?

    A. On a network server

    B. In a rule

    C. On an IDS

    D. On the firewall

14. Which of the following can help ensure that unauthorized users cannot gain access to a network-based IDS application?

    A. Enable physical security.

    B. Uninstall the software when it is not in use.

    C. Configure authentication.

    D. Use encryption for all communication.

15. An employee wants to defeat detection by a network-based IDS application. He does not want to attack the system containing the IDS application. Which of the following strategies can be used to defeat detection by a network-based IDS application?

    A. Create a network tunnel.

    B. Create multiple false positives.

    C. Create a SYN flood.

    D. Create a ping flood.

16. Which of the following should you consider when building a system that will house a network-based IDS application?

    A. The quality of the NIC

    B. The system's manufacturer

    C. The system's monitor

    D. The quality of the RAM

17. Serena has just purchased an IDS application from a company. This IDS application uses a manager/agent structure. She has installed one of these agents onto the network firewall. This firewall has been configured to forward information from other agents. What must Serena do to the agent that she has just installed?

    A. Configure the firewall to allow all connections.

    B. Ensure that it is using the same port number as the other agents.

    C. Change the default port number on the agent.

    D. Make sure the agent is using the same port number as the others.

18. Which of the following is not easily discovered and reported by a network-based IDS application?

    A. An X-Window connection by the root user

    B. A login to a router

    C. The use of the Windows NetLogon service

    D. The use of the su command.

19. Which of the following can be caused by a network-based IDS application that resides on one server, rather than by a host-based IDS application?

    A. System latency

    B. Network latency

    C. Additional login traffic

    D. Additional HTTP traffic

20. Which of the following describes anomaly-based intrusion detection?

    A. The rules of an IDS application are configured by a system administrator to detect unusual attacks.

    B. An IDS application creates a baseline of activity, and then responds to traffic that is unusual.

    C. An IDS application analyzes and responds to only unusual traffic activity.

    D. An IDS application analyzes and responds to legitimate traffic, not false positives.

Answers to Review Questions

1. **D.** Most host-based IDS applications require a fully functional DNS structure in order to operate properly. Proper operation includes the ability to listen for network traffic, as well as the ability to receive login traffic. If a manager or agent cannot obtain the proper DNS information, the manager/agent communication will fail, even if the agent is running and listening. In regard to this question, it makes little difference if the agent is listening on a hub or switched network, because the question is not addressing the agent's ability to listen for or respond to attacks. Rather, the question is addressing the ability for a manager to communicate with an agent. A firewall is not causing this problem, because the agent is on the same subnet as the manager.

2. **A.** A host-based IDS is capable of reporting almost any event that takes place on the local host. It cannot detect events on a remote system and is not the best choice for detecting network-based events, such as DDoS attacks.

3. **A.** When purchasing a manager/agent IDS application, a primary consideration is making sure that it encrypts all communication that takes place between them. Making sure that the agent can pass through a firewall is a configuration issue, and can be addressed once you are sure that your software communicates securely. Similarly, proper placement is not an issue when purchasing software.

4. **B.** An IDS application requires a properly configured rule to respond to an attack. A signature database does not determine how the IDS application responds to an attack. Rather, it determines whether or not the application recognizes the attack. Similarly, a host-based IDS application can read a log file to help it learn about attacks, but it does not use this file when responding to an attack.

5. **D.** A network-based IDS application places a system's NIC into promiscuous mode, and it uses some sort of packet sniffer to do so. Open source network-based IDS applications such as Shadow use `tcpdump` to listen for packets. Applications such as Snort, NetProwler, and eTrust Intrusion Detection use proprietary applications to obtain packets. A signature database (i.e., an attack profile) is not used to detect an attack. Rather, it is used to identify attacks.

6. **C.** A rule contains all of the above except for a log file entry. A host-based IDS application reads log files and then takes action when a particular log file entry is recognized as an attack.

7. **C.** Although it is important to define granular controls at all levels of a network, intrusion detection involves the real-time monitoring of traffic behind a firewall. An IDS application can also apply actions to rules, but so can a firewall. Furthermore, although an IDS application logs activity on a network's servers, so does a simple logging utility.

8. **B.** System hardening is the most appropriate answer. System maintenance implies many more activities that simply removing unnecessary services. It includes ensuring that all elements run properly. System management implies adding and removing system users, as well as maintaining the system. While physical security is always important, it does not address eliminating unnecessary services.

9. **D.** You do not necessarily have to rely on the vendor to obtain a new signature database. Simply define a new rule that detects this attack. Although shutting down a system might be an appropriate move, you likely will not have to obtain an entirely new IDS application.

10. **C.** A network-based IDS is not suited for detecting Trojan installation, because it does not review log files. Although it may be able to detect repeated login attempts, a network-based IDS is best suited for detecting network scans and denial-of-service attacks.

11. **A.** A rule determines how an IDS application will behave. It is not a separate application, nor is it a complete database. Furthermore, it is not a term regularly used in security policies when referring to what an IDS application can do.

12. **C.** Whenever an IDS application has mistaken legitimate traffic for illegitimate traffic, it is said to have generated a false positive. When an IDS application fails to detect illegitimate traffic, it is said to create a false negative. False positives always refer to applications, not individuals. Although a faulty IDS rule can result in false positives, the term *false positive* does not refer specifically to misconfigured rules.

13. **B.** All IDS application rules contain an action field. Actions can include closing a port, sending an e-mail, or issuing a page alert. It is

important that you properly configure the rule. The rule is configured on the IDS application software, and will reside wherever that software resides.

14. A. Although uninstalling the software when it is not in use will help ensure that unauthorized users will not be able to use it, the best strategy out of all of the answers listed is to ensure that the system is physically secure. This strategy is much more convenient, and it helps ensure that an unauthorized user cannot simply walk up to a system and begin monitoring connections. Configuring authentication and encryption are, of course, helpful strategies for securing network communication. However, they do not in and of themselves help limit access to an IDS application. After all, what happens if an authorized user has logged into the server and then walked away from the system? Keeping the system physically secure ensures that all of your other measures will work properly.

15. A. Most IDS applications are not capable of delving into an encrypted tunnel, or reading packets that have been embedded into another data stream. A properly configured network-based IDS application is more than capable of withstanding a SYN flood, or even a ping flood, if these are directed at the system. Furthermore, a network-based IDS application is uniquely suited to detecting these types of attacks on the particular network segment it is listening to. Finally, an IDS application creates a false positive, not a hacker. This is because the term *false positive* refers to the improper action of an IDS, not of a hacker.

16. A. Because a network-based IDS application sniffs packets off the network, its NIC is of paramount importance. System RAM and its ability to process information are also important elements. However, quality of RAM is often less important than its amount. The system's manufacturer and monitor are far less important concerns.

17. C. If an agent on the firewall is using the same port as all of the other agents, this port will be "busy," and the firewall will not accept and forward connections for other agents. Therefore, you will have to configure the agent to use a different port. Configuring the firewall to allow all connections will not solve your problem, and will reduce your network's overall security.

18. D. A network-based IDS application can fairly easily detect login traffic, including traffic made using the X-Window protocol and traffic involving the NetLogon service. However, the use of a specific command after login is less likely to be detected by a network-based IDS application. It would be remotely possible for a network-based IDS application to sniff a Telnet-based connection and note the use of the su command. However, if the session is encrypted, the network-based IDS application would likely not detect the command. Remember, a host-based IDS application reads the log files of a particular system, and most Unix/Linux systems will report the use of the su command to the /var/log/messages file.

19. A. A network-based IDS can easily overburden a system, especially if it is monitoring a busy network. This is because the network-based IDS application must process all of the packets on the network, and then reconstitute them so that they can be read. The activity of sniffing and processing all of those packets requires a great deal of processor speed. A host-based IDS application does not require nearly as many additional system resources, even if the application is installed on a busy server. This is because all the host-based IDS application has to do is read a log file. Furthermore, a network-based IDS application does not generate any additional traffic (login or otherwise). It simply listens to network traffic, which does not cause network slowdown.

20. B. Anomaly-based intrusion detection is a strategy whereby the IDS application listens for network traffic and then creates a database. The IDS then determines an average, or baseline, of activity. Whenever traffic exceeds this average, the application can treat this anomaly as an attack and act accordingly. While an IDS application should not report false positives, it should never respond to legitimate network traffic. Any IDS application that requires a systems administrator to configure a rule is signature based.

Chapter 14

Auditing and Log Analysis

THE CIW EXAM OBJECTIVE GROUPS COVERED IN THIS CHAPTER:

✓ Conduct log analysis, establish a user activity baseline, and implement auditing for various services and systems.

Perhaps one of the more challenging but critical aspects of security auditing is analyzing log files. Reading log files is a challenge because it requires a skilled individual to sift through a great deal of (sometimes) complex information. Checking log files is also a challenge because it is not one of the more glamorous tasks, and thus it is an activity that is often omitted. Checking files is always necessary; log files are the primary means of learning what has been happening on a network. As an auditor, you read log files to:

- Determine whether or not the network has experienced an attack in the past
- Learn more about how a past attack has occurred
- Identify normal patterns for a particular network
- Learn about the busiest systems so that you can spend more time and resources protecting them than you do other systems that are not as important
- Help make changes to systems designed to improve a network's overall security

Log files from various network resources (e.g., servers, routers, firewalls, and intrusion-detection devices) are the most efficient means of gaining information about your network. In this chapter, you will learn about key resources to audit, as well as some tools you can use to conduct your audit.

Baseline Creation

For the CIW Security Professional exam, it is important to understand that the first step in the efficient use of log files is to develop a network *baseline*, which is a measure of normative activity for your network. The goal of establishing a baseline is to provide a standard against which to measure and compare future activity. By creating a baseline, you will give yourself the ability to more easily identify *anomalies* in user behavior. Usage that falls outside this accepted norm needs to be examined closely. Security managers can obtain a baseline by conducting a *trend analysis*, which largely involves reading log files. Creating a baseline entails carefully examining the logs over an extended period, sometimes a month or more.

Searching for Normative Activity

During this baseline period, examine logs with the intent of determining your users' activity patterns. Start with broad observations. You can ask such questions as:

- What are the overall traffic patterns for this network?
- When are users typically logging onto critical network resources?
- What are the times when the network is busiest?

These questions may seem to be more relevant to systems administrators, but they are also important for an auditor to consider. As you conduct your baseline, look specifically for periods of heavy and light activity. Most organizations experience their heaviest activity first thing in the morning, around lunchtime, and again during late afternoon. However, activity patterns vary from network to network. As you take the CIW Security Professional exam, keep in mind that creating a baseline for your network is an essential step for an auditor.

Once you have identified normative traffic patterns, you can begin to search for traffic *anomalies*. Just remember that you can do so only if you have a clear idea of what constitutes "normal" activity for your particular network.

Detecting Suspicious Activity

The skilled hacker will attempt to camouflage his or her usage as legitimate system activity. However, telltale signs are often left behind, especially by less-talented hackers. It is your job to review log files and defeat such strategies. *Suspicious activity* can take many forms; here is a list of the most common types of anomalies:

Incomplete or garbled log-file entries Incomplete log-file entries can be evidence that a hacker has gained control of your system and has been able to at least partially alter log files. As you sift through log files, you might find illogical entries, such as those that suggest that a user has logged out of a system without first logging in. This type of partial log entry could be evidence that a hacker has been able to delete the initial login entry in an effort to thwart detection.

However, many operating systems (such as Linux) also generate a log entry showing when a user exits the system. If an operating system creates this type of log entry, a hacker would have to create an exit login script to delete it. Many newer hackers do not have such skills. Thus, if the log file shows only that a user has exited the system, you may have found evidence of an attack.

Similarly, if a series of log files is garbled or contains unexpected information, you may also have found evidence of an attack.

Changes in login times   Hackers often compromise legitimate accounts and then wait until after business hours to exploit them. Once you create your baseline of activity, you might begin to notice certain user accounts being accessed at unusual times. Such instances do not always suggest that a hacker has been able to compromise a legitimate account. However, you should carefully consider any anomalies. If you suspect a security problem, contact the owner of the account and ask if he or she has been using the account during the times you have noted. Emphasize that you are simply following up on usage patterns so that it does not appear that you are monitoring user activity.

Never take unilateral action if you find a suspicious login time. Do not lock out or delete the account, and do not forcibly remove the user from the network without proper instruction or authority. Although it is possible to set account login limits, do not set these limits either, unless you have permission to do so and have carefully weighed the ramifications of doing so. If, for example, any of your settings negatively affect the ability for your chief executive officer (CEO) to do business, you will likely have to change any settings you have put into place.

Repeated login and user-rights failures   Be especially careful to search for specific failure types, including login failures, file-access failures, and user-rights failures. Any of these instances might be caused by incompetent users, but they can also be evidence that a hacker has been trying to conduct a brute-force or dictionary attack against your system.

Repeated log daemon or service crashes When auditing a server or network resource, you might find that the log daemon has been stopped. At the least, this is a problem because the affected server can no longer report events. In other cases, a stopped log daemon could be evidence of tampering. Also, check the ownership and permissions of various log files. If they are set to be world writeable or have been moved to a new folder or directory, you might have found evidence of a hacker who has been manipulating log files.

System, service, or daemon restarts Many times, a hacker needs to restart a server or service in order to install a particular application or root kit. A server or service restart, especially at unusual times, should always generate a certain amount of suspicion. Often, a clever hacker will wait for a natural system or service restart by the legitimate system operators. Occasionally, he or she will be less patient and use either OS commands or a denial-of-service attack to restart the server and begin using hacking tools.

> **TIP** Ultimately, you need to create a baseline so that you can begin to suspect any activity that violates it. Although creating a baseline seems daunting, it is worth the effort.

Missing log files Just because a log file is missing does not necessarily mean that your system has been compromised. In fact, a missing log file could indicate a system misconfiguration. Still, less-talented hackers might not be able to alter log files, so they will simply delete them. Thus, if you discover a missing log file, you have grounds to suspect that the system has experienced a break-in.

Achieving Balance with Log Files

Logging (often called "auditing" in Windows 2000 systems) can present benefits and drawbacks. If you log too much traffic, the information you seek can become lost in a sea of records. Also, consider that *auditing subsystems* always requires more processing power. Therefore, it is possible for you to inadvertently cause the system to spend too much time logging traffic and too little time providing the network service for which the server was designed. You want your logging activities to affect normal operations as little as possible.

However, if you log too little traffic, you have insufficient information to create a baseline or detect anomalies. To achieve the best balance, consider the following strategies:

- Concentrate on perimeter devices (e.g., firewalls and routers).
- Carefully consider information from intrusion-detection system (IDS) applications.
- Audit only servers that are a priority for your network. If the server is of little interest or use, do not focus on it.

Analyzing Log Files

Once you establish a broad baseline through familiarity with your network activity, you can move on to the details. In the next section, we'll discuss which log files you should regularly search, as well as ways to filter log files so that you can receive definitive answers about network activity.

> **NOTE** Log files are useful only if you take the time to read and analyze them. Regularly schedule times to analyze log files to ensure that they are useful to you.

Firewall and Router Logs

When observing firewall and router logs, focus on the following tasks:

- Identify the source and destination interfaces.
- Discover the source and destination hosts.
- Trace usage patterns; on each interface, look for usage patterns that indicate scans from outside addresses. Patterns you discover could be evidence that someone is attempting to map the network.
- Search for nonproductive Internet use, which can include HTTP, RealPlayer, MP3, ICQ, Instant Messenger, and IRC traffic. Additionally, search for suspect ICMP, TCP, and UDP connections.
- Search for connections to suspect ports, such as 12345 (the default NetBus port) and 31337 (the default BackOrifice 2000 port, which a hacker usually changes to help avoid detection from IDS applications).

The most direct way to verify perimeter security is to search router and firewall log files. Reading a server's log file and detecting an intrusion from outside is an example of indirect proof that the perimeter device is having problems.

Additional Log Files to Search

Routers, firewalls, and operating systems are not the only systems that log events. As an auditor, consider the following sources of information:

- Telephony connections (including voicemail logs)
- ISDN and/or frame-relay connections
- Employee access logs (for logging physical access)

Operating System Log Files

The CIW Security Professional exam concentrates on the Windows 2000 and Linux operating systems. Next, we'll discuss the elements you need to know about in order to pass the exam.

Information to Search For

Regardless of the operating system being used, logging services and daemons will usually contain the following information:

- The username and UID of the user who has logged in
- Whether the login was local or remote
- The process ID of the login shell
- When the user logged out (e.g., the user's exit status)

Next, we'll examine how the Windows 2000 and Linux operating systems log entries.

Logging in Windows 2000 Systems

The native logging utility for Windows 2000 is Event Viewer. It allows you to control the EventLog service. You can access Event Viewer from Start ➢ Programs ➢ Administrative Tools ➢ Event Viewer, as well as through other snap-ins, such as Computer Management and Component Services.

Windows 2000 divides its logs into the following three categories.

System   This log records started and failed services, system shutdowns, and restarts.

Security   This log records events such as login activity, access and alteration of user privileges, and object access.

Application   This log records the actions of individual applications as they interact with the operating system.

Additional log types exist. However, they are added only if the service is present. For example, the DNS Server and Directory Service logs will be present if those services are added to the system.

Default Log-File Locations

Assuming that Windows 2000 resides on a C drive, you can find its system-wide log files in the following locations:

- `C:\winnt\system32\config\SysEvent.Evt`
- `C:\winnt\system32\config\SecEvent.Evt`
- `C:\winnt\system32\config\AppEvent.Evt`
- `C:\winnt\system32\config\DnsEvent.Evt`

Microsoft Internet Information Server (IIS) stores its log files in the `C:\winnt\system32\LogFiles\` directory. Each IIS service will create its own subdirectory. For example, the IIS FTP daemon will create a directory named `C:\winnt\system32\LogFiles\MSFTPSCV1\`. If a second FTP server is configured, the directory would be named `C:\winnt\system32\LogFiles\MSFTPSCV2\`, and so forth. If you wanted to check the IIS web server directory, you would therefore check the `C:\winnt\system32\LogFiles\W3SVC1\` directory.

> **Clearing Event Log Files in Windows 2000**
>
> Sometimes, it is necessary to purge the event logs—for example, if the logs have grown too large and are affecting system performance. To clear the event log files in Windows 2000, open Event Viewer, and right-click on the log file you want to clear. Then, select the Clear All Events option. You will be asked if you want to save these events. After you make your choice, all events will be cleared.

> It is wise to check Event Viewer to see whether event logs have been erased by an unauthorized user. Although most talented hackers will erase log files to cover up such activities, it is still worth checking your log files. Even if a hacker has deleted your log files from your hard drive, it is possible to store them on a remote device. See the section "Securing Log Files," later in this chapter.

Enabling Auditing in Windows 2000

In Windows 2000, you have to explicitly enable auditing to capture events. In a stand-alone Windows 2000 system, you enable system- and domain-wide policies in the Local Security Policy snap-in. Domain-based policies are enabled in the Domain Security Policy. Once you access this snap-in, you will see the Local Security Settings window. You have the choice of auditing successful events or failed events. The Audit Policy section of the Local Security Settings window is shown in Figure 14.1.

FIGURE 14.1 Viewing Audit Policy settings in the Local Security Settings window

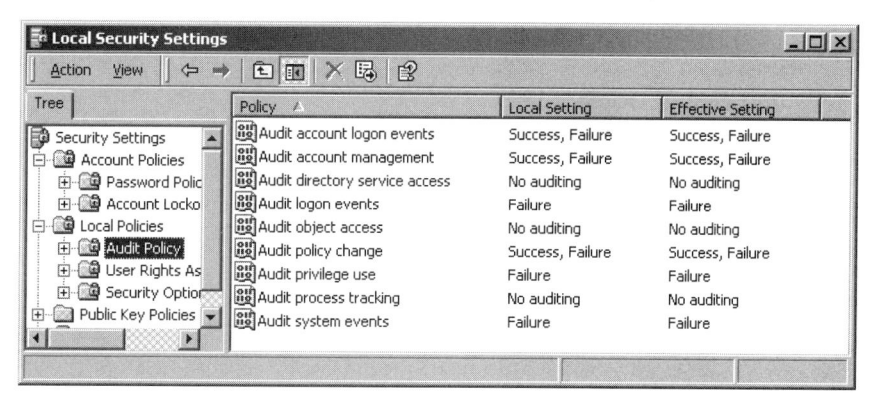

> **TIP** To activate auditing in Windows 2000 (or NT, for that matter), you must have NTFS enabled.

Once you have enabled object access auditing, you can use Windows Explorer to enable auditing on any file or directory you want. Simply right-click a file or folder, and then select the Properties command. In the resulting dialog box, click the Security tab. Next, click the Advanced button and select the Auditing tab. This tab, shown in Figure 14.2, allows you to select the users and groups to audit by clicking the Add button. For the CIW Security Professional exam, remember that the Everyone group includes even those users not defined on your host or domain, so choosing this group may be wise when adding groups and users.

FIGURE 14.2 The Auditing tab in Windows 2000

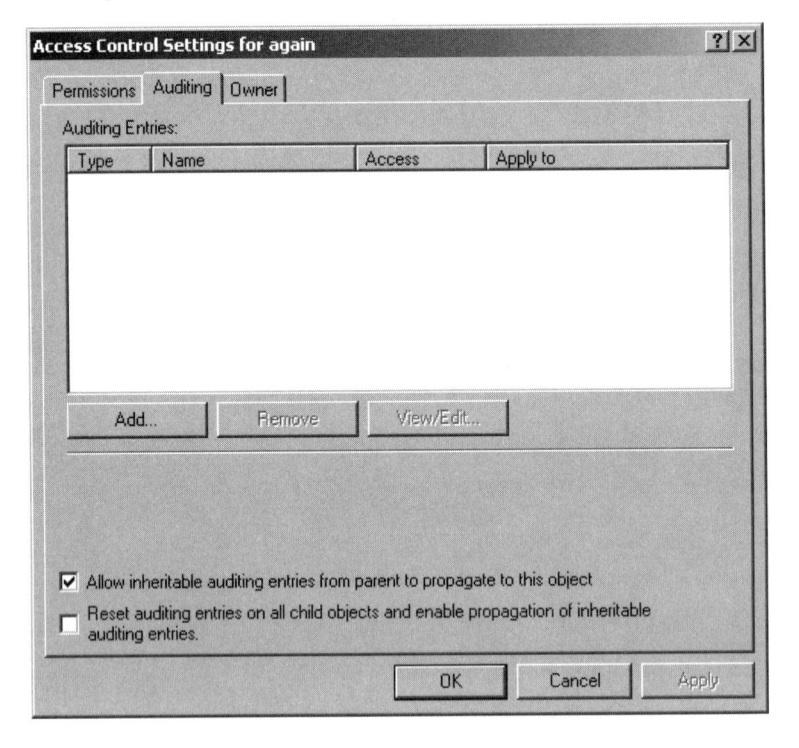

> **Comparing Windows 2000 to Windows NT**
>
> The CIW Security Professional exam does not explicitly cover the Windows NT operating system. However, comparing Windows 2000 to Windows NT might help those who are familiar with Windows NT. In Windows NT, you enable auditing in Windows NT by opening User Manager and selecting Policies ➢ Audit. In the Audit Properties window, enable auditing and select the events you want to monitor. As with Windows 2000, you enable auditing at the directory and file levels using Windows Explorer.

Important NT/2000 Events

Although the events to check for vary from system to system, at a minimum you should check for the events shown in Table 14.1. In Windows NT, these events have been in effect since Service Pack 4 (SP4). They are found in Windows 2000 by default.

TABLE 14.1 Significant Events in Windows NT

Event Number	Description
529	Signifies an unsuccessful logon (found in the Security log).
6005	Informs you that NT/2000 is restarting (found in the System log).
6006	Signifies a clean shutdown event (found in the System log).
6007	Signifies an improper shutdown request, due to inadequate permissions (found in the System log).
6008	Appears whenever NT/2000 has been shut down improperly (found in the System log). Also called the "dirty shutdown" event. Note: Some utilities, including sysprep.exe and shutdown.exe, cause NT/2000 to record this message in systems running SP4. Be sure to study each cause of this message.
6009	Records the operating system version, build number, service pack (if any), and information about the system's processor (found in the System log).
517	Announces the clearing of the event log.

You can read more about these events at the following URL:
http://support.microsoft.com/support/kb/articles/q196/4/52.asp

Figure 14.3 shows the "dirty shutdown" event from Windows 2000 Event Viewer.

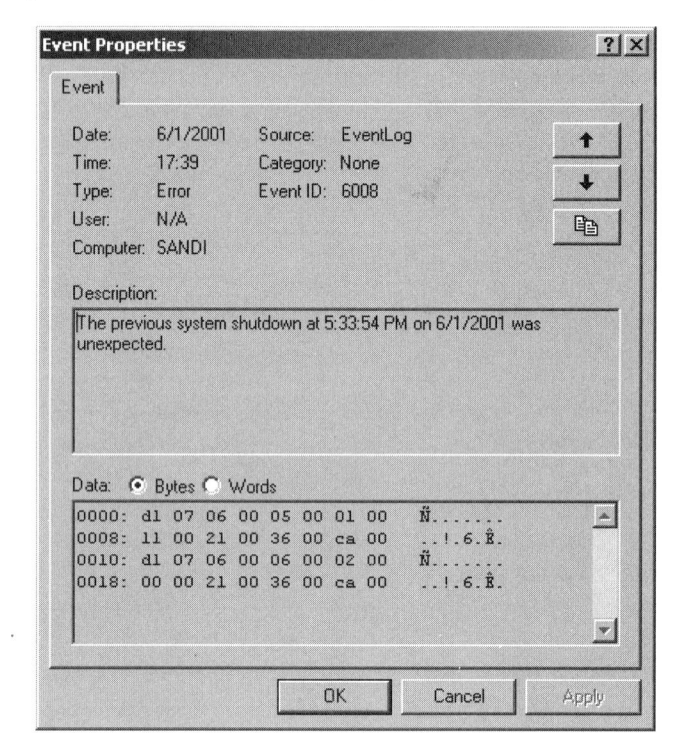

FIGURE 14.3 The "Dirty Shutdown" event in Windows 2000

Determining Service-Pack Level and Uptime Information in Windows NT/2000

You can use the Winver utility to determine the service pack installed on your system. Access the utility by choosing Start ➢ Run and then entering **winver**. While it is important to quickly verify a system's patch level, it is also important to identify when the system was last restarted. Unexpected system shutdowns and restarts are often evidence of hacker activity. You need a quick way to determine how long a system has been running. Although you can obtain system-activity time information from Event Viewer, you can also use the uptimei.exe utility. It is available at

www.microsoft.com/TechNet/winnt/Winntas/tools/uptime.asp

The uptimei.exe binary will give you a report similar to the following:

```
\\SANDI has been up for: 14 day(s), 16 hour(s),
   24 minute(s), 19 second(s)
```

You can also use `uptimei.exe` against remote Windows systems by specifying **uptimei servername**. The `uptimei /s` command informs you about multiple reboots. Additional options are supported; enter **uptimei /?** for more information.

Logging Linux Systems

In most Linux systems, `syslogd` is a daemon process that is configured to listen to logging actions by several systems and other daemons. It will then log these requests into a central file or repository for analysis. The `syslogd` daemon has a configuration file called `/etc/syslog.conf`, which tells the system to log a *facility/priority pair*. This pairing enables a Linux system to identify which daemon generated the traffic, and then allows the system to determine the importance of the traffic.

All Linux systems permit the use of the following facility keywords:

auth Informs you about local and remote logins, as well as when a user logs out.

auth-priv Records logins from remote systems. Generated by daemons that accept remote logins, such as SSH and FTP.

cron Informs you about messages generated by `cron`, the scheduling daemon.

daemon Captures information from network daemons installed on the system.

kern Logs information about the system kernel.

lpr Captures messages from the printing daemon.

mail Informs you about messages from the mail daemon (e.g., sendmail).

mark Informs you about internal system operations only.

news Records events from Network News Transfer Protocol (NNTP) daemons.

security Records authorization information. It is deprecated in favor of **auth**.

syslog Contains information about `syslogd`.

user Reports user-specific information.

uucp   Reports information on the Unix-to-Unix Copy Protocol, which is an older method of transferring files and information between systems across a network.

local0 through local7   Provides the ability to create custom-level entries.

Linux systems then allow you to assign a priority to the particular facility you want to log. You, as the security manager or systems administrator, can assign any priority you want to the information generated by a facility. Here are the codes, in increasing order of priority:

debug   Reports information that allows you to troubleshoot applications and daemons.

info   Sends messages that are for general consumption by end users, but are of only general importance.

notice   Sends messages about general system and daemon information to all users. Such messages are of higher urgency than those sent by the **info** facility.

warning   Reports information that the systems administrator or security manager can act on in case of an emergency.

err   Reports configuration errors.

crit   Denotes failures of essential daemons.

alert   Suggests that a break-in is in progress, or that an unacceptable condition has occurred.

emerg   Provides the highest alert, which is often used to mark information that may suggest a break-in.

The list does not contain the facility words **warn**, **error**, and **panic**. These three facility words have been deprecated for **warning**, **error**, and **emerg**, respectively.

Linux systems ship with an /etc/syslog.conf file that has default facility/priority settings applied. However, it is possible for you to customize this file to suit your own situation. A sample configuration file is shown in Figure 14.4.

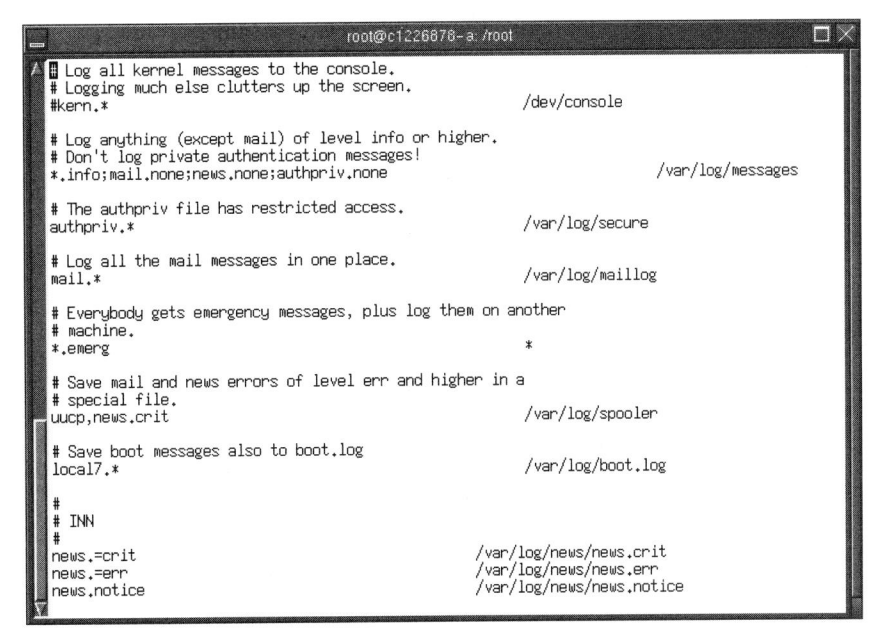

FIGURE 14.4 A sample configuration for the `syslogd` program

```
# Log all kernel messages to the console.
# Logging much else clutters up the screen.
#kern.*                                                 /dev/console

# Log anything (except mail) of level info or higher.
# Don't log private authentication messages!
*.info;mail.none;news.none;authpriv.none                /var/log/messages

# The authpriv file has restricted access.
authpriv.*                                              /var/log/secure

# Log all the mail messages in one place.
mail.*                                                  /var/log/maillog

# Everybody gets emergency messages, plus log them on another
# machine.
*.emerg                                                 *

# Save mail and news errors of level err and higher in a
# special file.
uucp,news.crit                                          /var/log/spooler

# Save boot messages also to boot.log
local7.*                                                /var/log/boot.log

#
# INN
#
news.=crit                                              /var/log/news/news.crit
news.=err                                               /var/log/news/news.err
news.notice                                             /var/log/news/news.notice
```

Important files to read in Linux systems include:

/var/log/messages Contains information generated by a majority of the facilities noted earlier, including `auth-priv`, `security`, `syslog`, `kern`, and others. This file will record local and remote logins, as well as messages from various daemons. Auditors often spend a great deal of time analyzing the contents of this file.

/var/log/secure Contains authentication information about remote logins.

/var/log/xferlog Records statistics about FTP sessions.

Additional Log File Locations

Here are some of the common locations of log files you should audit regularly on various Linux systems:

/var/log/cron Contains information about `cron` jobs that have been executed.

/var/dmesg Contains system boot information.

/var/log/acct Contains information for auditing processes, if enabled.

Additional log files for various daemons, such as Sendmail Apache Server and the lpr print daemon, exist in the /var/log/ directory.

Determining Patch Level and Uptime Information in Linux

The Linux operating system usually contains the `uptime` command. Standard versions of this command do not provide the ability to query remote operating systems; the command provides uptime information only for the local host. Here is an example of uptime information for a system named router:

```
12:31pm  up 22 days, 17:19,  1 user,
    load average: 0.02, 0.03, 0.00
```

For determining system-patch level, the Linux operating system provides the `uname` command, which can tell you the *kernel* version in use. The Linux kernel is the heart of the operating system. You can use the -a option for uname, which reports verbose information about the system:

```
host# uname -a
Linux router 2.4.2-2 #1 Sun Apr 8 19:37:14
    EDT 2001 i586 unknown
host#
```

In the previous example, the most relevant information is the kernel version. In this case, the system is running kernel version 2.4.2-2. Once you know the kernel version, you can conduct research to determine if updating is necessary. As far as daemons and applications are concerned, you will have to study each on an individual basis. If you are using the Red Hat Package Manager (RPM) utility, you can query various applications and daemons that have been installed. For example, if you need to determine the version of sendmail in use, issue the following command:

```
host# rpm -qa | grep sendmail
sendmail-8.12.2
```

This command runs the `rpm` command and queries the rpm database using the -q option. It then searches for all packages using the a option. The "pipe" command (|) then pushes all of the output through the `grep` command, which searches for the text string `sendmail`. As a result, only the version of the installed sendmail package will be reported. Using information from the `rpm` command, you can then determine if you need to upgrade the version of sendmail in use.

If you do not have access to the RPM utility, you will have to query each daemon individually. To determine the version of sendmail, check the daemon's configuration file (/etc/sendmail.cf), or use your Telnet client to access port 25 of the daemon. Many daemons provide simple ways to check their version. For example, to learn the version of Apache Server, you would issue the following command at a terminal:

```
host# httpd -v
```

Filtering Information

Logs can grow very large and can present complex information. You must know how to sift through log files to gain only relevant information. In this section, we'll discuss how to sift properly in Windows 2000 and Linux.

Filtering Logs in Windows 2000

Like any high-performance server, Windows 2000 enables you to filter your events. The event shown in Figure 14.5, for example, creates a filter that reports only entries related to the dates from 5/30/2001 to 6/1/2001.

FIGURE 14.5 Filtering Windows 2000 logs

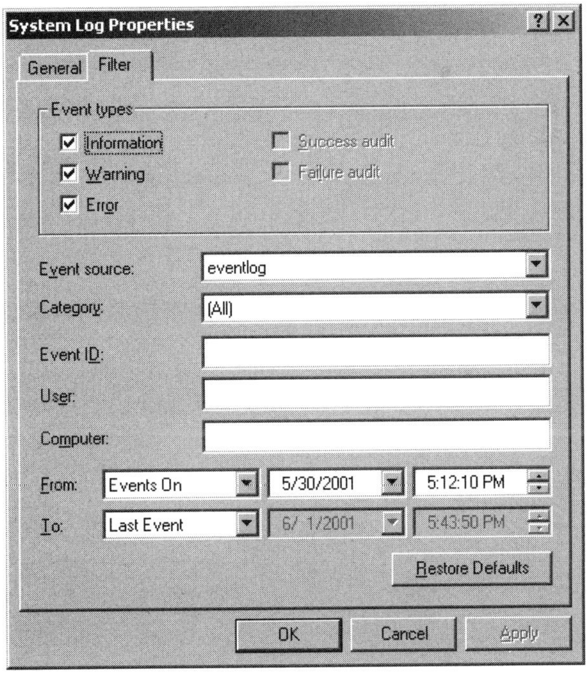

The Event Viewer log-filtering tool is very powerful. Exercise caution when using it, however, because only the events meeting your filter specifications will appear. Therefore, be careful that you do not create a filter that is too restrictive; any illegitimate activity that falls outside your parameters will not be shown.

Filtering Logs in Linux

Using `last` or `lastlog` without any arguments can provide too much information. Here are some ways to customize information:

last -x   Displays only entries about system shutdown and restart.

last -x reboot   Shows every system restart.

last -x shutdown   Shows every system shutdown.

last -a   Places all host information in the last column of the readout.

last -d   Shows all remote logins.

last -n *number*   Allows you to control how many lines `last` will display. For example, `last -n 2` shows only the last two most current entries.

You can combine commands. For example, `last -ad` displays the hostname and IP number of all non-local logins. It also automatically translates IP numbers back into DNS names, if possible. See Figure 14.6.

FIGURE 14.6   Using the `last -ad` command

```
[root@student10 james]# last -ad
user1     pts/0        Tue Mar 21 12:49   still  logged in    student1.classroom1.com
user2     pts/1        Mon Mar 20 19:17 - 19:20  (00:02)      student3.classroom1.com
ftp       pts/0        Mon Mar 20 18:05 - 20:21  (02:16)      s128-pm3a.ibm.com
root                   Mon Mar 20 18:04   still  logged in
james     pts/0        Mon Mar 20 17:46 - 18:04  (00:17)      334.aol.com
jamey     pts/0        Mon Mar 20 14:23 - 14:47  (00:23)      hacker1.hackers.com
jacob     pts/0        Mon Mar 20 14:12 - 14:21  (00:09)      system3.nsa.gov
joel      pts/1        Mon Mar 20 12:51 - 12:56  (00:05)      student15.classroom1.com
sandi     pts/1        Mon Mar 20 12:45 - 12:47  (00:02)      student13.classroom1.com
reboot                 Tue Mar 14 15:20          (2+03:19)    2.2.12-20
root                   Tue Mar 14 15:10 - down   (00:00)
reboot                 Tue Mar 14 15:05          (00:05)      2.2.12-20
ftp                    Thu Mar 16 12:39 - 12:39  (00:00)      student5.classroom1.com
serena                 Thu Mar 16 11:27 - 11:33  (00:05)      student10.nonetjames
james     pts/0        Fri Mar 10 09:42 - 09:50  (00:08)      english24.ucr.edu
davis     pts/1        Thu Mar  9 11:52 - 14:26  (02:33)      208.205.77.239
julie     pts/0        Thu Mar  9 11:44 - 13:57  (02:13)      208.205.77.239
paula                  Thu Mar  9 10:34 - 10:40  (00:05)      208.205.77.239
james     pts/3        Fri Mar  3 17:17 - crash  (00:03)      208.205.77.251
james                  Fri Mar  3 17:09 - crash  (00:10)      208.205.77.251
james     pts/2        Fri Mar  3 17:07 - crash  (00:12)      208.205.77.251
james     pts/1        Fri Mar  3 16:44 - crash  (00:35)      208.205.77.251
james                  Fri Mar  3 16:32 - down   (00:10)      208.205.77.251
root                   Fri Mar  3 16:17 - down   (00:25)
wtmp begins Wed Mar  1 12:22:21 2000
```

You can combine `last` commands with `grep` to further narrow searches. For example, `last -x | grep Tue | grep ftp` lists only events that occurred on Tuesday and that involve the use of FTP.

lastlog

The `lastlog` command reads the `/var/log/lastlog` file. `lastlog` accepts several arguments; here are the most pertinent examples:

`lastlog -t number_of_days` Allows you to specify the number of days that will be reported. For example, `lastlog -t 2` will print the logins over the last two days.

`lastlog -u login-name` Allows you to specify individual usernames to see when users last logged on.

> **NOTE** With `lastlog`, the -t argument overrides -u.

Using *lastb*

The `lastb` command reads the `/var/log/btmp` file. Normally, this file does not exist. To create it, issue the following command:

```
host# touch /var/log/btmp
```

Once you have created this file, `syslogd` will enter all failed logins to this file. `lastb` allows the same options as the `last` command.

Additional Logging Files and Commands

You can gain information about various services by reading the `/var/log/messages` file using the following command:

```
host# cat /var/log/messages | grep servicename
```

You can substitute Telnet, FTP, sendmail, and other services for *servicename*. You can also use `head` to sift through the first 10 entries in the messages file, and use `tail` to learn about the last 10 entries. You should also check the `/var/log/secure` file. The following command reads the file for any telnet connections:

```
host# cat /var/log/secure | grep telnet
```

You can substitute different terms, such as FTP, usernames (except root), `rlogin`, and `finger`.

Using the *tail* Command

The `tail` command allows you to read the last 10 lines of a particular text file (e.g., /var/log/messages). The `tail -f` command continually reads a particular file and reports additions made to it. Consider using this command as a way to read files such as /var/log/messages so that you can see the additions made by the logging daemon in real time.

> **TIP** You are not limited to using the `last`, `lastb`, `lastlog`, and `tail` commands. You can, for example, obtain log analysis applications from companies such as WebTrends (www.webtrends.com) and Webalizer (www.webalizer.org).

Securing Log Files

You have already learned how hackers target auditing logs. As an auditor, you are in a position to suggest ways to secure auditing logs. Possible recommendations include:

Replicating logs to a CD-recordable (CD-R) drive Many companies prefer storing log files onto a *write-once, read-many (WORM)* format, such as a CD-R device. This strategy is very effective; because the system stores the files, they cannot be altered. Traditionally, log files have been stored to a tape drive. Although this approach is also an option, it is easier to erase or alter information stored on tape.

Scheduling hard-copy backups Printing out all logs onto hard copy would waste an enormous amount of time, space, and paper. However, it is often useful to print out log information from critical servers to conduct spot checks on the information obtained by the log files. Automatic printout of log files at certain times can also help remind systems administrators and security managers that it is time to review log files. This activity should not stand by itself. The use of hard copies is only a supplement to the other techniques mentioned in this section.

Logging to remote systems is also a very effective strategy, as we'll see next.

Remote Logging

You have already learned that one auditing solution is to enable remote logging for systems. Remote logging is important, because it helps ensure that accurate log files still exist in case of a system compromise.

Remote Linux Logging

The Linux `syslogd` has the ability to log to remote systems. As with any client/server relationship, it is necessary to configure at least one Linux system to send logs and another system to receive them. Here are the general steps you would take to first send log-file entries to a remote system and then configure a remote system to accept these entries:

Sending log file entries to a remote system Open the /etc/syslog.conf file and enter a line to a remote system, for example: *.* @blake.romantics.com. This line has all traffic from your system logged to the blake.romantics.com system. You would, of course, substitute the name of a remote Linux system. You can, of course, be more selective; you can substitute *.emerg for *.*, if you want. Once you enter this value, be sure you use the /etc/rc.d/init.d/syslog restart command to have syslogd reread its configuration file.

Receiving log file entries from a remote system By default, Linux systems are not configured to receive logging entries from remote systems. Open the /etc/rc.d/init.d/syslog file using a text editor and scroll down to the enter start() section. Alter the daemon syslogd entry so that it has the -r and -h entries in addition to the -m 0 entry, as follows: daemon syslogd -r -h -m 0. The -r entry tells syslogd to listen for remote logging daemons. The -h option enables this logging daemon to forward these messages to other systems, should this forwarding be required.

After you make a change to syslogd, do not forget to restart it so that it reads the changes that you have just made.

> **Note:** One of the drawbacks of the above solution is that the logging daemon does not encrypt the logging traffic as it is sent between systems. One way to solve this problem is to enable IPsec between systems.

Remote Windows 2000 Logging

For remote logging in Windows 2000, using an operating system add-on such as Event Log Manager from Sunbelt Software (www.sunbeltsoftware.com) is an option. This type of application allows you to use one system to monitor Windows NT/2000 system log entries (i.e., the log entries found in Event Viewer) from multiple systems.

Operating System Add-ons for Logging Purposes

You need not rely on native logging utilities. You can use operating system add-ons such as Enterprise Reporting Server or WebTrends Firewall Reporting Center. Learn more about such products at www.webtrends.com. These applications are helpful, because they provide the following services:

- The ability to centralize log-file information
- Encrypted transfer of log-file information between systems
- One interface to read log files from multiple operating systems (e.g., Windows Internet Security and Acceleration Server [ISA] 2000 and Check Point FireWall-1).

Customizing Log-File Size

It is common for log files to grow rather large and affect system performance. If a system becomes unstable or you receive a report that disk space is low, consider checking the log files to learn how large they have become. In Windows 2000 systems, edit the log-file settings in Event Viewer so that the settings cannot grow too large. You can do this inside Event Viewer by right-clicking any of the individual log files (e.g., the Security log) you want to configure. You can then alter the log size or choose to overwrite events older than a certain number of days.

In Linux systems, /usr/sbin/logrotate, the logrotate application, is responsible for archiving old log files and creating new ones. logrotate is run automatically by the cron daemon, which can be used to schedule any number of applications or daemons. The process of archiving and creating new archive files is called *rotating*. The /etc/logrotate.conf file controls how often files are rotated. You can also edit this file so that log files are rotated. Here is an example of the /etc/logrote.conf file:

```
# rotate log files weekly
weekly
# keep 4 weeks worth of backlogs
rotate 10
# send errors to root
errors root
# create new (empty) log files after rotating old ones
create
# uncomment this if you want your log files compressed
compress
```

In this example, log files are rotated weekly, and 10 weeks' worth of log files will be stored locally. You could, if you want, change /etc/logrotate.conf to rotate logs daily, or even hourly. Error messages will be sent to the root account. Such messages often report that a particular file cannot be found when rotating logs. The create command tells the logrotate daemon to create new files after old ones have been archived. The compress command tells logrotate to use gzip to compress the log files. logrotate is able to compress the log file automatically because it was written to use gzip automatically. You do not have to specify anything else.

It is, of course, possible to modify existing entries, as well create your own entries. Creating your own entries is often necessary if you install a new daemon or application. If, for example, you install a new daemon to log port scans, you could add an entry to /etc/logrotate.conf so that the port-scanning-application log files are rotated and compressed daily.

Third-Party Logging

It is possible to use a third party to create and manage your log files. Such third parties are called *managed security providers*. Companies such as Symantec (www.symantec.com) specialize in providing managed security services that monitor and log sites to determine incursions, denial-of-service attacks, and any suspicious activity.

The Benefits of Managed Security Providers

Using managed security providers provides the following benefits:

More logging redundancy Not only will you be able to log connections, but your managed security provider will be doing so as well.

Trend analysis For a price, the managed security provider can read through your log files and inform you about any anomalous activity.

A quick, cost-effective start If you need to quickly improve your ability to log, detect, and respond to intrusions, a managed security provider can be your best choice. In all cases, installing an IDS, improving logging, and maintaining a firewall are all activities that take a great deal of time and training. Once you factor in the costs of training your own people and the time it takes to install and configure all of the software, choosing a managed security provider might provide the most cost-effective solution as well.

If you decide to use a managed security provider, be sure that you make available a single *point of contact* to the provider. A point of contact is a person or group who manages information that comes from and goes to the provider. The point of contact ensures that the provider contacts the right person in case of an emergency or a question. The point of contact also helps ensure that everyone is properly informed about the activities of the managed security provider.

Choosing the Right Provider

Most of the time, the teams organized by the managed security provider consist of talented, dedicated people. However, make sure that you have conducted research into the nature of the company. Use a provider that is financially stable and that has experience analyzing logs and providing security services. Also, make sure that the company you choose specializes in networks similar to your own. If, for example, your network is primarily Windows based, a provider that specializes in Solaris networks might not be your best choice.

> **NOTE** One of the more controversial topics relating to managed security providers is the use of "reformed" hackers. Some managed security providers refuse to hire anyone who has a record of hacking into systems. When contracting with a firm, ask about its policy concerning the background of the employees it hires.

Finally, be sure that you carefully coordinate your efforts with the managed security provider. The services offered by managed security providers can be quite expensive, if not managed properly. Use such providers only when you have specific demands.

Partial Implementation

You do not necessarily need to use a managed security firm to manage your entire network. For example, you might want the firm to provide support to only one part of your network. Or you might not need any help configuring and maintaining your firewall, but you could have problems maintaining adequate logging and intrusion detection in one particular high-priority subnet. In such cases, using a managed security firm can help you quickly solve your problem. After some time, you can then reevaluate your use of the firm. You may decide to continue using it in the same way, expand its use, or begin using your own team. Generally, as long as you can justify the use of an outside team and efficiently process the information that it provides you, consider using the managed security team. Consider expanding its use only if you are sure that the team can increase security in a cost-effective manner. If you find that the resources being protected by this team are no longer of primary importance, then consider dropping the managed security team or having them guard different resources.

EXERCISE 14.1

Auditing Boot and Login Entries in Windows 2000

In this exercise, you will study failed login attempts in Windows 2000.

1. Log on as Administrator.

2. Open the Local Security Policy snap-in.

3. Map to Local Policies ➤ Audit Policy, and configure each event as follows:

   - Audit Account Logon Events: Success, Failure
   - Audit Account Management: Success, Failure
   - Audit Logon Events: Success, Failure
   - Audit Policy Change: Success, Failure
   - Audit Privilege Use: Failure
   - Audit System Events: Failure

EXERCISE 14.1 *(continued)*

4. Log out of the system.
5. Fail login as Administrator several times.
6. Log back in as Administrator.
7. Open Event Viewer.
8. In Event Viewer, view the Security Log window.
9. Search for the correct number that records the failed login attempt (see the earlier list of items to audit, if you need guidance).
10. Log out, and then log back in as Administrator and view Event Viewer.
11. Clear the Security and System logs.
12. Now, restart Windows 2000 and log back on as Administrator.
13. Open Event Viewer and view the system logs.
14. Press the power button on your machine for more than five seconds. Windows 2000 will shut down abruptly.
15. Open Event Viewer and find the 6008 event.

Note: Consider the effect that auditing has on operating systems. What events would you choose to audit?

EXERCISE 14.2

Enabling Directory Auditing in Windows 2000

In this exercise, you will convert your Windows 2000 server's hard drive to use NTFS (if necessary). You will then enable file and directory auditing for various activities conducted by the Everyone group, including change of permissions, adding and deleting files, adding new services, and so forth.

1. Using Windows Explorer, verify that the system is using NTFS. If it is not using NTFS, open a command prompt and enter the following command:

   ```
   convert c: /fs:ntfs
   ```

EXERCISE 14.2 (continued)

2. You will receive a message informing you that the system can convert the drive only after restarting the system.

3. Enter Y to indicate that you understand the message.

4. Shut down and restart your system. As the system restarts, you should see the drive being converted into NTFS format. This conversion might take some time, especially because the computer will restart to finish the task.

5. After you have logged back on, open Windows Explorer.

6. Using Windows Explorer, create a directory named **Accounts**.

7. Right-click the Accounts directory and share it.

8. Now, create a new document named **private.txt** in the Accounts directory.

9. Right-click the Accounts directory and select Properties.

10. Click the Security tab, and then click the Advanced button. Select the Auditing tab.

11. Click the Add button, and then add the Everyone group.

12. You will see a list of auditing options. For this exercise, audit all successful and failed attempts for all categories. In a real-world situation, you would not audit all events; such volume can affect system performance. You would, for example, choose only Change and Delete permissions.

13. Make sure that in the Apply Onto field, the option This Folder, Subfolder And Files is selected. Enabling this setting ensures that all files and subdirectories are audited.

14. Repeat this process for the C:\InetPub and C:\Winnt directories.

    Note: These folders contain sensitive system files. The C:\Winnt\system32\config directory, for example, contains the files for the Windows 2000 Registry.

15. Open Event Viewer.

16. From the Log menu, select Security Log.

EXERCISE 14.2 (continued)

17. Using Windows Explorer, click any of the directories you selected for auditing.

18. Access the `private.txt` file. Add some content, save it, and exit the document.

19. After you have finished adding content to `private.txt`, access Windows Explorer and click any non-audited directory.

20. Now, view the Event Viewer Security log. You should see several events.

    Note: If you do not see the new entries, press F5 to refresh the screen.

21. Double-click the first entry, and then view each entry to see how Windows 2000 has been able to log each of the events you generated.

22. Clear the Security log.

23. View the Security log again. You should see one set of entries informing you that the Security log was reset.

24. Now, invoke a more reasonable auditing policy. Leave all the settings the same for all failed attempts. However, audit only successful Write, Delete, and Change permissions.

25. Log back in as Administrator, and then use Event Viewer to audit your activity. Now, think about what would happen if a hacker were able to erase these logs. Consider some of the solutions listed earlier.

26. Optional: Establish NTFS permissions on the directories so that only administrators can read them. Log out as Administrator, and then log back in as a standard user. Attempt to view the files and folders for which you have set permissions and auditing.

EXERCISE 14.3

Using Linux Log-Auditing Tools

In this exercise, you will use the `last`, `lastb`, and `lastlog` tools to audit a system.

EXERCISE 14.3 *(continued)*

1. Boot into Linux as root and use `last` without any arguments.

2. Now, use `last` with the appropriate arguments to display only entries on system shutdown and restart.

3. Use `last` to show only restarts and shutdowns.

4. Use `last` so that you see only remote logins, and where the host information is given in the last column.

   Note: You might have to use a remote system to log on to your system in order to obtain meaningful results.

5. Now, use `lastlog` to discover the accounts that have logged on.

6. The following steps will show you how to use the `lastb` command. First, issue the `lastb` command.

7. If you are using a newly installed Linux system, you should receive an error message that the necessary file cannot be found. Now, issue the following command:

   touch/var/log/btmp

8. Once you have created the touch/var/log/btmp file, create a new user named **linuxuser** using the useradd command:

   ```
   host# useradd linuxuser
   Make sure to give this user a password (use any
       password you like):
   host# passwd linuxuser
   Changing password for user linuxuser
   New UNIX password:
   Retype new UNIX password:
   ```

9. Now, log out as root, and then intentionally fail login as root, as linuxuser, and as a user that is not defined.

10. Issue the `lastb` command without any arguments. You should see a readout of failed login attempts.

Summary

In this chapter, you learned the importance of analyzing firewall, router, server, and IDS log files when performing a security audit. You learned how to create a baseline that establishes standard activity for your system, and you learned how to identify suspicious activity in your logs. Information such as this can help you establish an accurate security baseline.

Now that you have completed this chapter, you should be able to:

- Establish a baseline for your users' activities.
- Conduct log analysis.
- Filter events found in Windows 2000 and Linux systems.
- Establish auditing for logins, system restarts, and specific resource use.

In the next chapter, you will learn more about how to generate an auditing report and suggest changes designed to improve the security of your network.

Exam Essentials

Understand the importance of creating a baseline of user activity. There is no universal standard for "normal" network activity. However, it is vital for you to take the time to determine what is normative activity for your particular network. Study login patterns and make sure that you can identify anomalous activity.

Be able to identify anomalous activity. Examples of anomalous activity, in regard to the CIW Security Professional exam, include:

- Incomplete or garbled log-file entries
- Patterns of login and user-rights failures
- Failed login daemons
- System and service or daemon restarts
- Missing log files

Know the impact logging can have on a system. Log files on busy systems can easily fill up an entire partition. Additionally, the activity of writing log files to the hard drive can consume valuable CPU cycles. Achieve a balance between system performance and the information that you gain. Although it is possible to filter out unwanted information, carefully customize your systems so that they provide only necessary information in your log files.

Understand Windows 2000 and Linux logging subsystems. The Windows 2000 and Linux logging subsystems are examples of vital logging daemons, and the CIW Security Professional exam assumes that you understand common log file locations. Make sure, for example, that you know how to customize Windows 2000 Event Viewer, and that you know how to customize the /etc/syslog.conf and /etc/logrotate files in Linux.

Be able to filter log files and identify key incidents in Windows 2000 and Linux. Be able to identify when Windows 2000 and Linux systems have been shut down unexpectedly. Also, it is important that you know how to use Windows 2000 Event Viewer and commands such as last, lastb, and lastlog to filter events.

Know how to learn system uptime and determine patch levels. From the use of the uptime command in Linux to the Winver utility in Windows 2000, be able to quickly determine the state of your system. It is also important for you to explain the importance of verifying that you have updated your systems' applications and services to the latest, stable versions.

Be able to secure log files. Identify key ways to secure log files, including the use of CD-R drives, the creation of hard-copy backups, and remote logging. You will find that the use of CD-R drives and remote logging are the most effective methods, although using hard copies will help remind you to analyze the log files that you have kept.

Understand the benefits of using third parties to manage logging. Making sure that systems properly log events is difficult enough. Actually analyzing the log files is sometimes impossible. Be able to identify situations where using a third-party firm might help you gather and analyze traffic. Also, be able to explain why it is important to provide a single point of contact for the managed security firm.

Key Terms

Before you take the exam, be certain you are familiar with the following terms:

anomalies	managed security providers
baseline	point of contact
facility/priority pair	suspicious activity
kernel	write-once, read-many (WORM)

Review Questions

1. Which of the following is a common occurrence when auditing is enabled on a busy system resource?

    A. The system will slow down.

    B. The log daemon will issue an alert.

    C. The resource will crash.

    D. The log daemon will crash.

2. Which of the following can be used to read the /var/log/wtmp file?

    A. /usr/sbin/wtmpread

    B. /bin/cat

    C. /usr/bin/last

    D. /bin/wtmpread

3. Which of the following can be used in Linux to read the last 10 lines of the /var/log/messages file?

    A. tail

    B. last

    C. lastlog

    D. logread

4. What snap-in or application would you use to enable auditing on a folder in a stand-alone Windows 2000 server?

    A. The Internet Services Manager snap-in

    B. Windows Explorer

    C. The Computer Management snap-in

    D. Control Panel

5. Megan has been the victim of several attacks that have resulted in total compromise of her servers. She is certain that, among other measures, improving her logging security will help her detect future incidents more easily. Which of the following options is the most effective strategy for reducing the likelihood that log files will be altered?

   A. Enable remote logging to a central logging server's hard drive.

   B. Configure her logging daemon to log to a CD-RW drive.

   C. Configure her logging daemon to log to a CD-R drive.

   D. Enable the server to audit the logging daemon.

6. What daemon logs activity in Linux and most other Unix systems?

   A. syslogd

   B. rotate

   C. systemlogd

   D. logd

7. Serena wants to enable auditing on a Windows 2000 Server partition that is formatted with FAT32. She wants to ensure that data is protected on this partition, as well. Which of the following native commands should she use?

   A. convert

   B. ntfs

   C. format

   D. audfs

8. What is the meaning of the -n argument to last or lastlog?

   A. It places all host information in the last column of the readout.

   B. It allows you to control how many lines last will display.

   C. It displays only entries about system shutdown and restart.

   D. It shows all remote logins.

9. How should security managers begin the log analysis process?

   A. By requiring password aging

   B. By issuing all new passwords to users

   C. By developing a baseline

   D. By tracing usage patterns

10. In the Windows NT/2000 Event Viewer, what does Event Number 6007 mean?

    A. Unsuccessful logon

    B. Clean shutdown event

    C. Improper shutdown request due to inadequate permissions

    D. Operating system number, build number, service pack, and processor information

11. How can you determine what Windows 2000 service pack is installed on your system?

    A. By using the `uptimei.exe` utility

    B. By using the Start utility

    C. By using the Winver utility

    D. By using the System applet

12. Joseph wants to learn more about his network perimeter. Which logs should he first review?

    A. Firewall logs

    B. Server logs

    C. IDS application logs

    D. Remote system logs

13. On Linux systems, what file do you configure to modify `syslogd` behavior?

    A. /etc/syslog.conf

    B. /etc/syslogd.conf

    C. /etc/log.conf

    D. /etc/dlog.conf

14. Which snap-in allows you to activate or deactivate systemwide logging on a Windows 2000 system acting as a stand-alone server?

    A. The Local Security Policy snap-in

    B. The Services snap-in

    C. The Audit snap-in

    D. The Internet Services Manager snap-in

15. Which of the following is a valid log type found in Event Viewer in a Windows 2000 Server that has only the DNS service installed?

    A. Server

    B. IIS

    C. System

    D. Service

16. Why is it important in security to search for system restarts in a Linux or Windows 2000 server?

    A. Because they are evidence of a system misconfiguration.

    B. Because many Trojans and worms restart systems.

    C. Because system restarts are always part of a buffer overflow attack.

    D. Because logging failure often restarts systems.

17. You have been asked to obtain the log files for your company's FTP server. This server is a Windows 2000 Server, running IIS 5.0, and stores its log files on the C drive. Where would you obtain the most recent log file, assuming default log file locations?

A. From the C:\winnt\LogFiles\MSFTPSCV1\ directory

B. From the C:\inetpub\system\LogFiles\ftp\MSFTPSCV1\ directory

C. From the C:\winnt\LogFiles\MSFTPSCV1\ directory

D. From the C:\winnt\system32\LogFiles\MSFTPSCV1\ directory

18. Mary has noticed that the user account for the company president has been active several nights in a row between midnight and 3:00 A.M. She has become suspicious of this traffic. Which of the following has had the largest role in enabling her to become suspicious of this traffic?

    A. The logging daemon

    B. An IDS application

    C. Auditing

    D. A network baseline

19. You have enabled remote logging on all servers, which reside across three networks. The central logging server is stored on Network A. The other two networks are connected via a 56K connection. Which of these concerns should you first address?

    A. Whether or not the traffic is encrypted

    B. Whether or not the traffic will swamp the connection

    C. Whether or not the traffic will be properly logged by the central server

    D. Whether or not the log files will be read and analyzed

20. What must you do before using the `lastb` command on many Linux servers?

    A. Enable the program to run suid root.

    B. Create a file named /etc/lastb/btmp.

    C. Enable the program to run as a non-root user.

    D. Create a file named /var/log/btmp.

Answers to Review Questions

1. **A.** System slowdown can occur due to heavy auditing. The logging daemon will probably not issue an alert that the resource is too busy. Auditing will likely not cause the logging daemon to crash, unless other problems exist. Although a log daemon can crash due to overwork, such crashes are less common than simple system slowdown.

2. **C.** You must use the `/usr/bin/last` application to read the `/var/log/wtmp` file. Although you can use `cat` to read various text files, `/var/log/wtmp` does not format information in ASCII format, so `cat` cannot read it. There is no such command as the `wtmpread` command.

3. **A.** The `tail` command can be used to read the last 10 lines of a file. The `last` command does not read the `/var/log/messages` file, nor does `lastlog`. The `logread` command is not a standard Linux command.

4. **B.** Windows Explorer is used to establish auditing. The Internet Services Manager snap-in is used to manage the IIS web, FTP, and news servers. The Computer Management snap-in allows you to do many things (manage devices, obtain system information, manage users, and access Event Viewer). However, it does not allow you to enable auditing on a server resource. Control Panel enables you to adjust various Registry settings, including those for the network, Open Database Connectivity (ODBC), and other system elements.

5. **C.** Although logging to a central remote server's hard drive duplicates logging and thus makes it more secure, it is possible for a malicious user to alter the logs on this remote system. Logging to a CD-R drive ensures that information will not be erased. Logging to a CD-RW drive is also a good idea, and might save money, but because it is possible to alter or erase files on a CD-RW drive, it is not as secure an option. Auditing the logging daemon is helpful, but this setting can be altered by a malicious user.

6. **A.** The `syslogd` daemon is the standard daemon for most Unix systems. Unix systems often use `crond` to help rotate logs, but `rotate` does not log activity. Rather, it rotates old log files and creates new ones. No standard daemons named `systemlogd` or `logd` exist.

7. **A.** Windows 2000 Server cannot audit events unless NTFS is enabled on a partition. If your system uses a FAT32 drive, it must be converted to use NTFS using either the `convert` command or the Disk Management portion of the Computer Management snap-in. The `format` command would format the partition in NTFS, but all data would be lost. Windows 2000 Server does not have a command named `ntfs` or `audfs`.

8. **B.** The `-n` option allows you to control how many lines `last` will display. It does not place information in columns, nor does it display only system shutdown and restart entries or remote logins.

9. **C.** If you want to accurately determine the type of activity on your network, you first need to create a baseline of user activity. Doing so will help you identify anomalies in user behavior more easily.

10. **C.** An improper shutdown event is denoted by number 6007. You should check for such events, because they can help identify whether physical attacks have occurred. For example, if the server has been removed from its uninterruptible power supply (UPS) and shut down and restarted, this event will appear, as long as the UPS is configured correctly.

11. **C.** The Winver utility will tell you which service pack is installed on your Windows system. There is no System applet in a standard Windows 2000 Server system, and the `uptimei.exe` utility, available from Microsoft, does not provide service pack information. The Start utility by itself cannot provide service pack information.

12. **A.** Although consulting server, IDS application, and remote system logs can all indirectly help you determine the security of your network's perimeter, firewall logs are the most direct way to do so. This is because a firewall is used to create a perimeter between one network and the other.

13. **A.** The `/etc/syslog.conf` file contains all information for configuring the `syslogd` daemon. It is not named `/etc/syslogd`, and neither the `/etc/log.conf` nor the `/etc/dlog.conf` file is used as a standard, systemwide logging daemon configuration file. By editing `/etc/syslog.conf`, you can configure your system to maintain extremely detailed system logs, or to log only certain traffic for certain daemons.

14. **B.** The Services snap-in (along with the Component Services and Computer Management snap-ins) allows you to stop and start computer services, including the System Notification Event Manager). The Local Security Policy snap-in lets you configure certain auditing features but does not activate or deactivate logging. There is no Audit snap-in, and the Internet Services Manager does not allow you to configure system-wide auditing.

15. **C.** Windows 2000 has three default log types: Application, Security, and System. If you install additional services, it is possible for Event Viewer to contain additional log types.

16. **B.** It is common practice in Windows 2000 systems (and even in Linux systems) to have a worm reboot the system in order to install a particular Trojan or module meant to defeat security. Although improper system configuration can lead to a system restart, this issue is not a security issue, but one that will be addressed by IT workers. While a buffer overflow can lead to a system restart, not all buffer overflows do so. It would be rare for a logging failure to restart a system.

17. **D.** By default, the IIS FTP server stores its files in the `C:\winnt\system32\LogFiles\MSFTPSCV1\` directory. You can, of course, change this location, if you want.

18. **D.** A network baseline has allowed Mary to notice the change in login behavior. The only way to sense an unusual time is to first identify what is "usual" for your network. Although logging daemons, IDS applications, and auditing all can help, it is the network baseline that has truly enabled Mary to notice the anomaly.

19. **B.** Your immediate concern is whether or not your logging activities are going to affect the daily business operations of your company. If logging traffic causes an unacceptable slowdown, you will have to alter your plans. The next priority will be to encrypt login traffic so that no one will obtain information about your network. Proper logging of traffic should be assumed; you have already configured the systems to send traffic to the central server. You should not have to worry whether or not this setup is working. Ensuring that log files are read and analyzed is important; however, it is not an immediate priority in this case.

20. **D.** The `lastb` command on many Linux servers is configured to read the `/var/log/btmp` file. The `lastb` command will not work properly if this file does not exist. It is not necessary to use suid permissions on the `lastb` file.

Chapter 15

Recommending Solutions and Generating Reports

THE CIW EXAM OBJECTIVE GROUPS COVERED IN THIS CHAPTER:

- ✓ Identify ways to improve security policy compliance and create an assessment report.
- ✓ Install operating system add-ons, including but not limited to: personal firewalls, native auditing, and SSH.

A *network assessment* involves conducting a scan and recommending solutions to problems that you have discovered. It also involves generating a report. The CIW Security Professional exam requires knowledge of each of these concepts. You have already learned about conducting scans using various types of software, including port scanners and vulnerability scanners. In this chapter, you will learn about the specific recommendations you might have to make, as well as the technologies referred to in the exam. You will also learn about the importance of generating a report that addresses the proper audience. First, let's discuss some of the solutions covered in the CIW Security Professional exam.

Recommending Solutions

When you audit hosts, you will have to offer diverse solutions because each host will function according to unique business demands. Examples of auditing solutions include the following:

Improve perimeter security. Take steps to ensure that the network firewalls and routers are properly updated and configured to suit the business they are protecting.

Enhance intrusion detection. It is possible, for example, to enable promiscuous-mode detection to help learn more about what end users are listening to on your network.

Make operating system changes. You can place operating system add-ons, such as personal firewalls and encryption services, onto servers; clean up after poor installation practices; and implement native auditing.

Install compliance-monitoring software. If at all possible, use software to generate reports on systems that are not in compliance with your security policy.

Replace and update services. For example, you can replace Telnet with the SSH service, which can use public-key encryption to secure login sessions.

Improving Perimeter Security

When using firewalls, take the following steps:

Ensure that packet filter and firewall rules are appropriate and useful. Consider the firewall's default stance, and then make sure that all of the rules are appropriate.

Scan the demilitarized zone (DMZ) for problem hosts. An attacker from the outside will focus on servers that are in the DMZ, so concentrate your efforts in this area.

Restrict physical access to the firewall. Restricting access includes not only making sure the firewall is behind a locked door, but also taking measures to ensure that no one can simply walk up to the firewall and make changes to it. One way to do this is to remove the keyboard from the firewall whenever it is not needed.

As far as routers are concerned, consider the following strategies when taking the CIW Security Professional exam:

- Restrict physical access to the router.

- Obtain the latest operating system updates (for Windows NT/2000 systems acting as multihomed routers, as well as for dedicated router operating systems, such as Cisco IOS).

- Ensure that the router is not susceptible to forwarding denial-of-service attacks.

- Ensure that the router is not an unwitting partner in denial-of-service attacks.

Table 15.1 provides specific instructions on how to ensure that the latter two objectives are met.

TABLE 15.1 Securing Routers from Distributed Denial-of-Service Attacks

Procedure	Description
Enable effective ingress (incoming) and egress (outgoing) filtering	Configure your router to route outgoing packets only if they have valid internal IP addresses. Your routers should drop any outgoing packet that does not have a valid internal IP address. This action helps prevent your network from being the source of spoofed IP packets. Then, configure your routers to drop all packets stemming from addresses in Table 15.2. See Internet Draft ietf-grip-isp-07 (Security Expectations for Internet Service Providers) for more information.
Disable broadcast addresses	Many denial-of-service attacks, including the Smurf attack, work best if the hacker can take advantage of routers configured to conduct directed IP broadcasts. The easiest way to determine if a router is configured to respond to these addresses is to ping the network address (e.g., 192.168.4.0) or the network broadcast address (e.g. 192.168.4.255).

Table 15.2 describes some of the *egress and ingress filtering* addresses to consider when reviewing your routers.

TABLE 15.2 IP Addresses to Consider when Egress and Ingress Filtering

Category	Address
Historical low-end broadcast	0.0.0.0/8
Limited broadcast	255.255.255.255/32
RFC 1918 private network	10.0.0.0/8
RFC 1918 private network	172.16.0.0/12
RFC 1918 private network	192.168.0.0/16
The loopback address	127.0.0.0/8

TABLE 15.2 IP Addresses to Consider when Egress and Ingress Filtering *(continued)*

Category	Address
Link local networks	169.254.0.0/16
Class D addresses	224.0.0.0/4
Class E reserved addresses	240.0.0.0/5
Unallocated addresses	248.0.0.0/5

As you configure your routers, make sure that you control the historical low-end broadcast so that your routers cannot be used by distributed denial-of-service applications. For example, the Smurf attack, discussed in Chapter 3, can take advantage of low-end broadcasts. For more information, consult www.sans.org/dosstep/index.htm.

Enhancing Intrusion Detection

You might need to update the rules in your intrusion-detection system (IDS) application. Consider adding a rule, if necessary. For example, variants of old root kits and illicit servers are constantly being created. NetBus and NetBus 2.0 are exploits. However, it is possible for a talented hacker to come up with a new illicit server that your IDS application will not recognize. In such a case, you will have to research this new exploit and reconfigure your IDS application to identify its use. Unless you reconfigure rules to search for variants of old exploits, as well as new exploits, your IDS will never inform you about the attacks being waged on your network. In some cases, however, you might not have to add a rule to make sure that your IDS listens for the proper traffic; modifying existing rules could be an option, as well. However, if you modify an existing rule, you may end up modifying your IDS so that it finds a new attack but no longer finds older attacks that still can be waged on your network.

As an auditor, you will also have to determine if newly installed systems need to be protected by a host-based IDS application. Factors to help you determine this include:

The server's importance to the business   If the new server is vital to the daily operations of the business, then placing an agent on it should be a priority.

The server's exposure to public networks   Yes, it is possible to install an IDS application on a server that is exposed to the Internet. It is also a good idea to do this if you want to remain informed about all attacks waged against the server.

The server's attack history   It is wise to keep a written *attack history* for all server and network resources. This history should contain the time and date of the attack, as well as information on how the attack was waged. This history can help explain attack patterns. For example, it can help you learn if attacks have occurred internally, or from outside, which can help you place IDS applications in key places, as well as reconfigure firewalls.

You can also install additional applications to help you detect the illicit use of network applications, such as packet sniffers.

Detecting an NIC in Promiscuous Mode

In the proper hands, a packet sniffer is useful when analyzing the network. However, you do not want unauthorized employees to use one to eavesdrop on other employees. One way to ensure that employees are not doing this is to scan systems for NICs that have been placed in promiscuous mode. Programs such as AntiSniff and PromiScan use the following three tactics for *promiscuous-mode detection*:

- They detect changes in the NIC's electrical field that indicate promiscuous mode.

- They send out various packet types (ARP requests, ICMP packets, DNS queries, TCP SYN floods, and so forth). If returning packets from a particular host wait an unusual amount of time to return without any evidence that the packet has been read by the host, the program deduces that the host's NIC is probably in promiscuous mode.

- They wrap a false ICMP request into an invalid Ethernet header. All systems, except a host in promiscuous mode, will reject the header. Any host returning the false ICMP request is probably in promiscuous mode.

Regardless of specific tactics, all promiscuous-mode scanners work through deduction. In other words, they collect packets returned by remote servers and then analyze these packets. At some point, these applications must stop collecting and draw a conclusion about the information that they have gathered. Because these programs rely on limited data to draw a conclusion, false positives often result. Ways to reduce false positives include repeating a scan and using multiple systems to scan for promiscuous-mode activity. Another strategy for reducing false positives is to use a high-quality NIC recommended by the developer of the promiscuous-mode scanning software.

For more information about detecting an NIC in promiscuous mode, consult the following websites:

AntiSniff (www.securitysoftwaretech.com/antisniff)   As of this writing, AntiSniff binaries are available only for Windows NT, Linux, FreeBSD, and Solaris systems.

PromiScan (www.securityfriday.com)   This application will work on Windows 2000 Server and Professional systems.

> **NOTE**   Many enterprise-grade network vulnerability scanners have built-in promiscuous-mode scanners.

Now that you have a clearer idea of how to audit and augment existing intrusion-detection efforts, let's take a look at some of the operating system changes you need to know for the CIW Security Professional exam.

Operating System Changes

The most common changes to operating systems include:

Implementing native auditing   Auditing can be established at various levels. For example, if you enable auditing on a Windows Primary Domain Controller (PDC), the policies will apply to the entire Windows domain. Auditing can also occur at the operating system level. For example, you can audit for failed logins and system shutdowns, as you did in Chapter 14. You can also enable auditing at the resource level, which includes files and directories.

Fixing system bugs   Your job as an auditor is to find system bugs and then find ways to fix them. Operating system hotfixes and service packs are the primary means for fixing system bugs.

Changing old and default configuration settings   One of the recurring tasks of an auditor is removing unused accounts of former employees. Another is making sure that all employees are using strong passwords (e.g., passwords that have at least six characters, do not resemble dictionary words, and use special characters).

Installing personal-firewall software on workstations Personal-firewall software has become rather common for cable and Digital Subscriber Line (DSL) subscribers. It is also a good idea to recommend the software for company workstations.

We have already discussed auditing and fixing system bugs in earlier chapters (e.g., Chapters 8, 9, and 10). However, we have not spent much time discussing uses for personal-firewall software.

Personal Firewall Software

Although called personal firewalls, this type of software provides the following main services:

- Port blocking
- Connection traceback
- Alert messages
- E-mail attachment scanning

You can also block specific IP addresses. These programs are not actually firewalls. Also, most personal firewall software is not appropriate as a security solution for production servers.

Popular Windows Personal Firewall Vendors

Popular personal firewall software includes:

- Zone Labs' ZoneAlarm (www.zonelabs.com)
- Internet Security Systems' BlackICE Defender (www.networkice.com or www.iss.net)
- Norton Personal Firewall 2002 (www.norton.com or www.symantec.com)

WARNING Installing such systems on a Windows NT/2000 system will usually lock down all services, unless you explicitly allow them.

Although most personal-firewall products are meant for client systems, Internet Security Systems provides products suitable for high-capacity implementations: ICEpac Security Suite and BlackICE Sentry. The former is designed to protect your entire network, including your firewall, virtual private network (VPN) connection, and your servers. The latter is an example of network-based intrusion-detection software. ZoneAlarm Pro, by Zone Labs, is an enhanced version of ZoneAlarm that provides more configuration and reporting options. For example, it allows remote configuration, provides more scalable configuration options for Internet connections, and color-codes its alerts.

> **TIP** Many personal firewalls will reduce the speed of an Internet connection, even when you have configured them to not block connections.

Linux and Personal Firewalls

A user-monitoring application called `tcpspy` is available at `packetstorm.linuxsecurity.com`. It listens to all incoming and outgoing connections made by users on Linux systems. It can help you learn more about the connections that local users are making to remote systems. Once you have installed it, you can run it as follows:

`/usr/local/sbin/tcpspy`

`tcpspy` will monitor all TCP-based connections made by local users to remote connections. You can view those connections by using the `tail -f` command to read the `/var/log/messages` file. Each time a user connects to a remote system, `tcpspy` will record the connection. `tcpspy` will also record each time a remote user connects to your system. This application supports many options and arguments. Consult the `tcpspy` man page for more information.

Psionic PortSentry™ (`www.psionic.com`) is a popular tool to use on Linux systems. It has the following capabilities:

- It can log ICMP, TCP, and UDP packets.

- It can automatically detect port scans, including many scans conducted by `nmap`.

- It offers the ability to block hosts that have scanned the system. PortSentry can use `ipchains`, `iptables`, the TCPWrapper `hosts.deny` files, and the `route` command to block ports.

> **NOTE**
>
> Remember that you can also create a personal firewall yourself using `ipchains` and `iptables`. Although a firewall built in this way will not reconfigure itself automatically, it will nevertheless help secure your system and log connections.

EXERCISE 15.1

Installing a Personal Firewall in Windows 2000

In this exercise, you will install and configure the ZoneAlarm personal firewall. This exercise is designed to show you some of the capabilities of a personal firewall. This product is designed to protect client hosts (e.g., Windows 9*x* and ME systems). Like other companies, Zone Labs provides additional software designed for servers. However, as an auditor you will have to recommend personal-firewall software for installation on client systems, such as Windows ME. This exercise is written to version 2.6. If you use a different version of this application, you might have to alter certain steps.

1. Obtain the ZoneAlarm installation binary (`zonalm26.exe`) from www.zonealarm.com. Install the application using the installation wizard. You will be asked about the nature of your Internet connection. Give the appropriate answer according to your network's setup. Indicate that you want to start the program immediately.

   Note: If necessary, go to Start ➢ Programs ➢ Zone Labs ➢ ZoneAlarm to start the program.

2. ZoneAlarm will guide you through a series of tutorial windows. Read them, and then click OK until you see the ZoneAlarm interface, shown here:

EXERCISE 15.1 *(continued)*

3. Click the Programs button to view all the programs that are allowed to connect to and from your local system. You might be asked immediately whether a certain connection is allowed. ZoneAlarm will show you messages describing the nature of the connection. For this exercise, click Yes to indicate that you want to allow the connections. Here is the Programs window, with no applications listed:

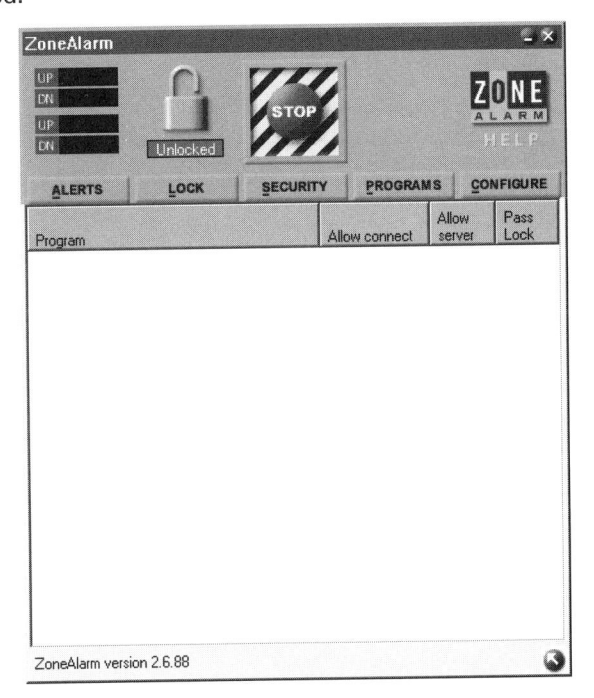

4. Open a web browser and access a site on the Internet or on the local network. ZoneAlarm blocks all activity unless you explicitly allow it. When ZoneAlarm detects a connection being made from the local host to a remote host, it will ask you if the connection should be made. ZoneAlarm might also ask you whether this system should be allowed to use your DNS server. Answer Yes.

EXERCISE 15.1 *(continued)*

5. When ZoneAlarm adds rules, you will see them in the Programs window:

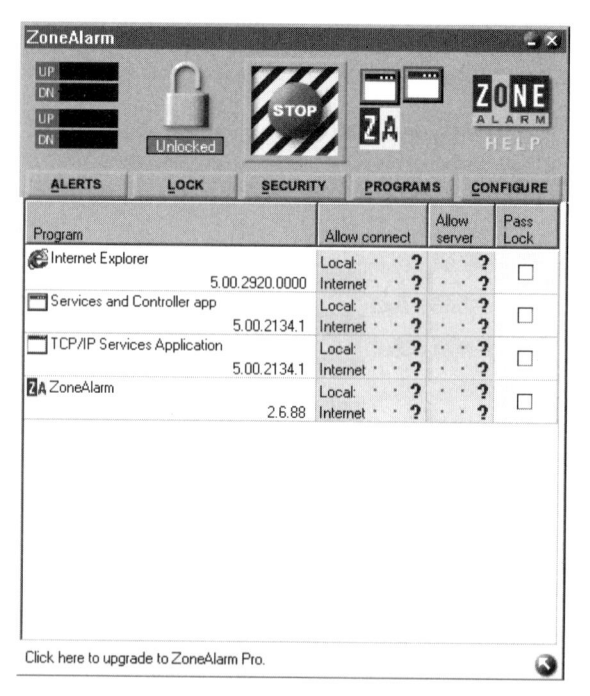

6. ZoneAlarm places connections into two categories: Local Network and Internet. ZoneAlarm defaults to asking you each time about a connection to the Internet. A black question mark next to an entry means that ZoneAlarm's default stance will be to ask you about each connection. A green check mark means that the connection will always be allowed by default. To allow all use of a web browser such as Microsoft Internet Explorer, highlight its icon, right-click it, and then select Internet ➢ Allow. Once you make this selection, all web-based connections will be allowed for Internet Explorer.

7. However, ZoneAlarm is very specific regarding the local applications it allows to use a certain port or service. Just because you have allowed Internet Explorer to access the Internet, this does not mean that Netscape Navigator would be allowed. Install Netscape Navigator and try to access the Internet. ZoneAlarm will ask if this application should be allowed to use the Internet. Answer Yes.

EXERCISE 15.1 *(continued)*

Netscape Navigator will be allowed to access the Internet this time only. To allow all subsequent access to the Internet, right-click the Netscape Navigator icon. Then, change the default stance for the Netscape application to access the Internet.

8. Open an e-mail client, such as Microsoft Outlook Express. Access a remote e-mail server. ZoneAlarm will ask you about this connection as well. Repeat Steps 6 and 7.

9. If necessary, maximize ZoneAlarm. Click the Security button. Note the default settings:

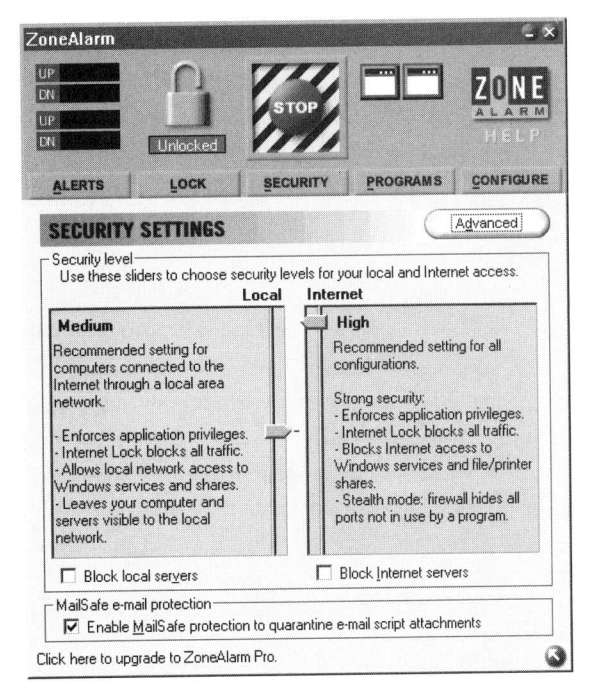

10. The default is to not allow Windows SMB networking to occur (e.g., you cannot connect to a share, nor can remote systems connect to your share). Test this rule by using Network Neighborhood, or by going to Start ➢ Run and entering a Universal Naming Convention (UNC) address to a remote host (e.g., \\neighbor_system\share).

11. Change the Internet setting from High to Low. Notice that the Local setting will automatically switch to Low as well. All systems will now be able to access shares on the network.

> **EXERCISE 15.1 *(continued)***
>
> 12. Change the Internet section to Medium, but keep the Local setting at Low. Verify that IIS 5 is running its web server, and have another person or system try to access your system's web server. This person or system will be able to connect.
>
> 13. Change the Internet section to High, and have a remote system try to access your server again. This system will not be able to connect, and you will receive a message about an illicit connection. Close ZoneAlarm by right-clicking its Taskbar icon.
>
> 14. Now, either disable ZoneAlarm or return it to settings that suit your particular situation.

Compliance-Monitoring Software

Compliance monitoring is the activity of ensuring that network equipment (e.g., servers, firewalls, and IDS applications) all adhere to standards as set forth by the security policy. Compliance-monitoring software uses a manager/agent architecture. Agents sit on resources and are (ideally) configured to detect problems in a network host's configuration. This type of software does not detect intrusions. Rather, it notifies a central system about systems that fall beneath certain policy thresholds.

For example, a compliance-monitoring program can be set to inform you about systems that have password-aging parameters set too low. Compliance-monitoring software is commonly used to search for the following problems, among many others:

- Accounts with no passwords
- System configuration issues that can lead to break-ins
- Patch levels on systems, services, and daemons

For several reasons, compliance monitoring is much more effective at discovering these types of problems than a vulnerability scanner. First, the agents reside directly on the server and can more closely monitor configuration issues. Second, this type of software contains native scheduling software that allows you to ensure that reports are generated regularly. Although it is possible to schedule a network-based vulnerability scanner to run automatically, the manager/agent software is specifically designed to fulfill such tasks.

This software is necessary in companies that require adherence to strict procedures due to contracts with other businesses and/or governments. It is important to understand that compliance-monitoring software is designed to help you focus on reducing vulnerabilities in a server according to instructions given by your security policy.

Examples of compliance-monitoring software include Symantec's Enterprise Security Manager (www.symantec.com) and PentaSafe's VigilEnt (www.pentasafe.com). For the CIW Security Professional exam, make sure that you understand that these types of applications are capable of issuing reports on problem configurations but that they cannot detect intrusions or block an intrusion from occurring.

When installing policy compliance monitoring software, consider the following issues:

Configure the software to comply with your security policy. Policy-compliance software will do little good unless you map it to your security policy. If, for example, you require your e-mail server to provide only IMAP and SMTP services, you can configure the agent residing on the server to send a report if another service or daemon is opened on that server. Or, if you decide that all servers—Linux, Windows 2000, or Novell—should use passwords with six characters, you can configure the agents on these servers to report any violations.

Be careful what you ask for. Depending on the quality of the software, it can return an enormous amount of information. Choose to search only those servers and vulnerabilities that you can address. You do not want to be overwhelmed by too much information.

Update the software to obtain the latest signature databases. Like vulnerability scanners and IDS applications, this software uses a vulnerability database to discover events.

Determine who will receive the reports. The reports from compliance-monitoring software will only be useful if they are analyzed and acted on. If the reports go to the wrong person (or to no person at all), you will have wasted time and money on software that is not helping you secure your network.

When monitoring compliance to the security policy, one of the more common activities is updating and replacing existing services. In the next section, we'll examine some of the more common steps you can take.

Replacing and Updating Services

The CIW Security Professional exam might expect you to know some of the following steps when updating or replacing a network service:

- Study the new product. Ask yourself if it is suitable for the network and/or business.

- Test the software on an isolated subnet. Then, once you are sure that the software behaves as you expected, you can then test it on a public network. Showing caution when installing software ensures that a seemingly simple addition of software into the network will not somehow cause too much network traffic or affect other servers.

- If you are installing an operating system add-on, make sure that you conduct any tests on a representative system. In other words, if you have been directed to install a personal firewall on all corporate workstations, install the software on a system with a configuration similar to these workstations.

- Determine how much time will be needed to implement the change.

- Test all updates thoroughly before applying them on production services.

- Consider how replacements and updates will affect other services. Most network hosts interact with and rely on additional hosts. Will the new service cause problems?

- Determine if additional end-user training is necessary. Whenever you are going to change an employee's work environment, always make sure that you explain the change thoroughly.

It is possible to recommend upgrades or replacements for any number of services. For example, it might be appropriate to recommend that a network upgrade from using the Network Information System (NIS) to Kerberos, or that a network move from Microsoft Windows 2000 systems using IIS 5 to Linux. However, always consider the needs of the business before making such a suggestion.

Now, let's take a look at two recommendations you can make: upgrading to IPv6 and implementing SSH as a replacement for Telnet.

Recommending IPv6

Updating TCP/IP usually involves making sure that the operating systems are using the latest applications and daemons. However, in some very specific situations, you will want to replace the standard IPv4 implementation and recommend the use of IPv6. IPv6 enables encryption and authentication, and is now supported by major operating systems such as Windows 2000/NT, Linux 7, and Solaris. As of this writing, choosing to use IPv6 as the only protocol can limit access to Internet services, but in some cases, it might be a more secure replacement for isolated LANs that need additional security.

IPv6 provides the following security features:

- Enhanced authentication (through the Authentication extension header) to reduce the possibility of spoofing and hijacking attacks

- Data encryption (through the Encrypted Security Payload [ESP] extension header) to reduce the possibility of sniffing attacks

If you need to improve security on an isolated network, using IPv6 might be a viable option for you.

Implementing Secure Shell (SSH)

Telnet, `rlogin`, and `rsh` are quite useful. They allow you to issue commands remotely on a server as if you were working directly at it. The `rexec` program allows you to execute commands remotely on a server without providing a password. However, these services transmit all information "in the clear." The most common replacement for these services is Secure Shell (SSH).

> **TIP** At one time, SSH servers had to be Unix based. In late 2000, SSH Communications (www.ssh.com) released an SSH server for Windows 2000. SSH clients for Unix, Windows, and Macintosh systems have existed for a long time.

Security Services Provided by SSH

SSH provides two fundamental services:

Data privacy In *data privacy*, the data channel is encrypted, because the server first sends its public key to the client. The client then encrypts all information to the server's public key. When the server receives encrypted information, it decrypts the information using its private key.

Strong authentication As far as *strong authentication* is concerned, using separate public keys from those we just discussed, two users can exchange keys that allow authentication based on the public keys. The benefit of this procedure is that username and password information is never sent across the network.

You need to understand that SSH first encrypts the data channel and then allows various methods for authentication. By default, Secure Shell uses port 22 and allows you to use public-key encryption. SSH2 uses the Digital Signature Algorithm, which is similar to RSA public-key encryption but is not proprietary. However, SSH2 can use RSA as well.

Encryption and Authentication in SSH

The encryption process begins when the server automatically sends its public key to the client. The client then encrypts all information to this public key, which the server can decrypt with its private key. All subsequent transactions between systems are then encrypted.

By default, SSH will first attempt to authenticate using *public keys*. These keys are stored in the $HOME/.ssh2 directory for each user. For example, if you have a user named james in Red Hat Linux 7, all keys (including james' public and private keys) are stored in the /home/james/.ssh2 directory. Note that this is a hidden directory. Also, if you use a different version of SSH, the directory name can have a different number, or may be simply .ssh, without a number at all.

If these keys or the identification and authorization files are not present, SSH will revert to using the standard usernames and passwords found in the /etc/passwd and /etc/shadow databases. The drawback to this procedure is that it transfers passwords across the network. Although the password information is encrypted, sending passwords across a public network is never as secure an option.

SSH2 Components

Table 15.3 provides a list of Unix and Windows NT/2000 SSH2 components.

TABLE 15.3 SSH2 Components

Component	Description
/usr/local/bin/ssh2	The Linux SSH2 client.
SSH Secure Shell Client	One of many SSH clients for Windows (available separately at www.ssh.com). One SSH client, F-Secure (www.datafellows.com), supports Windows and Macintosh systems.

TABLE 15.3 SSH2 Components *(continued)*

Component	Description
/usr/local/bin/ssh-keygen2	A component that generates key pairs for each user.
/usr/local/bin/scp2	A client that allows you to execute remote commands using the secure data channel created by SSH.
/usr/local/sbin/sshd2	The SSH2 daemon.
/usr/local/bin/ssh-agent2	A component that allows you to save public keys in memory. It enables logins without passwords, as long as you have established a trust relationship. Useful for multiple logins.
/usr/local/bin/sftp-server2	The secure FTP server run by sshd2. Certain Windows clients can also take advantage of the secure FTP server.
/usr/local/bin/sftp2	The secure FTP client.

Obtaining SSH

You can obtain SSH at various locations, including www.ssh.com, www.ssh.org, www.openssh.org, and www.rpmfind.net. OpenSSH is available free of charge.

> **NOTE** This chapter assumes the use of the Secure Shell server provided by SSH.com (www.ssh.com). The specific version is SSH2. For more information about SSH2, check the readme file that comes with the documentation.

Preparing SSH Components

As with any client/server product, you must first configure the server and client to communicate with each other. Doing so involves installation, as well as creating trust relationships. In Linux, installing the server also installs all client software. You will then have to generate and exchange public keys, as discussed in the section "SSH and Authentication: Establishing User-to-User Trust Relationships," later in this chapter. The server configuration process includes the generation of public and private host keys. These keys are automatically transferred during the *SSH handshake process*, which is where the server and the client exchange keys so that subsequent transmissions are encrypted. You must then start the SSH2 server by entering the following command:

/usr/local/sbin/sshd2

You can automate startup of `sshd2` by editing the /etc/rc.d/rc.local file or its equivalent. For Red Hat Linux systems, you would simply enter **/usr/local/sbin/sshd2** at the end of the file.

Logging in Using SSH

To log in using SSH, you can issue the following syntax:

/usr/local/bin/ssh2 -l username hostname

For example, to log on to a system named floyd as a user named pink, you would enter the following:

/usr/local/bin/ssh2 -l pink floyd

> **WARNING** You must have a working DNS structure to enable SSH. A proper structure includes full reverse DNS lookup. If you do not have a working DNS structure, SSH may fail authentication and/or behave unpredictably because most Unix systems, including Linux, require proper DNS to authenticate all connections.

EXERCISE 15.2

Installing SSH Server as a Replacement for Telnetd, *rlogind*, and FTP

In this exercise, you will install SSH as a replacement for Telnet and rlogin. This exercise installs the SSH server on a Red Hat Linux system.

Note: You must have a complete DNS structure in place for this exercise to work.

1. Obtain the SSH installation files from www.ssh.com. This exercise uses the installation of tarball files from www.ssh.com, which require you to unzip and untar the files, as well as use make.

EXERCISE 15.2 (continued)

2. Once you have obtained the zipped files, unzip them:

   host# gunzip ssh-2.4.0.tar.gz

   Note: Your version of SSH might differ slightly. The functionality will remain the same, however.

3. Now, untar the file:

   host# tar -xvf ssh-2.4.0.tar

4. Untarring the file should create the ssh-2.0.13 directory. Change to this directory:

   host# cd ssh-2.4.0

   Note: You may have a more recent version of SSH. If so, the version number might differ.

5. Once in this directory, compile SSH2 using the ./configure command:

   host# ./configure

6. Once the SSH configure command has run, issue the make command:

   host# make

7. After some time, SSH will complete installation. When you are returned to a command prompt, enter the following command to create the public and private keys for the Linux server:

   host# make install

8. Once you have created public and private keys for this host, start sshd2:

   host# /usr/local/sbin/sshd2

9. Open the /etc/rc.d/rc.local file using a text editor and enter the following code at the very end of the file:

   /usr/local/sbin/sshd2

   Inserting the above text ensures that Linux will start sshd2 when the host boots.

EXERCISE 15.3

Installing an SSH Client in Windows 2000

In this exercise, you will install an SSH client for Windows 2000 so you can use it to authenticate with the Linux-based SSH server you created earlier.

1. Completely disable the ZoneAlarm firewall.

2. Obtain the Secure Shell Windows client setup file from www.ssh.com.

3. Double-click the file and follow the installation wizard.

4. When the wizard is finished, a Secure Shell icon will appear on your desktop. Double-click it to start the client. Alternatively, go to Start ➢ Programs ➢ SSH Secure Shell ➢ Secure Shell Client to start the client. You are now ready to make a connection.

EXERCISE 15.4

Using a Windows 2000 SSH Client to Encrypt Transmissions and Authenticate with an SSH Server

In this exercise, you will use a client on a Windows 2000 system (known as the "SSH Client") to access a Linux system that is acting as an SSH server (known as the "SSH Server").

1. SSH Server: Make sure sshd2 is running properly. You should be able to execute ssh2d by using the following command:

   host# /usr/local/sbin/sshd2

   Also, you must have a complete DNS structure in place for this exercise to work. You must have valid forward and reverse DNS zones because Linux conducts reverse DNS lookups on many services, including Telnet, FTP, and SSH. If you do not have the proper DNS structure, you could receive inaccurate messages indicating that authentication has failed, when in fact, the connection has timed out due to a failed reverse DNS lookup.

EXERCISE 15.4 *(continued)*

2. SSH Client: Open the Windows SSH client, if it is not open already.

3. SSH Client: Press Enter or the spacebar to connect.

4. SSH Client: Enter the DNS name for your SSH server, as well as a valid username.

   Note: Do not attempt an initial connection to the remote Linux system as root. Connect as a non-root user, and then use su to assert root privileges.

5. SSH Client: You will see a dialog box that allows you to obtain the host public key, as shown here. Select Yes to accept the host key.

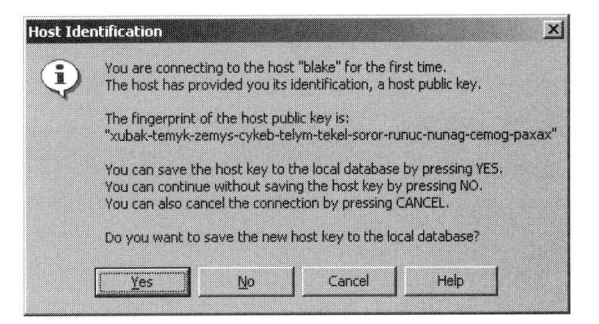

6. SSH Client: Once you select Yes, the client and the server will establish a secure channel. If you have supplied the correct username and password, you will then be authenticated. You should see something like a standard Telnet prompt that allows you to execute commands on this system.

7. SSH Client: Once you have finished with this shell, log out as you would at the end of any Telnet session.

8. SSH Client: Check to see if you have the host's public key. Select Edit ➢ Settings and highlight the Host Keys icon. You will see that the host's key has been transferred to your system, enabling secure communication.

> **EXERCISE 15.5**
>
> **Transferring Files with the SSH Secure FTP Client**
>
> In this exercise, you will use the SSH FTP client to connect to a remote Linux system.
>
> Note: You must have a complete DNS structure in place for this exercise to work.
>
> 1. Open the Secure Shell Terminal Client.
> 2. Go to Window ➢ New File Transfer.
> 3. The SSH Secure File Transfer client will appear.
> 4. Select File ➢ Connect.
> 5. Enter the hostname of the remote system and all other pertinent information (e.g., the user account name).
> 6. Click OK.
> 7. The SSH Secure File Transfer client will authenticate.
> 8. Use a packet sniffer such as Ethereal (www.ethereal.com) to test the difference between a standard FTP client and server and the SSH FTP client and server. Note that the standard FTP client transmits information in the clear, whereas the SSH FTP client provides encrypted file transfer.

SSH and Authentication: Establishing User-to-User Trust Relationships

The most secure SSH authentication option involves users creating a trust relationship by manually exchanging public keys. Each user must exchange public keys. In this section, we'll look at the process required to create key pairs that allow authentication. This process assumes that two users want to use SSH to authenticate using *public-key authentication*, a process where SSH uses public keys to authenticate users. Remember, the SSH server automatically encrypts the data channel. The client public keys provide authentication only. Each user would follow this procedure:

1. Using the /usr/local/bin/ssh-keygen2 program, create a key pair. As mentioned above, the ssh-keygen2 program automatically

creates a key pair that resides in the `.ssh2` directory off each user's home directory.

2. Change to the `.ssh2` directory that exists in your home directory. You then should rename the public and private key files. If you use the standard 1024-bit encryption, the files will by default be named `id_dsa_1024_a` and `id_dsa_1024_a.pub`. You can freely distribute the file ending in `.pub`. However, the file without the `.pub` ending must remain secret. In fact, you should make sure this file is readable by only you. You should also rename these files so you can keep track of them. For example, if your username is macduff, and this name resides on a system named page, you can rename the public and private keys as **macduffpage** and **macduffpage.pub**, respectively.

3. You then create two files named **identification** and **authorization**. The identification file contains the name of your own private key. The authorization file contains the names of all public keys of users you want to allow entry into your system. You can enter as many public-key names into this file as you want.

4. Enter the name of the private key into the identification file. The proper format is: `IdKey macduffpage`.

5. Each person who wants to authenticate securely will then exchange public keys. Remember, the private keys always remain private.

6. When you receive a public key from someone else, make sure the file is in the `.ssh2` directory. You must then enter the name of your partner's public key into the authorization file. The syntax is `Key keyname.pub`. Create a new line for each entry. If you entered Sandi's and Jacob's public keys into the authorization file, your authorization file would appear as follows:

```
Key sandi.pub
Key jacob.pub
```

7. Once you and at least one other person have taken these steps, each user can then use SSH2 to authenticate using public-key encryption.

> **NOTE**
>
> For these steps to work, the sshd2 daemon must be running. Remember, the sshd2 daemon provides encryption by automatically giving its public key to all who ask for it. Individual users are responsible for creating trust relationships that allow authentication. You must also make sure DNS is functioning properly.

EXERCISE 15.6

Establishing a Trust Relationship between Linux Clients

In this exercise, you will use ssh-keygen2 to create a public key pair on two systems. You will then rename your public and private keys and prepare a place to exchange keys.

Note: You must have a complete DNS structure in place for this exercise to work.

1. Log on to your Linux system as root. Make sure you are in the root directory.

2. Issue the following command:

   /usr/local/bin/ssh-keygen2

3. The ssh-keygen2 command will begin to generate a key pair.

4. When ssh-keygen2 prompts you, enter a password for your private key and then confirm it. For this exercise, enter **password**. In other situations, you are advised to use a strong password.

5. The ssh-keygen2 program has automatically created the hidden directory named .ssh2. Change to it now:

   host# cd .ssh2

6. List the files in this directory. Notice that you have two new files. One file should be named something similar to id_dsa_1024_a and the other should be named something like id_dsa_1024_a.pub.

7. Create a copy of the private key (id_dsa_1024_a); rename it using your first name. For example, if your first name is othello, enter the following command:

   host# cp id_dsa_1024_a othello

EXERCISE 15.6 (continued)

8. Copy the `id_dsa_1024_a.pub` key and rename it in a similar fashion:

   host# cp id_dsa_1024_a.pub othello.pub

   Note: Be sure to properly copy both keys. Do not confuse the public key with the private key. Use `cat` or a text editor to make sure you have actually copied the public key.

EXERCISE 15.7

Using Public-Key Encryption to Authenticate a Linux Client

In this exercise, you will create identification and authentication files, and then exchange your public key with a partner. You will then edit the authentication file so that it contains the name of your partner's public key. You will then authenticate using public-key encryption.

1. As root, change to the `.ssh2` directory of your own home directory.

2. Use touch to create two files named **identification** and **authorization**:

   host# touch identification
   host# touch authorization

3. Using a text editor, edit the identification file so that it contains an entry similar to this:

   IdKey james

4. Exit the text editor and save changes to the identification file.

5. Obtain your partner's public key. If necessary, create a central site that allows you to exchange keys. Otherwise, use FTP to obtain your partner's public key.

6. When you have received your partner's public key, make sure it is in the `.ssh2` directory.

EXERCISE 15.7 *(continued)*

7. Edit the authorization file so it contains the name of your partner's public key. For example, if your partner's username is sandi and the key's name is sandi.pub, you would enter the following into the authorization file:

   Key sandi.pub

8. Exit the text editor and make sure you save changes to the authorization file.

9. Make sure that /usr/local/sbin/sshd2 (the SSHD2 daemon) is running.

10. Now, issue the following command:

    host# /usr/local/bin/ssh2 -l root remote_machine

11. Notice that your computer will notify you that it is receiving your partner's public host key.

12. Your own system will ask you to provide the password for your private key. The password should be password. This message appears because your partner's computer has encrypted the authentication process to your public key, and you must use your private key to decrypt it. Once you enter the password to your private key, you will be authenticated and will receive a root shell on your partner's computer.

13. Log out from your partner's system, and then log back in using exactly the same sequence; however, when asked to provide a password for your private key, enter the wrong password. You will then be asked by your partner's system for the root password. This procedure is still encrypted, but it is no longer using the public keys for authentication. Enter your partner's root password to log in.

14. Establish a secure FTP session by issuing the following command:

    /usr/local/bin/sftp2 -S /usr/local/bin/ssh2
       remote_host_name

EXERCISE 15.7 *(continued)*

Note: You will be asked to enter the password for your private key. Upon successful authentication, you can then transfer files securely.

EXERCISE 15.8

Generating a Key Pair in Secure Shell Terminal Client for Windows 2000

In Exercise 15.4, you used the Secure Shell Terminal Client for Windows 2000 to access a remote Linux system. However, in that exercise, the Windows 2000 client was forced to access the system's /etc/passwd and /etc/shadow databases for authentication instead of using public keys because the users on the remote system had not created a key pair using their 2000 client, and because the other users had not modified the ./ssh2/authorization file on the SSH server. In this exercise, you will establish a trust relationship using your Windows 2000 SSH client.

Note: You must have a complete DNS structure in place for this exercise to work.

1. SSH Server: Launch into Linux as root.

2. SSH Server: Change the root password to `ciwcertified`:

   ```
   host# passwd
   New UNIX password: ************
   Retype new UNIX password: ************
   passwd: all authentication tokens updated successfully
   ```

3. SSH Client: Launch into Windows 2000 as Administrator. Open the Secure Shell Terminal Client.

4. SSH Client: Once in the program, go to Edit ≻ Settings.

5. SSH Client: Select the User Keys icon.

6. SSH Client: Click the Generate New Keypair button.

624 Chapter 15 · Recommending Solutions and Generating Reports

EXERCISE 15.8 *(continued)*

7. SSH Client: Follow the installation wizard, accepting all defaults, until you see the Enter Passphrase screen, shown here:

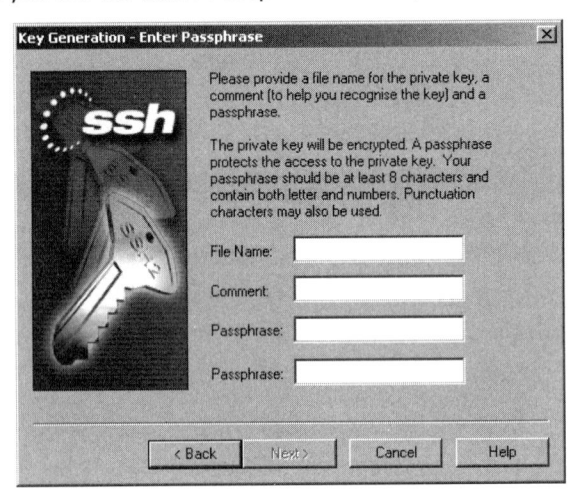

8. SSH Client: Enter **nt***yourname* in the File Name field, being sure to substitute your first name for *yourname*.

9. SSH Client: In the Comment field, enter **password** as the password, and then confirm the password. Click Next.

10. SSH Client: Read the message, and then click Finish.

11. SSH Client: Click OK to return to the main screen.

12. SSH Client: You need to make your Windows SSH client public key available to your partner. Go to Edit ➢ Settings, and then select the User Keys icon. Click the View Public Key icon, and then copy your public key to your desktop. Transfer this key to your partner's computer using FTP (your partner will be running Linux).

    Note: Make sure that you send your public key and not your private key.

13. SSH Server: Obtain the public key from the remote system's user (the account for SSH client), and place it in the .ssh2 directory of root's home directory (/root). Make sure you edit the authorization file so that it now contains the public-key name of the SSH client user.

14. SSH Client: Fill out the connection information; enter your partner's hostname and/or IP address, and then use **root** as the username.

> **EXERCISE 15.8 (continued)**
>
> 15. SSH Client: Click OK to connect to the SSH server.
>
> 16. SSH Client: Your client should ask you for the password for your private key. Enter the password (it should be **password** if you followed the instructions in Step 9).
>
> 17. SSH Client: You should be allowed access to the SSH server. You have now used public-key encryption to authenticate a Windows 2000 client. Notice that the SSH client user was able to authenticate using the word **password** instead of `ciwcertified`, which is the password stored in the /etc/shadow file. This is because SSH is using the key pair you generated instead of the /etc/shadow file.

Generating Reports

This book has shown you how to use several tools that allow you to conduct effective audits. One step remains, however: You must make detailed, written recommendations. Elements of a *security audit report* might include:

An overview indicating the level of existing security   You can note whether the level was low, medium, or high and include a quick summary of the equipment you monitored (e.g., mainframes, routers, Windows NT/2000 systems, or Unix systems). You can also include an estimate of how long it would take casual, experienced, and professional hackers to enter the system.

A quick summary of your most important recommendations   Be sure to include supporting material (e.g., reports from vulnerability scanners, routers/firewalls, and IDS applications).

A detailed outline of the procedures you used during the audit   Here, you can mention some of the more interesting items you found during the discovery, penetration, and control stages.

Recommendations about various network elements   You can make recommendations regarding the router, ports, services, login accounts, physical security, and so forth.

A discussion of physical security   Many networks have chronic problems with the physical placement of sensitive equipment. One company, for example, placed its file servers behind the receptionist's desk. Whenever the receptionist was away, the servers were exposed to a physical attack. In one instance, a security auditor picked up the server and walked out the door; he was even helped out by the security guard.

Evidence that you have carefully considered a variety of resources during your audit   It is not enough to simply forward a copy of a scanning report. Analyze the data thoroughly, and then provide a written report.

The Importance of a Written Report

Appendix A includes a sample audit report that contains both executive and IT-level reports. When you conduct an audit, your report will differ, but the sample in Appendix A offers a suggested format and structure. This document will report problems and suggest changes.

One thing that you must do in all cases is present a written report. It is not enough to simply inform someone through a phone call. It is vital that you provide evidence that you have carefully analyzed all scanning reports and other information, and the best way to do this is by writing down your findings.

> Auditing reports are often sensitive in nature. If you plan on delivering this report electronically, sign and encrypt the file using public-key encryption.

Making Auditing Recommendations for the IT Department

When making recommendations for your IT-level reports, consider the following six solutions:

1. Make sure that the company continues (or, in some cases, implements) efficient auditing so that you can readily determine the gap between security policy requirements and actual practice.

2. Confront and remediate virus, worm, and Trojan infections and system weaknesses.

3. Recommend the following changes and improvements, when appropriate:

    - Reconfiguring routers and/or network topology
    - Adding or reconfiguring firewall rules

- Upgrading the operating system patch level
- Replacing older and/or less secure services and operating systems
- Improving network auditing
- Automating and centralizing the administration of internal and perimeter security
- Adding intrusion detection applications
- Improving physical security
- Improving antivirus scanning
- Enhancing user-level encryption, such as PGP/GPG, and network-level encryption, such as IPsec
- Removing unnecessary accounts, applications, servers, and services
- Improving patch levels (i.e., installing all relevant hotfixes, operating system updates, system patches, and service packs)

4. Identify possible changes in the security policy.
5. Recommend end-user and IT professional training. For example, one of the best ways to avoid e-mail virus attacks is to have a well-trained staff who knows that they should not click on e-mail attachments irresponsibly. Remember that employees are your most important—and most vulnerable—resource. Regular training can help you ensure that your employee resources will remain effective and be less vulnerable to attack.
6. Inform the client about existing measures that are working well.

Now, let's look and see what you can do to help educate a company so that it does well in future audits.

Steps for Continued Auditing and Strengthening

It is possible that a company will not have a plan for conducting repeated audits. You should recommend these steps to any organization that wants to continue effective auditing:

1. Define a security policy, if necessary. Doing so should always be your first step.

2. Establish an internal organization to assign responsibility for specific tasks, including a hierarchical chain of command.

3. Systematically classify network assets.

4. Create security guidelines for employees.

5. Ensure physical security for personnel and network systems.

6. Secure the services and operating systems of network hosts.

7. Strengthen (or implement) access-control measures for the network perimeter, as well as network servers.

8. Ensure that the network meets business goals.

9. Measure compliance with the security policy.

10. Repeat the process.

If you want, you can include some (or all) of these steps in your audit report. If you are successful in convincing a company to begin the process of continually assessing and improving security, you can then call yourself a successful auditor and security professional.

Summary

In this chapter, you learned about ways to complete an audit. For example, it is vital to ensure that a network's perimeter and internal security are properly established and strengthened. You then learned how to recommend changes to the network when areas of vulnerability have been identified. Improving a server's security often requires operating system add-ons, such as personal firewalls. We examined the importance of replacing legacy services and daemons. Although your opportunities to recommend IPv6 will be relatively rare, you will often find the opportunity to replace Telnet with SSH.

Near the end of this chapter, you learned the importance of ensuring that your audit report mandates changes that are appropriate to the nature of the business you are auditing. You now have the knowledge and skills you need to recommend solutions to problems discovered during an audit.

Exam Essentials

Be able to identify perimeter and internal security solutions. If you are given a scenario, make sure that you can recommend changes to perimeter devices, including firewalls and routers. Also, be able to identify how to stop a Smurf attack at a router. You should also be able to identify when it is necessary to reconfigure internal IDS applications so that they can recognize new attacks.

Understand methods for detecting an NIC in promiscuous mode. Many IDS applications and network scanners are able to accurately deduce that an NIC is in promiscuous mode. Be able to explain, for example, that it is possible for software to detect changes in the NIC's electrical field, or send bogus network requests in an attempt to discover systems that are listening to packets.

Know the function of common operating system add-ons, such as personal firewalls. A personal firewall allows you to trace connections coming in and out of your system. It also allows you to block certain traffic and increase network security. Be able to explain some of the default behavior they exhibit. For example, some personal firewalls will block all traffic unless you explicitly permit it.

Be able to explain how Secure Shell (SSH) works, and identify the security services that it provides. SSH provides data privacy (i.e., confidentiality) and enhanced authentication. It is also important to understand how the server provides all clients with its public host key so that it can begin an encrypted session. Make sure that you are able to explain the difference between default SSH behavior (simply encrypting the connection) and more advanced ways to authenticate (e.g., using public keys). Finally, make sure that you are familiar with the port SSH uses (TCP port 22).

Know ways to improve compliance to a security policy. An organization's security policy enables you to focus on its most vital resources. Always consider what is mandated by the security policy so that you spend your time and money in the right places. Compliance software can be helpful in helping you comply with a security policy. Although this software does not replace workers, it does make it possible for one security employee to do the work of several.

Other ways to ensure compliance that might be mentioned on the exam include recommending additional user training, monitoring employee behavior, and ensuring physical security. In some companies that do not have security policies in the first place, remember that creating a security policy is one of the steps in auditing.

Be able to recommend solutions based on what you find in your audit. You have learned about how to identify vulnerabilities in previous chapters (e.g., Chapter 8 discussed operating system security, and Chapter 10 discussed how to assess and reduce risk). However, in this chapter, you learned how to recommend solutions in writing.

Understand the elements of an assessment report. An assessment report can include an executive-level summary and an IT-level report. The former is generally brief, and is designed to enable an executive to make strategic decisions. An IT-level report, on the other hand, is designed to enable a security manager or systems administrator to make changes to the network.

Key Terms

Before you take the exam, be certain you are familiar with the following terms:

- attack history
- compliance monitoring
- data privacy
- egress and ingress filtering
- network assessment
- promiscuous-mode detection
- public-key authentication
- public keys
- security audit report
- SSH handshake process
- strong authentication

Review Questions

1. Which of the following is a method used to determine if an NIC is in promiscuous mode?

    A. Wrapping a false TCP SYN request into an invalid ICMP header

    B. Wrapping a false ICMP request into an invalid Ethernet header

    C. Sending spoofed login packets

    D. Sending spoofed RARP packets

2. Which of the following security services does Secure Shell (SSH) provide?

    A. Non-repudiation

    B. Data privacy

    C. Data identification

    D. Anti-spoofing

3. Your web server continues to reject all connections via SSH. You receive an error message from the server stating that "All other authentication methods have failed." You can use SSH with all other servers on the network. What should you check first on this server?

    A. The server's SSH daemon

    B. The server's `hosts.deny` file

    C. The server's entries in DNS

    D. The server's public host key

4. What is the first step a security auditor should recommend to an organization that wants to continue effective auditing?

    A. Engage in penetration testing.

    B. Enable access control.

    C. Reconfigure the IDS.

    D. Read the security policy.

5. You have implemented Secure Shell on your server. You want to configure your system to authenticate a remote user using public keys. Where should you store the public key of the remote user?

   A. In your home directory

   B. In the `/etc/` directory

   C. In the user's home directory

   D. In the `/var/ssh/keys` directory

6. What security advantages does IPv6 offer?

   A. Enhanced logging and authentication

   B. Enhanced authentication and data encryption

   C. Built-in name resolution and encryption

   D. Enhanced authentication and connection tracing

7. Which of the following should be in a report sent to upper-level management?

   A. Details concerning the buffer overflow on a Solaris server

   B. Suggestions for packet-filtering rules on the screening router

   C. A summary of the network's existing security level

   D. A summary of the security policy

8. Janet has installed a personal firewall on an end user's workstation. After a day, the user calls her and informs her that he can no longer access e-mail. Before altering any settings, what should Janet do?

   A. Verify with management that the end user is allowed to receive e-mail.

   B. Explain how to adjust the personal-firewall settings over the phone.

   C. Go to the end user's workstation and adjust the personal-firewall settings herself.

   D. Go to the end user's workstation and teach the end user how to adjust the personal-firewall settings.

9. A Linux web server on your DMZ is responding slowly. This server is using kernel 2.4. You open up a packet sniffer and notice that ICMP traffic is being directed at the server from several remote hosts. What can you use to quickly keep these packets from reaching this server while still providing the services?

   A. Enter the IP addresses of the remote hosts into the `/etc/hosts.deny` file.

   B. Use `iptables` to drop the IP addresses of the remote hosts.

   C. Use the command `ifdown eth0`.

   D. Bring the server down to runlevel 1.

10. Mario works for a financial-services company as a security auditor. This company's security policy states that all servers should provide only one service at a time. This is Mario's chief concern. However, Mario is also the leader of a team dedicated to reducing vulnerabilities in critical company servers. While reading a report from a vulnerability scanner, he notices that the e-mail server provides the following network services:

    - SMTP
    - POP3
    - FTP

    The report also shows the following:

    - The FTP daemon is vulnerable to a remote exploit that could easily allow a hacker to obtain root access to the entire system.
    - The SMTP server (sendmail) is vulnerable to a local attack that allows a non-root user to easily assume root permissions on the server.

    To ensure policy compliance, what should Mario recommend for the e-mail server?

    A. Update the SMTP server.

    B. Update the FTP daemon.

    C. Shut down the FTP daemon.

    D. Update the security policy.

11. Wanda is the systems administrator over a web farm that contains 300 web servers and 30 database servers. She has determined that she needs to be notified when the patch level is too low. What software should she install on the servers in the web farm?

    A. Policy-compliance software

    B. A network-vulnerability scanner

    C. An IDS application

    D. A firewall

12. You have just installed security-compliance software on 50 company servers. Three of these servers are web servers, five provide e-mail services, and the remaining servers provide file and print services. As per company policy, the servers all use the Windows 2000 operating system. Which of the following steps is necessary to ensure that this software fulfills its primary function?

    A. Automating the software so that it constantly monitors the servers

    B. Mapping the software to the corporate security policy

    C. Identifying vulnerabilities in the most critical servers

    D. Generating a test report to verify that the software works

13. Tammy has been directed by the chief security officer of her company to choose a personal firewall product to be installed on all Windows XP systems. Before installing this software on all clients, what should Tammy do to ensure that she understands its behavior?

    A. Hold training sessions that show users how to configure it properly.

    B. Test it on a corporate server.

    C. Send an e-mail to users explaining its importance and how to use it.

    D. Test it on a workstation.

14. Which of these strategies can help a promiscuous-mode detector return accurate results?

    A. Repeat the scan.

    B. Specify the use of ICMP.

    C. Modify the scan.

    D. Specify the use of TCP.

15. What is the function of the server host public key in SSH?

   A. To enable authentication via public keys

   B. To enable encryption between a server and a client

   C. To authenticate the root user during a first connection

   D. To enable the server to encrypt its host key

16. Tim is auditing an Internet service provider (ISP). As he is scanning the DMZ, he notices a system with a low patch level. How should he report this vulnerability to his customer?

   A. Call the ISP and make the report orally.

   B. Give the report in person to management.

   C. Provide a report from his scanning application.

   D. Give the report in person to the IT manager.

17. Abdul has found that e-mail-based attacks are on the rise in his company. He has implemented antivirus software on his e-mail server, and has also secured his clients by installing antivirus software. What else can he do to improve e-mail security across the entire enterprise without affecting normal business operations?

   A. Reconfigure his IDS applications.

   B. Reconfigure packet-filter rules.

   C. Train company employees.

   D. Limit incoming e-mail.

18. After conducting an audit, you have discovered that the existing network authentication structure has fallen victim to packet-sniffing attacks. User-level security is minimal. What should you recommend as a solution?

   A. Implementing Kerberos

   B. Creating a policy entry forbidding packet sniffing

   C. Mandating password changes every day

   D. Installing shadow passwords

19. Which of the following configuration changes will improve physical security for information distributed across the entire enterprise?

    A. Using password-protected screensavers

    B. Unplugging the keyboard to the firewall

    C. Installing personal-firewall software

    D. Installing cameras in the server room

20. George wants to use the public-key feature in SSH to authenticate a remote user named Gracie. After generating a public key pair, what must George do in order to authenticate with Gracie's server so that he does not have to send his username and password across the Internet?

    A. Make his private key readable only by root.

    B. Send Gracie his public key.

    C. Obtain Gracie's public key.

    D. Store his private key in a hidden directory.

Answers to Review Questions

1. **B.** Wrapping a false ICMP request into an invalid Ethernet header is only one of the strategies used in promiscuous-mode detection. However, it is effective, because all systems except those in promiscuous mode will drop the request. It is not possible to embed a TCP packet into an ICMP header. Sending spoofed login and RARP packets does not necessarily help a system determine if an NIC is in promiscuous mode. Doing so might help the system to escape detection, however.

2. **B.** Secure Shell encrypts transmissions to provide encryption. It also has the ability to provide strong authentication. Non-repudiation is the ability to prove that a transaction has, in fact, occurred. SSH does not provide any special methods in regard to non-repudiation. Data identification and anti-spoofing are not concepts discussed in this book or on the CIW Security Professional exam.

3. **C.** SSH uses DNS to help its authentication process by conducting reverse lookups. If you do not have a proper DNS structure, authentication is likely to fail. If the SSH daemon were not running, no message would be returned by the system. Although it is possible to use a server's `hosts.deny` file, the server will not present a message about various authentication methods. Checking the server's public host key would not be revealing in this case.

4. **D.** An auditor should always read the security policy of the company to ensure that the audit looks for the most vital resources. Doing so ensures that you can measure compliance with the security policy. All other procedures, including performing penetration testing, enhancing access control, and reconfiguring the IDS, are secondary to this concern.

5. **A.** SSH requires you to store a user's public keys in the home directory of the user who wants to allow access. If you are using the commercial version of SSH (SSH2), the directory would be `$HOME/.ssh2`. Other versions of SSH, such as OpenSSH, would use the `$HOME/.ssh` directory.

6. B. IPv6 automatically encrypts transmissions and makes spoofing more difficult because it requires servers to identify themselves. IPsec for IPv4 provides many of the same services. IPv6 does not provide enhanced logging; operating systems (e.g., for workstations, servers, firewall, and IDS applications) provide logging. Also, IPv6 cannot trace connections. Connection tracing on a network is accomplished by using an application or daemon.

7. C. Generally, executives do not want to receive detailed technical information, nor do they want a rehash of existing policies. They do, however, require a clearly written report that allows them to understand the current level of the network. The summary can then categorize some of the areas that were checked. It is important that you do not provide too much information. You should use simple comparisons and clearly explain the ramifications of issues you have found.

8. A. Whenever you receive a call about connectivity after installing an operating system add-on, first verify that the end user is supposed to be able to access the resource. Janet should first check with the end user's manager; then, she can work with the user to adjust personal-firewall settings.

9. B. Using `iptables` to drop the ICMP packets from the offending remote hosts is the proper option, because entries into the /etc/hosts.deny file do not tell the kernel to drop ICMP packets. The /etc/hosts.deny file drops TCP-based connections to protocols such as FTP, Telnet, and SSH. Bringing down the eth0 interface will quickly solve the problem, but it will also completely shut down the network interface and deny services to all customers. Similarly, bringing the server down to runlevel 1 will shut down all networking for the server.

10. C. According to the question, Mario's chief concern is policy compliance, and the secondary concern is fixing vulnerabilities. So, he should see that the FTP daemon violates the security policy, which states that a server should provide only one service.

11. A. Policy-compliance software is designed to report compliance problems and is the best choice. A network scanner can also reveal a low patch level, but the most efficient choice here is the use of an agent that resides on the system and delves deeply into its inner workings.

12. B. The first step to take when installing security-compliance software is to configure it to support your security policy. Automated monitoring is a key feature in security-compliance software, but it is not the first step to take. Although this software can identify vulnerabilities, it can do so only if you configure it to work closely with your security policy. It is always important to generate a test report to verify that the software is working properly; however, you would generate a test report only after you have mapped it to your security policy.

13. D. The most important step in understanding the behavior of a piece of software is to first test it on a representative workstation. It is also a good idea to test this software on an isolated subnet and then expose it to the production environment. Although training end users concerning new software is always important, the question is not asking you how to make sure everyone knows how to use the personal-firewall software being installed.

14. A. Although specifying additional packet types is possible, the most effective strategy is to repeat the scan.

15. B. An SSH server always issues the server host public key when a new SSH client first connects. This key is essential for encrypting the session. The key has nothing to do with public-key authentication or authentication of any particular users. If you want to authenticate users via public-key encryption, you must use the ssh-keygen application.

16. C. When reporting vulnerabilities, do it in writing, and supply some form of proof. If the auditing job is large and supporting material becomes unwieldy, then make a note that supporting material is freely available and kept in a secure location.

17. C. Although reconfiguring an IDS application can help detect e-mail attacks in progress, the most effective strategy is to train company employees so that they know not to click on e-mail attachments irresponsibly. Reconfiguring packet-filter rules may eliminate all SMTP from entering the system, but this step would make it impossible to send e-mail, which would cause an enormous business problem. Limiting incoming e-mail might also help, but it can have a detrimental impact on business operations.

18. A. The most reasonable and effective solution is to implement Kerberos, which enables authentication to occur without having passwords cross the network (see Chapter 1). A security policy forbidding packet sniffing might reduce some attacks, but it would not end them, because determined hackers will ignore the policy. Mandatory password changes every day will likely introduce more problems than they solve, because users will begin to write down their passwords, due to the sheer inconvenience of having to change them every day. Also, this strategy will not eliminate the fact that passwords are traveling over the network. The installation of shadow passwords would not make the network secure from packet-sniffing attacks because users would still authenticate remotely using protocols that do not encrypt information or use strong authentication.

19. A. If all employees were to use password-protected screensavers, information would be more secure, because the screensavers would prohibit people from simply walking up to computers and improperly reading or manipulating information. Unplugging the keyboard to the firewall can be an effective solution for securing the firewall. It could be argued that this one change can improve security across the entire enterprise, because it helps ensure that the firewall cannot be manipulated as easily. However, this one step would do little to improve the physical security of all systems across the enterprise. Installing personal-firewall software will not solve physical security problems. Rather, it will help ensure that remote users will not be able to attack systems as easily. Installing cameras in the server room will help ensure that this particular room is safe, a change that indirectly affects all users who access these servers. However, installing cameras in the server room will not secure information that is distributed on the client workstations found in the enterprise.

20. B. In order for George to authenticate without using Gracie's /etc/passwd and /etc/shadow files, he must first send Gracie his public key. Then, during authentication, SSH will compare the value of George's public key with his private key and allow authentication to take place. If George obtained Gracie's key, Gracie could then authenticate with George's server. There is never a need to make a user's private key readable only by root. Also, George's private key will automatically be stored in a hidden directory; he will not have to do this himself.

Appendix A

Sample Security Audit Report

This appendix contains a sample security audit report. These reports generally include a compilation of the auditor's findings and recommendations for a company's security needs. Typically, you will use such reports for management purposes, both organizational and departmental. Note that this is just one example of this type of report.

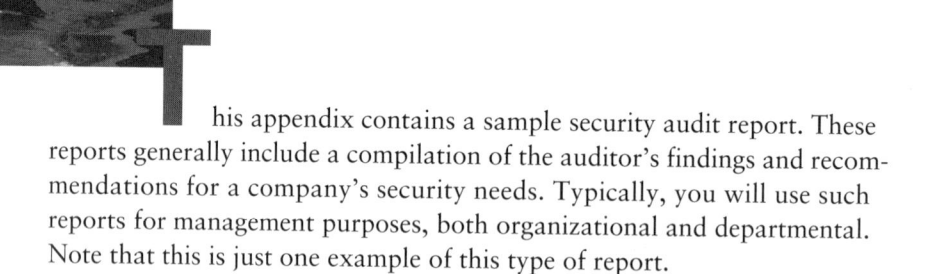

The assessment report contains an executive summary and a more detailed IT-level overview.

Executive Report

Overview

Overall security level was found to be low. Initial penetration of systems as administrator was achieved in less than 10 minutes. Primary security problems were the lack of good security filters and poor password selection on critical system accounts. These weaknesses allow relatively easy placement of tools such as packet sniffers, which allow examination of all traffic including that inside the firewall.

Perimeter Security

Your network does have a firewall, but you need additional rules. Also, several existing rules require editing to thwart newer attacks. Details about suggested rule configurations are given in a separate document titled "Firewall Rule Recommendations."

Internal Security

You do not, as of yet, have intruder-detection or probe software installed. Your host security is mostly adequate, though you need to improve your employee-training policy. You will find a discussion of these recommendations in the attached document, "Employee Training Recommendations."

Summary of Penetration Risk

Casual Attacker

Estimated time for a casual but determined attacker to penetrate security is less than two days with current security settings.

Experienced Attacker

Estimated time for an experienced attacker to penetrate security is less than one hour with current security settings.

Professional Attacker

Estimated time for a professional attacker to penetrate security is less than 15 minutes with current security settings.

Detailed Findings for the IT Department

Security Assessment Procedures

The external security assessment included several steps to determine the effective external level of security. To gain a true assessment of security from the perspective of an external attacker, we used the same methods and tools employed by the attackers. This process generally consists of three stages.

Discovery Stage

In this phase of the assessment, we use various tools to determine everything possible about the systems in the target network. This information is determined on a system-by-system basis. Once each system is located, it is individually scanned to identify elements, such as operating system version and patches, all software running on the system (again by version and patches), valid user and system accounts, complete system parameters such as system name, operating parameters, the system's role in the target segment, and security settings. Each running program is probed to determine the specific program configuration. By the end of the discovery stage, a complete map of the target network has been assembled.

Penetration Stage

We begin this phase of the assessment by examining the information from the discovery stage to select target weaknesses. All operating system and system software is checked against databases of known vulnerabilities. These vulnerabilities are individually tested on the target systems. The objective of this stage is to penetrate target-system security.

Control Stage

This phase begins after successful penetration of system security. In the target system, several activities take place. The entire target system is accessed, and any pertinent files and information are pulled. These files include complete security settings and parameters, log files, and system software configuration files. Other activities include creating back doors into the target systems and removing evidence of penetration. Once the target system is fully compromised, it is used as a staging point to penetrate security on the other systems on the subnet where this same process occurs.

Finally, to test the awareness levels of the systems staff, we launch a massive attack to trip any alarms and determine reactions.

Conclusions

The conclusions given in the executive summary are based on the following findings:

- Effective security filters are not employed at the external router.
- Strong passwords have not been employed on accessible systems.
- Unnecessary services have not been eliminated.
- Microsoft networking is accessible externally.
- SNMP information using the default "public" community name is accessible. Use Service Pack 6a on your Windows NT 4 systems to further enable SNMP options to allow read-only access to vital Management Information Base (MIB) settings. Your Windows 2000 systems already have this capacity. Consider using IPsec on your Windows 2000 systems to secure SNMPv1 transmissions, or use SNMPv3.

Note: SNMP often poses threats to network security, not only because it does not use encryption, but also because the code used to create the binaries has traditionally contained flaws. Activate SNMP only if you absolutely need it.

- Security auditing on accessible systems has not been enabled.
- File system security has not been fully implemented on accessible systems.
- DNS has not been secured.
- Windows 2000 system defaults have not been reconfigured.
- Critical Windows 2000 Registry trees have not been secured through auditing.
- System audit logs are accessible.
- Systems are readily susceptible to denial-of-service attacks.

Recommendations

First priority is the filtering of particularly vulnerable services at the outside router. Second priority is the proper securing of the individual NT/2000 systems. This includes properly securing accounts and services on the respective machines. Third, you need to introduce network-based intrusion detection in your DMZ. Host-based intrusion detection should be introduced at the 207.19.199.2, 207.19.199.3, and 207.19.199.5 systems.

The next phase of the security analysis is the onsite inspection of systems, software, and configurations. Additionally, key systems personnel should be interviewed to determine current procedures.

Immediate Recommendations (Medium to High Risks)

Implement packet filters at the external router:

- TCP/UDP 135 (RPC)
- UDP 137, 138; TCP 139 (Microsoft Networking)
- UDP 161, 162 (SNMP)

Note: Filters that implement the first two bullet points will stop over 80 percent of available tools for hacking Windows 2000.

Change all system account passwords to strong passwords.

Enable Windows 2000 security auditing on all machines. If possible, do the following:

- Audit all failures.
- Audit successful logons.
- Audit successful security policy changes.
- Audit successful startup and shutdown of system.
- Do not allow log overwrite.
- Save the audit logs regularly.

Enable strong password requirements for your Solaris and Windows 2000 systems.

Restrict anonymous logons.

Control remote access to the Registry.

Restrict access to the scheduler service.

Enable account profiles to lockout accounts, and enforce fresh passwords.

Enable administrator account lockout.

Rename the administrator account on Windows 2000.

Replace the Everyone group with Authenticated Users as appropriate.

Disable unneeded services as appropriate:

- RAS
- Unnecessary network protocols
- Server
- Alerter
- Messenger

Remove unnecessary subsystems, such as Posix and OS/2.

Secure IIS, including placing the FTP files on a separate partition.

You are running anonymous FTP with full read access. Although this arrangement is better than requiring password protection, you should ensure that the server does not allow itself to become part of a denial-of-service attack that can compromise root.

Network and Host-Level Security

Run an ACL reporting tool.

Encrypt the SAM password database.

Require the administrator account to log on locally.

Do not allow end users to restart the system.

Secure the /winnt/system32 directory with NTFS.

Long-Term Suggestions

Implement an active security monitoring system such as Snort, Symantec Intruder Alert, ISS RealSecure, or eTrust Intrusion Detection. A combination of a network-based and a host-based IDS would be ideal.

Install tripwires for hackers.

Create a dummy administrator account with heavy auditing and a login script that activates an alarm. If possible, install an application that systematically distracts and even punishes hacker activity.

Follow BS 7799 recommendations for antivirus control. You do not have a system in place for regulating and systematizing virus updates for all systems. Host 192.168.20.223 does not have any virus protection at all.

If you want, contact me for the eEye Retina log for the 192.168.21/24 subnet. None of the Windows 2000 servers is patched for the eEye IIS 5.0 buffer overflow hack. You can solve this by installing Service Pack 2 (or, alternatively, a post-Service Pack hotfix).

Configure your firewall to deal with IP spoofing and Smurf attacks. Also, your firewall is configured so that your network can become an unwitting part of a Smurf attack.

Your web server is vulnerable to both man-in-the-middle attacks and denial-of-service attacks. You can place your web server into a DMZ to further protect it. Also, you need to monitor its transactions more completely to determine whether it has become the victim of discovery and penetration attacks.

Remove sendmail banners from the following hosts: 192.168.56.129, 192.168.45.12, and 192.168.1.3.

Appendix B

A Sample Enterprise Scanner Report

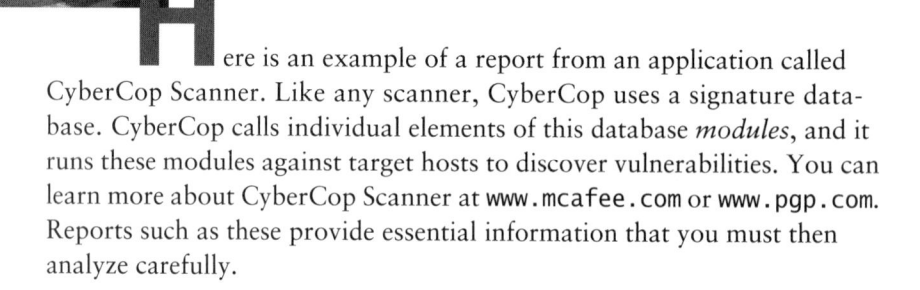

Here is an example of a report from an application called CyberCop Scanner. Like any scanner, CyberCop uses a signature database. CyberCop calls individual elements of this database *modules*, and it runs these modules against target hosts to discover vulnerabilities. You can learn more about CyberCop Scanner at www.mcafee.com or www.pgp.com. Reports such as these provide essential information that you must then analyze carefully.

Scan Results

Report for host: 127.0.0.1 (localhost)

Scan performed on Fri Apr 23 14:03:26 2001

Report generated on Fri Apr 23 16:09:30 2001

Hosts scanned: 1

12 vulnerabilities

Information-Gathering Modules

1007: sendmail Banners Check (Risk Factor: Low)

```
220-jacob.classroom11.com Microsoft SMTP MAIL ready at
    Fri, 23 Apr 2001 14:03:37 -0500 Version: 5.5.1774.114.11
220 ESMTP spoken here
```

This check collects the message displayed upon connection to the SMTP port of the target host.

Security Concerns

The SMTP port banner usually contains specific information about the version of SMTP agent you are using. This information can be used to launch specific attacks against software with known vulnerabilities. The most popular SMTP server for Unix, sendmail, has an extensive history of security problems. Knowledge of specific version information allows an attacker to predict what sort of attacks might be successful against your system.

Suggestions

Users of sendmail can modify banner information by editing the sendmail configuration file, /etc/sendmail.cf.

If you are running a version of sendmail prior to 8.8.8, we recommend that you upgrade sendmail; all earlier versions of sendmail have security problems. The latest version of sendmail is available from

www.sendmail.org

If you are not running sendmail as your SMTP agent, consult the documentation about modifying the version information displayed by your mail daemon.

Risk Factor: Low

1008: FTP Banner Check (Risk Factor: Low)

```
220 jacob Microsoft FTP Service (Version 5.0)
```

The FTP banner check attempts to gather banner information from the FTP daemon.

Security Concerns

If the FTP banner your host displays contains specific version information, an attacker can determine what attacks will be successful against your system.

Suggestions

If you are running a configurable FTP server such as WU-FTP or if you have access to the source code for the version of WU-FTPD you are using, consider making modifications to restrict the information displayed in the FTPD banner.

Risk Factor: Low

1009: Anonymous FTP Check (Risk Factor: Medium)

This check attempts to discern whether CyberCop Scanner can access an FTP server as an anonymous FTP user.

Security Concerns

If anonymous FTP has not been configured correctly, anonymous users might be able to extend their privileges beyond what you had intended. Consequences of an incorrectly configured anonymous FTP site can include:

- Remote compromise of your network
- Removal and modification of publicly accessible files
- The use of your site in the traffic of pirated software

Suggestions

Many Unix systems come with anonymous FTP set up by default. If you are not using anonymous FTP, disable it. Otherwise, ensure that anonymous FTP is configured correctly. The most important things to check are:

- The FTP account home directory is owned by the superuser.
- None of the directories in the FTP hierarchy are writeable by the FTP account.
- The passwd file in the ~ftp/etc/ directory does not contain passwords and lists only the few accounts needed for ls to map UIDs to usernames.

Risk Factor: Medium

1033: ICMP Netmask Check (Risk Factor: Low)

ICMP Netmask Reply: 255.0.0.0

This check attempts to obtain the remote system's network mask using the ICMP Address Mask Request and Reply packets.

1036: WWW Web Server Version (Risk Factor: Low)

Server: Microsoft-IIS/5.0

This module returns the version of web server running on the remote host, if it is available.

Security Concerns

Ensure that you are running the most current version of your web server software. An attacker can use the version information from your web server to determine if any known vulnerabilities are present.

Risk Factor: Low

SNMP Module

You have SNMP running. This version of SNMP is not patched and can be exploited by hackers. If at all possible, shut down SNMP services on this system. Otherwise, consult your vendor and patch this service.

20001: SNMP Community Check (Risk Factor: High)

```
'public': read-write
```

This module attempts to talk to a host's SNMP server using some commonly used community names. If a successful connection is made, the community is probed to see if it is read-only or read-write.

Security Concerns

SNMP access gives an attacker a wide variety of information from an SNMP-enabled device. This information ranges from the type and model of the device, to active network connections, processes running on the host, and users logged into the host.

SNMP write access allows an attacker to alter networking and other device parameters. An attacker with write access can alter the routing and ARP tables, bring network interfaces up and down, enable or disable packet forwarding, and alter several other networking parameters. In addition, vendor extensions can provide other control parameters that an attacker can manipulate. This level of access can lead to denial of service or the compromise of security or confidential information.

Suggestions

We suggest that you correctly configure your SNMP device to respond only to internal private community names. Write access should be disabled where not needed. Packet filtering should be used to limit the hosts that can communicate with the SNMP daemon.

Risk Factor: High

Port-Scanning Modules

21001: TCP Port Scanning (Risk Factor: Low)

```
TCP Port 21 (ftp) active
TCP Port 25 (smtp) active
TCP Port 80 (www) active
TCP Port 135 (RPC) active
```

```
TCP Port 443 (HTTPS) active
TCP Port 465 (unknown) active
TCP Port 554 (unknown) active
```
This check scans a target host for listening TCP ports.

Suggestions

The scanner will return which TCP ports are listening. You should check these ports to verify that they are running services you have approved. If they are running services that are undocumented, or that you do not want to run, we suggest that you disable them.

Many operating systems include numerous services that are not required for normal operation. In some cases, these services contain known or unknown security problems. Any services that are not required should be disabled.

Risk Factor: Low

21002: UDP Scanning Check (Risk Factor: Low)

```
UDP Port 135 (RPC) active
UDP Port 161 (snmp) active
UDP Port 162 (snmp-trap) active
```
This check scans a target host for listening UDP ports.

Suggestions

The scanner will return which UDP ports are listening. You should check these ports to verify that they are running services you have approved. If they are running services that are undocumented, or that you do not want to run, we suggest that you disable them.

Many operating systems include numerous services that are not required for normal operation. In some cases, these services contain known or unknown security problems. Any services that are not required should be disabled.

Risk Factor: Low

21006: RPC Scanning Direct (Risk Factor: Medium)

```
UDP port 756 program 100000 (portmapper) echoes calls
```
The RPC scanning direct check performs a UDP RPC scan of the remote host, attempting to find services by bypassing the Portmapper or `rpcbind`.

In many instances, the Portmapper (port 111), which translates RPC program numbers to port numbers, is being filtered at an organization's filtering device or firewall. By directly scanning for RPC services, you can obtain a full listing of RPC services running on the remote host and then contact them directly rather than querying the Portmapper first.

This check is unreliable over long-haul networks, due to the unreliability of the UDP transport layer. In cases when this check is being run over a long-haul network, some RPC programs that are actually running might not appear in the scan results.

Suggestions

We suggest that you review your filtering policy and prevent any RPC traffic from entering your network. RPC has a history of security-related problems, and many current implementations of RPC programs contain serious security vulnerabilities.

Risk Factor: Medium

Appendix C

Internet Security Resources

This appendix provides Internet addresses for many online security resources. Because of the constantly changing nature of the Internet, some addresses may no longer be valid.

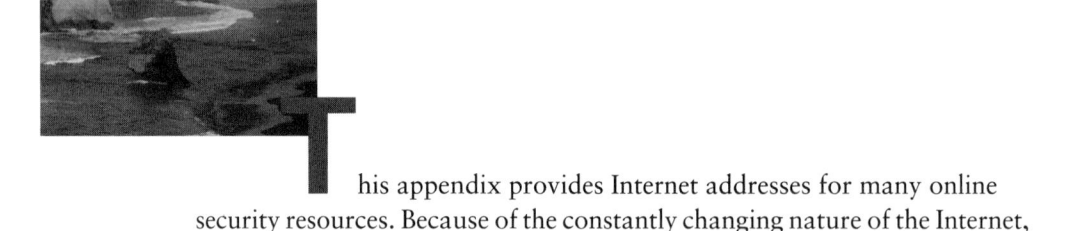

General

Computer Emergency Response Team (CERT)

CERT Advisories	https://www.cert.org/
CERT Security Tips	https://www.cert.org/nav/index_green.html
SANS Institute	www.sans.org/newlook/home.htm
Auditing Tips	www.securityauditor.net

Other Sources

Packetstorm	http://packetstorm.linuxsecurity.com
Internet Engineering Task Force	www.ietf.org
Internet Security Systems	www.iss.net
Symantec	www.Symantec.com
Helpful Operating System Hacks and Resources	www.securityfocus.com
International Computer Security Association	http://www.ncsa.uiuc.edu/

Third-Party Security Providers	www.itmtech.com
WebTrends	www.webtrends.com
Rainbow Series Online	www.fas.org/irp/nsa/rainbow.htm
Security Information, Stories, and Incidents	www.linuxsecurity.com www.slashdot.org www.linuxtoday.com
RSA Data Security—Encryption Information	www.rsasecurity.com
Secure Shell (SSH)	www.openssh.org www.ssh.com

Unix

BSD Bugs and Backdoors	www.freebsd.org
Linux Bugs and Backdoors	www.linuxsecurity.com
UNIX Security Tools	www.sourceforge.net
SCO Bugs and Backdoors	www.sco.com
Solaris Bugs and Backdoors	www.sun.com

Windows 2000

Known 2000 Bugs	www.ntbugtraq.com
Microsoft Security Advisory	www.microsoft.com/security
Windows 2000 Security Information	www.ntsecurity.com
Technical Downloads	www.microsoft.com/technet/download
Windows 2000 Security FAQ	www.ntsecurity.net
Miscellaneous Security Information	www.labmice.net/Security/default.htm

Glossary

A

absolute mode When using the `chmod` command, a way to assign permissions using the `chmod` command. Absolute mode uses the +, –, and = signs and options such as u, g, o, t, and s to assign permissions. Also known as *symbolic mode*. See *numeric mode*.

acceptable and unacceptable activity See *acceptable use policies*.

acceptable use policies Rules or regulations regarding authorized network and computer use and activities, including e-mail content. These policies are used to explain the activities that are acceptable and unacceptable in regard to network resources.

access control entry In Windows 2000, an entry in an *access control list (ACL)* that contains a user's or a group's *security identifier (SID)*, as well as the user's permission to access an *object*.

access control list (ACL) A list that defines the permissions for a resource by specifying which users and groups have access to the resource. See *access levels*.

access levels A term that describes a specific amount of access given by an *access control list (ACL)*.

access points A term often used to denote a secret *back door* created by a hacker. After a hacker compromises a system, he or she will create additional access points in case the systems administrator closes the original method of penetration.

access tokens Tokens given to user accounts by the operating system after successful authentication. An access token determines the parts of the hard drive that can be accessed, as well as the commands that the user can access for a particular session.

account reset The ability to have an account automatically reenable itself after a given interval. Often used with account lockout.

action In an IDS application, an action describes a specific response that the application will take. An action can include blocking a port, sending an e-mail, or sending a page to a security professional.

active open See *TCP handshake*.

adapter A device that provides connectivity between at least two systems.

address hiding The technique of using *network address translation (NAT)* to protect the network's topology.

Address Resolution Protocol (ARP) A Network-layer protocol used to convert a numeric IP address into a physical address, such as a MAC address.

Address Resolution Protocol (ARP) cache poisoning The ability to populate the ARP cache of a remote system with false information. Used as a strategy for sniffing traffic on a *switched network*.

Advanced Encryption Standard (AES) A replacement for the *Data Encryption Standard (DES)*, adopted in October 2000. AES is a symmetric-key encryption algorithm formerly called *Rijndael*.

agents Software that is installed on a network host and communicates information to a *manager*.

algorithm A particular procedure or process used to solve a problem. In server and network security, an algorithm is a mathematical function that allows information to be encrypted and decrypted.

amortization The practice of calculating costs over time.

analog A measurement format in which data is represented by continuously variable, measurable, physical quantities, such as time, frequency, or voltage.

anomalies Exceptions to *baseline* activity.

anomaly detection A strategy of a particular type of IDS application. In anomaly detection, the IDS application automatically creates a *baseline* of "normative" activity and then reports violations of that baseline.

anonymous FTP A method for legitimately accessing an FTP server without an assigned username or password.

antivirus software Applications that scan, detect, repair, and remove virus infections on a computer.

application An executable program typically used to perform functions on data, including retrieval, transmission, display, editing, and formatting.

Application layer 1) Layer 7 in the OSI/RM, responsible for presenting data to the user. 2) The top layer of the Internet architecture, corresponding to the Application, Presentation, and Session layers of the OSI/RM.

application layer proxy A firewall component that filters packets on a program-by-program basis and is capable of providing *strong authentication*. Also known as *application-level gateway*.

arp A utility that displays Address Resolution Protocol (ARP) information, including the physical address of computers with which you have recently communicated.

asset A network or server resource that requires protection. Assets also include information stored on network and server resources.

asymmetric-key encryption An encryption method using a pair of keys, one of which is made public and the other kept private. Also known as *public-key encryption*.

attack An incident in which a hacker or group of hackers attempts to compromise or deny service to a network or network host.

attack history A detailed list of server and network resources that have been attacked.

attack report A report that contains detailed information on a security event, including the nature of the event and actions taken by IT and/or security professionals.

attack signature database In an IDS application or vulnerability scanner, the collection of information that allows the security application to identify illicit traffic and vulnerabilities.

auditing The ongoing process of examining systems and procedures to determine their efficiency, including the ability to withstand hacker activity. Involves both manual and automated analysis.

auditor An individual who is authorized to test a network's security level. Auditors conduct tests to help them understand the network's ability to keep information secure and withstand various types of attacks.

audit report A written document designed to inform a specific audience about the security level of a network or network host. Audit reports are often directed at a specific audience (e.g., an executive or a senior IT worker).

authentication The ability to verify the identity of a person, host, or host process.

authentication header (AH) In *IPsec*, the data in an IP packet that allows a system to determine the identity of another system.

authentication package In Windows 2000, an item responsible for verifying credentials from a user.

B

backbone A network part that carries the majority of network traffic; usually a high-speed transmission path spanning long distances, to which smaller networks typically connect.

back door An undocumented opening in an operating system, daemon, or application that allows a user to defeat a system's authentication mechanisms.

bandwidth The amount of information, sometimes called traffic, that can be carried on a network at one time. Measured in bits per second. Many times, a *denial-of-service (DoS) attack* is designed to consume a network's bandwidth.

banner information Information presented by operating systems, services, and network daemons upon an initial connection. Such information can be used by hackers when discovering a system's vulnerabilities in preparation for system penetration and control.

baseline The activity of determining normative traffic and procedures for your network.

bastion A computer that houses various firewall components and services; it has one interface on a public network and another interface servicing a private network. Also known as a *bastion host*.

batch file A term used to denote a file that is run automatically under certain conditions. For example, a batch file can be created to run when a certain user account is activated. See *login script*.

binary file A file containing data or instructions written in terms of zeros and ones (computer language).

bind The act of attaching a networking protocol to a computer's operating system.

bitmap A graphics file format that assigns information to individual pixels.

black hat hacker A term used by security professionals to describe a hacker who gains illicit access to computer systems. See *white hat hacker*.

blind spoofing   An attack that occurs when a hacker manipulates a connection that exists on a separate physical line. See *non-blind spoofing*.

block cipher   An encryption algorithm that encrypts data in discrete blocks. See *stream cipher*. Also known as *block mode cipher*.

Boolean operator   A symbol or word used in Internet searches to narrow search results, or to include or exclude certain words or phrases from the results.

boot sector   A dedicated portion of a disk that contains the first parts of an operating system's startup files.

bottleneck   Any element (a hard drive, I/O card, or network interface card) that slows network connectivity rates.

bridge   A hardware device that filters frames to determine whether a specific frame belongs on a local segment or another LAN segment; uses hardware addresses to determine which segment will receive the frame.

broadcast addresses   IP addresses used to send messages to all network hosts. The broadcast address is typically 255.255.255.255.

brute-force attack   A method of network invasion that repeatedly tries different possible passwords from a *dictionary program* that contains obvious passwords and names in order to gain unauthorized access to network assets.

buffer   A cache of memory used by a computer to store frequently used data. Buffers allow faster access times.

buffer overflow   A condition that occurs when too much data is placed into a *buffer*, or when unchecked information is placed into a buffer that cannot properly process the data.

C

cable modem   A hardware device that connects a computer to a WAN, such as the Internet, using cable television lines. A cable modem works by demodulating transmissions from the cable network, modulating the computer's transmissions to the WAN, and using one or more channels on the cable television line for these transmissions.

cache   An area of RAM or disk storage used to store frequently accessed information for speedy retrieval.

caching server   An internetworking server that caches frequently accessed network data, such as web documents or streaming media.

capacity forecasting   The ability to plan the amount of bandwidth (and even server resources) required to provide services to future customers.

cascading proxies   See *proxy array*.

casual attacker   A hacker who discovers, penetrates, and controls systems for no other reason than curiosity. See *determined hacker*.

catastrophic event   The loss of information due to the failure of a server or network resource. The event can be a result of a natural disaster or human activity.

certificate authority (CA) In a *Public Key Infrastructure (PKI)* environment, a trusted authority that verifies authenticity of a host or person that requests a digital certificate. See *registration authority*.

certificate repository A server or series of servers and networks that house digital certificate information.

certificate revocation list (CRL) A list containing digital certificates that are no longer valid. Used in *Public Key Infrastructure (PKI)* implementations.

certificate server An internetworking server that validates or certifies keys. See *Public Key Infrastructure (PKI)*.

certification path A document listing the PKI servers responsible for creating a specific certificate.

chain In `iptables` or `ipchains`, a specific set of packet filter rules that allows you to block, allow, or redirect traffic. See *special chains*.

Challenge Handshake Authentication Protocol (CHAP) The de facto standard in dial-up connections. Used by many client operating systems when accessing a *remote access server (RAS)*. CHAP uses one-way encryption to help guarantee the security of the authentication process.

chargeback The ability to accurately determine costs for networking and security services provided. This concept is used by large corporations to track charges incurred when one department renders services to another.

checksum analysis 1) In network communications, the act of establishing how many bits have been transmitted during a session in order to determine if the session is complete. 2) In security, the ability to calculate the original state of a piece of data and then determine if the data has been altered.

choke point A single place where all traffic must pass through.

choke router A router that exists on a *demilitarized zone (DMZ)*. Specifically, it exists between the DMZ and the private network.

circuit-level proxy A firewall component that monitors and transmits information at the Transport layer of the OSI model. Also known as a *circuit-level gateway*. It hides information about the network; a packet passing through this type of gateway appears to have originated from the firewall.

Classless Interdomain Routing (CIDR) The ability to provide additional IP addresses by customizing the subnet mask for the IP address.

Classless Interdomain Routing (CIDR) notation The practice of referring to an IP address and its subnet mask. For example, the CIDR notation of 192.168.2.0/24 refers to the IP address of 192.168.2.0 on the 255.255.255.0 subnet.

client A system or application that requests a service from another computer (the server).

command-line interface A common method for accessing computers and operating systems that requires users to type and enter commands on a keyboard or console.

Common Criteria A security standard that unifies the Information Technology Security Evaluation Criteria (ITSEC) and the Trusted Computer Systems Evaluation Criteria (TCSEC). Discusses security levels, including D, C1, C2, and so forth.

Common Gateway Interface (CGI) A program that processes data submitted by the user through a web-based application.

Common Internet File System (CIFS) A term used to describe *Server Message Blocks (SMB)*.

community name In the *Simple Network Management Protocol (SNMP)*, a text string used to enforce authentication. The default community name is often "public."

compile A process used to convert programming code into machine code for an executable object or application.

compiled languages High-level programming languages that require a special program called a compiler to process statements written in a specific language; the compiler converts the language into code understood by a computer processor. Examples include C, C++, and Java.

compliance monitoring The act of determining compliance of server and network resources to a company's security policy. Often involves the use of compliance-monitoring software, which uses agents to report non-compliant resources to a security professional.

connection chain A series of connections made to systems across the Internet. Malicious users often log in to multiple systems before waging an attack. Connection chaining helps the user to avoid detection.

connectivity A term used to describe the ability for a client to communicate with a server, or for two or more networks to communicate with each other.

contingency plan A written plan that describes procedures to take when a firewall has been compromised or is no longer working properly.

control stage The stage of an attack in which the hacker is able to modify system settings and spread to other systems. See *discovery stage* and *penetration stage*.

cookie A small text file created by a web server that resides on a client's computer and preserves the state of a client-server session. May be used to store data, settings, and other information.

cracker A computer user who attempts to gain unauthorized access to another computer or network asset for nefarious purposes.

credential caching The ability for an operating system to store logon information, even after the user has logged off. Such credentials can be used to gain access to the network, even if the user's account is removed from a central authentication server.

cross-frame browsing bug A specific instance of a bug-based attack, the cross-frame browsing bug affected certain web browsers (e.g., Microsoft Internet Explorer 4). It allowed a malicious website to execute scripts on the end user's system. As a result, these hackers were able to gain illicit access to the systems of any user who visited the site.

D

daemon A Unix program that is usually initiated at startup and runs in the background until required.

database A file or series of files used to organize information by storing data in a consistent format so that users can search the files for specific information.

data confidentiality See *data privacy*.

Data Encryption Standard (DES) An encryption algorithm that was, until the adoption of the *Advanced Encryption Standard (AES)*, the de facto private-key encryption standard.

datagram A packet at the Network layer of the OSI/RM.

data privacy A term used to describe the ability to keep information secure. Encryption allows users and machines to ensure data privacy. Also known as *data confidentiality*.

data validation The process of checking or confirming data entered into fields by a user.

default gateway The IP address of the router on your local network.

default installations Hosts that have been placed onto a network and that have not been customized for their particular environment. Hackers often target systems that have default settings.

default shares Shares that automatically exist after system installation. These shares can be managed by right-clicking on the system's drive in a Windows 2000 system.

demilitarized zone (DMZ) A protected area between an external (i.e., screening) and internal (i.e., choke) router where public servers may be hosted.

denial-of-service (DoS) attack An attack meant to deny authorized users access to a network, usually by flooding one or more network assets with packets or messages that consume server resources.

destination IP address A term used in various security situations, including firewalls and IDS applications. It describes the IP address where a packet is going to be sent. See *source IP address*.

destination port A term that describes the port where a particular packet will be sent. This term is used in various situations, including the activities of configuring firewalls and IDS applications.

determined hacker A hacker who discovers, penetrates, and controls systems for a specific reason. Often, a determined hacker is motivated by financial gain or by a specific ideology.

dictionary attack The use of a *dictionary program* to wage an attack against a system. Such attacks are designed to defeat encryption. See *brute-force attack*.

dictionary program A program specifically written to break into a password-protected system. It has a relatively large list of common password names it repeatedly uses to gain access. See *brute-force attack*.

Diffie-Hellman The de facto method for exchanging public keys.

digital certificate A digital ID issued by a *certificate authority (CA)* to authenticate and validate Internet data transfers. A digital certificate is a specific form of an asymmetric key. See *Public Key Infrastructure (PKI)*.

digital signature The practice of using encryption (usually hash encryption) on data to show that it has not been changed. Also used to prove that data did, in fact, come from an authorized source. See *signing*.

Digital Signature Algorithm (DSA) An open source public-key encryption algorithm introduced by the *National Institute of Standards and Technology (NIST)*. An alternative to the *RSA* algorithm.

Digital Subscriber Line (DSL) A high-speed direct Internet connection that uses all-digital networks.

directory server An internetworking server that stores contact information for individuals in a database.

discovery stage The stage of an attack in which the hacker is able to research and scan systems to learn more about the nature of your network. Also includes *social engineering*. See *control stage* and *penetration stage*. Applications used during the discovery stage include ping and port scanners.

discretionary access control A term that describes how a server or network resource, or *object*, must have an owner; the owner should be able to determine who or what can access that object. Used with the *Common Criteria* (e.g., the C2 level enforces discretionary access control).

disk cache A storage space on a computer hard disk used to temporarily store downloaded data.

distributed denial-of-service attack (DDoS) A form of DoS attack that uses multiple computers to conduct a coordinated assault on a network asset.

Domain Name System (DNS) A system that maps uniquely hierarchical names to specific Internet addresses.

Domain Name System (DNS) poisoning The activity of populating a DNS server with false entries.

dotted quad A common term for describing an IPv4 address, such as 192.168.54.34.

dual-homed bastion hosts Firewalls that funnel traffic through a computer with two network interface cards (NICs). Software-imposed firewall rules help forward valid packets between subnets.

dummy accounts and files The use of seemingly valid accounts that in fact have no value. Often a component of a *honey pot*.

Dynamic Host Configuration Protocol (DHCP) An Application-layer protocol designed to assign Internet addresses, DNS servers, and gateway addresses to nodes on a TCP/IP network during initialization. Commonly used to configure workstations.

E

egress filtering The act of blocking outgoing traffic at a firewall or router. See *ingress filtering*.

e-mail (electronic mail) A system for transferring messages from one computer to another over a network. Messages may include data in text-only format or text with attachments.

Encapsulating Security Payload (ESP) The element of *IPsec* that allows data encryption. It provides data integrity and confidentiality to IP packets.

end entity A client in an *IPsec* or PKI implementation.

enterprise networks Networks that provide connectivity among all nodes in an organization, regardless of their geographical location, and run the organization's mission-critical applications. Enterprise networks can include elements of peer-to-peer and server-based networks. An enterprise network may consist of several different networking protocols.

/etc/nologin A text file that is designed to prevent users from logging into a system from a remote host. This file is found in Unix systems. The very presence of this file denies Telnet-based logins; its contents can include a message informing users that logins are denied, or it can be an empty text file.

/etc/securetty A text file found in Unix systems that lists the terminals the root user can use to log in to the system. The system's login program (usually `/bin/login`) reads this file. If the terminal is not listed in the file, then root cannot log in at that terminal.

Ethernet A set of hardware technologies and networking protocols for LANs, including MAC and CSMA/CD. Also defined as IEEE 802.3. First developed at Xerox PARC in 1972.

ethical hacker An auditor who imitates hacker activity. Also known as a *white hat hacker*.

execution control list (ECL) A list that determines what applications can be executed on an operating system or in an application. This list can apply to all users, or only to certain users.

extranet A network that connects enterprise intranets to the global Internet. Designed to provide access to selected external users to expedite the exchange of products, services, and key business information.

F

facility/priority pair In Linux and Unix systems, the values that allow `syslogd` (the system logger) to detect and report events.

false negatives Situations in which an attack has actually occurred, or where a vulnerability actually exists, but is not detected by a tool such as an IDS or vulnerability scanner.

false positives Situations in which a standard element of an operating system is marked by a security application (e.g., an IDS or vulnerability scanner) as a vulnerability, or on which legitimate network traffic is mistakenly marked a threat.

fault tolerance The ability of a system to respond gracefully to an unexpected hardware or software failure.

field A particular part of a firewall or IDS rule.

File Allocation Table (FAT) A Microsoft-specific format for a hard drive. The latest version of FAT is FAT32, which allows for larger partitions. It is not considered as secure a file system as *NTFS*.

File Transfer Protocol (FTP) An Application-layer protocol used to transfer files between computers. FTP allows file transfer without corruption or alteration.

flat-file database A database in which all information is kept in a single file. Also called *non-relational databases*. The Windows *Registry* is an example of a flat-file database.

forensic analysis The study of a computer that has been attacked. A forensic analysis can include "resurrecting" deleted files, analyzing log files, and any activity that helps determine the nature of the attack.

Fraggle attack The use of a flood of UDP packets sent from multiple hosts. See *Smurf attack*.

frame A packet at the Data-Link layer, used to traverse an Ethernet network.

freeware Software that is distributed free of charge.

front-door attack See *brute-force attack*.

fully qualified domain name (FQDN) The complete domain name of an Internet computer, such as www.ciwcertified.com.

functions Stand-alone, reusable segments of program code that are not part of an object.

G

gap analysis A study that determines the difference, or *gap*, between what is mandated by the security policy and actual employee practice.

gateway A device that converts signals from one protocol stack to another. Also called a "protocol converter."

GNU A variety of non-proprietary Unix-compatible software and operating systems. GNU software formed the basis for Linux. The acronym stands for "Gnu's Not Unix."

group identifiers (GIDs) In Unix systems, a GID is a number in the /etc/passwd file that identifies a specific group.

H

hacker In some circles, a computer user who knows an application, operating system, or hardware very well. As far as the CIW Security Professional Exam is concerned, a malicious user who tries to defeat authentication and gain illicit control over computer systems.

handshakes In host-to-host encryption (e.g., IPsec), the process of negotiating the proper dialects and encryption methods that will be used to begin a secure network connection.

hash encryption A type of encryption that converts information of any variable length into scrambled, 128-bit pieces of code called a *hash value*.

hash value A term used to describe what is generated when hash encryption is used against a piece of data.

Health Insurance Portability and Accountability Act (HIPAA) A security standard enacted by the U.S. government. It applies to all health care providers, and is designed to help guarantee the security of personal information stored on computers and transferred between networks.

hexadecimal A base-16 system that allows large numbers to be displayed by fewer characters than if the number were displayed in the regular base-10 system. In hexadecimal, the number 10 is represented as the letter A, 15 is represented as F, and 16 is represented as 10.

hijacking The process of taking over and controlling a connection. In a hijacking attack, a hacker is able to interrupt legitimate communications between two systems and then imitate one of the two systems. As a result, the attacker can gain access to valuable information.

honey pot A system (or series of systems) designed to trick a hacker into thinking that he or she has discovered, scanned, and penetrated valuable systems. Many times, such a machine is called a *sacrificial system*. A honey pot will then contain alarm systems that alert security professionals about an attack in progress. Another term for a honey pot is a *jail*. See *dummy accounts and files*.

hop One link between two network devices. The number of hops between two devices is considered a *hop count*.

host A generic term used to describe any machine that communicates on a network.

host-based IDS An application that involves the use of managers and agents to detect illicit network activity. See *intrusion-detection system (IDS)*.

host-based management model A security management model in which managers and hosts communicate with each other to provide security services. For example, compliance software often uses a manager/agent model to communicate the existing patch levels of a network server. See *network-based management model*.

host-based scanner Software that is installed on a network host, and that is capable of delving deeply into the system's inner workings. A host-based scanner can report low patch levels, system bugs, and problem system configurations.

hosts file A file that links IP addresses to alphanumeric names, such as nicknames and domain names. Before the DNS was developed, hosts files on each Internet computer contained a complete mapping of all registered Internet node names to their IP addresses.

hub A hardware device that connects computers in a star-configured network so that they can exchange information. Most hubs are active hubs; they have a powered supply and can act as repeaters. Also called a *concentrator*.

Hypertext Markup Language (HTML) The standard authoring language used to develop web pages.

Hypertext Transfer Protocol (HTTP) An Application-layer protocol for transporting HTML documents across the Internet. HTTP requires a client program on one end (a browser) and a server on the other, both running TCP/IP.

Hypertext Transfer Protocol Secure (HTTPS) An application-layer protocol used to access a secure web server.

I

illicit server Code that resides on a network computer that allows a hacker to bypass standard authentication procedures and control a system. Examples of illicit servers include NetBus, Girlfriend, and BackOrifice.

incident response team (IRT) A group of security professionals who use an *intrusion-detection system (IDS)* and other elements to identify and respond to attacks.

inetd The Internet daemon. A Unix network daemon that responds to received requests and starts an appropriate Internet service. Also called the *super daemon*. See *xinetd*.

information technology (IT) department An in-house computer and network systems department entrusted with the setup, operation, and maintenance of all computer systems within an organization. Often, security auditors and professionals are not a formal part of the IT department.

Information Technology Security Evaluation Criteria (ITSEC) The international version of the TSEC security standard that discusses security levels, including D, C1, C2, and so forth.

ingress filtering The act of blocking incoming traffic at a firewall or router. See *egress filtering*.

inheritance A term used to describe when a subdirectory is subject to permissions that have been set in a directory above it.

initial sequence number The number assigned to the first TCP packet during the *TCP handshake*.

inode In Linux and Unix systems, describes a file or directory on the hard drive. An inode contains information about files and directories. Such information can include location, creation times, modification times, and all associated permissions.

insider attacks An attack against a network asset mounted by an internal user of a computer network.

internal bastion host A bastion host that exists on an internal network. This type of bastion host is used to protect high-priority subnets from the rest of the company.

Internet The global wide area network (WAN) that uses TCP/IP and other protocols to interconnect other WANs, LANs, and computers.

Internet Control Message Protocol (ICMP) The troubleshooting Network-layer protocol of TCP/IP that allows Internet hosts and gateways to report errors through ICMP messages that are sent to network users.

Internet Key Exchange (IKE) In *IPsec*, the process of exchanging keys to create an encrypted network connection.

Internet layer The OSI/RM layer responsible for addressing and routing packets, using a protocol such as IP Layer 4 of the OSI/RM. Also known as the Network layer of the OSI/RM.

Internet Message Access Protocol (IMAP) A more sophisticated, powerful alternative to POP3. Allows sharing of mailboxes and multiple mail server access, and allows users to manage their files without first downloading them.

Internet Security Association and Key Management Protocol (ISAKMP) In *IPsec*, the protocol that negotiates the encryption type and authentication method used in a secure connection.

Internet Server Application Programming Interface (ISAPI) A web server extension that allows the server to execute other programs and scripts without the expensive processing associated with CGI. Supported on Microsoft operating systems and some third-party gateways.

Internet service provider (ISP) An organization that maintains a gateway to the Internet and rents access to customers on a per-use or subscription basis. Sometimes referred to as an *Internet access provider*.

Internet standard A protocol designated as an official standard by the *IETF*. Also called a full standard.

in the wild A phrase used to describe viruses that are currently being found in the Internet. Can also be used to describe hacker applications that are readily available.

intrusion-detection application An individual application, service or daemon that detects illicit activity. See *intrusion-detection system (IDS)*.

intrusion-detection system (IDS) A series of services, daemons, and applications designed to detect illicit activity that occurs on the company network. Two types of IDS applications exist: *host-based IDS* and *network-based IDS* applications.

IP address A numeric address that identifies a computer or device on a TCP/IP network. IPv4 addresses are 32 bits in length, and arranged in a dotted quad such as 127.0.0.1. IPv6 addresses are 128 bits in length and use eight sections of hexadecimal numbers, each delimited by a colon.

ipchains An application that allows a Linux system, for example, to create a packet filter rule. Newer systems use `iptables`. See *Netfilter*.

IPsec An authentication and encryption protocol that provides security over the Internet; it functions at Layer 3 of the OSI/RM and can secure all packets sent between two hosts.

IP spoofing The ability to forge IP packets so that they appear to originate from another source.

iptables In newer Linux systems (2.4 and higher), an application that creates packet-filtering rules.

J

jail See *honey pot*.

K

Kerberos An authentication system developed by the Massachusetts Institute of Technology (MIT). This system can authenticate users, network services/daemons, and hosts. Its chief benefits are that users can be authenticated without passwords crossing over the network wire, and that authentication can take place only for a certain period of time. Used in many authentication schemes, including Windows 2000 domains.

kernel The essential part of an operating system. Provides basic services and always resides in memory.

key A string of numbers used by software that scrambles your message from plaintext, readable by anyone, into encrypted text. Some software encrypts and decrypts with the same key (e.g., using *symmetric-key encryption*), whereas other software relies on a pair of keys (e.g., *public-key encryption*).

keylogger An application that can save keystrokes and then make them available to an illicit user (e.g., through e-mail, or by creating a world-readable file that the hacker can then obtain by connecting to an *illicit server*).

key pair A mathematically related set of values. Used in *public-key encryption*, one key is kept private, while the other can be distributed. See also *asymmetric-key encryption*.

L

land attack An attack involving the use of a spoofed IP packet to a target host. The spoofed packet has the same source and destination as the target host. Older Linux systems, for example, would subsequently crash.

latency 1) The delay caused when data is sent between two computers; each computer wastes time waiting to communicate, when that time could be used for actual computations. 2) In security, the measured impact that security measures can have on employees.

Layer 2 Forwarding Protocol A protocol introduced by Cisco systems meant to encrypt transmissions. See *Layer 2 Tunneling Protocol (L2TP)*.

Layer 2 Tunneling Protocol (L2TP) An IETF standard tunneling protocol primarily used to support *virtual private networks (VPNs)* over the Internet.

Lightweight Directory Access Protocol (LDAP) A protocol based on X.500 for transmitting data from a directory server to a client.

load balancing The process of distributing processing and communications activity evenly across a computer network so that no single device is overwhelmed.

Local Security Authority (LSA) In Windows 2000, a part of the security subsystem that is responsible for loading authentication packages, creating access tokens, and other services.

login script An executable file that runs whenever a user logs in. In a security context, often useful when creating honey pots. See *batch file*.

loopback A set of IP addresses used to test and diagnose network connections. The common loopback address is 127.0.0.1.

M

MAC address See *Media Access Control (MAC) address*.

managed security providers Third parties who can provide security services, including firewall configuration, intrusion detection, and management of vulnerabilities.

manager A piece of software used to communicate with an agent. A manager usually communicates with multiple agents and then stores information for retrieval by a security professional. See *agent*.

mandatory login A term used in security standards such as BS 7799 to describe the requirement for all enterprise-grade network operating systems to enforce authentication.

man-in-the-middle attack An attack in which a hacker manipulates packets being sent from one host to another. Specific man-in-the middle attacks include the use of a *packet sniffer*, *packet-injection attacks*, and *hijacking*.

masquerading The ability to rewrite private addresses in the IP address header so that private network transmissions can be forwarded across the Internet. See *Network Address Translation (NAT)*.

matrix A combination of individual methods, techniques, and subsystems meant to provide or improve network security.

media Any material that allows data to flow through it or be stored on it, including hard and floppy disks, wire, cable, and fiber optics.

Media Access Control Along with Logical Link Control, one of two sublayers of the IEEE 802.2 standard. Provides access to LAN media by placing the data on the network, and provides a physical address, hardware address, or Ethernet address.

Media Access Control (MAC) address A unique hardware address that is assigned and burned in by the *network interface card (NIC)* manufacturer. Can be used to identify a specific computer on a network.

mirroring A process that causes two sets of disk writes to occur for each original disk write that takes place. Uses a mirror set that is established between two or more physical hard drives or partitions.

mission-critical applications Applications that are absolutely essential for the day-to-day operation of a business environment.

modem bank A collection of modems that enable remote users to dial in to the network. A modem bank is often a target of attack by hackers who want to avoid the firewall and gain access to the private network.

multihomed bastion hosts A bastion host that has two or more NICs.

Multipurpose Internet Mail Extension (MIME) A protocol that identifies a file type, encodes the file using the file type, and decodes it at the receiving end to display properly. Used for e-mail attachments and by HTTP servers; file types are classified as MIME types.

municipal area network (MAN) A network used to communicate over a city or geographic area.

N

National Institute of Standards and Technology (NIST) An agency of the U.S. government that creates technology standards.

National Science Foundation (NSF) An independent agency of the U.S. government that promotes the advancement of science and engineering.

needs assessment audit A review of equipment to determine what equipment (e.g., software and hardware) is necessary in order to provide or enhance security.

NetBIOS The Network Basic Input/Output System, which allows systems to communicate over a network. Used by Windows systems (and Linux systems using Samba) to provide computer names over the network. See *Server Message Blocks (SMB)*. Often, NetBIOS is run over TCP/IP to enable network communications.

Netfilter A capability in newer Linux kernels (2.4 and higher) that allows more sophisticated packet-filtering rules.

netiquette A set of cultural standards for proper Internet usage, including the formatting and writing of e-mail and newsgroup messages.

netlogon service A Windows NT/2000 service that is part of the security subsystem. The netlogon service must be running in order for the operating system to authenticate users.

netstat A utility that displays the contents of various network-related data structures, such as the state of sockets.

network A group of two or more computer systems linked together.

Network Access Layer A layer of the Internet architecture that corresponds to the Physical and Data-Link layers of the OSI/RM. Includes the operating system's device driver, corresponding *network interface card (NIC)*, and physical connections.

network adapter card See *network interface card (NIC)*.

Network Address Translation (NAT) The process of mapping one or more external addresses to multiple internal addresses. Using NAT conceals the actual IP address of any computers behind the firewall.

network analyzer A software program that can intercept and decode network transmissions, including packets. Also called a *packet sniffer*.

network appliance A dedicated piece of hardware shipped from a vendor that has a specific security purpose.

network assessment The activity of conducting vulnerability scans, checking log files, and generating auditing reports.

network assets Network devices that include local resources, network resources, server resources, and information resources.

network-based IDS An IDS application that resides on one system and monitors the entire network. See *intrusion-detection system (IDS)*.

network-based management model A security model that uses sweep-based applications to discover the security levels of systems on the network. For example, many vulnerability scanners use this model. See *host-based management model*.

network client A generic term used to describe a host that is communicating with a server.

Network File System (NFS) A way for Linux (and Unix) systems to share directories across a network.

Network Information System (NIS) A centralized authentication system for Linux and Unix clients and servers.

network interface card (NIC) A hardware device installed in a computer that serves as the interface between a computer and a network. When you're using a cable modem, an additional cable connects your computer's NIC to the modem. Also called a *network adapter card*.

network latency See *latency*.

Network layer Layer 4 of the OSI/RM, responsible for addressing and routing packets, using a protocol such as IP. Also known as the Internet layer of the Internet architecture.

network map A detailed (often graphical) list of network resources. Can include servers, routers, firewalls, and wiring equipment (e.g., wiring closets).

network operating system (NOS) An operating system that manages network resources.

network perimeter The outer edge of the network defined by the firewall.

newsfeed A source that transmits newsgroup information and messages to NNTP servers.

newsgroups An Internet discussion group that allows users to read and post messages using NNTP.

New Technology File System See *NTFS*.

node Processing locations on a network, such as a computer, printer, or other device.

non-blind spoofing A situation in which a hacker manipulates a connection on the same subnet or physical line.

nonrepudiation The capacity to ensure that an individual party to a communication, agreement, or other contract cannot refute or deny the authenticity of their signature on a document or the sending of a message that they originated.

nonroutable An indication that a protocol cannot pass across a router. Also, private IP addresses are not routable across Internet routers.

NTFS A Microsoft-specific file system that allows for user-based permissions, auditing, encryption, compression, and larger partition sizes than FAT or FAT32. NTFS stands for *New Technology File System*.

null SMB session A session in which an anonymous user is able to retrieve information from a Windows system. A null session can be established either on Windows servers that have the Server service running, or on Unix/Linux systems that are using Samba. Information resulting from null sessions can include the server name and users defined on the operating system.

numeric mode A way to assign permissions using the `chmod` command. Numeric mode uses numbers, such as 544, to assign permissions. See *absolute mode*.

O

OAKLEY protocol In *IPsec*, a protocol that is used to exchange encryption keys.

object A specific resource on a network server. See *object reuse*.

object reuse Most network operating systems have the ability to reuse objects, and to protect the operating system from situations in which object reuse could cause a potential security problem. See *object*.

one-time password (OTP) A password that is never reused. An example of one-time passwords is the One Time Passwords in Everything (OPIE) project (`http://inner.net/opie`).

one-way encryption An encryption method that is used for information not meant to be decrypted. The encrypted message can be checked against a hash table of hexadecimal numbers to confirm its validity. Also called *hash encryption*.

online cataloging The process of creating a catalog of data; the catalog then becomes a searchable index that is available online.

open network A group of clients and servers that can freely access each other.

open source The act of providing free source code to the development community-at-large to develop a better product; Apache Web Server, Mozilla (a version of Netscape Communicator), and Linux are all open source creations.

Open Systems Interconnection Reference Model (OSI/RM) A seven-layer networking model used to break down the many tasks involved in moving data from one host to another.

operating system fingerprinting See *stack fingerprinting*.

organizational structure A term used to describe how to place IDS applications so that they help secure the most important resources.

out-of-process An executable program (EXE) that launches a separate process each time it is loaded or referenced.

P

packet Data processed by protocols so it can be sent across a network.

packet filter A router or firewall that screens packets based on their contents and discards offending packets. Packet filters operate at Layer 3 of the OSI/RM.

packet-injection attacks   Specific *man-in-the-middle attacks* that allow an illicit user to insert packets into an existing data stream.

packet sniffer   An application (e.g., `tcpdump` or `Ethereal`) that captures packets from the network. See *man-in-the-middle attacks*.

packet stream   A term used to describe packets of data as they flow across the network. Also known as a *data stream*.

packet trace   The activity of reviewing log files and records kept by intrusion-detection applications and then determining the origin of an attack. Can be foiled by *IP spoofing*.

packet type   A part of a packet-filtering rule that determines the type of packet that will be matched.

parallelization   The use of multiple processes, processors, or machines to work on cracking one encryption algorithm.

passive open   A part of the *TCP handshake*.

password aging   The configuration of an operating system to automatically request an end user to change a password after a certain period of time.

password lockout   The ability to have an account become disabled (permanently or temporarily) after a certain amount of time, or after a certain number of failed login attempts. Also known as *account lockout*.

password sniffing   A method of intercepting the transmission of a password during the authentication process. A *sniffer* is a program used to intercept passwords. Examples of packet sniffers include `tcpdump`, Sniffer Basic, and Ethereal.

patch level   A term used to describe the security of a particular operating system, service (i.e., daemon) or application. Whenever a security flaw is discovered, most vendors will issue code to solve the problem. This code is called a *patch*.

peer-to-peer network   A network formed by two or more computers that are linked to each other without centralized controls. Each computer can have as much control as the other over the network.

penetration stage   The stage of attack in which a hacker is able to use applications to defeat authentication. See *control stage* and *discovery stage*.

performance management   The process of determining the existing workload of systems on the network.

permissions   1) Instructions given by an operating system or server (or a combination thereof) that restrict or allow access to system resources, such as files, user databases, and system processes. 2) An owner's granting of the rights to another for the use of copyrighted or licensed intellectual property.

personal firewall   A combination of hardware, software, and policies designed to protect a personal computer from attacks launched through an Internet connection. Also known as a *desktop firewall*.

physical attack   A term used to describe the activity of gaining access to a network or network host by gaining entry to the server room. See *structure infiltration*.

physical-line trace An attempt to discover the origin of an attacker who has used a phone line.

ping flood The act of flooding a server with repeated pings, perhaps as part of a *denial-of-service (DoS) attack*.

ping of death An attack in which a hacker sends a packet larger than 65,536 bytes. Used on unpatched systems.

ping scanning The use of an application that issues ICMP packets with the intent of discovering systems that reside on a specific network.

plaintext Unencrypted text that can be easily viewed by the sender, the receiver, or an intermediary.

Pluggable Authentication Modules (PAM) In Linux, text files, binaries, and modules responsible for authenticating users and controlling access to system resources.

point of contact A designated person who will be notified in case of a break-in, or when information must be passed from a third party, such as a managed security provider.

Point-to-Point Protocol (PPP) An improved version of SLIP that allows a computer to connect to the Internet over a phone line. If an ISP offers you a choice of a SLIP or a PPP connection, choose PPP.

Point-to-Point Tunneling Protocol (PPTP) A protocol that encrypts transmissions and is capable of encapsulating (i.e., tunneling) other protocols. This protocol is often used to create a *virtual private network (VPN)* over public networks, such as the Internet.

port An address contained in the headers of TCP and UDP packets that identifies the appropriate communication process. Ports 0 through 1023 are referred to as the *well-known* port numbers. Ports 1024 through 49151 are known as the *registered* port numbers. Ports 49152 through 65535 are known as the *dynamic* port numbers.

port listener A piece of software that can listen in on connections made to a system. Often included in intrusion-detection and personal-firewall software. Malicious users can also use port listeners to "listen in" on other users who have begun sessions with the network host.

Portmapper A Linux/Unix daemon that listens on TCP port 111. It accepts requests and then maps them to various daemons, including the Network File System (NFS) and the Network Information System (NIS).

port redirection An activity that causes a system to send information from one port to another either on the local system or to a remote system. Often, port redirection is a valid activity. However, a hacker can attempt to redirect sensitive information so that it becomes available to the wrong parties.

port scanner A program designed to query remote hosts and discover any open ports that the system may have. An efficient port scanner has the ability to scan hundreds of systems very quickly, or even conduct a *slow scanning attack*.

Post Office Protocol (POP) A protocol that resides on an incoming mail server. POP sorts mail into the correct user mailbox for the user to download. The latest version is POP3. The standard POP3 port is TCP 110.

printer drivers Executable files used by print servers when processing print jobs. Through the years, improperly written print drivers have been responsible for successful attacks on systems, resulting in administrative access.

private key In encryption, the use of a single key to encrypt and decrypt information (e.g., a text file).

private NIC A NIC in a bastion host that is not exposed to the Internet.

proactive detection The attempt to anticipate attacks by using various methods, including honey pots, intrusion-detection systems, and employee awareness training.

process An executing program or task.

promiscuous-mode detection The ability for a system to detect if a remote system's NIC is capturing packets on the network.

proxy A generic term used to describe the ability for an application or service to accept requests from a client and then act for and in behalf of that client by passing the request on to another network or network host.

proxy array An arrangement in which several proxy servers have been chained together. Provides scalability, *fault tolerance*, and greater speed.

proxy cluster A collection of proxy servers. Proxy clusters are often used for *load balancing*.

proxy server An intermediary server that stands between a network host and other hosts outside the network. Provides enhanced security, manages TCP/IP addresses, and speeds access to the Internet by providing caching server functions for frequently used documents.

public-key authentication The use of *public keys* to verify authenticity. Allows authentication to occur without sending passwords across a network. *Secure Shell (SSH)* can be configured to allow authentication using public keys.

Public Key Cryptography Standards (PKCS) Standards that determine the proper behavior of PKI servers.

public-key encryption An encryption method using a pair of keys, one of which is made public and the other kept private. Also known as *asymmetric-key encryption*.

Public Key Infrastructure (PKI) The use of digital certificates to enable encryption and authentication for specific users and hosts. Often, PKI is used to refer to a collection of servers that create digital certificates.

public keys Keys generated by *Public Key Infrastructure (PKI)* tools. See *asymmetric-key encryption*.

public network A term used to describe a network that resides outside a firewall.

public NIC In a firewall, a NIC that is exposed to a *public network*.

R

real time A term that describes the capability of detecting events and responding to them as they occur. For example, firewalls and IDS applications can respond to as traffic as soon as it is detected and properly matched.

redundant logging The practice of duplicating a system's log files onto a remote system, or onto more secure media.

registration authority In PKI, responsible for verifying the identity of a person or host that participates in a PKI scheme. Often part of the *certificate authority (CA)*.

Registry In Windows systems, a flat-file database that contains vital system settings.

Registry subtrees The Registry includes subkeys that determine how the local system behaves.

remote access server (RAS) A server that accepts connections from remote systems and then provides access to a private network. A RAS can provide access to the network through dial-up connections, or through *virtual private network (VPN)* connections.

Remote Procedure Call (RPC) A protocol used in network-capable hosts that allows an application on one host to request a particular service from a remote host.

removable media Hard, floppy, and CD-ROM drives that can be attached or removed from a system, usually without a reboot. An example of removable media is a drive made available via Universal Serial Bus (USB).

replay attack An attack that involves resending or replaying a captured and altered message.

Requests for Comments (RFCs) Published documents of the IETF that detail information about standardized Internet protocols and those in various development stages.

reserved IP addresses Address ranges reserved by ICANN for use on private networks, including ISPs and LANs. These include 10.0.0.0 through 10.255.255.255; 172.16.0.0 through 172.31.255.255; and 192.168.0.0 through 192.168.255.255. The reserved address ranges are commonly referred to as the "private address ranges."

resource placement The act of determining where to place security tools (e.g., firewalls or IDS applications) so that they increase a network's overall security.

response field In an IDS, the particular part of a rule that allows the IDS application to take action (i.e., react to a perceived attack).

response policy A part of the corporate information security policy, which helps IT and security professionals react properly to attacks.

retaliatory measures The controversial practice of taking steps to punish a hacker for attacking a system.

Reverse Address Resolution Protocol (RARP) A Network-layer protocol that uses a node's hardware address to request an IP address. Generally used for diskless workstations and X terminals.

reverse proxy servers Proxy servers that receive connections from the Internet and then distribute connections to company web servers.

reverse scan A retaliatory measure, in which a system that you own conducts a scan on a system that has conducted a scanning attack. This practice is very controversial, because many attackers use *IP spoofing* to thwart attacks, and because it is rarely, if ever, acceptable to engage in attacks yourself.

Rijndael A symmetric-key algorithm that has been adopted as the *Advanced Encryption Standard (AES)*.

risk A term used to denote the amount of exposure to threats caused by vulnerabilities.

risk analysis The ability to determine how likely a specific threat can cause damage to your network. This analysis considers threats, and it also takes into account specific vulnerabilities found in your server and network resources. Also known as a *risk assessment*.

rlogin A series of applications and daemons that, once configured, allow a user to log on to a remote system without first providing a password. The rlogin series of daemons are generally not considered secure because they do not encrypt transmissions, and because they are too reliant on IP-based authentication.

root In Unix systems, a user account that has full administrative privileges.

root access 1) A term used to describe privileged administrative access to Unix systems (e.g., Solaris and Linux). 2) A generic term used to describe any administrative access.

root kit A collection of Trojans that replace legitimate applications, including `ls` and `passwd`.

round A discrete part of the encryption process; information is scrambled according to the key being used.

routable An indication that data can be forwarded through a router.

router A network device that determines the best path across a network for data.

routing The act of directing packets to their destination, using a router.

routing information table A database maintained by a router that contains the location of all networks in relation to the router's location.

RSA A public-key encryption algorithm owned by RSA Inc. (www.rsasecurity.com/rsalabs/). Invented by L. Rivest, Adi Shamir, and Leonard Adleman, and used in many public-key encryption applications. Many applications use the *Digital Signature Algorithm (DSA)*, because RSA is owned by RSA Inc.

rules Entries in a firewall or intrusion-detection application that determine how traffic will be handled.

S

sacrificial system In a *honey pot* (i.e., *jail*), a host that is designed to be an attractive target.

sandboxing A model and/or practice that limits a program's access to computer resources. One example of a sandboxed program is the *Java Virtual Machine*.

scalable A term used to describe a network solution that, by design, has the ability grow in size, and thus will not encumber users or suffer from frequent failures due to increased usage.

scanning attack An attack in which a utility is used to either discover hosts that are on the network or discover the nature of the services that a host is providing. Whenever a user scans another system he or she does not own, that person has conducted an attack on that system.

screened host firewall A firewall that uses a router to first filter out packets before they enter the DMZ.

screened subnet A complex firewall type that uses a bastion host to create a physical break in the network connection. It also uses two routers to screen incoming connections.

screening router A router that resides on the public side of the demilitarized zone. This router is the first to begin filtering traffic.

script kiddies Inexperienced users who employ downloaded scripts and programs to hack or crack into computers and servers, frequently by scanning many network computers to find machines that have a known security hole.

search path In any operating system, a value that determines the directories (i.e., folders) that will be searched whenever a process or end user issues a command for a specific file. Also known as the *system path* or simply *path*.

secure data backup and storage A phrase used to ensure that data has been properly stored. Includes using encryption to ensure data confidentiality and integrity, as well as offsite storage.

secure HTTP (S-HTTP) A method for encrypting HTTP traffic. The chief difference between S-HTTP and SSL is that S-HTTP occurs at the Application layer of the OSI/RM. See *Secure Sockets Layer (SSL)*.

Secure MIME (S/MIME) A secure version of MIME that adds encryption to MIME data.

securenets A file that controls which systems can use a Network Information Service (NIS) server.

Secure RPC An attempt to make the RPC protocol more secure. Secure RPC authenticates requests more thoroughly. This protocol also encrypts transmissions to help thwart sniffing attacks.

Secure Shell (SSH) A replacement to Telnet and the r-series of applications. SSH is capable of encrypting sessions and providing authentication that does not allow passwords to travel across the network.

Secure Shell (SSH) handshake process The process of obtaining the SSH server's public key and negotiating the encryption type for the session. When a Secure Shell client communicates with an SSH server for the first time, it will obtain the server's public key. A client always negotiates the encryption type when making a connection to a server.

Secure Sockets Layer (SSL) A technology, embedded in web servers and browsers, that encrypts traffic.

security A term that encompasses the safety and protection of information and network assets, especially from unauthorized users, hosts, and processes.

Security Account Manager (SAM) In stand-alone Windows 2000 and NT systems, the database that holds user and group credentials.

security association (SA) In *IPsec*, the exchange that uniquely identifies a particular host and enables encryption.

security audit report A written report directed at a specific audience designed to show the current state of the network. A security audit report can be directed to various parties, including executives and IT workers.

security descriptor In Windows 2000, a descriptor that holds the security settings for an object (e.g., a text file, a folder, or a database).

security identifier (SID) An identifier that represents a user, a user's group, or computer in a Windows 2000 system.

security levels A term used by the Trusted Computer Systems Evaluation Criteria (TCSEC) to describe the relative security level of a system. For example, a common security level is C2 (discretionary access control).

security mechanisms A term used in ISO 7498-2 to describe ways to implement security on a network. As far as ISO 7498-2 is concerned, wide and specific mechanisms exist. An example of a wide security mechanism is an audit trail; an example of a specific security mechanism is access control.

security roadmap A plan that allows you to manage and increase your network's security stance.

security subsystem In Windows 2000, the term used to describe the different applications and services used to authenticate users. Includes the Security Account Manager, Winlogon, and the Graphical Identification and Authentication DLL (GINA).

segment A part of a larger structure, commonly used in networking to refer to a portion of a large network.

Serial Line Internet Protocol (SLIP) A dial-up connection protocol that allows a computer to connect to the Internet over a phone line.

server farm A group of servers.

Server Message Blocks (SMB) A protocol that allows systems to share files and printers. Supported by Microsoft and Linux (using Samba). All systems that use SMB must first negotiate the specific form, or *dialect*, supported by both systems. More secure forms of this dialect encrypt transmissions. However, lower-grade dialects do not encrypt transmissions.

Server service A Microsoft-specific service that provides NetBIOS names for a system and allows the creation of shares. In many cases, the Server service can be deactivated to help secure an Internet-based server.

server-side include A piece of code written into an HTML page that activates programs and interpreters on the server. An include is designed to create active web pages and reduce server overhead.

service A method for providing information to network users.

session key A key that is kept secret; used to begin an encrypted session across a network.

setgid A Linux/Unix permission setting that allows an application to execute as if it belonged to a different group.

setuid A Linux/Unix permission setting that allows an application to execute as if it belonged to a different user.

shadow password In Linux, a file, readable and writeable only by root, that contains password hashes. One of the primary ways to begin to secure your Linux system is to ensure that all passwords have been removed from the /etc/passwd file and placed into the /etc/shadow file.

share points Folders where a share is provided on a network.

shareware Software that is distributed free of charge, but requests or requires payment of a registration fee if the user continues to use the software beyond a certain period of time.

shell A command-based interface, usually for an operating system.

shell account The command-line interface of a Unix server at the ISP. Shell accounts require users to enter commands to access and navigate the Internet.

shielded twisted-pair (STP) cable Twisted-pair copper wire that is protected from external electromagnetic interference by a metal sheath wrapped around the wires.

signature A specific entry in a program (e.g., an IDS application, vulnerability scanner, or antivirus application) that allows the application to detect illicit activity.

signature-based IDS application An IDS application (the most common type) that relies on a database of defined attacks in order to detect intrusions on the system. The opposite of an IDS that uses *anomaly detection*. See *intrusion-detection system (IDS)*.

signature detection See *signature-based IDS application*.

signing The use of a *digital signature* or hash code to help detect if data has been altered. Signing can also be used to verify information origin.

simple intrusion A term that describes a one-time intrusion that is limited to a single system.

Simple Mail Transfer Protocol (SMTP) An Application-layer protocol for transferring Internet e-mail messages. Specifies how two mail systems interact, as well as the format of control messages they exchange to transfer mail. The standard SMTP port is TCP 25.

Simple Network Management Protocol (SNMP) An Application-layer protocol that provides a standardized management scheme for managing devices on TCP/IP networks.

single-homed bastion host A firewall that uses one computer that acts as both a firewall component and the network interface.

single-purpose bastion host A bastion host that contains only one service or daemon.

slow scanning attack An activity in which an attacker discovers the ports of an individual system or the systems in an entire network over an extended period of time (e.g., several weeks or even months).

smart card A credit card-sized device that includes an embedded computer chip for storing and processing data.

SMB dialect A particular version of the *Server Message Blocks (SMB)* protocol. Some versions do not encrypt network transmissions. Others use relatively high encryption, depending on the patch level of the operating system.

Smurf attack An attack that involves an application that uses multiple systems to send ICMP packets to a target host.

social engineering An attempt to gain unauthorized network access by obtaining information from authorized users through simple psychological (rather than technical) tricks, like handing around a "personal survey" to obtain birth dates, children's names, and so forth.

socket The end point of a connection (either side), which usually includes the TCP or UDP port used and the IP address. Used for communication between a client and a server.

SOCKS A specific implementation of a *circuit-level proxy*. Also known as *SOCKS server*.

source IP address A term used when configuring firewalls, IDS applications, and so forth. Describes the IP address where a packet has originated. See *destination IP address*.

source port A term used to describe the port where a particular packet originated. Used when configuring various applications, including firewalls, personal firewalls, and IDS applications. See *destination port*.

spam A popular term for unsolicited commercial e-mail.

special chains In `iptables` and `ipchains`, built-in chains that can be used to block, allow, or redirect packets. Examples include INPUT, OUTPUT, and FORWARD.

spoofing attacks An attack in which a host, a program, or an application assumes the identity of a legitimate network device or host, in an attempt to gain information about a network asset. Also called a *masquerade attack*.

stack fingerprinting The practice of scanning systems and then studying the system's response to determine the operating system. By studying how the system responds to various network communication requests (e.g., connections on certain ports and responses to ping packets), the hacker can accurately determine the operating system being used on a remote system. Also known as *operating system fingerprinting*.

stand-alone services A service or daemon that is directly executed by the operating system. A stand-alone service or daemon is the opposite of one that is started by another daemon, such as *inetd* or *xinetd*.

stateful A protocol that requires a connection or state to be established before data can be transmitted. Also called *connection-oriented*.

stateful multiplayer inspection The ability for a packet-filtering firewall to detect a port scan.

stateless A protocol that can transmit data without a dedicated connection, using a "best-effort" technology that sends the information to the network, hoping that the data will reach the intended system. Also called *connectionless*.

stream cipher An encryption algorithm that encrypts data one bit at a time. Less common than a *block cipher*.

strong authentication The process of identifying an individual, usually based on a username and password, in which the requirements for selection and application of the username and password are designed to enhance the security of the authentication method.

strong password A password that cannot be easily decrypted or guessed. A strong password often involves the use of uppercase letters, nonstandard characters (e.g., @#$%^&), and/or numbers. Above all, strong passwords avoid words that can be easily guessed or that can be found in a standard dictionary.

structure infiltration A term used to describe activities in which a person works to gain entry to a building. See *physical attack*.

subnet mask A 32-bit number similar to an IP address with a one-to-one correspondence between each of the 32 bits in the Internet address. Distinguishes the network and host portions of an IP address, and specifies whether a destination address is local or remote. Also called a *netmask*.

super daemon See *inetd* and *xinetd*.

superzapping The use of one operating system or application to make changes to another target operating system. Such changes are not logged on the targeted operating system.

suspicious activity Any machine-based or human-based activity that falls outside of an established *baseline*.

switch A hardware device that directs the flow of information from one node to another. There are several varieties of switches that work at different layers of the OSI/RM.

switched network A network that uses a *switch* instead of a standard hub to connect systems. Often, a switched network makes it more difficult to engage in a *man-in-the-middle attack* (e.g., packet sniffing).

symbolic mode A way to assign permissions using the chmod command. Uses the +, −, and = signs and options such as u, g, o, t, and s to assign permissions. Also known as *absolute mode*.

symmetric-key encryption An encryption method that uses a single key to encrypt and decrypt messages. All parties must know and trust one another completely, and have confidential copies of the key.

synchronous A condition in which data is exchanged in character streams called message-framed data. The access device, such as a NIC, and a network device, such as a router, share a time clock and a transmission rate, and a start-and-stop sequence is associated with each transmission.

SYN flood A type of *denial-of-service attack* in which an unauthorized user initiates but does not complete the establishment of a connection-oriented session, called a *TCP handshake*. SYN is an abbreviated code for "synchronize," and is used in TCP to establish the connection-oriented session.

Syskey A Windows utility that allows a systems administrator or security professional to protect the Windows account database. Available in all Windows 2000 systems, and in Windows NT (Service Pack 4 and higher).

system accounts Accounts used by system services (i.e., daemons) and accounts; generally do not provide a login shell.

system bug A term used to describe a configuration error or an error contained in the code of an application or daemon.

system latency A term used to describe the amount of time it takes a system to respond to a request. Many times, security measures can have an impact on the performance of a network host. See *latency*.

system snooping The action of a hacker who enters a computer network and begins mapping the system's contents.

T

TCP handshake A three-step process in which a device attempts to create a connection-oriented TCP session by sending its TCP sequence number and maximum segment size to a recipient device, which responds by sending its sequence number and maximum segment size to the first device, which then acknowledges receipt of the sequence number and segment size information.

TCP/IP The standard protocol suite for breaking up data for transmission to another computer, using Transmission Control Protocol (TCP), and for specifying the destination address, using Internet Protocol (IP). See *Transmission Control Protocol (TCP)*.

TCPWrappers A collection of applications, or "wrappers," designed to protect daemons such as FTP, Finger, the r-series of applications, Secure Shell (SSH), and the trivial IP services. Once TCPWrappers is installed and enabled, it is possible to use the /etc/hosts.allow and /etc/hosts.deny files to control access to these daemons.

Teardrop A *denial-of-service attack* that manipulates UDP packets.

Telnet An Application-layer protocol that is the Internet standard for remote terminal connection service.

threat A possible attack that can be waged against your network. You have less control over the types of threats that face your network. See *vulnerability*.

time stamp Information on when data was last altered or sent from a network host. Can include exact times when data was created or altered.

topology Basic configurations that information systems professionals use to physically connect computer networks.

traceback The activity of determining the origin of a packet.

tracert A utility that can determine the path between the source and destination systems. An example is traceroute.

transaction 1) An event involving a financial exchange, such as a purchase in a store, or a withdrawal from a checking account. 2) An event that changes or alters one or more records in a database.

Transmission Control Protocol (TCP) A stateful Transport-layer protocol that ensures reliable communication and uses ports to deliver packets. TCP/IP fragments and reassembles messages, using a sequencing function to ensure that packets are reassembled in the correct order.

Transport layer The layer of the OSI/RM model responsible for building up and tearing down connections.

trap-door attack An attack on certain commands that open potential unauthorized access, such as a diagnostic account.

trend analysis The ability to differentiate between legitimate and illegitimate traffic by first establishing a *baseline* and then reviewing subsequent traffic.

tripwire 1) A generic term (lowercase) meant to describe an element of a *honey pot* or *jail* that automatically notifies a security professional of a possible security breach. 2) The name (Tripwire) of a Unix/Linux application that creates a *time stamp*, as well as checksums of information, and then issues reports listing any changes that have occurred on the hard drive.

Trivial File Transfer Protocol (TFTP) An Application-layer protocol used with BOOTP for initializing diskless systems such as workstations and routers by using UDP.

trivial IP services A collection of services, including quotd, chargen, echo, and echo, and others. These services are often used to troubleshoot network connectivity, and can often be disabled to enhance network security.

Trojan Also known as a *Trojan horse*. A file or program that purports to operate in a legitimate way but that has an alternative, secret operation. A Trojan is a specific program that destroys information on a hard drive.

trusted A term used to describe a proxy server's NIC that allows traffic from the internal network to enter the proxy server's system.

Trusted Computer Systems Evaluation Criteria (TCSEC) A security standard, specific to the United States, that discusses security levels, including D, C1, C2, and so forth. See *Information Technology Security Evaluation Criteria (ITSEC)*.

trusting A term used to describe the network and/or host that is allowed access to the network.

trust relationship The use of public-key cryptography to allow systems to authenticate with each other and encrypt transmissions.

Type of Service (ToS) A function in a router or even a firewall that allows you to give priority to certain types of traffic.

tunneling The act of encapsulating one data stream inside another. Tunneling can be legitimate (e.g., the authorized use of the Layer 2 Tunneling Protocol) or illegitimate (e.g., tunneling POP3 inside HTTP to defeat a firewall).

tunneling protocol A type of protocol that encapsulates data packets into another packet. See *Layer 2 Tunneling Protocol (L2TP)* and *Point-to-Point Tunneling Protocol (PPTP)*.

U

umask 1) A value on a Unix (i.e., Linux) system that indicates the permissions that a file will have by default when it is created. 2) A command that allows you to set the `umask` value.

Unicode A text and script character standard that can interchange, process, and display text of many different written languages.

Uniform Resource Locator (URL) A text string that supplies an Internet or intranet address, and the method by which the address can be accessed. The URL for the Sybex website is www.sybex.com.

unnecessary services Services or daemons that are running on a system, yet that do not fulfill any particular business role. Such services should be shut down in order to improve the network host's security.

unpatched A term used to describe a system that has a low patch level and that is susceptible to a *system bug*.

User Datagram Protocol (UDP) A connectionless Transport-layer protocol designed for broadcasting short messages on a network. UDP does not support acknowledgment messages. Also used for streaming media.

user identifiers (UIDs) A UID is a specific number on a Unix system given to each user. The lower the number, the higher the user's privilege. A UID of 0 denotes the "root" user. By default, Linux systems start UIDs at 500.

V

virtual network perimeter A term used to describe the outer area(s) of a series of networks after they are connected using a *virtual private network (VPN)*.

virtual private network (VPN) A method for allowing secure network access to external users through a firewall or remote access server using tunneling protocols.

virus A program that replicates itself on computer systems, usually through executable software, and causes damage to system files or to data that resides on the system.

Visual Basic The Microsoft graphical user interface (GUI) programming language used for developing Windows applications. A modified version of the BASIC programming language.

Visual Basic Script (VBScript) Scripting language from Microsoft, derived from Visual Basic; used to manipulate ActiveX scripts.

vulnerability A specific flaw or weakness in a network or server resource. You have the ability to take action against a specific vulnerability in order to reduce risk. See *risk* and *risk analysis*.

vulnerability scanner An application that scans remote or local systems to determine problems in configuration (e.g., low patch levels or unnecessary open ports). All vulnerability scanners use a database; they correlate data returned from a remote system with this database to determine the severity of the vulnerability.

W

war dialing A process in which a hacker uses specialized software to discover modems and then conduct dictionary and brute-force attacks to penetrate the network.

war driving A process in which a malicious user (e.g., hacker) drives from location to location with a wireless device to try to infiltrate wireless networks that have not been secured.

white hat hacker An individual who is authorized to test server and network resources for weaknesses. See *ethical hacker* and *black hat hacker*.

WHOIS An Internet utility primarily used to query databases to determine registered hosts.

wide area network (WAN) A group of computers connected over an expansive geographic area, such as a state or country. The Internet is a WAN.

window spoofing A particular web browser bug that allows hackers to imitate a legitimate site. The practice of window spoofing allows a hacker to send an end user to an illicit site, yet still make the end user think that he or she is accessing a legitimate web page.

Wireless Application Protocol (WAP) A communication protocol that provides a standard for wireless devices to access the Internet.

workstation A terminal or personal computer on a network; usually refers to a client.

worm A program that when executed on a computer, consumes more and more resources until that computer can no longer function. A worm can also spread to other computers.

Write Once, Read Many (WORM) The term used for any media that allows information to be permanently written to it. Once it accepts data, WORM media does not allow the information to be erased. To secure logging, it is often useful to write logs to such a medium (e.g., a CD-R disc).

X

X Window system A windowing system used with Unix, Linux, and other operating systems.

X.25 A WAN communications standard that ensures error-free data delivery by checking errors at many points along the data's path. Used for connecting automated teller machines, credit card transaction terminals, and point-of-sale terminals.

X.500 An OSI protocol used to manage user and resource directories; a hierarchical system that can classify entries by country, state, city and street, for example. See also *Lightweight Directory Access Protocol (LDAP)*.

xinetd A replacement for the original *inetd*. A network daemon that responds to requests and starts an appropriate Internet service. Also called the *super daemon*.

Z

zone file A file that contains name-resolution information for hosts that participate in the *Domain Name System (DNS)*.

zone transfer A process in which one DNS server obtains a *zone file* from another.

Index

Note to reader: **Bolded** page numbers refer to definitions and main discussions of a topic. *Italicized* page numbers refer to illustrations.

A

absolute mode, 371–372, **662**
acceptable activities, 20, **662**
acceptable use policy, **662**
access control, 33–35
    ACLs, **34–35**
    defined by ISO, 7
    ECLs, **35**
    enforcing, 157
    Everyone group and, 355–356
    exercise implementing, 36–42
    ntfs.txt settings, *358*
    overview of, 33–34
    specific security mechanisms, 8
access control entries (ACEs), **320–321**, **662**
access control lists. *see* ACLs (access control lists)
Access Control Setting dialog box, *357*, *357*, *396*
access levels, ACLs, 34, **662**
access points, 501, **662**
access tokens, **319**, **662**
accidental threat, 108
account module, Linux PAM, 326
account policies, Linux, 324
account policies, Windows 2000, **334–336**
    account reset, 335–336
    overview of, 334
    password aging, 334–335
    password lockout, 335
account reset, Windows 2000, 335–336
account security
    Linux
        password aging, 336–337
        strong passwords, 333
    overview of, 330

    passwords, 331
    timing out users, 336
    Windows 2000
        account policies, 334–336
        strong passwords, 331–332
accounts
    creating with batch files, *487*, 487
    hackers creating new, 501
    multiple, as hacker control strategy, 486–488
    removing, **337–338**
    renaming default, **338–339**, 408
    resetting, **662**
ACEs (access control entries), **320–321**, **662**
ACLs (access control lists), *320*
    defined, **662**
    overview of, **34–35**
    types of, 320
actions, IDS, 517, **519**, **662**
active auditing, 36
active threats, 109
activities, acceptable/unacceptable, **19–21**
adapters, **662**
Add Item dialog box, *213*, 213
address hiding, 407, **662**
Address Resolution Protocol (ARP), **662**
Address Resolution Protocol (ARP) cache, 112, **662**
administrative access. *see* root accounts
administrator Properties, Profile tab, *290*
administrators, security
    security policies and, **23**
    suspicion as characteristic of, 157
    training for, 163
Adore root kit, 137–138
Advanced Encryption Standard, AES (Advanced Encryption Standard)
Advanced TCP/IP Settings dialog box, *401*

AES (Advanced Encryption Standard)
   defined, **662**
   exercise using, 65–67
   overview of, **64–65**
agents, **527–528**
   defined, **662**
   manager-to-agent communication, 526, 528
   organization, 527–528
   placement, 527
   placing on servers, 599–600
   user/agent architecture, 442, *442*
AH (authentication header), **664**
alarms, proxy servers, 228
algorithms
   asymmetric, **69**, 91–92
   defined, **663**
   encryption and, 24
   rounds and, 57
   symmetric, 59–64
      AES, **64–65**
      Blowfish, **62**
      DES, **59–60**
      IDEA, **61–62**
      MARS, **63**
      others, 63–64
      RC2, RC4, RC5, and RC6, **61–62**
      Rijndael, 63
      RSA encryption, 60–61, *61*
      Serpent, **63**
      Skipjack, **63**
      Triple DES, **60**
      Twofish, **62–63**
Allow all traffic, firewall configuration, 204
amortization, **168**, **663**
analog, **663**
anomalies
   baselines and, 557
   common types of, 557–559
   defined, **663**
anomaly detection, IDS, 523, **663**
anonymous FTP
   defined, **663**
      information-gathering modules and, 651–652
AntiSniff, promiscuous mode detection, 600–601
antivirus programs
   defined, **663**
   preventing root kits with, 139
   protecting against keylogging, 133
Apache server
   authentication and access control in, 36–42
   information leakage in, 125–126
Apocalypso interface, 65, *65*, *66*
Application layer, **663**
application layer proxy, **197–198**, **663**
Application log, Windows 2000, 562
applications
   defined, **663**
   IDS, **517–519**, **674**
   mission-critical, **676**
   network discovery and server discovery, **454–455**
   NFS, 413–414
ARP (Address Resolution Protocol), **662**
ARP (Address Resolution Protocol) cache
      poisoning, 112, **662**
arp utility, **663**
assets, 7, **663**
asymmetric encryption, **67–69**, *75*
   algorithms, **69**
   authenticating Linux client, **621–623**
   backing up private key, 69
   defined, **24**, **663**, **682**
   overview of, 67–68
   proprietary algorithms, 91–92
   SSH and, 611–612
   web browsers and, 95
atd daemon, 417
ATM (Asynchronous Transfer Mode), 525
attack detection strategies, IDS, **523**
attack history, 600, **663**
attack reports, 296–297, **663**
attack response plan, **295–302**
   analyze and learn from incident, 300–302
   assessing the situation, 297–298
   documenting, 296–297

not panicing, 296
response policy
    executing, 298–300
    setting ahead of time, 295–296
    stopping or containing activity, 298
attack signature databases, 518, 663
attacks
    brute-force, 133–136
    bug-based, 123–128
        back doors, 124
        buffer overflows, 126–128
        trap doors, 124
    combining types, 128–130
    defined, 663
    DoS (denial-of-service), 116–122
        DDoS (distributed denial-of-service), 120–121, *121*
        land attack, 120
        ping-of-death/ping floods, 120
        preventing, 122
        recovering from, 121
        Smurf and Fraggle, *118*, 118–119
        SYN flood, 116–117, *117*
        Teardrop, 119–120
    exam essentials, 142–144
    fake e-mail, 130–131
    general categories, 108–109
    insider, 122–123
    key terms, 144–145
    keylogging, 132–133
    man-in-the-middle, 113–116
        connection hijacking, 114–115
        against DNS servers, 115–116
        types of, 113–114
    review answers, 152–154
    review questions, 146–151
    spoofing, 111–112
    system defaults and, 124–126
    Trojans, 136–139
    types of, listed, 109–110
    viruses, 139–141
    worms, 141–142

audit analysis, automated, 285–286
audit reports, 443–444, 664
audit trails, 8
auditing, 317, 434–480
    from behind firewalls, 445–446, *446*
    defined, 663
    discovery methods, 448–460
        DNS tools, 449–451
        finger command, 459
        network/server discovery applications, 454–455
        overview of, 448–449
        ping scanning, *451*, 451–452
        port scanning, *452–453*, 452–454
        SNMP, 459
        stack fingerprinting, 455–458
        Telnet, 458–459
        Trivial TCP/IP services, 459–460
    education and social engineering, 466
    eEye Retina, *467*, 467–470, *469*
    exam essentials, 470–472
    implementing native auditing, 601
    key terms, 472
    research, 466
    review answers, 478–480
    review questions, 473–477
    stages of, 446–448
        control, 448
        discovery, 446–447
        penetration, 447–448
    TCSEC definitions, 12
    types of, 35–36
    vulnerability scanners, 460–465
        information obtained with, 462–464
        list of, 460–461
        network scanning issues, 461–462
        reports from, 464–465, *465*
    Windows 2000 Registry, 395–396, 398–399
Auditing tab, Windows 2000, 563–564, *564*
auditors, 434–446. *see also* log analysis
    compliance analysis, 435–436
    defined, 434, 664

vs. hackers, 503
information obtained by
    host-level, 463–464
    network-level, 462–463
reading logs files, 556
reports, 443–444
risk analysis, 437–443
roles and perspectives, 444–446
auth module, Linux PAM, 325
authentication, 26–33
defined, 664
implementation exercise, 36–42
ISO definition, 7
methods, 27–29
    what you have, 27–28
    what you know, 26–27
    where you are, 28–29
    who you are, 28
misconfiguring Linux settings, 324
NIS weaknesses and, 413
proxy servers and, 228
as specific security mechanisms, 8
SSH and, 611–612, 618–620
TCSEC definition, 12
techniques, 29–33
authentication header (AH), 664
authentication package, 323, 664
autologout program, 337
automated audit analysis, 285–286
automated security scans, 283
automatic intra-operating system trust, 391–392
automatic key distribution, 57

B

back doors
    bug-based attacks, 124
    defined, 664
    hackers creation of, 501
backbone, 664
BackOrifice, 485

backups
    bastion hosts, 248
    log files, 574
    procedures, 161
    verifying, 160–162
    Windows 2000 Registry, 396
bandwidth, 664
banner information, 664
baselines, 556–560
    defined, 664
    normative activity, 557
    suspicious activity, 557–559
bastion hosts, 246–250
    defined, 664
    hardware issues, 247–248
    multihomed, 253, 253–254
    operating systems and, 248–249
    overview of, 199, 244
    services and daemons, 249–250
    single-homed, 252, 252–253
    types of, 246–247
batch files, 487, 487, 664
binary files
    defined, 664
    updating Linux, 415–417
bind, 664
biometrics, 28
bitmaps, 664
black hat hackers, 5–6, 664
BlackICE, 285
blind spoofing, 112, 665
block ciphers, 665
block mode, 57
Blowfish, 62
Boolean operators, 665
boot entries, failed logon and, 579–580
boot sector, 665
bottlenecks, 665
bridges, 665
broadcast addresses
    defined, 665
    Smurf and Fraggle attacks and, 119

brute-force attacks, **133–136**
   defined, **665**
   dictionary attacks, **134–136**
   John the Ripper/Crack and, 497–500
   LC3 and, 489–490
   overview of, 133–134
   types of, 110
buffer overflows
   bug-based attacks and, **126–128**
   defined, **665**
   susceptibility of browsers to, 489
   Unix vulnerability, 485
   Windows NT/2000/XP vulnerability, 391
buffers, **126**, **665**
bug-based attacks, **123–128**
   back doors, **124**
   buffer overflows, **126–128**
   trap doors, **124**
   types of, 110
business issues, **167–170**
   chargeback, 167–168
   Network latency and, 169–170
   risk analysis and, 440

C

cable modems, **665**
cache
   defined, **665**
   disk cache, **669**
caching servers, 228, **665**
capacity forecasting, **168**, **665**
CAs (certificate authorities), 93, 263–264, **666**
cascading proxies, 229, **682**
Cast 256 algorithm, 64
casual hackers, 5, 643, **665**
catastrophic damage, 160, **665**
CC (Common Criteria), **13**, **667**
CD-ROM drives, securing, 408
CD-Rs, replicating logs to, 574

CERT (Computer Emergency Response Team), 14, 299–300, 658
certificate authorities (CAs), 93, 263–264, **666**
certificate policy statement, PKI, 263
certificate repository, 263, **666**
certificate revocation list (CRL), 96, **666**
certificate server, **666**
certificates. *see* digital certificates
certification path, 263, **666**
CGI (Common Gateway Interface), **667**
chage command, Linux, 336, 337
chains
   connection chains, 502, **667**
   defined, **666**
   manipulating, 215
   special, 216
CHAP (Challenge Handshake Authentication Protocol), 261
chargeback
   defined, **666**
   determining security costs, 167–168
Check Point, FireWall-1, 230
checksums
   defined, **666**
   distracting hackers with, **287–288**
chgrp command, Linux, 374
Chief Information Officer (CIO), 23
Chief Technology Officer (CTO), 23
Chkrootkit, 486
chmod command, Linux, **371–373**
   absolute mode, 371–372
   command symbols, 373
   symbolic mode, 372–373
choke points, 245, **666**
choke routers, **203**, **666**
chown command, Linux, 374
CIDR (Classless Interdomain Routing), **666**
CIFS (Common Internet File System), 402, **667**. *see also* SMB (Server Message Block)
CIO (Chief Information Officer), 23
ciphers, 24

circuit-level proxy
    advantages/disadvantages, 199
    defined, **666**
    overview of, **198–199**
classifying systems, **16–18**
Classless Interdomain Routing (CIDR), **666**
clients
    defined, **666**
    FTP clients
        passive, 208–209
        SSH (Secure Shell), 618
        standard, 207–208
    Linux clients
        authenticating, **621–623**
        trust relationships, 620–621
    network clients, **678**
    Windows clients
        SSH (Secure Shell), 616–618
        trust relationships, 623–625
clobberd daemon, Linux, 337
command-line interface, **666**
Common Criteria (CC), **13, 667**
Common Gateway Interface (CGI), **667**
Common Internet File System (CIFS), 402, **667**.
    see also SMB (Server Message Block)
community name, **667**
compile, defined, **667**
compiled languages, defined, **667**
compliance analysis, auditors, 435–436
compliance monitoring, 597
    defined, **667**
    issues with, 609
    as recommended solution, **608–609**
    vendors, 609
Computer Emergency Response Team (CERT),
    14, 299–300, 658
conclusions section, audit reports, **644–647**
    immediate recommendations, 645–646
    long term recommendations, 647
    network and host-level security, 647
configuration settings
    changing defaults, 601–602

changing in Windows 2000, **406–408**
connection chains
    defined, **667**
    use by hackers to hide activities, 502
connection hijacking, **113–115**
connectivity
    defined, **667**
    dropping connections when hackers detected, 293
    risks and, 3
    securing in Windows 2000, **402–404**
containment, of attacks, 298
contingency planning
    defined, **667**
    firewall design and, 245
control stage
    auditing process and, **448**
    defined, **667**
    IT-level reports and, 644
control strategies
    actions of hackers after gaining control, **501–502**
    auditors vs. hackers, 503
    Crack, **497–498**
    creating multiple accounts, 486–488
    exam essentials, 504–505
    John the Ripper, **497–500**
    key terms, 505
    LOphtCrack 3, **489–497**
        cracking local SAM database, 490–492
        cracking remote SAM database, 494–496, *495*
        defeating password schemes, 489–490
        sniffing passwords, 496–497
        Syskey protection, *492*, **492–493**
    Pwdump3, **493–494**
    reporting methods, 503
    review answers, 511–513
    review questions, 506–510
    root access, **485–486**
    scanning server information stores, 488–489
cookies, **667**
costs
    chargeback and, 167–168
    security measures and, 169

Crack, **497–498**
crackers, **667**. *see also* black hat hackers
credential caching, 407–408, **667**
CRL (certificate revocation list), 96, **666**
cron, disabling, 417
cross-frame browsing bug, 488–489, **667**
CTO (Chief Technology Officer), 23

D

daemons, **668**. *see also* inetd daemon; xinetd daemon
damage, minimizing, 160–162
data confidentiality, ISO definition, 7
data integrity, ISO definition, 8
data privacy
    defined, **668**
    SSH and, 611
data validation, **668**
data verification, backups and, 161
databases, defined, **668**
datagrams, **668**
DDoS (distributed denial-of-service), *121*. *see also* DoS (denial-of-service) attacks
    defined, **669**
    overview of, **120–121**
    preventing, 122
    recovering from, 121
default accounts, renaming, **338–339**, 408
default configuration, changing, **406–408**, 601–602
default gateway, **668**
default installations
    defined, **668**
    security vulnerability of, 316
default shares
    defined, **668**
    disabling, 391
demilitarized zone. *see* DMZ (demilitarized zone)
Deny all traffic, firewall configuration, 204
Deny permissions, NTFS, 361
DES (Data Encryption Standard)
    defined, **668**
    overview of, **59–60**
    symmetric encryption, 24
design principles, firewall systems, 244–246
destination IP address, **668**
destination ports, **668**
determined hackers, 5, **668**
DHCP (Dynamic Host Configuration Protocol), **669**
dictionary attacks
    as brute-force attack, 134–136
    defined, **668**
    using LC3, 489–490
dictionary passwords, 333
dictionary programs, **668**
Diffie-Hellman, 69, **668**
dig command, 451
digital certificates, **263–267**
    creating, 263–265
    defined, **669**
    requesting and installing, 265–267
    SSL, 93
    SSL errors and, 95
    types of, 264
    uses of, 96
Digital Signature Algorithm (DSA), 69, **669**
digital signatures, 8, **669**
Digital Subscriber Line (DSL), **669**
directories, hidden, 137
directory auditing, Windows 2000, 580–582
directory server, **669**
"Dirty Shutdown" event, Windows 2000, 565–566, *566*
discovery stage
    auditing process, **446–447**
    defined, **669**
    IT-level reports and, 643
discovery tools, **448–460**
    DNS tools, **449–451**
    finger command, **459**
    network/server discovery applications, **454–455**
    overview of, 448–449
    ping scanning, *451*, **451–452**

port scanning, *452–453*, *452–454*
SNMP, **459**
stack fingerprinting, 455–458
Telnet, **458–459**
Trivial TCP/IP services, **459–460**
discretionary access control
    defined, **669**
    TCSEC definitions, 12
    Windows 2000 security, 317
disk cache, **669**
disk drives, securing, 408
distributed denial-of-service. *see* DDoS (distributed denial-of-service)
DMZ (demilitarized zone)
    defined, **668**
    firewall design options, *254–255*, *255*
    overview of, **203–204**
    scanning for host problems, *597*
DNS (Domain Name System), **669**
DNS names, *532*
DNS poisoning, 115–116, **669**
DNS servers, 115–116
DNS tools, discovery, **449–451**
documentation
    attack response plan, 296–297
    updating, 167
Domain Name System (DNS), **669**
DoS (denial-of-service) attacks, **116–122**.
    see also DDoS (distributed denial-of-service)
    defined, **668**
    effectiveness of IDS against, *524*
    land attack, **120**
    ping-of-death/ping floods, **120**
    preventing, 122
    protecting routers form, *598*
    purposes of, 116
    recovering from, 121
    Smurf and Fraggle, *118*, **118–119**
    SYN flood, **116–117**, *117*
    Teardrop, **119–120**
    types of attacks, 109
dotted quad, **669**

drive encryption, 92
drive partitioning, Windows 2000, **361–362**
drivers
    securing printer drivers, 406
    supporting Windows security, 323
DSA (Digital Signature Algorithm), 69, **669**
DSL (Digital Subscriber Line), **669**
dual-homed bastion, *253*, *253–254*, **669**
dummy accounts, **286–287**, **669**
dummy files, **287**
Dynamic Host Configuration Protocol (DHCP), **669**

E

e-mail, **74–96**
    defined, **670**
    drive encryption, 92
    exercises
        using GPG, 85–91
        using PGP, 78–85
    PGP and GPG encryption, 76, **76–78**
    proprietary asymmetric algorithms, 91–92
    Secure HTTP, **92–93**
    SSL, **93–96**
    step-by-step encryption process, 74–76
e-mail servers, latency and, 169–170
ECLs (execution control lists), **35**, **670**
education
    employees, levels of, **21–23**
    end user, 163
    social engineering and, 466
eEye Retina, *467*, *467–470*, *469*
    deploying, 468–470
    overview of, 467
    strengths, 468
EFS (Encrypting File System), 92, 133
egress filtering, *598–599*, **670**
elements, *15*
employees
    education, **21–23**
    insider attacks by, 123

Encapsulating Security Payload (ESP), **670**
encipherment, 8
Encrypting File System (EFS), 92, 133
encryption, **24–26**
   asymmetric, **67–69**, *75*
      algorithms, **69**
      backing up private key, 69
      overview of, 67–68
   categories of, 24–25
   e-mail, **74–96**
      drive encryption, 92
      exercise using GPG, 85–91
      exercise using PGP, 78–85
      PGP and GPG, *76*, **76–78**
      proprietary asymmetric algorithms, 91–92
      Secure HTTP, **92–93**
      SSL, **93–96**
      step-by-step process, 74–76
   exam essentials, 97
   hash, **69–73**
      implementing with MD5sum command, 72–73
      MD2, MD4, and MD5, **71**
      overview of, 69–70
      SHA-1, **71**
      signing and, 70
   key terms, 57–58, 98
   NIS weaknesses and, 413
   overview of, 24
   passwords, 335
   review answers, 104–105
   review questions, 99–103
   SMB and, **404–406**
   SSH (Secure Shell) and, 612
   strength of, 25–26
   symmetric, *58*, **58–67**
      AES, **64–67**
      Blowfish, **62**
      DES, **59–60**
      IDEA, **61–62**
      MARS, **63**
      others, 63–64
      RC2, RC4, RC5, and RC6, **61–62**
      Rijndael, **63**
      RSA encryption, **60–61**, *61*
      Serpent, **63**
      Skipjack, **63**
      Triple DES, **60**
      Twofish, **62–63**
      trusted relationships, **56–57**
end entity, 263, **670**
end user
   education, 163, 466
   resources, 6
enforcement of security principles, company-wide, 162
enterprise networks, **670**
Enterprise Reporting Server, 576
Entrust, 264
ephemeral ports, **204**
equipment
   placement of, 166–167
   selecting on basis of need, 165–166
ESP (Encapsulating Security Payload), **670**
/etc/host.allow, 420
/etc/host.equiv, 410
/etc/hosts.deny, 420
/etc/inetd.conf file, 419, *419*
/etc/nologin file, 329–330, *330*, **670**
/etc/securetty, 328, **670**
/etc/security, 325, 327
/etc/xinetd.d/, *418*, 418
Ethernet, **670**
ethical hackers, 445, **670**
eTrust Intrusion Detection, *520*, **536–543**, *538–541*
   gaining familiarity with, 537–539
   installing, 536–537
   as network-based IDS program, 524
   scanning for eTrust activity, 542–543
   viewing host network activity, 540–542
Event Log Manager (Sunbelt Software), 576
Event Viewer, Windows 2000
   clearing log files, 562–563
   filtering logs, 572
   as logging utility, 561

Everyone group, access control and, 355–356
execution control lists (ECLs), **35**, **670**
executive report, **642–643**
    internal security, 642–643
        penetration risk summary, 643
        perimeter security, 642
executive training, 163
experienced hackers, 643
Export Key to file dialog box, *82*
extranet, **670**

F

facility/priority pair, 567–568, **670**
fake e-mail, attacks, 129–131
false negatives
    audit analysis and, 285–286
    defined, **670**
    IDS issues and, 532–533
false positives
    audit analysis and, 285–286
    defined, **670**
    IDS issues and, 532–533
FAT (file allocation tables)
    converting to NTFS, 352–353
    defined, **671**
fault tolerance, **670**
fields
    defined, **671**
    exercise configuring rules, 211–214
    passive FTP clients, 208–209
    standard FTP clients, 207–208
file allocation tables (FAT)
    converting to NTFS, 352–353
    defined, **671**
file sharing, firewalls and, 209
file system security, 352–388
    exam essentials, 380
    key terms, 381
    Linux, 365–379
        chmod command, **371–373**

chown and chgrp commands, 374
    inode information, **365–366**
    ls command options, **366**, **366–369**
    permissions, **369**
    set bits, **374–376**
    setuid and setgid programs, finding, 376–379
    UIDs and GIDs, **373–374**
    umask command, **370–371**, *371*
review answers, 387–388
review questions, 382–386
Windows 2000, 352–362
    copying and moving files, **362**
    drive partitioning, 361–362
    NTFS permissions, assigning, 356–361
    NTFS vs. FAT, 352–353
    permissions, 353–356
    remote access control, 362–365
File Transfer Protocol. *see* FTP (File Transfer Protocol)
files, copying and moving, **362**
filter command, iptables, 218
filtering logs, **571–574**
    Linux, 572–574
    Windows 2000, *571*, **571–572**
finger command, **459**
firewalk, 484
FireWall-1, Check Point, 230
firewall logs, **560–561**
firewall system, 244
    bastion hosts, **246–250**
        hardware issues, 247–248
        operating system and, 248–249
        services and daemons, 249–250
        types of, 246–247
    common designs, 250–255
    design choices
        multihomed bastion host, *253*, **253–254**
        overview of, 250–251
        screened subnets, **254–255**, *255*
        screening routers, **251–252**
        single-homed bastion host, *252*, **252–253**

design principles, 244–246
exam essentials, 270–271
exercise
    configuring Windows 2000 for IPsec, 267–269
    requesting and installing certificates, 265–267
ICMP and, **255–258**
    ICMP message types, **256–258**
    overview of, 255–256
key terms, 272
PKI and, **262–265**
    certificate creation, **263–265**
    concepts, 263
    standards, 262
review answers, 278–280
review questions, 273–277
VPNs and, **258–261**, *259*
firewalls
    auditing from behind, 445–446, *446*
    concepts, 196–204
        bastion hosts, **199**
        DMZ, **203–204**
        NAT, **199–202**, *201*
        operating system hardening, **202–203**
        packet filters, **197**
        proxy servers, **197–199**
        steering and choke routers, **203**
    configuration defaults, 204–205
    exam essentials, 231–232
    functions of, 195–196
    IDS issues and, 531–532
    ipchains and iptables, **214–227**
        built-in (special) chains, 216
        examples of ipchains, 216–218
        examples of iptables, 219–221
        logging with, 221–222
        overview of, 214–215
        personal firewalls, creating, 222–227
        rules, 215
    key terms, 232–233
    overview of, 194–195
    packet filters, **205–210**
        advantages/disadvantages, 209–210
        overview of, 205
        rules and fields, **206–209**
        rules, configuring, 211–214
    penetration strategies, **483–484**
        avoiding firewalls, 484
        defeating firewall, 483–484
    personal firewalls, 222–227, **284–285**
    preventing unauthorized router programming, 483
    proxy servers, **227–230**
        advantages/features, 228–229
        configuring, 227, *227*
        disadvantages, 230
    restricting physical access to, 597
    review answers, 239–241
    review questions, 234–238
    risk analysis and, 440–441
    stateful multilayer inspection and, **210–211**
flat-file databases, **671**
floppy disks, securing, 408
folder permissions, 356. *see also* file system security
forensic analysis, 291, **671**
FQDN (fully qualified domain name), **671**
Fraggle attacks
    broadcast addresses and, 119
    defined, **671**
    as denial-of-service attack, *118*
    overview of, **118–119**
frame-relay connections, logging, 561
frames, **671**
FreeS/WAN, 269, 269–270, 528
freeware, **671**
front-door attacks. *see* brute-force attacks
FTP banner check, 651
FTP clients
    packet filter rules
        passive clients, 208–209
        standard clients, 207–208
    using SSH for file transfer, 618
FTP (File Transfer Protocol)
    defined, **671**
    replacing with SSH, 614–615

fully qualified domain name (FQDN), **671**
functions, defined, **671**

G

gap analysis, 435, **671**
gateways, **671**
Get Encrypted Passwords, LC3 Wizard, *496*
GIDs (group identifiers), 373–374, **671**
GNU, **671**
Gost algorithm, 64
GPG (GNU Privacy Guard)
    DSA algorithm and, 69
    e-mail encryption and, 76–78
    encrypting/decrypting files, 89–90
    exchanging and signing public keys, 87–89
    exercise using, 85–91
    generating key pair, 85–87
    Key Generation Wizard, *80*
group identifiers (GIDs), 373–374, **671**

H

hackers
    activities after gaining control, 501–502
    additional accounts, creating, 486–488
    attack response plan, 295–302
        assessing the situation, 297–298
        documenting, 296–297
        executing response policy, 298–300
        learning from incident, 300–302
        not panicing, 296
        setting response policy ahead of time, 295–296
        stopping/containing activity, 298
    vs. auditors, 503
    black hat types, 5–6
    control strategies, 501–502
    defeating firewalls, 484
    defined, **671**
    distracting
        checksums, 287–288
        dummy accounts, 286–287
        dummy files, 287
        jails, 290–291
        packet traces, 291
        physical line traces, 292
        tripwires, 288–290
    finding weaknesses by, 162
    gaining root access, 485
    penetration risk and, 643
    proactive detection, 282–286
        automated audit analysis, 285–286
        automated security scans, 283
        login scripts, 283–284
        overview of, 282–283
        personal firewalls, 284–285
    punishing
        methods, 292–293
        problems with retaliation, 294–295
        tools, 293–294
    scanning server information stores, 488–489
    use of auditing tools by, 466–467
    white hat vs. black hat, 4–5
handshakes, **671**
hash encryption, 69–73
    defined, 24–25, **671**
    implementing, 72–73
    MD2, MD4, and MD5, 71
    overview of, 69–70
    SHA-1, 71
    signing and, 70
hash values, 70, **672**
Health Insurance Portability and Accountability Act (HIPAA), **14**, **672**
hexadecimal, **672**
hijacking
    connection hijacking, 113–115
    defined, **672**
HIPAA (Health Insurance Portability and Accountability Act), **14**, **672**

HKEY_CLASSES_ROOT, 394
HKEY_CURRENT_CONFIG, 394
HKEY_CURRENT_USER, 394
HKEY_LOCAL_MACHINE, 393
HKEY_USERS, 393
HKLM subtrees, 395, 398–399
HNC algorithm, 64
Home Solutions, 171–172, *172*
honey pots
    defined, **672**
    functions and dangers of, 290
hops, **672**
host-based IDS, **525–528**
    agent organization, 527–528
    agent placement, 527
    attacks effective against, 525
    defined, **672**
    function of, 523
    manager-to-agent communication, *526*, 528
host-based management model, 442–443, **672**
host-based scanner, 443, **672**
host command, as discovery tool, 450–451
host-level security, 647
hosts, **672**
hosts file, **672**
hosts.allow, 420–421
hosts.deny, 420–421
hot fixes, 409
HTML (Hypertext Markup Language), **672**
HTTP (Hypertext Transfer Protocol), **672**
HTTPS (Hypertext Transfer Protocol Secure), **673**
hubs, **672**

I

I Love You virus, 392
ICMP (Internet Control Message Protocol), 255–258
    blocking ICMP packets, 255–256
    defined, **673**
    message types, **256–258**

    Smurf attacks and, 118
ICMP netmask check, 652
IDEA (International Data Encryption Algorithm), **61–62**
identification, TCSEC definitions, 12
identity theft. *see* spoofing
IDS (intrusion-detection systems), 516–554
    applications, **517–519**, **674**
    architectures, 523–529
        host-based, **525–528**
        network-based, **524–525**
    concepts, 517–523
        attack detection strategies, **523**
        IDS applications and rules, **518–519**
        IDS response actions, **519**
        incident response team (IRT), **521–522**
        redundant logging, **520–521**
        signatures and attack signature databases, **518**
    defined, **674**
    eTrust Intrusion Detection, *520*, **536–543**, *538–541*
        gaining familiarity with, 537–539
        installing, 536–537
        scanning for eTrust activity, 542–543
        viewing host network activity, 540–542
    exam essentials, 543–545
    functions of, 517
    issues with, 530–534
    key terms, 545
    list of, 441–442
    overview of, 516
    purchasing
        issues and questions, 534–536
        vendors, 536
    as recommended solution, 596, 599–601
    review answers, 551–554
    review questions, 546–550
    risk analysis and, 440
    rules, 529
    slow scanning attacks and, **529–530**
    testing prior to use, 531
    ways to defeat, 534

IKE (Internet Key Exchange), 260–261, **673**
illicit server attacks, *22*, 22–23, 485
illicit servers, **673**
IMAP (Internet Message Access Protocol), **674**
in the wild, **674**
incident identification, 517
incident response team (IRT), **521–522, 673**
inetd daemon
    configuring daemons launched by, **419**
    daemons controlled by, 417
    defined, **673**
    restarting after changing, 420
information-gathering modules, 650–652
    anonymous FTP check, 651–652
    FTP banner check, 651
    ICMP netmask check, 652
    sendmail banners check, 650–651
    WWW Web server version, 652
information leakage, **124–126**
Information Security Officer (ISO), 23
information storage resources, 6
information technology (IT) department, **673**.
    see also IT-level reports
Information Technology Security Evaluation
    Criteria (ITSEC), **9–10, 673**
ingress filtering, **598–599, 673**
inheritance
    defined, **673**
    moving/copying files and, 362
    permissions and, 356
initial sequence number, **673**
inode, **365–366, 673**
insider attacks, **122–123**
    as attack type, 109
    dangers of, 516
    defined, **673**
    social engineering and, 122–123
    terminated employees and, 123
integrated strategy, security principles,
    163–164
intentional threats, 108–109
internal attacks. *see* insider attacks

internal bastion hosts, 247, **673**
internal security, executive report and,
    642–643
International Data Encryption Algorithm (IDEA),
    61–62
Internet, **673**
Internet Control Message Protocol. *see* ICMP
    (Internet Control Message Protocol)
Internet Key Exchange (IKE), 260–261, **673**
Internet layer, **673**
Internet Message Access Protocol (IMAP), **674**
Internet Security Association and Key Management
    Protocol (ISAKMP), 260, **674**
Internet security resources, 658–659
    CERT (Computer Emergency Response
        Team), 658
    others, 658–659
    Unix, 659
    Windows 2000, 659
Internet Server Application Programming Interface
    (ISAPI), **674**
Internet Service Provider (ISP), **674**
Internet standard, **674**
Internet Threat Management Technology, 522
Intruder Alert, Symantec, 526, 528
intrusion-detection systems. *see* IDS
    (intrusion-detection systems)
IP addresses
    defined, **674**
    destination IP address, **668**
    reserved IP addresses, **683**
    source IP address, **688**
IP routing, 249
IP Security Monitor, 268
IP spoofing. *see* spoofing attacks
ipchains, **214–227**
    built-in (special) chains, 216
    defined, **674**
    examples of, 216–218
    logging with, 221–222
    overview of, 214–215
    personal firewall, creating, 222–224

rules, 215
switching to iptables, 221–222
tools for responding to hackers, 294
IPsec (Internet Protocol Security), **260–261**
communication between hosts, 528
defined, **674**
Internet Key Exchange (IKE) and, 260–261
overview of, 260
security associations (SAs) and, 260
Unix and, 269
Windows 2000 and, 264–265, 267–269
iptables, **214–227**
defined, **674**
examples of iptables, 219–221
logging with, 221–222
overview of, 214–215
personal firewall, creating, 224–227
rules, 215
switching to ipchains, 221–222
tools for responding to hackers, 294
IPv6, 610–611
IRT (incident response team), **521–522, 673**
ISAKMP (Internet Security Association and Key Management Protocol), 260, **674**
ISAPI (Internet Server Application Programming Interface), **674**
ISDN connections, logging, 561
ISO 7498-2, **7–9**
security definitions, 7
security mechanisms, 8–9
security services, 7–8
ISO (Information Security Officer), 23
ISP (Internet Service Provider), **674**
ISS Internet Scanner, 461, *461*
IT (information technology) department, **673**
IT-level reports, **643–644**. *see also* reports
control stage, 644
discovery stage, 643
penetration stage, 644
recommendations for IT Department, 626
ITSEC (Information Technology Security Evaluation Criteria), **9–10, 673**

J

jails
defined, **674**
functions and dangers of, **290–291**
John the Ripper
brute-force attacks, 497–498
control strategies, **497–500**
cracking passwords, 332
exercise cracking Linux, 498–500

K

KDC (key distribution center), **31**
KDE (K Desktop Environment), 376–377
kdestroy, **31**
Kerberos, **29–33**
advantages of, 30
defined, **675**
disadvantages, 32–33
how it works, 29–30
terms, 31–32
kernel, **215, 675**
key distribution center (KDC), **31**
Key Generation Wizard, *80, 624*
key pair
in asymmetric encryption, 67
defined, **675**
generating, 623–625
keylogging attacks, **132–133**
as attack type, 110
defined, **675**
functions of keyloggers, 132
protecting against, 133
keys
defined, **675**
encryption and, 24
kfind, 376–377
kinit, **31**
klist, **31**

L

L2TP (Layer 2 Tunneling Protocol), 261, **675**
LAN Manager authentication, 404–405
land attacks, **120**, **675**
last command, Linux, 572–573, 582–583
lastlog command, Linux, 573, 582–583
latency
    defined, **169**, **675**
    e-mail servers and, 169–170
Layer 2 Tunneling Protocol (L2TP), 261, **675**
LC3. *see* LOphtCrack 3 (LC3)
LC3 Wizard, 491, *491*
    Get Encrypted Passwords, *496*
    Start Sniffing button, *497*
LDAP (Lightweight Directory Access Protocol), **675**
Level I, security classification, 16–18
Level II, security classification, 16–18
Level III, security classification, 16–18
Lightweight Directory Access Protocol (LDAP), **675**
Linux. *see also* Red Hat Linux
    firewalls
        creating with ipchains, 222–224
        creating with iptables, 224–227
        implementing from floppy disk, 249
        personal, 603–604
    information resources for, 221
    IPsec, enabling, 528
    keylogging attacks and, 132–133
    Linux clients
        authenticating, **621–623**
        trust relationships between, 620–621
    Netfilter and, 214–215
    physical attack on, 174–176
    remote logging and, 575
    switching between ipchains and iptables, 221–222
    updating binaries, **415–417**
Linux, file system security, 365–379
    chmod command, **371–373**
    chown and chgrp commands, 374
    inode information, 365–366
    ls command options, *366*, 366–369
    permissions, **369**
    set bits, **374–376**
    setuid and setgid programs, finding, 376–379
    UIDs and GIDs, **373–374**
    umask command, **370–371**, *371*
Linux logging, **567–574**
    facility keywords, 567–568
    file locations, 569–570
    filtering logs, **572–574**
    important files to read, 569
    patch level and uptime information, 570–571
    prioritizing by facility, 568
    syslogd, 568–569, *569*
    using log-auditing tools, 582–583
Linux, OS security, 324–330
    account security
        password aging, 336–337
        strong passwords, 333
    /etc/nologin file, *330*
    /etc/security directory, 327
    PAMs, **325–327**
    poweroff command, restricting access, 328
    removing accounts, 338
    renaming default accounts, 339
    Telnet access and root account, 328–330
    vulnerabilities, 324
LKM (loadable kernel module), Linux, 137
loadable kernel module (LKM), Linux, 137
Local Security Authority (LSA), Windows 2000, 322–323, **675**
Local Security Settings, Windows 2000, 563, *563*
Local Users and Groups, Windows 2000, 338
log analysis, 555–594
    additional logs, 561
    balancing too much vs. too little, 559–560
    baselines and, **556–560**
        normative activity, 557
        suspicious activity, 557–559
    e-mail, detecting hackers, 292
    exam essentials, 584–585

exercises, Linux, 582–583
exercises, Windows 2000
 auditing failed login entries, 579–580
 enabling directory auditing, 580–582
filtering logs, **571–574**
 Linux, 572–574
 Windows 2000, **571–572**
firewall and router logs, **560–561**
key terms, 586
operating system logs, **561–571**
 information to search for, 561
 Linux, **567–571**
 Windows 2000, **561–567**
proxy servers and, 228
purposes of, 556
review answers, 592–594
review questions, 587–591
securing log files, **574–577**
 customizing log-file size, 576–577
 recommendations, 574
 remote logging, 575–576
security manager functions, 517
third-party logging, 577–579
 managed security providers, **578–579**
 partial implementation, 579
traffic, detecting hackers, 292
log daemon, anomalies in, 559
log files
 missing, 559
 securing, **574–577**
 customizing log-file size, 576–577
 recommendations, 574
 remote logging, **575–576**
logic attacks. *see* trap doors
login
 auditing failed login entries, 579–580
 disabling caching of logon credentials, 407
 hiding name of last user, 407
 interactive messages, 408
 log analysis and, 558
 mandatory in Windows 2000, 317
 using SSH for, 614

login scripts
 defined, **675**
 functions of, **283–284**
logrotate application, Linux, 576
long term recommendations, IT-level reports, 647
loopback, **675**
LOphtCrack 3 (LC3), **489–497**
 defeating passwords, 332, 489–490, 496–497
 SAM database
 exercise cracking local, 490–492
 exercise cracking remote, 494–496, *495*
 Syskey protection, *492*, **492–493**
ls command options, Linux, *366*, **366–369**
 ls -1 /dev/tty, 369
 ls -la, 368
 ls -la .rhosts, 368–369
 ls -ld, 366–367
LSA (Local Security Authority), Windows 2000, 322–323, **675**

M

MAC addresses, **676**
maintenance personnel, 171
man-in-the-middle attacks, **113–116**
 as attack type, 109
 connection hijacking, **114–115**
 defined, **676**
 against DNS servers, 115–116
 types of, 113–114
MAN (municipal area networks), **676**
managed security providers, 577–579
 benefits of, 578
 choosing, 578–579
 defined, 579, **676**
 log analysis, 578–579
 partial implementation, 579
manager-to-agent communication, *526*, *526*, *528*
managers, **676**
mandatory logon, 317, **676**
mangle command, iptables, 219

manual key distribution, trusted relationships, 56
MARS, 63
masquerading, **676**. *see also* spoofing attacks
matrix
    defined, **676**
    security system as, 159
MD2, MD4, and MD5 encryption
    encrypting passwords with, 335
    overview of, **71**
    as symmetric encryption, 24
MD5sum command, 72–73, 288
media, **676**
Media Access Control, **676**
media verification, backups, 161
Melissa virus, 392
Message Digest encryption. *see* MD2, MD4, and MD5 encryption
Microsoft, service packs and hot fixes, 409
MIME (Multipurpose Internet Mail Extension), **676**
mirroring, **676**
mission-critical applications, **676**
MISTY1/MISTY2 algorithms, 63
modem bank, 484, **676**
Modify permission, NTFS, 357
Msapsspc.dll, 323
Msnsspc.dll, 323
multihomed bastion host
    defined, 246–247, **676**
    firewall design options, *253*, 253–254
Multipurpose Internet Mail Extension (MIME), **676**
municipal area networks (MANs), **676**

N

names
    default accounts, renaming, **338–339**, 408
    DNS names, 532
nat command, iptables, 218
NAT (NetBIOS Authentication Tool), *135*, 135
NAT (network address translation), **199–202**
    defined, **677**
    masquerading and, *201*, 201

methods of, 200
    private and public NICs and, 202
National Institute of Standards and Technology (NIST), **677**
National Science Foundation (NSF), **677**
needs assessment audit, *165*
    conducting, 165–166
    defined, **677**
NetBIOS, **677**
NetBIOS Authentication Tool (NAT), *135*, 135
NetBus attacks, 22, 22–23, 485
Netfilter
    defined, **677**
    iptables and, 218
    Linux, 214–215
netiquette, **677**
netlogon service, 323–324, **677**
NetRecon report, *465*
netstat command
    defined, **677**
    SYN flood detection, 117
Network Access layer, **677**
network activity, being suspicious of, 157–158
network adapter card, **678**
network address translation. *see* NAT (network address translation)
network analyzer, **677**
network appliance, **677**
network assessment, 596, **677**
network assets, **677**
network-based IDS, **524–525**
    advantages/disadvantages, 524–525
    defined, **678**
    function of, 524
network-based management model, 441, **678**
network clients, **678**
network discovery applications, 454–455
Network File System. *see* NFS (Network File System)
Network ICE, 285
Network Information System (NIS), **411–413**
network interface cards. *see* NICs (network interface cards)

network latency, 531, *675*
Network layer, **678**
network-level security, IT reports, 647
network map, **678**
network operating system (NOS), **678**
network perimeter, **678**
network resources
    categorizing by type, *438*, 438
    prioritizing by department, *439*, 439
    resource categorization and, 6
network security, overview
    access control, **33–35**
        ACLs, **34–35**
        ECLs, **35**
        overview of, 33–34
    auditing, **35–36**
    authentication, **26–33**
        methods, 27–29
        specific techniques, 29–33
    elements of, *15*, 15
    encryption, **24–26**
        categories of, 24–25
        strength of, 25–26
    exam essentials, 43–44
    exercise implementing authentication and access control, 36–42
    hackers, **4–6**
        black hat types, **5–6**
        white hat vs. black hat, 4–5
    key terms, 44–45
    myth of complete security, 3–4
    resource protection, 6
    review answers, 52–54
    review questions, 46–51
    security policy, **15–23**
        activities, defining acceptable/unacceptable, **19–21**
        classifying systems, **16–18**
        determining administrator of, 23
        employee education, **21–23**
        overview of, 15–16
        risk assessment and, **18–19**
        risk factors, assigning, **19**
    standards, **7–13**
        Common Criteria (CC)q, **13**
        HIPAA, **14**
        ISO 7498-2, **7–9**
        ITSEC Document BS 7799, **9–10**
        TCSEC, **10–12**
networks
    asymmetrically encrypted information passing through, 93
    defined, **677**
    scanning, 461–462
New Technology File System. *see* NTFS (New Technology File System)
newsfeed, **678**
newsgroup, **678**
NFS (Network File System), **413–415**
    applications of, 413–414
    defined, **678**
    security weaknesses of, 414–415
NICs (network interface cards)
    defined, **678**
    private and public, 202, **682**
    promiscuous mode detection and, 600–601
NIS (Network Information System), **411–413**
NIST (National Institute of Standards and Technology), **677**
nmap, Unix, 454, 456–458, *457*
nodes, **678**
non-blind spoofing, 112, **678**
non-root users, Linux, 324
nonrepudiation, 8, **678**
nonroutable, **678**
NOS (network operating system), **678**
NSF (National Science Foundation), **677**
Nslookup, 449–450
NTFS (New Technology File System)
    assigning permissions, 356–361
    defined, **678**
    vs. FAT, 352–353
ntfs.txt
    access control settings, *358*

permissions, *358*, *359*
properties, *357*, *361*
ntsysv command, 417
null sessions
   defined, **679**
   SMB and, 403–404
numeric mode, **679**

O

OAKLEY protocol, 261, **679**
objects
   defined, **679**
   reuse, 12, 317, **679**
   Windows 2000
      controlling access to, 317
      primary types, 318
      security principles of, 318
one-time passwords (OTPs), 33, **679**
one-way encryption, **24–25**, **679**
online cataloging, **679**
open network, **679**
open source, 166, **679**
Open Systems Interconnection Reference Model (OSI/RM), 8, **679**
operating system logs, **561–571**
   Linux, **567–571**
      facility keywords, 567–568
      facility prioritization, 568
      file locations, 569–570
      important files to read, 569
      patch level and uptime information, 570–571
   type of information to search for, 561
   Windows 2000, **561–567**
      default log-file locations, 562–563
      enabling auditing, 563–564
      log categories, 562
      NT/2000 significant events, 565–566
      service-pack level and uptime information, 566–567
operating system security, 315–350

account security
   account policies, **333**
   overview of, 330
   password aging, **334–337**
   strong passwords, **331–334**
   timing out users, 336
exam essentials, 340–341
key terms, 342
Linux, 324–330
   /etc/security directory, 327
   PAMs, **325–327**
   poweroff command, restricting access to, 328
   Telnet access and root account, 328–330
   vulnerabilities, 324
removing accounts, **337–338**
renaming default accounts, **338–339**
review answers, 348–350
review questions, 343–347
vulnerabilities, 316
Windows 2000, 316–324
   components, **319–321**
   list of, 316–317
   objects, **317–318**
   security subsystem, **321–324**
operating systems
   detecting with discovery tools, **455–458**
   hardening, **202–203**
   recommended changes to, **601–609**
      overview of, 601–602
      personal firewalls, **602–608**
   solutions and reports, 596
organizational structure, **679**
OSI/RM (Open Systems Interconnection Reference Model), 8, **679**
OTP (one-time passwords), 33, **679**
out-of-process, **679**

P

packet alteration, 113
packet capturing, 113

Packet Filter dialog box, *212*, 212
packet filters, **205–210**
   advantages/disadvantages, 209–210
   configuring, *251*
   defined, **679**
   overview of, **197**, 205
   rules and fields, **206–209**
      exercise configuring rules, 211–214
      passive FTP clients, 208–209
      standard FTP clients, 207–208
packet-injection attacks, 113, **680**
packet sniffers
   defined, **680**
   SYN flood detection, 117
packet streams, **680**
packet traces, **291**, **680**
packets, **679**, **680**
page file, Windows 2000, 407
PAMs (Pluggable Authentication Modules), 325–327
   defined, **681**
   directories, 325
   entry format, 325
   /etc/nologin file, 329–330, *330*
   modules types, 325–327
parallelization, 57, **680**
partitions, 361–362
passive auditing, **36**
passive FTP clients, 208–209
passive open, TCP handshake, **680**
passive threats, 108
password aging, 334–337
   defined, **680**
   Linux security, 336–337
   Windows 2000 security, 334–335
password authentication, **26–27**
password lockout, 335, **680**
password module, Linux PAM, 325
Password Policy, Windows 2000, 332
password sniffing, **680**
passwords
   account security and, 331

Linux
   password aging, 336–337
   root account and, 333
   shadow passwords, 333
   programs for cracking, 332
   strong passwords and, 134–135
   Syskey protection, 178
   Windows 2000, 331–332
      enforcing strong passwords, 332
      password aging, 334–335
      password lockout, 335
      support of strong passwords, 331–332
patch level, 570–571, **680**
PATH variable, Linux/UNIX, 133
peer-to-peer networks, **680**
penetration risk summary, executive report, 643
penetration stage
   auditing process, **447–448**
   defined, **680**
   IT-level reports and, 644
penetration strategies
   firewalls, 483
      avoiding, 484
      defeating, 483–484
   removing evidence of penetration, 502
   routers and switches, 483
penetration testing, 484
PentaSafe, VigilEnt, 609
performance management, **168**, **680**
perimeter security
   executive report and, 642
   as recommended solution, **596**, **597–599**
   risk analysis and, 440
Permission Entry dialog box, *357*, *357*, *359*, *359*
permissions, 353–356
   basic, 353
   defined, **680**
   inheritance, 356
   Linux, **369**
   NTFS permissions, assigning, 356–361
   ntfs.txt, *358*, *359*
   remote access, 363

share permissions, **362–364**, *364*
Windows 2000, **354–355**
Windows 2000 Registry, 397–398
personal certificates, 264
personal firewalls, 602–608
    creating with ipchains, 222–224
    creating with iptables, 224–227
    defined, **680**
    functions of, **284–285**
    Linux and, 603–604
    services of, 602
    tools for responding to hackers, 293
    vendors, 602–603
    Windows 2000 and, 604–608
PGP (Pretty Good Privacy)
    e-mail encryption and, **76–78**
    exchanging encrypted messages, 84–85
    exporting and signing public keys, 81–83
    installing on Windows 2000, 78–81
    PGP home page, 76
    PGP keys, *81*
physical attacks
    defined, **680**
    Linux, 174–176
    strategies, 172–173
    Windows 2000, 176–179
physical-line trace, **292**, **681**
physical security, 170–173
    access logs, 561
    IDS issues and, 533
    maintenance personnel and, 171
    physical attack on Linux system, 174–176
    physical attack on Windows 2000 Server, 176–179
    physical attack strategies, 172–173
    security audit reports and, 625
    surveillance methods, 171–172
ping floods, **120**, **681**
ping-of-death, **120**
ping of death, **681**
Ping Pro, *454*, 454, 538
ping scanning, **451–452**, **681**

PKCS (Public Key Cryptography Standards), 263, **682**
PKI (Public Key Infrastructure), **262–265**
    certificate creation, **263–265**
    concepts, 263
    defined, **682**
    standards, 262
plaintext, **681**
Pluggable Authentication Modules. *see* PAMs (Pluggable Authentication Modules)
point of contact, **681**
Point-to-Point Protocol (PPP), **681**
Point-to-Point Tunneling Protocol (PPTP), 261, **681**
POP (Post Office Protocol), **681**
port listeners, **681**
port redirection, 501, **681**
Port Scan Attack Detection (PSAD), 294
port scanning, **452–454**
    anatomy of, 452
    defined, **681**
    software for, 453–454
port scanning modules, 653–655
    RPC, 654–655
    TCP, 653–654
    UDP, 654
Portmapper, 411–412, **681**
ports
    defined, **681**
    well-known vs. ephemeral, 204–205
PortSentry, 294
Post Office Protocol (POP), **681**
poweroff command, Linux, 328
PP (Protection Profile), Common Criteria (CC), 13
PPP (Point-to-Point Protocol), **681**
PPTP (Point-to-Point Tunneling Protocol), 261, **681**
Pretty Good Privacy. *see* PGP (Pretty Good Privacy)
principals, Kerberos, **31**
printer drivers
    defined, **682**
    Windows 2000, 406
private keys
    in asymmetric encryption, 67

backing up, 69
defined, **682**
private NIC, 202, **682**
proactive detection, **282–286**
    automated audit analysis, **285–286**
    automated security scans, 283
    defined, **682**
    login scripts, **283–284**
    overview of, 282–283
    personal firewalls, **284–285**
processes
    defined, **682**
    hidden, 137
processor speed, 248
professional hackers, 643
Profile tab, administrator Properties, *290*
PromiScan, 600–601
promiscuous mode detection, 600–601, **682**
Protection Profile (PP), Common Criteria (CC), 13
proxies, **682**
proxy arrays, 229, **682**
proxy clusters, **682**
proxy servers, **197–199, 227–230**
    advantages/features, 228–229
    application-layer proxy, **197–198**
    circuit-level proxy, **198–199**
    configuring, 227, *227*
    defined, **682**
    disadvantages, 230
    list of products and suppliers, 228
    vs. packet filters, 229
PSAD (Port Scan Attack Detection), 294
public-key authentication, **682**
Public Key Cryptography Standards (PKCS), 263, **682**
public-key encryption. *see* asymmetric encryption
Public Key Infrastructure. *see* PKI (Public Key Infrastructure)
public keys
    in asymmetric encryption, 68, *68*
    defined, **682**
    exporting and signing, 81–83

public networks, **682**
public NIC, 202, **682**
publisher certificate, 264
punishing hackers
    methods, 292–293
    problems with retaliation, **294–295**
    tools, 293–294
pwdump, 332
Pwdump3, **493–494**

Q

query architecture, *441*, 441–442

R

r-series commands, UNIX, 111
RA (registration authority), 263, **683**
RARP (Reverse Address Resolution Protocol), **683**
RAS (remote access server), **683**
RC2, RC4, RC5, and RC6 algorithms, **61–62**
real time, **682**
Red Hat Linux. *see also* Linux
    exchanging and signing public keys, 87–89
    generating key pair, 85–87
    physical attacks on, 174–176
    SSH server on, 614–615
    updating, 416–418
redundant logging, **520–521**, **683**
regedt32, 393
registration authority (RA), 263, **683**
Registry, Windows 2000, **392–398**
    auditing, 395–396, 398–399
    backing up, 396
    defined, **683**
    permissions, 397–398, *398*
    structure of, 392–395
    subtrees, 393–395, *395*, **683**
remote access. *see* VPNs (virtual private networks)

remote access control, Windows 2000, 362–365
remote access server (RAS), 683
remote logging, 575–576
    Linux, 575
    Windows 2000, 576
removable media, 408, 683
renaming default accounts, 338–339, 408
replay attacks, 683
reports. *see also* scanner report, example; security audit reports
    auditing recommendations for IT Department, 626–627
    auditors and, 443–444
    elements of, 625–626
    importance of written reports, 626
    recommendations for continuing and strengthening auditing, 627–628
    vulnerability scanners, 464–465, *465*
Requests for Comments (RFCs)
    defined, 683
    PKI and, 262
required, PAM flags, 326
requisite, PAM flags, 326
research, 466
reserved IP addresses, 683
resource placement, 245–246, 683
resource protection, 6
resources
    analyzing and prioritizing, 437–439
    categorizing by type, 438, *438*
    commonly attacked, 439
    prioritizing by department, 439, *439*
response actions, IDS, 517, **519**
response field, 683
response policy. *see also* attack response plan
    creating, 295
    defined, 683
    executing, 298
        notify affected individuals, 298–299
        notify CERT, 299–300
        notify service provider, 299
retaliatory measures. *see also* punishing hackers

defined, 683
    problems with, **294–295**
Reverse Address Resolution Protocol (RARP), 683
reverse proxy servers, 229, 683
reverse scans, 293, *295*, 683
RFCs (Requests for Comments)
    defined, 683
    PKI and, 262
Rhino9 Pinger, *451*, 451
rhosts file, 368–369
Rijndael encryption, 63, 684
Rijndael Encryption button, Apocalypso interface, 66
risk analysis, 437–443
    analyzing and prioritizing resources, 437–439
    business issues, 440
    checking for written policy, 437
    defined, 684
    evaluating internal and perimeter security, 440–441
    questions for, 438
    reporting on, 443–444
    security policy and, 18–19
    using existing management and control architecture, 441–443
risk reduction
    exam essentials, 422–424
    key terms, 424
    review answers, 430–432
    review questions, 425–429
    Unix, 409–422
        NFS issues, 413–415
        NIS issues, 411–413
        rlogin, disabling, **409–410**
        stand-alone services, **421–422**
        TCPWrappers, **420–421**
        updating Linux binaries, **415–417**
        vulnerabilities, 409
        xinetd and inetd, **417–420**
    Windows 2000, 390–409
        configuration changes, **406–408**
        Registry, 392–398

Registry, auditing, 395–396, 398–399
Registry, backing up, 396
Registry, permissions, 397–398
Registry, structure of, 392–395
removing unnecessary services, **399–402**
securing connectivity, **402–404**
service packs, **408–409**
SMB encryption issues, 404–406
vulnerabilities, 390–392
risks
   assigning risk factors, **19**
   defined, **684**
   recommendations for medium to high, 645–646
rlogin, Unix
   defined, **684**
   disabling, **409–410**
   replacing with SSH, 611, 614–615
root accounts
   control strategies, **485–486**
   defined, **684**
   Linux, 333
   Linux commands accessible to, 324
root kits, **136–138**
   defined, **684**
   examples of, 137–138
   how they get installed, 138
   overview of, 136–137
   problems caused by, 137
   repairing, 138–139
   tracing, 486
   Unix vulnerability to, 485
rotating log files, 576–577
rounds, encryption, 57, **684**
routable, **684**
route command, 294
router logs, 560–561, 560–561
routers
   defined, **684**
   egress and ingress filtering, 598–599
   penetration strategies, 483
   protecting from DoS attacks, 598
   security strategies for, 597

routing, **684**
routing information table, **684**
RPC (Remote Procedure Call)
   defined, **683**
   port scanning modules, 654–655
   Portmapper and, 411–412
RSA
   asymmetric encryption with, 69
   defined, **684**
   overview of, **60–61**
   symmetric encryption with, 24
rsh, 611
rules
   defined, **684**
   IDS, 518–519, 529
   packet filters, **206–209**
      configuring, 211–214
      sufficiency of, 597
Run dialog box, Windows 2000, 393

S

S-HTTP (secure HTTP), **92–93**, 685
S/MIME (Secure MIME), 685
sacrificial system, **684**
SAM (Security Account Manager)
   accessing remote database with Pwdump3, 493–494
   cracking local database with LC3, 490–492
   cracking remote database with LC3, 494–495
   defined, **685**
   physical attacks and, 177–178
   Windows 2000 security subsystem, **324**
sandboxing, **684**
SAs (security associations), 260, **685**
SATAN (Security Administrator Tool for Analyzing Networks), 445
scalability
   defined, **684**
   needs assessment and, 166
scanner report, example, 650–659

information-gathering modules, 650–652
    anonymous FTP check, 651–652
    FTP banner check, 651
    ICMP netmask check, 652
    sendmail banners check, 650–651
    WWW Web server version, 652
  port scanning modules, 653–655
    RPC, 654–655
    TCP, 653–654
    UDP, 654
  scan results, 650
  SNMP module, 653
scanning attacks
  defined, **684**
  effectiveness of IDS against, 524
Schannel.dll, 323
screened host firewall, **685**. *see also* multihomed
    bastion host; single-homed bastion host
screened subnets. *see also* DMZ (demilitarized zone)
  defined, **685**
  firewall design options, **254–255**, *255*
screening routers. *see also* packet filters
  advantages/disadvantages, 209–210
  defined, 205, **685**
  firewall design options, **251–252**
script kiddies, **685**
SCSI disks, reducing slowdowns, 248
search path, **685**
secure data back up and storage, **685**
secure HTTP (S-HTTP), **92–93**, **685**
Secure MIME (S/MIME), **685**
Secure RPC, 412, **685**
Secure Server (Require Security) Properties dialog
    box, 267
Secure Shell. *see* SSH (Secure Shell)
Secure Sockets Layer. *see* SSL (Secure Sockets Layer)
securenets, 413, **685**
security
  defined, **685**
  ISO definition, 7
Security Account Manager. *see* SAM (Security
    Account Manager)

Security Administrator Tool for Analyzing
    Networks (SATAN), 445
security associations (SAs), 260, **685**
security audit reports, 642–647. *see also* reports
  conclusions section, **644–647**
    immediate recommendations, 645–646
    long term recommendations, 647
    network and host-level security, 647
  defined, **686**
  elements of, 625–626
  executive report, **642–643**
    internal security, 642–643
    penetration risk summary, 643
    perimeter security, 642
  IT-level reports, **643–644**
    control stage, 644
    discovery stage, 643
    penetration stage, 644
security descriptors
  defined, **686**
  Windows 2000, **319–320**, *320*
security education levels, **21–23**
security identifiers (SIDs), **319**, **686**
security labels, 8
security levels, TCSEC, **10–12**, **686**
Security log, Windows 2000, 562
security mailing lists, 301–302
security managers, 517
security policy, **15–23**
  activities, defining acceptable/unacceptable, **19–21**
  advantages and functions of, 158–159
  checking for written, 437
  classifying systems, **16–18**
  determining administrator of, **23**
  employee education, **21–23**
  functions of, 16
  overview of, 15–16
  risk assessment, **18–19**
  risk factors, assigning, **19**
security principles, 155–191
  being suspicious of network activity, 157–158
  business issues and, 167–170

company-wide enforcement, 162
equipment, selecting on basis of need, 165–167
exam essentials, 181–182
exercises
    physical attack on Linux, 174–176
    physical attack on Windows 2000, 176–179
implementing, 180
integrated strategy, 163–164
key terms, 182
minimizing damage, 160–162
no system/technique is sufficient alone, 159–160
physical security, 170–173
review answers, 189–191
review questions, 183–188
security policy as foundation of, 158–159
training, 162–163
security recovery, 8
security roadmap, 436, **686**. *see also* security policy
security scans, automated, **283**
security subsystem, Windows 2000, *322*
    authentication package, 323
    defined, **686**
    Local Security Authority (LSA), 322–323
    Netlogon service, 323–324
    overview of, 321–322
    Security Account Manager (SAM), **324**
    security support providers, 323
Security Support Provider Interface (SSPI), 323
security support providers, 323
Security Target (ST), Common Criteria (CC), 13
"security through obscurity", 158
segments, **686**
sendmail banners check, 650–651
Serial Line Internet Protocol (SLIP), **686**
Serpent, **63**
server certificate, 264
server discovery applications, **454–455**
server information stores, 488–489
Server Message Block. *see* SMB (Server Message Block)
server room, protecting, 179
Server service

defined, **686**
disabling, 399
server-side includes, **686**
servers
    attack history, 600
    farms, **686**
    placing IDS agents on, 599–600
    resources, 6
service packs, **408–409**, 566–567
service providers, 299
servicename command, Linux, 573
services
    defined, **686**
    investigating anomalies in, 559
    list of services to block, 402
    removing unnecessary, 249–250, **399–402**
Services snap-in, Windows 2000, 399–402
session key, **686**
session module, Linux PAM, 326
SessionWall. *see* eTrust Intrusion Detection
set bits, Linux, **374–376**
    permission bits, 375
    setuid and setgid programs, 374–377
setgid
    defined, **686**
    exercise finding, 376–379
    overview of, 374–376
setuid
    defined, **686**
    exercise finding, 376–379
    overview of, 374–376
SHA-1, **71**
Shadow, IDS program, 530
shadow passwords, 333, **687**
share permissions, Windows 2000, **362–364**, *364*
share points, 363, **687**
shares, **362**
shareware, **687**
shell accounts, **687**
shells, **687**
shielded twisted-pair (STP) cable, **687**
SIDs (security identifiers), **319**, **686**

signature-based IDS, **687**
signatures
   defined, **687**
   detecting, *523*, **687**
   IDS and, *518*
signing
   creating signature files, *91*
   defined, **687**
   hash encryption and, *70*
simple intrusion, **687**
Simple Mail Transfer Protocol (SMTP), **687**
Simple Network Management Protocol. *see* SNMP (Simple Network Management Protocol)
single-homed bastion host
   defined, *246*, **687**
   firewall design options, *252*, *252–253*
single-key encryption. *see* symmetric encryption
single-purpose bastion hosts, *247*
Skipjack, **63**
SLIP (Serial Line Internet Protocol), **686**
slow scanning attacks, *529–530*, **687**
smart cards, *27–28*, **687**
SMB dialects, *403*, **688**
SMB (Server Message Block), **402–406**
   connection process, *403*
   defined, **686**
   encryption issues, *404–406*
   null sessions, *403–404*
   securing connectivity, *402–404*
   signatures, *405*
   sniffing SMB-based passwords, *496–497*
SMTP (Simple Mail Transfer Protocol), **687**
Smurf attacks
   broadcast addresses and, *119*
   defined, **688**
   overview of, *118*, **118–119**
sniffers
   configuring computer as password sniffer, *490*
   sniffing passwords with LOphtCrack 3 (LC3), *496–497*
   tools for responding to hackers, *293*
SNMP module, *653*

SNMP (Simple Network Management Protocol)
   defined, **687**
   discovery tools, **459**
   use by routers, *483*
Snort, *524*
social engineering, *122–123*, **688**
sockets, **688**
SOCKS, **688**
software certificate, *264*
solutions and reports, *596–624*
   compliance-monitoring software, **608–609**
   exam essentials, *629–630*
   examples of solutions, *596–597*
   intrusion detection, *599–601*
   key terms, *630*
   operating systems, changes to, **601–609**
      overview of, *601–602*
      personal firewalls, **602–608**
   perimeter security, **597–599**
   public-key encryption, **621–623**
   reports
      auditing recommendations for IT Department, *626–627*
      elements of, *625–626*
      importance of written reports, *626*
      recommendations for continuing and strengthening auditing, *627–628*
   review answers, *637–640*
   review questions, *631–636*
   SSH (Secure Shell), **611–620**
      encryption and authentication, *612*
      FTP client, *618*
      obtaining and preparing, *613–614*
      services provided by, *611–612*
      SSH client on Windows 2000, *616–618*
      SSH server on Red Hat Linux, *614–615*
      SSH2 components, *612–613*
   trust relationships, **618–625**
      between Linux clients, *620–621*
      user-to-user trust relationships, *618–620*
      using Windows 2000 client, *623–625*
   update services, **610–611**

source IP address, **688**
source ports, **688**
spam, **688**
special chains, **688**
specific security mechanism, 8–9
spoofing attacks, 111–112
    as attack types, 109
    defined, **674, 688**
    traceback and, 112
    types of, 112
SSH (Secure Shell), **611–620**
    defined, **685**
    encryption and authentication, 612
    FTP client, 618
    logging in with, 614
    obtaining and preparing, 613–614
    replacing rlogin with, 410
    services provided by, 611–612
    SSH client on Windows 2000, 616–618
    SSH server on Red Hat Linux, 614–615
    SSH2 components, 612–613
    Windows 2000 terminal client, 623–625
SSL (Secure Sockets Layer), **93–96**
    defined, **685**
    digital certificates and, 93
    security of, 94
    sequence of, 94
    typical errors, 95–96
SSPI (Security Support Provider Interface), 323
ST (Security Target), Common Criteria (CC), 13
stack fingerprinting, **455–458, 688**
standard FTP clients, 207–208
standards, **7–13**
    Common Criteria (CC), **13**
    HIPAA, **14**
    ISO, 7–9
    ITSEC, 9–10
    PKI, 262
    TCSEC, **10–12**
Start Sniffing button, LC3 Wizard, *497*
stateful, **688**
stateful multilayer inspection
    defined, **688**
    firewalls and, **210–211**
    Unix risk reduction, **421–422**
stateless, **688**
Station-to-Station (STS) protocol, 69
steering routers, **203**
storage
    procedures, 161
    securing media, 408
    securing site, 161
STP (shielded twisted-pair) cable, **687**
strace command, 486
stream cipher, 57–58, **689**
strong authentication, 611–612, **689**
strong passwords
    defined, **689**
    dictionary attacks and, 134–135
    Linux, 333
    types of content in, 331
    Windows 2000, 331–332
structure infiltration, 173, **689**
STS (Station-to-Station) protocol, 69
su command, Linux, 328–329
subnet masks, **689**
subtrees, Registry, 393–395, *395*
sufficient, PAM flags, 326
super daemons. *see* inetd daemon;
    xinetd daemon
superzapping
    defined, **689**
    example of, 176–179
    physical attack strategies, 172–173
surveillance methods, 171–172
suspicious activity, 557–559, **689**
switched networks, **689**
switches, 483, **689**
Symantec
    Enterprise Security Manager, 609
    IDS services of, 522
    Intruder Alert, 526, 528
    as managed security provider, 577
symbolic mode, 372–373, **689**

symmetric encryption, *58*, **58–67**
   algorithms, **59–64**
      Blowfish, **62**
      Data Encryption Standard (DES), **59–60**
      IDEA, **61–62**
      MARS, **63**
      others, 63–64
      RC2, RC4, RC5, and RC6, **61–62**
      Rijndael, **63**
      RSA encryption, **60–61**, *61*
      Serpent, **63**
      Skipjack, **63**
      Triple DES, **60**
      Twofish, **62–63**
   defined, **24**, **689**
   exercise using AES, 65–67
   overview of, 58–59
SYN floods
   defined, **689**
   effectiveness of IDS against, 524
   overview of, **116–117**, *117*
synchronous, **689**
Syskey
   defined, **689**
   password protection with, 178, 335
syslogd, Linux, 568–569, *569*, 575
system accounts
   defined, **690**
   login scripts and, 284
system Administration, Networking, and Security (SANS), 14
system bugs
   defined, **690**
   fixing, 601
system defaults
   attacks and, **124–126**
   information leakage, **124–126**
   overview of, 124
system elements, 157
system latency
   defined, **690**
   IDS issues and, 530

System log, Windows 2000, 562
system logs, checking, 180
system snooping, **690**
system updates, 180
systems, classifying, **16–18**

T

tail command, Linux, 574
tape backup devices, 248
Target of Evaluation (TOE), Common Criteria (CC), 13
TCP handshake
   connection hijacking and, *114*, 114–115
   defined, **690**
TCP/IP, **690**
TCP (Transmission Control Protocol), 653–654, **691**
TCPD daemon, 420
TCPWrappers, 412, **420–421**
   components of, 420
   defined, **690**
   syntax for hosts.allow and hosts.deny, 420–421
TCSEC (Trusted Computer Systems Evaluation Criteria), **10–12**
   defined, **691**
   Level C2, F-C2, and E2 requirements, 12
   security levels, 10–12
Teardrop/Teardrop2, **119–120**, **690**
technology, keeping current with, 180
telephony connections, logging, 561
Telnet
   defined, **690**
   denying access with /etc/nologin file, 328–330, *330*
   discovery tools, **458–459**
   Linux, 328–330
   packet filter, 206
   replacing with SSH, 611, 614–615
   scanning port 80 for web server, *458*, 458
TFN (Tribe Flood Network), 524

TFTP (Trivial File Transfer Protocol), **691**
TGT (ticket-granting ticket), **31**
third-party logging, 577–579
    managed security providers, **578–579**
    partial implementation, 579
threats
    accidental and intentional, 108–109
    defined, **690**
    ISO defintion, 7
    ITSEC definition, 10
ticket-granting ticket (TGT), **31**
tickets, 31
time stamps
    checksum analysis and, 288
    defined, **690**
timing out users, 336
topology, **690**
TOrn root kit, 138
ToS (Type of Service), **691**
traceback
    defined, **690**
    spoofing attacks and, 112
tracert, **690**
traffic
    balancing amount logged, 559–560
    detection, 517
    identifying suspicious, 503
    interference of IDS system with legitimate, 530
    logging, 292, 540–542
    padding, 8
training, security principles, 162–163
transactions, **690**
Transmission Control Protocol (TCP), 653–654, **691**
Transport layer, **691**
trap doors, **124**, **691**
trend analysis
    baselines and, 557
    defined, **168**, **691**
    managed security providers and, 578
Tribe Flood Network (TFN), 524
Triple DES, **60**

Tripwire program, 133, 139, 288
tripwires, **288–290**
    concerns with, 289
    defined, **691**
    exercise, setting tripwire script in Windows 2000, 289–290
    functions of, 288
Trivial File Transfer Protocol (TFTP), **691**
trivial IP services, **459–460**, **691**
Trojan attacks, **136–139**, 287
    defined, **691**
    repairing root kits, 138–139
    root kits, **136–138**
    types of attacks, 110
trust relationships, **56–57**
    automatic key distribution, 57
    defined, **691**
    Linux clients, 620–621
    manual key distribution, 56
    overview of, 56
    user-to-user trust relationships, 618–620
    Windows 2000 clients, 623–625
trusted functionality, 8, **691**
trusting, **691**
tunneling, **691**
tunneling protocols, 258–259, **691**. *see also* VPNs (virtual private networks)
Twofish, **62–63**
Type of Service (ToS), **691**

U

UDP (User Datagram Protocol), 654, **692**
UIDs (user identifiers), Linux, 333, **373–374**, **692**
UltraScan, 453
umask command, Linux, 370–371, *371*
    defined, **692**
    more value bits, 370
    role in file creation, 371
    testing, 378–379
unacceptable activities, 20–21, **662**

unauthorized zone transfers, DNS servers, 115
Unicode, **692**
Uniform Resource Locator (URL), **692**
Unix. *see also* Linux
    file system, 365
    host command as discovery tool, 450–451
    Internet security resources, 659
    IPsec and, 269
    nmap discovery tool, 454, 456–458, *457*
    as operating system of choice for bastion hosts, 249
    r-series commands, spoofing and, 111
    removing services of, 249
    root kits and, 137
    stack fingerprinting and, 455
Unix, risk reduction, 409–422
    NFS issues, **413–415**
    NIS issues, **411–413**
    rlogin, disabling, **409–410**
    stand-alone services, **421–422**
    TCPWrappers, **420–421**
    updating Linux binaries, **415–417**
    vulnerabilities, 409
    xinetd and inetd, **417–420**
unnecessary services, **692**
unpatched, **692**
updates, **610–611**. *see also* SSH (Secure Shell)
    issues with, 610
    replacing IPv 4 with IPv6, 610–611
    SSH and, 597
    system updates, 180
URL (Uniform Resource Locator), **692**
user/agent architecture, *442*, 442
User Datagram Protocol (UDP), 654, **692**
user identifiers (UIDs), Linux, 333, **373–374**, **692**
user-rights failures, 558
userdel command, Linux, 338

V

VBScript, **692**
vendors
    compliance monitoring, 609
    IDS systems, 536
    personal firewalls, 602–603
    proxy servers, 228
VeriSign, 264
video surveillance, 171
VigilEnt, PentaSafe, 609
virtual network perimeter, 258, **692**
virtual private networks. *see* VPNs (virtual private networks)
virus attacks, **139–141**
    types of attacks, 110
    types of viruses, 140
    virus behavior, 140–141
    vulnerability of Windows NT/2000/XP, 392
viruses, defined, **692**
Visual Basic, **692**
VPNs (virtual private networks), **258–261**, *259*
    defined, **692**
    overview of, 258–259
    protocols uses by, 261
vulnerabilities
    vs. attacks, 109
    defined, **692**
    ISO definition, 7
    ITSEC definition, 10
    minimizing, 157–158
    operating systems, 316
    Unix, 409
    Windows 2000, 390–392
vulnerability scanners, **460–465**
    defined, **692**
    equipment placement and, 166
    information obtained with, 462–464
    list of, 460–461
    network scanning issues, 461–462
    reports from, 464–465, *465*

W

WAN (wide area networks), **693**
WAP (Wireless Application Protocol), **693**
war dialers, 245, **692**
war driving, **693**

web browsers
    security problems of, 488–489
    use of public-key encryption by, 95
Web servers, 35
WebTrends Firewall Suite, 483, 576
well-known ports, **204**
white hat hackers, 4–5, 445, **693**
WHOIS, **693**
wide area networks (WANs), **693**
wide security mechanisms, **9**
window spoofing, 488–489, **693**
Windows 2000
    Encrypting File System (EFS), 92
    exchanging encrypted messages, 84–85
    filtering logs, *571*
    Internet security resources, *659*
    IPsec and, 264–265, 267–269
    key pairs, generating, 623–625
    personal firewalls on, 604–608
    PGP on, 78–81
    physical attack on, 176–179
    public keys, exporting and signing, 81–83
    remote logging, *576*
    risk reduction, 390–409
    Run dialog box, *393*
    SSH client on, 616, 616–618
    tripwire script in, 289–290
    WinRoute on, 211–214
Windows 2000, file system security, 352–362
    copying and moving files, **362**
    drive partitioning, **361–362**
    NTFS permissions, assigning, 356–361
    NTFS vs. FAT, 352–353
    permissions, **353–356**
    remote access control, **362–365**
Windows 2000, logging, **561–567**
    auditing failed login entries, 579–580
    Auditing tab, 563–564, *564*
    compared with Windows NT, *564*
    default log-file locations, 562–563
    "Dirty Shutdown" event, 565–566, *566*
    enabling auditing, 563–564

    enabling directory auditing, 580–582
    filtering logs, **571–572**
    Local Security Settings, 563, *563*
    log categories, 562
    NT/2000 significant events, 565–566
    service-pack level and uptime information, 566–567
Windows 2000, OS security, 316–324
    account security
        account policies, 334–336
        strong passwords, 331–332
    components, **319–321**
        access tokens, **319**
        ACEs, **320–321**
        ACLs, *320*, 320
        security descriptors, **319–320**
        security identifiers, **319**
    list of features, 316–317
    objects, **317–318**
    removing accounts, 338
    renaming default accounts, 338–339
    security subsystem, **321–324**, *322*
        authentication package, 323
        Local Security Authority (LSA), 322–323
        Netlogon service, 323–324
        overview of, 321–322
        Security Account Manager (SAM), **324**
        security support providers, 323
Windows 2000, risk reduction
    configuration changes, **406–408**
    Registry, **392–398**
    Registry, auditing, 395–396, 398–399
    Registry, backing up, 396
    Registry, permissions, 397–398
    Registry, structure of, 392–395
    removing unnecessary services, **399–402**
    securing connectivity, **402–404**
    service packs, **408–409**
    SMB encryption issues, 404–406
    vulnerabilities, 390–392
Windows File Protection (WPF) utility, 139
Windows NT
    logging, compared with Windows 2000, *564*

service-pack level and uptime information, 566–567
significant log events, 565
WinRoute, 211–214
Wireless Application Protocol (WAP), 693
workstations, 693
World Wide Web (WWW), 2
worm attacks, 110, **141–142**, 693
WORM (Write Once, Read Many), 693
WPF (Windows File Protection) utility, 139
WWW Web server version, 652
WWW (World Wide Web), 2

X

X Window system, 693

X.25, 693
X.509 standard, 262, 693
xinetd daemon
    configuring daemons launched by, **417–419**
    daemons controlled by, 417
    defined, 693
    restarting after changing, 420

Z

zone files, 693
Zone Labs Zone Alarm, 285
zone transfer, 693
ZoneAlarm, *604–605*, 604–608, *607*

Sybex Covers CompTIA CERTIFICATION PROGRAMS

From self-study guides to advanced computer-based training, simulated testing programs to last-minute review guides, Sybex has the most complete CompTIA training solution on the market.

Study Guides

Designed for optimal learning, Sybex Study Guides provide you with comprehensive coverage of all exam objectives. Hands-on exercises and review questions help reinforce your knowledge.

STUDY
- In-depth coverage of exam objectives
- Hands-on exercises
- CD includes: test engine, flashcards for PCs and Palm devices, PDF version of entire book

Virtual Trainers™ software

Based on the content of the Study Guides, Sybex Virtual Trainers offer you advanced computer-based training, complete with animations and customization features.

- Customizable study planning tools
- Narrated instructional animations
- Preliminary assessment tests
- Results reporting

Virtual Test Centers™ software

Powered by an advanced testing engine, Sybex's new line of Virtual Test Centers give you the opportunity to test your knowledge before sitting for the real exam.

PRACTICE
- Hundreds of challenging questions
- Computer adaptive testing
- Support for drag-and-drop and hot-spot formats
- Detailed explanations and cross-references

Exam Notes™

Organized according to the official exam objectives, Sybex Exam Notes help reinforce your knowledge of key exam topics and identify potential weak areas requiring further study.

REVIEW
- Excellent quick review before the exam
- Concise summaries of key exam topics
- Tips and insights from experienced instructors
- Definitions of key terms and concepts

*Look to Sybex for exam prep materials on major CompTIA certifications, including A+®, Network+™, I-Net+™, Server+™, and Linux+™. For more information about CompTIA and Sybex products, visit **www.sybex.com**.*

CompTIA. One Industry. One Voice.

SYBEX®
www.sybex.com

Sybex—The Leader in Certification

JumpStart™ Your Career!

Take your career in high-tech to the next level.

The JumpStart™ series from Sybex® has all the answers. JumpStart books provide the firm grounding in computer and network topics you'll need to approach certification training with confidence. In each JumpStart book you'll find:

- Clear and concise explanations of complex technical topics
- Review questions to help reinforce your understanding
- Real-world insights from expert trainers

Once you've covered the basics, you'll be ready to start down the road in pursuit of certifications such as Microsoft's MCSE, Cisco's CCNA, and others.

CCNA JumpStart: Networking and Internetworking Basics
ISBN: 0-7821-2592-1 • US $19.99

TCP/IP JumpStart: Internet Protocol Basics
ISBN: 0-7821-4101-3 • US $24.99

MCSE 2000 JumpStart: Computer and Network Basics
ISBN: 0-7821-2749-5 • US $19.99

Coming Soon:

A+ JumpStart: PC Hardware and Operating Systems Basics
ISBN: 0-7821-4126-9 • US $24.99

Network Security JumpStart
ISBN: 0-7821-4120-X • US $24.99

SYBEX®
www.sybex.com

THE MOST COMPREHENSIVE
MCSA Study Solution
from Sybex

The Microsoft® Certified Systems Administrator (MCSA) is a new certification from Microsoft developed to address demands from the IT industry for a mid-level Microsoft certification. No matter what combination of exams you decide to take, Sybex has the study tools you need so you can approach the exams with confidence.

MCSA Virtual Lab software
by James Chellis
ISBN: 0-7821-3030-5
US $199.99

MCSA: Microsoft Certified Systems Associate Exam Requirements

Pass ONE Client OS Exam

Installing, Configuring and Administering Microsoft Windows 2000 Professional
—OR—
Installing, Configuring and Administering Microsoft Windows XP Professional

Pass TWO Networking System Exams

Installing, Configuring and Administering Microsoft Windows 2000 Server
—OR—
Installing, Configuring and Administering Microsoft Windows .Net Server (available 2002)

Managing a Microsoft Windows 2000 Network Environment
—OR—
Managing a Microsoft Windows .Net Server Network Environment (available 2002)

Pass ONE Elective Exam

Implementing and Administering a Microsoft Windows 2000 Network Infrastructure

Installing, Configuring, and Administering Microsoft SQL Server 2000

Installing, Configuring, and Administering Microsoft Exchange 2000 Server

Installing, Configuring, and Administering Microsoft ISA Server 2000

Supporting and Maintaining a Microsoft Windows NT Server 4.0 Network

CompTIA's A+ and Network+ Combination

CompTIA's A+ and Server+ Combination

MCSA/MCSE: Windows® 2000 Network Management Study Guide
by Michael Chacon, James Chellis, Anil Desai, and Matthew Sheltz
ISBN: 0-7821-4105-6 • US $49.99

For a list of all Sybex products that will help prepare you for any of the MCSA exams, visit **www.sybex.com**, or train online at **www.sybexetrainer.com**.

SYBEX®

TELL US WHAT YOU THINK!

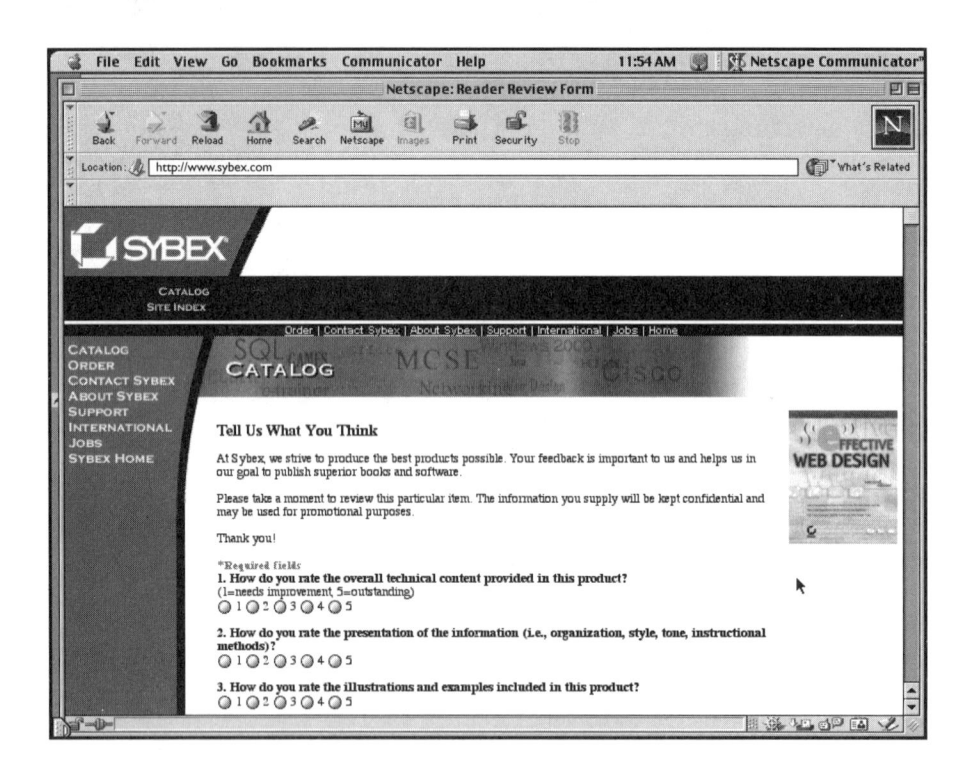

Your feedback is critical to our efforts to provide you with the best books and software on the market. Tell us what you think about the products you've purchased. It's simple:

1. Visit the Sybex website
2. Go to the product page
3. Click on **Submit a Review**
4. Fill out the questionnaire and comments
5. Click **Submit**

With your feedback, we can continue to publish the highest quality computer books and software products that today's busy IT professionals deserve.

www.sybex.com

SYBEX Inc. • 1151 Marina Village Parkway, Alameda, CA 94501 • 510-523-8233

Sybex + ProsoftTraining = CIW Success!

The CIW (Certified Internet Webmaster) program from ProsoftTraining™ is the most widely recognized Internet-specific certification. Sybex and ProsoftTraining™ have teamed up to bring you high quality Study Guides that will provide you with the skills and knowledge you need to approach the exams with confidence!

Endorsed by ProsoftTraining™, each CIW Study Guide from Sybex® is based upon the official ProsoftTraining.com courseware and comes packed with additional study tools for your benefit.

CIW Associate

The CIW Associate certification is the entry point for those pursuing the "Master" CIW designations. The Foundations exam validates the basic hands-on skills and knowledge that an Internet professional is expected to understand and use. Foundations skills include basic knowledge of Internet technologies, network infrastructure, and Web authoring using HTML.

Exam Name	Exam #	Sybex Products
Foundations	1D0-410	*CIW: Foundations Study Guide* ISBN: 07821-4081-5

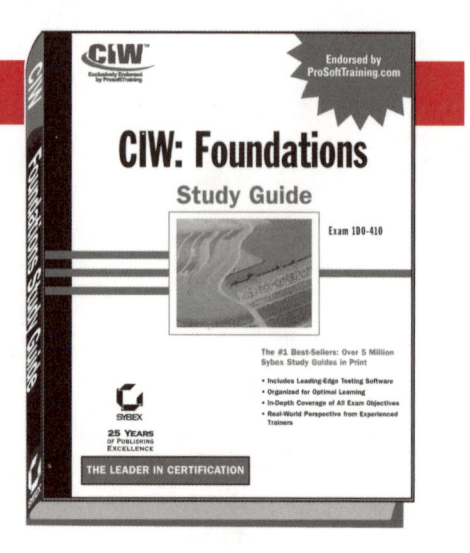

Master CIW Designer

The Master CIW Design certification requires candidates to pass two exams in addition to Foundations. The Site Design exam validates skills relevant to designing, implementing, and maintaining web sites using authoring languages and content creation tools. The E-commerce exam tests knowledge of web marketing and purchasing methods, inventory control, shipping and site performance.

Exam Name	Exam #	Sybex Products
Site Designer	1D0-420	*CIW: Site and E-Commerce Design Study Guide* ISBN: 07821-4082-3
E-Commerce Designer	1D0-425	